Roy T Menlo[ve]
received this book
from Darrell Menlove
Christmas 1997

Journey to Zion

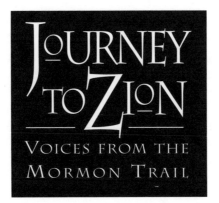

CAROL CORNWALL MADSEN

DESERET BOOK COMPANY

SALT LAKE CITY, UTAH

Library of Congress Cataloging-in-Publication Data

Madsen, Carol Cornwall, 1930–
    Journey to Zion : voices from the Mormon trail / by Carol Cornwall Madsen.
        p.   cm.
    Includes index.
    ISBN 1-57345-244-0
    1. Mormon Trail—History—Sources. 2. Mormons—West (U.S.)—History—Sources. 3. Frontier and pioneer life—West (U.S.)—Sources. 4. West (U.S.)—History—Sources. 5. West (U.S.)—Biography. I. Title.
F593.M257   1997
978—dc21   97-2043
                                                                             CIP

Printed in the United States of America   72082

10   9   8   7   6   5   4   3   2   1

The journey from Nauvoo

to these valleys will stand

in bold relief as the main key

of the Mormon history

of the nineteenth century.

—Wilford Woodruff

CONTENTS

CONTENTS

CONTENTS

FOREWORD

FOR MORE THAN a century, historians of the American West
have lauded Brigham Young's accomplishments in leading the
Latter-day Saints to the Salt Lake Valley and in expanding
Mormon settlement across a broad western landscape. From the
perspective of western settlement history, two observations commonly emerge in telling the story of the westward trek and sub-
sequent colonization of the Intermountain West. First, historians
note that The Church of Jesus Christ of Latter-day Saints succeeded in moving tens of thousands of emigrants west during a
twenty-year pioneering period because of the organizing skills
of President Young. Second, they note the importance of the
unity of the Saints—their commitment to a common purpose
and their willingness to sacrifice personal needs for the greater
good.

Both of these characteristics were evident in the Church long
before the Saints sold their farms and homes in the Nauvoo area
and elsewhere and fitted out for a journey into the wilderness
beyond United States boundaries. Brigham Young and others
had experienced the benefits of traveling in well-organized
migrant companies. They had marched under military style in
Zion's Camp from Kirtland, Ohio, to Clay County, Missouri,

under the leadership of the Prophet Joseph Smith in 1834. Many of the Saints migrated to Missouri in organized companies. Members of the Quorum of the Twelve helped organize the removal of the Saints from Missouri to a new place of refuge in the Nauvoo area. They did so by creating a committee to manage resources and people. In addition, during their mission in England, the Twelve structured the Saints into branches and districts with spiritual overseers and regular procedures for reporting.

These experiences taught the Twelve that, like the biblical children of Israel, the Lord's modern people were willing to follow their leaders because of testimonies that bound them to a common objective. The Saints who gathered to the designated Zion across the Rocky Mountains during the last half of the nineteenth century believed that the Lord had picked that place for refuge. In every step they took, the Saints moved westward with faith. They longed to gather with other believers, and they looked forward to the opportunity to build a temple to replace the Houses of the Lord left behind in Kirtland and Nauvoo.

The word and will of the Lord to Brigham Young, given in Iowa in January 1847, confirmed the use of principles tried and tested over a dozen years by faithful members. The Saints understood and accepted the organizational pattern set forth by the Lord: "Let the companies be organized with captains of hundreds, captains of fifties, and captains of tens, with a president and his two counselors at their head, under the direction of the Twelve Apostles" (D&C 136:3). The carefully structured emigrant camps offered inexperienced travelers the safety that comes from sharing talents and resources. It allowed the Saints to cooperate in establishing Zion and fulfilling its purposes of gathering believers to temple cities, offering them saving ordinances, and performing those same ordinances by proxy for deceased ancestors.

Brigham Young's inspired guidelines for the westward trek

emphasized that organization, orderliness, cooperation, and discipline on the trail encompassed spiritual as well as temporal principles. Latter-day Saint emigrants were "organized into companies, with a covenant and promise to keep all the commandments and statutes of the Lord" and to "walk in all the ordinances of the Lord." If the Saints would share their goods with the poor, the widows, and the fatherless "with a pure heart, in all faithfulness," the Lord promised to bless them in their journey to "a land of peace" (D&C 136:2, 4, 8, 11, 16).

Here, then, is the key to understanding the individual experiences of pioneering. Each diary kept, letter written, and reminiscence penned carries within it the seeds of faith. The westering Saints were preparing a people to receive the risen Lord when he returned to claim his people. They emulated in their lives the Christian principles of faith, charity, and hope. They sought the blessings of eternal life in temples, and they wanted their ancestors and their children to enjoy the same blessings. The organized migration was a means to a faith-filled objective.

In the fine collection of personal documents assembled by Carol Cornwall Madsen in this volume, the generation that pioneered a western headquarters for the Church through their personal sacrifices preserved a message for later generations. As a worldwide church remembers their faith in a time of commemoration, that message of faith carries new meaning. Those early Saints accepted the Lord's reminder: "My people must be tried in all things, that they may be prepared to receive the glory that I have for them, even the glory of Zion; and he that will not bear chastisement is not worthy of my kingdom." That promised glory would be theirs, the Lord explained—in words just as true today—"if ye are faithful in keeping all my words that I have given you, from the days of Adam to Abraham, from Abraham to Moses, from Moses to Jesus and his apostles, and from Jesus and his apostles to Joseph Smith, whom I did call upon by mine angels, my ministering servants, and by mine own voice out of the heavens, to bring forth my work; which foundation he did lay, and was faithful" (D&C 136:31, 37–38).

The first generation of Latter-day Saints set in motion the Lord's work of bringing his church out of obscurity (see D&C 1:30). When Mary Fielding Smith, the wife of Hyrum Smith, left her husband incarcerated at Liberty Jail in 1838 and set out from Far West, Missouri, to find a new place of refuge in Illinois, she understood these same principles. To her brother in England, she wrote, "I feel but little concerned about where I am, if I can but keep my mind staid upon God; for, you know in this there is perfect peace" (*Millennial Star* 2 [June 1840]: 41).

Glen M. Leonard

PREFACE

THIS VOLUME REPRESENTS the contributions of many people. An invitation from Sheri Dew of Deseret Book to make a collection of Mormon trail diaries and reminiscences for the 1997 Sesquicentennial Celebration initiated the project. The cooperation of Richard Turley, William Slaughter, Linda Haslam, and other staff members of the LDS Church Archives greatly facilitated locating the documents. The excellent research assistance of Joe Richardson, Rex Griffiths, Marianne Griffiths, and Sheri Slaughter in Salt Lake City, and Brigham Young University students Becky Dodds and Kimberly Dray, helped enormously in the selection and preparation of the accounts. Special thanks go to research assistants Kami Wilson and Rebecca Hopkins, who gave enthusiastic and meticulous service in the final preparation of this volume. Typists Marlise Paxman and Sariah Wilson were essential contributors. I am also indebted to my colleagues at the Joseph Fielding Smith Institute for Church History for their support, especially our director, Ronald E. Esplin; William G. Hartley, an expert on the Iowa trail; and Marilyn Parks, our secretary, whose assistance and advice were invaluable.

Of particular help in enlarging my understanding of the trail experience were the numerous studies by both LDS and western historians. Recent research, especially, has yielded new information about the geography of the Mormon Trail, the Mormon way stations in Iowa and Nebraska, the "down and back" companies, the early plans for eventual western settlement, and the impact of the Perpetual Emigrating Fund. New views of the handcart companies and their rescue, the flight from Nauvoo, and the sojourn at the Missouri have also enriched our knowledge of this significant period of Mormon history. All have been useful in helping me provide a context for the personal experiences related in this compilation.

My deepest gratitude is for those pioneers whose writings comprise this volume. The heart of the experience is what they have chosen to tell us. Without their words, we can trace their footsteps, view their wagons, open their trunks, handle their tools, and know the cold of winter and heat of summer and many of the other inconveniences and difficulties of the trail, but we cannot fully appreciate how they functioned within these external dimensions or what emotions and responses were activated by the circumstances of their trail experience.

This is primarily a book about people, and in the interest of those who may be looking for references to their own pioneer progenitors in these accounts, I have attempted to identify all of the names mentioned. Some names eluded that search, and if there are cases of mistaken identity I take full responsibility. I have also provided biographical information on each of the writers, more readily available for some than for others. Its accuracy is based on the sources available.

I cannot make claim to any preconceived notion or pattern of selection of documents beyond choosing writings of both men and women with selections spanning the entire pioneer period, from 1846 to 1869. Legibility and accessibility of the documents were certainly factors. Some accounts have been published in one or another of Kate B. Carter's series on pioneer history or in other collections, but whenever possible, I have used original documents, some of which vary from the published versions. The sheer number of reminiscences and interviews, especially by women, suggests that many were written at the urging of historians or collectors, such as Kate Carter, as well as descendants. Many more volumes could easily be compiled from the numerous extant accounts. Needless to say, it was difficult not to include all those that I had opportunity to read.

Original spelling and punctuation have been left untouched except when it was necessary to alter them for better reading and comprehension. Brackets have been used occasionally for intended words. Words struck through were struck through in the originals. Words in angle brackets indicate words inserted above the line in the originals. When only typescripts were available, the accounts are generally rendered in common usage.

The chapter titles, as Latter-day Saints will readily recognize, are taken from the great Mormon hymn, "Come, Come, Ye Saints," by William Clayton. Though written just two months after the first Saints departed Nauvoo and well before Clayton's 1847 trek with the vanguard pioneer company, it nonetheless encompasses the spirit of the pioneer experience and quickly became the anthem of the trail. Taught by rote from company to company throughout the pioneer years, it expressed their hopes, their determination, their steadfastness, and most of all their faith, the faith that carried the Saints to their Rocky Mountain home and enabled even those who found they would not make it all the way to declare, "All is well, all is well."

Carol Cornwall Madsen

"This Tale to Tell"

HISTORY REMEMBERS BRIGHAM YOUNG
as the charismatic leader and skillful organizer of
the Mormon westward migration, settling a significant portion of the Rocky Mountain region and
establishing a permanent presence in the West. But Brigham
Young thought of himself as a parent in that great undertaking,
calling his children to "come home." "I feel like a father with a
great family of children around me in a winter storm," he wrote
to his friend Jesse Little in February 1847, "and I am looking
with calmness, confidence and patience for the clouds to break
and the sun to shine so that I can run out and plant and sow and
gather in the corn and wheat and say, Children, come home,
winter is approaching again. . . . I am ready to kill the fatted calf
and make a joyful feast to all who will come and partake."[1]

---

1. Brigham Young to Elder Jesse C. Little, 26 February 1847, reprinted in James R. Clark, ed., *Messages of the First Presidency*, 3 vols. (Salt Lake City: Bookcraft, 1965) 1:318.

To the thousands of Saints waiting at the Missouri River, throughout the states, and in countries abroad, Brigham Young was indeed the father of the Gathering. Though not yet sustained as the prophet when he wrote this letter, as president of the Quorum of Twelve Apostles he carried the burden of fulfilling Joseph Smith's vision of establishing a permanent home for the Church. Within the next two decades, he would shepherd seventy thousand Saints to the Salt Lake Valley in as ordered and safe a manner as possible. Even the ten experimental handcart companies, with misfortune befalling only two of them, brought nearly three thousand Saints to Utah.[2]

The "peculiar" and "distinguishing" doctrine of the Gathering spurred the faithful westward, tested their commitment to the work of the restoration, and strengthened both the temporal and spiritual foundations of the Church. More important, it created a nucleus of Saints to whom the Lord could reveal the saving ordinances of the Gospel, which, in Nauvoo, had blessed the Church with "privileges and power she otherwise could not have had," explained Thomas Ward, editor of the *Millennial Star,* to the waiting converts in Great Britain.[3]

Many new members responded to their own inward call to gather, touched individually by "the spirit of gathering." But whatever its source, the call to come home reordered the lives of thousands of people, conjoining them in one of the great epics of western American history and at a pivotal point in the history of the Church.

Ironically, when Brigham Young wrote his letter to James Little, he had not yet been to the "home" to which he was call-

---

2. Estimates range between sixty and eighty thousand Mormon pioneers who traveled west between 1847 and 1869. Though many other western travelers used covered wagons after completion of the transcontinental railroad in 1869, traditionally the terms "pioneer" and "pioneer period," in the context of western travel, have been arbitrarily reserved for those who traveled west before 1869. Clearly, the term is applicable in a wide range of contexts and periods.

3. *Millennial Star* 8 (15 July 1846): 11.

ing the Saints. Its specific western location, however, really made little difference. It was not as much where it was to be as what it was to be that interested Brigham Young and his followers. Of importance to them was that it would be a place of God's choosing, not theirs, and that their prophet would know it when he saw it. In the early 1830s Joseph Smith had talked of the far west as the "region blessed by the Lord as the land of Zion,"[4] and in 1842 he had prophesied that the Church would eventually move there.[5] When the Saints left Nauvoo, recalled apostle Erastus Snow in 1873, all they knew about their destination was that they "were seeking a country which had been pointed out by the Prophet Joseph Smith in the midst of the Rocky Mountains in the interior of the great North American continent."[6] Thus, while the starkness of the Salt Lake Valley caused the settlers some dismay, the knowledge that the Lord had designated it as the new Zion reassured them. There, the Lord had said, they would find a haven, a refuge, a place "in which [He] designed to hide His people."[7] There they would be safe from the destruction of the wicked, the persecutions of their enemies, and the temptations of Babylon. A decade after settling there, Brigham Young confirmed it as "a good place to make Saints" and "a good place for Saints to live; it is the place the Lord has appointed, and we shall stay here until He tells us to go somewhere else." He was not apologetic in saying, "I want hard times so that every person that does not wish to stay, for the sake of his religion, will leave."[8] And hard times they had.

---

4. *The Evening and The Morning Star*, October 1832, as quoted in Ronald K. Esplin, "'A Place Prepared': Joseph, Brigham and the Quest for Promised Refuge in the West," *Journal of Mormon History* 9 (1982): 85–111.

5. Frederick A. Norwood analyzes the Mormon exodus as a fulfillment of Joseph Smith's prophecy in *Strangers and Exiles, A History of Religious Refugees*, 2 vols. (Nashville & New York: Abingdon Press, 1969) 2:241.

6. 14 September 1873, *Journal of Discourses*, 20 vols. (Liverpool: Latter-day Saints' Book Depot, 1874, reprint copy 1966) 16:207.

7. *Deseret News*, 1 May 1861, quoted in *Exodus of Modern Israel, From the Diary of Orson Pratt and Others*, comp. N. B. Lundwall (Salt Lake City: N. B. Lundwall, n.d.), 91–2.

8. 17 August 1856, *Journal of Discourses* 4:32.

But turning back was far from Thomas Bullock's mind in July 1847 when he first gazed on the shimmering salt sea and empty sweep of land edging it. "Hurra, hurra, hurra," he was moved to exclaim, "there's my home at last."[9] Neither the reassuring familiarity or material comforts generally associated with home provoked his cry of thanksgiving. Nor did Patty Sessions see anything familiar or comforting—or even beautiful—when she saw the Valley a few months later. Yet she also viewed the scene as a joyful homecoming: "My heart flows with gratitude to God that we have got home all safe, lost nothing, have been blessed in life and health. I rejoice all the time."[10] Ann Agatha Pratt was another. She wrote, "My soul was filled with thankfulness to God for bringing us to a place of rest and safety—*home*."[11]

While the Saints did not ignore their desires for comfortable shelter and adequate food, productive work, and at least some of the amenities of life, the image of home that drew them west was spiritual, not temporal. The personal stories in this volume attest to that reality. They show the eager response of the Saints to answer the call to come home, and they reveal the steadfast faith that enabled them to do it. For if conversion changed the worship of these early Saints, it also altered their pattern of life, especially evident on the trail. Mormonism was nourished by a principle that persistently privileged the general welfare and community goals over individual gain and personal ambition. The millennial hope was to establish Zion and build a spiritual kingdom on earth worthy to receive its heavenly ruler. Recognizing the depth of their devotion to this collective mission is the key to understanding the Saints' willingness to undergo the personal suffering and sacrifice it entailed. Nancy Tracy articulated this commitment. An early convert, she wrote at

---

9. Diary of Thomas Bullock, 22 July 1847, holograph, Archives, Church of Jesus Christ of Latter-day Saints, Salt Lake City, Utah, hereinafter referred to as LDS Church Archives.

10. Diary of Patty Sessions, 24 September 1847, holograph, LDS Church Archives.

11. "Personal Reminiscences," *Woman's Exponent* 21 (15 March 1893): 139.

the end of a long life that took her from New York to Ohio, Missouri, Illinois, and finally Utah to follow the Church, "My life, ever since I became a Mormon, has been made up of moving about, of persecutions, sacrifices, poverty, sickness, and death. Through all my sufferings I never doubted but felt to cling to the gospel."[12]

The Mormon hegira was an epoch in LDS history. It underscored Mormonism's collective purpose and gave the pioneers a religious and historical identity that distinguished them from other western travelers.

Moreover, the trek west was not only a geographic bridge between the City of Joseph and the city built by Brigham; it was also a psychic bridge, a defining and coalescing period for the Church and its members. It marked a transition from the esoteric, charismatic leadership of the revelator Joseph Smith to the pragmatic, administrative leadership of implementor Brigham Young. It served as a significant institutional rite of passage as well as a personal pilgrim's progress.

Time has tended to telescope the trail accounts into a single story, a monolithic tale beginning with the exodus from Nauvoo and proceeding, after a brief interlude at Winter Quarters, on to the Salt Lake Valley. The voices we hear from this volume tell a much more complex and far more dramatic tale. The 1846 crossing of Iowa offered challenges different from those experienced by the handcart pioneers who crossed Iowa a decade later, and the journey beyond the Missouri little resembled the Iowa segment for many of the Saints. Though more than three times farther, it was better organized and equipped, and for many veterans of the Iowa trail, much easier. Those who went west in the 1860s found that the railroad, reaching ever farther westward, cut wagon travel by hundreds of miles. Moreover, the European

12. "Life History of Nancy Naomi Alexander Tracy Written by Herself," typescript copy in Special Collections, Harold B. Lee Library, Brigham Young University, Provo, Utah.

7

emigrants added thousands of nautical miles to their journey west and tell another story altogether.

The Nauvoo exiles were distinctive in their own way. They were true refugees, *forced* to leave their homes, too many of them unprepared. With their destination still vague, they were wanderers, scarred by what lay behind and apprehensive of what lay before. But their primary difference was that they were the only ones of the seventy-thousand Zion-bound Saints during the pioneer period who had received the blessings of the temple. The fifty-six hundred endowed men and women, led by the nine apostles who held all the keys of the priesthood,[13] left Nauvoo as a "kingdom of priests, and an holy nation," the Lord's covenant people (Exodus 19:6). As covenanters, they knew at the outset that their true destination was spiritual, not geographic, and they would go where the Lord led through his prophets. Their endowment was as assuring to them of God's presence and purpose in their lives as was the pillar of cloud by day and fire by night to the ancient Israelites.

Hundreds of personal writings remain to tell the story. Company clerks and many company captains kept travel records. Others wrote for their own reasons, and while far more reminiscences than diaries have been preserved, many remembered accounts convey the same sense of immediacy as diaries. While the underlying motive for their being on the western trail suffuses the spirit of these accounts, their stories dwell on the particulars of their trail experience. Some historians have noted the similarity in men's and women's trail observations. Both, for instance, show the same concern for order in the companies and for environmental conditions. Both note the importance in

---

13. Nine apostles stayed with the Church during this period and eventually went west: Brigham Young, Heber C. Kimball, Orson Hyde, Parley P. Pratt, Orson Pratt, John Taylor, Wilford Woodruff, George A. Smith, and Willard Richards, all of whom had previously coalesced into a cohesive quorum as missionaries in Great Britain. They faithfully served the Prophet Joseph, receiving from him the fullness of the priesthood upon their return to Nauvoo from England.

selecting the right campsites, the availability of water, the difficulty of river crossings, the methods and amount of food distribution, the feed and condition of the oxen, the success of hunting trips, the nature of the terrain, and the spiritual interventions. Other historians have emphasized gendered perceptions, noting, for instance, the difference in men's and women's reaction to Indians, women's sensitivity to the personal needs of their traveling companions, women's emphasis on the web of friends and family and tasks within their company, and some women's conscious notation of the graves along the way.

Mormon journals confirm both findings. But even more than gender differences or similarities, the readers of these narratives may find that the personality of the writers, their level of literacy and writing skills, their individual interests, their motivations for writing, and even the year in which they traveled made the primary difference in their style or content. Moreover, the age of the writers played an important role in their perception of the experience. For men, the middle years were among their most active, and they carried the burden of the physical labor of trail travel. For women these were the childbearing years, a period of physical vulnerability. The travails of pregnancy and childbirth in a wilderness and the relentless watchcare of infants, toddlers, and adventurous teenagers, with sometimes the additional care of aged parents, engendered a far different trail experience from what single, childless young men and women or older dependent adults encountered.

It is the combination of these experiences that tells the full story of the Mormon trek. Each account brings its own individuality to bear and in so doing enlarges and reifies the story for us. The personal experiences collected in this volume can show the value of such life writings to later generations. They are our heritage as Latter-day Saints.

Besides historians, a number of playwrights, movie makers, song writers, poets, novelists, painters, and sculptors have discovered the great drama in this westward move of a whole people. Each company of emigrants was a microcosm of human character and experience waiting to be expressed in some artistic fashion. Along with the leaders and followers, there were the optimists and the grumblers, the dreamers and the pragmatists, the courageous and the fearful, the resourceful and the dependent, the strong and the weak. To this diversity may be added the range of ages and variety of family relationships, nationalities, and economic circumstances. The challenge for the artists in this human medley is to capture its recurring theme—the shared vision and faithful discipleship of its participants. Some have succeeded.

Writing or painting the trail experience, however, is one thing. To claim a pioneer in one's pedigree is another, tantamount to claiming a pilgrim father or Revolutionary War patriot in one's ancestry. The popularity of the complementary organizations, the Sons and Daughters of Utah Pioneers, attests to the enduring pride of noble descent. From such veneration has come a library of pioneer histories, well-preserved diaries, and multitudes of reminiscences written for proud children and grandchildren. This written legacy is beyond price.

But the majority of Church members today cannot trace their lineage to these pioneers. Can the story have meaning to them? Perhaps their own spiritual separation from Babylon and the blazing of their own religious trail, not to a Zion of place but to one of heart, connects these latter-day pioneers to their nineteenth-century counterparts in ways that only those who have known this life-changing experience can truly share or understand.

The persistent and pervasive celebration of this epic event each July has tended to mythologize it, initiated by the pioneers themselves. For them the Nauvoo exodus found its prototype in the flight of ancient Israel. The fleeing Saints called themselves the Camp of Israel; their Sinai was Nauvoo; the freezing of the

Mississippi, the parting of the Red Sea; their sacred books and records, the Ark of the Covenant; and the miracle of the quail among the poor camps, the appearance of the quail to the Israelites. They were the Lord's covenant people delivered from their enemies by a modern Moses and led to a promised land where they would build a temple to the God who had preserved them.

Years of commemorating the trail story have enhanced and entrenched its mythic elements. Yet they have not molded the story into the traditional mythology of invention but rather into one that has risen from "real stories that appeal to the consciousness of a people by embodying its cultural ideals or by giving expression to deep, commonly felt emotions."[14] For many Church members, the pioneers are avatars of the highest and best of Latter-day Saint ideals. It is the reverence with which they regard these spiritual progenitors that has tended to transform them from real people to mythic figures, a transformation aided by the romanticized paintings of Frederick Piercy, the heroic murals of C. C. A. Christensen, and the works of other artists. Some years ago Wallace Stegner warned that "piety and ancestor worship are not the best foundation for the study of history."[15] That is undoubtedly true. It is, however, the words of the pioneers themselves, more than the works of historians, that have sustained the mystique of the trail and invited such worship. Moreover, if "myths are clues to the spiritual potentialities of the human life," as Joseph Campbell has asserted,[16] then such veneration serves an important function in affirming Mormon cultural and religious ideals. Their tales are modern-day records of how God's purposes are brought about, and their preservation,

---

14. This definition is from the *American Heritage Dictionary* (Boston: Houghton Mifflin Company, 1969).

15. Wallace Stegner, *The Gathering of Zion* (New York: McGraw-Hill Book Company, 1964), 296.

16. Joseph Campbell, with Bill Moyers, in *The Power of Myth*, ed. Betty Sue Flowers (New York: Doubleday, 1988), 5.

in the words of Alma, "have enlarged the memory of this people
. . . and brought them to the knowledge of their God unto the
salvation of their souls" (Alma 37:8).

We miss the reality of the pioneers' lives, however, if we allow
the mythic elements of the trail to cloak its human dimensions.
Though they were of another century, facing circumstances
unfamiliar to most people today, the pioneers were not of
another species, their heroism understandable only because we
think of them as different from us. Their words remind us that
underneath their seeming stoicism, their tenacious faith, and
their persistent courage lay their all-too-human fears and sorrows, their discouragement and annoyances. The frequency of
accidents and disease, of harassment and persecution, of separation and loss did not inure them to pain and suffering. They
were not less fearful than we are when hunger theatens and disease decimates, nor less awed by nature's power to harm as well as
to please. Nor did they mourn less because death came more
often.

In their lifetime as well as in ours, the pioneers were revered
as a distinct generation, bonded by their shared experience. One
company of ten made that connection permanent. Strangers at
the outset, by journey's end they vowed to stay together. They
built their homes and reared their families near each other, continuing the familial relationship they had developed on the trail.
The faith they shared in traveling to Zion endured in their
shared lives thereafter.

In answering the call to "come home," the pioneers wrote a
moving and powerful chapter in Mormon history. Theirs is a
sacred story. In their own words they have shown in the most
vivid of terms the power of faith and the extraordinary dimensions of the human spirit.

1

THE IOWA
TRAIL

"Fresh

Courage

Take"

*J*N 1846, 4 FEBRUARY WOULD HAVE BEEN just another cold, gray, midwestern winter day had it not been the day Charles Shumway chose to drive his lumbering, loaded wagons down Parley Street in Nauvoo, Illinois, to a waiting flatboat on the bank of the Mississippi River. There Charles, his family, and their wagons and livestock were ferried across the river to the friendlier shores of Iowa. Charles Shumway assured himself a place in Mormon history that winter day as he led out in the slow exodus of Mormon refugees, reluctantly leaving the City of Joseph, which had been their home for seven years.[1]

Never had Nauvoo been more prosperous. The previous year a steady stream of British emigrants had swelled the population

---

1. The story of Charles Shumway and, through his experiences, the tale of the trail west and settlement in the Great Basin are effectively told in Joseph E. Brown, *The Mormon Trek West: The Journey of American Exiles* (New York: Doubleday, 1980). The narrative account is beautifully illustrated with photographs by Dan Guravich. Like Wallace Stegner's *The Gathering of Zion* (New York: McGraw-Hill, 1964), the text is not footnoted, nor does it include a bibliography, though the diary entries used to tell the story are all credited.

with skilled craftsmen, artisans, and eager workers. Public buildings along with sturdy brick homes replaced log cabins and frame
huts. The city now boasted a Seventies Hall, music and cultural
halls, and even the beginnings of a university.[2] As the Saints prospered, tithing had increased, and the temple rose steadily skyward.
Ann Pitchforth, newly arrived from England in May of 1845, was
thrilled with her new homeland. "We are as comfortable as can
be," she wrote home to her parents. "Nauvoo is a quiet, peaceable
place, & we are not in the least afraid of anything."[3]

The death of Joseph Smith a year earlier had stunned his fol-
lowers. His enemies were certain it would mark the end of
Mormonism. Instead, it spurred efforts to complete the temple
as a monument to their fallen leader and a symbol of the fulfill-
ment of his mission. Nothing could have united the Saints more.
"There appears to be the most union that has ever been," Zina
Jacobs observed. "The faithful are determined to keep the law of
God. . . . The Temple prospers."[4]

By the end of that year, however, their dreams of permanence would once again come to a dismaying end. Though plans
had long been entertained for eventual settlement in the West,[5]
Church leaders had hoped that Nauvoo might remain intact as a
"temple city" and "a corner stake of Zion."[6] But that was not to

---

2. See letter of Brigham Young to Wilford Woodruff, 27 June 1845, in Joseph Smith, *History of the Church of Jesus Christ of Latter-day Saints,* 7 vols. (Salt Lake City: Deseret News, 1932) 7:431.

3. Ann Hughlings Pitchforth to Father & Mother, May 1845, holograph, Special Collections, Harold B. Lee Library, Brigham Young University, Provo, Utah.

4. Diary of Zina Huntington Jacobs (Young), 10 March 1845, Archives, Church of Jesus Christ of Latter-day Saints, Salt Lake City, Utah, hereinafter cited as LDS Church Archives. Brigham Young elab-
orates on this theme in his letter to Wilford Woodruff, 27 June 1845, in Joseph Smith, *History of the Church* 7:430–32.

5. An excellent study on the early references to the Rocky Mountains as a refuge for the Saints is Ronald K. Esplin, "'A Place Prepared': Joseph, Brigham and the Quest for Promised Refuge in the West," *Journal of Mormon History* 9 (1982): 85–111. For a larger study, see Lewis Clark Christian, "A Study of Mormon Knowledge of the American Far West Prior to the Exodus (1830–February 1846)" (Master's thesis, Brigham Young University, 1972); a shorter version is Christian, "Mormon Foreknowledge of the West," *Brigham Young University Studies* 21 (Fall 1981): 403–15.

6. Joseph Smith, *History of the Church* 6:406. This and other references to the place Nauvoo would fill in the ultimate expansion of the Church can be found in Esplin, "'A Place Prepared,'" 85–111, esp. 95–96.

be. The peace and calm that Ann Pitchforth enjoyed in the spring of 1845 were gone by fall.

First a few and then a flood of families sought shelter in Nauvoo when mobbers began burning Mormon homes and barns in the outlying communities. The county sheriff, J. B. Backenstos, admitted defeat in trying "to raise law and order citizens to quell the mob," and he advised Brigham Young to raise his own defense.[7] It was becoming ever more evident that Illinois was going to be a replay of Missouri. But Brigham Young gathered resolve from the events. "The mob seem determined to drive us to our duty in gathering," Brigham Young wrote to Sheriff Backenstos, "and then drive us to carry the fulness of the gospel from among them and carry it to Israel."[8] In the larger plan for the Church, Nauvoo was only a way station on the journey to that undefined place in the West that Joseph had envisioned as early as 1832. The time was clearly at hand to give substance to that vision. When hostilities between the Mormons and mobbers escalated to bloodshed and a general conflict seemed imminent, Church leaders agreed to remove the Saints from the City of Joseph the following spring.[9]

At the final conference in Nauvoo in the fall of 1845, Church leaders revealed their agreement to vacate the city. Their task was to kindle the Saints' commitment to sacrifice once again their material welfare for the sake of the gospel. George Whitaker, a British convert, remembered that everyone voted to leave,[10] but many wondered how they would be able to do it. "However much the people may seem disposed to not go," Amasa Lyman explained, "the sails are set, the wind is fair, and we are

7. Joseph Smith, *History of the Church* 7:444.

8. Joseph Smith, *History of the Church* 7:445. Israel, in this instance, referred to the Indians, or remnants of the Lamanites, descendants of the house of Israel.

9. When the Nauvoo Charter was revoked some months after the death of Joseph Smith, the citizens renamed Nauvoo the City of Joseph.

10. "Life of George Whitaker, A Utah Pioneer, as written by himself," 8, typescript, Utah State Historical Society.

bound to weather the point, whether we will or not; for we are not at the helm."[11] For Louisa Pratt the news fell on her ear "like the funeral knell of all departed joys." Her husband, Addison, was halfway around the world preaching the gospel in the Society Islands; like many others, she caught the vision of a new Zion in the West but without any assurance of how she was going to get there with her four young daughters. "What could I do," she thought, "with my little means and my helpless family, in launching out into the wilderness. I had no male relative to take charge of my affairs." When no immediate help was proffered, she met the challenge with her usual display of spirit: "I will show them what I can do." That feisty self-reliance carried Louisa and her daughters all the way to Salt Lake City on their own.[12]

Anticipating a spring exodus, Church leaders organized the Saints into twenty-five traveling companies of a hundred families each, with subdivisions of fifties and tens and a leader assigned to each division. Over the next six months, under the direction of the captains of hundred, Nauvoo became a builder's workshop.[13] Wagon shops were set up in buildings throughout the city, and wheelwrights, carpenters, and cabinetmakers became overnight "foremen wagon makers."[14] Untrained workers prepared timber to build the wagons, and women sewed wagon covers, quilts, tents, and clothing. The feverish industry became a study in contradiction.[15] While such activity showed the Saints' intention of leaving, work steadily continued on the temple, a powerful symbol of permanence. But their divided efforts made

---

11. Joseph Smith, *History of the Church* 7:468.

12. Reminiscences of Louisa Barnes Pratt (1879), LDS Church Archives.

13. Bathsheba W. Smith described the city as "one vast mechanic shop, as nearly every family was engaged in making wagons. Our parlor was used as a paint-shop for the wagons. All were making preparations to leave the ensuing winter." In Edward W. Tullidge, *The Women of Mormondom* (New York, 1877; reprint, Salt Lake City, 1975), 321.

14. Joseph Smith, *History of the Church* 7:535.

15. Joseph Smith, *History of the Church* 7:535–36. See also "Life of George Whitaker," 9.

sense: if they were to be materially dispossessed, at least they would not leave spiritually deprived.

The temple was not wholly finished until May of 1846, after many of the Saints had already left Nauvoo, but they left endowed. Brigham Young had dedicated the attic story on Sunday, 30 November 1845, to enable the Saints to begin receiving the saving ordinances.[16] On 10 December, Mary Ann Young, Vilate Kimball, and Elizabeth Ann Whitney, who had received their endowments from Joseph and Emma Smith, began administering the ordinances in the temple, joined later that day by Brigham Young and Heber C. Kimball.[17] Others were appointed to assist in the work. So anxious were the Saints to receive their endowments that some willing workers stayed each night to administer the ordinances around the clock. By the time the last endowment was given in early spring, fifty-six hundred members had received their temple blessings. For Sarah Pea Rich, those blessings made the westward trek possible. They "caused us joy and comfort in the midst of all our sorrows, and enabled us to have faith in God, knowing He would guide us and sustain us in the unknown journey that lay before us. For if it had not been for the faith and knowledge that was bestowed upon us in that Temple by the influence and help of the Spirit of the Lord, our journey would have been like one taking a leap in the dark, to start out on such a journey in the winter as it were, and in our state of poverty, it would seem like walking into the jaws of death."[18] For some it was.

---

16. As early as May 1842, Joseph Smith had introduced the temple ordinances to several of his closest associates, and before his death as many as sixty-five men and women had received all of the temple ordinances. Frequently noting that he might not live long enough to teach the endowment ceremony in the temple, he presciently endowed these trusted followers in preparation of performing the saving ordinances to the body of the Church. For details of this selected "endowment group," see Andrew F. Ehat, "Joseph Smith's Introduction of Temple Ordinances and the 1844 Mormon Succession Question" (master's thesis, Brigham Young University, 1982).

17. Joseph Smith, *History of the Church* 7:541–42. The temple was dedicated privately by Joseph Young on 30 April and publicly from 1–3 May by Orson Hyde. Thousands of Saints attended the services. Wilford Woodruff addressed three thousand Saints at the temple on 10 May.

18. Reminiscences of Sarah De Armon Pea Rich (1885–93), LDS Church Archives.

This was an undertaking of immense proportions. Approximately thirteen thousand Latter-day Saints lived in Nauvoo and its satellite communities.[19] Hundreds more were scattered about the states. And thousands had accepted the gospel in the British Isles, waiting to join the Saints wherever the gathering place was to be. Not all would choose to go west that year, and some not at all, but to lead a people of such vast number over more than thirteen hundred miles of hazardous trails to a destination that was more a direction than a place took both enormous courage and limitless faith. Brigham Young had both. Those who followed needed a comparable faith. These men and women had every opportunity to doubt the mission he so eloquently pronounced, to reject the call to the unknown, or to question the strength of their own conviction—but most did not. "My faith is to gather with the people of God," wrote Eliza Cheney to her family in New York, "and though I might swim in wealth if I returned . . . I could not be happy there."[20]

Among the throngs of Americans going west, the Mormons were distinct. As one historian noted, unlike other westering people, the Saints were responding to the push of continual persecution and to the pull of a free, unsettled region that could offer a permanent gathering place.[21] It was not material wealth they were seeking but a spiritual haven. Theirs was a whole community on the move, carrying not only individual and family possessions but also their community records and the documents, histories, minutes, and other artifacts of their sixteen-

19. From a variety of sources, Susan Easton Black sets the Nauvoo population at eleven thousand in 1845, but there may well have been several thousand more throughout Hancock County and environs and in Iowa settlements along the Mississippi River. See Black, "How Large Was the Population of Nauvoo?" *Brigham Young University Studies* 35, no. 2 (1995): 91–94.

20. Eliza Cheney to Parents, Brothers and Sisters, January 1848, in Historical Letters and Sketches, 1841–1919, Eliza Jane Rawson Collection, LDS Church Archives.

21. Frederick A. Norwood, *Strangers and Exiles: A History of Religious Refugees,* 2 vols. (Nashville: Abingdon Press, 1969) 2:246.

year-old religion.[22] Even the Nauvoo temple bell went west, reclaimed from the belfry of the Methodist Church in Nauvoo, where it had been taken after the first contingent of Saints left the city.[23]

What most set them apart from other migrants, including the emigrant Saints, however, was the spiritual endowment they had received in the temple. This became their motivation and resource when times were grim. "We go as Abraham went," Sally Randall wrote to her parents and siblings, "not knowing whither we go but the Lord will go before us, and be our front and [our] rearward."[24] These Saints were also set apart from other westering people by their commitment to aid all who wished to gather to Zion. In the last conference of the Church before they left Nauvoo, the Saints, assembled in the temple, made a covenant with their leaders that they would "give all to help to take the poor; and every honest industrious member who wants to go." Sometimes referred to as the Nauvoo Covenant, it was invoked many times throughout the long period of emigration.[25]

The restless mobs and false rumors of government troops poised to intercept the Saints' planned exit in the spring became

22. In November 1845, Willard Richards, Church historian, made a plea to the Saints to collect and bring to him any records, documents, maps, charts, books, or information of any kind relating to the Church and requested all missionaries to submit a written report of their experiences if they had not done so, all to be included in *The General History of the Church*. See Joseph Smith, *History of the Church* 7:526. Eliza R. Snow preserved the minutes of the Nauvoo Relief Society, which she carried with her throughout Utah territory when she organized Relief Societies in 1867–68. These minutes were of special value to the women of the Church, containing the carefully recorded words of the Prophet Joseph Smith to them, outlining their responsibilities, position, and privileges within the Church.

23. The Nauvoo Temple bell was crafted in England, cast in bronze, and sent under the care of Wilford Woodruff to hang in the tower of the temple even before the temple was completed. When the Saints abandoned Nauvoo, the bell was taken down and hung in the belfry of the Methodist Church, from which it was later removed by a group of Mormons who carried it safely to Winter Quarters and from thence to the Salt Lake Valley in the first company to follow the pioneer company. It was finally installed in a campanile on Temple Square under the auspices of the Relief Society in 1942, the hundredth anniversary of that society's founding. For more information, see Mary Grant Judd, "A Monument with a Message," *Relief Society Magazine* 29 (January 1942): 12, and Lois Leetham Tanner, "Old Bell, Temple Bell," unpublished paper in author's possession.

24. Sally Randall to Parents, Brothers and Sisters, 1 June 1846, in Letters of Sally Randall, LDS Church Archives.

25. *History of the Church* 7:464–65.

worrisome. To buy time for the anxious but unprepared Saints and to show compliance with their agreement to leave, Brigham Young decided to lead out from Nauvoo with just the Twelve and their families earlier than the time agreed upon. Then, when better prepared, the rest of the Saints were to follow in the spring and summer. He found, however, that the great demand for temple ordinances delayed his departure.[26] While he was thus occupied, some of the Saints, worried and unwilling to wait until spring, crowded the streets leading to the river, awaiting a chance to cross and expecting their leaders to follow immediately.[27] Few had been able to acquire the extensive store of supplies itemized by Parley P. Pratt or to get proper teams and wagons to carry them. They came anyway, in whatever conveyances they had, bringing whatever provisions they had collected. Thus it was that on 4 February, Charles Shumway, not Brigham Young, crossed the Mississippi and led out in the great western exodus that would continue from Nauvoo for the next eight months. On that same day, a small band of Eastern Saints, 70 men, 68 women, and 100 children, began an odyssey of their own. Urged by Apostle Orson Pratt to "flee out of Babylon either by land or sea," as the Nauvoo Saints had been warned to do, they gathered their belongings, paid $50.00 for their passage, and sailed out of New York harbor on the four-hundred-fifty-ton chartered ship *Brooklyn.* Samuel Brannan presided over the company.[28]

Besides its passengers and their belongings, the ship carried a wide range of equipment essential to establishing a community somewhere yet unknown to these waterway pioneers. Flour mills,

---

26. Joseph Smith, *History of the Church* 7:578–79.

27. Helen Mar Whitney, "Our Travels Beyond the Mississippi," *Woman's Exponent* 12 (1 December 1883): 83. Her account is made up of her own reminiscences and the daily journal of her husband, Horace Whitney, as well as other pertinent documents and personal accounts.

28. Samuel Brannan, born in 1819 in Maine, was baptized into the Church sometime in the 1840s after becoming acquainted with William Smith, the Prophet's brother. Supporting William Smith's claim to succeed Joseph Smith as prophet, Brannan was disfellowshipped but later reaffiliated with the Church. In New York he published first *The Prophet* and later *The Messenger* before his appointment by Orson Pratt to lead the *Brooklyn* Saints to California. He died in California in 1889.

crockery, tents, farm implements, medical supplies, food, a printing press and paper, books, and even some farm animals accompanied them on the six-month-long journey. The twenty-four-thousand-mile voyage took the *Brooklyn* as far west as the Hawaiian Islands before circling round to Yerba Buena, the seaport that eventually became San Francisco.[29] On 31 July, the company disembarked on land recently claimed by the United States, while the army continued the campaign against Mexico south of Monterey. By this time, the Mormon Battalion had begun its long march to California to do its part in the campaign.

The *Brooklyn* Saints, with their extensive amount of equipment, set up a thriving settlement, doubling the population of Yerba Buena. They anticipated a meeting with the displaced Nauvoo Saints the next year. When Samuel Brannan learned the following spring that Brigham Young did not intend to settle in California, he hastened to meet him on the trail and persuade him of the advantages of a California settlement. Unsuccessful, Brannan returned to the West Coast, became a wealthy and influential man for a period, but relinquished his ties to the Church. Though some remained in California, many of the *Brooklyn* Saints eventually rejoined the body of the Church in Utah.[30]

The early departure of the Nauvoo Saints upset the carefully planned order of travel as families rushed across the Mississippi to the relative safety of Iowa. No orderly procession of white-topped wagons filed over the ice-bound Mississippi, as so many artists have depicted. All manner of vehicles lined up at the river front waiting to be ferried over on flatboats. Some were the required heavy-duty wagons, whose specifications had been care-

29. All but twelve of the original voyagers reached California, with two additional passengers born on the way.

30. "The Ship Brooklyn Saints," in Kate B. Carter, *Our Pioneer Heritage*, 20 vols. (Salt Lake City: Daughters of Utah Pioneers, 1960) 3:473–587.

fully outlined, but others were smaller farm wagons, and many people traveled in horse-drawn carriages and buggies. Oxen, mules, cattle, and horses were all part of the flatboat cargo until the river froze over later that month. Animals sometimes bolted, upsetting the wagons and spilling their contents into the river. Thomas Grover lost two oxen and most of his belongings when someone spit in the eye of his startled ox, causing it to stumble overboard.[31]

Many in these early companies were inadequately prepared, and families were sometimes separated as husbands went ahead as teamsters, guards, or company clerks or else stayed behind to sell their homes and property while sending their families on. Some women awaiting childbirth preferred the uncertainty of the city to the unfamiliarity of the trail.[32] Trustees of the Church also stayed to sell the Church's property and oversee the exodus of the remaining Saints. More than two-thirds of the Saints remained in Nauvoo after the rushed winter exodus, following at intervals during the spring and summer months. Only the very poor, unable to acquire the means to leave, were still in the city by autumn, when the mobs forced their exit.[33]

Charles Shumway and the Saints following after him col-

---

31. Susan Easton Black describes this and other unfortunate incidents during the Iowa portion of the exodus in "Suffering and Death on the Plains of Iowa," *Brigham Young University Studies* 21 (Fall 1981): 431–39.

32. The oft-told story of nine women giving birth at Sugar Creek or one of the other temporary campsites is difficult to corroborate since there are no contemporary accounts. Eliza R. Snow is credited with being the original source, having "heard" that nine babies were born one fearful night, a statement quoted in Tullidge, *The Women of Mormondom*, 307. Her account is defended by Richard Bennett in "Eastward to Eden: The Nauvoo Rescue Missions," *Dialogue: A Journal of Mormon Thought* 19 (Winter 1986): 107. Carol Lynn Pearson argues that additional evidence suggests that the event took place not in Sugar Creek in February but instead in October 1846 among the "Poor Camp." See "'Nine Children Were Born': A Historical Problem from the Sugar Creek Episode," *Brigham Young University Studies* 21 (Fall 1981): 441–44.

33. William G. Hartley has identified these three distinct migrating periods and noted that many of those who left in the spring, as planned, made it to the Missouri before those who had left in the winter. See Hartley, "Spring Exodus from Nauvoo: Act Two in the Mormon Evacuation Drama," in Susan Easton Black and William G. Hartley, eds., *Iowa Mormon Trail: Legacy of Faith and Courage* (Orem, Utah: Helix Publishing, 1997), 61–84. The later groups did not have the company of Church leaders, for the most part, and traveled in collections of family groups. Many traveled independently.

lected across the river at Sugar Creek, about seven miles from
Nauvoo, awaiting Church leaders, most of whom were, ironically, still in Nauvoo. In another season Sugar Creek would have
been a camper's delight, and even in February, before it snowed,
it was an inviting shelter in a wooded grove by the creek.
Eighteen-year-old Emmeline Whitney's first view of the camp,
at sunset on 27 February, reminded her of a romantic biblical
painting: "It looked like pictures I have seen of the ancients
pitching their tents and journeying from place to place with their
cattle and their goods."[34] Helen Mar Whitney found camp life at
Sugar Creek, at the outset, a novel experience and "even a pleasant one compared with what was laying before us." Most of the
campers had brought tents, and their wagons and whatever provisions they had with them made life fairly comfortable at that
point. During the almost month-long wait before moving on,
however, the Saints began to lose their studied cheerfulness. A
heavy snowfall and dropping temperatures, leaking tents and
wagon covers, and memories of warm rooms and comfortable
beds began to take a toll on their goodwill. The arrival of the legendary William Pitt and his brass band was a welcome sight and
lightened the mood of the disheartened exiles. "Everyone danced
to amuse ourselves as well as to keep our blood in proper circu-
lation," Helen Whitney remembered.[35] As Wallace Stegner
observed, "Music was their gift and their blessing, an expression
of their oneness in the hostile wilderness."[36]

Brigham Young's powerful presence and rousing oratory was
what worked the miracle, to be repeated many times before this
long journey was over. When he arrived in mid-February, he
reorganized the companies and unified the travelers by creating

---

34. Diary of Emmeline B. Wells, 27 February 1846, Special Collections, Harold B. Lee Library,
Brigham Young University, Provo, Utah.

35. Helen Mar Whitney, "Our Travels Beyond the Mississippi," 83. William Purdy presents a brief
history of Pitt's band in "They Marched Their Way West: The Nauvoo Brass Band," *Ensign* 10 (July 1980):
21–23.

36. Stegner, *The Gathering of Zion,* 81.

an orderly network of communication and responsibility. The people stirred up their faith and renewed their resolve to move on with courage and hope. It took until the first of March for all available Church leaders to assemble at Sugar Creek, but then the Camp of Israel, now several thousand strong with five hundred wagons, began to roll.[37] Their troubles were just beginning.

Accounts of the three-hundred-mile Iowa crossing reveal why it was the most difficult part of the whole westward trek for these Nauvoo exiles. At first they followed primitive country roads uncomfortably close to the northern border of Missouri. But in the Missouri settlements, more numerous than in Iowa, they could exchange their possessions and especially their labor for supplies. As historian Stanley B. Kimball has noted, the Camp of Israel was like an industrial army marching through Iowa, its men stopping off to work as rail-splitters, cornhuskers, and handymen.[38]

But their own needs were only part of their concern. Until growth of the spring prairie grass, their animals depended on the corn and other feed found only in the settlements. Orson Pratt recalled, "It became quite a difficulty to sustain our numerous cattle and horses, for it required many hundreds of bushels of grain daily to keep them from perishing."[39] Once again the William Pitt band proved its value to the wandering Saints. Besides bolstering Mormon spirits, the band entertained settle-

---

37. An accurate count of the company assembled at Sugar Creek is impossible. According to Stanley B. Kimball, a historian of the trail, there were likely about three thousand individuals and five hundred wagons, with close to ten thousand Saints left in Nauvoo and the surrounding area. Most of them would follow by the end of September. See Kimball, *Historic Resource Study: Mormon Pioneer National Historic Trail* (Washington, D.C.: United States Department of the Interior/National Park Service, 1991), 36–37. The term *Camp of Israel* was usually applied to this first group of pioneers. Eliza R. Snow perpetuated the name as well as the Israel analogy through her series of poems written on the trail entitled "Camp of Israel." See *Eliza R. Snow, An Immortal* (Salt Lake City: Nicholas G. Morgan, Sr. Foundation, 1957): 247–51. She also left a legacy of comfort poems memorializing the many deaths that occurred along the trail.

38. See Stanley B. Kimball, "Social Life on the Mormon Trail and the Meaning of the Camp of Israel: An Essay," in Black and Hartley, eds., *The Iowa Mormon Trail*, 85–104.

39. N. B. Lundwall, comp., *Exodus of Modern Israel, From the Diary of Orson Pratt and Others* (Salt Lake City: N. B. Lundwall, n.d.), 19.

ment residents along the way and earned money needed to purchase corn and grain.

Nothing impeded their progress more than the weather,
however. The winter departure exposed the travelers to the chill-
ing cold of the humid climate, and spring brought heavy rain,
pelting them in torrents, turning their tents and wagon covers
into sieves. Spells of dry weather brought out snakes and other
insects, alternately frightening and harassing the vulnerable travelers and their animals. For nearly four months this vanguard
company trailed on to the Missouri (later companies would make
the crossing in four weeks). For a third of those months, they
faced either heavy snow or drenching rain. Some days the camp
could travel no more than three miles.

By late April almost all of Iowa was an open prairie of tall
grasses, flanked by groves of oak and hickory trees, but the heavy
rainfalls softened the ground, and wagon wheels and animals
sank deep into the muddy trails. The thick, deep, muddy pits
required double- and even triple-teaming to get the wagons
through. The riverbanks and steep bluffs adjoining them, made
slippery by the spring rains, slowed travel even more. Jean Rio
Baker (Pearce) described the road her wagon train followed a few
years later as "a perfect succession of hills, vallies, bogs, mudholes, log bridges, quagmires, with stumps of trees, a foot above
the surface of the watery mud, so that without the utmost care,
the wagons would be overturned, 10 times a day."[40]

Fording the swollen streams was backbreaking work as men
and boys using heavy ropes pulled the teams and wagons across. If
the rivers weren't too deep, women and girls tied up their skirts
to wade across. Everyone stayed wet until they could dry their
clothes later by campfires. All had to help. Joseph Fielding
remarked on the cooperation he saw at one river crossing: "One

---

40. Journal of Jean Rio Griffiths Baker Pearce, 2 May 1851, typescript, LDS Church Archives.

might have taken us for two Armies encamped on either Side of the River waiting the Signal for Conflict, but how different was the Case when we saw almost the Whole Strength of the one wading through the River from one to 3 feet in depth to help their Friends."[41]

The daily round of domestic tasks proved especially burdensome. Lucy Smith recalled the difficulty of preparing a meal on a blustery, freezing day. The howling wind continually threatened to put out her campfire and blow sparks on her tent, and when dinner was over, washing the dishes was no easier. "When I would wash a dish and raise it out of the water, there would be ice on it before I could get it wiped," she recalled.[42]

With an eye to those who followed, company clerks kept careful records of the best campsites. Sugar Creek, Richardson's Point, the Chariton River, and Locust Creek were all favored stopping places for the first part of the journey. But Locust Creek was the setting for a historic event not shared by the others. On 15 April, William Clayton, company clerk and historian, was resting after a difficult night on guard, when he heard the news that his wife, Diantha, who had stayed in Nauvoo expecting her first child, had given birth to a son. The happy announcement warranted not only a grand celebration, again featuring William Pitt and his band (of which William Clayton was a member), but it also inspired Clayton to write that great hymn of hope, "Come, Come, Ye Saints." If any one expression could define the spirit that animated this wilderness journey, it was this hymn. It became the pioneer anthem and is known worldwide as the great hymn of the Latter-day Saints.[43]

---

41. Diary of Joseph Fielding (December 1843–March 1859), 149, LDS Church Archives.

42. "Original Historical Narrative of Lucy Meserve Smith" (1888–1890), LDS Church Archives.

43. Details surrounding the writing of this famous hymn can be found in Paul E. Dahl, "'All is Well . . . ': The Story of 'the Hymn That Went around the World,'" *Brigham Young University Studies* 21 (Fall 1981): 515–27. Dahl notes that while William Clayton wrote that Ellen Kimball (wife of Heber C. Kimball) brought him the news of his new son, having read it in a letter she received from Nauvoo, Helen Mar Kimball Whitney claims credit for breaking the news to Clayton. See ibid., 518.

Each morning the Camps of Israel were reluctantly roused by a bugle call. "A morning in camp," Emmeline B. Wells remembered, was "not very amusing." Often when the campers awoke, they were missing horses and cattle, which sometimes took days to find, or they suffered from minor annoyances such as kettles upsetting and drenching the morning fire. Tents leaked or blew over in the night, and fresh snow greeted the travelers on many mornings. Despite such incidents, she recalled, "Somehow we always felt safe." "There was order in the camp, men stood guard at night and we slept soundly in the open air." But she also found the Iowa trek difficult to talk about even fifty years afterwards. "The wonder is," she wrote, "how we had the courage, the perseverance, the endurance to accomplish it."[44]

As they pushed farther west and northward from the Missouri border, provisions gave out, settlements disappeared, and sickness spread, prompting them to establish a temporary resting place where those unable to go farther could stop, put in a crop, and regroup for later travel to the Missouri. Here the Nauvoo covenant came vividly to life. The Saints remembered their pledge to "not cease their exertions until every individual of them who desired, and was unable to gather to the Rocky Mountains by his own means, was brought to that place."[45] This settlement was its first test. It would not only provide food and rest for those needing them then, but it would also be a way station for the thousands of Saints yet to come. When the site was chosen, about a hundred forty-five miles from Nauvoo, workers began immediately to lay out the settlement, erecting fences, building cabins, and planting crops. They called it Garden Grove.

George Whitaker marveled at the cooperation that built this small hamlet. When they decided on the place, he wrote, "the whole camp was then reorganized. It was concluded that we would

---

44. "A Morning in Camp," *Woman's Exponent* 29 (15 July, 1 August 1900): 17–18.
45. In Andrew Jenson, "Church Emigration," *The Contributor* 13 (December 1891): 80.

fence in a large field of about six hundred acres and plant it in corn and vegetables. Every man was put in his proper place to work. Some worked at cutting house logs, some at building houses, some at cutting timber for rails, some at splitting rails, some at plowing, some at planting corn and vegetables, while others commenced to put up the fence, and a certain number were sent out to herd and take care of the stock. Every man went to work with a will. There were no idlers amongst us. We were all full of life and spirit. We had almost forgotten our trials and troubles of our two month's journey. . . . In about 14 or 15 days we had quite a little town built up."[46]

Almost as soon as the settlement took shape, Brigham Young organized a branch of the Church with Samuel Bent as president and David Fullmer and Aaron Johnson as his counselors. They would be both the temporal and spiritual leaders of the small group who would winter there. But Garden Grove struggled to meet its lofty purpose. With families passing through daily hoping to be reprovisioned, the drain on the community's resources was heavy. Supply simply couldn't keep up with demand. And those uncontrollable plagues of pioneer life, disease and death, swept through the settlement. President Bent, an early victim, died just three months after his appointment.[47]

Prospects for the nearly six hundred Saints who had settled for the winter in Garden Grove were grim. One of them, Luman Shurtliff, worried that there were "only provisions enough to last until April as prudent as we could possibly be and clothing very scant. From April to July," he feared, "we should be in suffering conditions."[48] The generosity of their Iowa neighbors and

---

46. "Life of George Whitaker," 19. See also Lundwall, *Exodus of Modern Israel*, 24.

47. Information on Garden Grove is taken from Leland H. Gentry, "The Mormon Way Stations: Garden Grove and Mt. Pisgah," *Brigham Young University Studies* 21 (Fall 1981): 445–61; and Karla Gunzenhauser, "The Settlement at Garden Grove, Iowa," *The Nauvoo Journal* 6 (Fall 1994): 14–44.

48. Autobiography of Luman Shurtliff, typescript condensation of original journal, 89, Special Collections, Harold B. Lee Library, Brigham Young University, as quoted in Gunzenhauser, "Settlement at Garden Grove," 17.

their own resourcefulness helped them survive that first year. Ensuing years brought more fruitful crops. While Garden Grove never really prospered or grew much beyond its original dimensions, it nonetheless provided an essential resting and recruiting place for the Mormon exiles.[49]

After preparing the Garden Grove settlement, those who chose not to stay moved on in a more northwesterly direction, where they established another way station on a fork of the Grand River, about forty miles beyond Garden Grove. Well situated on the brow of a hill that opened on to grassy vales interrupted by occasional gentle slopes, the new settlement was given the biblical name of Mount Pisgah by Parley P. Pratt. Here another settlement was laid out and a branch of the Church organized to care for the Saints who would winter there. William Huntington was appointed president with Charles C. Rich and Ezra T. Benson as his counselors. Sixty-three-year-old William Huntington was a worthy but reluctant president. He wondered how in his straitened circumstances he was to care for his large family while also shepherding the Saints at Mount Pisgah. He had "much to discuss with the Lord" when he retired with his counselors to a private area beyond the town site, where they pitched a tent, dressed in their temple robes, and asked for divine help. For William Huntington, the struggle soon ceased. Like President Bent at Garden Grove, he died just three months after his appointment and was buried at Mount Pisgah.

Mount Pisgah became a travel hub for Mormons, some going on to Council Bluffs, others returning east as far as Nauvoo to gather up families, and some settling in for a season in the camp or on its outskirts. Daily, wagons were arriving in the massive spring exodus of some ten thousand Saints from Nauvoo. As

---

49. Gentry, "Mormon Way Stations," 445–53. More information about Garden Grove can be found in the journals kept of the Iowa trek. An early study of Garden Grove is Lynn Robert Webb, "The Contributions of the Temporary Settlements of Garden Grove, Mount Pisgah, and Kanesville, Iowa, to Mormon Emigration, 1846–1852" (master's thesis, Brigham Young University, 1954).

Eliza R. Snow observed, "Companies were constantly arriving
and others departing; while those who intended stopping till the
next spring were busily engaged in making gardens, and otherwise preparing for winter—sheltering themselves in rude log huts
for temporary residence." She noted that camps were strung
along for several hundred miles across Iowa, both temporary and
semi-permanent.[50] Despite the facade of bustling industry, the
Saints at Pisgah suffered from the inevitable appearance of disease and death that stalked frontier settlements; by late summer
the "autumnal ague" held the newcomers in its grip. When Emily
Partridge Young arrived in late August, the natural beauty that
surrounded the town could not offset the sickly pallor and
squalid look of the fledgling community. She declared it to be
"the most like nowhere" of any place she had ever been.[51] It did
not remain so, however, and sheltered more than two thousand
Saints during its six years of existence. By 1852 it had served its
purpose and passed quietly into oblivion, except in the diaries
of the people who once passed its way.

The Saints were now in Indian country. Yet, in all the time
they spent at the Missouri and during their many years of travel
on the overland trail, they had few serious skirmishes with the
various Indian nations they encountered. They were especially
welcomed by the Pottawattamies, who claimed a kinship with the
Mormons in their common exile. Their chief, Pied Riche,
reminded the Mormons that the Pottawattamies were also a dispossessed people, driven from their homeland in Michigan years
earlier. "We must help one another," he said, "and the Great
Spirit will help us both. Because one suffers and does not deserve

50. As quoted in Tullidge, *The Women of Mormondom*, 314–15. A splendid compilation of Eliza
R. Snow's personal writings with detailed annotation is Maureen Ursenbach Beecher, *The Personal
Writings of Eliza Roxcy Snow* (Salt Lake City: University of Utah Press, 1995).
51. Emily Partridge Young to Brigham Young, August 1846, quoted in Dean C. Jessee, "Brigham
Young's Family: The Wilderness Years," in *The Exodus and Beyond: Essays in Mormon History*, ed.
Donald Q. Cannon and Lyndon W. Cook (Salt Lake City: Hawkes Publishing, Inc., 1980), 29.

it is no reason he shall suffer always. We may live to see it right yet. If we do not, our children will."[52]

Though the first vanguard of Saints did not reach the Council Bluffs area on the Missouri River until 15 June, Brigham Young still hoped to push on to the Rockies that summer. But he now planned to recruit only a company of young, healthy men who, with the Twelve, could travel rapidly to the West, establishing way stations and planting crops for the body of Saints who would follow the next spring after a much-needed rest and reprovisioning at the Missouri. He therefore sent messengers to Mount Pisgah and Garden Grove requesting as many volunteers and supplies as could be spared.

But this plan, too, would be abandoned. At the same time that he began recruiting for his advance company, a U.S. Army representative, Captain James Allen, appeared in Mount Pisgah, also requesting a volunteer company of young, healthy Mormons to go west. But Allen wanted them as soldiers, not pioneers. He promised each volunteer clothing, rations, a stock of guns, and some advance payment for one year's service in the war against Mexico. The request seemed ludicrous to most Saints, who at that time felt little loyalty to their government. The notice was first given to William Huntington, Mount Pisgah's branch president, who commented that Captain Allen delivered an "address to the brethren appropriate to his foolish errand." President Huntington responded with an address of his own "by way of commendation or as the old proverb says answering a fool according to his folly."[53] He then sent Captain Allen on to Council Bluffs to confer with Brigham Young. Sarah Rich voiced her reaction to what so many felt was a gross insensitivity to the Mormon plight. "A

52. Statement appears on a monument at Mount Pisgah, Iowa.
53. William Huntington, "A Brief Sketch of the Travel of William Huntington and his Family in Company with the Saints Who Left Nauvoo in the Winter of 1846," 26 June 1846, Special Collections, Harold B. Lee Library, Brigham Young University, Provo, Utah.

more cruel demand could not have been made upon us at this time of our affliction and poverty," she explained.[54] Some even feared a plot: that after taking the best men away, the rest of the camp would be destroyed on the plains, or if the Mormons refused to cooperate, the army would attack "and put an end to Mormonism."[55]

What few knew was that six months earlier Jesse C. Little, president of the Eastern States Mission, had been negotiating in Washington, D.C., with President Polk for financial help to relocate the Mormons in the West. While this plan of volunteer military service, which President Polk proposed, was not quite what Church leaders had hoped for, it would serve government interests and show Mormon loyalty while providing the Church much-needed revenue through the soldiers' pay. It would also be a means of transporting at least five hundred of the Saints to the West. Recognizing the benefits of the proposal as well as the hardships it would impose, Brigham Young agreed to it and promised to assist the hard-pressed families of the volunteers to go west, where they would be reunited with their men.[56] Nevertheless, many battalion wives were left to fend for themselves while the soldiers' advance pay bought community supplies and general provisions for the forthcoming trek. Fannie Parks Taggart, for instance, had no home of her own at Council Bluffs but resourcefully exchanged her nursing services for housing, moving from place to place as she was needed.[57]

It was no easier for the volunteers to leave than for their families to see them go. Reluctant volunteer Henry Standage was typ-

54. Reminiscences of Sarah Pea Rich, 28.

55. See "Narrative of Lucy Meserve Smith."

56. B. H. Roberts, *A Comprehensive History of the Church of Jesus Christ of Latter-day Saints*, 6 vols. (reprint, Provo, Utah: Brigham Young University Press, 1965) 3:60–121. Many studies have been done on the Battalion. See John F. Yurtinus, "A Ram in the Thicket," 2 vols. (Ph.D. diss., Brigham Young University, 1975); Norma Baldwin Ricketts, *The Mormon Battalion, United States Army of the West, 1846–1848* (Logan, Utah: Utah State University Press, 1996).

57. Carter, *Our Pioneer Heritage* 11:386–88.

ical. He was able to provide his wife and mother with a cow and three dollars, but they had neither a house nor a tent. He found housing for his widowed mother with a family willing to take her in, but his wife had to manage on her own.[58]

Within a month's time, the requested number of men answered the call to serve their country. The irony of their situation was not lost on the Saints. "It must ever remain a truth on the page of history," wrote Brigham Young, "that while the flower of Israel's camp were sustaining the wings of the American eagle, by their influence and arms in a foreign country [Mexico], their brothers, sisters, fathers, mothers, and children, were driven by mob violence from a free and independent state of the same national Republic."[59]

The volunteers were mustered in on 16 July. Before they marched away to California, the Saints treated them to a farewell ball. William Pitt was on hand to provide music for dancing. The party was so festive that no one noticed the lack of decorations or refreshments. The merriment could not hide the apprehension of families about to lose their menfolk, however. Drusilla Hendricks attended the dance with her son William. With Drusilla's husband crippled since the Haun's Mill incident, William was Drusilla's mainstay. But William wanted to go with the battalion, and Drusilla struggled to decide what to do. The next morning she watched him go about his work. "I got ready to get breakfast," she wrote, "and when I stepped up on the wagon tongue to get my flour I was asked by the same spirit that had spoken to me before, If I did not want the greatest glory and I answered with my natural voice, Yes, I did. Then how can you get it without making the greatest sacrifice, said the voice. I answered Lord, what lack I yet. Let your son go in the Battalion,

---

58. *The Pioneer*, January–February 1994, 14.

59. General Epistle from the Council of Twelve Apostles, 23 December 1847, *Millennial Star* 10 (15 March 1848): 82.

said the voice. I said it is too late, they are to be marched off this morning. That spirit then left me with the heart ache. I got breakfast and called the girls and their Father to come to the tent for prayers. William came wet with dew from the grass and we sat down around the board and my husband commenced asking the blessing on our food, when Thomas Williams came shouting at the top of his voice, saying "Turn out men, Turn out, for we do not wish to press you but we lack some men yet in the Battalion." William raised his eyes and looked me in the face. I knew then that he would go as well as I know now that he has been. . . . I went to milk the cows. . . . I thought the cows would be shelter for me and I knelt down and told the Lord if He wanted my child to take him, only spare his life and let him be restored to me and to the bosom of the church. I felt it was all I could do. Then the voice that talked with me in the morning answered me saying, It shall be done unto you as it was unto Abraham when he offered Isaac on the altar. I don't know whether I milked or not for I felt the Lord had spoken to me."[60]

By the end of the year, more than ten thousand Latter-day Saints had reached the Missouri River, setting up camps on both sides, nearly four thousand of them settling Winter Quarters on the west side of the Missouri. Hundreds more were scattered in the camps and settlements throughout Iowa. Until forced to move back to the Iowa side of the Missouri in 1848, Winter Quarters was the headquarters of the Church at the Missouri.[61] From 1848 to 1852, Kanesville, formerly Miller's Hollow, on the east bank of the Missouri, served as the center of Church activity at the Missouri.

---

60. "Historical Sketch of James Hendricks and Drusilla Dorris Hendricks," typescript copy, 26–27, LDS Church Archives.

61. Kanesville, Iowa, even more than Winter Quarters, played an important role in the history of the Church while the Saints occupied land by the Missouri River. Little published material is available on Thomas L. Kane, after whom Kanesville was named. Studies currently available are Albert Zobell, *Sentinel in the East: A Biography of Thomas L. Kane* (Salt Lake City: Nicholas G. Morgan Sr., 1965) and Leonard J. Arrington, "'In Honorable Remembrance': Thomas L. Kane's Services to the Mormons," *Brigham Young University Studies* 21 (Fall 1981): 389–402. Kane's papers now reside in Special Collections of the Harold B. Lee Library at Brigham Young University.

After settling the Saints at the Missouri, Brigham Young once again turned his thoughts to those still in Nauvoo. Nearly a thousand Saints still remained in the city, and news of increasing hostilities prompted Young, in response to the covenant made in Nauvoo, to send a rescue team with wagons and provisions to bring them to Winter Quarters. Captain Orval M. Allen headed an eleven-man corps. They left 14 September, poorly provisioned themselves but commissioned to invite contributions along the way. They were particularly heartened when they came across the Joseph Fielding company, which included Joseph Fielding's sisters, Mary Fielding Smith and Mercy Fielding Thompson. "Sister Mary Smith met us with a how do you do, and her other hand was full of charity of the right kind," Captain Allen wrote. He was touched by her concern for the impoverished Saints backed by her contribution of fifteen dollars and sixty pounds of flour. Her sister Mercy also gave him money to purchase supplies. "We ask the Lord to bless them," Captain Allen noted in his journal.

When the rescue party finally reached the Mississippi on 6 October, they found about three hundred of the evicted Saints scattered along its west bank in temporary campsites, unable to go further. Some of the refugees had families in various places across Iowa whom they hoped to join, but some were alone, like Louisa Norris, and dependent on generous friends. Louisa had watched her father die defending his family in the battle of Nauvoo and then found herself orphaned when her mother and infant sister died in their camp on the Mississippi. Allen's heart went out to these Saints, who were sick, hungry, ill equipped, poorly clothed, and dubious about joining the Camp of Israel at the Missouri, which they had heard was no better off than they were already.[62] His task was thus not only to rescue them but also

---

62. Richard E. Bennett analyzes the rescue efforts of the "poor camps" in "Eastward to Eden: The Nauvoo Rescue Missions," *Dialogue* 19 (Winter 1986): 100–108.

to revitalize their spirits. Within three days he had gathered up 151 people, about half the number waiting for help but all that he could transport. A second rescue team arrived soon after to collect the rest.

No one who kept a record of that perilous time failed to note in their recollections or diaries what Captain Allen described as a "direct manifestation of the mercy and goodness of God." As the first rescue team was preparing to leave with its band of sickly Saints on the morning of 9 October, a large flock of quail flew into the camp, startling the company. "Some fell on the Wagons, some under, and some alighted on the Breakfast tables," Captain Allen recorded. "The brethren and children ran after them and caught them alive with their hands. . . . There were so many killed that every man, woman, and child had them for their dinner." The quail returned again and again that day, circling the camp and alighting so the Saints could easily catch them, even the sick lying in their wagons. "Thus was showered down upon the poor persecuted Saints a sufficiency," Allen noted. "The brethren and Sisters praised God and glorified his name."[63]

The rescue teams that returned to the Missouri were surprised to see that a new city of several hundred cabins and sod houses had sprung up in their absence, all carefully laid out in neat square blocks. The town would number eight hundred dwellings before the Saints abandoned it. The roads between them were often muddy, and most of the houses offered little more than basic shelter, but they were full of hospitality and well situated for neighborliness. No one boasted of truly comfortable quarters, but a disparity was clearly visible. Helen Mar and Horace Whitney, newlyweds when they left Nauvoo, were happy

---

63. Diary of Orval Morgan Allen, 9 October 1846, microfilm of holograph, LDS Church Archives. Thomas Bullock also details the experience in his diary and in a letter to Elder Franklin Richards published in the *Millennial Star* 10 (15 January 1848): 28–29 and republished in Carter, *Our Pioneer Heritage* 8:237. Carter has collected many other accounts of this event, which are published in her various series of pioneer stories.

for a room of their own in a row of houses built by Helen's father, Heber C. Kimball. With a door, a window of four panes of glass, a dirt floor, and a smokey fireplace, it was similar to many other dwellings (except for the glass panes). But she was happy to lay down pieces of carpet that had weathered the Iowa journey and hang up curtains to partition the room into separate spaces for cooking and sleeping. She was pleased that her rocking chair had also managed to survive the journey intact.[64] Some managed to build two-story and multi-roomed houses with shingled roofs and puncheon floors, but many others had to make do with leaky tents and the damp, dark, sod houses that were little more than dugouts with roofs.[65] Bathsheba Smith reported that her husband, George A. Smith, built four cabins and a dugout for his family of five wives and several children. But Jane Richards and her sister wife, Elizabeth, whose husband Franklin was in England on Church business, shared a one-room cabin "just large enough for two little beds and a fireplace."[66]

In a letter to her relatives in the East written 5 July 1847, Fanny Young Murray noted the variety. "Some are good log houses," she observed, "and others about the medium sort and many poor indeed, but better than none." The surrounding hills, she found, were "really beautiful," and she was sanguine enough about the town's appearance that she told them, "If you could sail up the river and take a peep at our place, you could say it was romantic and grand."[67] A closer look might have yielded a

---

64. Helen Mar Whitney, "Scenes and Incidents at Winter Quarters," *Woman's Exponent* 13 (15 February 1885): 139.

65. For more concrete details about the layout and living conditions of Winter Quarters and vicinity, see Richard Bennett, *Mormons at the Missouri: 1846–1852* (Norman: University of Oklahoma Press, 1987), 68–90. While population figures vary from study to study, those used here have been taken from Bennett's calculations. Bathsheba W. Smith provides a good description of the housing at Winter Quarters and some of the early activities in Tullidge, *The Women of Mormondom*, 322–23. Mary Haskin Parker Richards's diary is another good source. See Maurine Carr Ward, *Winter Quarters: The 1846–1848 Life Writings of Mary Haskin Parker Richards* (Logan, Utah: Utah State University Press, 1996).

66. Reminiscences of Jane Snyder Richards, holograph, LDS Church Archives.

67. Fanny Murray to Gould and Laura Murray, 5 July 1847, in Helen Mar Whitney Papers, LDS Church Archives.

different impression. Nevertheless, in its two years, Winter Quarters was a lively, friendly community where sorrow and joy, privation and plenty freely intermingled.

The social organization of Winter Quarters mirrored the orderliness of its physical layout. Twenty-two bishops in Winter Quarters and ninety bishops across the river in Iowa monitored the spiritual and temporal welfare of the Saints.[68] Police chief Hosea Stout and his aides also helped the Saints maintain order and guarded the settlements against Indian thefts.

These stopover communities quickly developed beyond mere subsistence. School was held on both sides of the river, and socials, dances, singing schools, and parties kept the Saints entertained. They implemented a postal system primarily to keep in touch with the trustees still in Nauvoo[69] but also to maintain close contact with the far-flung Saints waiting for another season to move westward. Industrious Saints also constructed a prosperous ferry, flour and corn mills, and stores, which sold goods purchased in Missouri. At both Winter Quarters in Nebraska Territory and Miller's Hollow, the Saints' main settlement in Iowa, they also built temporary council houses for meetings and socials. They knew, however, that their sojourn at the Missouri was only a hiatus on their journey to Zion. Amelia Slade Bennion inadvertently described their situation when she commented on her first view of the river. "The Missouri," she wrote, was "just one big river of mud, flowing out of somewhere, sluggishly past, and on to nowhere."[70] Her sentiment was an apt metaphor for the Mormon refugees, especially during the winter of 1846. Nauvoo was somewhere, but the vast western expanse was more like nowhere as they tried to envision their new home in the West. Life between the two points was indeed sluggish for

68. Bennett, *Mormons at the Missouri,* 119.
69. The three trustees were John S. Fullmer, Joseph L. Heywood, and Almon W. Babbitt.
70. Carter, *Our Pioneer Heritage* 2:224.

the Saints as they awaited spring and the renewals of their journey west.

With several thousand Saints residing somewhere besides Winter Quarters in settlements stretching up and down the river, no one story can tell the tale of the Mormon sojourn at the Missouri. Some things, however, the Saints had in common. If the Lord required a "tried" people, he could easily claim these exiled folk as his own. The Missouri encampment was a scene of suffering and hardship that first winter. Even the well-prepared soon exhausted their provisions as they shared their goods with the needy, and buying or trading in Missouri and Iowa settlements for supplies required something to barter. With nothing left to sell, faith was their only stock in trade. Sarah Rich made good use of it. Left without means but with the responsibility to provide for her husband's large, extended family when he returned to Nauvoo, she set out to find food for them armed with nothing but her faith. An attempt to borrow a few dollars was unsuccessful, but a prompting to call in at Sister Ezra T. Benson's cabin yielded her a welcome cup of tea and a silver dollar, which bought her "a little sugar, and a little coffee, and tea." That was not all. On her way to the store, Sarah met Brother Ezra T. Clark carrying a sack of flour and a bushel of potatoes. It was for her, he announced. Then, before she arrived home, Brother Flake, a perfect stranger whom she met on the street, gave her a quarter side of beef. Sarah's faith produced not just one but several small miracles. It proved to be her best bartering tool.[71]

Women used their skills as well as their faith to provide for their dependents or to help their husbands. If they had not been resourceful before, these women learned to be so now. Lucy Smith, a young plural wife of George A. Smith and a model of self-reliance, attended a school in Kanesville, then taught in the

---

71. Reminiscences of Sarah Pea Rich, 32–33.

school and finally went to Bellevue, across the river in Nebraska Territory, to teach at the Pawnee Indian mission school for six months. She was proud to earn her own money to take her west.[72]

Martha Pane Thomas, whose husband and son had gone west with Brigham Young in the first company, learned to manage alone very quickly. Having sent virtually all of the family's provisions along with her husband, Martha found that she and her remaining children "were very near in fashion with Father and Mother Eve." But Martha was a weaver. All she needed was some cotton yarn and dye, and then she could weave "all the plain and striped stuff for dresses I had a mind to." Taking two lanterns, her only tradeable possessions, she bartered for cloth and dye with a Mr. Stootesman, a storekeeper. Mr. Stootesman gave her what she needed, let her keep her lanterns, and assured her of a ready market for her dresses. She wove more than two hundred yards of cloth that season and one bolt of forty yards for wagon covers. When her husband and son came back to Winter Quarters the next year to retrieve their family, she had managed not only to provide for her children in her husband's absence but also to weave sufficient cloth to last her family for several years.[73] They were well outfitted for the trip west.

Sarah Allen also learned to be self-reliant. A Mormon Battalion "widow," her first year alone was discouraging. First, the arrangements her husband had made for her to draw provisions from a trading post did not materialize. Then she could find only a small shanty to live in, which offered little more protection than her wagon. Finally, her only cow, the milk supply for Sarah and her two young children, wandered off. The outlook brightened, however, when a family settled nearby and helped her build a decent cabin. They also willingly shared their

---

72. "Narrative of Lucy Meserve Smith."
73. "Martha Pane Jones Thomas," in *Daniel Stillwell Thomas Family History* (Salt Lake City: Kate Woodhouse Kirkham, 1927).

provisions throughout the winter. Sarah took over her own support the next year by teaching school while preparing for her
husband's return. Finally, in the spring of 1848, a group of former battalion men returned to Winter Quarters. She eagerly
sought them out, only to learn that her husband had been killed
by Indians in the California mountains. His friends had
retrieved a small bag of gold dust marked with his blood. With
the little bit of gold and four more years of hard work, Sarah was
ready to travel on to the Salt Lake Valley on her own.[74] As Helen
Mar Whitney observed, "They [the women] were a nation of
wonderful managers. . . . Their art availed them in their changed
affairs."[75]

The legendary Mary Fielding Smith also proved resilient in
preparing to travel west. The oft-told incident in which her faith
and prayers enabled her to find her lost oxen occurred during
her stay in Winter Quarters. She and her brother, Joseph
Fielding, her mainstay from Nauvoo to Salt Lake City, and her
young son, named after his uncle, made frequent trips to St.
Joseph, Missouri, to buy supplies during their stay at the
Missouri. On one of these trips her oxen strayed, and neither of
the Josephs was able to find any trace of them. Finding his
mother deep in prayer when they returned, young Joseph
learned the power of faith when his mother then went out to
search and found the lost oxen.[76] Mary Fielding Smith's experience is only the most well known of such faith-revealing
instances.

Disease was a major enemy to the Saints while they waited at
the Missouri, especially the dreaded scurvy. With diets short of
fruits and vegetables, these wilderness sojourners were vulnerable
to this unrelenting, often fatal disease. Cholera, dysentery, and

---

74. "Sarah Beriah Fiske Allen Ricks," in Carter, *Our Pioneer Heritage* 11:135–44.
75. "Travels Beyond the Mississippi," *Woman's Exponent* 13 (1 October 1884): 105.
76. "Mary Fielding Smith," in Carter, *Our Pioneer Heritage* 19:212.

the ague also took their toll of health and lives. The Saints had few resources either to prevent or to cure them. Their diaries tell harrowing stories of their physical and emotional ravages, and statistics show their pervasiveness. In the first year, from September 1846 to September 1847, the death rate, just for Winter Quarters, according to the available records, was 82.1 per thousand. Even in frontier Utah three years later, another vulnerable period, it reached only 50 per thousand. Confirming sad diary accounts, nearly a third of these deaths were infants.[77] This was Winter Quarters' darkest hour, but it did not demoralize the Saints. There were "many happy seasons after the mighty struggle with the destroyer was over," Helen Whitney testified.[78]

A people who never let difficulties extinguish their pleasures, they used their council houses for dances, concerts, plays, and celebrations as well as meetings and conferences, which drew Saints from all around the vicinity. "We are indeed in the wilderness," wrote Thomas and Sarah Colburn to their family in New York, "but still our ears are saluted with the sound of mirth."[79] Eliza Cheney also found some good times that winter. "We have good meetings and good music," she told her family, "and we are all as brisk as larks."[80]

Unless Mary Haskin Parker Richards was unlike her circle of family and friends in Winter Quarters, she was not immune to the discomforts of living in a tent for a year or insensitive to the illnesses that afflicted those around her. She was herself alone, her husband serving a mission in England. But she too found pleasure attending singing school, listening to William Pitt's band

---

77. Statistical accounts vary. Some historians feel that the figure of six hundred deaths most often quoted is inflated, basing their claim on existing cemetery records. The figures used in this study are taken from calculations made by professional demographers and published in an excellent study of Winter Quarters by Maureen Ursenbach Beecher, "Women in Winter Quarters," in Beecher, *Eliza and Her Sisters* (Salt Lake City: Aspen Press, 1991), 89–91, esp. fn. 40. Certainly the personal accounts show that the Saints themselves were devastated by the heavy death toll that seemed to touch every family.

78. "Scenes and Incidents at Winter Quarters," *Woman's Exponent* 14 (15 February 1886): 134.

79. Thomas and Sarah Colburn to Daniel Bown, 6 September 1846, LDS Church Archives.

80. Eliza Cheney to Parents, Brothers and Sisters, January 1848, LDS Church Archives.

concerts, and "dancing almost every figure & a mixing round at a great rate" at the dances held in the council house. There were family parties and anniversaries to celebrate and time to appreciate the beauties of the countryside as she walked on the bluffs and along the riverside of her temporary home.[81] Ann Cannon, a young orphan living with her uncle John Taylor in Winter Quarters, remembered picking strawberries, wading in the stream when helping with the family wash, and dancing every night in a large tent assembled between the houses occupied by Wilford Woodruff's and John Taylor's families. When the water running the grist mill froze, she ate boiled wheat with milk, which wasn't bad eating, she remembered, and unlike some others, she always had sufficient if not necessarily savory food. Attending Church meetings, sometimes twice a week, was a pleasure to Ann and the source, she felt, of the lifelong testimony she left to her children.[82]

But underscoring the bright allegro moments as well as the sobering hardships of those who wintered at the Missouri was the loneliness felt by women left to care for themselves or families while husbands dutifully served missions, conducted trading excursions into Missouri, served in the battalion, herded livestock for months at a time, or traveled west before their families. As a result, Winter Quarters and most of the area bordering the Missouri River was permeated by single-parent families. As in Nauvoo and other close-knit settlements or towns, the women living at Winter Quarters, because of their close proximity, could visit and meet together more easily than women scattered in the various campsites away from the center of Church activity and unattached to the leading families. For the first time, polygamous

81. The journal of Mary Haskin Parker Richards is often cited in the various accounts of Winter Quarters. A brief but insightful review of the journal is Maurine Carr Ward, "A Journey in the Wilderness: The Life of Mary Haskin Parker Richards at the Missouri River, 1846–1848," *The Nauvoo Journal* 7 (Fall 1995): 17–23. See also Ward, *Winter Quarters: The 1846–1848 Life Writings of Mary Haskin Parker Richards.*

82. Ann Cannon Woodbury in *Cannon Family Historical Treasury,* ed. Beatrice Cannon Evans and Janath Russell Cannon (Salt Lake City: George Cannon Family Association, 1967).

wives could associate freely together, and the sister wives of Brigham Young, Heber C. Kimball, Newel K. Whitney, and other Church leaders found solace, companionship, and assistance in these familial networks. After the heads of most of these families left in 1847 with the first pioneer company, their wives spent hours together sharing household tasks, attending the sick, socializing, and revitalizing their faith through blessing meetings. In these small, spiritual gatherings, usually but not always attended only by women, they renewed a practice they had begun in Nauvoo, exercising various gifts of the Spirit, such as prophesying, casting out evil spirits, blessing, and healing one another. Their diaries recount a great surge of spirituality accompanying these shared experiences; Eliza R. Snow and others established their unique spiritual leadership in these quiet but profoundly uplifting gatherings.[83]

The journals and reminiscences of those unattached to these families, however, contain few references to sisters' meetings or to the exercise of spiritual gifts, and many Saints still were unaware of the practice of polygamy. But these Saints also received spiritual manifestations, often in private and sometimes in simple but nevertheless miraculous ways. Sister Benson's kindness to Sarah Rich, the unnamed couple who befriended Sarah Allen, the comforting voices that sang to Lucy Smith in her dreams, and the cake of cornmeal that multiplied itself to satisfy the hunger of Rhoda Fullmer's six children—all of these small miracles confirmed their faith in the course they had chosen.[84]

---

83. The diaries of Eliza R. Snow and Patty Sessions contain the most complete accounts of these gatherings. Helen Mar Whitney also describes such meetings in the Kimball family after Eliza R. Snow left for the West in June 1847. See Beecher, "Women in Winter Quarters," 93–97; Beecher, *The Personal Writings of Eliza Roxcy Snow*, 112, 166–77; and Whitney, *Woman's Exponent* 14 (1 January 1886): 133. Patty Sessions' diary, edited by Donna Smart, will be published soon by Utah State University Press, part of a series under the general editorship of Maureen Beecher.

84. Journal of Rhoda Ann Marvin Fullmer, 4–5, LDS Church Archives. Rhoda provided for her family for two years before leaving for Salt Lake Valley in 1850 with the assistance of the Perpetual Emigrating Fund. She met her husband at a ferry crossing of the Platte River, where he had been assigned to work. He was able to provide the means for her and their children to continue the journey "with comfort and plenty."

They gained confidence and strength from one another. Barbara Evans and the other fatherless families camped with her on Starvation Creek (their husbands were seeking teams and provisions in Missouri) remembered that though they all suffered from hunger and cold, "we did not complain," she wrote, "for we were united; we truly lived the order; we all shared alike."[85] Sharing their misery often lessened it.

The most significant event of the Missouri Valley hiatus was the sustaining of a new First Presidency. For more than three years the Church had been governed by the Quorum of the Twelve Apostles under the leadership of Brigham Young, president of the quorum. The time had come to reinstitute a First Presidency. Following the unanimous decision of the quorum to sustain him as president with Heber C. Kimball and Willard Richards as counselors, Brigham Young, upon his return from the Salt Lake Valley, called a special conference. On 27 December 1847, in the newly constructed log tabernacle, the Saints ratified the action of the Quorum of the Twelve.[86] Following a sermon by the newly sustained president, Pitt's brass band played, and the congregation celebrated with the hosanna shout led by apostle George A. Smith: "Hosanna, Hosanna, Hosanna to God and the Lamb. Amen! Amen! Amen!" Historian B. H. Roberts wrote, "It is impossible to stand unmoved on such an occasion." When the hosanna shout is given, he noted, "it seems to fill the prairie or woodland, mountain wilderness or tabernacle, with mighty waves of sound; . . . It gives wonderful vent to religious emotions, and is followed by a feeling of reverential awe—a sense of oneness with God."[87] One

---

85. Journal of Barbara Ann Ewell Evans, in *Bishop David Evans and His Family* (Provo, UT: J. Grant Stevenson, 1972), 49–53.

86. At this point, the Quorum consisted of Brigham Young, Heber C. Kimball, Orson Hyde, Orson Pratt, Willard Richards, Wilford Woodruff, George A. Smith, Amasa Lyman, and Ezra T. Benson, who were together at the Missouri. John Taylor and Parley P. Pratt were with the Saints in Utah, and Lyman Wight was in Texas.

87. Roberts, *Comprehensive History* 3:317, fn. 19.

can well imagine the sounds of that shout echoing across the bluffs, reaching the ears of Saints who had not participated in that momentous meeting. Throughout the Church, the action taken in this conference was sustained: first by the annual April conference held four months later in Kanesville,[88] then by the 18,000 Saints in Great Britain in August 1848, and finally by the nearly five thousand Saints settled in the Salt Lake Valley in October 1848.

By 1852 virtually all of the Saints had left their temporary dwellings by the Missouri River. Brigham Young had issued the call to "come home," and they had followed. Kanesville became Council Bluffs, and a site a few miles north of Winter Quarters became the Nebraska town of Florence. During most of the pioneer trail period, Florence served as a major outfitting post for Mormon travelers to the West.[89] Except for their cemeteries, Mormon traces soon disappeared.

Later travelers, no doubt preoccupied with their own pilgrimages to Zion, seldom mentioned Mormon origins of these town as they passed through. Sarah Birch, however, in 1853 noticed traces of "huts and dugouts" and felt "solemn and thoughtful" as she "walked upon the ground where there had been so much death and suffering."[90] A decade later, John Lingren was also moved as he walked the paths of the once-thriving Missouri River town of Winter Quarters. "Here," he wrote, "were relics of different natures; a house that Brigham Young had lived in, a well that Heber C. Kimball had dug and the remains of the dugouts, camping places and other sacred memories of gone-by times." This eighteen-year-old Swedish con-

---

88. When the Saints moved their headquarters from Winter Quarters on the west bank of the Missouri in early 1848 to Kanesville on the east bank, they dismantled and then torched their buildings and little remained of Winter Quarters except the cemetery.

89. For details, see William G. Hartley, "The Great Florence Fitout of 1861," *BYU Studies* 24 (Summer 1984): 341–71.

90. "Sarah Birch Waters," in Carter, *Our Pioneer Heritage* 11:164.

vert, for whom the flight from Nauvoo, the horrendous trek across Iowa, and the sacrifices at the Missouri could have been little more than a distant story, felt the impact of that great drama played out on the soil beneath him.[91]

A place is hallowed, John Lingren knew, by what transpires there. If ever places were sanctified, they were Winter Quarters, Kanesville, and their neighboring settlements, where all the small incidents of individual human courage, patience, and steadfastness combined to define a people and clarify in bold relief their devotion to their mission. The Camp of Israel had survived its first wilderness test and was ready to make a new Zion in that western land beyond the Rockies.

In the caravan of exiles that crossed the Mississippi River during those eight crucial months of 1846, the Saints were focused on leaving Nauvoo and escaping their intransigent enemies more than on their ultimate destination.

George Whitaker, a young convert from England, arrived in Nauvoo just a year before the Saints left. He drove a wagon for Parley P. Pratt in the Nauvoo exodus and found the association eventful and pleasing. His sister Sophia became a plural wife of John Taylor, which gave George entry into another of Mormonism's prominent families. His reminiscence shows a lively sense of detail as he describes the many tasks required to make a settlement, even temporary ones like those at Garden Grove, Mount Pisgah, and the Council Bluffs area.

---

91. "Autobiograhy of John Lingren," in Kate B. Carter, comp., *Treasures of Pioneer History*, 6 vols. (Salt Lake City: Daughters of Utah Pioneers, 1952–1957) 1:238.

G E O R G E   W H I T A K E R [92]

IT WAS NOW GETTING TOWARDS the fall of the year [1845]. The war clouds began to gather around. The mob threatened and swore they would drive the Latter-day Saints from Nauvoo. The [Nauvoo] Legion was called together often, and the guards were sent out in greater numbers. They (the mob) were afraid to come to Nauvoo as they knew we were ready for them, but they began to harass our brethren in the outside settlements by burning their houses and stacks of wheat, threatening women and children, and frightening them and driving them from their homes. Their husbands and fathers had to get out of their way or they would have been killed. Hundreds of families came into Nauvoo destitute. We prepared ourselves for self defense the best we could, but the mob dared not come into Nauvoo. They were afraid some of them would get hurt. They knew they were in a bad cause. The Latter-day Saints were on the defensive to protect themselves, their wives and children and their property. Business was paralyzed, excepting the work on the Temple, which was going on very rapidly. The authorities of the Church felt determined to get the walls up and the roof put on. Hundreds of men were working on it. Some of the leading men of the state and the authorities of the Church held councils. It was agreed that the mob should cease their hostilities and that the Saints should go somewhere beyond the Rocky Mountains when the spring opened. After this treaty was made,[93] the mob

---

92. "Life of George Whitaker, A Pioneer, as written by himself," typescript, Utah State Historical Society.

93. This was the treaty, signed 16 September 1846 by the Quincy Committee, which called for the removal of the Saints from Nauvoo and an end to hostilities.

to some extent ceased their burnings and drivings in the outside settlements.

At the October Conference a great many people gathered
together. We did not know until then what the authorities of the
Church had done. We knew that some important business would
be transacted. We were told that the spirit of the mob was so bitter against us that we would have to leave the confines of civilization and go beyond the Rocky Mountains into Mexican territory.
It was better to leave our houses, our lands, our temple, and our
beautiful city than to stay there and fight the mob, and many of
us perhaps would lose our lives. They thought the life of a good
man was worth fifty bad men's lives. This was put to a vote, and
we all voted to leave; if they gave us anything for our property to
help us out it was all right, but if they did not we would go anyway. Counsel was given to go to work and finish the temple
according to the revelation given to Joseph Smith, so that we
might receive our washings and anointings and the keys and powers of the Holy Priesthood, and also the Holy Anointings and
Sealings that the power of God might rest upon His servants. It
was also prophesied that in less than five years we would be a great
deal better off than we were at that time, and many more things
were told us that came to pass according to the words that had
been spoken. The name of the city of Nauvoo was changed and
called the city of Joseph, being called after the Prophet Joseph
Smith. A great many things were done at that conference that I
cannot write. Suffice it to say, the Spirit of God was with the
people and the blessings of the Almighty were upon them.

When the conference was over we went to our homes and
began to prepare for the great journey before us. The thing on
hand was the finishing of the temple. There was a great deal of
work to be done in a little time. Meetings were called in different
parts of the city to organize companies for manufacturing wagons. Men went into the woods to get out timber, and seasoned
it the best way they could, while every man who could use a tool

worked at some part of the business. My brother Moses went to work in the blacksmith shop making the irons and setting the tires on the wagons. I went to work on the temple. I turned all my labor in on tithing.

The greatest portion of our summer's work was lost. The kiln of bricks which we had made we could not sell. Everybody wanted to sell their property, therefore nobody wanted to build or improve their property. The Saints in Nauvoo were as a general thing very poor. Some thousands had emigrated from England and from the Eastern States, and had spent most of their means in getting here. We lived mostly on corn meal and milk, vegetable, and sometimes a little meat and flour. Our enemies tried to starve us out by stopping everything they could from coming into Nauvoo. Money was very scarce. I never got one cent in money from the time I arrived at Nauvoo until I left.[94]

About the last of November the temple was so far along, having the upper rooms finished, that they began to give endowments. Those [who] had paid their property tithing, that is, one tenth of the property they had brought with them, and also one-tenth of their increase or labor, had the privilege of going through the temple. Everyone seemed to be trying to work and settle up their tithing that they might have the privilege of getting their endowments in the space of about ten weeks. I paid my property tithing and also my labor tithing and got my receipts for it, and had the privilege of going through the temple and getting my endowments a few days before they closed. They were at work night and day from the time they commenced until they closed, which was about the sixth day of February, 1846.

About this time the Twelve Apostles and all those who had teams were making preparations to cross the Mississippi River into Iowa. I with two other young men was working at Brother

---

94. He arrived at Nauvoo from England 27 March 1845 and left 9 February 1846.

Parley P. Pratt's. He came to us and said he wanted two or three young men to drive teams for him to the Rocky Mountains or wherever the Saints were going. He told us he could not give us any wages, but would give us something to eat. We all told him that we would come. He then told us to bring what bed clothes we could as he had a large family and needed all the bedding he had. He told us to be there next morning. This was rather short notice for me to start on so long a journey, but I had told him I would come and I was going to do as I had agreed.

I went home and told the folks what I was going to do. They were a little surprised but concluded that it was a good thing for me to do as I was single and had nobody to take care of but myself. My brother Moses had got married. We were all living at my sister's.[95] They were not prepared to go at this time and they thought it would be best for me to go as I would be a pioneer for them. I put my clothing in a large box I had brought from England. My brother gave me his temple garments as I did not have any, and also a mattress. My sister gave me some bed clothes. I left a few things with them that I had brought from England, circular saws, scythes, and spades, and also a box of clothing which my sister Harriet sent with me. I left the kiln of bricks and told my brother he was welcome to what he could make out of them. I bade them good-bye and was down at Brother Pratts in good time in the morning.

I was the only one of the three that came. I did not know them and never saw them after. Brother Pratt had a horse team ready for me. I had never driven a team in my life before, but I thought I could drive as they did not seem to be very spirited. Brother Pratt got into the wagon to show me how to drive as he knew by this time that I was an Englishman and had never been used to handling the lines. We went around gathering up some

---

95. Mary Ann, his only wedded sibling at the time, married Richard Harrison in 1836 in England.

things that we needed for our journey. He then sent me alone to get some more things. I thought I could drive as well as he could. He told me not to whip the horses and let them take their time. I got along very well until I began to think they were not going fast enough. I gave them a little whip which made them start up in a hurry, and the fist thing I knew they were on the full gallop. I thought they were going to get away with me, but I held on to them with all my might until finally I brought them to. This was one of my first lessons in driving a team. I told him I thought I had done first-rate. I did not tell him of the runaway. I got along very well after that. We were very busy in loading up our wagons. All was hurry and bustle. Brother Pratt looked at my large English box. He thought he would not be able to take it, but he finally put it into the wagon. I thought a good deal of my box and the things that were in it, but it was not long before I had to leave it behind.

On the 9th of February, about noon, we started. We had four wagons. We got down to the river and found it frozen over. We crossed over it with our wagons on the ice. It was full three quarters of a mile across the river. After crossing the river we camped for the night. The snow was three or four inches deep and still snowing. We set up a large tent and swept the snow away. We did not make any fire or cook any supper although it was very cold. Brother Pratt had six or seven wives and quite a number of small children. Everyone seemed to be cheerful, although complained a little of the cold. We ate some cold victuals and laid our beds down in the tent. Most of the family slept in the tent that night. We went to bed at an early hour. I did not sleep very warm as my bed was by the tent door and the wind blew in very cold. I did not say anything as I thought I would get used to it in time. We all got up about daylight next morning. Brother Pratt was up and around the first. He asked us how we had slept. I did not hear any complaints. I did not make any myself. We made a fire and got our breakfast. We all felt to rejoice and felt first-rate.

Bro. Pratt had very recently built him a large and commodious brick house. It seemed as though there was something more than human nature which caused them to feel so joyful and happy to leave their comfortable homes and to go out in the dead of winter with so many young children to face the cold and the storms, and not even knowing where they were going. It seemed to me that we must be in possession of some power besides the power of man.

I soon got acquainted with the women folks. I tried to do all I could for them and in return they were very kind to me. I was very quiet. I did not say much. They would often ask me questions. Sometimes they would think I felt bad, and would ask me how I was feeling. I always told them I felt first-rate which cheered them up and made them feel good.

We were late before we got a start that morning on account of the snow and the cold. The women were a long time packing up and getting their children comfortably fixed. I thought if we did not make more headway we would be a long time getting to the Rocky Mountains, but finally we made a start. We traveled slow. Sometime in the afternoon we reached the tithing office in Iowa, where there was a branch of the Church.[96] There was plenty of corn there and we thought we would stay. We were then about four miles from Nauvoo. That was our first day's travel. We drove our teams into the yard and gave our animals something to eat as they had had but very little since we had left Nauvoo. The women and children went into a log cabin. There was already a good fire made for them and we spent the evening very comfortable. It was quite different to the evening before, which we had spent on the banks of the Mississippi River. We spent the evening in talking and chatting and looking forward to the time when we should be at the end of our journey. There was nothing said in

---

96. The tithing office was probably near the Ambrosia Branch, a few miles west of Montrose.

regard to our homes and our pleasant places we had left in Nauvoo. We had given them up never to see them again. We felt we were going to a better country where we could live in peace, free from mobs and strife, where we could worship God according to our own conscience, none to molest or make us afraid.

We had a very good new milch cow, which gave ten quarts at milking. Brother Pratt gave her in charge of me. We lived on milk and cornmeal. We would have milk and corn dodger for breakfast and mush and milk for supper. I got to like it so well I could sooner have it than anything else. The fact was, there was very little of anything else for us.

President Young and the main body of the camp had crossed the river a day or two before us. They were about four miles ahead of us camped on a little stream called Sugar Creek. He intended to stay there until the weather moderated so that we could travel with more comfort, and also to stay until the companies had gathered up that were going that winter. He was organizing them into companies for traveling, and placing over them captains of fifties and captains of ten, and also a company of men to go ahead as pioneers with axes and spades to cut down the brush and make the roads, and also a company of men to guard the camps.

Brother Pratt and family were still at the tithing office in Iowa. Brother Pratt went often down to the camps to counsel with the Twelve. He would come back in the evening. After supper we would all sit around the room on our boxes or anything we could get for a seat and Brother Pratt would then begin to talk to us and teach us a great many good things. He told us some of his experiences in the Church, about his early history, the persecutions of the Saints in Missouri, the expulsion of the Saints from Jackson County, the great phenomena that was seen in the heavens in the shooting of the stars on a bitter cold night as they were camped on the banks of the Missouri River, men, women, and children, without any covering but the heavens, driven by a ruthless mob. He told us about the Exterminating Order of Governor Boggs, how they had to leave the state of Missouri—the murders and robberies that were committed, their expulsion in midwinter, their hardships and poverty. He told us of the massacre at Haun's mill, how that eighteen men and boys were shot down in cold blood and many more were wounded; how they had to be thrown into an old well with their clothes on, while those who remained had to get away fearing the mob would return and kill them. He also told us of the battle at Crooked River where David Patten was killed and other brethren. He told us how he and other brethren were taken to prison and their miraculous escape, how he traveled many days in the woods and by paths with very little food until he got to the Mississippi River. All these things were very interesting to us. I thought he was the best man I ever saw. I felt that I would like to stay with him all my life. He told about the Rocky Mountains and California and spoke of the prospects of the future, and also prophesied of the final destiny of the Latter-day Saints. We listened to what he said with great satisfaction. We felt to thank God that we had left our homes and got away from our enemies. Brother Pratt would then call upon us to take the lead in singing a hymn. We would then have prayers and retire to rest.

As I had nothing much to do, and only about four miles from Nauvoo, I thought I would like to see the folks before the camp moved away from Sugar Creek, as we expected to move on in a few days. I told them I would like to go over to Nauvoo and see my brother and sister before we went away. They rather got the joke on me as they thought I wanted to see someone else besides my brother and sister. That was true. I was engaged to a young lady, Evline P. Robinson. I had taken her through the temple and we had got our endowments. Her father went to the state of Maine to get some money he had there. They expected to start in May, and we had agreed to get married when we met again. We could not tell when that would be, but we hoped to meet again. This was all arranged before I left.

After eating breakfast one morning I started on foot for Nauvoo. I came to the river. It was still frozen over. I got over the river very well and made for my sister's about two miles distant. I found them all well. They were very glad to see me. I stayed two days as I had promised not to stay over that time. I bade them all farewell, hoping we would meet again sometime in the future. I wended my way towards the river. Upon arrival there I found the ice had broken up. I could not cross and I did not know what to do. I thought it would not do to go back home as I had stayed my full time. They would be expecting me at the camp, and the Saints were almost ready to start when I left. I wanted to go with them. I had no desire to go home. The camp of the Saints was my home. Where they went I wanted to go. I had the spirit of emigration and there was nothing in the world that would stop me excepting sickness or death. I walked up and down the banks of the river for some hours watching for a skiff or boat to cross the river. Many thoughts passed through my mind. I was sorry that I had left the camp and crossed the river. I was worried, and being a stranger I didn't know how to apply to get over. I waited for hours, until finally I saw two men some distance from me up the river. I made for them. They had a little boat and were going across the river. I asked them if they would take me. They said they would if I would pay them. I told them I had no money, and they said they could not take me. I told them my circumstances, how I had left the camp to go to Nauvoo to see my folks, and I had promised to be back in three days. I told them who I was living with, and that I expected the camp was ready to start. I told them that anything I had on or about me they could have. The most valuable things I had in my pocket were a silver penholder, which I had brought from England, and a pocket knife. They said they would take me over for the penholder. I was very much pleased with the trade. I got into the boat and we made our way to the other side. We were a long time getting across on account of the ice. I felt to thank God that I was safe across. I made the best of my way to the tithing office. It was night before I got there. I found them all well. Brother Pratt and family were pleased to see me back. I was very glad to get back. I gave them a little synopsis of my visit—how I was detained on the banks of the river through the breaking up of the ice, and how lucky I was in getting across. They laughed at me, they thought I had very little experience, and that I had a great many things to learn, as I soon began to find out.

When I got back I found that Sister Mary Ann Pratt, Brother Parley's first wife, had packed up her things and gone back to Nauvoo to see her father and mother. She had said she would come back again. Brother Parley went over to get her before the camp started, but she would not come; she said she would come along in the spring with her parents. She had three little children, two girls and a boy about six months old. So far as I know her she was a very good woman. When we had started for the West she had asked that I should drive her team. Some ten years after she came to Salt Lake.

While we were staying at the tithing office we had overhauled our wagons and provisions and put everything in a better shape for traveling. We had three horse teams and one ox team. Brother Pratt's family consisted of seven wives and quite a number of small children; three or four under one year old. Parley was his oldest boy. He was eight years old. His mother died about the time he was born.[97] Another family was with us by the name of Rogers,[98] his wife and two children. They came from New York. They had money and helped to get the necessary outfit, such as horses, oxen, and wagons, and provisions for the journey. There

---

97. Thankful Halsey Pratt died in giving birth to Parley 25 March 1837 in Kirtland, Ohio.

98. Possibly David Rogers, who was converted to the Church during Parley P. Pratt's mission to New York.

were two teamsters besides myself, Wm. Pratt, Parley's brother, being one of them. Brother [William] Leffin[g]well, who kept the tithing office, and family concluded to pack up and go with us. It had been about three weeks since we had left Nauvoo. I had become very well acquainted with Brother Pratt and his family. I did everything I could to make them comfortable, and they thought a great deal of me. They did everything they could for me. If I had been their brother or their son they could not have done more.

On the first day of March 1846 we started, drove to Sugar Creek, about four miles and camped. We found that President Young and company, about fifty wagons had gone. Quite a number were there and preparing to go. Next day we caught up with Brother Young. It was very cold and had been snowing. The pioneers had gone ahead and had prepared a camping place. As there was plenty of wood and timber there they had hauled it in piles. When we got into camp about dark, there were thirty or forty large fires burning, which cheered us up very much. Each family or two or three small families would be put to one fire. Everything was arranged in the best of order. I went to make the mush. We had not traveled above six or eight miles that day. When our supper was ready and we had taken our mush and milk, we all got around the fire and talked about our day's journey and had the prospects before us. We all felt very happy and joyful. Our camp ground took up some acres of ground. We could see grouped all around the camp fires men, women and children; some were singing, some were dancing, some were playing music, everyone seemed full of life and joy. We felt as though we had been released from bondage and were free, where there was no one to make us afraid.

After we were through with our conversation, Brother Pratt called upon me to start a hymn. They were all good singers and we made a very good choir of ourselves. After singing we had prayers, every family in camp doing the same, as we were all

60

instructed to call upon the Lord morning and evening, that he would bless us with health and strength and that he would lead us and guide us to the place of our destination, and also to bless our cattle and horses that they might be strong so that they might perform the work that they had to do, which was very hard. The men put down their beds in the tent on the wet ground. The women and children slept in the wagons. We had a large family wagon fixed so that six or seven could lie cross-ways in the wagon. We all slept soundly. At day break when we got up, the whole camp was astir in making fires and getting breakfast and preparing for our day's journey. The cow was milked. We had corn dodger and milk for breakfast. After breakfast we took down our tent, put all our things into our wagons, got our teams hitched on and all ready to start. The pioneers rolled out first and went ahead so as to look out and make ready a camping place for the night. I should judge there were about one hundred wagons. It was late in the forenoon before they had all left camp. We traveled about the same distance that day as we did the day before, and camped at night in the same [unreadable]. Our progress was rather slow on account of our heavy loads and [unreadable].

On the fourth day we came to the Des Moines River and also a little town called Farmington. The river was from seventy-five to one hundred yards, while it was not more than two feet deep. We forded the river as there was no bridge. We all got safely across and camped a few miles from town. We traveled a few days in this way. We were making very slow progress on account of so many wagons in one company. Some were heavily loaded and had very poor teams and seemed to be in the way of others that had good teams. We had to travel in line one after another. Very often the wagons that had the poor teams would get stuck in a mud hole and would have to be helped out, as no one was allowed to pass another thus situated. Therefore it became very trying to a good many. We all needed a great deal of patience. Things did not go along as pleasantly as some had expected. It was a new thing to most of us, and we found many things to contend with. It seemed very pleasant to me. I was young and strong and always willing to put my shoulder to the wheel and help my brethren.

The slow traveling did not suit Brother Pratt and a number of others. They thought they would make a company and go ahead of the others. I suppose it was the counsel of President Young. I should imagine we had traveled then about forty or fifty miles. About twenty or thirty wagons started out, Brother Pratt in the lead. We soon got ahead of the main camp, but there seemed to be a serious difficulty before us. We were getting where the old settlers were not so thick and only a log house here and there. The pioneers had got some money from the camp and had been buying corn to feed our animals, and as we did not expect any grass for two or three weeks that our stock could feed on, it would not do to get out of the settled country altogether. We had but very little money with us and we thought we would stop a few days, rest our teams, as they raised little else but corn. We soon found some work in building log houses and barns. Corn was only about 15¢ or 20¢ a bushel. We could put up a log house in a day and this would buy corn enough to last us several days. Brother Pratt thought that he would overhaul the wagons to see if there was anything that he could leave behind that we did not really need, as our teams were becoming very weak and he was afraid they would give out. He soon came across my big box that I thought so much of. He told me that he could not carry it any further on account of the weakness of the teams, and that I must put my things in sacks. I could see that there was reason in this and I consented. A brother that was there said he would bring it for me, but that was the last I saw of it. Sister Elizabeth Pratt gave me a very small old trunk and I put the rest of my things in sacks. The main camp did not come up with us. I suppose they were stopping for the same purpose.

After staying two or three days we again started. We were now getting to the outside settlements. We had to make our own roads as there were none. We traveled in a western course as near as we could. It was now about the middle of March. We had only traveled about sixty miles. The weather was cold and very rainy. It rained almost every day. Brother Pratt and myself had to be out in the rain mostly all of the time. Fires had to be made, water had to be brought, cows had to be milked, and cooking had to be done, and the teams had to be seen to. The women could not get around much on account of the rain and mud, although they wanted to get out of their wagons and help around, but I told them I would get supper, which consisted in cooking a large kettle of mush. I was willing to do all I could for the comfort of the women and children. The other men did not feel so interested as they might have done. They kept in their wagons as much as they could to keep out of the rain. Brother Pratt was always around doing all he could and when he wanted help he always called on me. He was always in a good humor and would be singing and talking and encouraging us all he could. I always felt very cheerful, although it was very cold and disagreeable. We would go to bed in our wet clothes as there was no chance of drying them. It seemed as though the Lord was with us and His angels around about us to keep us from getting colds and from sickness, as we were all well and hearty.

We were traveling through a rolling country, and we had to cross little hollows and valleys. As our company was in the lead we had to pioneer and make our own roads, traveling west as near as we could. In crossing these little hollows, having had so much rain, our wagons would sink down and there we would have to stay until we were helped out. Some of the wagons would turn out of the track and try to cross at another place, but would sink down and there were times when there were as many as half a dozen stuck at once. We would then double teams and get the company across, and then get those out that were stuck in the mud.

We traveled in this way all through the month of March and

part of the month of April. The rains were almost incessant. We could only travel a few miles a day. Our teams were weak and we made very slow progress. We would travel a few days and then would stop and rest our teams a day or two if it was a good camping place. As Brother Pratt was always busy and wanted to be doing something, he would have all hands turn out and cut down some timber and build a log house or two. He said it might be a resting place for somebody. He was thinking about those who would follow, and as there was good land there, he thought perhaps some persons who could not get any further would stay there and cultivate the land and the houses would come in very useful, and which we found out afterwards was the case.

At one of these camping places on a small river called the Sharidon [Chariton], Brother Pratt, Brother Rogers, and myself, thought we would have a day's shooting, as there seemed to be plenty of game in that neighborhood, such as ducks, geese, and wild turkeys. We took our guns and ammunition, crossed over the river, traveled two or three miles until we came to a small lake. There were plenty of ducks and geese on it, and we thought that this was a good place to try our skill at shooting. I had never been at the business before and I did not know much about a gun. I had learned how to load a gun and that was about all. I thought I had a nice little rifle that shot bullets and had great faith that I could kill something as we stood in great need of something of that kind. We separated and got around the lake at different points and lay down waiting for chances. There seemed to be plenty of chances and plenty of shooting, but we could not hit anything. We frightened all the game away. [unreadable] waited several hours and then concluded we had better go to camp. I had expected Brother Pratt and Rogers to get something, but I had not to do much. I was not satisfied—I did not want to go to camp without anything as they were expecting to have a feast on what we should bring home. Brother Pratt and Rogers said they would go home as they were tired. I told them I would go

64

into the woods and get a turkey and take it to camp. They wished me success and went home. It was getting towards evening when I struck into the woods, about the time that turkeys were going to roost. I had thought but very little how I should find my way back to camp. I was very anxious to take a turkey home. I looked up in every tree as I went along. It was getting dark. I happened to see a fine turkey on the top branches of a small oak tree. It was a splendid shot. I rested my rifle on one of the low branches and taking good aim I fired away. The turkey rose as though there was nothing the matter and flew away. I thought surely there must be something the matter with my gun as it would not shoot straight. The greatest difficulty then was to find my way to the camp. I wandered about for about two hours, and as luck would have it, I came in sight of the camp fires. I came down to the river opposite the camp and called to them, and they sent over a little boat and took me over.

We had a small cooking stove in one of the wagons to keep the children from freezing. Brother Pratt thought they could do without this stove as the weather would soon be getting warmer and it would lighten our load a little. Our horse teams were getting very weak as we were out of the settlements and could not get any more corn, and the grass had only just begun to spring up. We had to cut down cottonwood trees for our cows and cattle to browse on, and thus they were kept alive for two or three weeks. Our horses could not stand it so well as our cattle, so what little corn we had we gave to the horses. Brother Pratt thought we had better trade our stove and a span of horses for some corn. We hitched up a span of horses to a wagon, put the stove into it (although the women were very loath to part with it) and traveled about twenty miles. We came to a farm house. They had a good farm and plenty of everything around them that they could raise on the farm. They were a long way from any market and from settlements, and only here and there a farm house. We drove up to the house and told them our business. They were pleased to see us as they had not seen anybody for a long time. They took care of our horses, and gave them all the corn they could eat. We told them that we wanted to trade the stove and horses for some cattle. They seemed to want the stove very badly as they did not have any. We had not seen a stove in any of the houses of the settlers throughout the country. They had large, open fireplaces where they could roll in logs and make large fires.

It was late in the afternoon when we got there. They invited us into the house and seemed very pleased to see us as they did not see strangers very often. We had supper there, which consisted of pork and dogger (corn bread), butter and milk, which was quite a feast to us. This was pretty much what they lived on all through that country. We did not see any flour bread and very few vegetables. They made us very comfortable for the night. About the middle of the night we were awakened by the family. It explained that a skunk had gotten into the house and was under the floor. I did not know what a skunk was. I thought it was some horrible beast that would kill some of us, but I soon found out what kind of animal it was. After getting the skunk out, we returned to bed and slept until morning.

After breakfast we began to talk business. They did not want the horses but they very much wanted the stove. They finally concluded they would give two yoke of oxen for the horses and stove. We decided to accept the offer as we had no choice in the matter and we could not go anywhere else to trade. We yoked up our oxen and started for camp. Brother Pratt was pleased with our trade. They had been there several days; the cattle had browsed on all the cottonwood trees and they wanted to move.

Next morning we broke camp and moved on. Brother Pratt went ahead on foot to look out the best road. We traveled on the ridges or along the divide as much as we could as the land was much drier and our wagons went easier. My wagon made the first track following after Brother Pratt, he traveling west as near as he could. We traveled this way for a number of days, bridging small streams as we went along. The way we bridged the streams was by putting strong poles across and brush and dirt upon that. It would not take us more than two or three hours to bridge a small stream.

About the first of April we camped in a beautiful place. The timber was scattered and it looked to me like an English park. Everything was looking green and beautiful. The grass was three or four inches high. We thought there would be green for our stock from this time on. Brother Pratt named the place Paradise. Brother Pratt thought we had better stop there until the main camp came up, as we had not heard from them for some time. While staying at this place some of the people concluded to send some things they thought they could spare down into Missouri to trade for some cows, as we needed milk and butter. Sister Rogers sent her feather bed. Sister Pratt sent their crockery and many other things. A man was appointed to go and do the trading. Some other men, little Parley Pratt, a boy above nine years old, and myself were appointed to go with him. We were camped on the Madison River, a branch of Grand River that ran through the state of Missouri. We loaded up two wagons with such things as they thought they could spare, although we had nothing that we could really spare, but we had to get some more cows as we mostly depended on our cows for a living.

We started on our trip. There were no roads to the settlements. We got on the ridges or divide and made our way as we thought towards Grand River, where we expected to find some settlements. In four or five days we came to Grand River. We found some few scattered farm houses. We traded our things with the settlers and some had nothing left. We had taken things that the settlers needed, and they sold very readily, while we were well satisfied as we had about twenty cows to take back. We started back to the camp. Nothing particular happened on our way back. Sometimes we would have to go out of our way to get across the head of a creek or bridge it over.

One little incident I will mention. There were a great many rattlesnakes in that country, I had charge of little Parley Pratt, his father having given me particular instructions to take care of him and to bring him safely back. As we were traveling he found a large rattlesnake. He got a short stick and began to play with it. The snake curled up and began to strike at him. I happened to see him and took hold of him and pulled him away, telling him that if the snake had bitten him he would have died. He did not seem alarmed. I took him away and let the snake go. The man that had been appointed to do the trading was taken very sick. He was so sick that he had to leave his horse and ride in the wagon. A day or two after arriving at camp he died. We had been gone about ten or twelve days. The people were well satisfied with their cows. We then had plenty of milk and butter for our corn meal. We had traveled a little more than one hundred miles through mud and rain, making a new road and bridging the streams. Our horses and cattle had stood the journey very well. None of them had died although they had been very much exposed to the rains and storms and were very poor in flesh. We would tie them to trees at night and in the morning they would be up to their knees in mud; but the season had come when everything began to look fresh and green, and our animals began to do better, and it also put new life into the Saints as the weather became warmer. They felt happy and rejoiced in the Lord their God.

It was now getting toward the middle of April. The main body of the camp had come up and had passed along before we came back from trading. Brother Pratt was very anxious to be on his way to catch up with them. We gathered up our teams, hitched them to our wagons and started out. We traveled along on their trail about six or seven days, traveling about 50 miles and caught up with them at a place which President Young called Garden Grove. It was a beautiful place for a settlement. The Twelve held a council and decided to stay there about two weeks and make a settlement for the benefit of those who were coming who could not get any further that season.

The whole camp was then reorganized. It was concluded that we would fence in a large field of about six hundred acres and plant it in corn and vegetables. Every man was put in his proper place to work. Some worked at cutting house logs, some at building houses, some at cutting timber for rails, some at splitting rails, some at plowing, some at planting corn and vegetables, while others commenced to put up the fence, and a certain number were sent out to herd and take care of the stock. Every man went to work with a will. There were no idlers amongst us. We were all full of life and spirit. We had almost forgotten our trials and troubles of our two month's journey; how we had traveled through cold and snow and rain and mud, and that we had traveled only about 150 miles. When we had completed our work for the day and had finished our suppers, we would have music and dancing, singing and any other recreation that we thought proper. The weather was splendid and all was joy and happiness. In about 14 or 15 days we had quite a little town built up. We had about 600 acres of land fenced in, plowed and planted. The brethren kept coming in about every day.

It was now past the first of May and orders came that those who had a good outfit with provisions and teams could go west, and all those who were not provided with those necessities should stay there and reap the benefit of our labors and go when they got ready. Brother Pratt was a "go ahead" man, and he was very glad when the word came out to start. He and a small company were appointed to go ahead and look out another location as there were no settlements in that part of Iowa Territory. We got our wagons packed and everything ready to travel and soon started out taking the lead. Bro. Pratt had no horse to ride, therefore he went on foot ahead of the teams. My team was the first to follow him. Sometimes he would get into the wagon and ride for an hour or two and show me which way to go. I became so well acquainted with the country that I could travel for hours without his assistance. We always kept along the divides on the highest land when it ran in the right direction. We traveled this way for about eight days. We never traveled on Sunday. We always rested on that day. We would put on our Sunday clothes and have a meeting. We always tried to camp by a grove of trees on a Saturday night so that we could meet in the shade on Sunday. We enjoyed our meetings just as well as though we were in a fine meeting house. We had traveled about eight days through a beautiful open country with patches of timber near the small streams. We came to a place which Brother Pratt thought would be a good location for a settlement. He was half a mile ahead of my wagon. He traveled back and met us and told us there was a good location for a settlement and he would call it Mt. Pisgah. It was at the end of a divide on which we had been traveling. We camped on the side of the hill. Below us was a small stream with plenty of timber near by. We concluded to stay here until President Young and the main body of the camp came up. The main body could not travel so far in a day, as a good many of their teams would give out and they had to send back teams to get the others into camp. Brother Young would not leave any teams back, but would have them all in camp at night. A great many of their teams were overloaded, and they soon found out they would have to leave a great many things behind, as they were so overloaded they could not travel.

Brother Pratt said we had better commence to lay the foundation for a settlement. We commenced building houses, fencing in and making gardens as though we were going to stay there. In about four days President Young and his company came up. Pisgah is about 100 miles from Garden Grove, as near as I can recollect. After we left it became quite a large settlement. Brother Pratt had a son born to him at this place and he was named Heleman. He was the first child of Sister Mary Wood Pratt. Soon after he was born Sister Pratt wanted me to come and see him.

Being young and bashful, it was sometime before I could find the courage to go into the wagon and see the baby, but when I did Sister Pratt seemed very cheerful and was glad to see me. I can say that the Sisters Pratt were all very good and kind to me and did everything for me that lay in their power just the same as if I was one of their own family, and also Brother Pratt was like a father to me. Neither Brother Pratt or his wives ever gave me one cross word, and I do not know that I was ever angry or cross with them.

President Young called a meeting of the brethren and spoke to them in relation to our traveling and getting over the Rocky Mountain that season. We had then been on the road about three months and had only traveled about 225 miles. President Young wanted the brethren to fit out the Twelve and make up a company large enough to travel in safety through the Indian country, cross the Rocky Mountains and form a colony that season, but the people did not see it in this light. They did not seem willing for him to go ahead without them, and he was not willing to go with such a large company, so many women and children, as he knew they were not fitted out for a journey of a thousand miles. Quite a number of the Saints could not travel any further, and so it was decided that a settlement should be made there and that it should be a resting place for the Saints until they were able to continue their journey. Brother Charles C. Rich was appointed to preside.[99]

President Young and the rest of the company started out for the Missouri River which was supposed to be about 75 miles. It was now past the middle of May. We traveled about ten or twelve miles a day through a beautiful and well watered country. The streams were very much swollen on account of the great amount of rain that had fallen. It was very difficult to bridge some of the

---

99. William Huntington was called to preside. Charles C. Rich was his counselor.

streams. It took a good deal of time and labor. One stream in particular we had to bridge several hundred yards as the river had overflowed its banks. We were three days bridging this stream with more than 100 men at work.

In July we arrived at Council Bluffs, overlooking the valley of the Missouri River. President Young and most of the companies camped on the bluffs. Brother Pratt and a few of his friends went down a hollow and camped by a beautiful large spring of water. Here we discovered acres of large wild strawberries. We could sit down and get our fill without moving far. This was a luxury that we had not thought of finding. [. . .]

About this time the young lady whom I had taken through the temple at Nauvoo, arrived with her father's family. It was on Sunday. After the meeting was over, I took her to our tent and introduced her to Brother Pratt's family. I asked her where her father was camped but she could not tell me. She thought it was two or three miles from there. I know the country around there very well, so we started to find the camp. We made for the large spring where we had found so many strawberries and we found them camped right by the spring. They were very glad to see me and made me welcome. Her father's name was John Robinson. He had been a sea captain and master of a vessel. They had started from Nauvoo in May with a good outfit consisting of three wagons, six yoke of cattle, some cows and quite a number of sheep. They had lost all but about six of their sheep and they lost the remainder before they left the spring. I went back to camp in the evening.

I will now say something about the movement of the camps. The lateness of the season, the poverty of the people and above all, the taking away of the 500 of our best men [to the Mormon Battalion], finally compelled us to abandon any further progress westward till the return of another spring. The camps therefore began to prepare for winter. We sent a small company of men down to the Missouri River to get lumber to make a flat boat to carry us across the river. Bro. [Frederick] Kesler, who was afterwards Bishop of the Sixteenth Ward, Salt Lake City, was appointed to superintend it. The camps all moved down to the river to a place which was called the Point, where some Indian agents lived who kept supplies for the Pottowatamie Indians, living about 30 miles east from there. They were the first Indians I ever saw and they seemed to be quite intelligent. They wanted to know where we were going. We told them we were going beyond the Rocky Mountains, that we were driven out from the United States and were seeking a home far away in the west. They seemed to be very friendly and thought it very strange that we could not live with the white people. We showed them the Book of Mormon and told them it was a record of their forefathers. They seemed very pleased and wanted to know more about it. Some of those Indians had been to Nauvoo and had seen Joseph Smith, who had told them a good deal about the Book of Mormon, that it was a record of their forefathers and that they were once a white people like unto us. They did not stay there many years after that as the Government took their lands and they moved to Indian Territory. (I have strayed a little from my narrative, but as I had missed this little incident I thought it was a good place to put it in.)

We went down to The Point, did a little trading at the store, camped on the banks of the Missouri about two weeks until the boat was completed, and then commenced to ferry across the river, which was about one quarter of a mile wide, being narrower there than in many other places. They kept the boat going night and day and still could not complete the crossing of the camps till late in the season. We had a very steep hill to go up from the river to get on the bluffs which made it very hard pulling. We traveled a few miles on the bluffs up the river and camped. As we were going to stay there a few days, I concluded to cross the river, go back and get Miss Robinson, as we had agreed before I left Nauvoo that when we met we would get mar-

ried. I spoke to Brother Pratt on the subject and he told me I had
better go back and bring her along.

I took my horse and carriage, crossed the river and found
them camped on the bluffs. I made my errand known to them
and she was willing to go with me and share with me in anything
we would have to go through. I stopped with them that night.
Next morning she gathered up the few things that she had and
put them into the carriage. We bade the old folks good-bye and
started for the river. The boatman knew it was Brother Pratt's
carriage. I told them I was on urgent business so they put me
across in quick time. In going up the hill from the river we both
had to get out and walk. The hill was very steep, our horses were
not very strong and the carriage was very heavy. I began to fear
we could not get up. I told Miss Robinson to drive and I would
push behind and block the wheels, but as she was no driver that
would not work. The carriage went back instead of going ahead.
I got a hold of the lines and told her to block the wheels. We
managed to get along by going a few yards and resting, and in this
way finally got to the top of the hill. We had taken the things out
of the carriage and left them half way down the hill. I had to go
back and carry them up. This took me sometime and I was very
nearly exhausted, but we finally got started for camp which was
only about three or four miles, arriving there in safety. The
Sisters Pratt were very pleased to see us and began to make preparations for our wedding. It was decided that Brother Pratt should
marry us the next day. On the evening of the 27th of July, 1846,
all of the family dressed in their best, and Brother Pratt performed the ceremony. Hymns were sung, a good supper was
served, and we all felt happy.

As before stated, it was now getting too late in the season to
pursue our journey to the mountains, and as we had eaten a good
portion of our provisions and had to get fresh supplies,
President Young thought we had better stay somewhere in the
vicinity until another season. The object now was to find good

winter quarters. We traveled about 16 miles further up the river and camped near a large grove of timber which place was called Cutlers Park in honor of Father [Alpheus] Cutler. We remained there some three or four weeks, plowed and fenced in several acres of land and planted it with turnips which matured before the winter set in. This was about two miles from the river. President Young was looking for a location for us to winter. He did not think this place was suitable. He decided that we should go to the bluffs. We moved down there and pitched our tents. This was sometime in September.

The next great question was where we could winter our stock as we had several thousand head. The prairie grass was drying up and we could not feed them on that, and the only plan that could be devised was to send them up the river about 100 miles on the river bottoms and winter them on the bushes. Men were sent up the river to look over a good place, and most of our horses and cattle were sent away, with the exception of a few that were wanted for our immediate use, and also our milch cows. Quite a number of men went to cutting hay and stacking it up. The hay was not very good as it was cut too late in the season, but it was thought it would save the lives of some of our stock. Some of the men, including myself, were appointed to take some stock about 20 miles up the river to herd. A wagon was unloaded and some provisions put in. My wife and myself with some other families fitted out in the same way with horses to ride, went up the river to herd. It was a very nice place. We found plenty of honey made by wild bees in hollow trees. We always collected the honey at night when the bees were sleepy. We had all the butter, milk and honey that we wanted to eat with our bread. It was that time of the year called Indian summer and it was very pleasant.

One evening I was gathering up the stock. I had strayed several miles from camp. It became dark and I lost my way. I wandered about for several hours. At last I saw a little glimmer of light. I went toward it and it proved to be the camp. I found my wife crying. She thought the Indians had taken me and that she would never see me again. The Indians on that side of the river were very bad. They would steal all they could put their hands on and if they caught a white man alone very likely they would kill him as they did in one or two instances.

Towards the last of October I was called to go to the main camp, or as the place was called, Winter Quarters. Although I had spent a very pleasant time herding, I was glad to go back. I took all the honey that I could collect back with me. They wanted me at Winter Quarters to help them to erect houses as they were preparing for cold weather.

I will say that before I went up to the herd, Brothers Pratt, [Orson] Hyde and [John] Taylor were called to go to England to settle some difficulty in relation to Elder [Reuben C.] Hedlock and the joint stock company.[100] It had caused a good deal of trouble and dissatisfaction among the Saints in England. Brother [John] Van Cott was left in charge of the family.

When I arrived at Winter Quarters I was greatly surprised to see over 500 log houses put up, making quite a city, as when I had left to go with the herd there was not a house of any kind. The streets were laid out at right angles which formed it into squares. Brother Pratt's houses were not put up. Two or three men, including myself, went up the river, made a raft by boring holes and fastening them together by pegs. When we had secured enough, we got on to the raft and floated down the river, landing opposite the city. It took us about four days. We then hauled them to the place where we were going to build and were soon working on the houses. White cloth was used for windows as we

---

100. Reuben Hedlock, the presiding elder in London, organized an "Emigration Fund" in which English members contributed funds for stock. The members were promised that the money was being used to help poverty-stricken emigrants, but Hedlock and two partners were using the money for their own personal use. Parley P. Pratt had to remove Hedlock and straighten out the Church's financial affairs in England.

did not have any glass. We thought the houses were very comfortable as we had been without houses for nine months.

It was now getting towards the last of November. We had very fine weather, but now it began to get very cold. The snow began to fall and it froze very hard at night. Brother Pratt ~~and~~ <had> 21 in his family and I was the only one to see to things out of doors. There was wood to be hauled and chopped up to keep the fires going, and many other things to do. Our provisions also were getting very scarce and little or no money to get any more. As Brother Pratt was away in England, the family had to do the best they could, and although Brother John Van Cott was left in charge, yet 21 in a family was a great many for him to see to as he had a family of his own. He was a cousin[101] to Brother Pratt and was well provided for. He had not traveled with us through the spring and summer, but had come right along from the states with three loaded wagons, and had overtaken us at Winter Quarters. The brethren and sisters kept coming along all summer as fast as they could get teams, wagons and provisions to fit themselves out. Some came to Winter Quarters while others remained on the Iowa side of the river choosing for themselves the best location they could find. They were scattered for a good many miles up and down the river. [. . .]

Quite a number went to the neighboring settlements and got work while those who were left were taken to Winter Quarters. The cold weather had now set in. It was the hardest winter that had been known for years. The ice on the river was three feet thick. Teams traveled back and forth across the river for three months.

When December arrived we had used up most of our provisions. We had a little corn that was not ground, and there was no mill within 100 miles. Brother Van Cott had brought with him a large coffee mill. We set a post in the ground and the mill was fas-

101. John VanCott's mother, Lovinia Pratt, was a sister of Parley's father, Jared Pratt.

tened to it and was used by the Saints to grind their corn. We had no more flour until the next spring. The corn meal was very coarse, but when we got used to it, it went very well. The greatest trouble was that we did not have enough of it. Sometimes we would have a little molasses to eat with it, sometimes a little butter and milk. It was quite hard to be out grinding corn when the thermometer was several degrees below zero. I spent most of my time through the winter hauling wood and grinding corn. President Young and those who came from Nauvoo when we did lived in about the same way as far as I could learn. We never tasted vegetables from the time we left the Mississippi River until we raised some in the valley of Salt Lake. When we became very hungry we would go down to the river and dig a few artichokes and what we did not eat raw, we brought home and cooked, and thought they were very nice. I do not know how we would have lived through the winter if the soldiers who had joined the Battalion had not sent us some money. When the Battalion got down to Ft. Leavenworth they had a certain amount of money given to them out of their pay to send to their families, which amounted to several thousand dollars. It was sent to President Young late in the fall. He thought it would be the best plan to send some competent man down to St. Louis and have him bring things that were needed for the camp. Bishop [Newel K.] Whitney, who was the first bishop in the Church, was selected for the purpose. Besides this money there was some collected from persons who had it, as they thought money would be of no use to them after leaving the frontier. Bishop Whitney went down to St. Louis and purchased a boat load of goods and provisions and returned early in the spring.

There was a great deal of sickness in the camp during the winter, partly on account of not having the proper food and partly from hunger and exposure. The disease of scurvy was prevalent. Hundreds died and were buried on the hill above the city. It was a time of mourning among the Saints. A great many of the middle aged and old people were taken from us. [. . .]

Sometime in February I was sent to the herd, about 30 miles up the river on the opposite side, to get a horse and to take one up there that was almost starved. I started as early as I could and crossed the river on the ice. I had never been up there and had to find my way the best I could. I thought I could get there by dark, but my horse was so poor that I could not get him along. After traveling about 20 miles, I found that I could not get to the herd that night. It was no use traveling after dark as I did not know the place, and there was no road. I had been directed to travel along by the edge of the timber, as there was timber all up the river about a mile, while outside of that was open country. As I could not make the herd camp that night, my horse being tired out, I turned into the timber. The snow was on the ground about six inches deep. I had a buffalo robe with me. I tied my horse to a tree and selected an old dry log to camp by. There was nothing to eat for myself or horse. I gathered up some dry wood and made a fire. It was now dark. The wolves began to howl around me. I became quite alarmed. I had nothing to defend myself with, neither gun nor pistol. It was the first time I had ever been alone, and I had to make the best of it. I had read that wild animals would not approach where there was a good fire. I knew that would be the only thing that would save me. I gathered some more wood, as there was plenty all around. I got my horse, that I had tied some little distance away, tied him pretty close to the fire. I sat on the log for some hours listening to the howling of the wolves. Many thoughts passed through my mind. I did not feel afraid, although I felt very lonely. The howling of the wolves began to cease a little. I began to get sleepy. I knelt down by the side of the log, lay down on it, wrapped myself up, and in a little while I was fast asleep. I slept until an hour before daylight. I got up, found my horse all right, made up a good fire, warmed myself, saddled my horse and started out. I found I was about six miles from the herd camp. I got there about 10:00 o'clock and turned my horse loose to get something to eat as he had not had anything from the time we left Winter Quarters. I remained there that day, found the horse I wanted, started for home early the next morning, and managed to reach there about dark.

We had many meetings through the winter. Our meeting house was a double log cabin that would hold from three to four hundred. We received excellent teachings from President Young and from the Twelve Apostles. Meetings were held once or twice a day on Sundays, our house being so small it would not hold nearly as many as wanted to attend. A great many quorum and council meetings were held to find out the best course to pursue in regard to our organization and travel the coming season. There were now some thousands gathered at Winter Quarters and many hundreds camped up and down the river and on the bluffs. All were anxious to know what they should do. Spring was now opening upon us. A great many of the Saints had lost part of their stock during the winter, some of it having been stolen by the Indians and some having died. This naturally broke up the arrangements of a good many who had intended to cross the plains that season, and they were compelled to get what little stock they had left and go to farming or anything else they could do and wait until they could get another outfit.

A brother by the name of John Neff and family from Pennsylvania, came to Winter Quarters early in the spring. He was a miller and farmer, and had acquired considerable means. President Young thought it would be a good plan to build a grist mill on a little stream that ran on the north side of the town, as it would make work for a great many men who had nothing to do and very little to eat. The mill was needed to grind our wheat and corn that we were to take with us the ensuing summer. He wanted Brother Neff to take hold of it and build it, which he agreed to do. Accordingly, quite a number of men were wanted to go to work. There was a dam to be built across the creek to hold the water. Brother Frank Pullen and myself were appointed to super-intend that work. There was also a mill race to be dug, two or three hundred yards long and from eight to twelve feet deep. Carpenters, millwrights and sawyers were employed. They had to saw all the lumber by hand or what we would call pit sawing. This work seemed to revive and stimulate people. We now had more provisions and the people felt better as the spring opened. It had been a very severe winter, such a winter as I had never experienced before and have not since, over 30 years.

On the sixth day of April 1847, the annual conference was held. Many thousands were gathered together to know and understand what was to be done the coming season. President Young said he wanted a company of men with a good outfit to go with him as pioneers to find a location for the gathering place of the Saints. He had but very little idea of where he should go as he knew nothing about the country, but thought he would locate somewhere beyond the Rocky Mountains, and he wanted to start as soon as the company could be gotten ready. He chose a good many young and middle aged men, including all of the Twelve that were there, as the Brothers Pratt, Hyde and Taylor had not returned from England. Quite a number volunteered, and the company was made up numbering 143 men and three or four women. About the 12th of April they started on their journey.

We were looking for Brother Pratt and the brethren that were with him to return as we had heard they were coming and were not far away, and that my sisters were with them, Harriet, Sophia and Elizabeth. In a few days after the pioneers had left, Brother Pratt came home. Everybody was very pleased to see him. All our troubles, tribulations and privations which we had suffered during the long cold winter were for the time forgotten. Now life and joy rested upon us. He had been away just about nine months. He found an increase of one in his family.[102]

The day after he got home he told me he wanted me to go

---

102. Parley P. Pratt's wife Sarah Huston had given birth to Julia on 1 April, seven days before Parley arrived home.

and meet my sisters and to get the carriage ready and he would go with me. He had brought two young ladies from England whom he intended to make his wives.[103] The next morning I got everything ready, and we started on our journey down the river. We traveled some 25 miles and stopped for the night. The next day we had not traveled a great distance before we met them traveling with a team. It was a very happy meeting and almost unexpected. I knew they had made their calculations to emigrate to Nauvoo in one year from the time I left England, but as we had been driven from Nauvoo and were in the wilderness and traveling to an unknown country I did not know when I should see them again. I did not know that my youngest sister [Elizabeth Whitaker] was married until I met them. She had married a young man by the name of Joseph Cain about the time they left Liverpool. Brother Pratt put his two young ladies in the carriage and drove towards home, leaving me to return with Brother Cain and my sisters. We traveled slow and got to Winter Quarters in about three days. Soon after we got to Winter Quarters my Sister Sophia was married to John Taylor. My sister Harriet and Brother Cain and his wife went to live in a dug out which one of the brethren had left. As many as could fit themselves out and could follow the pioneers were making preparation.

About this time Brother Pratt told me that it would not be convenient for him to take my wife and myself across the plains as he had many wives and children of his own and my wife was likely to be confined in a short time and would want a wagon and he would not have any to spare. He said he was very sorry to lose me as I had been of so much help to him and his family, but that circumstances had changed. He thought I would be able to get some help and would get along all right. I thanked him very kindly for

---

103. Parley met Martha Monks and Ann Agatha Walker in England and married both on 28 April after returning to the United States.

his good feelings towards me and was glad to hear that he was satisfied with my labors.

I had been working on the mill dam and helping to dig the mill race for five or six weeks and was making a dollar and a quarter a day. I had taken that home to the family and it was a great help in supporting them, but now that work was all done. We gathered together what few things we had at Brother Pratt's and took them to my wife's father's who lived a short distance from us.

I now began to study what I should do. I could not see any way open for me to go that season. I did not think my sisters had any more than would take them. Brother Cain had just returned from a mission to England and he had but little or nothing. My wife's father did not make me any offer, nor give me any encouragement and my wife and myself were too independent to ask him for any help. I was young and strong and able to work, and I thought I could get along very well, although I wanted to go very much and would do or sacrifice anything to go. I had been a Pioneer from Nauvoo and I would very much like to go with the first companies, but my way did not seem to open up. I had nothing to do at this time. I wanted to be at work. I commenced to dig up some land for a garden and put in some seeds such as radishes, lettuce, peas and many other small seeds. I could not get it out of my mind but that I should go, still I could not see any way by which I could go. I had no provisions, no money to get any with, no team and no wagon. My clothes that I had brought from England were pretty much worn out, and I was not in a very good condition to go a long journey, but those things did not trouble me if I could get a chance to go.

It was now about the first of May. I went over to my sister's and we began to talk about the journey. She said Brother Cain and herself were going to try to go, and they would like it very much if I could go with them. She knew my circumstances and knew I wanted to go. She suggested that my wife's father would probably help me some and she would help me and I should do all I could to help myself. I then began to feel I was going. My sister and her husband had some things they could part with that they had brought from England and also a little money. It was concluded to fit out a team and go to Missouri and trade those things away and get our provisions and some cows and what we needed for the journey. We got up a company consisting of five or six wagons. My wife's father sent a wagon and one of his sons. I was to go with the outfit with Brother Cain. My mother-in-law gave me $5.00 and my wife told me to get some flat irons, bake kettle, shovel and tongs.

The company started down to Missouri about the beginning of May. We traveled down to St. Joe about 150 miles. Nothing particular transpired on our way. We would trade as we went along, if we saw anything we wanted. Sometimes we would go out of our way to farm houses to see if they had any wheat or corn for sale. So many of the brethren had been down there before us that the country had been pretty much cleaned out for grain. Brother Cain offered a saddle for sale. They said it was the very thing they wanted. Brother Cain wanted $10.00 for his saddle. They told him they would give him 60 bushels of corn for it. He soon closed the bargain and we got our corn. We also got our wheat, took it to the mill and had it ground into flour, bought two cows, did our other trading, loaded up our wagons and started back for Winter Quarters and arrived there about the first of June.

On arriving home we found my sister Harriet very sick. She had been chopping wood and had broken a blood vessel which caused her to come very near dying, but by the administration of the elders and the goodness of God, she got well very fast.

The grist mill that we had expected to use in grinding most of our wheat did not begin to run before the first of June. It was lucky for many that they got their flour down in Missouri, or they would have been very late in starting. The mill did very good business for one run of stones. When they got it going they kept it running almost night and day.

We now began to prepare for our journey west. We had but one wagon and two yoke of oxen. My sister Harriet traded different things for another wagon. We then wanted two yoke of oxen. Joseph Cain made out to get one ox. My wife's father saw that we had done all we could. He then furnished us with three oxen, making all together two yoke for each wagon. We had to get so many pounds of flour for each individual, 350 pounds for each person, if not, we were not allowed to go. There were men appointed to inspect each wagon to see if we had the requisite quantity. We knew that we were going into a country where we could not buy any. We had to take enough to last us fifteen months, or until we could raise it. We had to take our seed grain, farming implements, cooking utensils, and such things that we could not do without. Some would take a few chickens fastened on behind the wagons, and some would take a little pig. We had our wagons all loaded up and inspected and pronounced all right.

On the 10th of June we left our Winter Quarters, traveled about ten miles on to a large open plain. There we remained two or three days to be organized into companies. Brothers Pratt and Taylor were with us. They took a prominent part in the organization. Before President Young had left he had appointed some of the captains of hundreds. We were organized into companies of hundreds, fifties and tens. To each of those divisions was a captain. Bishop Edward Hunter was the captain of our hundred. Brother Joseph Horn was the captain of our fifty and Brother Abraham Hoagland was the captain of our ten. [. . .]

Brother John Taylor traveled with our fifty. I will say that those brethren whom I have named [the heads of families in his group of ten] traveled together all the way and settled down very near together, and have loved one another as brothers ever since.

Eliza Partridge Lyman, the daughter of Lydia Partridge Huntington, widow of Edward Partridge and later married to William Huntington as a plural wife, did not travel with her mother's family. Both were, however, assigned to the Amasa Lyman company. Eliza, a plural wife of Amasa Lyman, left Nauvoo with his company on 9 February, one of the first groups to cross the Mississippi. Eliza occasionally saw her mother along the journey, but their families traveled apart from each other, and it was not until Lydia reached Winter Quarters, after William Huntington's death in Mount Pisgah, that mother and daughter reunited. Eliza, like many women diarists, fills her diary with the friends and family with whom she shares the vicissitudes of the Iowa trek and Winter Quarters. The woman's world she lives in and recreates in her writing is rich with companionship, domestic ties and tasks, and much patience in suffering.

E L I Z A   M A R I A   P A R T R I D G E   L Y M A N[104]

I WILL GO BACK to the time when I left Nauvoo on the 9th of Feb, [1846] and write from my private journal. It will not perhaps be very interesting to anyone but myself, but it shows more particularly how we were situated and the hardships we endured in accomplishing the journey. On Feb 9th 1846 I bade adieu to my friends in Nauvoo and in company with my Husband

104. Journal of Eliza Maria Partridge Lyman, 1846 February-1885 December, LDS Church Archives.

Amasa Lyman, Daniel P. Clark and wife [Sarah Melissa Hakes Clark], Henry Rollins, and Dionitia W. Lyman (one of my husbands wives) started westward, for some place where we might worship God according to the dictates of our own consciences.

We went about one mile to the Mississippi river, waited about three hours, then succeeded in procuring a boat, onto which we put our horses and waggons, and as there was no prospect of Father Huntington crossing the river that night, we took my mother [Lydia Clisbee Partridge Huntington] and sisters Caroline and Lydia and Br Edward with us and crossed the river.[105]

When we were about midway [of the stream] we saw a boat at some distance from us, sinking, with no one near to assist them, but fortunately for them they were near a sand bar so that they were not drowned, and soon a boat reached them and took them safely to shore.

Our boat got into the ice which hindered us about an hour but did no damage. We went to Br Sidney Tanner's where a part of us staid all night and the rest staid at Nathan Tanners [sons of Father John Tanner].

Tuesday 10th We are all alive and well. Dionitia, Caroline and I slept in one bed and as I was very tired I did not sleep much. Br Lyman is going back over the river to visit his wife Maria.[106] I cut and made a dress for Sister Tanner.

Evening Br Lyman has just returned bringing his wife Maria with him. I was heartily glad to see her. I went (by invitation) with them to visit her father. Father Huntington and mother and brother Edward also came there and staid all night. Mother Tanner[107] prepared an excellent supper for the company.

---

105. The marriage of William Huntington, a widower, and Lydia Partridge, Eliza's mother, linked two prominent Mormon families.

106. Louisa Maria Tanner Lyman, daughter of John Tanner.

107. Probably Eliza Beswick Tanner, third wife of John Tanner whose first two wives had died before the family moved from New York.

Wednesday 11th Br Lyman went back to Nauvoo to see how the children were getting along as his wife left them while she visited us. The rest of us remained at Father T. during the day and night Br L. came back in the evening reporting all well.

Thursday 12th Br Lyman took his wife Maria to the river and saw her safely landed on the opposite shore, then returned to us feeling very well. Mother Tanner gave us the privilege of making some mince pies, and assisted us to do so.

Friday 13th Br Lyman went to the camp. Took me with him as far as Sidney Tanner's where I staid all day till br L- came back. Went back to Father Tanner's.

Saturday 14th Arose in the morning and found the ground covered with snow, continued snowing all day.

Sunday 15th The weather quite pleasant. Went to the river with br Lyman to see my sister Emily,[108] Found her in a tent surrounded with mud. Came home in the afternoon. Wrote to Sister Maria Lyman in the evening.

Monday 16th Took breakfast with Aunt Polly Cook.[109] Twisted some thread for Mother,[110] Came back and finished a dress for Mother Tanner.

Tuesday 17th Mother Tanner gave br Lyman twelve yards of factory[111] to line his waggon cover, which I made in the morning. About two o clock we started for the camp where we arrived about sundown, prepared our tents, took some refreshment, and retired for the night, but did not sleep much on account of the horses, we not being accustomed to their noise. When we left Father Tanner's he gave us a few lbs fresh beef butter, 6 or 8 lbs

---

108. Emily Partridge was a plural wife of Brigham Young and traveled in his company.
109. Polly Beswick, sister of John Tanner's wife, Elizabeth, married Edward Cook in 1844 in Nauvoo.
110. The process of twisting thread is employed after spinning to obtain greater strength and smoothness, increased uniformity, or novelty of effects.
111. A term for the gray cotton muslins made in American mills.

some pork and some mince pies, and to Father Huntington a fine calf, which he killed for veal.

Wednesday 18th The sun shines warm and the weather is very fine. I can set in the waggon and write with all ease without fire. Father Tanner and family came to camp and made a short visit. Albert Tanner [son of Father John Tanner] brought a load of hay and some potatoes from his father's.

Thursday 19th Arose in the morning and found the ground covered with snow. Snowed all day which makes us very uncomfortable as the wind blows the snow in every direction and our fire is out in the storm so that we can not get warm by it. I am almost frose, so shall go into the waggon and make my bed and get into it as I can not get warm any other way.

Friday 20th The weather is somewhat pleasanter than it was yesterday but is very cold. Our family consists of seven persons, namely Amasa Lyman and his wife Dionitia, Daniel P. Clark and wife, Henry Rollins, Albert Tanner and myself.

Saturday 21st The sun shines warm, but the air is cold. We received a load of corn from A. Lyman's farm.

Sunday 22nd We have had a very cold night, but the sun this morning with his genial rays warms the earth and all nature revives again. Received another load of hay from Father Tanner's.

Monday 23rd The weather cloudy and cold. Received word from Nauvoo that Sister Maria Lyman was very sick. I started about two o clock in company with br Lyman to go and see her. When we had gone about three miles our buggy broke down and left us in the mud. Fortunately a waggon came along and took us to Montrose. Found the ice running in the river so that it was impossible to cross that night, except in a skiff which br L- succeeded in doing with great difficulty, leaving me on this side w/ Sister Daniels' to stay all night.

Tuesday 24th Br L- came back this morning, said he found his wife more comfortable than he expected, had a fine son which they call Amasa. He took dinner at Sister Daniels' then went back to Nauvoo to stay till tomorrow. I staid at Sister D's till nearly night when Albert Tanner came and took me back to camp where we arrived about dark.

Wednesday 25th In the morning, assisted in preparing breakfast, and through the day made preparations for starting on our journey on the morrow. Br Lyman came back in the afternoon, brought a sheet iron stove to put in the tent which will make us more comfortable.

Thursday 26th The weather cold. Br L- went to Father Tanner's and staid all night.

Friday 27th As we are yet in camp I have concluded to go to Nauvoo and visit Sister M[aria]. Lyman. Went with Henry Rollins and Dionitia Lyman. Crossed the river on the ice. Found Sister L- quite smart but her son Marion[112] was sick with measles. Staid with them all night.

Saturday 28th Staid with Sister L- all day looking for Br Lyman who expected to have visited us this afternoon. About three o clock H. Rollins came and said the camp had orders to move tomorrow, consequently br L- could not come over but had sent him to bring us back, which was a great disappointment to Sister L- I then bade my friend good bye and went back to camp where we arrived about seven o clock in the evening. We were stopped by the guard in sight of our own fire, and were obliged to wait till br Lyman came and took us over the line. We found the brass band assembled around our fire making some very good music.

Sunday 1st The camp are preparing to leave, but we shall stay till tomorrow.

Monday 2nd Left camp at 15 minutes to ten. Had in company br R[oswell]. Dana and family, Wm. Huntington Sen. and family, A Lyman and family, D[aniel].P. Clark and wife,

---

112. Amasa's and Louisa Maria's second child Francis Marion. He was born 12 January 1840.

H[enry]. Rollins, A[lbert]. M[ills]. Tanner, H[enry]. B. Jacobs, S[anford]. Jacobs and J[ohn Lowe]. Butler. Traveled on the Farmington road. Camped at 5 o'clock. Our ox team arrived at sundown.

Tuesday 3rd Up at six o clock, traveled 10 miles. Camped three miles above Farmington. Camped before sundown.

Wednesday 4th Staid in camp all day. Washed, ironed, baked.

Thursday 5th Up early in the morning, and ready for a start. Br Lyman took his wife Priscilla Turley into his waggon, and she will live with us for the present. Traveled the most muddy road I ever saw. Went about 6 miles. A little before night, Uncle John Smith's waggon upset with himself, wife and daughter, did but little damage. Several teams gave out before night. We reached the prairie a little before dark, and camped in company with Br H. C. Kimball, we made no fire but ate some cold meat and bread and went to bed.

Friday 6th Arose in the morning and made a small fire of bark and made some coffee to drink with our bread. After breakfast started again on our journey, went about seven miles, found the roads very good. Stopped about 10 o clock near Br B. Young's camp on Indian Creek and staid the rest of the day. One horse died belonging to B. Young's company. Br Lyman has brought a rabbit, J. H. Rollins 2 prairie hens, and D. P. Clark a bird, which will make us a very comfortable meal.

Saturday 7th Up in the morning before sunrise, eat breakfast and left Indian Creek at 1/2 past 8. Traveled 8 miles and camped on the farm of Dr [John] Elbert where some of the brethren are at work. Stopped at 15 minutes past 1 o clock, pitched our tents and made ourselves as happy as possible. The Boys killed some hens, rabbits, etc. The weather very warm and pleasant.

Sunday 8th Quite unwell through the night, better this morning. Br L- and J. H. Rollins have been to the main camp, and learned from the President that we are to join them this afternoon.

Evening: We are comfortably camped again with the main body. Have found the rest of our company, namely, Sidney and Nathan Tanner with their families.

Monday 9th Staid in camp all day.

Tuesday 10th Made all preparations to start. Part of the teams went on, but it soon commenced raining which hindered us from going. It rained all day and is very muddy. Two of the Pioneers, J[ohn]. Brown and Si Dayton[113], commenced boarding with us.

Wednesday 11th Still raining.

Thursday 12th The ground is very muddy, we cannot step without getting over shoe top in mud. We have been obliged to move our camp to a better place about a quarter of a mile.

Friday 13th Washing Etc.

Saturday 14th Ironed etc. Bro Lyman and Rollins killed a mess of squirrels which were very good.

Sunday 15th The weather fine, but the wind very high, can hardly keep our tents right side up.

Monday 16th The sun has risen in all his splendor and the weather is very fine. Br Rollins took his team and started back to Nauvoo. Father Huntington and Nathan Tanner went away to trade horses for oxen.

Tuesday 17th This morning br Sidney Tanner's youngest child named James Monroe died and was buried in the afternoon.

Wednesday 18th Went over to the other camp to see my sister Emily Young. Staid most of the day. While there Br Edwin Little's corpse was brought in for burial.

---

113. John Brown joined Brigham Young's pioneer company in April 1847 and was the chief hunter of the caravan. Si Dayton is probably Lysander Dayton, the son of Hiram Dayton. Lysander went to Utah in 1847 in advance of the rest of his family. He was a member of the Mormon Battalion.

Thursday 19th The camp have mostly moved on leaving us here waiting for teams. Received a letter from Sister Maria Lyman by R[obert]. Cliff. Br N. Tanner has returned from his trading expedition having exchanged one span of horses for a yoke of old cattle, one yoke of steers, a cow, a gun, and a steel trap. Father Huntington came back having made no effectual trade.

Friday 20th Very high winds. N. Tanner took Father H's horses and started off this morning to trade for cattle. He succeeded, and returned in the evening with 2 yoke of oxen. Our men busy fixing yokes etc. in order to be ready to start on again in the morning.

Saturday 21st All well. Weather fine. Started at 11 o clock to pursue our journey. Traveled about three miles, when Br Young and Evan Green[114] came up with us, from Nauvoo bound for the camp of Israel just on express they said. Traveled 9 miles this day, camped on the south fork of the Cheques [Chequest] River.

Sunday 22nd Awoke in the morning and found it had been raining. Started at 8 o clock, traveled 18 miles and camped for the night in the edge of the woods near Fox River.

Monday 23rd There was so much rain fell during the night that we were obliged to lay by this day. Had quite a hail storm in the afternoon. Our men took a job of splitting rails for corn, three bushels to the hundred.

Tuesday 24th The rain continues to pour down upon us with some snow. The ground is very muddy, almost impossible to get about without getting mired.

Wednesday 25th The ground covered with snow, continued to snow all day. Br. Lyman killed 2 ducks and one rabbit.

Thursday 26th The sun shines and every thing seems pleasanter than on yesterday.

---

114. Evan Melbourne Greene served as postmaster at Kanesville, Iowa, from 1849 until 1852, when he left for the Salt Lake Valley.

Friday 27th Cold and cloudy. The boys have commenced another job of rail making for which they get corn and pork.

Saturday 28th Weather pleasant. Boys off to work. Captain gone hunting, girls washing, and I am doing a little of every thing, and not much of any thing.

Sunday 29th Edward Dusset[115] and family arrived here on their way to the camp. Br Lyman and others made up a load of goods and sent them to the camp on Chariton river by Br Sidney Tanner.

Monday 30th Weather fine. Br Lyman 33 years old to day. He has been hunting and killed 3 ducks and two squirrels.

Tuesday 31st We had an excellent dinner of our ducks and squirrels. I started with D. P. Clark to go to Bloomfield a distance of 3 miles. Went two miles, came to Fox river, could not cross, so went back home to camp. Br S. Tanner came back in the evening.

Wednesday 1st Packed up our things and started again on our journey, Came to Fox river found the crossing very bad. I undertook to walk across on a log with br L- holding one hand and D. P. Clark the other. Unfortunately for Brother L- he stepped on a rotten limb which broke and let him fall a distance of ten or more feet into the water, but I more fortunate held fast to Br Clark and thus saved myself from falling and reached the other bank in safety. After the trouble of changing wet clothes for dry ones, and lifting wagons out of mud was got along with, we went ahead again for about a mile when Dionitia hurt her foot in the double trees of the waggon. Traveled 15 miles this day and camped for the night.

Thursday 2nd Started early in the morning. Traveled 12 miles and came to the Chariton river took in the rest of our loading and crossed over. Went on to the bluff on the opposite

---

115. Edward Duzette was a drummer in the Nauvoo Legion and a noted band major in the Nauvoo Legion Band. He served a mission in Michigan before leaving for the Valley in 1848.

side and camped for the night. Two brethren from Br Pratt's camp met us before we crossed the river, with seven yoke of oxen to help us on the rest of the way to their camp, a distance of 7 miles on the west side of the east fork of Shoal Creek. At the river we came across Henry Jacobs wagon in the mud, his wife <Zina> sick in bed on the top of the load, so near the wet cover that she could hardly raise her head, a babe in her arms but a few days old, and no other wagon near or friend to do any thing for her except her husband.

Friday 3rd Started early. Traveled a short distance, met Bro P[arley] P. Pratt, and G[eorge]. A. Smith coming to see what had become of us. Went to their camp, for the rain was pouring down in torrents. Pitched our tents in the mud and water. It continued to rain all day. It was almost impossible to get any thing to eat as we had to cook it out doors in the rain, over shoe in mud.

Saturday 4th Arose from our beds some time in the fore noon and found them and our clothes quite wet with the rain. After breakfast we commenced to dry our bed clothes by the fire in the rain where one side got wet while we were drying the other.

Sunday 5th The ground a little frozen, but the sun has risen and shines pleasantly. Washed, cooked etc. as we expect to start again tomorrow.

Monday 6th Awoke in the morning and found it raining which prevents our traveling to day. Rained all day.

Tuesday 7th We had a severe storm of rain and wind with sharp lightning. Br James Scott came to our camp this morning from a camp 3 miles ahead of us where Brs [George] Miller, [Newel K.] Whitney and [Heber C.] Kimball are. Just heard that President Young wishes us to move on as fast as possible so we expect to start again tomorrow.

Wednesday 8th Started on our journey in company with Brs P. P. Pratt, and G. A. Smith and their companies. Traveled 7 miles across a very wet prairie, the wagons settling into the turf nearly to the axle trees the most of the way. Reached Locust creek about dark, crossed over, ascended the hill, and pitched our tents in a very wet place. Found Br Kimball and the rest of the camp at this place ready to start on the morrow. We had thought that our teams must do without corn to night, but to our great satisfaction Br Kimball had some corn for us, which was a great blessing to our teams after their hard days work.

Thursday 9th Started early in the morning, and were obliged to double teams before we could get off our camping ground. Roads were very bad indeed. There were few teams that could go half a mile without help. Commenced raining about 12 o clock, and we in the midst of a large prairie with no prospect of reaching timber this day and consequently could have no fire let the weather be what it might. Continued raining very hard. Roads getting worse and worse. The best of the teams cannot move their loads without help. Br Lyman told me to drive on with the buggy till we came to a fire if we could find one, as there was no prospect of the teams getting much farther to day, and it seemed as if both the people and the teams must perish if they stopped there. We accordingly went ahead (that is Dionitia and I) some two or three miles, when we came in sight of tents not far from the road, went to them and found my Mother and family there with Father Huntington which made us feel quite at home although it was a most uncomfortable place, but we were wet and cold and glad to get any <place> where there was a fire. Their fire however did not do us much good as the rain continued to pour down which spoiled our chance of drying our clothes. Br Lyman came up about dark with one team, but the one with our beds and provisions was left out in the prairie with D. P. Clark and wife and Priscilla [Turley] Lyman [wife of Amasa] without fire or feed for their teams. We had to sleep as best we could which was anything but comfortable, some lying on boxes, some on chairs, and others in wet beds. I laid across a box in Father Huntington's waggon, with my head on his and Mother's bed with my feet on the front end board and my clothes wet about a quarter of a yard deep about my ankles. I do not know why I did not freese, for I had no bed and very little covering. It must be that there was not room in the wagon for the frost to get in, it was so full of folks.

Friday 10th Arose in the morning and found the mud so deep that we could not get from the wagon to the tent without getting nearly mired. Found the beds in the tent wet through. After much ado we succeeded in getting some breakfast. The brethren then took all the teams they could raise and went back to help those who were left out last night, they returned towards night with some of the families but left several to stay another night in the prairie The weather is very cold and they have no fire and very little food.

Saturday 11th The brethren have gone again to the prairie to render assistance to those who have not yet come up. Washed some of our wet clothes.

Sunday 12th Br Lyman has gone to attend a council of the twelve. Distance 5 miles. He returned towards evening almost crazy with the toothache.

Monday 13th Took all the teams in the company and part of the wagons and went 5 miles to stay while the teams went back for the rest.

Tuesday 14th The teams came up and went on past us 3 miles then came back for us, we started about 3 o clock came up with the main camp before dark Found sister Emily and babe[116] well.

Wednesday 15th Traveled 7 miles and camped in the edge of the prairie.

Thursday 16th The most of the company have moved on and we shall remain here while our teams are being sent off to trade. N. Tanner and D.P. Clark having gone for that purpose. We expect teams from the other camp to help us along tomorrow.

Friday 17th The teams have come for us but it is so late in the

---

116. Edward Partridge Young, son of Emily and Brigham Young, was born 30 October 1845 in Nauvoo.

day and Br G.A. Smith is here destitute of teams, that we have concluded to stay another night. Br Lyman, Hutchinson and Driggs[117] have gone turkey hunting, will stay all night.

Saturday 18th Our hunters have come in bringing one turkey and 1 chicken. Started on our journey again. Traveled 8 miles and camped in the timber.

Sunday 19th A most beautiful morning. All well except Br Lyman who is very sick with bowel complaint.

Monday 20th April I am 26 years old to day. Br L- very sick. Received a letter from Sister Maria Lyman.

Tuesday 21st Answered Sister L.'s letter. Br L- is not as well to day as yesterday. Suffers much pain. One of our horses very sick.

Wednesday 22nd Br L- some better. The weather very warm.

Thursday 23rd Brother L- same as yesterday. Dionitia taken sick.

Friday 24th Brother L- able to dress himself and leave the wagon.

Saturday 25th P[arley].P. Pratt and family left us and went on to Grand river.

Sunday 26th The weather pleasant. Folks getting well.

Monday 27th Woke in the morning and found it raining, it rained all day

Tuesday 28th It has rained all night and is raining yet.

Wednesday 29th The weather cloudy with some rain.

Thursday 30th Still raining.

Friday May 1st The weather more pleasant. Bros Tanner and Clark have just returned from their trading expedition.

Saturday 2nd Br Johnson and family came up with us, just from Nauvoo.

---

117. Probably Jacob Flynn Hutchinson. Jacob traveled in the Edward Hunter company of 1850 to the Valley. The name Driggs could refer to any one of the sons of Uriah Driggs and Hannah Ford, including Lorenzo Dow, Samuel, Shadrach Ford, and Starling Graves.

Sunday 3rd Had a severe storm of rain.

Monday 4th A fine pleasant morning. We had designed to start on our journey again but the rain has prevented us.

Tuesday 5th Weather extremely fine. Br Wm. Edwards very sick. The rest of our men preparing for a game of ball.

Wednesday 6th We are again hindered from pursuing our journey by a most violent storm which visited us last night, and we have another to day, a most furious storm.

Thursday 7th The morning cloudy, but a prospect of better weather.

Friday 8th Weather fine. Br Edwards some better but not able to sit up. Sister Lydia 16 years old to day. We have plenty of squirrels and wild turkies here and at night we are blessed with the music of the wolves.

Saturday 9th Started on our journey at 1/2 past 8 in the morning. At 12 stopped to feed our teams. Br Edwards very sick and so crazy that it is almost impossible to keep him in the wagon. Traveled 8 miles and camped for the night.

Sunday 10th Traveled 9 miles.

Monday 11th Traveled 7 miles and came up with Br Young's camp at the farm on Grand river. I staid with Sister Emily all night. The rest of our company went on 2 miles farther. Left Br Wm. Edwards at Father [James] Allred's.

Tuesday 12th Br Lyman came back with the buggy for me. Sister Emily and babe went with us and she staid with me all night.

Wednesday 13th The ground quite wet with last nights rain. Traveled 12 miles, and camped in the prairie and looked for a storm. Heard that br Edwards died this morning.

Thursday 14th The looked for storm came about dark last night and a harder rain we have not had this spring, almost every thing we have is wet, but the prospect is fair for a pleasant day. Br B. Young has just arrived and camped near us. We have traveled none today.

Friday 15th Traveled 6 miles and camped in the prairie.

Saturday 16th Traveled 6 or 8 miles across the prairie and camped near a skirt of timber.

Sunday 17th Staid in camp all day.

Monday 18th Went to Grand river. Found Brs P.P. and O[rson]. Pratt encamped

Tuesday 19th Br Lyman went in company with B. Young and others to look at the country around us. Two Indians came to our camp looking for a stray horse.

Wednesday 20th Rainy morning. It is thought best for some of the families to stop here for the present and raise crops this coming summer. They have named the place Mt Pisgah.

Wednesday 27th Father Huntington is moving his family to a house that he is building, and will not move any farther this year.

Sunday 31st Attended meeting in the grove.

Tuesday June 2nd [1846] Br Lyman has started back to meet his wife Maria and family. They are about 30 miles from here.

Saturday 6th Br L- has returned with his family and Father John Tanner and family.

Thursday 11th We are now ready to start on our journey again after having staid nearly a month in this place. I here leave my Mother and sisters Emily and Lydia and little brother Edward with the rest of the family excepting sister Caroline who is also Br Lyman's wife, she is going with us. Cornelia Leavitt Lyman (also one of Br Lyman's wives) has joined our family and is going west with us. Started about four o clock, traveled about four miles and camped for the night.

Friday 12th Traveled till night; then camped in the prairie, so far from wood that we could have no fire and of course not much supper.

Saturday 13th Arose early, ate some rusk[118] and milk and started

---

118. A light, soft, sweetened biscuit.

on our journey at 6 o clock. At 12 we came to some timber made a fire and prepared breakfast. Staid till 3 then went on till night.

Sunday 14th Weather pleasant. Br E[zra]. T. Benson took breakfast with us, on his way from Mount Pisgah to Council Bluffs. Traveled till noon, stopped near a small creek where we found an abundance of ripe strawberries. Camped in the ~~timber~~ <prairie> a short distance from timber.

Monday 15th The cattle could not be found till 11 o clock. We started about 12. Traveled till 3, stopped to bait. Met with one of the Potawotomie Indians. We carried wood from this place to where we camped in the prairie.

Tuesday 16th The morning pleasant. Traveled 16 miles. Passed an Indian village on the Nisheam Botany [Nishnabotna] River.

Wednesday 17th Weather fine, roads very dusty. Met several Indians who were out hunting. They had venison on their horses. We camped at night on the bank of quite a river.

Thursday 18th Some rain through the night, also plenty of mosquitoes. Br Benson met us this morning. Took a letter for me to my Mother at Pisgah. Traveled 16 miles. <~~Traveled~~> Camped on the bank of the [West Nishnabotna] where we had plenty of mosquitoes.

Friday 19th Traveled 8 miles. Passed a dead ox in the road.

Saturday 20th Traveled 10 miles. Came up with the main camp 7 miles from the Missouri river. Passed another dead ox.

Sunday 21st Had meeting in the grove.

Monday 29th We have had quite a great deal of hard wind and some rain during the past week. Wrote to my friends at Mt Pisgah this morning. Sent it by Br Pratt.

Tuesday 30th Br Lyman with his family of 16 persons left the camp and started for the river which the twelve expect to cross to day. Traveled about 6 miles came to some bad mudholes which they were obliged to bridge so that we did not reach the river this day, but camped for the night in the bottoms a short distance from Brs Young and Kimball.

Wednesday July 1st The sun shines pleasantly this morning. We were much annoyed with mosquitoes during the night. Came to the river at 12 o clock were detained till almost night then crossed over ascended the hill and went to the prairie a distance of 2 miles.

Thursday 2nd Went to Br [George] Miller's camp four miles from the river. Upset one wagon into the mud but not much damage done. Made some trouble drying and washing clothes that were wet and muddy.

Sunday 14th My first child was born here, in a wagon. I have named him Don Carlos. I am very uncomfortably situated for a sick woman. The scorching sun shining upon the wagon through the day and the cool air at night, is almost too much of a change to be healthy.

Wednesday 15th Br Lyman went over the river. It was about this time that the Mormon Battalion was called for.

August 9th Since I last wrote I have been very sick with child bed fever. For many days my life seemed near its end. I am now like a skeleton so much so that those who have not been with me do not know me till told who I am. It is a fearful place to be sick with fever in a wagon with no shade over except the cover and a July sun shining every day. All the comfort I had was the pure cold water from a spring near by. But the Lord preserved my life for some purpose for which I thank Him. My babe in consequence of my sickness is very poor but as I get better I hope to see him improve. Left the spring and went up the river about 12 miles.

Sept. 14th Wrote a letter to Mother sent by Father [Amos] Tubbs.

Monday 21st Visited Father [Cornelius Peter] Lotts [Lott]. Had a baked goose for supper. In the evening we were alarmed with the cry that a mob was near us but it proved to be false.

Tuesday 22nd Don Carlos 10 weeks old to day and as bright a little fellow as ever was.

Wednesday 23rd In the evening attended the wedding of Wm Martindale and Rebecca Ann Haynes.

Saturday 26th Removed to our Winter Quarters on the bank of the Missouri river.

Sunday 27th Staid at home.

Monday 28th The wind blows very hard. Several tents were blown down. Received a letter from Mother. Br Sidney Tanner moved from the Bluffs to the river bank.

Tuesday 29th Br S. Tanner's wife Louisa died leaving a babe three months old.

Wednesday 30th Sister Tanner buried. Father and Mother Tanner here, staid all night.

Thursday October 1st Br Lyman and other brethren gone up the river to cut house logs.

Saturday 3rd Br Lyman and company came home with a raft of logs the first that has been brought here.

Sunday 4th Staid at home and tended Baby.

Monday 5th Br Lyman and others went up the river again for more logs.

14th Don Carlos three months old to day and weighs eleven pounds.

15th We have taken possession of our log house today. The first house my babe was ever in. I feel extremely thankful for the privilege of sitting by a fire where the wind cannot blow in in every direction and where I can warm one side without freesing the other. Our house is minus floor and many other comforts but the walls protect us from the wind if the sod roof does not from the rain.

25th Caroline wrote a letter to Mother. My hair has nearly all come out, what little is left I have had cut off. My head is so bare I am compelled to wear a cap.

29th Took breakfast within the walls of our house It is now about 7 months since we have eaten in a house till now.

Nov 9th Daniel Weden Clark died this morning aged 3

weeks. He was the son of D.P. and Sarah M. Clark, and were living with us.

Nov 14th Don Carlos weighs 13 lbs, having gained 2 lbs during the last month. He is a great comfort to me.

Dec 6th My Baby sick and getting worse. Has cried all day but I cannot see what ails him.

12th The baby is dead and I mourn his loss. We have done the best we knew how for him, but nothing has done any good, he continued to fail from the time he was taken sick. My sister Caroline and I sat up every night with him and tried to save him from death for we could not bear to part with him, but we were powerless. The Lord took him and I will try to be reconciled and think that all is for the best. He was my greatest comfort and nearly always in my arms. But he is gone and I cannot recall him, so I must prepare to meet him in another and I hope a happier world than this. I still have friends who are dear to me, if I had not I should wish to bid this world farewell, for it is full of disappointments and sorrow, but I believe that there is a power that watches over us and does all things right. He was buried on the west side of the Missouri on the second ridge back, the eleventh grave on the second row counting from right to left, the first row being farthest from the river. This will be no guide as the place cannot be found in a few years.

Friday January 22nd 1847. Br Lyman has gone to visit the Brethren on the other side of the river in company with G[eorge].A. Smith and Lyman [Luman] Calkins.

Sunday 24th I went to Nathan Tanners to take care of his wife who is sick.

Wednesday 27th Sister Caroline attended a party at the Council house in company with D.P. Clark and wife.

Friday 29th I visited Br Young's wife Louisa[119] and others.

---

119. Brigham Young married Louisa Beaman in the fall of 1846.

Monday Feb 1st Br Lyman came home in good health and spirits.

Tuesday 2nd I am not able to stay with Sister Tanner so have come home to stay awhile. Priscilla [sister wife] has gone to take care of her a day or two.

Wednesday 3rd I am making a dress for Priscilla. Sister Caroline is writing to Mother.

Wednesday 10th Attended a Bishop's party at the Council house in the evening in company with Bishop L. Calkins and wife. Had a very pleasant time. There were many good brothers and sisters present and also some of the twelve, who seemed to enjoy themselves very much.

Friday 12th Dionitia has moved her bed to her brother in law's house where she will stay for the present to take care of his children, as they have been deprived of their mother by death.[120]

Thursday 16th Visited in the afternoon at E. K. Fuller's with sister Maria Lyman. Br L- came in the evening bringing news that J[ohn Harvey]. Tippetts and Br [Thomas] Woolsey had returned from the army (Battalion).[121]

March 19th After so long a time Mother and family have nearly arrived, they are on the opposite side of the river from us and so much ice in the river that they cannot come over. Mother's husband died at Pisgah so she is and the children are alone.[122]

20th I went to the river and saw my friends on the other side but could not speak to them. Sister Caroline went across but not without danger.

Sunday 21st The river is clear of ice on the other side and a road cut for the boat on this side, so that Mother has crossed.

---

120. Dionitia (also spelled Diontha) Walker Lyman's sister Nancy Reeder Walker died 28 January 1847 at Winter Quarters. Her husband Horace Martin Alexander was left with four children.

121. John Harvey Tippetts and Thomas Woolsey, members of the Mormon Battalion, left the Battalion site at Pueblo to bring the Saints at Winter Quarters money, mail, and dispatches. After fifty-two days of hardships, including an attack and capture by the Pawnee Indians, they reached Winter Quarters.

122. William Huntington died just three months after his appointment as president of the Mount Pisgah settlement.

and I am much rejoiced to meet her again, and hope we shall never be separated again untill death.

April 8th The wagons of the Pioneers started this afternoon They are going west to look for a location for the Latter Day Saints and have no idea where that is but trust the Lord will lead them to the place.

9th Br Lyman started but expects to come back before leaving entirely.

Monday 12th Brother L- returned to spend a day or two before he leaves.

Tuesday 13th Went to the creek and washed.

Wednesday 14th Brother Lyman has now gone with the Pioneers and we do not expect to see him again this summer. I took my turn with the rest of the girls in taking care of Sister Tinney for the rest of the month.

May 1st Took some wool of Sister [Sarah] Summy to spin on shares. Picking, washing, carding and spinning for half. Spent a great part of the time making garden.

Saturday 8th Sister Caroline and I walked several miles over the bottoms, hunting one of our cows, but did not find her.

Sunday 9th Went to meeting.

Monday 10th Spun wool and worked in the garden.

Tuesday 11th Carded wool.

Wednesday 12th Took our clothes to the creek and washed.

Thursday 13th Went to Father Lott's and borrowed a little wheel to spin wool on, and spun the rest of the day.

Friday 14th Carded and spun.

Saturday 15th The same as yesterday.

Sunday 16th Rainy day. Had to keep within doors.

Wednesday 19th Visited at sister Lenora Morley's with Sister E. R. Snow and others.[123]

---

123. Leonora Morley was Eliza R. Snow's sister and plural wife of Isaac Morley.

Thursday 20th Am engaged in making clothes for Sister Spicer,[124] who is very sick.

Friday 21st Sister Spicer died leaving two small children to the care of her sister.

Sunday 23rd Went to meeting. Heard brs Pratt and Taylor preach.

Monday 24th Rainy day.

Tuesday 25th Sisters Emily and Lydia visited us in the afternoon.

Wednesday 26th Made a cheese.

Friday 28th Washed at the creek.

Saturday 29th Worked in the garden.

Sunday 30th Forenoon rainy. Went to meeting in the afternoon.

June 1st Sister Elvira Homes' [Holmes] babe died.

Wednesday 2nd Received an invitation from Sister Holmes to come and spend the day with her which I accepted. Visited with her the grave of her child.

Thursday 3rd Am spinning wool for Sarah P. Rich [wife of Charles C. Rich].

Sunday 6th Staid at home and took care of Sister Maria Lyman's babe while she went to meeting.

Wednesday 9th Mill dam broke away.

Saturday 19th One of the people shot by the Indians while coming from the Horn, died next day.[125]

July 6th My brother Edward started for Missouri with br Flake. This is the first time my brother has been so far away from his Mother. He is 14 years old and over.[126]

October 5th Since I last wrote I have been busy at all kinds of work the time having been passed with out anything of note

---

124. Anna Smith Spicer, the wife of John Spicer.
125. The Horn refers to the rendezvous point at the Elk Horn River. The man was Jacob Weatherby. The incident is mentioned in several journals.
126. Edward Partridge, Jr., was born 25 June 1833 in Independence, Missouri.

having occurred. D.P. Clark and wife started for St. Joseph, Missouri.

Oct. 16th Went to the farm and dug potatoes.

17th Went to the farm again and dug potatoes Cornelia Lyman [sister wife] started for Illinois with her uncle.

18th 19th 20th Did housework

21st Went and dug potatoes all day. When we came home at night we met Myron Tanner [son of John Tanner] just come from the mountains. We were much rejoiced to see him and those who were with him as they had been out long and suffered much.

22nd Myron went with us to the field and helped us dig 18 bushels of potatoes which we brought home at night and put in the cellar.

23rd Myron helped us again to day. We dug 23 bushels to day, making 57 bushels of potatoes that we have put in the cellar. We live mostly on vegetables, with but very little bread, corn plenty, but no grinding of account. Br Tinney very sick.[127]

Sunday 24th D.P. Clark and wife have returned from Mo-

28th Thursday evening. Br A. Lyman returned from the valley of the great Salt Lake, He staid at home till Saturday, when he with others started with provisions and corn to go back and meet camp. They met them this side of the Horn.

29th Br L- and the Pioneers came home, having found the place that the Lord designs for his people to gather to.

Monday Nov 1st Br Lyman made a dinner for some of his friends who had endured many hardships on their journey. Had a party in the evening of the neighbors who seemed to enjoy themselves well. My sister Caroline and I have been trying to build a log house for ourselves as we do not feel quite comfortable where we are. We first got possession of an old house which

---

127. Possibly Thomas Tinney. Thomas was a member of the Church in Kirtland and endured the mob persecutions in Missouri.

we pulled down and had the logs moved to a spot where we wanted it put up again. As we could not get any one to lay it up for us, we went at it ourselves and laid it up five or six logs high when some brethren came and laid it up the rest of the way and put a dirt roof on it. Then I built a fire place <and chimney> till it was about as high as my head and some brother topped it out for me. We had one window of 3 panes of glass. Now we have a house, with out floor, or roof that will keep the wet out. We divided the room with a wagon cover, and let D.P. Clark and wife have one part as he had helped to build it. We had each room enough to put our beds by having the foot of the bedsteads come together and about 6 feet square from there to the fire.

Nov 19 We have commenced house keeping in our 6 by 10 or 12 house. That is Sister Caroline and I, and we feel very comfortable to what we have sometimes.

Sunday 28 During the last week I have made a coat for D.P. Clark and a dress for Maria Lyman. Spent the day at Mother's.

Monday 29th Helped sister Eveline Rollins quilt.

Tuesday 30th Washed etc.

Dec 1st Attended a sewing party at Mrs. Elisa Hakes.[128]

Thursday 2nd Helped Maria Lyman wash. Had company in the afternoon.

Friday 3rd Helped Dionitia wash. Br Lyman started over the river to attend a conference.

Saturday 4th Called on Sister Lucy Morley [wife of Isaac Morley] who is quite sick.

Sunday 5th Spent the day at Mother's.

Monday 6th Washed for sister Hakes for which I got a bushel of corn to feed Mother's cow.

Friday 10th Mother and I visited Sisters Emily and Louisa Young.

---

128. Eliza Amanda Beebe Hakes, the wife of Weeden Vander Hakes, was the mother of Sarah Melissa Hakes, the wife of Daniel P. Clark, mentioned throughout this account.

Saturday 11th Wrote a letter for Mother Walker.[129] Brother Lyman returned from the conference. He expects to start on a mission soon to the southern states. Ten of our Brethren arrived here to day from the Mormon Battalion.

Thursday 16th Paulina [Eliza Phelps] Lyman [sister wife] became the mother of a fine son which she has named Oscar Morris. Mother and child comfortable.

Friday 24th Br Lyman started on his mission south. Daniel Clark gone to the rushes.

Sunday 26th D.P. Clark came back bringing 2 turkies.

29th A young girl by the name of Emily Cox left her Mother's house with a seducer by the name of Long. They say they are married but she will not be likely to stay with him long.

Lines composed by Sister E. R. Snow on hearing of the death of my babe, Don Carlos.

Beloved Elisa, do not weep
Your Baby sleeps a quiet sleep
Although in dust its body lies
Its spirit soars above the skies.

No more upon your throbbing breast
It lays its little head to rest
From all the pains of nature freed
Your fond caress he does not need.

Sweet was its visit, but its stay
On earth was short, 'twas called away
By kindred spirits to fulfill,
Its calling and Jehovah's will.

---

129. Possibly Nancy Cressy Walker, wife of Oliver Walker, and mother of Dionitia Walker Lyman. Oliver died 13 April 1843. Nancy was thereafter sealed to Brigham Young.

Then soothe your feelings, do not mourn
Your noble offspring will return
With all its loveliness again
And with its friends on earth remain.

Feb 27th 1848. Ruth Adelia Lyman died. She was the daughter of Amasa and Maria Lyman.

April 6th Went over the river to attend the general Conference.

8th Came home again.

June 29th Since I last wrote we have been very busy in making preparations for our intended journey to the valley of the great Salt Lake, where we hope to live in peace and serving God as he commands us. Br Lyman has returned from his southern mission accompanied by quite a number of saints who will travel westward with us. Among them are John Brown, Wm Crosby, Wm Lay and Wm Bankhead. We are some better fixed for traveling than when we left Nauvoo but our outfit is very scant. Have provision enough to last a few months after we get there, but not enough to last till we can raise more. But we go trusting in the Lord who never forsakes his people. Sister Caroline [and I] have one waggon for our use to cook and eat by ourselves. We have a bedstead laid on the projection so that our bed do not have to be moved about.[130] We have room for a chair which is a luxury for me under the circumstances. My Mother's wagon is next to mine. My sister Emily has gone on with her husband B. Young and the rest of his family, so I am leaving none of my near relatives behind which is a great satisfaction to me. We started on our journey and traveled 6 miles and camped for the night.

July 1st After staying in camp two nights we started again for

---

130. On some wagons an overhang on either side increased the living space within.

the Horn river, but were detained another night in consequence of the rain.

2nd Crossed the Horn and waited till the 7th for Dr Willard Richards, when both camps left and went to the Platte river.

15th Crossed the Loup Fork, and went 4 miles and camped on the Pioneer's old camping ground.

16th Our men and teams went back and helped the Dr's company cross the Fork. Saw the first Indians here since we started.

August 20th Platte Dealton Lyman born, at about 6 o clock on Sunday morning. This is the second son that I have had born in a wagon and I still think it is a most uncomfortable place to be sick in. He was born on the east bank of the Platte river, opposite Fort John or Laramie. The journey thus far has not been very pleasant to me, as I have been very nearly helpless all the way, but it is all right, we are going from the land of our oppressors where we hope to raise our children in the fear of the Lord and where they will never suffer by the hands of our enemies as we have done.

21st Crossed the Platte river. The rocks in the bottom are so large that it seemed sometimes as if they would tip the wagon over. I held fast the baby and Sister Caroline held fast to me so that I was not thrown quite out of bed.

Oct 17th Reached the place of our destination in the valley of the Great Salt Lake. I have been quite as comfortable on the journey from Laramie as could be expected under the circumstances. Some of the time the weather has been very cold with rain and snow, so that I could not be comfortable any where as I had no stove in the wagon, but I and my child have been preserved through it all and I feel to give thanks to my Father in Heaven for his kind care over us. We are now at our journey's end for the present. The weather is beautiful. The country barren and desolate. I do not think our enemies need envy us this locality or ever come here to disturb us.

Emmeline Whitney (later Wells) was one of the fortunate Saints to be able to walk over the frozen Mississippi River when she left Nauvoo late in February 1846. As a plural wife of Bishop Newel K. Whitney, she traveled in his company, which included his first wife, Elizabeth Ann, and their children (Horace, married to Helen Mar Kimball Whitney; Sarah Ann, married to Heber C. Kimball; Mary Elizabeth; Orson; John; Joshua; Don Carlos; and Mary Jane), all mentioned in Emmeline's diary. Only one of Bishop Whitney's other plural wives is noted in the diary, although he took several others shortly before leaving Nauvoo. Traveling close to Brigham Young and other Church leaders, the eighteen-year-old Emmeline seems intrigued and delighted and comments frequently on their meetings and visits. A life-long diarist, Emmeline Whitney ends her account abruptly when she reaches the site that became Garden Grove, Iowa.

EMMELINE BLANCHE
WOODWARD WHITNEY WELLS[131]

FRIDAY FEB 27. 1846. Mrs. Whitney Sarah Ann and myself crossed the river to go to the encampment of the saints. Br. Lot and his wife took Mrs. W. and myself in their carriage. We crossed the river a part of the way on foot, and then went on to the encampment about 7 miles beyond; we reached the destined place about

---

131. Diary of Emmeline B. Wells, holograph, Special Collections, Harold B. Lee Library, Brigham Young University, Provo, Utah.

Sunset when we came in view it looked like pictures I have seen of the ancients pitching their tents and journeying from place to place with their cattle and their goods. We repaired immediately to Mr. H[eber].C. Kimballs tent took supper and slept for the first time on the ground. There was a snow storm without yet all was peace and harmony within.

Sat. Feb. 28. This morning Mrs Whit. felt troubled about the little children and Br Kimball prophesied they should all arrive today in safety. About twelve o'clock Joshua came on his [horse], and immediately after John, with grandmother, Olive [Bishop, a plural wife] and the two little children [Don Carlos, 5; Mary Jane, 2]; Orson [16] soon followed on the colt, bringing word that his father was behind with the teams; the band [Pitt's Brass Band] then started out, together with several other carriages to escort Bishop Whitney to the en-campment he having stayed in Nauvoo so long after the rest came away: he came about five o'clock, pitched his tent, Joseph also pitched his, put up his stove, we put down the carpets and soon had a comfortable place to pass the night.

Sun. March 1. In the morning I awakened out of a sound sleep and saw Mary Elizabeth [18] was preparing breakfast and the word was be ready to go at twelve of the o'clock we took breakfast, picked up and packed off as soon as possible, I rode with Orson in his wagon, about one o'clock we took up a line of march and left Sugar Creek, travelled over a very bad muddy road, reached the encampment about four o'clock, formed a line with the wagons, pitched their tents, made their fires and soon had a place fitted and prepared to pass the night. We are all happy and contented as yet and determined to go ahead.

Mon. March 2. 1846. This morning was warm and sunny the most pleasant day we have had since we left the city we started behind the principal part of the teams. the first hill we came to a balking horse they had in the family wagon began to show his obstinacy and hindered us considerably we went on about seven miles and camped in a hollow with Br. Kimballs company Josephs teams had gone on with the company ahead of us. and he was obliged to tent with his father. Sarah and I had a bed in the wagon and slept first-rate.

Tues. March 3. This morning we arose early and Sarah Ann taking her mother in her carriage and Joseph on horse back beside them. went on to over take their teams. After breakfast Loenza Maria and I took a walk in the woods just behind the tent we found stems of strawberry leaves green and fresh I intend to keep them as a memorial of the time when we returned we found they were about starting Ann and I came up the hill which was very long on foot seated ourselves on a prostrate log and here I am at the present time scribbling. We reached the place of encampment about noon having travelled 3 miles finding almost all of the teams had gone we proceeded on our journey together with Joseph he having waited for our coming. about < > miles ride brought us to Farmington a very pretty Western town. Here we saw thirty or more loafers loitering around the Grocery's &c. Porter Rockwell on his mule rode up among them all armed and equipped which seemed to excite some of them considerably there being those there who knew him and they were overheard talking by themselves in a low tone of shooting &c. saying there would never be a better chance however nothing occurred of consequence.[132] From the village we had a very bad road it was so dreadful muddy and crooked. Some of us walked along on the bank of the Desmoine [River] considerable distance the roads being so exceedingly bad the horses could scarcely draw their loads. It was after dark when we came in sight of the camp and a dismal looking it is the tents are all huddled in together and the horses and wagons are interspersed some are singing and laugh-

---

132. Porter Rockwell, famed for his rough ways and dramatic exploits, had served as a bodyguard to Joseph Smith and at this time acted as emissary between the Camp of Israel and those remaining in Nauvoo.

ing some are praying children crying &c. every sound may be heard from one tent to another; it is late and I must retire.

Wednesday March 4. We have stopped all day in order to recruit the teams they being nearly tired out after dragging through the mud. We have washed mended visited &c. It has been a very pleasant day.

Thursday March 5. This morn. we started at ten o'clock. I walked perhaps a mile and a half along the shore of the Desmoine river when Porter came riding on his mule and said that one of Mr Whitney['s] wagons had broke down I then went back to the wagons they were not yet up the first hill they took the load from the broken wagon and put it on another and hitched on the horses. We travelled about three miles and came to the village of Bonaparte a very pretty Western town here we forded the river; it was very bad travelling and continued to grow worse; we went about a mile farther and camped on the bank of the river where we have an excellent view of Bona. The rest of the company have gone on about two miles farther there are only the two families camped here.

Friday March 6. This morning at ten o clock we were again on the road which we found very muddy and bad until we came to the prairie there it was better. We arrived at the camp about three in the P.M. having travelled about eight miles the teams were very tired and so were some of the folks. we found they were on very damp ground by the side of a little muddy brook. After the tents were pitched Mr Whitney and Orson made a rustic bedstead of poles for Sarah.

Saturday March 7. This morning about the time we were ready to start a man by the name of Cochann came and laid claim to a yoke of oxen belonging to Mr W. said they strayed or were stolen from him three years before to avoid trouble Mr. W. paid him his price which was thirty dollars in gold. This day we have had rather better roads we travelled about nine miles and camped in a pleasant valley by a small stream of water about three miles from the principal encampment.

Sunday March 8. Today we have been detained in consequence of Sarah's being sick she has a fine boy her father has named this place the Valley of David in honor of the child it is situated 2 1/2 miles East of Richardson's Point, Chequest township Van Buren Co. Iowa. At evening Brigham & Heber came down from the camp with their wives, Mary Ann Young & Vilate Kimball took supper and blessed the child; it has been a lovely day, warm and beautiful.

Monday March 9. About noon William Kimball came with an easy carriage, to convey Sarah to the camp; she started about two of the o'clock Horace[133] and I rode in the buggy behind them, the teams followed after, all arrived in safety about four o'clock. Pitched their tents on the side hill, next to Br. Kimball; the tents here in rows like a city; it is really a houseless village. Just at dusk the band commenced playing and some of the young people collected and amused themselves by dancing.

Tuesday March 10. This is a stormy day, a part of the camp intended to have moved on but it [is] impossible; it is very muddy without yet the tents seem to be quite dry. Tuesday night at twelve o'clock the tent hooks on one side gave way and the tent pole leaned but Orson being on guard saved it from falling. The rain is pouring down in torrents here and there it sprinkles through the tent yet we keep a good fire and are quite comfortable.

Wednesday March 11. Today I slept till one o'clock after being up all night the rain had beat through the tent and wet my pillow and the quilts but I did not take cold Mrs. W. has been quite unwell all day Sarah gets along finely. Horace has gone to Keosauque to a concert I am sitting up again tonight.

---

133. Horace Whitney was honeymooning with his new bride, Helen Mar Kimball Whitney, daughter of Heber C. Kimball.

Thursday March 12. It has been an unpleasant day at times a slow drizzly rain and then thick clouds gloomy and dismal they are all asleep around me Sarah is not quite so well to night We continued in this place being prevented by the mud until Thursday the 19. we then proceeded on our journey Sarah had an ox wagon fixed to ride in we left about eleven o'clock we had not gone far before Sarah began to grow sick from the easy rocking of the wagon and she was no better until we arrived at the stopping place Sarah has sunk to sleep.

Friday March 20. This day has been cold and chilly we had a stove fixed in the horse wagon and a bed for Sarah; her mother and I rode there with her we had pretty good road all day travelled about fouteen miles stopped in a mean damp place Sarah stayed in her wagon and had a fire all night.

Saturday March 21. This morning we started at ten o'clock had a pretty decent road most of the way travelled eleven miles and camped in a pleasant place almost at the outside of the camp it has been a dark gloomy day.

Sunday March 22. This morning about nine o'clock we left the camp went about a mile and came to the [river] bottoms they were not so bad as we had anticipated after we got across the bottom we went into the wood came in sight of the camp crossed the Chariton river here the scene was indescribable some in a boat teams wading through and men dragging them up the hill with a long rope the banks were very steep and muddy and the road very bad for a mile beyond one very long steep hill where they had to double teams just at the top of the hill was the camp we came on beyond all the rest so we might be a little more retired. it is quite a pleasant situation here we all rejoice that we came over the river today for it rains very hard we have had some thunder and lightning this evening we have only travelled about five miles. This is Sarah's birthday [21].

Monday March 23. This has been a stormy day we were obliged to tarry on account of the weather about two in the afternoon we had some hail they fell as large or larger than buckshot it continued to rain through the night.

Tuesday March 24. Today as yesterday is rainy and unpleasant very exceedingly muddy at evening Sarah thought it being so very wet and damp it would be more comfortable in her wagon so they prepared it and about four in the afternoon she left the tent

Wednesday March 25. Last night considerable snow fell this morning was quite cold some snow has fallen during the day very muddy Mrs. Whitney has taken up her abode in the family wagon two or three doors from Sarah this evening Horace has been playing on his flute sounded very melodious at a little distance.

Thursday March 26. This has been a pleasant day the first one we have had this week Mrs. Whitney has been quite sick all day better this evening I am with her now.

Friday March 27. another fair day not quite as muddy as it has been Orson and George Sexton started this morning on a hunting excursion Mrs. Whitney is better has visited Sarah they are now in the tent together it is the first time Sarah has left the wagon since Tuesday she stayed in the tent until after dark took supper there and then went back rested very well all night.

Saturday March 28. This morning I feel first-rate it is spendid the sun shines brilliantly the ground is some what frozen it is rather cool; the sick ones are all better.

Sunday March 29. This has been another warm sunshine day we are still here nothing new except Mr [Stillman] Pond has returned from a trading excursion in the country has sold the riding colt for one yoke of oxen and another horse for another.

Monday March 30. another fine day Sarah has been taking a ride today for the first time. Spencer has given Loenza a young squirril which she intends to tame.

Tuesday March 31. Today has been a pleasant day nothing occurred of consequence we are still here cooking and eating.

Wednesday Apr. 1. nothing happened worth mentioning.

Wednesday [sic] April 2. Porter Rockwell arrived from Nauvoo having been there and returned since our departure he brought several letters but none for me We had written letters to send back I wrote one that night to send to my sister[134] pinned it to his coat pocket said it should not be moved until he saw her we intend to pursue our journey in the morning. Brigham and his company have started on today Mrs Whitney gave them some cakes as they passed to night we are to put away everything we are not using and be ready to take an early start

Thursday [sic] Apr 3. we started about eight or nine o'clock found pretty good roads to the next camp here we came up with Brigham it was in a wet prarie or moist ground not pleasant for camping at all we got there a little after noon stopped and rested until Br. Kimball came up he having been detained to mend a wagon they then concluded it would be better to go on it looked like rain we went on They found a man who had some corn to sell gave them an order to go and get it the company sent three teams from this place we had rather bad travelling most of the way we camped by ourselves about twelve miles from where we started it was about five oclock when we stopped cold and windy night

Friday [sic] Apr. 4. This morning Brigham passed us and went on. Three of Mr Whitneys oxen were missed sent three men on horseback after them found them about four miles off a man driving them as soon as they were found we began to get ready to start it had rained all the morning and by this time began to be very muddy Joseph had considerable trouble in starting his horse in the buggy broke a thill and cross piece it rained as if it would wet everything on earth about three miles brought us to Millers

---

134. Emmeline's mother, two sisters, and a brother were still in Nauvoo. They did not leave until forced to evacuate the city in August. Her mother died soon after leaving the city. Her two sisters traveled with other families to the Valley while her brother joined Emmeline and the Whitney family.

camp here we crossed a small creek and ascended a very steep hill and are safely harbored all in good spirits.

Saturday April 4. It still continues to rain they say there is no crossing the creek now it has risen so high. They have sent the cattle away to browze and men to watch them.

Monday April 6. Br. Kimball came into our wagon and related the following circumstances On Saturday evening he went into the woods by himself offered up the signs of the Holy Priesthood and prayed to the Lord that the storm might abate and the sun shine forth in his Majesty and for the health prosperity and salvation of the Camp of Israel. About twelve o'clock the storm ceased the sky became clear and was so light we could see to pick up a pin froze a very little. At morning the sun rose brilliantly and we had one of the most pleasant days we have had since we started on our journey although the ground was wet and muddy. About eleven o'clock they called the camp together and also Elder [William] Clayton's company and [on] a dry eminence of ground and there gave them some instruction with regard to their team and [said] they should stop here until the weather and the roads would enable us to pursue our journey with more ease and pleasure taught them the necessity of union patience meekness forbearance etc. in order to make us happy. Bishops Miller and Whitney were present Miller said he had been out seven miles found the roads so bad it was impossible to pass. Elder Lorenzo Young gave a short exhortation and some remarks from Br. [Peter] Haws. They adjourned at about one o'clock had a good time the brethren felt the spirit of union and blessing instructed the Captain of each ten to call their comp. together and administer bread and wine in his own company and also in Elder Clayton and Pratts Bishop Miller had a glorious time he thinks he has never seen the brethren and sisters more cheerful gave out an appointment for the Captains of tens to come together at 6 o'clock to take into consideration the propriety of sending after corn They assembled on a high eminence about half way between the three camps it was thought proper to send for corn enough to last to Grand river as there is no corn to be bought between here and that place for less than three bits a bushel and but very little at that price. Br. Kimball concluded to send five teams Captain Clayton four teams Bishop Miller one the distance to inhabitants is twelve miles we being camped in an entire wilderness in the timber of Shoal Creek the timber being almost wholly walnut or hickory one or two Missourians came into the camp in the course of the day. The camp retired to bed pretty early rose very early on Monday morning the sixth found it had commenced raining the forest looked dark and dismal The rain poured down in torrents About seven in the morning ten wagons with four yoke of oxen each started for corn making in the whole forty yoke of oxen and twenty men we feel much for those who have gone as it is now twelve o'clock and it has not ceased raining one moment it continued raining until night when it stopped and looked like clearing away early in the evening or between seven and eight a noise was heard afar off in the air and soon after the wind commenced blowing a perfect hurricane overthrowing tents scattering fire and almost taking away our breaths the first blow lasted about twenty five minutes during which time the rain commenced pouring down in torrents wetting beds through wagon covers etc. etc. the rain continued nearly all night with considerable wind and cold too.

the morning of the 7 Tuesday found us all destitute of homes almost [illegible] only here and there a tent had stood the wind of the preceding night and now they were frozen so it was almost impossible to raise them the wind continued high through the most part of the day the ground was frozen they talked of starting in the morning to go on but the teams they sent after corn did not arrive that night.

Wednesday morning of the 8th was pleasant but quite muddy did not seem very favorable for going across the prarie towards noon Bishop Whitney on horseback went out with some others to examine the roads came back and said it was impossible to go that day we had better stay where we were on half rations than try to go on soon after the teams they sent for corn arrived bring only [. . .] bushels of corn finding no more to be sold this is all the corn we can have for our teams until we get to Grand river this is hard for the poor horses and cattle to drag through the mud with scarcely anything to eat they said likewise that the roads were very bad indeed they called a council and concluded to start the next morning Towards night P. Pratts O. Pratt and Bishop Millers company came up the hill to be ready to start in the morning also G[eorge A.] Smith and Amasa Lyman.

Thursday morning the ninth was damp and looked like rain about eight o'clock we were all in our wagons one company following after another went on we found roads very muddy had not gone far before it commenced raining this made the roads worse than before we crossed some very bad sloughs and got stuck once we went on to Br Kimballs company about seven miles from where we started in the open prarie everything wet a mile and a half from any wood it was a long time before they could start fires of our families only Joseph with his family wagon and buggy and the Bishops one horse wagon are here there is five of us in one wagon and three of them in another to sleep or stay we happened to have a biscuit with us or we would have been supperless the rain runs into our wagon it has wet the bed &c. Bishop Whitneys cow happened to come along so we had some milk for the children. it is the first time we have camped in the open prarie and the first time we have been separated.

Friday morning the tenth it still keeps on raining and has rained all night the mud is very deep Joseph took a horse and went back to see where the folks were found them in a perfect mudhole several of their teams stuck fast so it was impossible to get them out last night this is a new era the most trying time we have had Br. Kimball and some others are about starting on going to double teams and take some through to the timber about five miles and then return with the teams for the rest. Joseph went to his fathers camp several times in the course of the day and two of the Bishops wagons were brought up with one more of Josephs.

the next morning Saturday eleventh about nine o clock William Kimball[,] Horace and some other[s] returned with teams to take on the last of their wagon[s] and also Josephs and some few more we all arrived at the camp in safety about noon or one o'clock it is a splendid camping ground the corner of a prarie skirted with wood I hope we may stay here until good travelling Br. Brigham is camped three miles farther on but is here now with Br. Kimball.

Sunday 12. A pleasant day quite warm several men came down from Br. Brighams camp with him to hold a council here they are to dine with us people are putting on their summer clothes today it is so warm Bishop Whitney and Joseph have sent back teams after their wagons left behind and Lyman's about eleven o'clock the council sit in the open air and continued until about two o clock they then took dinner and Brigham with his men returned to his camp soon after Br Kimball called the people together and administered the sacrament giving them some counsel and &c.

Monday 13. another beautiful day almost every one is washing Men are mending broken wagons fixing ox yokes repairing harnesses &c &c Tomorrow we are to leave this beautiful sequestered spot and go we know not whither

Tuesday Apr 14. We put out this morning about nine o'clock travelled five miles and camped on a hill above a pleasant wood near Brighams camp we have had some bad roads to day although very pleasant overhead picked whole bunches of wild flowers in the wood and fields there are two or three camps in view quite a scenery

Wednesday April 15. We have spent this day in our camping ground [Locust Creek] Loenza and her father have received let-

ters from home bringing word from Nauvoo of all manner of
wickedness dancing schools grog-shops and billiard tables and
everyone supporting himself at the expence of his neighbor also
bringing tidings that Diantha Farr had a fine son [in] consequence of which on the same evening the band gave a christening
giving music first with the brass band and then with drums and
violins several songs also were sung this commencing soon after
dark was kept up until after twelve o'clock.[135]

Thursday Apr 16. We have had an April shower during the
night just enough to cause the grass to spring up without doing
much injury to the roads we have travelled to day 6 or 7 miles of
prarie and camped in the middle of it about two o'clock Brigham
and the band have camped in sight of us. Eight rattlesnakes have
been killed in the course of the day two oxen have been bitten
and one of William Kimball's best horses there is some little grass
for the horses and cattle here some one discovered a bee tree and
took from it several pounds of wild honey which has been divided
between the different families it is the first wild honey I have ever
seen tastes considerably of wild flowers it has been almost
uncomfortably warm during the whole day.

Friday April 17. A cool cloudy morning about nine o'clock
we commenced our day's journey travelled across the praire the
distance of eight miles once while walking with several other girls
we saw a large rattlesnake the first I had ever seen we camped in a
thick forest just above a creek we arrived here about one o'clock
but some of the company had gone on to another camp through
mistake families were divided some here and some there. after
dinner Br. Kimball thought best to go on as there was a bad place
to cross he would like to be on the other side before a rain about
three o'clock we left this place just across the creek some one had

---

135. Diantha Farr was the wife of William Clayton. Her son's birth gave rise not only to a celebration of his safe delivery but also to the hymn "Come, Come, Ye Saints," penned by William Clayton on
that occasion.

set the prarie on fire how we were to cross this was a question it ran like lightning through the grass making a crackling among the bushes resembling the noise of burning crackers however they put out the fire the width of a road so we could just pass through the ground was black and the white ashes flew in our faces as we crossed about a mile brought us in sight of the camp just on the border of a prarie here we joined the rest of our company and camped for the night it is rather damp wet prarie. To night we had a little black wolf here some one had taken from a hollow tree in the woods it moans piteously.

Saturday 18. Br Kimball this morning before breakfast went on about a mile and a half and selected a new camping ground on the border of a prarie just above a creek on the other side of which is a thick wood he then returned and directed us to come here Br [John] Taylors company are camped on an opposite hill this afternoon the boys have been fishing in the creek and caught some little chub fishes such as abound in the streams of New England.

Sunday Apr. 19. A pleasant day many of the brethren went this morning to Br. Brighams camp to meeting at 4 o'clock we had a meeting by the creek to administer the sacrament preaching by Br. Kimball and Br. Taylor a warm day and night in meeting time Porter and Edwin Cutler returned from Nauvoo bringing letters for several one for me from Maria [her sister].

Monday Apr. 20. A council has been held to day at Brighams camp in which the brethren have decided that those who are sufficiently prepared will cross the mountains while others will make a location on Grand river and there the brethren who have left their families in Nauvoo are to stop and put in a crop and then return and bring their families to it that they may have something to come to [and] not be destitute when they arrive there. They also decided that we should all be put on rations of half a pound of flour a day with other things this is I believe all I have heard at dusk Br Kimball called the company together to get corn for their horses it having come as they expected thirty five ears a piece for horses none for oxen some rain fell during the night.

Tuesday Apr 21. another pretty day some rain in the course of it part of Kimballs company have moved on today his own teams could not they some of them being gone for corn we intend to move on in the morning. Brigham[,] Miller and several other companies have gone on today about six miles.

Wednesday Apr 22. We are still here because some of the teams sent for corn have not yet arrived this morning two families by the name of Tracy left the company without giving any notice Br. Kimball sent after them and bought their oxen and cow yesterday I forgot to mention that I wrote several letters to Nauvoo to send by Porter today I believe Mr Whitney finished a trade with father Durphy [probably Jabez Durfee] for his oxen giving him Lot's horses tomorrow morning early we are to move on. just after dark a storm came up the wind blew thunder rolled and lightning flashed the storm continued all night.

the morning of Apr 23 found us here Br. Durphy started about seven o'clock and about ten Porter Rockwell William Reuther and Br Pond started off before Porter went he came and treated us with wine in a twin bottle about two o'clock found us ready for a start we went on without interruption until five o'clock when it began to rain slowly we saw dozens of rattlesnakes in passing along we camped about 4 miles from where we started just on the edge of a bank or cut on the other side there is a wolf's den it has rained some but not much they say there is excellent feed for cattle here we are without wood and no bread cooked at all now the seabread comes in play to night we all made a supper of sweetened water and seabread.[136]

Friday Apr 24. this morn. is cool and beautiful I have picked some blue violets which remind me of New England here four

---

136. Seabread, sometimes called ship biscuit, sea biscuit, or hardtack, was a hard biscuit or bread made only of flour and water.

of Br. Kimballs best horses have strayed away and men have gone on horseback to find them Br Markham came to our camp about nine o clock bringing with him several yoke of oxen which they put before Br. Kimballs wagons and took them to the next camp it was a pleasant place the corner of a prarie after dark W. Kimball and those who went with him returned with the horses found them about eight miles off. There we passed the night the next morning pursued our journey travelled about five miles stop and let the cattle feed for about two hours and then went on five miles farther and camped for the night.

Sunday Apr 26. We arose early and started as soon as possible considerable rain having fallen during the previous night the roads in some places were very bad about five miles brought us to the camp three miles from Grand river Brigham. Miller Taylor Pratt Amasa Lyman and several other companies had arrived here before us. This is the place where they intend to put in a crop. This afternoon I crossed the creek or river found the most beautiful spot I ever saw viewing it from the opposite bank the gound was covered with a carpet of green and interspersed with flowers which might have done honor to the Elysian bower Today Br. Brigham told them from the stand that no one should return to Nauvoo with his consent until they had done something towards helping build up this place to help those who stay and those who shall come after they made some arrangements for work making fence[s] building log houses &c &c

Friday May. 1. Robert More one of Mr. Whitneys teamsters started to go back to Nauvoo nothing has happened since we arrived here worthy of notice it has rained most of the time retarding the progress of work of all kinds.

Sunday May 2 [3]. Meeting was held in the forenoon a few remarks by Orson Spencer afterwards by Br. Brigham he said we should not go from this place until there was something accomplished he wanted houses built for those who remained so we might take all the tents along with us a fence made around the field.[137]

Monday May 4. Tonight when the horses and cattle were brought up one of the horses Old Bill we call him had been bitten by a rattlesnake in three or four places about his nose being the first one of Mr. Whitney creatures that had suffered by accident on the journey he applied to the Indian Tindel [?] to try his skill in relieving him he exerted every means in his power and though the wound was very badly swollen yet on Wednesday he was partially recovered so as to eat some they gave him some corn at night he appeared to be very restless getting up and laying down alternately the next morning they let him go to feed and about noon they brought word that he was dead he fell dead upon the log as he was attempting to cross on it This was Thursday the 7th. of May we greatly regret his death for he has been a great use to us he was very large and strong and always true to his place Thursday night we had a tremendous shower attended with wind awful thunder and fearful lightning. [End of Journal]

William Huntington left a prosperous life in New York to follow the Church first to Kirtland, then to Missouri, and back to Illinois. At age sixty-two, he was once again called to leave all behind and start over in some unfamiliar region in the West. Appointed as a captain of ten, he traveled with his three plural wives and their children in Amasa Lyman's hundred. With all his responsibilities, he somehow kept a daily journal, a detailed chronicle of the hazardous trek across Iowa. The journal ends at Mount Pisgah, where he was

---

137. This settlement was called Garden Grove, the first of the way stations in Iowa designed to be a place of recruitment and reprovisioning.

appointed to preside, and where he died three months later. While his spelling and lack of punctuation impede the ease of reading somewhat, they do not obscure his thoughts and feelings.

WILLIAM HUNTINGTON[138]

*F*EBR 9TH 1846 A brief scetch of the travel of Wm Huntington And his family in company with the saints who left Nauvoo In the winter of 1846

Febr 9th I left my house in the City of Joseph at 12 oclock PM, with my family, I crossed the massipi 9 oclock at night stayed on the bank of the rivver my self that night-my family went in company the same night to Father Tanners[139] I followed them the Next day in company with my sone John we remained there one week in the same time the church have Continued to cross the river day and knight and Encamped 6 milds from the river on shugar crick-on Tuesday 2 oclock P.M a solm event transpired one of the Flat boats that was imployed in carrying the brethren Across the river spran a leak, with some 30 persons co[n]sisting of men women and children with one waggon two yoke of oxen two cows one calf-the boat sunk rested on a sand bar in 5 feet water the loading all floated in the river one yoke of oxen was drowned with the calf All the people ware saved with the remainder of the cattle much of the goods ware Lost Thomas Grover[140] one of the high council was the principal

---

138. "A Brief Sketch of the Travel of William Huntington and his Family in Company with the Saints who left Nauvoo in the winter of 1846," Archives, Harold B. Lee Library.

139. John Tanner (known as Father Tanner) joined the Church in New York in 1833. He was one of the earliest elders of the Church and lived through the Kirtland and Missouri persecutions. Nathan, Sidney, and Albert Tanner (mentioned in this document) are Father Tanner's sons.

140. He was the father of Emeline Rich, whose account is included in this volume.

sufferer-at the same time the alarm of fire was given at the temple the roof of the temple was discovered to be on Fire A mighty exertion was made the fire was [s]oon Extinguished. burned a hole throgh the roof 10 ft square All things remain calm and peacible in Nauvoo through the present week-I have ben over to Nauvoo twice in the week-my sone Dimmick B Huntington with his family crossed the river went in to the Tanner neighbor-hood[141]-it was thought best for him to return back and come on in the spring in company with my sone Wm D Huntington and my daughter Presend Buell of Lyma[142]

Febr 14th saturday night stayed with my sone Wm D Huntington, my family all well-Sunday morning my family yet at Father Tanners-

monday 16th went to the camp in company with A[masa] Lyman was counciled to move our families to the camp [Sugar Creek]

Tuesday 17th we all movd to the camp on shugar crick which was the main camp

wensday A more full organiseation was entered into with the camp myself and family ware organized in to Amasa Lymans company-this day the artiltery arrived in camp-all Is pleasant good order in camp-no opposition from the inhabetants The camp are wating here for some brethren to come from Nauvoo-brother [Newel K] Whitney and [William] Claton not over-my family all in good health

18th this day President Brgham Young went back to Nauvoo on business

19th A severe snow storm commenced and snowed 24 hours

---

141. In mid-March of 1840, the Tanner family moved to Iowa and settled upon the "half-breed" tract, about four miles from Montrose. They cultivated a large farm and lived there for six years.

142. William Huntington's daughter Presendia married Norman Buell in January of 1827. They lived in Lima, Adams County, just south of Hancock County, near Lima Lake. Norman Buell apostatized during the Missouri period. In 1846 Prescindia married Heber C. Kimball for time in Nauvoo. She was sealed to the Prophet Joseph Smith.

20th verry cold snow 6 inches Deep-more pleasant the brethren in good health and in good spirits Brother Brigham still in Nauvoo—

Saturday 21st all well in camp

22d 23d 24th 25th weather cold with some snow the health of the people in Camp remains good in camp through the week

Febr 28th my family all in good health-this day I went to Nauvoo visited my children they ware all in good health Left Nauvoo for the last time for the present

March 1st this day an order was given to leave the present encampment accordingly the twelve with most of the camp struck their tents and rolled out-went 6 milds and Encampt for the night—weather pleasant Amasa Lymans company remain on the ground through the night in conciquence of two teams not being in camp-

monday morning 2d weather good our company Left the camp 15 minutes before 10 traveed 15 milds Camped on a small crek on the farmington road found People friendly gave us straw for our cattle

3d Tuesday morning weather good- our teams bocked [balked], [our leaving] hindred Left camp 1/2 past 10 overtook the main bod[y] of the camp which left shugar crick saboth evening and took a more suthern rout we fel in with them at farmington 1/2 past 2 oclock-arived on the camping ground with President Young 1/2 past 5 we camped on a piece of Land the brethren took to chop the timber and fence the same—

wednsday 4th wether good—orders is to remain here this day

5th and rest our teams and wash

Friday 6 orders Again for the first company to move on Left camp 15 minutes past 10 crossed the Dismoin at Bonapart 5 minutes past one had an extreme bad road on the bottom and Up the bluff President John Smith[143] turned over his Waggon

143. John Smith, uncle to the Prophet Joseph, was made president of the Nauvoo Stake on 7 October 1844. He also presided over a branch of the Church in Lee County, Iowa.

damage but trifling injured Sister Smith [Clarissa Lyman Smith] slightly Camped on the paraie had no fire—eat a cold supper pitch[e]d our tent had some straw from a sitzen [citizen]

~~saturday 7th~~ [sic] travilted 6 milds

morning 7th moved on arived at Indian crick 15 minutes before 11 stayed all night

Saturday morning 8th Left camp 20 minutes before 9 traveed 8 milds arived at Doctr Elberts plantation[144] 30 minutes Past one pitched our tents in his timber spend the night Pleasantly A Lyman A[lfred] Bybee and H[enry] Rollins went in Company with Doctr Elbert to the camp whare the band had stopt-the Doctr and other Gentlemen ware well Pleased with the performance of the band,

sunday morning weather pleasant, A Lyman and H Rollins left Went to visit the camp on a head whare president Young was to get inteligence as to further operations wa[s] councilled to move on the same day, left Elberts 30 minutes past one passed bishop [Newel K.] Whitney Camp At a crick whare Joseph Kingsburys wife [Dorcas Adelia Kingsbury] was confined on the 8th with a fine sone-Arived in camp at Richardsons Point Vanburen County Iowa teritory 15 minutes past 5 Capt. Alfred Bybees company of the ten which he had the charge of or the 2d ten of A Lymans Company Arived in camp withe us 30 minutes past 6, I will note here that I have the charge of the first ten and A Bybee the 2d in A Lymans company, I note here Also that the camp have taken Jobs of different Kinds of work such as building houses Chopping timber Splitting rails husking corn &C. for which we have recievd such things as was Necessary for the sustainace of man and our teams

monday 8th [sic] weather good an order given for all the men who ware Able to chop and split rails to go to work at the above mention

---

144. Dr. John D. Elbert, a friend of the Mormons, appropriated a section of land in Iowa for a Mormon encampment and provided the Mormons with corn in return for clearing his land.

Tuesday 10th orders came for George A Smith and Amasa Lyman companies to move on 15 milds Acordingly we sent of[f] A Bybees ten as they ware principally ox teams soon after they set out it began to rain the remainder of the companies Remained it continued to rain tuesday Wednsday And thursday-thursday our camping ground was Over flowd with water and mud we removed our Camp to Dryer ground 12th

Friday morning wind north more cool winday through the day mud dryed fast our boys this day are husking corn by the Job have 12 bushels of corn and dinner for husking a certain pile of corn 13th I will mention our boys husked Yesterday which was thursday thoug it rained some 407 stooks of corn for the fodder and 4 bushels of corn

Saturday 14th weather good the camp still remain here

Monday 16th myself and Nathan Tanner left with 5 horses to trade them For oxen traveled from Vanburen Co North Crossed the Dismoin North into Jefferson, Co. I returned on thursday evening I made no trade for oxen on my return at Chequest Crick met with two men proposals ware made for a trade on the day following accordingly my sone John and Nathan took my horses and Went to affect a trade

Friday 20th I will mention here that on thursday 19th the camp most of it left this point for the Flats on the sharidon [Chariton] river, Amasa Lymans Company most of it remain on the ground and expe[c]t to untill Saturday-I will mention that on tuesday morning the 17th of March a sone of Sidney Tanners [James Monroe Tanner] of About 18 months of age Expired this is the first death in A Lymans Company there has ben two other deaths brother Edwin Little a nefew of brother Brigham Youngs,[145] and Sister Spencer the wife of Orison Spencer all have

---

145. While Edwin Sobieski Little (the husband of Harriet Hanks, whose account is included in this volume) was aiding wagons across the Mississippi River, the ice broke, causing him to fall into the freezing water. He contracted lung fever shortly thereafter and died 18 March 1846 near Richardson's Point.

dyed while the camp has ben here at Richardsons Point.[146] my family all in good health. my daughter Zina[147] Left on Thursday with the camp that left this place-wather cool roads are improving fast, Mar[c]h 20th

Sauahterday 15 minutes past eleven A Lymans company left the cam[p]ing place and set out fo[r] the sharidon bo [sic] bottoms I will mention my sone and Nathan Tanner returned from exchangeing my horses they affected a trade returned with two yoke of oxens which enables me to go on with my loading we traveled Saturday 9 milds stoped at Mr Locks plantations on the South fork of Chequest river we had a slight rain in the night

sunday morning March 22d left camp 15 minutes past 8 weather Cool and cloudy. 12 oclock sunday we are now in davis county-traveled this day 18 milds weather Cloudy through the day-sunday night encampt at Mr Easleys grove on fox river commenced to rain in the evening rained moderately through the night-

monday 23d showrey through the day could not go on our journey-took A job to make 500 rails for 15 bushels of corn we are to make the rails for Mr Easley- rained and blowed through the night

tuesday 24th continues to rain and snow throug the day up to 30 minutes past one

Wednsday 25th snowd and rain through the day-wind shifts to west at sunset-roads impassable

thursday 26th wind west sunrises clear snow melts fast our men at mackeing rails to finish the job of Mr Easleys-this day was visited by brother Richard Thorn who is camped 2 milds up the

---

146. Catherine Curtis Spencer (wife of Orson Spencer) died 12 March 1846 at Indian Creek near Keosaqua, Iowa Territory, at age thirty-four. She had not fully recovered from childbirth a few days earlier when she had to endure the cold of the journey. She was taken back to Nauvoo to be buried.

147. Zina Diantha Huntington married Henry Bailey Jacobs 7 March 1841 in Nauvoo and had two sons from this marriage, Zebulon Williams Jacobs and Henry Chariton Jacobs. Zina was sealed to the Prophet Joseph Smith on 27 October 1841. After Joseph's death, she married Brigham Young for time in 1846 and had one child by him, Zina Williams Card.

river with a small Camp of brethren-herd [heard] by brother
Thorn from the main Camp who are on th[e] sharidon river or
they are across the river on the bluff brouseing their Cattle[148]-my
Family all in good health who are with me. Zina is on ahead with
the main camp I expect—

Friday 27th weather Cold ground frose spits snow thaughs
out throug the day our hands commence a job to macke 3000
rails are to recieve pork and corn-myself and Sidney Tanner
made one hundred rails this day which finishes the job for Mr
Easley thus ends this day all is well in our camp-

Saturday 28th wind west cool and winday pleasant for march-
this day I am 63 years of age am in good health made a pare of
oxboes [bows] have the care of a company of ten in Amasa
Lymans company our camp are yet at Mr Easleys timber in township of Bloomfield Davis County Iowa Teritory on fox river
about eighty milds from Nauvoo-

Sunday morning 29th weather more pleasant this morning
we sent two of our teams in company with Brother Edward Duset
[Duzett] on to the main camp-our teams took a part of our loads
so as to lite our loads expect our teams will return before we leave
to join the main Camp-my wife Caroline and Lydia[149] spend
their time at this Place mackeing palm leaf hats. all well except
John who is troubled with the bowel complaint -

Monday morning 30th weather plasant our hands gone to
their job A Lyman and John a hunting ducks and sqirrels-now
11 oclck A. M.

Tuesday 31st weather good all hands at work myself and
Nathan Tanner made a yoke for apiece for our Oxen our hands
finished the rail job this day-we had a birth day dinner at A
Lymans tent mad[e] of ducks in commemoration of him self our

---

148. Where there was little feed, branches were cut from tall bushes and trees so the cattle could eat
the leaves.

149. William Huntington married Lydia Clisbee Partridge (Edward Partridge's widow) in 1840 in
Nauvoo. Caroline and Lydia are her daughters.

teams returned from the camp request sent from brother Brigham For A Lyman to hasten on accordingly his camp Left Easleys

Wednsday April 1st 30 minutes past 9 oclock Crossed the Fox river at twelve oclock traveled 15 milds camped on Little indian creek on 17 mild paraie [prairie] at a pleasant place good water all well in Camp

Thursday morning weather pleasant 2d April 10 minutes past 6, Left our encampment this morning 10 minutes before 8-crossed the Sharranton [Chariton] 3 oclock P. M. arived on the bluf 30 minutes past 4 encamped on the ground the main Camp Left the day before-windy night-

Friday morning high east winds looks licke rain 12 oclock cross shoal creek Thunder shower rains arived on the ground the main Camp left the day before 30 minutes past 1 rains hard Encamp with P[arley] P Prat[t] and George A Smith rains hard the afternoon wind east 12 oclock at night wind west, rains hard through the night wind blowed down brother Tanners tent verry muddy unpleasant time streams high all well-

Saturday morning 4th Cloudy light rain or mist 3 oclock PM. John gone a hunting-we are now As we suppose in Missourie on the bluf of Shoal Crick or in other words we are now on the disputed tract under the jurisdiction of Missourie[150]- John has returned with brother Rice helped brother Rice to bring a Venison had one quarter of the same rains this evening-

Sunday 5th clear and pleasant-John went out before brakefast shot a fat turkey brother [Theodore] Turleys arived in camp this day who have ben behind from Shugar creek 3. oclock P. M.

monday 6th commenced to rain at 6 oclock A M.-rained all day wind South wind shifted into the wist [west] at ten in the evening, thundered and rained in torents wind blew a gale it was

---

150. The camp was traveling at this point along the northern border of Missouri on land not yet clearly assigned to either Missouri or Iowa.

with difficulty the brothren could hold their tents up brother Ricees tent blew down-Doctor Braleys horse mired by his waggon chilled and died, had a disagreable night-

Tuesday morning 7th wind high ground frose our teams much chilled-held a meeting of the Company at P P Prats tent revced instruction relative to the organiseation of the camp or that of a fifty aluding More perticular the organiseation of the 3d fifty consisting of the families or companies of P Prat Orison [Orson] Prat George A Smith Amasa Lyman and the Spencors Daniel and Orison-which is calculated will macke 50 waggons in all No corn for our teams have fed all to them this morning our Commisaries have gone out this morning in persuit of More-now 3 oclock P M. Clear and cool high wind—

Wednsday 8th Commsaries[151] returned yesterday no corn for the camp this morning have orders to rooll out wether pleasant I left the camp 10 minutes before 9 this camp is on the north fork of Shoal creek roads bad traviled 8 milds encamped on the south fork of Shoal found my daughter Zina with a fine sone borne in a tent on the bank of the Sharaton [Chariton] River[152] encamped for the night

thursday 9th orders to rooll out this morning 10 minutes before 8 loocks licke rain road extreme bad-Heber Kimballs company first. the other companies consisting-of Hause [Haws], Harvey, and Miller rooled out rather in confusion that is, thos first redy roolled out first acordingly my team was a head of the three last companies-from the north fork the two days of bad roads I had no help from any team while scarcely a team but what had help at 12 oclock P M. it commenced to rain with some 200 teams then scatered over the wet flat Pararies for throee milds the rain increased the roads soon become impassable teams were stauled in every direction men Doubling and thribling teams but to no effect with many waggons were left stalled in the mud in

---

151. Some men were assigned to be commissaries of their companies to oversee the food supply.
152. Zina named her boy Henry Chariton.

every diretion many families remained on the pararie over the night with out fire with their clothing wet and cold—high wind all night Heber Kimballs company travilled 8 milds encamped 1/2 mild from timber in the cold west Pararie- the three remaining companies, those of them that ware not stauled on the pararies, turned off the road 1/2 a mild encamped on Elmpoint Spent one of the most uncomfetable nights that so many of the church ever suffered in one night rained steady all night verry cold and a high wind the ground filled with water the mud ne [knee] deep around our tents and Little or no feed for our teams one cow through fatieuge Laid down by the waggon on the paraie chilled and died A general Sene of suffering for man and beast-

Friday 10th the sene of suffering still continues-Frequent showers through the day gales of wind throwing down tents upset brother Theodore Turleys buggy injured the top-teams were sent out on to the paraie to bring in families who had staid over Night my team went out twice after waggons, a gale of snow at 4 oclock P M. friday night frose hard

Saturday 11th cool Cloudy day sent out teams to helped in all the families Sent after corn-we are browseing our cattle by cutting down elms trees-have no grain to feed our teams

Sunday morning 12th weather Pleasant—a request sent from President Young for A Lyman and my self to attend a council consisting of the twelve the high Council and others Leading men such as bishops &C met at Heber C Kimbals Camp at 10 A.M. council decided that A company of men should leave this week Consisting of the twelve[,] pioners and others to the amount of 50 should go up to the timber on Grand River some 30 milds and macke farm of some one hundred acers fen[c]e plow and put in A crop and build Sone cabbins[153]-another com-

---

153. Stephen Markham and an advance party were sent to a site on the east fork of the Grand River, about 145 miles from Nauvoo, that would be a temporary settlement for incoming Saints. This would be Garden Grove.

pany to Go to Grand river to join[?] Millers Mils to Labor for corn And provision[,] other to exchange in horses and other Property for oxen and provision &C. decided also that the camp should not go through the Missourie settlement but that we would go from the farm on grand River which is in contemplation to be made direct to Council bluff Council adjourned I took dinner with brother Yearsley-returned holme—

monday Morning 13th weather good-struck our tents rooled out from Elm Point which is in Missourie Putnam County on Blackbird crick left 1/2 past 11 A M. Arived at the camp of Heber C Kimbals 1/2 past 2 P M. we are on the north fork of Locus [Locust] crick in Putnam Co. on the disputed tract

Tuesday 14th weather pleasant orders from Brigham for all the Camp to cross the bottoms of the Locus crick this day accordingly All the [oxen] are put in requisetion by doubling teams to Cross the bottoms-my team has come this morning from Elm point with Albert Tanners waggon as he helped me yesturday up to this place and are now gone to the camp of Brighams am expeting them back every Minute now 3 oclock P M. Left the cam[p] at 4 P M. rooled Across the bottom of Locus crick one of the wort peaces of road that Could be found in a wet time but ha[v]ing had 3 or 4 dry days the road improved much we arived on the bluff about sunset whare we joined the main camp as butiful a site as ever was seen in this region of cuntry a city of tents and waggons inhabitated by the saints of the last days

Wednesday 15th weather pleasant orders given for most of the camp to roll out according at about 11 oclock A M the line of march was tacken up here one of the most splendid sights I ever witnessed so great a number of wagons spread out on one of the most splendid wide paraies that ever was seen-we took a western coruce [course] on the divid between the Locus and Gound Medicine river intending to hit the timber on Grand River where it is intend to macke a farm traviled 7 milds encamped on a small

fork of Locus crick whare thare was wood and water-John Taylors
company encamped near us it loock licke rain it is now a bout
sundown-John is out a hunting-John returns

thursday 16th weather pleasant our company most of them
roll out a company of three or foar go on a trading expedition
to exchange horses for oxen George A Smith and A Lyman
remained on the ground untill teams could be sent back for
them as their teams ware sent off for trade we arived at our
cam[p]ing ground 1/2 past foar after rolling over the most beautiful paraie grass in the ravens [ravines] is up so as to give our
Cattle something to eat wather warm agrowing time we encamped
on one of the North forks of medicine river a beautiful situation

Friday morning 17th wather good. teams ware sent back for
the brethren behind the day is spent in tackeing care of our teams
and araingings our camp—

Saturday morning 18th wather good a councill called met at
Brighams camp as all of the companies are encamped near each
other A council is called to commence fitting a company for the
mountains all the teams Put into the camp by individuals to help
off the church ware called for. orders was Given by President
Young, for all waggons Loaded with families drawn by publick
teams to be onloaded and broat to him on monday morning next
to be Loaded with Publick property and the families to be helped
up to the contemplated farm and there be left untill such times as
they can fit them selves for the mountains here I have one of the
most trying sens I ever have had as I have not team nor waggon
here of my own. I expect on monday morning to onload the waggon I have ben useing, put my goods on the ground and be
helped up to the stopping place, having agreable to councel previous to leaving nauvoo given a deed of my lot to the trustees in
order to fulfill my covenant made at October confernee As also
all the church to do all we could to help the church-therefore I
am now according to the Presidents order to be left on the camp

ground and my affects to be carried up to grand river settlement
and fit out myself[54] John has killed 6 turkeys this week-

Sunday morning 19th woather good the brethren are agreable
to appointment this morning a going to meeting met at Brighams
camp - this is the first meeting held since we left Nauvoo ware
addressed by Brigham and others on the propriety of emigrating
on corect principals, our meeting was I think held without a person
but what was on the journey we are not on the disputed tract [of
Missouri territory] near the north line on a wide paraie where there
is no road but that made by the church it was recommended by
President young that we hold meetings every week as we journey a
pleasant or an interesting meeting a good spirt prevailed in the
camp Brothers Lee Bybee & Mark Hall arived here from Nauvoo
came here for the express purpose to tacke Back towo of our waggons mine and Henrys an arangement was made to Leave them

Monday 20th A council called this morning at 9 oclock A
M. A report of all the members of the tens as to their means to
go on their journey to the mountains in order to select a company of such as could fit themselves-this day in council President
Young said to me that I might have the team and waggon to go to
the mountains if I could fit my self with provisions it was recommended for all the fifties to send out men with waggons Loads
of such Property as could be spared such as beds Chest and all
unnecessary property for the journey and exchange it for oxen
cows and provision accordingly I [s]ent of my Portion of property to exchange it for cows and my sone John went with the
teams this day I recieved a Letter from brother Ari Brower[155]

---

154. At this point Brigham Young still intended to send an advance party all the way to the Rockies.
Those traveling with wagons and teams provided by the Church were to relinquish them for this enterprise and remain at Garden Grove until they could prepare themselves to continue.

155. Ariah Coates Bower traveled to the Valley with John Taylor's company in 1847. He was a pioneer printer, foreman of the *Times and Seasons* in Nauvoo, and foreman of the *Deseret News* in Salt
Lake City. He also published "Emigrant's Guide from Salt Lake to Sacramento" with Joseph Lain. The
wife whose mother died is Margaret Elizabeth Hussey, daughter of William Tucker Hussey and Mary Ann
Johnson Brower Hussey.

anounceing to me the death of his wifes mother whose name was Mary Brower she died the 27 of March and was buried on my Lot [in Nauvoo] with my first wife[156]-

Tuesday morning 21st weather Cloudy Loock licke rain. the great part of the camp rolled out this morning For Grand river. some of our men have gon to Loock for work to procure provisions while the waggons and my sone which I spocke of yesturday set out this morning to macke an exchange of property it is now 1 oclock P M. my family all well

wednsday 22d wether warm a growing time Look for showers Some of the companies have Rolled out for Grand river Brighans company traveled 10 milds and gained 5 we are now a waiting for Nathan Tanner[157] to return from a tower of trading together with Amasa Lyman who is sick I spend my time herding my team and doing chores-at dusk this evening it Lightened Looked Licke showers at ten it thundered heavy at the same time two of our company ware A hunting turkeys set out to come to camp Lost their course Fired guns and hallord ware answered from the camp got in as the rain commenced-a frightful Looking cloud sharp Lightning one tree was struck with Lightning near our camp thundered and Lightned all night-but Little rain

Thursday 23d Cloudy some thunder this morning-P P Prat has this mornin[g] set out to Look a nearer road to Brighams Camp it is now 10 oclock A M.-

Friday 24th weather pleasant-we all remain in camp Yet waiting for the traders to return have ben gone more than a week-I have finished me a yoke for my lead oxen made me a whip lash am Getting all things redy to roll out at order-now about sundown

Saturday 25th weather pleasant this day we built a bridge

---

156. William Huntington married Zina Baker 28 November 1804 at Merident, New Hampshire. She died 8 July 1839 in Nauvoo.

157. Nathan Tanner was appointed commissary. He brought news from the camp every one to three weeks while also buying, selling, and trading for the camp.

across one of the forks of Medcisne [Medicine] river to get a Higher rout to grand river settlement as the brethren have began to gather at the place whare It is the calculation to macke a farm president Brigham has arived on the farm P Prat set out this day with his ten for grand river, my family all well-

Sunday 26th thunder shower this morning-Brother Lorenzo Snow set out this morning as he belongd to P Prats ten for grand river Shederick Roundy arived in our camp this day from Nauvoo on a special mision from the trustees in Nauvoo to the twlve in camp to assertain whether it would be expedient to sell the temple as proposals had ben made by the methodists in St Louis to purchase the same-hard times in Nauvoo no sales of conciquence—the mob Are driveing the brethren in from the out skirts of the county-the brethren are crossing the river as fast as possible are scatered on to the Shariton [Chariton] river-now 1 oclock P M.

monday 27th no infermation from the brethren out a trading as yet, this a rainy day cloudy dark day-rains all night streams high

Tuesday morning 28th still a raining the flood has carried away a part of the bridge we made this day is cloudy rains some— it is a dark time with me as to my situation in every respect as regards my going to the mountains having no team or waggon of my own and what mackes it more unpleasant is I am now out of provision or I have none of conciquence have no meat no flower no meal save a few quarts of pearched Corn meal no milk have a few crackers-how I shall be provided for the Lord knows I do not

Wednesday 29th after haveing rained all last night the water in the streams is high this morning Wind west cloudy through the day we are anxious to have good weather-no intelligene as Yet from our brethren who are out a trading-we are here in idleness impossible to travel it is so wet and we nee[d] addition to our teams as we have sent off a number of our Horses to exchange for oxen-my family in good health as also the brethren in Camp

Thursday April 30th weather yet cloudy with mist of rain through the day we are all here as yet in idleness (wating) fo[r] the return of the brethren from trading no inteligence as yet my health is not as good now as it has ben as i am afflicted with a bad Cold. we are a wating for intelligence from the main camp at Grand River-thus ends the month of April at this time my family are much scattered, my eldest sone Chauncey in Rutland Jefferson Co. N Y. D (B) Huntington and Wm D Huntington in Nauvoo if they have not set out [on] their journey for the west my daughter Precendia Buell I expect is at Lyma [Lima,] Handcock [Hancock] though I expect she will come with my sones at Nauvoo My sone John is of[f] on a trading voyge with the brethren in Misorie-Oliver B Huntington is in Cambra Niagra Co N Y. while Zina Jacobs is here with me in camp with her husban Henry B Jacobs-I will say to my joy and that of the camp that a little before sundown my sone John Arived in camp after an absence of ten days had for the most part of the time rainy weather, streams high, bad trailing-disposed of most of the Property they took with them John sold our bed and got me a cow the brethren in company with my sone come to a crick in a mild of the camp and encamped for night and John come in to the Camp for to get refreshment for the brethren who ware much fatiegued I went in company with John to the brethren with refreshment and returned and left them for the next day—

May 1st weather cloudy we went with our company in the morning and helped the brethren [bring] their oxen and cows to the camp—on our return to the camp ware informed A brother had stayed with brother Nathan Tanner who was back to Locus crick and would be in cource of the day accordingly they arived in camp at 2 oclock with 25 head of cattle old And young-brother Wm Edwards who my sone went with broat old and young, 13 head which made a grat addition to us [. . .] as also to the accomodation of milk-at the same time P P Prat Arived here from Grand river from the main camp informed us the expedition to the mountains this season in part is given up that is a small Company of men would go and no women that other companies would Locate in different places as council should dictate

May 2d this morning the sun rose clear thoug it rained before 12 oclock, our men are mackein ox yockes and boes for our new teams-brother John Gleason Arived here ~~from~~ this day from the main camp on his way to Nauvoo to turn the brethren from the road which has ben traveled by the Saints on to the divide between fox and dismoin rivers to council bluff and from there acrss the missourie and up grand river 150 mild and there macke a Late crop[158] this appears to be the council from the present our men ware out this day a hunting for a deer which had ben wounded the day before a dog in company with them wa[s] attacted by a wild hog drove, the dog scared the horse a young man rode, throw him from the horse[,] the dog seased the hog- while the father of the young man shot the hog, they left the hog untill the next morning—

Sunday 3d weather pleasant the forenoon pleasant—the men went out and got the Hog we dressed it and divided the same in the company the hog wd 200 lbs we spend the day in mackeing preparations to set out for grand river 2 oclock P M. it has commenced to rain this afternoon we now want good weather that we may go on our journey tomorow if the weather is good John went out this morning and shot a turkey it commenced to rain thunder and lighten about 4 P M. and rained in torents untill bout sun down filled the earth with water for which we shall not go on for some days

Monday 4th wather Pleasant through the day-brother Wm Edwards one of the comisaries for our company one who had the charge of the trading company sent out Last from our company the company With whom my sone John went[,] in conciquence

---

158. The extraordinarily lengthy trek across Iowa, lack of food and provisions, and the general malaise of the Saints prompted several alternate plans for continuing the journey.

of the heavy rains being in the wet fording streams And much fatiegue returned sick[,] is now verry sick, is much deranged in mind, is thought to be dangerous-this day a company of three, my sone John one of them went on a hunting Expedition to be gone two days

Tuesday 5th weather still good ware visited last evening by Brother Caleb Balding [Baldwin] from the main camp on his way to Nauvoo to get his family[,] brother Edwards is no better this morning now 9 oclock A M. the weather through the day Verry hot appearance of rain sundown thunders at 10 oclock the hunting company returned with 3 turkeys and a pail full of honey in the comb immediately on their return it commenced to rain in torrents more water fel through the night than at any Storm we have had since at this place the streams the hightest

Wednsday 6th Weather Loocks for rain-this morning have recieved inteligence from Grand River roads impassible for Loaded teams-so wet at the camp stops plowing-times look Dubious for the saints-John off a hunting this forenoon others herding cattle on the Paraie-Edwards more comfortable now 2 P M. a black cloud made its apearance in the west about 3 oclock P M. at 5 it comenced blowing raining and hailing we had a Great rain the stream ware high[h]er than they have ben since we have ben here carried of[f] a bridge which had withstood all the rains before-not much rain through the night

Thursday 7th weather cloudy brethren from the main camp the great rains hinders the work on the farm the roads are impassable for loaded teams-Andrew Cahoon Arived her this afternoon from Nauvoo-said times are much as they have ben for some time the temple has ben dedicated the work on the house is done the house it is hoped will soon be sold if it should be it would help the church much[159]-said Portir Rockwell was

---

159. The "house" is the Mansion House, built for Joseph Smith. It was hoped both the Mansion House and the temple would sell at favorable prices and bring the Church much needed revenue.

147

arested by the troops from carthage on the first day of May was tacken to Quincy Gail-rains again this afternoon-now 20 minutes of 6 P M. Edwards is a failing it is dobtful whether he will recover—

Friday 8th weather good this morning Edwards more comfortable this day-the roads are improving fast as there is a brisk wind from the north-three waggons rooled out from here this morning not of our company we expect to go on tomorow Andrew Cahoon left here this morning For the main camp now 10 minutes past 1 P M.

Saturday 9th we at Last after staying 3 weeks and 2 days have ben favored with weather to roll out we left 1/2 past 8 A M. traveled 8 milds encamped at a convenient place on a small crick which em[p]tied in to grand river weather pleasant through the day met 5 brethren from the main camp

Sunday morning 10th of May weather fine our teams are well rested we calaclate to roll out soon 7 oclock A M. [Monday morning] 1/2 past 8 oclock A M. we commenced to roll out had bad roads though the roads improved [h]ourly in conciquence of its being verry warm traviled 8 milds encamped one mild beyond the main camp on grand river or in other words the East fork of grand river at a pleasant place on the paraie near a point of timber left brother Edwards in main camp at James Alreds tent

Tuesday mor[n]ing 12th weather good we shall remain in camp whare we are untill brother Amasa returns from the main camp as he has gone this morning to get council with respect to those of us as have no means to go on any further as some of our company have no team or means to go any further as this is my case I cannot go any further with out help now 1/2 past 8 A M. this evening thunder showers round us a light rain on us this evening brother Wm Edwards died at Brighams Camp this morning 1/2 past 1

Wednsday morning 13th looks for rain we rolld out 1/2 past 7 a shower on us at ten stoped after trailed 5 milds at a beautiful sit-

uation for camping Brothers George A Smith was there in camp
with a small portion of Peter Hauses [Haws'] camp. weather verry
warm, at this time it is thought wisdom for us to roll out 5 milds
this afternoon 1 oclock P M this day on our travils we beheld as
beautiful a sight as I ever have seen of the licks [likes] that is the
most beautiful rolling paraie spread out in a[l]most every
Direction as far as the eye could extend with something licke one
hundred waggons strung out on the paraie for some 6 or 8 milds—
the weather this afternoon is verry warm a sultry heat loock licke
showers Clouds run low at foar commenced to thunder in the west
at 5 we pitched our tents at 7 it commenced to rain at 8 it rained in
torrents wind blew a gale and continued to blow for hours we had
in my tent to get out of our beds dress ourselves my self wife John
and Edward and hold our tent from blowing Down the rain beat
in our waggons and wet our loading more than it had done in any
storm we have had on the journey the great Number of waggons I
have spocke of all ware over tacken on the open paraie by the storm
had to stop and experiened a tedious night had no fire and got
verry wet through the night as it rained about all night-

thursday morning 14th the storm cleard off at about 8 in the
morning—President young arived here this mor[n]ing with about
ten of his waggons camped here with us this day as the road was so
bad it was thought not best to go on for a day or two-President
young witt [with] George A and A Lyman went on to explore
found a camping ground for the next days travel

Friday 15 weather good the camp rolled out this morning had
a beautiful Day traviled 6 milds encamped on a small crick on
the paraie built bridge stayed all knight fell in company with
Solomon Handcocks [Hancock] Company who came the
Northern rout from fox river—[160]

Saturday 16th weather good are calculating to roll out early

---

160. A more northerly route proved to be easier traveling.

this morning 5 oclock A M Camp rolled out at 7 camp scattered in great confusion witt [sic] the exception of Preisdent youngs company A Lymans and George A Smiths we took a Northwest cource built a bridge crossed over traviled this day 6 or 8 milds encamped on a small crick which is on one of the small forks of the Shariton a convenient place for camping

Sunday 17th no meeting this day the twelve and others have gone to Look a camping Place as it looks for rain if it should our bridge would be liable to be carried off therefore we are now getting up our teams so as to be redy to cross over if necessary on the return of the brethren who have gon[e] to Loock the road now 20 minutes past 11 A M. the brethren returned at three Brigham Heber C Kimbal and most of the brethren crossed over the crick this afternoon except A Lymans company for some reason known to himself he would not go over accordingly we all remaind throug the night—

Monday 18th loocks for rain brother Lyman took it to his head to build a bridge some 20 rods abovve the one church had built and passed over in order to tacke a nother divide and get a nigher [higher] rout to the main camp but failed in his calculations got a worse road and further, we over took the main camp at 12, built a bridge the camp joined P Prats company at 5 P M. on the middle fork of Grand river whare it is expected the church will make anoth[er] farm [Mount Pisgah]

Tuesday 19th loocks for rain thunders this morning the twelve and other have gone out this morning to see if they can find a location for a mill on the fork and find the best location for a farm—now 1/2 past 11 P M. the men are getting timber for stocking plows John returned this afternoon from a hunting he shot and broat in a good turkey and a sand hill Crain—

Wednsday 20th rains this day all day all business Stop for the wett—

thursday 21st ~~thursday~~ this day is attended with showers the camp called to gether and organised A council or presidency of which I was appointed by the Church in council to preside over that portion of the Church that stop here [Mount Pisgah]-am to preside over spiritual as well as temporal things brothers Ezra T Benson and Charles Rich are to act as presidents with me—

Friday 22d weather pleasant we are this day commencing to organise our business as to plowing fencing and other matters pertaining to our stoping in this place this day I delivered the team concisting of two yoke of oxen which I have had the use of from Nauvoo to the Rockey mountains am wholey destitute have no[w] made a sacrifice of all things as to property my hands are now completely tied as my time will necessarily be taken up in the oversight of the concerns of the church—

Saturday 23d weather warm six houses this day have ben commenced two of them for my self I had the first house [any] body put up in this place-we are here on the middle fork of Grand River some 70 or 80 milds from Davis County in Missorie or Adam on diah [Adam-ondi-Ahman] we are now on a tract of Land sold by the Potawatomi tribe of Indians the Land has ben sold by the indians to government is by contract to be evacuated by the indians next fall

Sunday 23d rains this morning clears off meeting at 12 ware adressed by President Young on the grat subject of the gospel the work of gethering of Zion in the tops of the mountains and other subjects pertaining to temporal affairs as well as spiritual addresses from a numbr of others. spoke myself on the subject of our present organiseations in temporal affairs—this has passed off it has rained a most every day we have made some fence plowed some twenty acers and planted it with corn-the waggons have ben rolling in 20 or 30 a day through the week-the twelve have ben ingaged this week in mackeing preparations to roll out for council bluff—

On saturday the 31st of May the twelve and some others myself and my council that is brothers Ezra T Benson and Charles C Rich wen[t] onto the paraie some two milds north

pitched a tent Clothed ourselves according to the order of the
priesthood had for the first time a prayer meeting in which such
thing as we stood in kneeds of

May 31st weather in the morning pleasant had meeting in the
grove near my house resolved the meeting should be made use of
as a special Confernce accordingly the meeting proceded to business At 10 A M., at 12 it commenced to thunder and soon rained
in torants most of the day much business however was done this
is expected to be the last meeting we shal have with the twelve at
this Place which is called Mount pisga indain lands Potawatama
Nation

June 1st monday morning cool and rainey but little business
Done here this day high wind this afternoon a number of waggons have gone over the fork this afternoon for the bluff—

2d Tuesday weather cool and pleasant the men commence
business this morning in their different branches—I will mention that on sunday 31st of May brothers Noah Rogers[161] died with
a fever

wednsday 3d this morning at the riseing of the sone I parted
with my sone John who has gone back to Nauvoo to work this season to get cloths as he is verry Destitute of clothing—the brethren
are rolling out for the blufs-we are building fence and plowing,
the bretheren are comeing in hourly-

thursday 4th all business is rolling on this day—My daughter
Presenda Buell arived here this day from Lyma she ran away from
her husban[d] who is a discentor and abused his wife she broat
with her her youngest sone and left her oldest Sone with his
father who will eventually come to the church-my daughter was
broaght here by a brother by the name of Furgerson who went to
Lyman in the Night at the risk of his life and took her and her
sone and broat them away She was hid three days in the wood

---

161. Noah Rogers had recently returned from Tahiti where he had helped open the land for missionary work.

while her husban[d] serched the cuntry for her but invain she
could not be found by him—

Friday 5th

Saturday 6th all business is rolling on with us here this day
with animation My Sone Dimmick arived here with his family—

Sunday 7th Orison Hide [Orson Hyde] arived here gave a
lecture to the saints stayed two or three days and went on—

Monday 8th weather good this week has passed off pleasantly
the waggons have continued to roll in by hundreds through this
week—A Lyman rolled on Thursday

Saturday 13th brother Ezra T Benson left this place for the
main camp or for the twelve as there was business of importance—

Sunday 14th Charles C Rich and myself crossed over the
river went two milds to See Col John Scott who has the charge of
th[e] artillery-meting this day here at the grove had a good congregation and good teachings this day on many subjects—

monday 15th business lively this day Brother Wilford
Woodruff Arived here this day-also my Sone Wm D Huntington
arived here this day much to my joy This week has passed off, the
flood of emigration ha[s] continued to roll on through this week
all business has ben prosporous—

Sunday 21st this day my sone Wm Huntington left this place
for the Bluff

monday business lively through this week emigration not so
Grat

thursday 25th two men by the name of Carter and Mc
Kinney Came here from Davis County Mo stayed with me that
night

Friday 28th this Day a united states officer From Fort
Levingsworth [Leavenworth] arived here with instructions from
Colo. Carney [Colonel S. W. Kearny] commanding officer at
that point with an invertation from the president of the united
states to inlist 500 mormons to ingage in the war between the

united states and Mexico I was introduced to the gentleman [Captain James Allen] had a pleasant interview with him-called the brthren together Capt Allen delivered an Address to the brethren appropriate to his foolish erand-I followed him with an adress by way of commendation or as the old proverb says answering a fool acording to his folly I gave him a letter of intro-duction to the authorities of the church at the bluffs he left the same day-[162]

sunday morning 28th had a meeting ware addressed by Elder Wilford Woodruff And others on various subjects—

monday 29th brother woodruff left

tuesday 30th all business lively the brethren are constantly rolling in from the east.

Wednsday July 1st 12 ocl[ock] P M. brother P. P. Prat arived here 48 hours from the Mo. River on the bluff with instructions From the council there informing us a company must be raised from 3 to 500 men, without women with teams seeds mill irons farming utentials provusion &C. A meeting was called the people came to gether at 5 ocl P M a good number volunteered money to A considerable amount was paid in teams and provision given sufficient to fit the men out for the bluf.[163]

all left on thursday 2d of July brother Parley left 1st of July with brother Ezra T Bentson who has recieved an appointment to tacke the place of John E Page in the corum of the twelve[164] brother Bentson and family left for the bluf the same day with P P Prat—this evening two men arived in camp from Mo. as spies under pretext to seell us bacon stayed with me all night left this morn[i]ng

Friday 3d I will mention that I reciesed a communication

---

162. William Huntington's response to this call for military volunteers reflected the feelings of most of the Saints.

163. This was the call of Brigham Young for a well-provisioned company of young healthy men as an advance company to the Rocky Mountains in anticipation of the rest of the Saints following the next spring.

164. John E. Page was excommunicated.

from President B Young requesting me to come with my family to the Mo river I had made my calculation to roll out the next day after the Arival of brother Prat-but was counciled by him to remain for the Present at Mt Pisga as brother C C Rich would have ben left alone-this day my Sone Dimick B Huntington left this Place with his family for the bluf—the brethren are a rolling out from this place fast on for the bluf-this day I have had the most rest that I have had since I first recvid my appointment July 3d

Saturday July 4th this day all the business has moved on in good order the Emigration has this day ben great-the saints here ha[ve] cebrated the forth of July in poverty and tribulation on our journey into the wilderness

Sunday 5th this day to joy and satisfaction of the saints we ware addressed by Elder Little who presides over all the Churches in the eastern States is now on his way from Washington to the camp at the Mo haveing a message to the twelve—

monday 6th this morning brother C C Rich left here for the bluf they traveled about 6 or 8 milds and met brothers Brigham Young Willard Richards Heber C Kimball they all returned to the camp at sundown

tuesday morning at ten oclock we had a meeting president young laid before the meeting the object of his mission was to raise 500 men to go the mexican war by way of santifee [Santa Fe] raised in all at this point about 80 men-

Wednsday 8th all hands came to gether adjourned untill thursday we sent a man of[f] to Nauvoo—

thursday 9th this morning those men who had inlisted with their baggage waggon took up a line of march for the bluf whare they expect to find Capt Allen who on raiseing the requeed [required] number of men will be promoted to a Liet. Colon. who will tacke the charge of the mormon troops—this day the twelve all that had ben or came has left this morning for the bluf-

I expect my self and brother C C Rich will be under the necessity of staying her[e] untill fall

thursday 9th my self and brother Rich went with the twelve out on the road for the bluf as far as brother Cutters Camp there we parted with the twelve

Friday Saturday passed of[f] pleasantly

saturday 11th to my great Joy my sone Johne returned with Brother Levy E Riter—I expect my sone will continue to the bluf with brother Riter—

Sunday 12th had a meeting brother Benjamin Clap spoke to the people—

monday Tuesday Wednsday all things move on in good order this day my sone went on with brother Riter-

Thursday 16th weather Verry cool last evening brother Bent[165] arived here from the lower farm or Garden grove—

friday Saturday Sunday 19th weather Cool and dry. all the affairs move on in good order through the week past this day held a meeting had three Mosorians [Missourians] to hear. brothers Campbell Rich and my self spoke on the first principals of the gospel

monday Tuesday Wednsday this day after some weeks of dry wether it began to rain and rained so as to wet the ground well which is of grat good to our crops this day also brother Hyrum Spencors corps [corpse] was broat here for interment he died some one hundred milds from this back near Soap Creek a sudden and Unexpected death his family up at the bluf—22d

Thursday 23d weather warm after the rain a growing time some Sickness in this place this day brother Hare died—

Friday 24th

Sunday 26th held a meeting in the grove Erastus Snow gave an apropriate discource followed by C Rich and myself

Monday 27th this week has passed of[f] nothing of note has

---

165. Samuel Bent presided over the settlement at Garden Grove.

transpired through the week except much sickness in the camp brother rich and myself spend most of our time visiting the sick- ague and fever and chill and fever is the great difficulty with the saints in Mt Pisga[166]

August Sunday 2d this day held a meeting in the grove ware adressed by Elder Caleb Balding followed by C C Rich and myself-this day two aged sisters died at Mount Pisga much sick- ness in this place

---

Lucy Meserve Smith was one of the six wives of Apostle George A. Smith. A deeply spiritual woman, twenty-nine-year-old Lucy was also highly self-reliant and endowed with a good sense of humor. Her experiences crossing Iowa and especially in Winter Quarters did not give rise to much levity, however, though her optimism and other qualities are clearly apparent in her brief account.

LUCY MESERVE SMITH[167]

ON THE 9TH OF FEBRUARY 1846 we crossed the Mississippi and started to go, we knew not where, but [arrived at the Missouri River] after tedious traveling through snow and mud and slush for at least three months.

After leaving Nauvoo, in crossing the Mississippi river we were obliged to

---

166. Late summer and early fall brought on these complaints. Many had experienced the same sick-ness in Nauvoo.

167. "Original Historical Narrative of Lucy Meserve Smith" (1888–1890), LDS Church Archives.

roll up both our wagon covers as the wind blew so strong. The large cakes of ice were running so fast that it seemed hazardous to undertake a crossing, never the less we were compelled, to leave our comfortable homes and flee into the wilderness by order of the State authority, as a mob had control. We encountered some very severe cold weather with very strong high winds and as a matter of course our fires had to be built so the wind would blow the sparks from the tent, I cannot forget how cold I was standing in the tent preparing food and washing dishes for our big family. When I would wash a dish and raise it out of the water there would be ice on it before I could get it wiped. I could not get warm from morning till night and night till morning. I lay down in the bottom of the wagon with a thin bed under me as I must leave my bed at home as teams were scarce and to start out the 9th of February to go I knew not where. At one time we traveled through rain, mud and slush all day and when night came the mud was six inches deep and the men were completely drenched. Brother P.[Parley] P. Pratt was along with us. they came into our wagon and tried to dry his clothes as we had a little stove in our wagon. He said he would give Brother Orson [Pratt] his birthright for a comfortable place to lay down that night, as he was so tired. and nearly frozen. It was a sad night. Our teamsters had to make their beds down in the mud as there was no other alternative, the women could not get out of their wagons for days. One day the wind came up very suddenly and took off nearly every wagon cover as quick as a minute, the dishes and brooms went whizing through the camp. We named the camp ground Windy Hill. It was so cold some nights after the men would get to bed a sudden storm of snow and wind would come up, strike the camp and away would go the tents. Then the boys would get up and out in their night suits shouting and singing at the top of their voices, till they pinned the tents down again. They would get very wet, but never seemed to mind it. In the morning the bed covers would be frozen stiff and tight to the wagon cover, and across their chins.

It was a great labor to bake a batch of bread, as the wind would take the coals away as fast as we could put them under our dutch ovens. While we were at a camping ground called Mt. Pizgah, Sister Zilpha and Nancy and babe and Sarah [Sarah Ann Libby], the mother of John H. [John Henry-born Sep. 18, 1848 in Kanesville], Hannah [Hannah Maria Libby], the mother of Charles W. [Charles Warren-born 1849-Council Bluffs], was with us[168] and my brother David, altho his wife was back in Nauvoo. Sister Sarah traded and got a pair of bullocks and brought the rest of the sisters along. Sister Zilpah's baby died before she got to Mt. Pizgah, it was a sad meeting for us all, as we expected to see the dear little baby, but Sister Nancy's baby was as pretty as a pink. Her papa thought so.

A number of our company stopped at Garden Grove in order to raise crops, so that the companies coming after could have recruits, also a number stopped at Pizgah and sowed and furnished food for others as they came after.

Before we got to the Bluffs Colonel [Thomas L.] Kane rode into our camp, having traveled days and nights to make known the plans at head quarters concocted to destroy our whole camp on the plains. He said their [U.S. Government] plan was that if they got a battilion of our best men the rest of us would die on the plains, and if President Young refused to give them up they would massacre the whole camp and that would put an end to Mormonism. I had this from the lips of George A. Smith. The result was that President Young was ready for Col. Allen, when he made his wants known. His answer was you shall have your Battalion if it has to be made up of our Elders. So the Elders were called out and mustered into service. I had a chance to know

---

168. Zilpha, Nancy, Sarah, and Hannah were sister-wives of Lucy Meserve Smith.

the truth of this affair, as my brother David Smith was called to go, and he must leave his wife to get along as best she could, and it left me to drive my ox team alone hundreds of miles and the following September 1st., I gave birth to my son Don Carlos, on the 11th of August 1846, at a place called Cutler's Park. Soon we went into Winter Quarters and Brother Amasa Lyman's folks kindly took care of my brothers wife as I was not situated to do it myself.

The next spring my brother died at San Lewis Ray [San Luis Rey], California, in 1847.

We moved down to Winter Quarters when my babe was two weeks old. There we lived in a cloth tent untill December, then we moved into a log cabin, ten feet square, with sod roof, chimney and only the soft ground for a floor and poor worn cattle beef and corn cracked on a hand mill, for our food. Here I got scurvy, not having any vegetables to eat. I got so low I had to wean my baby and he had to be fed on that coarse cracked corn bread when he was only five months old. We had no milk for a while till we could send to the herd and then he did very well till I got better. My husband took me in his arms and held me till my bed was made nearly every day for nine weeks. I could not move an inch. Then on the 9th of February I was 30 years old. I had nothing to eat but a little corn meal gruel. I told the folks I would remember my birthday dinner when I was 30 years olde. My dear baby used to cry till It seemed as tho I would jump off my bed when it came night. I would get so nervous, but I could not even speak to him. I was so helpless I could not move myself in bed or speak out loud. One incident which happened while I was sick with scurvy, when I got so I could raise up to my elbow I took to bleeding from my throat and nose a stream the size of a knitting needle. I must have bled a quart when a strange woman came in and said, dear child, are you bleeding to death, and I said I expect I am, said she, Have you any candle wicking, they gave her a ball and she tied it around my fingers and thumbs losely, and the bleeding stopped. She said had it not stopped she would have tied it around my wrist and toes and ankles and around my neck, as she never knew this remedy to fail stopping the worst bleeding from a cut. This receipt is easy to be obtained.

One evening a grim old man appeared at my bedside and said that we were very sick last fall but we must give it up now, but I knowing him to be an evil spirit by his having a black necktie about his neck, altho the rest of his clothing was white, I never saw any good angels with anything black about them, so I sneered at him turned my head and said I shant die. When I got better I had not a morsel in the house I could eat, as my mouth was so sore. I could not eat corn bread and I have cried hours for a morsel to put in my mouth. Then my companion would take a plate and go around among the neighbors and find some one cooking maybe a calf's pluck.[169] He would beg a bit to keep me from starving. I would taste it and then I would say oh do feed my baby. My appetite would leave me when I would think of my dear child. My stomach was hardening from the want of food.

The next July my darling boy took sick and on the 22nd, the same day that his father and Orson Pratt came into the Valley of the great Salt Lake my only child died.[170] I felt so overcome in my feelings. I was afraid I would loose my mind, as I had not fully recovered from my sickness the previous winter. I went away from home to nurse a sick woman untill she died, then I took care of her sick baby till his papa got married again.

The next summer I attended school at Kanesville then I assisted in the school for a while, I was sent for, to go to Bellevue to teach the Pawnee mission school. I went and taught the Indian

169. The internal organs of an animal.
170. George A. Smith was a member of the first company to leave Winter Quarters the previous April.

children for six months. They, the Missionaries offered me double wages if I would stay longer as I had such good control over the old folks as well as the children, but not with standing that they treated me with great respect, yet I could not stay. They presented me with a number of pretty moccicon [moccasins], but I did not forget to send them presents when I got home. I boarded with a missionary family and ate in the same room with the indian children and they helped prepare the food for the tables. The old folks would often crowd around the stove in the morning and pick live vermin off their bodies and eat them. I must confess that it weakened my stomach so that I got thin, but my hostess discovered it and she took great pains to fix some little extra food for me which I could eat with relish, knowing she had prepared it herself. I was determined to stay six months, for I was proud to earn money to purchase my necessaries to prepare for the vallies, and then the children took such interest in their stud-ies and they thought so much of me that it helped to while away lonesome hours. Altho I was far from home, but yet I was in the way of my duty and my heavenly father comforted me, with dreams and visions. At one time three voices sang an anthem to me. these are some of the words, Glory to God who hath made us etc., one was on my bed and the other a distance away, but their voices accorded perfectly, and Oh, how charming, and then my little son appeared to me. I tried to hug and kiss him, but I felt no substance, but I said to him why did you leave mother dear, he answered and said because I had a greater work to do some where else. I said God bless you dear and he disappeared and left me as wide awake as I am at this moment. His answer was a great consolation to me as I couldn't understand why my heart should be so keenly pierced as to be compelled to give my only child up.

I once heard Pres. Young say these providences of the Lord Almighty we cannot understand. How true this scripture is, no one knoweth the things of God but by the spirit of God. Then how necessary it is that we should so live that we can have his holy spirit always within our hearts.

While at the Mission I dreamed an holy angel appeared to me, bowed gently offering me his hand in an inviting position. I dropped my hand into his. He said thou art blessed of the Lord and thou shall have your inheritance with Abraham, Isaac and Jacob. He then stepped back, bowed gently, and a veil dropped which hid him from my view. I could not relate this dream for a long time without feeling that same heavenly influence which I felt in the presence of the angel.

The Indian children used to contend on[e] with another to see who should comb my hair and get water in the morning, indeed they were very kind to me. They wrote me a kind little token saying I love you well as my own people. You such good lady, sorry you go to valley. Wish I go to valley with you. You teach us long time to read, write, and study geography and Atlas. I had many gentlemen from the East to visit my school. I used to exhibit the writing books, cut out hard words, ask questions on the Atlas, etc. The gentlemen declared they never saw it equalled in any white school. Then Indian agent, Mr. Miller, and the interpter, Mr. Saunsisee used to visit my school often. They took delight in hearing the children sing. I taught school five and one half days a week and Sabbath School on Sunday. When my six months was up I bade adiew to the Paunee Mission and went home. I then made preparations with the rest of the family and started for the Salt Lake Valley. Our family included a teamster, hunter and cowboy [and] numbered 19 souls. Sister Bathsheba Smith [George A. Smith's first wife] and myself did the work for fourteen with the help of Philyneas Dailey [Phineas Daley][171] at the wash tub and Thomas Adshead[172] to help bake the bread.

---

171. Phineas Daley, a twenty-year-old single male, traveled in the George A. Smith company.

172. Twenty-one-year-old Thomas Adshead, like Phineas Daley, was unattached when he traveled to the Valley with the Smith company.

Sister Sarah and her baby, John Henry and Sister Hannah and her baby, Charles Warren and teamster was a separate family. Sister Sarah being quite feeble in health. Sister Hannah had to do most of the work for their portion of the family.

We left Kanesville June 22nd., 1849, crossed the Missouri River July 11th., and crossed Elk horn the 17th., and had a cattle stampeed and it was a lot of bother to get them together again. Apostle George A. Smith, captain of 50, Elder Myron Tanner captain of ten, each ten had a captain. The first Welch Company of Saints helped to compose our fifty.

One of the most faithful and expressive life writings is the reminiscence of Sarah DeArmon Pea Rich. The first wife of Apostle Charles C. Rich, she and her children traveled in his company from Nauvoo to Mount Pisgah where they spent the winter of 1846 and then on to the Salt Lake Valley the next year. Her sister wife, Emeline Grover Rich, also left a reminiscence of the journey, much shorter but also anecdotal and detailed. Emeline, who had no children at that time, did not travel with the Rich family. As one of Thomas Grover's seven motherless daughters, she traveled with her siblings and her father's plural wives, driving a wagon from Winter Quarters to the Valley. The family group, almost all female, depended on the women and some children to be their teamsters. The different personalities of Sarah and Emeline (as well as their different ages and responsibilities) are clearly evident in their colorfully written narratives.

EMELINE GROVER RICH[173]

WE STOPPED ABOUT EIGHT YEARS in Nauvoo - when we were again driven from our homes which we had made comfortable - just beginning to enjoy the fruits of our labor. Our family were considerably scattered by this time through necessity - but the inborn love and affection for our parent and our dear little orphaned sisters[174] were still burning in our bosoms - like an unquenchable fire, as the love we have for our dear mother seemed to be centered on our father - who was very loving and kind to his motherless children.[175] He was truly a handsome man - called by most people the handsomest man in Nauvoo. I always looked upon my father with admiration. In 1846 about the 10th of February he with three teams oxen and waggons left all that was near and dear to us in Nauvoo, Ill. and started on our journey into the wilderness, crossing the Mississippi river on the ice with snow clad ground for our beds, or, on which to make our beds, with nought but sky for our covering. Women and children have to walk, and that through snow, mud and rain - wet through for days and nights together - traveling as far in a day as our teams could stand to travel - from one to six miles was an average distance per day and sometimes we have waded and pulled through mud-hole-deep to our wagons and camped not more than half a mile from where we started - and here let me say (strange as it

---

173. "Journal of Emeline Grover Rich and History of Grover Family Written by Emeline Grover Rich, 1890," photocopy of original in author's possession.

174. Caroline Whiting Grover, Emeline's mother, died 17 October 1840 in Nauvoo, leaving seven daughters: Jane (9), Emeline (8), Mary Elizabeth (6), Adeline (4), Caroline (2), Eliza Ann (18 months), and Emma (about 9 months), their ages at the time of her death.

175. After the death of Emeline's mother, her father married Caroline Eliza Nickerson. She did not go west with the family.

may seem) that not a word of repine or grumbling was heard in our camps, but singing praises to God for his deliverance from the midst of our enemies.

In April we camped near the State<line> of Mo. Teams worn out, provisions exausted and sickly season commencing. Some of the men went into Mo. to work for provisions while our teams rested and recruited.

In a few weeks we jogged onward until we came to a good location for a longer resting place - and so it proved to be to hundreds of the worn out Saints, We stopped at this place, (since known as Mt. Pisgah) until the following Spring or at least, some of the companies stopped and some went onward until they came to the Mo. river (now Omaha) and there stopped for winter quarters. My father had a good outfit compared with most of the saints.

The following Spring, - in March the Saints, who remained back, (or at least those who had not succumbed to Malaria) came up to Winter quarters, rested awhile and prepared to continue their journey to the Rocky Mountains.

In the meantime it became necessary to send a company of men in advance and on ahead of the companies as pioneers - to look out the roads - build bridges construct boats on which to cross the Streams etc. My father was selected as one of the party to go. He left his family, with no boys or men folks to come on afterward with the company later on.

I will here relate an incident which happened to my father and family when crossing the Mississippi river The ice at the time had parted and broken away at a point of an Island on Sand bar - So that [he] had to drive onto a flat boat for a part of the way. They were going along nicely enough when a young fellow on the boat (for want of something better to do I suppose) spat ambier (tobacco juice) into an ox's eye he commenced to plunge and jump, breaking a hole in the bottom of the boat - the ox jumped over board and was drowned also another yoke of cattle and three cows shared the same fate The boat went down, until one end struck the point of the sandbar which left a part of the wagon above water - some of the family were in the covered wagon - My sister Eliza Ann who was about seven years old and a babe six months old. The front end of the wagon was pitched down into the water until the <wagon> stood almost on end, the water was filling up the wagon and she kept climbing for the uper part She happened to think that the little boy Thomas was somewhere in the bedding under water She immediately plunged down into the deep water, caught the babe by his dress by one hand while she used the other to help her to climb back on up where she could hold herself by one hand hold of a wagon bow <with> just her head out of water holding the babe so that his head was also out of water. All this time the mother was standing on the bank, looking on thinking her babe was gone - and not being able to render any assistance - until at last when some of the excitement was over some one chanced <to> think that some one was in the wagon when my father with his pocket-knife ripped a hole in the wagon cover and liberated the almost perished prisoners. Well now, this was a cold bath - in Feb. not a dry thread on them or in the wagon - and in the middle of this large river - help from the shore was rendered as soon as possible what was to be done? was an important question. They lost no time in getting across the river - There was no house nearby - they made a fire on the river bank, dried their clothes as quickly as posible and made themselves as comfortable as they could - and strange to say they were none the worse as far as their health was concerned than before it happened. but in goods - cattle - books etc. they suffered a great loss. My father was compelled to yoke some of his cows up with the oxen and travel on with what they had left after laying by a few days to dry bedding and clothing etc. etc. Suffice it to say there was no lives lost. My fathers family record with many other valuables went to the bottom of the Miss. River During the past four or five years several changes had transpired in my fathers family which I've omitted to write - but will mention some of them. His wife [Caroline Eliza Nickerson] in consequence of being in delicate health concluded to return to Iowa where she had relatives, stop there until the next season, when she would be in a better condition to travel. my father divided his teams and provisions in fact - gave her half of all he posessed, hired a man to drive her team to where she wished to locate - She took with her, her only living child (Persia) belonging to my father, and went back to her folks. It proved to be a final separation - he married other wives - had many children born to him of whom I know but little as I was not one of his family at these times, and was interested in my own affairs <of> which I shall mention later on.

Commencing with my fathers travels and that of his family across the plains, will say that my father started <from Omaha> early in the spring of 1847 in company with many others, (50 I think) to explore and find a road to the Great Salt Lake basin of which they had an idea existed somewhere - but road or even a trail, there was none. There was a great amt. of rain that spring which made their progress slow and also very disagreeable for their families who were left camped out on the banks of the Missouri river, where Omaha is now located. His wife Hannah[176] was confined while living in a covered wagon - had a daughter called Hannah, I well remember the night the rain poured down in torrents, I was kneeling on her bed all night trying to keep her bed dry by scooping the water with my hands first down one side - then the other so that it would follow down the course of the cover and wagon bows instead of pouring straight through - would occasionally take off some of the bed covering and wring it then lay it on again to catch the water that we could not divert into channels down the cover or into pans basins etc. of which

---

176. A plural wife, Hannah Tupper. They were married in 1844. Hannah's sister, Lodoiska, married Thomas in January 1846.

there were several on the bed to catch the unruly streams as they poured in, in almost torrents.

I think it was on the 14th of June <1847> that we (a number of large companies) started on our journey across the plains - some with cow teams, some with wild steers yoked with cows - while some had good, ox teams, and there were a few horse teams, and the beauty of this was, (If I may be allowed the expression) that of the teamsters of this motley outfit - there were 9 out of 10 who were girls, women, or children. I can but laugh now, when I look back upon that picturesque scene (for be it understood that I was one of those teamsters) and at the time it was no <laughing> matter but real, reality in the full sense of the term - Some there were who was equiped with big ox whip 6 or 8 feet long who I doubt not had never seen, much less handled a whip of this kind - and knew not gee from haw perhape had been raised tenderly and who owing to scarcity of male members in our camp had to take the whip in hand and drive their teams - walking of course as they couldn't drive their unbroke ox teams and sit in the wagon, else when they espied a spear of grass out side the road (of which there was but a faint track made by the pioneers) they would sometimes turn off and break the wagon tongue - all these things we had in our camps. But as I was going to say, it was owing to the scarcity of men in our camp in consequence of five hundred of our best men being called upon by our dear Unkle Sam. to go to (Mexico - which was all right enough of course,) and then 500 men going out as pioneers These were heavy draughts on us at that time owing to our condition.

One incident which happened while we were camped on the Platt river of a laughable nature I must here relate. (for I can tell you we had to laugh sometimes) - we drove up to our camping ground which our capt. had decided was a good place to stop (posibly because our teams had given out as was often the case) and we girls ~~unyoked~~ unhitched our teams <from the wagons> -

drove them to the river to drink, a [illegible] chum of mine just my age 16 - drove her team just a head of mine - they of course were thirsty and tired - so they went out into the stream - half way across - they drank and then stood there as though they were in no hurry to come back -. The girl called to them they seemed to look happy and contented to stay where they were - Oh, dear what shall I do - I cannot wade out to them?- I looked around and espied a young man coming with his team to water them - I said wait a minute just as she was about to wade into the water See - there is a young man coming perhaps he will ~~take~~ have pity for you. Oh! no he is out - it isn't likely he'll wade into the river for my cattle - well I said lets wait and see. He came up to us and of course could see what was our trouble - he said Shall I fetch your cattle out ladies? - She said if it's not asking too much of you - after he had started in after them - she said to me, Who is that young man? I told her I had never met him before - She replied I am going to set my cap for him, and sure enough they were very good friends all the way on our journey ever after this occurrence, and after the journey was ended they were married and have live[d] a long happy life together.

We travel'd on through a wild Indian country meeting with no serious trouble except now and then loosing some of our cattle or sheep. Dont think we had a death in our camp on the journey. When we arrived at Fort Bridger we found a Mountaineer, Bridger by name, living with a little Squad of Indians - here we met my father and some of the Pioneers returning, after, or to meet their families, we were overjoyed to meet worn out as we were to hear them say that they had found and located a stopping place for the Saints, for we had been three months on our journey and had began to think we were pretty good teamsters, Still all were willing to surrender the ox whip to its owner whenever demanded by its owner - as they returned from their Pioneer life, and the men also had a time of rejoicing on meeting with their familys Capt. Bridger gave us but little encouragement concerning our new home he told my father that he would give him a thousand dollars for every bushel of wheat that was raised in Salt Lake Valley.

This did not in the least have a tendency to discourage us - We were also told that we had the hardest and roughest part of the journey to travel - I wondered how this could be, for I could picture nothing in my mind that could be worse than what we had passed. we had walked 2 and 22 miles per day - and driven our ox teams sometimes one yoke and sometimes two - yoked and unyoked them, and then cooked our food and attended to camp work besides And now to be told that the hardest part of our journey was just on a head - but we were still equal to the task - of course we were [illegible] over those two ranges of mountains Walked up and down with [rod?] in hand haw here and gee there until at last we reached the goal <of our anticipations> and were made happy about the 28th of Oct 1847 By entering and locating in Salt Lake Valley.

Now we thought - our labors at an end on this we were sadly disappointed - it was late in the season - winter approaching - no houses - canals, sheds barns etc. Scarcity of clothing, children all barefooted - Snow began to fall, we knew not how deep - it might fall - we were short of provisions - Some families were entirely out before arriving in the Valley. The Saints counselled together and considered the best method of procedure to adopt in order that none should starve Some there were, who had a sufficiency for themselves and some to spare. It was decided that the breadstuffs in all our camps should be weighed - an estimate made, to see if there was enough to allow half pound per capita - it was ascertained that by rationing ourselvs very closely we had scarcely enough to last the winter through - Say nothing about until harvest. There were poor cattle killed to eat that I do not think, if cooked all up would have made a grease spot on a silk dress. We had no milk to help out until Spring and very few had any then. We commenced our rations on half lb [two illegible

words] – that did very well – but we could see that such extravagant rations would not do, we were getting low in "our meal
bags" – we had to frequently divide with those less fortunate, and
were entirely without bread or anything else to eat – Some per-
hapse, who would not ration themselves, but eat all they wanted
too. Then it was that people grumbled – but it made no difference people must not starve – but many there were who boiled
ox hides and lived on them for weeks together.

Men, women and children turned out and went into the
canons [canyons] to pick up wood for fire and helped to get out
logs to build shantees to protect them from the stormy blasts of
air ice covered region – for many of the Saints were without tents
or wagons – brought through by some person who wished their
services perhape and were set down with the cold earth for a bed
and the sky for covering.

Some of the more favored in camp succeeded in getting rude
log huts – thatched with grass and covered with earth, or as we usually say with dirt roof. My father was one of this class. As soon as
Spring opened, and bare ground was in sight, the more energetic
of the brethren began looking over the Valley for the purpose of
selecting a place for a home, and farm – It was not counsel for men
to take their families away from the forte – for they had made a
temporary fort during the winter to protect us from the Indians
– of whom there seemed to be thousands My father located a farm
10 miles north of Salt Lake City. He moved his family too, for he
had no help except women and children but he worked hard, as
did all his family his labors were crowned with success, he was one
of a very few who raised corn and wheat to ripen the first year – he
had a sufficiency for his own use and some to spare As for sickness
and deaths, they were few and babes were born, children were fed
and clothed in the usual way, and people prospered. I never knew
of any body dying from hunger or cold.

SARAH DeArmon Pea Rich[177]

[Iowa - 1846]

The Temple was finished and dedicated unto the Lord, and the work of given endowments commenced. President Young chose many brothers and sisters to come to the temple and assist in given endowments among those chosen was Mr. Rich and my self We ware to be thare at 7 in the morning and remain untill work was done at ten or twelve o'clock at night if necessary. So we got a good girl Mary Phelps a wife of my husband to stay and take care of the children and we helped in the House of the Lord to give endowments for four months untill the house was closed and we as a people commenced to prepare ourselves to depart for the rockey mountains for by this time the Devil was mad and the lives of many of our brethern ware sought by the mob that had assassinated our brethern, Joseph and Hyrum, but many ware the blessings we had received in the House of the Lord which has caused us joy and comfort in the midst of all our sorrows and enabled us to have faith in God knowing he would guide us and sustain us in the unknown journey that lay before us, for if it had not been for the faith and knowledge that was bestowed upon us in that temple by the influence and help of the Spirit of the Lord our journey would have been like one taking a leap in the dark. To start out on such a jearney in the winter as it ware, and in our state of poverty it would seam like walking into the jaws of death but we had faith in our heavenly father and we put our trust in him feeling that

---

177. Reminiscences of Sarah DeArmon Pea Rich (1885–1893), holograph, LDS Church Archives.

we ware his chosen people and had embraced his gospel and enstead of sorrow we felt to rejoice that the day of our deliverence had come, so I set to work to prepare my self and family to be as comfortable as we could with what little means we had for we wanted to start out with the first company as president Young wanted us to start in the first company the same as him and family ware going in. We had no team of our own; all we had in that line was one horse and 2 cows but those that had means and teams came forward and offerd to assist those that ware going in the first company for there was only a few hundred familys going to start out in this company. Others were to follow on from time to time as it should be thought wisdom for them to do so. I will now mention one good brother that came forward and offerd to assist us with a waggon and team, and his young son to drive our team untill we come to a stopping place where the team and boy could be sent back. It was Brother Joel Ricks, and the boy he sent at that time was his son Thomas Ricks now president of Rexburg Idaho[178] he being at that time only 16 or 17 years old. Other brethern allso turned out teams to help carry provisions tents and other things necessary for such a jearney. I went to work and had some cloth wove and the sisters turned out and helped me to make up clothing for my children and family and it was not long untill I could say I am reddy for a start but as I am a little a head of my story I will go back to some things that took place in the temple we are about to leave. As the gospel with all its fullness had been restord to the earth through the Prophet Joseph Smith of course all the former ordenences were restord. Allso among other things celestial marriage was restord and the ordenences there onto ware performed in the temple just eluded to. So when my husband and my self had this doctern explain and taught to us in its true light by those that had a right to teach it

178. Thomas Ricks was the first president of the Bannock Stake in Rexburg, Idaho.

174

we both saw the propriety of the same and believed it to be true and essential to our future glory and exaltation heare after. We accepted the same and like old Sarah of old I had in that temple given to my husband four other wives which ware sealed to him in that temple by the holy order of God by one having athority to do the same. There names ware Eliza A. Graves, Sarah J. Peck, Mary A. Phelps and Emeline W. Grover; they ware all that was seald to him at that time. So this enlarged our family to be a few more in number to prepare for the jearney west. Many may think it very strange that I would consent for my dear husband whome I loved as I did my own life and lived with him for years to take more wives. This I could not have done if I had not believed it to be right in the sight of God and believed it to be one principal of his gospel once again restored to the earth that those holding the preasthood of heaven might by obeying this order attain to a higher glory in the eternal world and by our obedience to that order we ware blessed and the Lord sustained us in the same for through obedience to that order my dear husband has left on this earth a numers posterity like the ancient Apostles and Servents of God. Now I will again return to our preparing for the moov west and when we got every thing reddy for the start teames ware reddy for us to load up and we started on the 13th of Febuary. We crossed the Mississippi river on the ice with our waggons and horses. We had 3 waggons one was drove by Mr Rich, one by brother Thomas Ricks and the 3rd by a young man that had volenteared to go with us by the name of George Stailey. We allso had a young boy given into our care by his father his mother being dead. His father wished him to go with us to the mountains and we ware to look after him the same as our own. His name was George Patton of whome I will speak more about later on. Two or three of the brethern crossed the river with us and assisted us as fare as my fatherinlaw 12 miles away from Nauvoo in iowa. In Nauvoo on this the 13th day of february I parted for the last time in this life with my dear mother Elizabeth Pea allthough we both expected at that time that her and my father [John Pea] and sister Jane [age 27] would follow on the next season but death deprived me of ever meeting my mother again in this life.[179] Brother charles pendleton was one of the good brothers that kindly assisted us to my fatherinlaws and he returned to Nauvoo and waited for a year or too and followed on. President Young, Kimball and others had allso crossed the river with a few hundred familys and ware camped on a stream called Sugar creek. There they waited until all the companyes came together and they all became organized. Mr. Rich went back and forth to Nauvoo to help other of the brethern to start while we remaind at his fathers also to git ox-teams to hall [haul] our provision. So we had to leave our house and furniture all unsold, left stoves chairs bedsteds clock and all our furniture standing in the house not sold. So the time came for us to roal [roll] out into camp and we bid our friends goodby and started for camp. It snowd all that day and when we pitched our tent at night we had to sweep away the snow and make our beds on the coald ground for there was not room for us to sleep in our wagons. We remaind in camp a few days. I there was taken verry sick through being exposed in the storm and as my Charley was then a nursing baby it was verry hard on me to be sick but by good care and the kindness of my husband and his young wives and the administering of the brethern I was restored to health again and able to travel with the rest of the company but before we left camp my father and sister Jane rode over to see us and again bid us good by. Father [Joseph] Rich and mother [Nancy O'Neal] Rich also rode out to camp to see us and again bid us good by and left us for good at that place expecting to join us some time in the future when we would find a resting place Mr. Rich returned from Nauvoo on the 25th, fixed up the wagons and made them comfortable as he could for

---

179. Elizabeth Knighton Pea died 30 December 1847.

the jearney and at 3 o'clock that afternoon we started on our jearney. Traveled five miles and camped on lick creek a little after night. There was snow on the ground 3 inches deep and we had a coald night of it having to sweep away the snow, strech our tent and make down our beds on the coald ground. We had a lot of rag carpet which came in verry handy to lay on the ground under our beds but yet it was coald and uncomfortable for us having 3 little children one a babe at the breast. My health was not verry good but I was blessed of the Lord by my obediance in receiving the law of polygamy for as my husbands other wives ware all young girls and 3 of them ware then with me they assisted in the work and helped me with my children, a blessing which I acknowledge was from the Lord. One of them Mary A. Phelps Rich to[ok] all the care of my children at night except the baby and when the wether was bad I stayed in the wagon with my babe and my meals was handed in to me as all the cooking had to be done by a fiar built up in open air, rain, snow or shine. Meals had to be prepard in this way, and all this time those dear girls waited on me and done the work without a murmur or complaint. On the 26 of feb we started on and traveld on threw a little place called farmington. Here Mr. Rich got some coffe sugar leather and other things to help us on our jearney, then went up the desd-mine [Des Moines] five miles and camped on Reeds crick. Here we found brother bishop miller and company and some of the pioneers who were apointed to travel with each company to assist to build bridges, make roads and to help us along in case of need. They ware young men or men that had volunteard to go with us some hundred miles and then return and bring their familys. Bishop Miller had here taken a contract of a setler that lived at this place of clearing ten acres of land in order to git grain and bread stuff for the jearney and it being Saturday Mr Rich stoped over Sunday and had his men help Bishop miller out with his contract. On Sunday 29th Mr Rich helped to bury brother Smiths child, one of the brother millers company. My

husband and bishop miller preach the funearl sermon there
being a number of setlers present who paid good attention to
there preaching and in the afternoon my husband went to visit
Mr. Neal, an old acquaintence from Kentucky. I was quite sick
that afternoon and could not go with him. Monday March the
2nd I was much better. Mr. Rich went to a place called bonapart
2 miles away and got some horse shewing done and returned and
brother youngs company came up and all stoped and rested awhil
for the roads ware so muddy as the rain had melted the snow and
the roads ware horrible. The mud was so deep we would only
travil a few miles a day and stop and camp and sometimes would
have to stay in camp several days waiting for the roads to get better; then we would start on and pass other camps waiting as we
had done for the roads to git better but we had to take courige
and endure the hardships before us through rain and mud. We
past brother orson Spencers camp. Sister [Catherine] Spencer
was verry sick and afterwards we heard she had died. She was a
noble faithfull latter day Saint and was a kind mother to her
beautiful children who ware left motherless by her death. She was
a lady in every respect and left a beautiful family of children who
kept all together and the daughters thought [though] then small
managed to do the work and ware united together and became
honerable sisters in the Church and the sons became honerable
men and are all now living to do good.[180] We still traviled on as
fast as the wether would permit only travling a few miles a day and
then perhaps stop for a day or two waiting for the rain to stop,
camping and sleeping in our tent on the damp ground at night
and when there was a chance the men folks would git jobs of work
from the farmers as we passed along and the pay would enable us
to git things most needed to make us comfortable on our jearney for we ware verry poor and needed maney things that we had

---

180. One of her daughters, Aurelia Spencer Rogers, initiated the idea of the Primary Association
in 1878.

to deny ourselves of, but notwithstanding all our hardships we felt cheerful knowing our reward was in the future and if we ware faithfull our lives would be preserved and that we ere long find a stoping place where we could rest and help to build up the kingdom of our God for when we imbraced His Gospel we had a claim upon His promises. We continued on our jearney all through the month of march, stoping when there was a chance to git work and our brethern would do the work while there wives and children would cook, wash, iron and then parch corn and grind it on our coffee mills and then when we had our meals we would eat the parched corn meal in milk and when milk was scarce would do as most of our milk men do now a days, put in a little water. This is how we poor mormons had to do while jearneying from civilization to find a home in the mountains where we could serve our God in peace for a season. Each company had a few cows to give us milk but often these cows had to be yeoked up and help to draw our wagons and of course they could not give us much milk. We also before starting out west got squashes and cooked them up as dry as posible and then made them out in small thin cakes and dried them in our stoves and put them in clean sacks and they too ware used in milk and oftimes when we stoped for a few days we would make them into pies by soaking them in milk, but we did not have eggs to put in them to make them nice, but we did the best we could and called them squash pies. Young ladys of today, what would you think of one of our squash pies of those days? Now we started on our jearney traveld about 4 miles and camped on fox river near the camp of father [Samuel] Bent, and a number of the high council were camped here. We again stoped while Mr. Rich and others took a job to make some shingles for a farmer near where we stoped and the next day being Sunday brother John Taylor and his family came to our tent, made us a visit. Brother Taylor held meeting, spoak of what lay before us, told us to be humble and patient and all would be right. After meeting, him and the portion of his family that was with him returned to our tent and took dinner with us and cheered us up with his lively joaks. Mr. Rich then visited the main camp to attend a council meeting. I and Sister Mary Rich went with him to visit some of our friends in that camp. We returned and the next day fixed up our things and again set out on are trip. Started, traveld up the divide between Soap creek and fox river and camped at brother orson pratts camp. We that day had traveled about 17 miles. We ware then in about 3 miles of the main camp where president Young and kimball ware camped. The next day we traveld about 12 miles over bad road stalled in the mud and had to unload one wagon. The main camp was travling just ahead of us, so we overtook them at night in camp and struck our tent and camped near by. The next day our company started on, leaving the main camp where it was crossed over the pararia [prairie], traveld 12 miles, crossed the Shariton [Chariton] River, camped on the west bank. Here we again found brother orson Pratt and brother [Charles] Shumwais company camped. Here Mr. Rich and other took a contract to clear one acre of ground. This they accomplished in one day and got 23 bushels of corn for we had to feed our teams all this time. While the brethern were doing the work the main camp came up, crossed over the river and camped on the hill a half mile from our camp. Here I will make mention that while crossing this river in a waggon our wortha brother Chariton Jacobs[181] was born and they named him after that river. He now is a wortha man of a family and lives in Salt Lake City. We tarried here a few days, also all the camps. Brother Taylors company was camped near us and one evening brother Taylor, Mr. Rich and myself together with Sister Harriet S. Kimball visited the camp on the hill. The brethern met in council and about ten o'clock at night Mr. Rich brother Taylor and myself returned to our camp.

---

181. Son of Zina Diantha Huntington Jacobs (Young).

Sister H Kimball [Vilate] remaind in her own camp as she had
only come to our camp on a visit, having lived with me at the
time she was married to brother Kimball. By the time we started
back to camp it had commenced raining and was very dark. We
missed our way and by the time we reached camp we were wet and
in mud over our shoe tops, but notwithstanding our mud
brother Taylor cheered us up and kept us a laughing all the way to
our tent. It was a very wet desagreeable time and while here in
camp Sister Mary Rich one of my husband's wives came down
with the measles, also one of the young men of our company
brother Bartina. We all felt verry bad for it was a bad time to git
measels in our camp and I had a baby about a year old that soon
after came down with the same complaint. Hear at this place the
companys ware all organised for our final march into the wilderness as it then seamed to us and many of our pioneers returned
to Nauvoo to prepare to bring on there familys and friends, and
on April the 2nd we left the Shariton on our march towards the
rockey mountains leaving all the Settlements behind, so from
that [time] on we had to pick our way without aney road only as
we maide it. Soon after leaving this place my little baby Charley
took down with the measles and was verry sick for a weak or more
but we still traveld on sleeping in our tent at night. Some times
the rain would poor down and all would be damp and wet but
still the Lord blessed us and our little one and Sister Mary recovered from the measels and no one seamed to take the disease
from them for which we thanked the Lord for his kindness, for
to have the disease spred in so large a camp while travling would
truly be distressing, but the Lord is all wais mercifull to those who
puts there trust in him. We still continued our jearney, could
only travil a few miles a day on account of the bad roads. [F]rom
Shariton river we continued our jearney west only being able to
travil but a few miles every day on account of mud and the bad
roads. It rained part of the time and at other times it would snow
and sleet notwithstanding it was in the month of April. About

the 9th of April we got to a dry Elm grove in the praira; here we found some of the companeys that was a head of us camped having passed president Youngs company on locus [Locust] creek. Here we camped in Elm grove and stayed over Sunday the 12th waiting for the rest of the companys to come up. Here the brethern met in council at brother kimballs tent and decided to go by council bluffs and stop and make a settlement on grand river. While here the boy that was with us George Patton [Patten] was taken verry sick with the mountain fever so we tarried untill Wednesday the 15th and travild on the divide, leaving the main road. Travild about eight miles and camped in a small grove and on the next day traveld on leaving part of the companys still in camp. After a hard days travil reached a branch of the medisan [Medicine] creek. Here again the company tarried and helped up the other companeys for when it was so muddy they would, the brethern that was a head, would take there teams from there waggons and go back to those behind us and double teams and help them up, for we ware then like one family in our feelings towards each other and conciquently we had to travil slow in order to help each other along. We got all together and traveld on a few miles and again camped in a body and stoped on a small stream and waited over Sunday as we did not travil on the Sabbath. Here our brethern held meeting and afterwards met in council and to find out how much provision was on hand and on the 22nd some of the companey started on while our company and some others had to stop on account of some teams of our teames being sick and the boy that was with us still was verry sick. We stopped untill fryday the 24th having lost an ox by death. We started on and traveled 16 miles and camped and on Saturday the 25th we reached a grove which they named garden grove. Here the main camp all arrived. Here it was decided that some of the companeys was to stop at this place and fence in a large field and put in a crop altho late in the season. This was a beautiful place, plenty of timber and water. Brother [Samuel] Bent was apointed to preside over this place with Daniel fullmer and Aaron Johnson his 2 councilers. Here we stoped untill the 22nd of May, stoped in our tent. Our boy George Patton still got worse and became as helpless as a babe, was out of his head and to all appearence could not live. Our beds had to be made down in the tent; one was fixed comfortable for the sick boy. All our family done all they could for him. Mr. Rich and a brother Russell Brownell took charge of him and watched with him at night. Brother brownell was travling with us to help us along. George Patton the boy was put into our charge to look after the same as one of our own children. He had by this time become unconchious. Mr. Rich and brother Brownell ware compleately worn out. Mr. Rich came to my bed and called to me and wanted to know if I could watch over the boy awhil for he must have a little rest, so I got up, went to the bedside of the sick boy while my husband and brother brownell could have a little rest. They both thought the boy could not posibly live maney hours, so I took my seat beside the poor sick boy and began to reason with myself. My reasoning was something like this. I thought to myself this poor dying boy was put into our charge to watch over the same as one of our children. Could we give up one of our own children to die without using all the faith within our reach to plead with the Lord to spare the dear one and not take it away from us? This boy had no mother living to plead with the Lord to spare his life to meet his dear father again at our hands. I said no to myself, I will not give him up as long as there is life. I will pray and ask the Lord to tell me what to do for him. I neald down while all in the tent was asleep and plead with the Lord to spare his life and to impress it upon me what to do for poor George for he was a good boy and we all loved him, so when I got up from praying I was led by my feelings to put a teaspoonfull of concicrated oil in his mouth. His tonge was drawn fare back in his mouth and was verry black and his breathing rattling and heavy and his eyes to all appearence set in his head. I did not see that he swallowed the oil so I anointed his face and head with the oil asking the Lord to bless the same, then in a little while gave him another teaspoonfull of oil asking the Lord at the same time with a humball heart to spare the boy and accept of my feeble efforts in his behalf. I felt broken hearted before the Lord and to my great joy I noticed that George had swallowed the oil. I then took couriage, got some viniger, swabbed it and with a soft swab I rubed his tounge and mouth in order to remove the black crust that was forming in his mouth and throut. I then gave him a little branda and watter; he swallowed that. I then made some tea of what we called horse mint; he also swallowed that. I then washed his face and hands in watter and soda and thus I worked with that dear boy until daylight all alone for the rest was all asleep. Having been up so much they slept verry sound, and about daylight to my great joy George opend his eyes and looked upon me as though he was astonished. I said George do you know me? He spoak in a whisper, yes. O how glad I felt. By this time Mr. Rich had waked up and enquired how the boy was, saying afterwards that he allmost feared he was gone. I said to him come and see. The boy looked at him and smiled which astonished Mr. Rich so much that he turned to me and said what has caused such a chainge. I said to him prayr and faith and hope in our father in heaven. So I told my husband what I had done and how humble I felt while praying to the Lord to spare the boys life. My husband was truley affected and told me the boys life would be spared to yet be a blessing to me in some future time, and from that time on the dear boy continued to mend slowley and got well and prooved himself to be a blessing to me and my children maney years afterwards when My husband was away from home on a mishion and me and my children ware destitute and needed help, for he grew to be a man, helped to bring his father to Salt Lake Valley, married, and settled in Payson, Utah, prospered and was blessed with plenty, raised a large family and at this time is still living and many has been the time that he would bring me loads of provision butter

Eggs and grocererys when Mr. Rich would be off on mishions to forward the work of the Lord, and when George would help me he would allwais say mam, for that is what he calls me, he would say mam I owe my life to you, for your faith and prayrs saved me from death. This same boy is now brother George Patton that lives in Payson, Utah and he will give his testimony that what I write is the truth.[182]

Well I will now return to our travels from garden grove to our next stopping place called Mount Pisgah. We left garden grove May the 22nd. At this place snakes ware verry bad and many of our cattle and horses ware bit by them. Our horse, the only one we had of our own, was bitten by a rattle snake. Mr. Rich docturd him with sweet oil and harts horn and he recoverd. It was no uncomon thing to find snakes quoiled up under our beds when we took them up in our tent in the morning. So on the 22nd of May we took a part of our things and started for our next stopping place, having to leave a part of our things to be brought on at some other time as Brother Thomas Ricks had to return to Nauvoo from this place to help his fathers family on the next season. So that left us one waggon and team short so it took us about 7 days to reach the place we ware to stop at for the ballence of the summer and the next winter. It was only 40 miles from garden grove but we had to travil slow. We arrived in camp on the 26th of May. On reaching this place we found that father William Huntington was appointed by President Young to stop here and preside over the place and that Esra T Benson and C C Rich to be his councilers. The brethern that had went a head of us to this place and ware appointed to stop here had allready commenced to raise small log houses, so we lived in our tent and waggons untill our men could put up one log house and cover it with bark

---

182. George Patten was born 26 October 1828 in Chester County, Pennsylvania, the son of William C. and Julianna Beach Patten. He was baptized in Nauvoo in 1843. A builder and colonizer, he served the Church throughout his long life.

and dirt and we had a dirt floor, but our wagon boxes were taken off of the wheels and turned into bed rooms; allso our tent was used as a room. The men folk went to plowing and planting late as it was and putting up as good fences as the[y] could to keep the cattle out of the crops. So it was not long until the brethern of this place had got in about one thousand acres of ground into grain corn mostly and potatoes squashes and seads of all kinds such as we had with us and the[y] had it partly fenced then they went to work to prepare to fix up places to live in for the winter. All those that had means to go on further had done so leaving orders for all that came after was to stop at this place untill further orders from the first presidency that had went on to council bluffs on the Misouri rivers. Thare they stoped for the winter in order to prepare to start in the next spring for the Mountains. About the middle of June brother Benson started to council bluffs with the mail from pisgah and returned and about the last of June brother Benson was called to be one of the twelve apostles to fill the place of John E. Page who had apostatized, leaving the burthen [burden] of the place on father Huntington and Mr. Rich to see to affairs as best they could, for there was a great care resting upon them at that time, and about the 20th of June we were visited at this place by Cornel [James] Allen of the Army of the West. He wanted our people at this critticle time of our travels to raise five hundred men as voluntears to go to the mexican war to help fight mexico. Father Huntington and Mr. Rich sent him on to headquarters to where the first presidency was. So my dear readers you can see notwithstanding we had been driven and ware jearneying in poverty to seak a place to rest we ware followed and this cruel demand made upon us. So in a few days brother parley p. pratt was sent from headquarters by President Young and council for President Huntington and Rich to rais fifty men in this place as the heads of the Church had concented to have the five hundred men raised to fill the demands of the government from whence we ware driven, thus showing to the world that they ware loyel to the government. A more cruel demand could not have been made upon us at this the time of our affliction and poverty. The men was raised and sent and their famileys had to be looked after while they were gone. About this time the brethern president Young, Kimball and Richards, J[esse] C[arter] Little and others had concluded to come and make us a visit and see about raising the men. The[y] said what Brother Huntington and Rich had done in the matter was all right. They stayed a few days, preached to the people, gave good council, had a dance on the bare ground out doors, seamed to enjoy there visit. So the brethern left their blessing with our camp and returned to winter quarters. Their visit to us at that time was encouraging, for they left a good impreshion among the Saints which gave them new courage to persevere and prepare themselves for what was ahead of them. Along about the first of July our brethern found they must go to work and stake and rider their fence in order to secure there crops from unruley cattle. Now I expect maney of my readers will not know what stake and rider fences mean for they do not see much of that kind of work in this day, but they put up stakes cross ways on each end of there poles and then laid an other pole on top of the old fence, which made the fence some higher than it was so the cattle could not jump over the fence.

Well now about this time sickness set in among the different parts of the camp and many were down with chills and feavers which kept our bretheren on the go all the time administeren to the sick. And Aug 5th brother Benson and Sidwell called on us on there way to the east from winter quarters. At this time brother Huntington was allso taken with chills. He was our president and it was hard to have him prostrated with sickness. Brother Benson and Mr. Rich and others met in council and prayed for and administered to him before brother Benson departed for the East, but our dear father Huntington continued to grow worse until the 19th of August when he died. Great was the sorrow of the camp at the loss of so good and kind President. All was done to save him that was in our power to do, but he was called for and had to obey the call. Thus passed away one of our most useful and noble men. Maney were the achaking hearts left to mourn his loss after he was laid to rest in that lonely spot. The burthen of looking after the Saints in that place then rested on my husband as he then was the only Counciler left in that place as Brother Benson the first councilor had been called to the apostleship. Sickness increased in the place and on the 23rd, four days later, Mr. Rich was taken with the chills; 2 of my children ware also down with chills and feaver. So my dear readers you can give a little gess how his family felt at that time to see our leading brother laid away and then his counciler on whom rested all the burthen of that place stricken down and others of the family sick and us in a fare of [far off] land. It truly was a time of sorrow. Mr. Rich lay sick about 2 weeks. During this time there ware maney death[s] amonge the people left at this place and other members of our family were taken sick and suffered much for maney necessarys which we could not git at that place being 40 miles from any settlement, altho a number of our brethern had gone into the west part of misouri to git work in order to lay in a few needful things for there familyes through the coming winter. So by the good care which Mr. Rich received from the hands of his kind family and the faith and prayrs of the brethern he was restored to health again and though verry weak he was able to attend to the affairs of the place, but about this time nearly all of our family ware taken down sick so much so that there was scarcely enough of well ones in our family to see to the sick. Mr. Rich done all he could for the sick and poor for by this time the familyes of the soldiers that had gone to Mexico were in want and maney of them sick. They were calling on my husband for help and he called on those that had means to donate and assist him in this the hour of affliction to help the sick and poor that was in this place. Sickness continued to increase and nearly every boddy was sick and many died. I think about eighty died at Mount Pisgah and among

that number was father Joseph Knight, one of the first members of
the Church of Latter day Saints one that assisted the Prophet
Joseph Smith to means to soport his family while he was translat-
ing the book of mormon. So in this lonely spot in the graveyard
at Mount pisgah in what was then called potowatama lands lies one
of the noble benifactors of the prophet of Joseph who will come
forth in the mourning of the first resurection to meet the prophet
as well as all good Saints. Allso there lies that Noble father and
president William Huntington, allso Hyrum Spencer and many
brothers and sisters and dear children, also brother and Sister
Judson and little daughter, all burried as it were in one grave.[183]
The little girl was burried one day and on the day following her
father and mother died and there was so maney sick that they could
not find well ones enough to burry them for 4 days and they ware
both laid in one grave, leaving 3 small children. One died soon
after and the other 2, Timothy and Mary Jane, Mr. Rich and I
took them and brought them to Salt Lake. Mary Jane Judson
remained with us untill she married William Hanson by whom she
has raised 4 sons and 3 daughters. Timothy remain in our family
about 2 years and one of his older brothers came on and lived with
us one year and then him and Timothy went to California and are
still thare. Well after the sickness of pisgah and so many deaths had
passed over a little, our brethern had to look after there crops and
secure the same to help them through the coming winter. Mr.
Rich had two rooms built down on the river where we would be
handy to wood for the winter and where we ware living we had to
use spring watter which was suposed to be what was called mineral
watter and caused so much sickness and on the river we could use
river watter. It was a branch of grand river. So we with Mother
Huntingtons family[184] and a number of other familyes moved on

---

183. This is Samuel Judson and Arilla Rice Judson of Pinsky, Iowa.
184. Lydia Huntington, widow of William Huntington, had several unmarried children still in her
care.

to the river a mile or so from the Hill where we lived through the summer, but before we moved on the river Mother [Phebe Palmer] graves and her daughter Eliza Graves Rich came on as Eliza was one of my husbands wives that had to be left back in Nauvoo on account of her confinement on the 11 of february before we left Nauvoo on the 13th. So she had to be left; her and her babe ware left with her mother and came on in the fall company. She allso with her mother lived on the river and at this place Sister Sarah J. Peck Rich, another one of Mr. Richs wives, had a fine son born about the 26 of october.[185] After this Mr. Rich was again taken sick with a feaver and was verry sick for a long time and it turned to the chills. He was sick in bed when I was confined on the 15th of December when I had a son born [John Thomas Rich]. There we were in one little small room with a bark roof and a bark floor, for the oak and other trees would peal easey and the bretheren would peal off large peaces of bark and spred them out and make floors and cover the house with the same. Brother Lorenzo Snow and family had also come on to pisgah and stoped for the winter. He lived near us and himself and family ware so kind to us in our time of sickness and administered words of comfort and cheered us up in our affliction, and at this place we had many testamoneys that the Lord had not forsaken us and that he was mind full of His people who put their trust in him. One item of which I will make mention. The poor ware coming to us all the time for help and this one circumstance I will mention showed the hand of the Lord so plain that I want to leave it for my children to read and think upon so that they may put there trust in the Lord in some future time when they may have the chance of learning for themselves, as we did at that time. Well, as I was going to relate, a poor woman, one of the wives of one of the men that had went with the mormon betalyon to mexico, came to my husband who

---

185. Hyrum Rich was born 8 October 1846 at Mt. Pisgah, Harrison County, Iowa.

was still sick in bed and told him she had no bread for her children to eat I by this time was able to be up and see to my little babe. This Sister was crying and told us how destitute she was. My husband turned to me and said let this Sister have some flower. This was a puzzel to me knowing we did not have 20 pounds of flower in the house and none in the place to buy and not a cent of money to buy with. So I said we have not got 20 pounds of flower in the house and none in the place to git. He looked at me and smiled and said, Sarah let her have all there is in the house and trust in the Lord to provide for us. I arose and done as I was bid but knew not how our children was to get bread. When the Sister was gone Mr. Rich said I know the Lord will open the way for us to live so do not feel uneasy for there will be a way opend for us having a loaf of bread in the house. I too began to ask the Lord to open the way for us to live and along towards evening we saw some coverd waggons coming down the hill towards the house, so the man in frunt drove up and came into the house; it proved to be the brother Sidwell that was with brother Benson that had called on us as they went east. Brother Sidwell said he wished to stop over night with us. My husband told him he could do so. He then turned to Mr Rich and said to him, the Spirit tell[s] me you are out of money and tells me to help the[e], as he was a Quaker he used the word the[e], and handed Mr Rich fifty dollars. Mr Rich turned to me, handed me the money saying, now you see the Lord has opened the way for us to git flower, for he was quite overcome with thanks in his heart. Brother Sidwell after understanding our cituation said we have bread in our waggons enough for tonight and in the morning and we passed a waggon load of flower a little way back that will reach here either tonight or in the morning. So you can be suplyed with bread stuff. So we both burst into tears to think the Lord had so blessed us for blessing the poor Sister and her little children. So when the wagon of flower arrived Mr Rich not only laid in a suply for our own family but got a lot to give out to others that were sick and poor and in want. Brother Sidwell allso bought some flower and left with us to give to the poor of that place; he allso let us have some grociryes. He was a weltha batchler, was on his way to winter quarters and there assisted others to start to the mountains. So I want my children and all that reads this when I am laid to rest in my grave to see how the Lord blessed his Saints while travling from Nauvoo to the valleys of the mountains and how he has blessed them and sustained them after the[y] reached this valley when our provision was short and we had to live on rashions and verry small at that for over two years. Well now I will return again to our pisgah home. After my husband had got means from this good brother to provid for his family and for others he commenced to git better. Brother Snow and others ware verry kind to us and assisted Mr Rich to many things. He had got brother Snow and brother York to see to the bretheren of the place and look after buisness and by the 3rd of febuary he had so much recoverd that he was able in company with brother James S. Haleman to start to winter quarters to council with the brethern about what was best to be done concearning our moove to the west, having prevous to this appointed brother Snow as his first counciler and A.M. York as 2nd counceler. Mr. Rich and brother Haleman arrived at winter quarters after 4 days drive, staid near a week, got back to pisgah on the 16th, found all well at home. Brother Snow and Mr Rich held several meetings and then he began to make preparations for our moove to winter quarters, allso to help Sister Huntington to go. At the same time we ware to go she was to go with her family. About this time brother Orson Pratt and Brother [Joseph] Horn[e] had arived on important buisness concerning organising and preparing for the jearney to the west. Before we left pisgah the brethern and sisters got up a party for our benefit; it was held in brother Orval Coxs shop. There ware about one hundred people there. Mr Rich was helped to some meanes to assist us on our jearney. We had a good time and good feelings prevail; all was sorry to part with us. We prepared for the trip and on the 12 of March we started with all our

family. Allso Mother Huntington and her family as president
young had sent a team and Charles Decker with the team to assist
Sister Huntington with her family to winter quarters. It was coald
wether and continued so nearly all the way. We traveld 15 miles and
camped on the big prairiea and on the 13th we crossed the big
prairiea and reached brother Ivens camp, 26 miles. Here we
stoped for one day as it was so coald and on the 15th we started
again, traveld 25 miles and camped within five miles of indian
town[186] and on the 16th we went to big ishnabotoney [Nishna-
botna] 30 miles. 17th we traveld 17 miles and camped on Cay creek
and on the 18th we traveld 18 miles and got within 4 miles of camp
and on the 19th of march got to the Missouri river, found we
could not cross and here we had to remain three days. It was coald
and winday and virry disagreable especialy for the little babys we
having 3 of them in our family, the eldest of the 3 a little over one
year old, but we all felt good natured and made all hands as comfortable as posible. We finely crossed over the river in a flat boat
and arived safe in winter quarters and the brethern that was there
soon found us an empty house to stop in for a while. After resting Mr Rich arranged things for us so that he could return to
Nauvoo and dispose of what little property we ware compelled to
leave when we left Nauvoo. We found on arriving at winter quarters that the 12 and maney others ware preparing to start west for
the mountains and my husband was anxious to allso go west that
Spring. So on the 16th of Aprail Mr Rich left winter quarters for
Nauvoo committing his family into the hands of the Lord, at the
same time telling the family if they would pray for Sarah D his wife,
meaning my self, that I would see that they would have enough to
eat until his return as he was not able to leave enough on hand to
last untill he would return and no means to buy with but on his
going back at that time depended our prospect to go with the first

---

186. A Pottawattamie settlement on the west bank of the Nishnabotna River.

company across the plains. He bid us good by and started for Nauvoo. At that time we had brother James Leach and wife [Isabella Daniels Leach] with us to help us along on our jearney as they had no children and could not have a fit out of their own. So it was not long before what we had in the house to eat had give out and when we went to bed at night we did not know where our brakfast was to come from. So when we got up in the mourning I called on Brother Leach to attend family prayrs; he did so. I then told Mr Richs other wives that was with us to put on the tea kettle and set the table. I then said to brother Leach, come go with me. I put on my bonnet and shall and asked Sister Leach to see to the children and I and Brother Leach would go and get somthing for brakfast. Brother Leach looked at me with astonishment knowing I had no money to buy aneything with but we started out on faith. I was directed to 2 of the brethern that I thought I could barry 2 dollars of in order to git something for my family to eat but they both were hard up and were preparing to start west and could not spare the money as they expected to be on the moove before Mr Rich would be back. So I started on. Brother Leach by this time wondered how I could be able to git aneything to take home but told me afterwards that he was praying in his heart all the time to the Lord to help Sister Rich to be able to suply her family with something for brakfast. I was by this time at the gate of Sister Esra T Benson. Said I to brother L, we will call in here. Sister [Pamelia] Benson was very glad to meet with me. After setting a few minites she said Sister Rich have you been to breakfast? I said No. Then she called to her sister, Addaline[187] to make me a cup of tea. I by this time felt as though a cup of tea would do me good. Before I had time to tell her my buisness out she said have you anything at home to eat? I said no Sister Benson but I soon shall return home with something. She threw a silver dollar into my lap and said go to

---

187. Pamelia Andrus Benson's sister Adeline was also married to Ezra T. Benson.

brother [Stephen] Winchesters and get some grocerys for he just
got in last night with some grocerys to sell. He has been out to the
settlements to work and got grocerys. By this time tears could be
seen both in my eyes and brother Leachs. I thanked Sister Benson,
told her I would replace the dollar as soon as my husband got back.
She said I should do nothing of the kind. So we drank a cup of tea
and started for Brother Winchesters. We had not gone far before
we met brother E[zra] T[hompson] Clark with a sack of flower and
a bushel of potatoes in his waggon enquireng where I lived, said it
was for me so I sent him on to my house with instructions for the
girls to hurry up brakfast and we would soon be there with some
grocerys. We went and got a little shugar, a little coffee and tea. Of
course a dollar would not git much but we ware so proud to get a
little. We then started for home, passed brother [James M.] Flakes
whome I had never seen. He was just finishing dressing a calf.
Some on[e] present observed to him that there went Sister Rich.
He turned and called to me and said Sister Rich send that man
here and git a quarter of this calf. I did so and reached home with
plenty to eat, found the family reddy to thank the Lord that they
had prayed for me and that the Lord had blessed me in my efferts
to git something to live on until Mr Rich would return. So my
friends I write this that you me [may] see the result of trusting in
the Lord in time of need. Pray unto Him with a humble heart and
he will answer your prayers as he did ours at this time of need, and
it is this same good father in heaven that sestained and helped His
Saints to come to these valleys and provided means whereby we
could live after we got here for our lott was then cast in great
poverty and in all our trials the Lord has been near to answer the
prayers of those who put their trust in Him. Who can doubt this
work of the Latter day Saints after passing through what I have
passed through for forty-five years. One thing which I omitted to
menshion I will relate here and that was after we reached winter
quarters and before my husband started for Nauvoo him and
myself and the girl that had lived with me so long went to presi-

dent Youngs office as had been preaviously arainged with president and Mr Rich and the girl, Sister Harriet Sargent, and myself, that being the day apointed by the president for us to come. We went to his office, I think it was the 12th day of April, and Sister Harriet Sargent was sealed to my husband as his wife for time and all Eternity by president Brigham Young and returned back, and afterwards he returned to Nauvoo and desposed of what property we had left, visited our friend together with my father mother and sister, left them in Quincy Illinois. He then started for our camp in the west, fell in with a company of Saints coming out to winter quarters and traveld with them. They ware men of means and had there familys with them and were verry anxious to come to the valley with the first company. So they arrainged with Mr Rich to help him out with his family so we could all come together. So when they reached winter quarters they found the companys fast preparing for a start and all went to work together and we all got fitted up for a moove west with what my husband had and what those brethern helped him too, part as a lone to be replaced again and part as a donation. We were fitted up as comfortable as we could be with waggons and teams and provision besides some cows and sheep and teamsters and some to drive the stock for all that had loose stock brought it along. The names of those 2 brethern that so kindly helped us to be able to come with the first company were Zasabel Shoemaker and Aaron Cherry. Them and us traveld together in the same company all the way to the valley.

Leonora Cannon Taylor was one of those women who resolutely and unpretentiously supported the work of the Restoration and their husbands' crucial role in that work, no matter what personal sacrifice it entailed. Quiet and unassuming despite her prominent position as wife of Apostle and later

President John Taylor and faithful to the core, she left only a brief diary and some letters, but they reveal much about the personality and dogged faith of this remarkable and little known woman. Original spelling and lack of punctuation reflect her limited writing skills, but the content reveals a sensitive, caring, and observant diarist.

LEONORA CANNON TAYLOR[188]

LEFT NAUVOO to go on our Journey to California the 15th of Feb 1846. went down to the River on Sunday to camp. the Wind was so high we returned, and slept at Br Hirum Kimbals.[189] Mon 16 crost the River and went on to Sugar Creek where the Bretheren were campt while there I was very sick with inf. Ruimutism we were visited by many of our Nauvoo friends. had very severe Wether. Snow Storm & wind we made a Family Bed all over the tent floor

Left Sugar Creek 2 of March I campt on the Desmoine 16 miles from our first encampment on the 3d we removed a mile. 4th went through Farmington traveled about 9 miles. 5th went through Boneypark [Bonaparte] & crossed the Desmoine. went 10 miles stopt with company a Mr Packs join us on a Mile next day at Indian River went 13 miles. 6th overtook the camp 7th

---

188. Leonora Cannon Taylor, Personal Diary, 1846–47, in George John Taylor Collection, LDS Church Archives.

189. The home of Hiram and Sarah Kimball was near the ferryboat crossing, and several diarists made note of staying with the Kimballs while waiting to cross the river. The Kimballs did not leave Nauvoo until 1851.

joined the Atilary at a place cald Gospel Valley we are here pret-
tyly situated the Rain has come on and spoild our floors we slept
last Night with the wind blowing into our wagon so[190] hard. Mr
T[aylor] could scarse catch his breath 17th went 3 Miles campt
near Fox River 18th remained in camp William[191] went back 19th
traveled 18 Miles stopt near Bloomfield 20th 11 Miles through
wet Prarie got into camp in the night. George[192] got the Mumps
Saturday 21st traveled 15 miles good road acros'd the Shardon
[Chariton] River in campt on its bank a very pretty situation a
sever Snow storm Sunday 22 Monday cleared an acre of Ground
Tuesday 23 snows Wedday 25 Thurd snod severe snow

27th Fri cold and fressing [freezing] 28 Sat cold Sunday 29
Mon. 30th clear warm Tues 31 April 1st a warm day 2'd left
Shardon [Chariton] traveled 13 miles, campt Shout [Shoal]
Creek campt on a hill near Brother [Heber C.] Kimball. 3'd
went on traveled 4 miles overtook Bishop William - crosed over a
creek campt on a high hill on Prairie Sat 4th went 8 miles of very
bad road campt on the Prairie sand 5 traveled 5 miles with double
Teams campt on a branch of Locust Creek. walk over on a log

Monday 6th 16th anniversary of the Church about 171 miles
from Nauvoo Tuesday bad roads. Wed 8th same Thursday 9th
traveled 3 miles, double teams cariage broke down I had to walk 3
miles, through mud all the way 12th we were the first on the Road
near a mile beyond Br Brigham Mr T[aylor] went back to council, a giant storm came on our tent blown down, heard the night
we left our last encampment the ground was quite overflown and
People who had gone there to stop had to leave in the Night 11th
our Ox Died, a very cold day some snow Mary Anne[193] cooked

---

190. The preceding material has been put here in chronological order although the sentence beginning "Left Sugar Creek" and extending to the phrase "blowing into our wagon so" appears on the left-
hand page of the diary facing the page noting their departure from Nauvoo.

191. Probably William Taylor, the brother of John Taylor.

192. George John Taylor was the twelve-year-old son of John and Leonora. George Q. Cannon,
Leonora's nephew, also traveled with the family.

193. Mary Ann Oakley was a plural wife of John Taylor.

some artichokes with potatoes & onions and found them very good. while we were at Locust Creek Br Benson came to borrow [crossed out] borow a couple of Oxen after he got them he met Joseph[194] & asked the childs age he told him he was 7 years old, he put him on his leader horse and made him ride 2 Miles to the Camp then sent him home with the oxen through mud that would take a man to his knees, the[y] run into the Woods he followed them, and cried all the way home, the dear Child was cover'd with mud from head to foot, he several times lost sight of the road but would not leave his Oxen Sunday 12th a windy day Mr T went with Gen Rich to Br Kimbals camp back 4 miles back to counsel I sat in the girls[195] tent all the afternoon. Mond 13th a fine day very unwell myself, had the blacksmith forge up to mend the Carriage Tuesday 14th dry & windy Father not well. sick Myself 15th went 7 miles 16 went 4 Miles stay'd all night on a Wet Prairie heard 3 Wolves Bark around us cookd in Boneypark oven

Frid 17th 3 Miles before breakfast of [illegible] Sat 18th campt on a Locust Creek near Br Kimbal on Thrd 19th Mr Taylor went to meeting to Br Youngs camp 2 miles back Mr. T & Kimbal preached in the afternoon Mond 20 Mr T. went to a counsel, Tuesday 21st good rain for the Grass Br Spencer campt on the oposite point on the forks of Medcine [Medicine] going to start for Grand river tomorrow if all is well wrote twice to George Cannon [her brother] had two letters from him had a letter from Elinor [her sister][196] dated Jan 12th 1846 Liverpool, no account of my

Brother John or David[197] since George left Liverpool[198] 22nd

---

194. Joseph was the seven-year-old son of John and Leonora.
195. "The girls" refers to the plural wives of John Taylor.
196. Elinor eventually came to Utah after her husband died.
197. Her brothers John and David left England and went to Australia.
198. After Captain George Cannon, Leonora's father, died at sea in 1811, his son George left the family home at Peel, Isle of Man, off the coast of Great Britain and sailed to Liverpool to seek work in order to help the family's financial situation. He eventually traveled to America where he died in St. Louis in 1844. Leonora brought George's orphaned children to Salt Lake City.

Wed round 7M stopt on Medcine Thursd 23 Mr. Kimbal and a Missourian came and stopt all night 24th Frid traveled 8 miles Mr T & [illegible] Harpes bit by Snakes threw Quoity + in the even [evening] stopt at a place where we found a Fire and tent ground prepared beside a creek Father fished. 25 Sat overtook the whole camp on the forks of Grand River. 26 Sund all went to a Meeting Mr T & O Pratt spoke. raind Mon raind Tuesd 23 rain'd Br Romney[199] came from Nauvoo he and [illegible], Slept in the Tent 29th Wed Rain Th'd 30 Rain. 1st of May Friday moved to the point + Mr T pact the girls things went with them and left the Children & I to scramble through the mud how we could 2nd Sat Mr T started on [with] Mary [Anne] along with Father [John] Smith[200] & Br Spalding[201] to Nauvo 3 Sund Br Smith came back to look for B. Bs. horses who had run away, we went [to] meeting heard Br Spencer preach & Br B. Young after him we had a good time it was a great storm in the afternoon. Mary Anne stay'd at Br Y's. and got wet coming home 4th Mond Br Smith went Back took Mr Ts knife and Pistol he had forgotten Cool day 5th Tuesd very warm, cariage horse bitten badly by a Rattle Snake.

applied Murtahor & oyle & a poltice of salt and onions a thunderstorm in the Night [illegible] 6th Wed a storm gathering the Boys had just returned home in the afternoon when a huricane came on, blew down the tentz and Trees. all around us. Through the mercy of the Lord no one was hurt, Joseph ran away from the tent in the midst of the storm for fear of the Trees I went out to seek him Br Jones got hold of the tent pole and said the Wind would find it had to beat or [illegible] if it beat him. very soon after the roof pole came down and the tent was soon

---

199. Probably Miles Romney, the master builder of the Nauvoo Temple. He traveled to the Valley in 1850.

200. John Smith, uncle to the Prophet Joseph, was the fifth presiding patriarch of the Church.

201. Probably Ira Newton Spaulding. He traveled to Utah with the Brigham Young company, reaching the Valley 24 July 1847.

prostrate we then fled to the Wagon & I got the children in when the[y] cryed out ther is a Tree coming down the Men ran and by there united efforts gave it a diferund direction, or it must have crushed the cariage and large Waggon both. the storm continued with great violence Br Rich cut down a Tree that was split and ready to fall on his tent all had to leave it in the Rain, several very large Tress fell near Br Youngs tent, one fell on a cow one on a Mule one on a Donkey yet none of them were killed I have heard no further perticulars it is getting late the Storm has abated Sgt Johnston[202] has got within a few Miles we hear there are many on the road Jane Glen was here yesterday She told me that some men here had workd without food for two days. 7th Thd. Storming 8th Fd fine I went with George to the camp saw A. Calhoun[203]. he had seen Mr T on the road he said Porter Rockwell[204] was in Prison in Quincy.

I wrot to Mr Taylor, the Duchman Stable Horse taken Sick, cost 300 Dollars. Sprained my knee getting out of the cariage, this is a fine Moon light Night a Violin playing & a Dance by Gen Richs tent. This place is called Garden Grove and a lovely place it is. 9th a very warm morning the Horse still very sick, my knee very bad, sat a while wit the Girls 10th Sun fine warm day J[edediah]. Grant preached all went to meeting but Joseph and I, my knee very bad indeed. We had Sacrament in the Eve B.Y. spoke 11 Monday had a very bad night, could not get into the tent without help Doc Spraige[205] cald in & told me to keep on a bandage wet with Whiskey and water it gave me some relife. 12 Tued Stil bad with my leg. 13th Wed no word of Mr Taylor 14th Br Hayley came from Nauvoo he said Mr T was there the week before & was to Preach on Sunday 10th in the Temple I hope while there, he

---

202. Possibly Andrew Johnston, chairman of the Quincy Committee, which pushed for an end to hostilities in Nauvoo.

203. Probably Andrew Cahoon, a son of Reynolds Cahoon.

204. Porter Rockwell had been a bodyguard to Joseph Smith and acted as a courier for the traveling Saints and Nauvoo during this time.

205. Dr. Samuel Lindsey Sprague was, in 1848, the first physician to arrive in the Salt Lake Valley.

will do me Justice and contradict the Stories his B.W. and Robins has told which he himself knows to be false. on Thee my blessed Savior I would cast my care, my deep Sorrow and distres Thy eye alone has seen all

15th Frid the traders came back brought 2 Yoke of cattle 2 cows one Calf traded of[f] Rate which belonged to George, my Side Saddle a Man's Saddle and Mare blind of one eye gave four dollars & a half with them, Sat my leg a little better 17th Sund Meeting back of the Waggons I laid on Sis [Isabella] Horn[e]s Bed to hear I could not sit up my Leg so bad I have tryed many things for it had hands laid on by Br Rich Br [Joseph] Horn[e] & Curtis. Sund night never slept with pain in my leg 18th Mond very Sick with pain and want of rest 19th packed up to move. Jones stopt at the Farm got two new Teamsters left in the camp with Br Horn & Oakley[206] campt on an Ant Hill

Wed very wet Morning Sis Midleton[207] came to rub my knee & Georges which was hurt with dears [deer's] horn traveled in rain all day.

[3/4ths of page left blank to bottom. 2/3rds of a page left blank from top.]

June 5 left Mount Pisgah crossed middle fork of grand River went about 4 miles Amos Fielding stayed with us all night on his way to Nauvoo from B.Y. Camp the[y] were 27 Miles ahead 6th Br Amos left on his way to England to buy what provision we should need the[y] went to travel down the ridge between the Ottawa and Stream called one hundred & two, the country was really lovely, gently rolling and divided in long ridges & those on each side all Marked like the Quarters of an orange, the[y] appear like little chanels to convey the water into the long ones & those into longer and deeper all covered with rich grass and lovely flowers every few Miles there is a creek and a little Grove

---

206. Probably Ezra Oakley, a pioneer of 1847, or one of his sons.
207. Possibly Mary Heedy Butler Middleton, wife of William Middleton.

of Trees where we stopt tonight one of the Pottawatomy Chiefes came to us on a lovely little poney black as Jet and dresed as fine as it could be so was the Chiefe we gave him some biscute and Tobacco he let the children ride on his pony & said he lived 4 Miles of[f]

we started at 8 had a shower of rain traveled about 7 miles at 12 campt untill the rest of the company came on in the evn Br. Bird joind our company - Sund June 7th rested in the afternoon we had a meeting a very good one Mr. T preached we put a tent to the end of ours had quite a Company present in the evning Br. Horn Both Br. Oakleys came on, we went to meet them. Sister O—. Mary Ann & Jane Maggy took super with us Mon 8th started at 6 8 oclock fine weather, excellent Roads, the prairy covered with beautyfull flowers Prairy 18 Miles across traveld about 15 Miles Stopt about 6 oClock June 9th Tuesday started early before breakfast had to go 4 miles before we met with Wood & Watter had a meeting to send of [off] traders traveled until 6 oclock Camped in a bottom where there was Wood & wr the creak was called the hundred and two Wed 10th June set of [off] at 8 this day we traveled 13 Miles we campt on the bank of a Stream called by the Indians Otawee some brethern were campt there who said B. B. Y had preached to the Indians, on the Sun'd before the [they] had a town five Miles north of where we campt Th June 11th sent of [off] Brs. Mot & Evans to trade the[y] took two span of horses to trade for Cattle and sent. [. . .]

Frid 12th June we moved at 8 oclock went through a love[ly] Praiarie about noon came in sight of an Indian Village on a hill it lookd like a storm our cariage was behind the Wagons, we had met Uncle John Smith who had told us August, his son Johns wife, was very Ill, I stayd about an hour with her, but could do her no good so went on I was delighted to see the Indians, Squase, & papoces, all dressed up so smart painted Feathers, beads, blankets, & every thing fantastical they could put on, there was a kickapoo present who talked a little English a very good

looking Man & dressed in a large Shawl Nanny[208] fell in love With
him. his wigwam was 18 miles of[f] he said there was a very wide
creak there which our brethern had made a temporary Bridge
over of logs. I dare not look at them cross least I should see them
break through I walkd over & found a party of Indians busily
ingaged playing card[s] a Chiefe came up to me and shook hands
very freindly They called the River Visnibotney [Nishnabotna] it
forked about that place first was bridged the other we for'ded it
was wide and rapid the Indians followed us in great numbers to
the side of a hill where we campt the princes all road on Poneys
decorated in every possibly way there were, Kikapoos,
Pottawatamies, & Ottawas severale Chiefes came to our tent but
they could understand very little that we said there interpreter
was at councl Blufs for which we were very sory. Mr. T. talked to
several and answered there Questions (which were very numerous) as well as possibley told our reasons for leaving our homes &
wandering with our poor children in the Wilderness the Squaws,
brought salt to trade a[nd] green mustard and beads the[y]
wanted ribons & whiskey.

we gave them some thing to eat and mild for there papposes
there was one a month old, a fat little thing swathed to its bazket
which I ornamented with yellow bows, the[y] all seemed much
pleased we staid with them severale hours we left them campt on
a stream went about 14 miles that day we had some trouble on
account of our cattle getting mired in the creeks on this Road,
Sunday 4th June a very pleasant looking Indian came to our tent
he said he was by birth an Ottawa but had been adopted into the
Pottowatamie tribe & had married a chiefs Daughter he ate with
us got some tabaco and left well pleased

in the afternoon we had a meeting opened by John Oakley
Mr. T. cald on Br. Bird to make some remarks he made some

208. Nanny was the Taylor's hired girl.

very sutable was followed by Mr. T. who gave us faithfule exhortation [illegible] and then tryd to comfort and give us a glimps of what we should be if faithful and patient, our situation does require all the grace we can muster I pray the Lord give us all that is needfull that I may never bring a reproach on his cause or people. 15th June set of[f] again Br. T[homas]. Butterfield stayd behind to look for a strayd ox our cariage went on first we past through wood at the end we found a very long bridge built by the Brethern on drift wood after getting on the hill on the Prairy we saw a Grave carefully built around and covered with logs belonging to the Indians we saw.

Br. Cooledge campt with us at night he had just got on Br. Birds [illegible] both very sick. F. ten miles crossed another creek cald Nishreb [?] went over a lovely Prairie coverd with popis and other Flowers 16th traveled 18 miles Mr. T took us a head looking for a camping place we had to go out on a point a distance from the Road to get wood and watter Wed Jn 17th Started at 8am reached the camp on the Bluffs we passed very uneven land all hills and hollows I went to sister Youngs Waggon The children came to know if the[y] might go for Strawberrys with L.Y. Family. M[ary]. A[nn]. & Annie[209] went & brought us back some delightful berrys we got our camp all in order before evening Mr. T. went to the trading Village[210] along with the [illegible] to see the U.S. Agent he is placed here to see that the Indians are not imposed on his name is Major [Robert B.] Mitchell We saw the chief his name is McClure a half Breed a very Gentlemanly man, he informed them that the principal part [of] them were gone of[f] to a medicine dance or religious ceremony in which no one

---

209. Annie Pitchforth was the five-year-old daughter of Ann Hughlings Pitchforth, a plural wife of John Taylor. When her mother died soon after leaving Nauvoo, Annie traveled with her older brother Sam and his wife Mary, her sister Mercy (14), and her sister Sarah (11). Annie was described as "the camp pet; bright-eyed and happy, she was thoroughly spoiled by everyone."

210. Near the Mosquito hill encampment where the main body of the Saints was camped was a Pottawattamie agency known as "Trading Point."

is allowed to partake exap [except] the[y] are known to be good men the[y] had been ingaged two days and Nights the[y] Mr.T. & the rest came home in the evng—- Thd 18th went with the Girls & children about two miles in the cariage to an encampment of the Brethern to get Strawberrys the[y] were more plentyfull there than any place I ever saw they gathered them by Bushels Fri John drove Nanny and the children to get Strawberrys I went to visit Sister Kimball Mr. T. was very busy at home June Sat 20th Mr. T. drove Mary Anne [daughter] & the girls to a concert at the trading Village B- and Lane went out trading, numbers of the Bretherin went down the band went with them. We had a very pleasnt time indeed.

about seventy persons dined at Major Marshals [Mitchell's] [they] had quite a dance There was a number of half breed Squaws danssed very well indeed, we went to the store and got some things we needed had some songs from Br. Kay[211] and a deal of musick upon the whole we spent a very pleasant day Jane [Ballantyne - sister wife] lost her boy with M[ary]. A[nn]. Oakley. [illegible] into it and a looking glass at the Village we all Rode back with the band playing the Villige is a situated on the creek of the Missouri River[212] it did me good to look upon houses & a good wide river once more after living in a tent or Waggon going on five months through rain frost & snow Deprived of many comforts we had been accustomed to suffering with pain, and the knowledge that others was a great deal worse of[f], with out necesarry foods or warm clothing! how long oh! Lord! how long are the wicked to bear rule and thy afflicted people to be oppressed Sund 21st) went to meetting in the grove[213]

---

211. John Moburn Kay, a member of the Nauvoo Brass Band and a singer, was often invited by the Prophet Joseph Smith to assist in entertaining guests. During the Saints' exodus from Nauvoo, Elder Kay helped sustain his company by giving numerous concerts in Missouri and donating the proceeds to the company.

212. She may be referring to Mosquito Creek which flowed into the Missouri River.

213. There was a large bowery near the Taylor's camp on a creek emptying into Mosquito Creek where the brethren held their meetings.

P[arley].P.P[ratt]. prayed & O[rson]. Hyde spoke after him A[masa]. Lyman very profitable part of it, walked of[f] the hill home in afternoon Sis Tipion[214] came staid untile Night Mr T went to many meeting & staid to counsel Mond 22d fine day, sewd and wrote in Journal very windy night Tus 23d) Nanny & Annie Jane Glen June B. went down to wash in the waggon it raind all day & the[y] stopt in it Mr. T [J.W. 2. to 7. O.A.M. fellows left——this line is largely illegible] Wed 24th Noah Packards son came rain'd most of the day, sewd & knit I could not dry the cloths Thur 25 pouring down Rain, Mended Fathers coat made an Apron altered dress knit in Sister [Isabella] Horn's tent Mr. Pinkham came in, S.H babe 3 weeks old[215], Sis Woodworth[216] making the boys jackets Fri 26th) pouring rain cut a pair of trousers for Father & began them

Road out in the carriage the girls, & Mr. T went along Sat 27 This day two years since, poor Br. Joseph & Hyrum were murdered & Father shot all most to death in Carthage Jail,[217] where shall we be or how situated, this time next year the Lord only knows. Sund 28) went with Father to meeting Br. Young spoke met Br. Norton & Family & manny others from Nauvoo,[218] Rained in the afternoon Bretherin met at five, propose to have the 12 go over the Mountain leave all there Familys behind, very high Wind every thing wet in the Waggon Mon 29) Doct. [Willard] Richards said that day two years [ago] he brought the bodyes of Br J[oseph]. & H[yrum] into a people fild with

---

214. Possibly Sally Sipion, wife of Elijah Sipion.

215. Elizabeth Ann Horne, daughter of Joseph and Mary Isabella Horne, was born 3 June 1846. It is interesting to note that the Horne's next child, born in 1849, was named Leonora Taylor Horne.

216. Possibly Phebe Watrous Woodworth, wife of Lucien Woodworth who traveled through Iowa about the same time as the Taylors.

217. During the gunfight that resulted in the martyrdom of Joseph and Hyrum Smith, John Taylor was shot in the left knee, the left arm, and twice in the left thigh, one shot of which tore the flesh away from his hip the size of a man's hand. The shot aimed at his chest struck the watch in his vest pocket, thus protecting him from further harm.

218. Many Saints who left Nauvoo in the spring crossed Iowa in three or four weeks, arriving at Council Bluffs at about the same time as the first companies in the Camp of Israel.

mourning & woe a fine day Father apointed to take his horse dutch man & go out fourteen miles & compell the foulks to come in that were campt around. Br. [William] Blackhearst foulks came into camp

I knit & sewd in the tent all day took a long walk in the evening with Father a lovely night. Tues June 30th) got up at 4 oclock to get Wagons all tyied [tied] the wagons loaded up & to cross over the Misouri River Bro Young & Kimbal started and a very hard storm came on we remaind another Night

July 1st Got up very early loaded, got all our cattle up Father started on horseback to the River, & met Br. Young & Kimbal coming to Meet all the Brethern by our tent. The Brn dined with us & then held a meeting, slept in the little Tent at night 2d July went part of the way down to the River with, Father in the cariage found a wagon apart in the creek every thing driping wet

water 2 feet over the Bridge I durst not cross. Father went on held a meeting along with O. Prat[t], spoke about Vollonteering to the People 500 of our Brethern has volunteed to have 10 Dollars per month for one year there Arm U.S. July 3d Father about home all day Sat July, 4th the band came went with Father to Col [James] Allens Tent²¹⁹ [illegible] went & the children a number of halff breeds from the River came we had quite a concert they run there Horses after & made a great noise we had a very violent storm of wind & rain. Friday 5th Br. Hyde spoke so did P.P. Prat Mon Prat & Evans came back from traiding made no trades came back worse than if the[y] had not gone

we are now in the Wilderness our Property which was worth ten thousand Dollars is gone, all except the Necessaries we have with us, we have been obliged to sacrifice it to the Mob if the Lord will suply us with food & raiment I care nothing about what we have left. Br. Stewart lent us 50 Dollars for which I sincerily

219. Colonel Allen of the United States army was sent to raise 500 volunteers from the Mormon ranks.

thank the Lord.[220] July 7th Wed. wagons getting ready Wed 8 went down to the River with the Girls and Mary Ann July 9th moved our camp a mile nearer the River near Musquito Creek, Br. Woo[d]ruffe came on and campt near us which is a great comfort to me Fri July 10th fixing the Wagons 11th Indians left

July 12th Sund, we held a meeting under a bower near our tent Mr. T & Br. Woodruff Preachd Br. Young & Kimbal Richard & [Jesse] little returned from Mount Pisga Col Cain [Thomas L. Kane] arrived with power from the President 13th had a dance under the Bower 14 the [illegible] all day. men volunteering 15 Mon Shelly maried to Nanny Turquas by Father he was one of our teamsters She was our hired girl 16th still Musick. Volunteering, dancing very evng Mr. T. came here along with Avone smith all most crasy about his wife who had left him to Join the Church July 19th had a meeting at our Camp again [illegible] stopt with [us] as usual (20) sent of[f] a wagon with Br. W. Mitches [Miller] to go across the Mountains[221]

21 the twelve came over 22 apointed twelve Men to take charge of the Church on the Bluffs father went with the 12 up the River July 23'd 25 Sat had a dreadfull storm a cow kild by lightning Grandmother[222] Children and I all dripping wet in our Waggon all Night there Tents blew down and every thing scattered by the Wind Sund July 26th Br. [Ezra T.] Benson[223] & Mr. T preached Mod July 27 Very bussy had a very severe Storm Tents down our Wagon tipt of[f] the Blocks everything wet & uncomfortable 29 heard of Fathers Mission to England[224] very stormy

---

220. Because of the lack of success of the trading expedition, the Taylor family found themselves without provisions sufficient for the journey. John Taylor recorded his thankful relief at the fifty dollar loan provided him by Brother Stewart. He recorded, "I felt thankful to the Lord that He had opened my way, as He always does in time of need."

221. Brigham Young instructed George Miller and his company to camp some miles west of the Missouri River while the other camps settled on the east side of the Missouri River.

222. Agnes Taylor, mother of John Taylor.

223. Ezra T. Benson had been ordained an apostle on 16 July, just ten days earlier.

224. John Taylor, Orson Hyde, and Parley P. Pratt were sent to England to correct the abuses of Reuben Hedlock and the joint stock company.

30th stormd dreadfully Doc [Willard] Richard[s] & Br. [Jesse] little Slept in the little Tent it blew down the Doc got under the bed the Watter found him there he & Br. Little walkd about the camp with Grandmother bed Clothes around them it took a long time to gather things a gain, all coverd with mud Br. Mot [?] went back with his Wagon which he had volnterd to take us to over the Mountains in Musquitto Creek has overflowed the Bottom is a Sheet of Watter 31st Br. Pratt, Hyde, Pierce & little came to go with Father the Briges were all caried away and the[y] could not go on land so went in our Cariage Down to the River Br. Bird drove the cariage I watched it back & went to meet him [illegible]

July 31st the[y] had taken a macanaw [?] boat and would go untill they met a Steam Boat [blots] busy all day 1st Sat August Br. Henry busy at the Waggons Sunday Aug 2 Br. George Smith preached I came 4 pm near half dressed Mond 3rd Still at the Wagons 4th Tue Started for the River, campt near the River, the Road very bad indeed 5th Wed the sand burning hot Joseph run away down the River & made me very anxoious we crossd in the evg & walkd up the hill to the Prarie we Joind part of our camp that was in the Prairy we stopt there 2 nights 6th thursd 7 Frid Sat 8th moved to the generals Camp our Comp Campt on a hill 9th Sun went to meeting in the Cariage took Grandmother S. Horne S. Woodworth and the Girls cald to inquire for Col Kain on our way P.P. Prat returnd brough[t] a letter from Father home cald at J. Woodrufs, & S. Young Mond 10 washing, Tuesday 11th moved into Br. Young's inclosure the Camp is divided, into two divisions Br. Young & Kimbal we went into Br. Young & occupy one side of the square. Wed 12th Making Pens for the cattle Th'd 18[13]th the same Fri 14th I feel very sick Sat 15th Sund 16th Sent all to Meeting stayd at home alone Mond 17th home Washd.

Tued 18 Anne Sick John Dixon sick Doctored them, & hope they will soon be better, a great number sick in the Camp Wed

19 went with S.G. Smith to Br. Kimbals camp left her there promised to go back in the cariage, my head ach'd so I could not think of it Thusd made Beer for Sis Sipions, who was very sick

Thusd 20th John is better, Sis Woodworth sick Fr. Nany Sick 21st Sat went to vissit the sick 100 sick in the Camp two men died since we have been busy Br. [Newel K.] Whitney is going to St. Louis to purchase Goods for the Brethern I sent for 20 Dollars worth. by him Sund 23d Br. Jed[ediah] Grant preached a good many cald.

in the evng, went Sis Woodruff & Smoot to visit the sick, letter came to Sister [Elizabeth] Arrowsmith.[225] Grandmother opened it stated that Grandfather was Sick Agness's [Agnes Taylor Rich] child died & that he had put William [Taylor] & Agness into Prison for helping his wife and children of[f], who are now, on there way here Mond 22d Sis. Rupell came & took Diner, I went with her to Br. Whitneys in the eveng vissited the sick a great many sick in the Camp I am very unwell myself headach all the time the twelve went over the River to council with the Brethern a few days since and have not returnd. Br. Bird went with others to wait upon

Six [Sioux] Indians Ottow[a] Nation Cheif came the Indians to know if we might remain here, this winter.[226] Tuesd 25th our Tent came down Mr Farrer very sick with chills [illegible] G. Cannon Wed 26 herding the Cattle, came home in the Evng & put it up [the tent] Thur 27th let a Horse go to fetch the Indians Br. Rockwood came for Flower to make Bread for the Indians he let us have Beef for it we kild our White Calf. and sent a peice to the Girls, F. ashbys, Johns, Br. Horns, T. Puikka [?] B. Smoot, F. Bawlding, Levi Richards, B. Blackhurst, Br. Abot, in the afternoon 30 Indians of the Omehaw [Omaha] Tribe came

225. Elizabeth Taylor Arrowsmith, wife of William Arrowsmith, was the sister of John Taylor.
226. Cutlers Park, the first settlement on the west side of the Missouri, and later Winter Quarters were situated on Indian Territory.

Pitched a large & small tent on the hill for there oposite our Tent the Girls George and John went with me to see them ate there super [supper] I was very sick all night and am still Br. Kimbal brought a trunk from the bluffs that Father sent to the Children Fri 28th a pair of shoes a piece [of] calico for a Dress for myself [illegible] (Mary Ann) [illegible] for Trousers for the boys & some Tea I thank the Lord and him for remembering us, Five Ottow chiefs Dined on a Large Veale Pie I made for them in the afternoon Sis Green[227] spent the Evening I visited sick, and made Soup for them took it around, B. W[illey] Br. P.P.s & Smoot & Snow Sat 29th the Bretherin Br. Smith gone to look out a camping place the omohaws told them of a great number of wagons coming in from Nauvoo Lorinsa [Lorenzo] Young sent to say we might send for a peice of Beefe I sent [last line on page scratched out]

30th Aug Sund fine Morn, Indians all gone, visited the sick boys had Horses of[f] herding, had to go to meetting late, B. Woodruff & Young spoak O. prat, Doc Pattens Daughters rode home with us Grand mother came back to diner in the Evening, Sis W., Jane B, and G. Cannon, went with me to see Br. Larson, to inquire about those on the Road going to send back Teamsters to fetch on those who are sick over the River Br. Hunter, & all his Family sick at the [illegible] 31 Aug Mon Boys mowing vissited a great many sick S. Smoot very bad so is Sis. Oakley

Tue Sep 1 Boys hay making I visited Sick & gave medicine Wed. 2 the same washing Thd 3d went up to the uper Camp to see Sister Hunter. She had moved down, saw doctter Patten & Bro. brewer Br Snow. & Woolly Fri 4 Storming visited sick Sat Sep 5 busy, visited sick, boy's making hay Sun 6th took the Girls, Grand Mother Mary & Anny in the Cariage, to Meeting Mon 7th Boys hunting cattle vissiting sick Tus 8th Clark & Bunels [?]

---

227. Possibly Susan Kent Greene, wife of Evan M. Greene.

left, Grandmother fell over a trunk and hurt her back Wed 8th
[9th] a great Storm of Wind & Rain, blew down a great many
tents ours Stood fast B. Y. brought a letter from Mr. T. dated
New York Th 9th [10th] stormed all Night Fri 10th [11th] Sis
Smoot came & spent the day met S. Young at S. Woodruffs had a
conference Sat 12th Sick People & Children came to the tent
went to see a number of sick

Sund Feb 13th went to see Br. Young about Babtisms [bap-
tizing] Sister Mitchel who is quite crazy, met with S.Y. in the
Wagon a while, went to see S. Woodruff who is very sick the girls
went to meetting along with B. horn S. O. Pratt cald & B. P. Br
Woodruff cald, I went to see the sick Mond 14th S. Mitchell very
Crazy, got a comfortable dress that was washed Br Young calld
about the Stray trunk, got S. Mitchell Babtised, Tud 15th
returned the things I have got a dreadfull headach George went
to herd the Cattle got thrown from his horse one he had caught
& put his whip acrost his mouth he got scared the lash came of[f]
the handle of his whip and threw him, on his Arm & Split the
Bone I took ime [him] to Doc Sprauge I bath it with wormwood
and Whiskey I had a presentiment all morning something was
going to happen [to] him and spoke of it before he came home
Wed grand mother better Phinas Young called told us about the
foulks on the Road, Rain'd G.C. read to us while we worked. Br.
G. Smith cald, his foulks all sick Thurd 17th Cows all of[f] put
our ox in to be Butchered 18th Boys at hay talk of moveing nearer
the River 19th Sat very busy 20th I was very Sick S.W. went to
meetting Mond vissited sick 22tud Grandmother able to get out
of her Wagon Wed boys still of[f] to the Hay camp moved

24th Thud moved near the River to a place cald Winter
Quarters Ground laid out in seperate divisions ours the 8 [or 9]
in a very good situation 25Fr moved our tents a little Sat all at
work 27th Sunday went to Meeting with S. Woodworth S. Smoot
& S. Kimble Br. & S. Kimball grand mother went over the River
took Super with us had a very good time 28th Mond the Boys

hauling the fence down Grand Mother got home & brought Elizabeth [Taylor Arrowsmith] hir two Children Agnessez [Agnes'] 3 Children and Williams Wife all sick of Ague W W was well the[y] had one Wagon & a tent Grand Father and Agness is still back tud 29 Boys hunting Cattle & hauling rails Wed 30th build the Counsel house in the Yard Sep Thd 31st I went with John over the River, Br. Bremer [Brenner?] went along I took the Girls to gather Grapes and Sis Woodworth we could not get Cattle until evening [?] got over the River and Campt all Night Oct 1st got to the indian Village got some onions, Potatoes, Aples Box of Raisins from Fathers I bought cacke [cake] & Beer for the Girls drove to the counsel point took super & remaind all night, after breakfast set of[f] for the Grapes found a great many Mother Alldred[228] & her Daughter went with us the Cattle went of[f] I went into the woods & prayed that the[y] might be found John walkd all day & could not find them it was near Sun down he gave them up & went to borrown a Yolk of Cattle to take the Wagon to the point, when he was gone I asked the Girls to go with me into the Woods to look for them we found them without any trouble we returned with a Barell of Grapes a bag of Hops & very happy at having found the Cattle[229] got Super and went on about four miles when it became dark. we lodge for the night on the Prairie where John cut grass for the Oxen, next day we got our wheat & started home arived there in the Evening found all the Childrin well, delighted to see me again. Sun 4th Oct there was meeting I was not well enough to attend, S. Woodruff cald with S. Smoot, Mond John set of[f] up the River wtih the Company to cut logs Nanny went down the River with Br. Woodruff & his foulks to get grapes She came back on Wednessday got a Letter from Mr. Taylor datted New York

---

228. Elizabeth Warren Allred, wife of "Father" James Allred.
229. Her story of an answered prayer is similar to Mary Fielding Smith's, who also prayed to find her lost cattle when the menfolk could find no trace of them. Both women enjoyed an immediate answer to their prayers.

8th Oct 1846 Elder babbit here full of himself and all that
he is famous for Jane Ballentine over heard S. Babbit give a nice
description of what people thought of her Sister She Stood to
listen outside of Sister Horns tent I tryd to make the best of it,
which Jane had to acknoleg 9Sat, John came back Sund it
stormed all day 12th Oct Mon John set of again to cut logs this
Week nothing particular ocur's [excepting?] a wind storm which
tore our tent Br. Woodruff got hurt by a Tree falling on him
which he was cutting for house Logs Sat 17th a fine day I have a
bad head ache 18th went to Mulling all about how we could guard
against the Indians who are stealing every thing they can and
killing our cattle. it is proposed to build a wall around the
Houses Mond 19th all the Camp of[f] Hunting up Cattle
Tuesday the[y] went of again after them the Prairies on fire
Started by the Indians Wed Oct 21st John went with the Bretherin
to raft down the logs Sister hyrum Smith arrived S.T. & Elizabeth
Caine came wtih them, Mrs Benbow came along very sick went
to Br. Woddrufs Camp Br Kimbal brought C. here Sund 25 had
a meetting Mon 27 hauling the logs out of the River got our
Bricks from Br Patten Tued 28 went to spend the day with Sister
Benbow, to Nurse her She is very sick Wed with Sister Benbow
nursing her all day Th 29th Ballantines came to the River Br
Wight & Sister Simons from Nauvoo.

Fri 30th [crossed out] George C & William went over the
River to go for a load to Missouri John hauling Hay littlefield
came on from Nauvoo after the Boys had started I went I was to
crop[?] with them to see if Ballantine had brought us anny Flour
he said he got 40 Dollars of Br Phelps he had bought me some
groceries laid out part of it for himself and gave Br. Wright part,
who says he never got a farthing of it what shall I do for Bread for
the Family this Winter my Father only knows I should have had
8 Barrels of Flour purchased with that money Fri Johns drawing
logs for the House Sat went to see Sis H. Smith & d Kimball

E. babbit brought me a Letter from Mr. Taylor dated New

York Sep 3d he was to sail for Liverpool on the 8th I have heard
there was a great Storm soon after that date, I wrote him a long
letter by Br. Orson Spencer who is going to England on a
Mission Br. Elias Smith has to go along with him.

Nov 1st Fathers Birthday today 38 years old I would give
something to know where & how he is this day, Br Young, B.
Clap [Class?] preached I felt as if I could weep all the time of
meetin that unfortunate girl of Ballantines came over the River
to meeting I am sorry to see Mary Anne Oakley Seen with such a
one Mond 2d Now Sis Arowsmiths child hannah Died. I went up
and took callico and made a shroud and cap on tuesd 3d had the
cariage and took Grand Mother Elizabeth and the girls Br.
Holdman & 3 children were buried the same day We 4th devid-
ing the Hay I was at G.[rand] Mothers Br Wright came very sick
Br Lymon [Amasa Lyman] came to the Division Thud 5th raind
all day John sick W Father is getting better, he has been sick 10
weeks Fri Br Horn kild a Beef John helpt him. I made calves feet
jelly for Sister Benbow Sat 7th sent 7 Cows in the comity [com-
munity] herd we had a Beef kild very fat indeed I made ginger-
bread for S. Benbow Sund 8th Nov. [The diary ends abruptly
with that partial date.]

---

*Three women who did not leave Nauvoo until May, none with husbands to
accompany them, made their own way to the Missouri. But their stories are
very different. Louisa Barnes Pratt, at first chagrined that no special help
would be provided even though her husband was serving the Church far away
in Tahiti, pulled up her boot-straps and soon acquired the means and gradually the courage to lead her four daughters into the western wilderness.
Encouragement from Brigham Young strengthened her resolve, and putting*

"all her energies to the test to get ready," she hired a teamster and triumphantly made her way to the Missouri and on to Utah. Her journal reveals a woman successfully overcoming fear, lack of confidence, and a tendency to worry by reconfirming her trust in God's presence and power in her life.

LOUISA BARNES PRATT[230]

IN THE AUTUMN OF 1845 the Saints entered into a treaty to leave Nauvoo the ensuing spring. No pen can paint the anguish of my heart when I heard the news. It fell on my ear like the funeral knell of all departed joys. What could I do I thought, with my little means, and my helpless family in launching out into the howling wilderness: I had no male relative to take charge of my affairs. My brother-in-law and family were not prepared to go at the time, were struggling hard to make preparation. I was almost in despair when I reflected on the burden I had to bear, and my companion on the opposite side of the globe.[231] An indescribable melancholy came over me at times, when I thought of my devotion to that beautiful City! My mind wandered back to the poor Jews, when they were compelled to leave their beloved City! Oh! how sorrowful I was! But the watchword was "go!" Like the pilgrim, "take your stuff and travel on." I had yet some property remaining in Indiana. A house and Lot in the village of Pleasant Garden. I sent by letter and sold, gave a bond for a deed, which I wrote out

230. Reminiscences of Louisa Barnes Pratt (1879), LDS Church Archives.

231. Addison Pratt left Nauvoo to serve a mission to the Pacific Islands 1 June 1843. He was released in May 1847.

myself according to my best judgment. A yoke of cattle and wagon were sent me, which enabled me to launch forth on the fearful, and more than dreaded journey. To others it did not appear forbidding. Women who had husbands and sons, prospects of the journey seemed romantic. We were going away from our enemies. Little did we think how soon they would follow us.

Late in the fall I took a young lady boarder, by the name of Catherine Philips. She had come from Pittsburg with a widowed mother. She was a delicate girl, not able to do hard work; had no means to pay her expenses. She could help me some; was affable, orderly, and exceedingly neat and clean in habits.

It was a real comfort to have a companion in my house who could keep every article in its proper place. When the church left Nauvoo she went back to Pittsburg, to join her mother, who went before her. The Temple was completed ere she left Nauvoo, and she received blessings therein which greatly rejoice her heart; lonely and desolate as she felt.

After very great suspense, I was called to the Temple to receive my blessings, where I encountered grievious disappointment, Not in the charter of the blessings, but in not being permitted to remain through the day as I had anticipated. The house being crowded, the overseer requested us to withdraw and make room for others. I remonstrated, but all in vain. I retired with a heavy heart. Afterwards I had frequent opportunities of attending the different exercises in the House, and felt that all was made right. It was a glorious sight to go through the Stately edifice and examine the varied apartments, the architecture of which we all believed was dictated by the wisdom of God.

At length the time came that we must leave our beloved Temple, Our City, our homes. I forbear to dwell upon the solemn dread which took posession of my mind. Almon Babbit called to see me. I asked him if he could divine the reason why those who had sent my husband to the ends of the earth, did not call to inquire whether I could prepare myself for such a perilous journey, or if I wished to go or stay? His reply was, "Sister Pratt, they expect you to be smart enough to go yourself without help, and even to assist others." The remark awakened in me a spirit of self reliance. I replied, "Well, I will show them what I can do."

Early in the spring of 1846 men came up from Indiana bringing to me the remaining avails [items of value] for our farm. There were cattle and a new wagon, well covered. It did indeed look like encouragement to undertake the journey. An order came on Almon Babbitt committee of church sales, for fifty dollars to be paid me. I saw the way opening, still I did not wish to go. My heart drew me towards my childhood's home where my parents still lived. I asked counsel of Orson Hyde; he said, "If the Spirit directs you to go to visit your kindred, go: and it shall be well with you and be overruled for the best." I was on the point of selling my team and wagon for the money to go. In the meantime the authorities (First Presidency) and a portion of the Church had started: were camped on the west side of the Miss River; suffering with cold, much deep mud. As I did not feel quite clear in my mind, I wrote to President Young, told him my intention to go back to my kindred. He did not write an answer, but sent it by a brother who was present when my letter was read. His reply was, "Tell Sister Pratt to come on; the ox team salvation is the safest way." He says, "Brother Pratt will meet us in the wilderness where we locate, will be sorely disappointed if his family is not with us."

Upon this I nerved up my heart, and put all my energies to the test to get ready, determined to follow the Church, come life or death. Men came in from the country to buy furniture and purchase other property. I had a good lot, well fenced, a house which had cost at the least $300, three hundred all I was offered was eighteen doll's [dollars]. I refused; would choose to make a full sacrifice. The first thing I sold was my stove, which cost sixteen dollars; all I was offered was 50 pounds flour and two blankets: in amount, $7.00. I accepted, though in one hour repented my bargain. The buyer was an insolent fellow said so many insulting things about the people who were forced to sell their property for the merest trifle, tantalizing and abusing them for being subject to the wills of brutal men, and himself one of the same kind. The weather soon became very cold, and never did I need anything more than I did the stove. I was obliged to sit by my kitchen fireplace, a poor miserable hearth, and my heart accorded with the surroundings. It was gone and I must dispose of all my furniture as quickly as possible, which I did for less than a quarter its real value. My wagon was packed, ready to start, when a man came from the country; said he would buy my house and lot and give me a yoke of oxen. I snatched my pen and paper, sprang into my wagon, made out a quit claim deed according to my own judgment, without any guide. Just as I finished it, brother Joseph L. Haywood[232] came up. I read the deed to him asked if he thought it would do. He replied, "If you had consulted a dozen lawbooks you could not have made it more to the purpose."

He then inquired if I kept a daybook. I replied in the affirmative. "Well," said he, "write it down, that your posterity after you may know what a smart mother they had." As we finished the conversation the old gentleman's son came up and interfered with the trade; claimed the cattle, and the bargain fell through. I swept out my pleasant house, closed the doors and bid farewell to it. I had sold one yoke of cattle for forty-five dollars; fifty, Mr. Haywood paid me, which fitted us up for provision and clothing. I had two yoke of oxen, two cows, and a good new wagon. I was comparatively rich; and by this time began to be in fine spirits. Several of my neighbors who were not ready to start, escorted me to the river, and sincerely wished me good fortune.

As I was passing down the streets of Nauvoo, I cast a lingering look at the beautiful Temple; I felt inclined to say as the poor

---

232. Joseph Leland Heywood was one of the three trustees left in Nauvoo to manage the care and disposal of Church property.

jews said of Jerusalem. ["]When I forget thee, Oh Nauvoo: let my right hand forget her cunning, if I prefer not thee above my chief joy." I began by this time to feel comparatively happy. I am another woman compared with her who groped about the house two days ago. I believe that was the worst day of all my life. My grief was of a peculiar nature. I did not feel willing to disclose the whole cause to anyone.

The boat not being ready to cross that night I went to Sister Hiram Kimball's and slept there. I had called at the P.O. as I came down and found a letter from Mr. Pratt, on the far distant isles of the South Seas. This gave us all great joy: for many months had passed away and not a word had we heard from him. I carried my letter where I went to spend the night, and they all rejoiced with me.

The letter contained good news. The kind man wrote, he was sending money to his family; by one Capt. Hall, who belonged in Boston. He had agreed to forward it to the church. Moreover it informed us that my husband had received two letters from me which had been written two years [ago]: the first he had heard from his family in that length of time. He says he will never leave us so long again, that if he returned and is ever sent back, he shall insist on taking his family.

As I had failed in getting the cow as I had expected on the west side, the river, I went back to Nauvoo to obtain one from the tithing office. I went direct to Brother Haywood's as he was the man who had charge of business. I was agreably surprized in finding a pleasant company assembled to celebrate the fifth anniversary of their marriage. I was on the point of making apologies for intruding, Brother Haywood placed me a chair at his right hand, at the same time repeating the passage of scripture which runs thus: "Sit thou on my right hand until I make thine enemies thy footstool."[233] I felt honored and free to par-

---

233. Psalms 110:1.

take of their bounties which were large. I spent the night, obtained a good cow to take back: a man going over the river kindly offered to drive her, and every thing conduced to banish gloominess from my mind and make me reconciled to undertake the ambiguous journey. I reached my home which was on wheels: found the children all cheerful.[234] Brother Busby informed me that the company had been waiting sometime for him and were disposed to start on and leave me, but he told them he would not move till I was ready to go.

May 31st—Pitched our tents between Farmington and Boneparte. At the latter place we bought flour best quality, $1.25 per hundred. Bought Ellen a shawl $2.50. Across the Des moine River the boat was drawn by pullies. I was in great fear that the ropes would break. We got safely over, and my driver called to see his mother; whom he had not seen for some little time, having been with his father in Nauvoo. She was opposed to his going on with me, unless the family were ready and could join our company. A scene ensued I plead with his mother: told her I thought it would be unjust to detain him there and leave me without a teamster, when his father had given his full consent for him to go with me. Tears were shed by both parties, till at length my pursuasions prevailed and we moved on with the company, which was then small. That night camped where there were forty wagons. It looked cheerful after travelling all day over a desolate country and intolerable roads, to salute a large company of our brethren.

It became necessary to have my wagon overhauled, goods repacked. For that purpose everything was taken out and put in the tent. It being late in the afternoon, there was not time to replace them before the dusk of evening. No signs of rain till we were all locked in the arms of morpheus, then suddenly loud

---

234. Louisa's four children, ages fourteen to six in 1846, were Ellen Sophronia, Frances Stevens, Lois Barnes, and Ann Louisa.

thunders began to roar! Fierce lightning flashed! I knew my tent would not shed rain, and I dreaded the consequences of a hard shower more than I ever did in my life. I prayed most fervently that the storm might pass over and do us no harm! Suddenly the clouds began to disperse, the thunder rumbled in the distance, I looked abroad and saw a clear sky. I felt a glow of gratitude I shall long remember.

I found great pleasure in riding horseback. By that means I could render some assistance in driving the stock. There was in the company a comical fellow by the name of Ephraim Hanks.[235] He had charge of the loose cattle, was a dashing rider, gave me some lessons in that art till I became very expert. He assumed the name or title of Captain, gave to me that of Commodore. I was quite proud of my title; arose early in the morning, mounted my horse to help gather up the stock. It was air and exercise besides amusement which kept my spirits brisk.

We camped on a creek which I shall name Musketae [perhaps Locust] creek, for the want of a more suitable name and that could not be for the insects are worse than the locusts of egypt. Our friends who were behind overtook us at this place, and the camp was organized. The brethren met by themselves, organized, and chose a president without the aid or counsel of the women. This evening the sisters proposed to organize themselves into a distinct body, to prove to the men that we are competent to govern ourselves. If they set the example of separate interests, we must help carry it out.

June 6th—We started early, thought to accomplish a good days drive. The loose cattle were very unruly and hindered us. We have in our company a young man whom the girls have named "Green Horn." He blundered into a mudhole and broke

---

235. Ephraim Hanks, nineteen, served in the Mormon Battalion and as a scout and post rider. He traversed the plains many times and participated in the rescue of the Willie and Martin handcart companies.

his axle tree. So here the whole crowd must be hindered to wait for repairs. My eldest daughter said to him, "had your head been right side up, you might have saved us all this delay." He submitted to the jokes very patiently, as the loss was general. My two cows are very docile and willing to be driven, but we have one in the herd our Capt. says is not a Mormon; she has nothing of a gathering spirit, seems determined to go back, and he says, "If she was mine I would never take her to Zion." While waiting to repair the broken wagon one of my cows had a young calf: this was an amusement to the children as for a few days he would have to be carried along in the wagon: a beautiful creature he is! white as snow, with a few red spots. While the company was staying encamped, I took a horse back ride to visit a Camp of Saints two miles ahead: found them to be a company from Laharpe Ill. They invited me to eat and drink with them when they learned who I was and treated me with true politeness. On my return I found a good kersey[236] blanket in the road. When I reached camp and gave a history of my adventures, I was highly complimented. Thus something in the line of social enjoyment was continually transpiring to cheer our hearts amidst all the trials. My horse came back on the gallop, which occasioned some meriment, as he was very dull on going out.

7th day. Nearly ready to start again. Phineas Young passed our camp this morning, in from C[ouncil]. Bluffs on his way to Winter Quarters. Last evening the ladies met to organize. Mrs. Isaac Chase [Phoebe Ogden Chase] was called to the chair. She was also appointed President by a unanimous vote. Mrs. L[ouisa]. B[arnes]. Pratt, counsellor and scribe. Several resolutions were adopted: 1st. Resolved: that when the brethren call on us to attend prayers, get ingaged in conversation and forget what they called us for, that the sisters retire to some convenient place

---

236. Kersey is a heavy fabric made of wool or a wool and cotton mixture.

pray by themselves and go about their business. 2nd. If the men wish to hold control over women let them be on the alert. We believe in equal rights. "Meeting adjourned, sic ne die [sine die]."

We have to let our "calf baby" ride in the front of the wagon, but he is so very handsome, and so gentle, he is no annoyance.

8th day Yesterday we travelled over the most intolerable roads! It was a query in my mind how the first company, going as they did in the Spring, ever forced their way through so much mud! I was led to exclaim, what is there in all the world, the Mormons will not attempt to do? We were compelled to create our own amusements. When we camped near a level spot of earth where water had been standing and dried away, the young men would propose a dance. The older ones feeling the absolute need of diversion would accede, as it would cost nothing and would most likely cheer and enliven us on our wearisome journey. In the midst of our amusements we did not forget our prayers. We have large campfires around which we all gather, sing songs, both spiritual and comic; all very appropriate.

9th day—Last evening Brother [Stephen] Markham camped with us on his way back to Nauvoo, to bring on a load of provisions. He informed us the "Twelve" had gone on to Council Bluffs. We have very little hopes of overtaking them. I begin now to admire the country: such a beautiful rolling paradise:

10th day—Last night we camped on the bank of a creek about a hundred miles from Nauvoo: the last house we shall see for the present, and that not a house, a hut, where the inmates keep ardent spirits, and bacon. The spelling on their sign is "flower" for flour, "baken" for bacon. We laughed at their lore. Have just struggled through a three mile mud hole; and have arrived again at a mormon city of tents and wagons, white with black spots, emblimatical of the lives we live in this world of change. We work hard to live, and we earn our enjoyments by the sweat of the brow. What a pity that any poor man should be without land to till, when there is so much lying vacant, so beautiful, good, and productive: Sister Eldridge[237] and myself have had a long ride on horseback, taking a view of the country, and admiring it. Sometimes I feel cheerful: again it comes suddenly to my mind, how far I am going from home, parents, and every relative I have in the world! But the Lord has called us, and appointed us a place; where we can live in peace, and be free from the dread of our cruel persecutors!

12th day—Yesterday for the first time my wagon had to be dug out of the mud. One wheel ran off a bridge. It made racking work, broke my table, which was tied on behind. This morning our company broke up; three started back to Bonaparte after flour, left their families encamped to wait for their return. The rest pursued their journey as usual, are now 55 miles from the main camp. Last evening there was great sport in our camp. The young man we call Capt., dressed in woman's attire, danced to amuse us. Several in the crowd did not know who it was; thought it was some strange lady who had come in from another company.

June 15th—We have at last arrived at Mount Pisgah. The tents are scattered every where. I am going to look around to find myself a location. Poor people here; they are in the sun without houses. I pity them. May the Lord reward for all their sacrifices! I have just returned from a long walk have been taking a survey of the place entire. On the Bluffs is a beautiful grove of oak trees; beneath the towering branches we can pitch our tents and be sheltered from the sun's scorching rays. Several little cabbins begin to make their appearance. The Post Office is laughable, a little log pen, 10 by 8, covered with bark.

18th day—I have at length got my habitation moved into the mount. My tent pitched under the shade of three oak trees. The children are delighted: A pleasant family by the name of Hallet[238]

237. Probably Betsy Ann Chase Eldredge, wife of Horace Eldredge.
238. Thatcher Clark and Phebe Bray Hallet and their children.

are very near: The man is gone with the Pioneers, and the poor woman is sick.

23rd day—The wind is blowing a heavy gale; it seems as though the very heavens would come down to earth! The tent is pinned down or it would be carried away. The elements are in great commotion, and my mind is dark and dismal! I think, "what if we have to wander forty years in the wilderness, as the children of Israel did!"

25th day—We have just experienced one of the severest storms of thunder and rain I ever knew. We are all drenched out, so here we are wading in mud over shoes, trying to get our breakfast. We moved our beds into Mrs. Hallet's tent the succeeding night where slept quite dry.

4th day of July—Went to a wedding party; had music and dancing; a thunder storm to wind up the celebration.

5th day—Elder [Jesse C.] Little arrived from New Hampshire: he came to my wagon early in the morning, informed me he had brought the money my husband had sent me from the Islands. This was good news, as I had been waiting for it to pursue my journey.

8th day—Sister H. Silver and myself went across Grand river to visit Mrs. Bullock. We invited Brothers Benson and Little to accompany us. We had a fine agreeable visit, came home by moonlight. The ensueing morning I invited to breakfast Messrs. [Brigham] Young, [Willard] Richards, E[zra] T Benson, and J[esse] C Little. H. Silver was with me, and we rehearsed the incidents relating to our visit the preceding day, which occasioned some mirthfulness and made the time pass pleasantly away. Soon after, we had an evening party in the open air. The said gentlemen took an affectionate leave of us all and went on to the Bluffs. A little before their departure, recruiting officers came there to enlist men for the Mexican war. 500 men were demanded; quite a number were taken from that place. The young man who had driven my team to that point remained there; as his parents had arrived. I had engaged another by the name of William Sterritt, a kind and faithful young man. I was in great fear that he would be called to go as a soldier to the war. I made a request of brother Heber C. Kimball that his name might not be written on the list. He promised me it should not. "Father Huntington" and C C Rich were the presidency there, two as good men as ever took upon themselves the name of Latter-day Saints. When I was imposed upon, they interposed, and caused restitution to be made. When I heard the news of Father Huntington's removal from this sphere, I said, "A righteous man has gone to receive his reward for all his noble deeds, his integrity and faithfulness!"

16th—Last evening I called on Sisters [Hannah] Markham, E[liza] R Snow, and Dana.[239] They all seem resigned to the times and circumstances. I wish I could: I pray earnestly for submission. Here preparing to leave Mount Pisgah. People all around me are taking chills and fever.

July 29th—A sorry time it is; many are sick. Sister Hallet is very low. I have for some time had charge of her babe, seven months old. Last night I had a serious exercise with her, was up and down alternately. She refused all consolation. At length my bedstead (one I had made myself) broke down. I then made my bed on the ground. There was a bottle of bitters standing near. I thought perhaps a few drops might lull the child to sleep. She struggled much under the opperation. I then gave her a dose of cream. I thought if the poor child could speak she would tell me I would kill her with kindness. I felt sorrowful on leaving the sick woman and the babe, as the other members of the family were also in the same condition not able to help each other.

Aug. 1st—Left Mount Pisgah with an agitated mind, sorrow for the afflicted ones and regretting that any one should wish to wrong me, and have to be compelled to act justly.

---

239. Probably Margaret Kennedy Dana, first wife of Charles Root Dana.

3rd day—Camped by a beautiful stream, where we found a spring of clear, cold water. O how delicious! The first cold water I have tasted since my arrival in Mt. Pisgah. At that place the water was fearful! It oosed through marshy ground where it was supposed buffaloes had been mired and buried. We met brother Hallet on the way returning from the Bluffs, informed him of the sickness of his family; entreated him to make all possible haste to get back home! He seemed much affected with the news, assured us he should lose no time, neither did he, but was soon taken sick, and the first news we heard, he was gone! Likewise a little girl twelve years old, and the babe! Oh! the sickness was terrible. The next place was an Indian village. They flocked around us with corn and cucumbers; it looked delicious in our sight. We purchased of them, paid them in sea bread.

9th day—Sabbath. Camped on the broad prairie near Brothers [William] Felshaw and Wooley. Not a tree to shelter us from the scorching sun; it seemed that we must dissolve with the heat! Our cattle left us and we were obliged to remain through the day. The next day found the cattle, went on a few miles. The young men were sick, not able to drive teams or cows.

11th day—For the first time my cows were missing. I found them lying down in the bushes after going over a great portion of the range. Camped on "Musketoe Creek," nearly eaten alive with insects. The creek is miry; cattle drink with great difficulty; this country never could have been designed for human beings the water is so poor: here and there we find a little spring.

10th day—We are through with another musketoe night, were just on the moment of starting when J[esse]. Fox's horse took to his heels and away he went. How long we shall be detained is uncertain. I intended to have described a bridge we crossed a little west of Indian Village. Not much to the credit of the many teams which have passed over, or rather their owners. It is very long, made of large logs, very uneven; one side being two feet higher than the other. It took one team a quarter of an hour to cross over. In the midst of all the perplexities, my health continues good, and that of my children, who seem to enjoy the journey. My oxen and cows do not incline to stray at all: they really appear to understand that they have a duty to perform. I have much to be thankful for.

Winter Quarters, September 26, 1847—A long time has elapsed since I have written in my journal. A crowd of cares caused by extreme sickness in my family has prevented me. When I last wrote I was on the road between Mt. Pisgah and Council Bluffs. We traveled in company with brs. Truman[240] and Fox. I have mentioned the death of brother Hallet and two children. I now hear that his wife has followed him, likewise a sister Gould,[241] a member of the same family, (who were my pleasant neighbors beneath the oak trees) both gone to their long home! Brother Sterritt was faithful and good to us; we got along smoothly till some began to be taken sick. Brother Fox was first attacked with intermittent fever. At the Bluffs his sister and niece were both laid on beds; the latter died with only a week's illness, a girl 15 yrs. I was also seized with the same disease brought on by washing in the hot sun without a shelter, others besides were taken: and we were all admitted into a sister Henderson's house, a kind lady she was! We were in the woods, low on the bank of the river, we could feel no air stirring. We had no cool water; the warm river water was sickening. I offered to pay five dollars to any one who would go to a certain cold spring and bring me a jug of water. They said it was too far to bring it, it would get warm on the way. I believed warm water would cure me. I believe it now.

When I had partially recovered, we started to go to the main camp 18 miles on the west side of the Missouri. There were so many teams ahead of us we had to wait nearly the whole day for our turn. I was extremely weak! There was great confusion on the

---

240. Possibly Jacob Mica Truman.
241. Probably Ann Rosary Gould, a wife of Clark Hallet.

boat, the cattle were frightened, I was terrified, and it caused my fever to return. There was a dreadful hill to climb as we drove off the boat, deep mud, and at the top, thick woods. It was dark and we dared not drive on: had no place to pitch the tent, so there we must remain till morning, mosquitoes beyond endurance. I with a raging fever, the four children with me on the bed. The ferryman's wife lived at the top of the hill in a little cabin. At twelve o'clock that night the good woman hearing groans of distress, came with a light to my wagon. Had a light shone down from heaven it could not have rejoiced me more! She instructed the elder daughters to remove things from the front end of the wagon, set them outside on the mud and make themselves a bed separate from mine, that their "mother might have some chance to rest." They did as she directed and I was more comfortable. Besides, she brought me a cup of warm coffee and something to eat, which greatly revived me; and enabled me the better to fight musketoes. The driver was out herding the cattle; came to us early in the morning. No poor mortals were ever happier to see daylight appear! We told him our adventures during the night, and we all pronounced blessings on the good samaraton. That day we drove on, camped at night by some cold springs. Now thought I, will be a good chance for me to get all the cold water I can drink: I resolved to make up for past sacrifices. The children were told to bring a large coffee pot full and place at the head of my bed in the tent. I felt that a great luxury was to be enjoyed. I drank lavishly through the night: the following day was conveyed to camp half dead with cholera morbus! The sisters thronged about my wagon, all anxious to do something to relieve me. One proposed brandy and loaf sugar. I told her if she would bring it in a glass tumbler with a silver teaspoon I would take it, but would not drink it from a "tin cup!" She laughed heartily and made haste to bring the medicine according to directions. It had the desired effect, and I was better. But that was not to be the end of my sufferings. The shaking ague fastened deathless fangs upon me, from which there was no escape! I must bow my head, and submit to my fate. I shook till it appeared to me my very bones were pulverized! I wept, and I prayed, I besought the Lord to have mercy on me. The sisters were moved with sympathy; they assembled at my tent, prayed, annointed me with oil, and laid their hands upon me. Although I was not wholly restored, I was comforted, and enabled to bear more patiently my distress. I had money to hire a good nurse a faithful one she was. She was always cheerful, even merry, which was better than medicine. Sometimes myself and children would all be shaking at once. The nurse would go from one to another to administer relief in every possible way; held the watch to let us know how the time passed. We knew the moment when the agitation would cease, and our systems became tranquil. Then the fever would succeed, which would last nearly as long but less pain to endure.

I, at length, got my chills broken, was relieved for a short time, but a cold rainstorm and exposure caused a relapse. I was in my wagon, my children all sick in the tent, except the youngest daughter, six years, who escaped it all and was able to wait upon the others, which she did to the admiration of all who knew how faithful and brave she was. A cold dreary winter was before us. I hired a man to build me a sod cave; he took the turf from the earth, laid it up covered it with willow brush and sods; built a chimney of the same. I hung up a blanket for a door, had three lights of glass to emit light. I built a fire, drew up my rocking chair before it, and that moment felt as rich as some persons (who have never suffered for want of a house) would to be moved into a costly building. Thus we learn to prize enjoyments by sacrifices.

I paid a five-dollar gold piece for building my sod house, 10 x 12. An old ox with a lopped horn had the habit of hooking everything that came in his road. Greatly did he annoy me by throwing down my chimney: it had several times to be rebuilt. Sometimes just as I was preparing a meal and almost famishing for refreshments, down would fall my chimney. I knew not which to condemn, the brute or his owner. I tried to refrain from cursing either. My mind was wholly occupied about my diet. I had so far recovered that I desired nothing on earth so much as to satiate my appetite with some luxury. There were no vegetables in the camp; for this reason nearly all were afflicted with scurvy a terrible disease! I pined for vegetables till I could feel my flesh waste away from off my bones. I would have given a yoke of oxen for a cheese, had one been brought to my door.

About the middle of winter I began to recover my health. I could walk a half-mile. I went forth from my cave in the earth, gazed abroad on the face of nature, and breathed a new atmosphere! I went to the store of Messrs. Whitney and Wooley[242] to get articles I had sent money to St. Louis for. By then they had lost the bill and would not let me have the goods. Returning after dark, I fell on the frozen ground and sprained my knee. I had to be helped home and was thrown on my bed for two weeks only being removed to have my bed made. My limb swelled to an astonishing size! continued swollen during the winter. The pain I endured I will not attempt to describe. For several weeks I went about on crutches. At length my chimney entirely failed, and I moved into what is called a dugout five feet underground. It was a very damp, unhealthy situation: there I had the scurvy.

A long cold rain storm brought more severely again the chills and fever. These with scurvy made me helpless indeed. The air in my cellar was too confined. I resolved never again to complain of a cold house and fresh air. I had willows laid upon the ground, then a thick carpet spread double, straw bed, and lastly, feathers. I could feel dampness through them all. On examination I found my carpet and straw bed were quite wet. I left the place and determined to sleep in it no more. I went into my wagon; a long heavy

---

242. Newel K. Whitney and Edwin Dilworth Woolley. Both had been previously engaged in the mercantile business and both were involved in obtaining goods for the Saints who had left Nauvoo.

rain came on. I was forced to keep closely covered which caused me to sweat profusely for three days. This broke my chills and I began to recover. Oh! how sweet is sympathy to a poor afflicted soul!

While living in my "den" under ground, Brother Anson Pratt (P.P's brother) came to see me: when he saw the condition I was in, with my four young children on my heart and hands; he sat down and wept a long time. His tears seemed to comfort me. He says, "I will go and see if a room cannot be found for you." There was none to be had. In the midst of our sufferings there was something always to cheer us. The most of the Twelve had gone with the first Presidency to explore a country beyond the Rocky Mountains. The leading men who remained did everything in their power to keep life and spirit among the people. Picnic parties were encouraged; the poor brought out to eat and drink; the best the place afforded was set before us. We listened to the strains of cheerful music, met and conversed with old friends whom we had known in days brighter and happier than those; our hearts were made to rejoice in anticipation of a time to come when we should greet each other in a goodly land, away from our cruel opposers.

I have determined to add one more to my many efforts to buy me a dwelling above ground. Some were beginning to go to the mountains with their families. I found a cabin to be sold for five dollars. I made the bargain and moved into it. I thought in that I could keep dry in a rain storm, but I was mistaken. The first thunder shower I caught a barrel of water in my fireplace. I went about making repairs. I hired a floor laid of split logs hewed, which cost six dollars. So there I dwelt in an eleven dollar house. I had a six-lighted window and felt quite exalted! I had cause to look up, I was well. My daughters also were by this time in good health. The eldest (14) could teach a juvenile school, assist me in providing for the family. The second daughter (11) was unusually smart to do outdoor work: she could make a gar-

den, take care of the cows in winter. Sometimes, when charity
was cold, she chopt the wood, with a little help from the kind
neighbors.

Many of my friends sickened and died in that place, when I
was not able to leave my room: could not go to their bedside to
administer comfort to them in the last trying hours; not even to
bid them farewell: neither could I go to see their remains carried to their final resting place: where it was thought I would
shortly have to be conveyed. The Lord had more work and suffering in store for me: and I lived; with all my children, to be a
witness of his faithfulness to those who trust in him.

I had a bowery built in front of my house where I could seat
twenty five pupils; which my daughter and I taught with pleasure
and profit. In speaking of the faithfulness of God towards those
who trust in him, I now recall an instance I would not forbear to
mention: which took place while I was destitute, and unable to
labor. On a time when I was out of means to buy food, I went to
Col. Rockwood[243] with a request that he would buy a featherbed
of me, which I offered for $12.00. He was preparing to go to the
mountains with the pioneers, had not the means to spare. I
remarked to Sister R that I had nothing in my house to eat. She
replied, "You do not seem troubled; what do you expect to do?"
I answered, "Oh, no, I do not feel troubled, I know deliverance
will come in some unexpected way and when I see you again I will
inform you how it came." I walked home, and on my way called at
Brother J. Busby's: said nothing of my circumstances. He began
inquiring about an old-fashioned iron crane, I had brought
from the state of New York. Said he, "If you will sell it, I will give
you two bushels of corn meal, and take one to your place this
evening." I then mentioned what I had said to Mrs. Rockwood.

Thus in many instances have I been relieved, when appar-

---

243. Probably Albert Perry Rockwood.

ently there was no prospect before me of help from any quarter. Many there were who would divide their last morsel with me in want; but humbling it is to an independent mind to ask of those who have nothing to spare. I make a record of these things, that my children and others who may read these memoirs may be admonished to trust in the One who is all-powerful to save, almighty to deliver. At times the weight of cares I have upon me, the anxiety for the proper training of my daughters, seems unsupportable. I nerve up my heart and determine to live till my husband returns. That I may have one more day of rejoicing, in my toilsome and weary life.

After I had been deprived the privilege of attending publick worship for eight months on account of ill health, I at length was permitted to go. It seemed to me the heavens were smiling upon me! In the afternoon I attended a prayer meeting. The sisters laid their hands upon my head and blessed me in a strange language. It was a song; a prophetic song! Mrs. E[meline]. B. Whitney was interpreter. She sang in our tounge that I should have health, and go to the vallies of the mountains, and there meet my companion and be joyful! I was then fully expecting him to come to that place, before I could with my family undertake such a journey. I still desired to hold that belief, but was admonished by those who heard the prophesy to accept the contrary, and strive to be reconciled. I felt the undertaking to be impossible: I see no way whereby I could obtain means to fit my children out with what [would] be indispensable.

President Young said I must go, that I must do what I could, and he would assist me. When I had decided to go, and asked strength and courage of the Lord, means came flowing into my hands. Things I had thought of no value, that I should throw away, were sold for a fair price to those who were not of our faith, or who were not prepared to go at that time. The Pres't ordered my wagon made ready, a thousand pounds of flour was allotted me; a yoke of oxen, in addition to what I owned; a man hired to drive my team. Fifty dollars worth of store goods was appropriated to clothe myself and children: this with what I obtained by my own economy made me very comfortable. I began to feel myself quite an important personage! It was hard for me to wave the dread of, (as I felt,) a never ending journey!

I gave my eleven dollar house to a neighbor. who moved it across the river to Canesville [Kanesville]. I started on the dreaded journey with a saddened heart, affecting to be cheerful as possible! My good teamster was not permitted to continue with us, having been sent back to Iowa to bring on families left behind. The one hired was a stranger. The question whether he would be companionable or agreeable could not be a consideration; however important it might be to us, so immediately concerned. We were organized in President Young's fifty wagons, with captains of tens; a head commander over all. Six hundred wagons in the whole company, travelling three abreast. As we made our own road, we could easily make a wide one. We camped at Elkhorn River more than two weeks, waiting for others to join us. We were thirty miles from our starting point. While we lay encamped, a sister, by the name of Taylor, died with the measles, it was a sorrowful affair! She left a husband and four children to bewail her loss! To make a lone grave by the wayside at the beginning of our journey caused our hearts to flow out with sympathy for the poor young girls, left to pursue the wearisome route over the deserts without a mother!

The company were generally healthy; even those who started on beds were soon able to enjoy the amusements accessible to all, such as climbing mountains and picking wild fruit. The gloom on my mind wore gradually away. When I had been three weeks on the way there was not a more mirthful woman in the whole company. The grandeur of nature filled me with grateful aspirations. The beautiful camping grounds which were so clean that one was led to conclude no human foot had ever trodden there!

So green was the grass, so delightful the wildflowers, so umbrageous the grounds on the banks of the rivers!

The Pres't counselled us to rest from travelling on the Sabbath day. He said, "Write it in your day book when you travel on Sunday, then notice your success through the week and you will find more time lost through accidents than you had gained by travelling on the day appointed for rest." Sometimes the whole camp of six hundred wagons would be within visiting distance, then indeed it was like a city of tents and wagons. The cheerful campfires blazing at night, far away from the civilized world reminded us that our trust must be in the Lord. He who clothes the lillies of the vallies and notices even the little sparrows would assuredly watch over us.

When we came to the buffalo country, we were full of wonder and admiration. Nothing could be more exciting than to see them in large droves or herds, marching as orderly as a company of soldiers; nothing seemed to daunt them. If they were headed towards our traveling companies, we would make a wide passage for them to cross our path and they would march along so majestically, with their great bushy heads, turning neither to the right nor left, not seeming to notice us at all, while we would stare at them with breathless anxiety, thinking how easily they might crush our wagons, and do us great injury were they to become furious. The men would not fire upon them when they were near us, but follow them to their haunts, capture one, kill it, and haul it to camp with two yoke of oxen. The meat would keep sweet without salt till perfectly dried. Nothing I had ever seen amused so much as watching the bufaloes. As well as I loved the meat when I saw the men pursuing one intending to kill him I always wished in my heart he might elude them and escape with his life. I have seen them wade into the deep water almost over their backs knowing the men could not follow them: prompted by instinct they were impelled to strategy like human beings. I felt it a crime to destroy the life of such a knowing animal.

The Platte River country was beautiful! The women, in small companies, were often seen walking on its banks by moonlight, bathing in its waters: our hearts, at the same time, glowing with wonder and admiration at the beauty and sublimity of nature, alone in a great wilderness, far from the haunts of civilization; none but an occasional red man wandering along in search of game to gaze on the beautiful scenery and pluck the wild fruit. On the Sweetwater we camped for two weeks or more to recruit our teams; but it proved fatal to many. There being alkali in pools about on the range the cattle drank it and several of them died. While we remained there teams were sent by pioneers from S Lake to meet our company and help us on our journey. This gave us new courage. My daughters wore out their shoes; I made them mocasins of buckskin. We had many rambles on the steep hills where we could overlook the surrounding country. The men talked of the great future when the "Iron Horse" would be wending his way over the silent vallies and through the Rocky Mountains; and thus pave the way for teeming multitudes to locate on the beautiful prarees!

We travelled hundreds of miles without seeing a single tree. When, at length, we came to a lone cedar tree, we stopped our teams, alighted, and many of the company walked quite a distance for the pleasure of standing a few moments under its branches. Looking up we saw something lodged among the thick boughs, apparently for concealment. The boys tore it down. Wrapt in a thick buckskin or rawhide was an Indian papoose. There was a horn of powder and, I think, a knife. The men caused it to be replaced. A strange idea of a burial have the poor savages.

Independence Rock was another novelty. The size was immensely large and rather difficult of ascent. A thousand names were inscribed on the rock, which proved we were not the first adventurers. Freemont had been there; also the pioneers to Salt Lake valley. We left our names with the rest, and as we descended in a crevice of the rock saw water dripping down into a spring. With much exertion we crowded through a narrow passage, and got to the spring, and drank our fill of the sweetest, coldest water I have seldom tasted. O! how delicious to the taste in a hot day! After being for months obliged to drink river water, (and sometimes from sloughs) to come to a cold spring to quench our raging thirst was a luxury we could appreciate. Although we had been compelled to leave Nauvoo we did not feel like outcasts. We realized that our Heavenly Father had made a beautiful world, and desired his children should enjoy it; and if our enemies would not allow us to remain neighbors to them because of our being peculiar in our religious views we found by launching out into the wilderness, how much romance and beauty there was in nature, where she dwelt alone! We found there was room for all, it is wisely ordered that those who are not congenial to each other can seperate and live not as enemies.

As we drew nearer the place of destination, our hopes began to brighten. Rumors from the camps already landed in Salt Lake valley came out to meet us with cheering news. A little Scotchman told us that soldiers from the Mexican war were on their way home, coming in the north route from California, that intelligence had reached the pioneers that Elder Addison Pratt was in their company. He says to my daughters, "I shall hasten my return, and go out to meet the battalion boys, shall see your father before you will; shall have the pleasure of informing him that his family are in the company and will soon be in the valley." Our hearts began to swell with joy in view of the prospects that were before us.

Aug. 19th day—Still travelling through canyons, deep mudholes, willow brush, big rocks, steep hills, objects that seem almost unsurmountable, still nothing impedes our progress! Slowly we move along, gaining a little every day. We find an opening every night for camping, clean and pleasant. I feel now as if I could go another thousand miles. Frances, our second daughter, makes her fire the first of anyone in the morning: it is her greatest pride to have people come to her to borrow fire, and praise her for being the lark of the company. Going through the willows, a slat was torn off the chicken coop, and the only surviving hen was lost out. We did not miss her till we camped at night. When the children found she was gone they could scarcely be restrained from going back on foot to recover the lost treasure. "Such an extraordinary hen, that knew the wagon where she belonged, and laid all her eggs in it; and had travelled a thousand miles!" [And so her travel journal ends.]

Ursulia Hastings Hascall ("Haskell" preferred by some family members) and her daughter Irene Pomeroy also left Nauvoo in May, a much more seasonable time to travel in Iowa, although also subject to heavy rain. Ursulia's husband left Boston on the sailing vessel Brooklyn *the previous February, planning to meet his family at their final destination in the West. Ursulia and Irene were not as destitute of help as either Louisa Pratt or Jane Richards, however. Irene's husband Francis and Ursulia's teenage son Thales eased the way for them. With the spring weather, ample provisions, and a well-worn trail to follow, their journey to Winter Quarters turned out to be pleasant. Ursulia's natural cheerfulness and desire to put a good face on her experiences may have colored the letters she wrote back home, but compared with many others, her travels through Iowa and her stay at the Missouri were relatively uneventful.*

URSULIA HASTINGS HASCALL[244]

CAMP OF ISRAEL, Sept 19 1846

Dear sister, In the wilds of North America is the residence of your affectionate sister. Not unhappy and suffering, no, far from it, nor none of our family. There is nothing that would induce me to leave the company of the saints of God, unless it is the salvation of my friends and dear relative[s]. O how gladly would I rend the thick veil of darkness, traditions and sectarianism, that covers their eyes and hearts so they might understand the plainness of the gospel while they have the open bible in their hands searching out their sabbath school below. I am sure you would like to be placed in the right way if you knew certain which it was, look about you and see if your preacher tells you things as they are in the bible, exactly, not I believe so, I think so, it is my opinion, and such stuff, it is of no consequence, if he does not know a thing, we can all guess and think as well as he, when a preacher says he knows a thing, and I shall find it so, when I meet him at the bar of God, and I find it agrees with scripture, there is no room for doubt. We have meetings every sabbath in a place fitted up in the woodland about a mile from the prarie where we are camped with our waggons and tents. We have it fixed expecting to stay until spring. There is two companies on ahead of us. One is stopped 150 miles from here the other has gone on, there is about 800 waggons in this company with brother Brigham Young and brother Heber Kimball at the head, and more adding daily.

Now I will give you a history of my journey or a sketch of it, We started from Nauvoo the 30th of May. Had as good a waggon

---

244. "Letters of a Proselyte, The Hascall-Pomeroy Correspondence," *Utah Historical Quarterly* (April 1957): 133–51; (July 1957): 237–57.

as any of them, three yoke of oxen with flour enough to last us one year, ham, Sausages, dry fish, lard, two cans hundred pounds of sugar, 16 of coffee, 10 of raisins, rice with all the other items we wish to use in cooking. I will describe our waggons and tent as well as I can. I wish I could make you know exactly how they look. The waggon is long enough for both our beds made on the flour barrels chests and other things. (Thales and I sleep at the back end, and F[rancis] and Irene at the forward end while we were traveling if we camped too late to pitch our tent.) It is painted red. It has eight bows eighteen inches apart, a hen coop on the end with four hens, we had two webs of thick drilling. We put on one cover of that, then three breadths of stout sheeting over that and then painted it, the heaviest showers and storms does not beat through only a few drops now and then. Our tent is made of drilling sixteen breadths in the shape of an umbrella. A cord three feet long on the end of every seam and a pin on that to drive into the ground. The pole in the middle that holds it up carries it three feet from the ground, then a breadth of sheeting put on the edge to let down in cool weather and fasten with loops and pins in the ground.

Now we start (every one is councilled to start as soon as ready morn or eve) saturday four oclock in the afternoon and went down to the Mississippi river [and] found a boat to convey us across. Landed safely on the other side, went three miles and camped for the night. Chained our oxen to the wagon after baiting, eat some bread and milk and piece of pie and went to bed in our wagon, never slept better. In the morning made a fire had a good cup of coffee, went eight miles, found a camp of fifty wagons and tents [and] stopped for several days waiting for others, we found some of brother Fars [Farrs] family,[245] pitched our tent

---

245. The family of Winslow and Olive Hovey Farr was converted to Mormonism through the efforts of missionaries Orson Pratt and Lyman Johnson in Charleston, Orleans County, Vermont. In 1837 the family left Vermont to join the Saints in Kirtland, Ohio.

waited two days for them, and then commenced our journey in
earnest. It was not many days before we bid adieu to the last
house we expected to see until we had them of our own. We travelled for hours and saw nothing but the wide expanse of heaven
and the waveing prairie grass not a tree or bush. Then we came to
timber and water [and] camped for the night, do our cooking
and washing all that wish to start the next day take wood and water
enough to make our coffee for breakfast and hastepudding[246] and
milk for dinner. We always found wood and water as often as
once in twenty four hours but not always at the right time. The
company we were in killed several fat calves they always gave us
some, we had the old fashioned soups with a light crust. We have
had every thing on the way to make us more comfortable than
any one could possibly expect, and in this way we travelled until
we came to council bluffs on the Missouri river (you can find it
on the map) There we found the camp of Israiel with its leaders
(or some of them I might say) waiting for a boat to be built to
carry us across the river here we camped two weeks, then the boat
was ready. All crossed as fast as possible, came on twenty miles
this side of the river and stopped a while, finally Brother Young
the president of the church said the best way was to stay here this
winter, and let those that are ahead break the way and we start
early in the spring. They consented to it, went to work. cut grass
and made such big stacks of hay as I never thought of, for the
cattle, building log cabins for their families. Some split the logs.
Francis split his. They make boards and shingles here by hand.
They brought saws and almost every thing else. They brought a
carding machine. I think they will need it there is seven hundred
sheep in one drove that is church property, there is lots of fat
cattle killed, one or two every day this six weeks. We have some
every week, Francis and Thales got a lot of honey the other day

---

246. Hasty pudding is a mush made of cornmeal. It is so named because it is quickly prepared.

equal to Daniels,[247] the warm biscuit and honey [and] a good cup of coffee is not so mean. Do not worry about us, I think we shall get along with as little trouble as other people that live in painted houses and carpet floors. The Mexican war is no trouble to us at present. It is rather a benifit. President Polk sent two officers to our President Young for five hundred able bodied men to take [to] Santa Fee and he might have it for a location. Polk would find everything [and] pay seven dollars and a half per month to the soldiers 40 to the Capt and so on to officers, President Young started out immediately from camp to camp, soon enlisted his five hundred men, sent them on to fort Leavenworth there to receive orders from your President. They stayed there a while, received there money sent home to there families considerable of it. They do not need of it at present, and they put it into President Youngs hands for the benifit of the church. He sent one thousand dollars to St Louis to buy goods of all kinds.

We are all well and have been excepting a few days. Francis had an ill turn and so did Irene. Francelle [grand daughter] is a beautiful child. She has had the whooping cough the old fashioned way. [It] took of her flesh some, [but she is] pretty much over it, Thales stands all kinds of w[e]ather. He has had only one ill time since [we] started that was bowel complaint. For two or three days [we] did not take anything but peppermint. I do not see but he is as contented as he would be there. He would like to have one play with the boys he used to play with. He began a letter – he said it would be all mistakes and he would not write. His business is herding cattle with several other boys. He says he is a sick of it as finds [blank] he says he rather they follow him than to go back. He has a peck of filberts he picked. [. . .]

When I left Nauvoo I gave fifteen cents to brother Thompson to take your letter and send it to mount Pisgah. That

---

247. Probably Daniel Andrews, Jr., Ursulia's brother-in-law. Daniel lived in New Salem, Massachusetts, the town Ursulia and Irene left when they gathered with the Saints.

was the second camp. There they took the name of every man that passed through the gate, then when a letter came it was forwarded to him. I began to think if you had written it was lost but at last it was cried on the stand a letter for F[rancis]. Mr. [Stillman] Pond he went and got it, how the last came is quite remarkable. Dr [Willard] Richards was at some office where he found it paid the postage and cried it on the stand at meeting. Some families that have arrived within a few days have suffered with sickness. All sick at a time. There has been over twenty deaths since we were on the way and since. We talked [to] Brother [George B.] Wallace [who] said he had made seven coffins. [. . .]

I feel as if I narrowly escaped from Babylon with a mighty effort, it is not my wish to return. The Indians are very plenty here. They are here begging every week. Sometimes [they] steal a tin cup or garment if it lies in there way. Brigham Young has made a treaty with them. They are to have our houses and all the improvements when we leave. We found one tribe that had several that had been baptised by Joseph. They would say "me mormon"

Direct your letters to Huntsuckers postoffice Atchison County Missouri.

U. B. H.

there is no end to them black walnuts in abundance hundreds of bushels of grapes orchards of wild plumbs, fifty bushels in a place, you never saw anything better [to] make pies and preserves.

Camp of Israiel, Winter quarters
Indian Territory April 1847
Dear Brother, and sister, I fear you have not received my last letter as I have not received an answer, I went to the office found a letter I thought it must be from you, but it was from Francis mother, I was disappointed. I assure you the time has now arrived that we are preparing to pursue our journey. Expect to arrive at our place of rest, before we stop again, only

for repairs &c, about two hundred pioneers started two weeks ago, they calculate to get there and put in seed of various kinds long before we get there, the teams were mostly mule and horses. Francis was among the number and Thales is to be our teamster. He thinks he can manage three yoke of oxen. Irene says he is a young man, he has grown tall and stout, his flesh is hard and health good. If he only had Albert[248] here to go hunting with him he thinks they should kill lots of prairie hens wild turkeys geese ducks and maybe a deer or buffalo, his business this winter past has been chopping the wood at the door, and the care of one cow. Our other cattle have wintered on rushes forty miles up the Missouri river with five or six hundred others. There was ten men chosen to herd them, and keep the indians from killing them, Francis was one of the ten, had 2 dollars per head. We have lived in our log cabin through the winter very comfortably. We have a brick chimney and hearth, (two thirds of the people have them made of sods and they do very well), a window with four lights of glass 10 by 12, gave eight cents a light, the furniture consists of sacks barrels chests trunks and two wild bedsteads with curtains from eaves to floor, my chest for a table, We have had plenty of provisions except vegetables, we have had beans enough and some potatoes, this spring there is abundance of wild onions and artichokes first rate, there is a store opposite of us with every necessary, English and west Indies, goods coffee sugar, salaratus all fifteen cents per pound. First best sugar house mollasses one dollar per gallon, I think we shall get along first rate, there is companies organized of hundred, and Captains of fifties and tens, we are going in brother Wallace's company of fifty.[249] The Woodburys are going with the same company. They are twenty miles from here. Thomas has been here and staid over night. Where

248. Albert F. Haskell, Thales' cousin from New Salem, who was about his age.
249. George B. Wallace was a captain of fifty in the A. O. Smoot company.

William is they do not know.[250] Brother [Samuel] Aikins family are at Garden Grove some distance back, Samuel [Aikens] came on with brother Ponds family and died here away from father and mother, I suppose you have heard of deaths in brother Ponds family. The children are all dead but Elizabeth [and] Loenza,[251] when they were on the way here they turned from the main road into a settlement where he and Samuel could earn two dollars per day with their teams. It proved to be an unhealthy place, They were all taken sick and they came away as soon as they could, but they were unable to take care of themselves on the road and suffered for the want of care, Lowell died before they arrived, the rest lived to get here and then dropped away one after another, Sister Pond has not recovered and I fear she never will,[252] Brother Ponds health is very poor. Sister Clark died on the way here.[253] She wore her self out with hard work I think, I never saw a female that could live and do as she did, The children came on with P[orter]. Rockwell they have the first rate families to live in. Hiram lives in the same family with Emiline. She thinks them the best people in the world. She is as happy as a queen, has everything to eat, drink [and] wear. She instructs the children has the care of their clothes and does as much or as little as she pleases.[254] Tell mother sister Murdock is here with her family.[255] Where brother Harris is we do not

---

250. Joseph Jeremiah and Mary Ann August Woodbury and their family were fellow converts with the Hascalls in North New Salem, Massachusetts. Thomas Woodbury married Irene Pomeroy's cousin, Catherine Haskell. William, age eleven, is their son.

251. The Pond and Aikens families were fellow converts with the Hascalls in New Salem. Elizabeth Almyra Pond was the wife of Newel K. Whitney.

252. The Pond children who died included Abigail Augusta, a daughter from Stillman's first marriage to Almyra Whittemore, who died in 1833 in Massachusetts. He subsequently married Maria Louise Davis. All the children from this second marriage died of malaria. Maria became consumptive and died 17 May 1847.

253. Sister Clark is Diadama Hare Woodward Clark, the mother of Emmeline B. Wells, who was then married to Newel K. Whitney. Emmeline married Daniel H. Wells after Bishop Whitney's death in 1850. Diadama Clark and Emmeline's three younger siblings, Maria, Ellen, and Hiram, migrated from North New Salem to Nauvoo in 1845 and left Nauvoo with the "poor Saints" in the fall of 1846.

254. Emmeline lived with the Newel K. Whitney family.

255. Sister Murdock is Sally Stacy Murdock, a friend and fellow convert from north New Salem. Her husband, Joseph Murdock, died in 1844, so she crossed the plains with her two sons in the Ira Eldredge company of 1847.

know.[256] Sister Brimhall is well. She did not grieve much for the Prichards loss. We have now and then a newspaper from New York. Shall we believe the cracking asunder of the Union of the United States, Yes, sooner or later the Lord will avenge the blood of his martyred Prophets and persecuted Saints, Unless they repent and restore their right. Irene read President Polks message. It's as harmless as milk and water. I think he is as Eliza Smith said about my going to singing school—I should not do any hurt if I did not any good. The ship Brooklyne has landed we hear and printed a paper.[257] I suppose Uncle Sam has received one by this time. I expect Francis will see [my] husband before we shall. [. . .]

Give my respects to Grandfather and mother Andrews. Tell them the mormons have built one of the best grist mills that ever was seen in the States. Although this is the indian territory when they leave it the next company will use it and so on untill all the mormons have passed along. It ground twelve bushel of corn an hour the first few hours. but they took it down to six bushels when they made a business of it. You spoke about dancing. I filled my other sheet before I thought of it but now I will tell you. The Mormons (as they are vulgarly called) do not have any guess work, in their exercises, they have a rule and the order of God, for all their movements, Thales attended dancing school this winter, they open their school with prayer and so they always do at their dancing parties or feasts. They have all the good and fat things they can procure for supper, I never saw a larger supply at any place. Each grade had a feast until they went through the

---

256. Brother Harris very likely refers to Elias Harris, the first father-in-law of Emmeline B. (Harris, Whitney) Wells. He and his wife, Lucy Stacy Harris, did not stay with the Church. Lucy Harris eventually returned to New Salem and remarried. Elias Harris' date of death is unknown.

257. Sam Brannan began publication of the San Francisco Bay's first newspaper, *The California Star*, on 9 January 1847. This paper was a general newspaper with occasional supplements devoted to special interests of the Church. Ursulia Hascall had personal interest in the voyage of the *Brooklyn*, since her husband, Ashbel Green Hascall, was among the Saints aboard. He died, however, before reaching Salt Lake City.

camp, I went with the wives of the elders that are sent on missions, widows and soldiers wives. There is some of the smartest and best men and women here there is in the world, They dress superior to your New Salem people if they have had to winter in log cabins. I send this [letter] by a sister that is going to Boston to visit her friends. [She] returns in october. Her name is Sabra Granger. direct your letters to Francis M. Pomeroy Huntsakers Ferry Austin postoffice Atchinson County Missouri, to be forwarded to the Camp of Israel.

Your affectionate U B H

I send you a piece of my new sun bonnet the handsomest one you have seen.

The following letter is from Irene Pomeroy and written from the Salt Lake Valley. It describes the family's experiences after leaving Winter Quarters.

IRENE HASCALL POMEROY[258]

ADDRESSEE: Miss Ophelia M. Andrews
North New Salem
Franklin County
Massachusetts
(Care of Col. Wilson Andrews)
Postmarked:Kane Io. [Kanesville]
May 16 1848
Great Salt Lake City March 5th
1848.

---

258. "Letters of a Proselyte: The Hascall-Pomeroy Correspondence," *Utah Historical Quarterly* 25 (July 1957): 241–45.

Cousin Ophelia, having a little leisure from domestic cares I thought [I would] write you a few lines knowing you would be very anxious to hear from us. We are all well contented and happy. We have a log house made of hewed logs sixteen by eighteen and covered with planks and slabs. Our fireplace is made of clay pounded into one corner and the fireplace cut out just such shape as you please. The rest is sticks plastered outside and in which makes it quite nice. We have quite a nice door made of fir boards which were sawed since we arrived. We have nothing but the boards of our wagon for floor yet. We have a window with five squares of ten by twelve glass and one of cloth pasted on. There is two beds at the east end of the room and curtains drawn across the room in front of the beds and a little chamber floor over the beds where we keep our provisions. Picture to your self Irene sitting in such a room as this writing on her same chest which stood in her chamber in Mass. Mr. [Frances] Pomeroy and Thales have gone to what is called the Cotton woods for poles to fence the land. Francelle is filling the little creampitcher (your mother and mine used to play) with water and washing it in the washdish. Mother is knitting. (I will fill this page with family concerns now I have come so near it, and tell you on the next how we came hear and what kind of place it is). We have two yoke of oxen, two cows two heifers (two years old) a pair of horses three hens two chickens and a dog. We have killed one yoke of oxen for beef. We expect to have a garden in front of our house. Our farming land is five or six miles from hear. The houses are built adjoining each other and in the form of squares enclosing ten acres each. It was thought wisdom to have them in this manner for this season because we could better defend ourselves from all kinds of danger.[259] When the companies arrive next Summer we expect to commence a brick house. There will be a city laid out then and

---

259. She is describing the fort built in Salt Lake City for protection from the Indians.

each building will have land for all necessary purposes and a large garden and the farming land will be with out the city.

When Mother wrote you at Winter Quarters we were preparing for our journey still farther west. Thales went down into Missouri with Br Wallace and bought a new supply of provisions and we left Winter Quarters June 17th and I can assure you we passed through a variety of scenes a distance of ten hundred and sixty miles from W. Q. Rivers, brooks, mudholes, mountains, plains, woods, broken waggons Indians, Buffaloes, wolfs, deer, antelope, wild dogs, bears &c. The Indians were very friendly. They do not hurt if we kept strong guard out so they could not steal our horses and cattle in the night; We passed through some places where it [was] almost impassable, mountains of cragged rocks seeming as it were bending over us on either side of the road, at another time we would be on the side of a mountain below us on one side of the road 50 or 100 feet straight down as Grandmother says, on the other side a mountain and seeming every moment as if the waggon would be upset. This was the last part of the road. The first 1000 miles was mostly praries, see nothing but land as far as the eye could reach; You can look on the map and see where we came; We came nearly the whole of the length of the Platte river and camped on its bank most every [night]. We walked a great part of the way where there were bad roads (Catherine says tell them I could walk 10 or 15 miles per day). We generally travelled from 10 to 15 miles in a day sometimes 20 and once or twice 25. We did not travel on sundays on the whole we had quite a pleasant journey. We would (about half a dozzen) go on ahead of the waggons, find some place of curiosity and wait for the teams to come up. How many many [times] mother and I would say how Aunt Samanthy would love to see this and that.[260] Grandmother might have come if she had

---

260. Samantha Olcutt Hastings Andrews was Ursulia's sister and Ophelia's mother.

thought so. There is some older than she here. I presume you
have heard of Richardsons bitters. The old man's son is here and
his sons mother came from Vermont. Emeline is yet in W. Q.
When we came away she was teaching school in the same family
where she has been.

There was about 600 waggons came last summer.[261] Such
only came as could buy provisions, the rest staied to raise it. We
expect a much larger company this season. Well after all this long
journey, when we were coming over mountains and between
them all at once a little narrow passage between the mountains
(called a cannian [canyon] I think I have not spelled it right)
opened into a beautiful valley. This is our place of residence. It is
in the midst of the rocky mountains surrounded on every side
by impassable mts. and just one passage in and another on the
west side which will not take much labor to stop an army of ten
thousand. Now let the mobbers rage. The Lord has provided this
place for us and if we are faithful the troubles and calamities of
the Gentile nation will not harm when all is past, we will step
forth from our hiding place the secret chambers spoken of in the
bible. I wish you would come and stay with [us]. You would if you
[could] see the future. But live in darkness, we know this is true,
what you call mormonism. If we ever meet in the resurrection
you cannot say I never told you, What I say to one I say to all who
shall here it, and read it to every one you can (this part if nothing more) for I say it again I know it is truth and I say it by the
spirit of God. I would die in one minute for this gospel if necessary or required of the Lord. Remember what I say to you, I
expect Augustus before long. He said he should come when he
was twenty one.[262] The journey does not seem to us now as it did
in Mass. Why we [would] not think any more of coming back

---

261. Between the middle of September and 10 October 1847, 2,095 Saints arrived in the Valley.
262. Augustus Haskell was Irene's cousin and the brother of the aforementioned Albert. Although
he was twenty-one in 1848, by 1850 he was still living in New Salem.

than we used to do of going to New York city. There is a large salt lake lying in the northwest part of the valley called on the map lake Timpanagus. Its water is more highly impregnated with salt than those of the ocean. They make some of the nicest salt you ever saw. They can shovel up bushels of coarse [salt] on the bank. The mountains near the city are covered with vegetation. Those at a distance look rough and rocky. The timber is mostly on or near the mountains. Streams of beautiful water run from the mountains and empty into a river called Jordan which empties into salt lake. Some of the mountains are covered with perpetual snow. The climate is thought to be warmer here than in New England. The winter has been very pleasant. Feed for cattle all winter. Those that ran at liberty were grew fat all winter.

People have commenced plowing and planting some but it freezes a little [at] night. We have not had any snow to last long. There are some maple trees here, poplar fir cotton wood oak birch spruce and a species of hemlock. Br. Woodburys family are here and all much better than when they left Nauvoo. Catherine is well and children. Elizabeth and Loenza are well send love, Loenza [Pond] is married to Joseph Kingsbury. I [suppose] you know that Abby is dead.[263] When they left Nauvoo they went off the road into a very sickly town because they could get great wages and thought they would earn something. They were all taken with chills &c. and none but Br Pond E[lizabeth] and L[oenza] survived the disease. Br Aikins family are yet at W. Q. and William W[oodbury]. was on his way there last we heard from them and Mrs. Russel Maria, Ellen and Hiram Clark. W[hile] at winter Q. H[iram] lived with Emeline. You have heard of dressing in skins. I will send you a specimen. Francis has a coat and pantaloons and Thales pantaloons. We can wash it and stretch it while it dries. Thales says he wants to see George & Waldo Albert and the rest

---

263. Abigail Pond, eighteen-year-old plural wife of Newel K. Whitney, died of "chills" on 7 December 1846.

of the boys very [much]. He is almost a young man, taller than I. We have heard father is on California shore and have wrote to him and expect he will come here this season. Tell Grandmother she would laugh to see Francelle talk and motion it out with her head like Aunt Phebe. Francelle has been putting my ink on her hair calling it oil. Mother says tell Grandmother and S. she [has] not been out of coffee yet and drinks it most every day. We have got company a lady from Cape Cod. I know you are a good scholar so I think you can read this. I have not time to read my letter you must guess at what is not here. It is a very healthy place.

I have not much room for compliments. Love to all who know us. I think perhaps you are married. If you are love to your husband. Write as soon as possible. When you write pay postage or it will not come.

Irene

The following excerpt by Jane Richards is one of the more poignant accounts of the Iowa crossing. Like many other wives of missionaries and Church leaders, she and her sister-wife were left to make their way on their own, depending on their own resources and the help of friends and family. Sickness, however, added to the burden of self-dependence while tying lives together in mutual caring and shared suffering.

JANE SNYDER RICHARDS[264]

EARLY IN THE WINTER of [18]45 it was decided by President Young that the church should move farther west the temple was still being built according to the revelation. But was not entirely finished untill spring. A portion of it was dedicated by President Young during the winter and meetings held there. Late in the spring and after Pres Young and the majority were gone it was finally dedicated.[265] It was in Feb and March that the greater portion of the population had succeeded in crossing the Miss River crossing on the Ice in order to save ferriage. poorly fitted out and travelling but a few miles at a time. We were among the last to go. The mob harrassed and threatened and tried to arrest Brigham Young and he thought it expediant to leave.

Among my woman friends at Nauvoo I must mention Mrs. Julia Farnsworth, Mrs. [Sarah] Leavitt[,] Kind and motherly always ready and helpful Whenever my husband or I was sick. Mrs [Hannah] Fish Mrs Bilate [Vilate] Kimball Mrs Jeannetta Richards very intelligent and kind and respected by everybody. Mrs John Taylor. Mrs Phobe Woodruff and Mrs [Nancy] Rockwood Mrs Jeannetta Richards died just before our start from Nauvoo.

My Husband [Franklin D. Richards] returned to nauvoo when my baby was ten months old, about a week after Joseph

---

264. Reminiscences of Jane Snyder Richards (1880), holograph, Archives, Church of Jesus Christ of Latter-day Saints, Salt Lake City, Utah.

265. On 30 April 1846 the Nauvoo Temple was privately dedicated by Joseph Young. A public dedication was held the following day.

Smiths death.[266] He went to work as carpenter at once on the temple and on our house. Which as I said was completed only three months before we were oblidged to leave it. While my husband was away I spent part of my time with his parents and part of the time with my Mother [Lovise Comstock Snyder]. I had met Mr Richards parents for the first time this winter. They had just come to Nauvoo. Father Phineas Richards I found was a man of strong character firm in his religious convictions and consistent In Mother Richards [Wealthy Dewey Richards] I found a noble hearted woman. Who gave me a Daughters place in her home. and in her love. I was also very warmly attached to the Brothers and sister of my Husband.

A few months previous to Joseph Smiths death he had recieved a revelation in reguard to Polygamy and Hyram Smith had talked of it in confidence with my husband who mentioned it to me. Though I spoke of it to no one. It seems that Joseph Smith had taken some more wives during these months. But the revelation required that he should do it without publicity at this time, as the mob spirit was already so much excited without this having been thought of at all. It was not on this account he was persecuted as it was not known untill after his death.

The celestial marriage or sealing were not solemnized untill it could be done in the temple although with Joseph Smith it neccessarily was done elsewhare as the temple was not then ready for use. During this winter and previous to the company starting, Mr Richards took his second wife, Elizabeth McFate. Polygamy was now made known to us for the first time and while the majority of the Church were made acquainted with the doctrine it was only practically entered into by few. In my case it came at first thought as a strange thing and I was uncertain as to

---

266. Records show that Franklin D. Richards had left for a mission to England during the spring of 1844. In New York he received word of the Prophet's death. He did not return to Nauvoo, however, until 2 October 1844. Wealthy Lovisa, the Richardses' daughter, was born 2 November 1843.

the result. But was satisfied that it was a sacred revelation and that my religion required its acceptance. This wife Elizabeth was young (about 17 and pretty) and amiable very considerate and kind to me Never in our associating together was there an unkind word between us. I was in delicate health and from the time she first entered my home three or four days after her marriage she seemed only concerned to relieve me of trouble and labors. She was ready to take hold and do any-thing always asking me for direction. We lived in our two story brick home she occupying the upper portion.

To those in the church who knew of the doctrine. I always spoke of her as Mrs Elizabeth Richards. but even now it was not publicly talked about. I knew of other families at this time living in Polygamy. But as yet it was a new thing. I was sick some of the time and Elizabeth would be very attentive and kind and inter-ested to do what she could for my little Daughter Wealthy. We lived happily together and indulged no evil or Jealous feelings towards each other. In the latter part of May we sold our house which we had built with shuch sacrifice denying ourselves in every way to save enough to build and now we sold it for the paltry con-sideration of two yoke of half broken cattle and an old wagon. Taking with us two cows one trunk of clothing but little Furniture and scanty provisions to last if Possible untill next spring. Principally bread stuffs no tea or sugar or luxuries of any kind A neighbor a Gentile Mr Cheesbro very considerately gave me one pound of tea which through sickness and great suffering was about all the subtenance I had for some time.

We left our home before we were ready to start on our jour-neying for the mob was so threatening that I dared not remain longer. We camped out on the other side of the River for six weeks and about July 1st started West. Our cattle was not broke. One yoke had been stolen from us. On the morning of starting I was alone with my little Girl in the wagon when the cattle becomeing frightened at the crack of the whip jumped up and ran over a level plain for a mile and a half at a frightful speed But as they reached a rough stumpy piece of land stopped of their own accord This start was not very assuring

We reached sugar creek twelve miles distant the first night and there my husband left us to go on a mission to England. I[t] was a great trial to us all. I was very feeble. We did not know how Wealthy would stand the trip Elizabeth seemed the only strong one in our family and yet she died on this trip. One teamster was Philo T. Farnsworth.[267]

Before leaving us Mr Richards called us all together as a family and prayed with us and blessed us. I felt as though it was doubtful if I was living on his return. And it was a sad parting.

Matters grew worse Elizabeth was taken very sick with chills and fever. Wealthy was taken sick the day after her Father left and continued ill from this time untill her death the 14th of Sept In the meantime exposure and anxiety hastened my illness and I was confined in the wagon on the 23rd of the month. My baby a little son whom we named Isaac Phinese [Phineas] died an hour after his birth.

Our situation was pitiable my little Daughter was dangerously ill. I had no suitable food for her and nothing for myself for the past twenty four hours. The severe rain prevented our having any fuel for cooking and we could scarcely keep the dampness out of the wagon. On the third day after my confinement we started again on our journey. I was very eager to reach Mt Pisgah where I might burry my baby. We were now on the 23 day of July only sixty miles from our starting point. I should have mentioned the devoted care that my sister [Sarah] Mrs [Benjamin Prince] Jenne gave me. She was with me in my troubles as much as it was possible for her to be as her own family of little ones required her time as well as myself.

---

267. Twenty-year-old Philo Taylor Farnsworth became the first bishop of Beaver, Utah, a probate judge in Beaver County, and a member of the territorial legislature.

On the fifth of August I reached Mt Pisgah very ill. My little Girl still very sick. Here many of our church people were waiting twelve of the Elders[,] Father Richards, Father Huntington and Father Bent and Charles C. Rich among them, came to see us and sympathized with us. The Elders gathered around our wagon, rolling the curtains up and evidently thinking that I had little chance of living. They annointed Wealthy and myself and prayed earnestly for us. Everything was done for us that kindness could suggest and my baby was buried here.

We seemed to get strength and improved slowely and though it was not untill Cutlers Park[268] that I had strength even to walk. When I reached Council Bluffs one hundred miles beyond [Mt. Pisgah]. Pres Young heard of my situation and came back some fifteen miles to counsel me.

He was distressed to find me so ill and to see Wealthy so feeble and he then said if any one had passed through tribulation I had. and if he had known my circumstances he would not have required Mr Richards to have gone on this mission. Then he gave an order allowing our team to pass on across the ferry before the rest some two hundred waiting in turn and then I was once more with my Mother and friends.

Cutlers Park where Brother Brigham was stopping was three hundred miles from Nauvoo, and here was my crowning affliction. At last my little Daughter after suffering almost incredibly for weeks on the 14th of September passed from us. There was a time when I had thought she might live and then it seemed as though all I had suffered would seem but a dream. Her life being spared. Now she was taken my own life seemed only a burden. My Husband was to be away for two years and the hardships he might suffer made his return seem most uncertain. I only lived because I could not die.

---

268. The encampment at Cutlers Park was later moved to a better location that became known as Winter Quarters.

An instance of inhumanity should be recorded while on our travels we passed a house with some farming about it. this was the last of civilized life untill we reached Cutlers Park. Just previous to this my little Daughter had asked for some potato soup and said she had not eaten anything since Papa went away (which had been eight or ten weeks.) and that would taste so good. How eagerly we welcomed the returning apetite and the potato field just in sight. My Mother went to the house and stating our circumstances asked for some potatoes for my dying child. A rough woman heard her story impatiently through and putting her arms on her shoulders marched her out of the house. saying "I wont give or sell a thing to one of you damned Mormons." And I turned in my bed and wept as I heard the Grandmother trying to comfort my little one in her disappointment.

While at Cutlers Park there was a great deal of sickness. My child died beside me in the wagon, I being unable to move without being lifted. At this time my two Brothers were also sick. Mrs Elizabeth Richards was very ill in the tent. Just ahead of me and I could hear her screaming in her delirium and she wanted to see me. I was carried to see her a few hours after Wealthys death. My sister Mrs Jenne lost her baby that fall also. Most of our people were sick. In fact the call for five hundred able bodied men from Council Bluffs for Mexico by the Government deprived us of about all our strength. We must have lost at least one hundred of our company by death while at winter quarters. Cutlers Park now called Florence in Nebraska was on shuch an elevation as to be too exposed for winter life. So we settled upon the flats. Near the Missouri River which were called winter quarters.

Elder Willard Richards had been a Physician in Boston and he was very kind and able in his treatment of me. His wife Amelia was a noble woman and was shuch a support to me, in keeping up my spirits. She was bright and cheerful and dearly loved. Mary Richards was Samuels wife and she kindly consented to remain with me and help me through my trouble.

During our travelling the heat increased our sufferings for there was but a thin covering of cotton cloth to our wagon which was our only protection from the sun rain and dew. The bolt of cotton cloth I brought with me. I was obliged to dispose of in exchange for the necessaries of life or to pay for services rendered me. that was intended as extra covering to the wagon.

At winter Quarters my provisions were nearly exhausted. During my illness, I could not take care of them. but in my helplesness would tell those who did services for me to help themselves to what they pleased as compensation. Now there was little that remained. Elizabeth had recovered from the illness that she previously had and needed strengthening food. We were oblidged to grind corn and live on that for awhile. It was cold and our wood exhausted. Our log House like those about us was small, about twelve by fourteen. Just large enough for two little beds and a fire place. We had no furniture worth mentioning. We would sit by the fire on the beams that extended out towards the fire place. Though we each had a rough chair. The floor was of rough boards hewn from logs. But preferable to the damp ground. I would sometimes go to my sister-in-law and say, "shall I freeze or ask you for wood," and so we lived. Often my clothe[s] would be frozen stiff about my anckles remaining so day after day that you could hear them rattle as they struck against any-thing. What was there to thaw them out Scurvy broke out in our Camp and the death rate increased.

Elizabeth was taken ill again and at last confined to her bed. I was now arround and able to take care of her lifting her from her bed and in her chair. Untill she died. I wanted proper nourishment for her. But there was nothing left to barter for food. A nephew of Brigham Young came to see me and asked me what he could do for me. I told him what I needed. But I had nothing left but my Husbands violin and nobody wanted that. He replied he would take that. But all he had was about a gallon of wine that had been given him in exchange for goods while at Council

Bluffs. That I eagerly took and Elizabeth lived on it for some time. When she talked to me of dying. I felt I could not have it so. Then I should be entirely alone. Perhaps my husband would feel that I had not done everything that I could for her. Perhaps others would think so. Though my own conscience was satisfied.

But on the 29th of March she was taken and I was left. My brother had been to the Rushes one hundred miles distant where the cattle were left for the winter but he returned previous to Elizabeth's death and was devoted in his care. assisting and relieving me in the lifting of her and in the responsibility.

I should have mentioned the roofs of the houses. they were made of logs laid across with flags spread over them. and earth spread over these.

This was partial protection from the rain. But when once it was soaked through in a heavy storm. Then we were at the mercy of the rain.

About the first of april Brigham Young and several other pioneers started out to find for us a new home. We hoped now to get away so far that we should never be molested again by civilization. They found Salt Lake on the 24th of July and there decided to settle. some few remaining among whom were Mrs Lorenzo Young and one of Brigham Young's wives Ms Van Cott and her husband.[269] Others joined them from the battalion returning from California and others from another delegation which came on from the co[a]st.[270] They sowed some little grain and made some preparation for a permanent home Pres Young and the others returned to us in November and we had happy anticipations for the future.

In May 1848 Pres Young again started for Salt Lake this time with the majority of the people those left behind were to be com-

---

269. Her memory is faulty here. Harriet Decker Young (Mrs. Lorenzo Young), her daughter Clara Decker Young (married to Brigham Young), and Ellen Sanders Kimball were the three women who accompanied the original pioneer company and remained in the Valley.

270. A group of Saints from Mississippi also arrived in time to spend the first winter in the Valley.

pelled by the Government to vacate the winter quarters and go across the river to council Bluffs. However two hundred more wagons formed under the leadership of Dr Willard Richards and started west on the 1st of July. My Husband had now been with us six weeks. Our corrispondence had been very irregular. The first he recieved several months after he left me. containing news of the birth and death of his little son. And of the death of his little Daughter and of all the sickness it entailed. His first letter reached me in april he had left me the previous July and in that he told me that he was taking care of his Brother who was down with small pox. What could I expect but to hear next that he himself was dead from that desease.

Now we were starting well provisioned and comfortably provided with clothing. The english branch sending us generous donations of clothing and my Husband bringing me a good supply. Philo Farnsworth had been in Missouri with others working and earning enough to get the neccessary provisions for a years suply. My Husband had brought in a company of Saints from England. All being in readiness we started I soon was taken ill again. And untill we reached salt lake city on the 19th of october. I was unable to walk for three weeks. The whole party were obbliged to wait over on my account; and as before it seemed impossible I could live.

When we reached salt lake we made the best use of our opportunity and time. Our people went into the old stockade. Our wagons brought into correls for a day or two. then we moved on to the city lot. The tops or wagon boxes were taken off the running gear. and placed on the ground. In these we lived untill we had some kind of houses built. Our house was like most of the rest built of abode [adobe]. Mr Richards sold his cloak which he brought from England for abodes [adobes] the side of the house was completed. But the roof had to be made of boards made of green lumber. Which shrunk and made a poor protection. This was covered with hay. But the frozen earth prevented the addition of a covering of earth.

In february even my poor roof was destroyed as our poorly constructed chimney set it on fire On the 20th of June my son Franklin was born. when the baby was a week old the rain came through in torrents. on to my bed for three months Since april we had scarcely any bread. All through one company the scarcety of bread stuffs had been so much felt that at last Pres Young advised that every family ascertain just what amount of bread stuffs they had and report to the council. This was on the 1st of April. Then each family was counselled to make calculation of just the amount that could be used each day from now till harvest time most of them were able to ration themselves off two and 1/2 pound a day. But many like Dr Richards were limited to four oz. a day.

I had started off well provided as I said but sickness had again laid me aside. and others suffering for food had been supplied from my store. Which easily accounts for my present difficulty. We had plenty of beef and milk but no vegetables of any discription.

We had no furniture but what was manufactored now. and no lumber. for we as yet had no saw mill. I needed an easy chair which was made by Elder Appleton Harmount [Harmon] as my health made that necessary this was obtained in exchange for three paris of woolen stockings. The wool was carded then spun and knit by me and in that chair I rocked my boy to sleep many a time and all the rest We now commenced having traffic with the outside world though we had hoped to keep aloof from it altogether.

The parents of Scottish convert Robert Gardner, Jr., emigrated to Canada, where they lived for several years before traveling to Nauvoo. They arrived soon after the exodus began, stayed only long enough to outfit themselves for the journey west, then crossed the river and eventually joined a group calling itself the Canada Company. Robert's relatively brief account gives a perspective on the Iowa experience from one who had not lived in Nauvoo but traveled with the Nauvoo exiles. His journal describes the need all the travelers had for trading with Missourians and the tasks men assumed in making the settlements at the Missouri habitable for the Saints.

ROBERT GARDNER, JR.[271]

WE STAD IN NAUVOO a few days and bought our fit out for the mountains flour and partched corn meel and such things and seed as we would need on the way and after we got to our resting place. that was a good place to camp for The Saints had nerley all left that was able and there houses was standing emty in unsold we could have ether brick frame log or stone houses with chars bedsteads I dont know but by looking we might have found coock stoves for the people were driven away and what they could not sel nor take with them they had to leve for they [had] but five teems and had to lad[en] them with provisions. We had no time nor desire to stay there longer then to get our fitout.

---

271. Journal and Diary of Robert Gardner, Jr., microfilm of holograph, LDS Church Archives.

we crosed the Mississippi river and pased Montros and went
to the blufes a few miles north of Montros and camped I then
went up in Iowa trying to trade my horses for oxen. I found oxen
had been bought up and were hard to find I had one Canadan
horse that was very bad with the heves but I was told it soon left
them in the west. I came acros a man one day whom I [asked] if
he had any oxen to trade me for that horse he said no but he had
a fine mare he would give me for him I went to see her but rod
my horse very slow lest he would begin to heve his mare was a very
fine one but I had to give him 14 dolars to boot but I did not
want to stay long lest Pat would begin to heve so I got on my mare
and thawght I had dun it I rod about 2 miles and pased another
man he asked me if I had bought that mare I said yes wasn't she a
fine one he said yes but she was stone blind that took me down a
notch but I did not go back for old Pat I had been fooled but
there might be some more fools out on my track so I went on.
Shortly I met a man with a fine team and fine bugy wel drased
with every thing gay I thought he was precher or a judge or a
Lawer or some smart so he stoped for he had his eyes on my mare
and I got min on his horse So he bantered for a trad he said his
horse had no fault but to much life, and what was the caractor of
mine I told him he must be his own judge for I had jusd got her
so he tock out his spectels and exemened her clos and pro-
nounsed her good so he tock of his harnes and I tock of my sadle
and we was bothe soon of the trade ground

After this I traded that horse for one yok of oxen and bawght
another yok of oxen and one cow went back to camp we then
riged up our ox teems in place of horses and started west we traveled about 12 miles and camped for the night. here my son
William was born in my wagon.[272] it raned so hard all night that
the water was up to our boottops around our wagons. this was in

---

272. William Gardner was born 22 May 1846.

Lee County Iowa next morning we fixed up my wife [Jane McKeown] and her baby as comfortable as posable and started on for the coumpanys from Nauvoo was all a head at Bonapart next we lodid [loaded] in more flour for we had strenthned our teems. and we ware pushing on for the Missouri river, expecting to overtake the mane camp of Saints there by this time our coumpeney had got the name of the Canada Coumpaney for we traveled pritty nere to gither.

there was: John Park, William Park, Daved Park, and famleys; James Hamilton and famley James Rilfyol and famley, Samuel Bolton and dawghter James Crage John Baroman, George Correy and famley, Andrew Correy and famley Bro Johnes and famley, my Brother William and famley, Archibald and famley, my father and mother and myself and famley, and John Smith & famley.

Iowa was a nue and thinley setled teratory and (many of) the Saints being poor not haveing teem sufisent to [t]ravle ware counseld to stop where the land was not taken up and put in crops til they could help themselvs they had seteled a place caled garden grove one called Pisco [Pisgah] and other places some of our camp began to drop of at thes places and the rest went on. we overtook what was known as Orson Hides [Hyde's] camp nere Miskete [Mosquito] Crek clos by the Missouri river.

here I began to see some of the sufering of the Saints. the furst night we came to Hides camp, there came up a terable rain storm with terable thinder and wind next morning it was paneful to see the Saints with there tents blown down and wagon covers torn of[f] socked in the rain I went to one tent where the tent had ben and found a woman siting on the ground with a young baby both shaking with the agu. and a number of the larger children siting around her in there wet clowes all shaking with the same diseas no one able to help the rest. I asked the woman where her husband was. She said he was caled of to go to Mexico to fight for Uncle Sam that had driven us to the wilderness to endure thes suferings. I tryed to gather up her tent but I could not, it was wore out and torn to peses. they had ben driven from Nauvoo in the dead of winter in the depth of poverty traveling threw deep snow the men having to leve part of there famley by the way and travel perhaps for a weak and then leve that part and go back for the rest with the same teem til themselves and neerly every [thing] they had was wore out and many died by the way from hardship.

We next travld on a fue miles to the man [main] camp at the liberty pol[273] on Misketo [Mosquito] Creck where President Young and Councle was making up the rest of the 500 men of the Mormon batalun. to go to Maxaco they were soon rased and started of, leving there family in wagons and tents where they had them. for some ware without. and that in the middle of an Indain country thes things made me feel like asking O liberty, and freedom, where hast though [thou] fled for this demand was made a trap thinking we would not comply. then they could slay us as trators that was what was wanted and they ware very much disapointed when President Young rased the conmpy

the next thing was to cros the Missouri river the furst coumpanes had bilt a bot when my Bro William got his teem and wagon on the bot, one yok of wild stears jumped into the river with the yoke on and turned to come back. he jumped in caught there tales heded them round and swam them to the other side by there tails.

we then traveled about a half a day to camping ground ner a grove of timber which was caled Cutlers park. the seson now being fur spent and so maney of our best young men gon to Mexaco President Young thawght best to go no further this faul,

---

273. The Liberty Pole most commonly referenced in the diaries was erected on 4 June, near Fremont, Dodge County, Nebraska, one-fourth mile northeast of the Platte River. The second company of pioneers erected a large cottonwood pole to mark the staging ground where Brigham Young brought the pioneers together to further organize them for the journey ahead. Robert Gardner may be referring to a different marker erected on the Iowa side of the river or he may have meant the Platte River rather than the Mosquito.

but find winter quarters cut hay for our stock and start on erly in the spring.

A town site was Selected down on the river caled winter quarters Streets blocks and lotts was layed out and given out to the peple and in a fue days a town of houses was in site large stacks of hay was cut, stock taken to herd growns, a large log meeting house was bilt (and) a good grist mill was bilt to grind the corn and wheat the peple had brawght with them. houses and wood had to be provided for the famlies of them that had gon in the batalyon a meat markit was erected saveral blacksmith shops sue shops chare makers, and nerly all kind of work as if the peple was going to stay for years. men that could work had to worrk nerly night and day for many of the older men was taken with a disese caled the black leg [scurvy] and was entirly helples and many died with it here legs from the nes [knees] down would get as black as a col my father [Robert Gardner, Sr.] and oldest brother [William] and brotherinlaw[274] brothers onley boy big anough to help him,[275] all had it. this left the work of five famles to Archey and me

Maney a evening I have visited the familes of men that had gon in the Batalyon in time of snow storms and found them in open log houses without any chinken and it snowed as fast in side as it did out side and nothing but green catten wood to burn I would go and cut them some dry wood help them all I could. but it semed hard times but there was no one there to blame for men was so scarce. and so maney sick and dying that I have had to go and help the sexson to biry the dead yet the athoratis [authorities] keept up there meetings and now and then would have a dance to keep up the spirits of the peple.

on account of having to stay there that winter and use up there provisons many had to go to Missouri to work and trade for pro-

---

274. Roger Luckham, husband of Robert's sister, Mary.
275. Probably William's son John, born 24 October 1831.

visons and seed to thake with them acros the plains for it was the intantion to start west erly in the spring, butt the Fyrst Presidents and the 12 thawght it would be best to start a small coumpney of pinaneres [pioneers] a head of the general coumpney to look out a location and try to get in some crope [crops]. So they with others started about the 5 of April this was in the spring of 47

I will here go back to our stay in Winter quarters. my brother myself and James Cragee [James Craig] one of the pininears [pioneers] got out the timber for the grist mill I menshened. I dun the huing with the bradax while doing so I was taken with fever and ago [ague] but thawght I wouldnt give up but I had to one day I went home and went to bed and was crasey all day. when my brother and Crage came home I got them to adminester to me next morning I was well and at work by daylight and kept so till we got to the horn [Elk Horn] just menshened.

Barbara Ewell Evans and her family found their own way to the Missouri, working their way westward with the stragglers slowly drifting out of Nauvoo. Though not quite as destitute as those forced to leave Nauvoo in the fall, the Evans family still had to stop at different points over several years before eventually reaching Winter Quarters. For Charles Smith and Barbara Evans and the others like them, traveling on their own, the leaders were always "way out in front," unseen but always present in their minds. Without the daily association with their leaders or the companionship of the other Saints, their perseverance is all the more remarkable.[276]

276. Accounts such as Charles Smith's and Barbara Evans' and the hundreds more not included in this volume form the basis for the moving tribute to the lesser known "supporting Saints" given as a conference address by J. Reuben Clark, Jr., and published in book form under the title, *To Them of the Last Wagon* (Salt Lake City: Deseret News Press, 1947).

BARBARA ANN EWELL EVANS[277]

MY FATHER AND MOTHER left that state [Virginia] when I was nine years old [1830] and moved to Bedford County, state of Tennessee, where we remained three years. In 1833 we moved to Ray County, Missouri. There I witnessed the falling of the stars, November 13, 1833.

It was in my father's [Pleasant Ewell] house that I first heard the sound of the everlasting gospel, preached by Brother Jacob Foutz. The next elder I heard was David Evans. My mother [Barbara Fauber Ewell] being first to believe, she was baptized by David Evans, and the family soon followed.

We remained in Missouri until the Saints were driven from that state. My mother and sister [Sarah Ewell Packer] were very sick when we left, and they both died shortly after our arrival in Illinois,[278] and in the course of a few months another of my sisters [Elizabeth Hill Ewell Thornhill] died, each leaving a small child[279] which I had charge of in connection with my father's family. This consisted of two brothers,[280] two sisters,[281] my father, myself and the two small babies of my sisters. I had charge of all, I was only 18 years of age at that time.

I was baptized by Elder David Evans, and confirmed by him June 10, 1837, and I was married to him on the 23rd of November, 1841.

---

277. In *Bishop David Evans and His Family* (Provo, Utah: J. Grant Stevenson, 1972), 49–53, Library, Church of Jesus Christ of Latter-day Saints, Salt Lake City, Utah.

278. Sarah Ewell Packer died 1 June 1839 in Hancock County, Illinois, and Barbara Fauber Ewell died 28 June 1839 in Nauvoo.

279. Elizabeth's son, Pleasant Thornhill, was born in 1839, and Sarah's son, Nephi Ewell Packer, was born 27 July 1838.

280. The two brothers she refers to are possibly William Fletcher Ewell (30) and Thomas Maxey Ewell (27).

281. Mary Daliney Ewell (14) and Pirene Brown Ewell (10).

I saw Joseph and Hyrum Smith after their martyrdom. It was a solemn day among the Saints. We felt like a flock of sheep without a shepherd, but the Lord had another shepherd to lead his Saints. It was Brigham Young. I was present the day he was set apart to lead the church. No Saint could dispute it for it did seem when he spoke as though it was Joseph's own voice that was addressing us. I never shall forget that day nor how the Spirit of the Lord was poured out upon the people; it came so mild, yet so penetrating that every heart beat with joy to know we had a man of God to lead the Saints. Oh, what a consolation it was to know we were not forgotten.

I remained in Illinois until the exodus from that state, which was in 1846. Some of the Saints had neither teams or wagons. The brethren united together and made wagons for those that had none; by that means all had wagons, but not teams, and we were obliged to get away, as the mob was howling around, and Nauvoo was threatened. So my husband, being bishop of the Eleventh Ward, concluded to take the teams they had and move as many as they could. We made a start with what teams we had, crossed the Mississippi River, went a day's journey, and set the families down on the prairie. The next day they took the teams and brought the rest.

Soon after the men got employment breaking prairie and doing other work. We took oxen and milk cows so in the fall all had teams and provisions for winter. I did considerable spinning in the tent, also quilted several quilts. One great blessing, we were generally well. We did not have many luxuries, still we felt thankful for what we had. We then started for Council Bluffs, but it was late in the fall, winter had set in, and we stopped on the headwaters of the Nodaway. The men cut hay and put up log huts. My husband made a sideloom, and I did considerable weaving that winter. The cattle could not live on the frostbitten hay so they commenced to die; our provisions began to get short; and we were obliged to leave in the month of February, 1847. We started for Missouri and lost our way. Our teams that were left gave out, and we had to kill and eat them to save our lives.

My husband and two other men, Joseph Smith (of Lehi) and Shaw,[282] went down to Missouri to get fresh teams and provisions, while they left their families camped on a small stream which was called Starvation Creek. We suffered from hunger and cold, but we did not complain, for we were united; we truly lived the order; we all shared alike. My husband came with fresh teams and provisions. I tell you it was a day of rejoicing. We had not heard from them since they left. They had had hard work to get teams. The people were so prejudiced against the Mormons, they were almost to return without anything. My husband told the people he would return and die with the rest of the people. One gentleman spoke and said, 'Can't you do something for these men; they seem to be honest?' The men began to volunteer, and he soon had all the provisions and teams he wanted.

We then made another start for Missouri. The snow had fallen to a great depth, and we could not keep on the divide. After wallowing in the snow for four or five days, camping on the prairie without fire, we arrived in Nodaway County, Missouri, March 1, 1847. My son, Joseph, was born April 7th, in a house without doors, windows, chimneys or floor. My food was corn bread ground on a hand mill; we had bran for coffee. We stayed there three years, had plenty of work, made a good outfit and started for Utah, May 15th, 1850. My baby was ten days old when we started. After the company got together, Bishop Evans was appointed captain. They were organized, and on June 15 we made a start for Utah.

The cholera soon broke out in camp. People were stricken down on every side. There were five deaths in our company, my husband's oldest daughter, Mrs. Ira Hinckley, was one among

---

282. Possibly John Shaw, a pioneer of 1848, or Samuel A. Shaw, a pioneer of 1847.

them. That was a trying time. I had six small children, but none of them had the dreaded disease. Had it not been for that we would have had a pleasant journey. After we arrived at Laramie, we all enjoyed good health.

In the year 1850, September 15th, we arrived at Salt Lake Valley, and lived there until February 15, 1851. We then moved to what was called Dry Creek, which was later called Lehi, and we have made our home in Lehi ever since.

Mercy Fielding Thompson, widow of Robert Thompson, was among the late refugees from Nauvoo. Her brother Joseph Fielding helped her prepare, but she needed a driver for her wagon. Charles Smith answered her call. He left his wife and young children camped near Bonaparte, Iowa, while he traveled to Winter Quarters with the Fieldings, including Mercy Thompson and her daughter, Mary Fielding Smith and her family, and Joseph Fielding and his family. In return the Fieldings offered him the use of a wagon to retrieve his family and take them to the Missouri settlements. Despite their generosity, Charles did not have enough provisions to take his family to Winter Quarters that year, and he had to leave them frequently during the next two years while he worked on a riverboat and in Missouri earning the means to continue the journey. After much difficulty, sickness, and disappointment, he and his family finally reached the Missouri in the spring of 1848.

CHARLES SMITH[283]

IN CONSEQUENCE OF POVERTY which was the lot of the saints generally i was retarded in procuring a fit out for the west i managed however to procure a waggon during the winter and following summer on the 13th of August about 4 o clock on thursday morning 1846 my wife [Sarah Price] was delivered of another Son we called his name Charles Edward. on the saturday following i was taken sick, but in a few weeks gained my original Strength, during my sickness however the mob had again began to collect in the neighbourhood of carthage i was unable to attend in the musters of my brethren in consequence of Sickness however a few weeks before this i was assisting in the search for those brethren who had been kidnapped by the mob party,[284] but without effect they were however released and returnd to their familie and friends about the latter part of August Sister Thompson [Mercy Fielding] made a propisition that if any one would go and drive a team for her to the camp on the Missouri river they should have a team to come back with to remove their family i accepted of the offer myself and made my arraingments accordingly the house which took me considerable labour to build besides paying 35 dollars for the lot, i sold for ten dollars after paying twelve dollars more for the lot that adjoined it, in order to make one lot of it, and make mine saleable the waggon which cost me so much time and expence; sold for about one half what it cost me however with the promises of the psalmist David

283. Reminiscences and Diary of Charles Smith (1842 March–1905 June), photocopy of typescript, LDS Church Archives.

284. They were Richard Ballantyne, Phineas Young, Brigham H. Young, and James Standing.

before me Gather yourselves together you that have made a covenant with me by Sacrafice[285] being prepared according to holy writ i assisted sister Smith[,] Hyrums widow[286] accross the Mississippi and on monday the 7th of Septr 1846 i took my family over the river to sister Smiths encampment on wednesday brother clifford[287] and i borrowed a skif to cross the rver with to assist in bringing over the balance of the cattle on wednesday after noon we commenced loading the boat by about dark we were ready to take our last cargo accross the river we started and got about a hundred yards from shore the cattle not likeing their position began to be unruly and presently every one of them was over board i jumped into the skif and rowd to shore to turn the cattle into the yard again but it had gone so dark that i could not see them all but i securd part of them. the next day i returnd over the river with the skif leaving brother Feilding[,] Clifford[,] George mills,[288] amasa Bonny[289] and brother in law to look after the cattle in a day or two we movd three miles beyond Montrose where we remaind a few days we then took up our line of March for the camp when near Farmington i took my family or rather a brother by the name of phelps was going to Farmington from Evans camp and he took us with our goods in his waggon as i had to look up some one of the brethren with whom to leave my family whilst i went to camp we had our things set down on the side of the road in a little while brother Richard Ralphs who had been to Farmington with a waggo[n] was returning to bonaparte he gave me some information respecting some brethren near Saw mill creek two miles from bonaparte we were loaded up again in

---

285. See Psalms 50:5, "Gather my saints together unto me; those that have made a covenant with me by sacrifice."

286. Mary Fielding Smith.

287. Possibly Elijah Clifford.

288. One of the original pioneers of Utah. Little is known of George Mills except that he died of cancer about 1854 in Salt Lake City.

289. Amasa Bonney, born in 1865 in New York state, was a member of the Kirtland Safety Society in Ohio and a member of the second quorum of seventy.

a few mintutes and on our way for saw mill creek where we reachd
in safty i found two familys campd here from them i derived the
desird information however it was got to late in the day to remove
my family any furthur, we pitched our tent or rather fixed some
rails up against a fence throwing over it a quilt under which we
made our bed on the ground and retired about midnight we were
awaked by the noise of distant thunder we re-moved our bed into
the tent in the morning brother George Edwards brought a cart
to remove us to brother Griffiths[290] after breakfast i took leave of
my family and friends and proceeded to join sister Smiths camp
i met them at bonaparte but the waggons had gone on five miles
furthur, the next morning the Sheep strayed away which detaind
us four days we then proccdded for the camp at winter quarters
in which we arrived about six weeks, i staid ere about a week,
being councild by brother Heber C Kimball to return without a
team to my family i did so i returnded with brother Robert Stuart
who had hired a team to go to Bentons port[291] for flour we arrived
in bonapar two weeks from the day we left winter quarters, i[n]
the road back i [met] brother Harrington[292] who authorized me
to go to Nauvoo and get a waggon he left there after remaining
at bonaparte a few hours i went to my family found them well, i
staid at home a few days then went to Nauvoo, for the Waggon. I
stayd a few days in Nauvoo to assist in repairing this waggon which
i found very much out of Order i crossed the waggon over the
river on monday 23 of November the Steamboat called the Iron
City was then laying at Montrose i learnd that brother George
Black was on this boat i went to see him he persuaded me to go as
a hand on the boat i did so as i foresaw that i must be diligent

290. Joseph Griffith left Nauvoo when the Saints were expelled and lived in Iowa until his trek to
the Valley about 1851.

291. The settlement of Bentonsport was northwest of Bonaparte, along the Des Moines River.

292. Probably Leonard Ellsworth Harrington, who came to Utah with the Edward Hunter company and later served on the judiciary committee in the Utah legislature, as mayor of American Fork, and
as trustee of Brigham Young Academy.

before the Lord in procuring means to remove with the church i was on this boat three days and a half while i went to rock Island and back i then proceeded to Saint Louis being prosperd on my way thither, i remained in Saint Louis all winter in the spring returnd to my family but not hav[ing] sufficient means to remove west i returnd to St Louis i stayd there six weeks then returnd to my family i staid at home a few weeks then returnd to Saint Louis after i had been here a few [?] i sent for my family they arrived in Saint Louis about the middle of August my wife was sick with the chills and fever and my little one of the diarrehea i also lay sick upon my bed with the chills and fever this was a distressed time, but the Lord was merciful and we were soon raised up i went to my daily labour as soon as i possibly could though very weak in body yet the spirit of persivance rested upon me to pre-pare to go west Soon after this i was discharged from my employ-ment this spread a gloom over my preperations but it turned out for the best, as a shop had been vacated in Second Street brother [James] Frodshaw [Frodsham][293] and my self took this shop for six months we were prosperd in it and by spring i was prepard to go west although not in affluent circumstances we started from St Louis on the 25 day of March 1848 on the Edward bates Steamer bound for Keokuk we arrived ere on the 27 we were met by brother Griffiths with a team to remove us to his house my wife was taken Sick through exposure on the river with the chills and fever we started from Keokuk in a few hours, we traveld about twelve miles and then camp for the night within a few miles of Nauvoo in the night the horses broke loose and started for hom a distance of about twenty miles Brother Griffiths followd them and returnd about ten o clock the next night the next morning we proceeded my wife being very sick we breakfasted at charleston and then proceeded. arriving at brother Griffiths in

---

293. James Frodsham, like Charles Smith, was a watchmaker by trade. James Frodsham continued in the business of watchmaking in Salt Lake City and later in Provo, Utah.

the evening. in a few days my wife got well i then began to make preperations to go westward i purchasd a yoke of cattle and a cow and on the eight of April started i got brother Griffiths to assist me through the woods, when within a mile of reaching the prairie one hind wheel gave way breaking three or four spokes i concluded to have a new wheel made, brother Griffiths returnd to Bonaparte with the wheel this detained us until monday having got all ready we started again brother Griffiths when [went] with us about a mile we then bad him farewell, to give all the details of this journey would be all most superfluous but i would say that breaking down and mud holes in which we were stuck became almost an every day occurrence when i arrived at pisgah i had another new wheel made i also staid ere four days to recruit my cattle we then traveld on to winter quarters

Joseph Fielding and his sisters were among the earliest members of the Church and the most loyal. Joseph Fielding was one of the first missionaries to open the field in the British Isles in 1837, where he also served as president of the mission. He took full responsibility for his two widowed sisters' removal from Nauvoo, though finding sufficient means to provide for his own family was a struggle and the reason for their late August departure from Nauvoo.

JOSEPH FIELDING[294]

JAN. 29, [18]46 Last Eve called at the Temple. Many were receiving their Endowment, and Numbers waiting to be sealed; all things dark around us. It is generally expected the County is to be put under Martial Law. Affidavits have been made at Washington by Rigdon, or William Smith and Adams, or all, that we intend to go and bring on the Indians against the Government, and the Design is to prevent our going by putting us under Martial Law and to hem us in on all Sides, and then to torment us with Writs, etc. It is hard to think of our Brethren leaving us while is going so well, especially in the Temple.

Feb. 18 For about the last 2 Weeks the Saints have been busily crossing the River Mississippi with their Waggons, etc., and having a great deal of Public Property, such as Cannons, Guns and other Weapons, and Ammunition Printing Press and other Mechanical and farming Implements, and the Church Records, etc., Seed Spring Wheat, also intending, if possible, to put it into the Ground in the Spring. These, with a suitable Supply of Provisions, at least as far possible for such an unknown Journey, have taken all the Teams that could be mustered, both Horses and Oxen. suppose they have over 200 Teams, they cross the River in Flat Boats. They have about 1 1/2 Mile to go on the Water and it is hard Work to row them across the Stream. The Wind has often been too strong for them, and they were obliged to wait. I suppose by this time they are all on the other Side.

6 Days ago I went over to see the Camp, which is 5 or 6 Miles from the River. The Camp Ground is by Sugar Creek where they

---

294. Diary of Joseph Fielding, holograph, LDS Church Archives.

have plenty of Wood and Water; a good Place for such a Purpose. On the Night of the 13th the Snow fell and covered the Ground, and the 14th was a very Rough Day, snowing all the Day long. I felt much for them. Some had Tents and some Waggon Covers, and some, neither of them. This Day is also rough, snowing all the Day from the North, but it is not very cold. When I think that Men, with some Women and Children, should be so exposed

The Camp travailed slowly, the [road] being bad and Weather rough and cold, sometimes having to put 8 or 10 yoke of Oxen to a Waggon till they came to what they called Garden Grove, about ___ Miles from Nauvoo, where they commenced ploughing and planting; and after staying there a While the greater Part of them moved on, a Distance of ___ Miles, where they arrived in time to put in other Crops, some of which came to Perfection, but some did not. They fenced in a large Field, having Grand River as a Fence on the West Side; this Place they [called] Pisgah. Both of these Places seem to have been very sickly and have proved to be the Home of many of the Saints; many of them are there mingled with the Dust, before they had time to reap the fruit of their Labours, the main Part of the Camp again moved westward till they crossed the Missouri River, about 3 miles, from which the[y] encamped and went to work at getting Hay for the winter, and in the Fall of the Year they moved on to the Bank of the River. They had been compelled to barter their Property, Horses, Harness, Beds and Cloathing, etc. to the Missourians for Provision, and made great Sacrifices. Brother Samuel Bent was left as President in Garden Grove and Brother Charles C. Rich in Pisgah, but during the Summer the former was called home,[295] having done his Work, I believe, to the satisfaction of all the Saints. He had long been President of the High

---

295. Samuel Bent, presiding elder at Garden Grove, died 16 August 1846.

Council, and the Latter was General of the Nauvoo Legion: a Man of unblemished Caracture.

But to return to Nauvoo where I spent the Summer for want of Means to get away. I sold my House and 20 Acres of Land for 200 Dols in Trade, taking 2 Horses, a Waggon, a Coat Cloth, and a few (4 1/2 Dol) in Cash. The Land was in good Cultivation; 120 Rods of good Rail Fence; a Frame House 16 feet by 24 filled in with Bricks; a pretty Garden; a Number of Apple Trees and Peach Trees just ready to bear Fruit; and an excellent Well 21 feet deep, not 2 Miles from the Temple. I paid for the Land in its wild State 160 Dol's, built the House, etc., so that the Price of the whole would not near pay the cost One of the Horses I took for the Place I soon found to be bauky, and I only got in trade for her a small yoke of young Oxen.

The last Harvest we had in Nauvoo was uncommonly great, the Land in general bringing forth in abundance as much as 60 Bushels of Corn to the Acre. I had about 600 Bus. on 10 Acres; in short, the whole Place was as the Garden of the Lord for fruitfulness. This was, of Course, a great Blessing to the Saints, but still it made the Sacrifice appear the greater. Soon after, I sold my Place I removed my Family and goods to the House on my Sister's Farm, called Brother Hyrum's, where my Sister thought of planting some Grain, but we found it to be useless, and I did not so much as plant the smallest Garden Stuff.

The Enemies all around were breathing out threatenings against the Saints, till at one time, as eight Men were reaping Wheat for the Members of the Church (Siros Davis), about 12 Miles from Nauvoo, a Company of about 80 armed in Carriages and on Horses came upon them, took them one by one a short Distance to the Place where one of their Friends had been killed the year before, and they supposed, of Course the Saints had killed him, and there gave each of them a severe whipping, took some of their Guns off and broke others of them. The Eight made the best of their Way to Nauvoo, and as soon as they had made the matter known, the new Citizens, (they being the Officers of the City) in union with the Saints, determined at once to endeavour to bring the Ring leaders of the Mob to Justice, and the next Day towards Evening a Posse left Nauvoo, and went to the House of Captain McCalla[296] in the Night and took him and 2 others and a gun which they found in his House which they had taken from the Eight Men, and brought them home to Nauvoo to take their Trial. But in a few Days we were informed that the Mob had kidnapped 4 of our Brethren and one of the New Citizens, 5 in all, and that they had them in a Place called Pontusuck [Pontoosac], 14 Miles off.

The Sunday after, about 50 Horse and foot Men, armed, formed a Posse left Nauvoo in the Evening, traveled in the Night and came to Pontusuck by Day-Light in the Morning; I was one of them. The first thing we saw was a couple of Mounted Men as a Picket Guard. Some of our Party chased them for some Distance. One of them sprang through the Brush and got into the Field, but the other they pursued and overtook him. He said there were about as many of them together in the Village as there were of us. A little before we came to the Place we saw Men's Heads starting up in the Brush wood on the Side of the Road, and we could not tell how many there might be concealed. We halted, and Brother Wm. Anderson, the Captain of the Posse, called out and told them his Authority, that he had been legally authorized and sent with a Posse to apprehend such as were not subject to Law.

We had been very private about coming to this Place, but still our Coming was expected there, and just as we got to the Village we were in loud voices commanded to halt, and we beheld a Body of Men partly concealed in the Brush. Some of the foremost of them called out to us to halt or they would instantly fire upon us;

296. Probably John McCauly, an anti-Mormon leader.

we were then within gunshot of them. Each of us had his gun cocked and ready to return the Fire if they fire, but Wm. Cutler, one of our Captains, told them our Authority, etc., and no gun was fired. Some of them were very mad and swore bitterly, and we began taking some of them Prisoners, and finally we took 14 of them, and after searching several of the Houses to find the Captives, we brought them to Nauvoo. On the Way, we were joined by a small Company who had left Nauvoo in the Morning to come to our Assistance if we should need it. We brought them [to] Nauvoo, and there was some Rejoicing in the City.

The next Day we went off in a Posse in Search of the five Captives, and that Night we Slept on the open Prairy. The Night was cold, and we had nothing to cover us, or but little. At one the next Morning we started, divided into two Companies, and searched several Houses to find, if possible, either the Captives or those that took, but the former were taken off by those that held them for fear we should find them. At the time we went to Pontusuck they had them within hearing of us, a little out of the Village, but on finding that we were there they marched them off, but we found their Stuff: a double horse Waggon containing Flour, etc. belonging to Phineas Young, who was on his way home from the Mill, and a Buggy. These we took home. The Names of the Captives were Phineas Young, and Brigham, his Son, James Standing, [Richard] Balentine, and—

When we thus went out in a Posse it put all of them [in] fear, and we could scarcely find a Man at his home by Day or by Night. We did not return home till Saturday Eve, but our Labor was in vain. The Mob Party took every way they could to deceive us and lead us on the wrong track. As we learned afterwards, they were taken from Place to Place every Day through the woods, etc., having eight Men to guard them, who hurried through the woods, some of them being sick with Ague, but they were often told that if they faultered or stopt they would instantly shoot them. Several times they had fixt a time and Place to do it, and were on the

Point of it, but were prevented through fear, through the Mercy of God. We searched for them all this week and most of the next Week, going as far as 30 or more Miles, some times going all Night, and sometimes but little to eat. Our Horses were much reduced, and we were weary. This was just in Wheat Harvest, and so were the People in fear of us that many large fields of Wheat were destroyed for want of cutting, for the[y] durst not be seen, but some of them said they would wait upon after Harvest.

After being in Captivity over 2 Weeks they all returned safely home, being let go by a fresh guard to whom they had been committed til the old ones attended a Meeting in Carthage. They were gladly received home to their Wives and Friends; indeed it was far more than we expected, ever to see them again.

Not long after this the Mob began to collect and to threaten us with destruction; first at Goldings [Golden's] Point to the Number of 200 or 300, from whence they dispersed through fear, but soon began to gather again near Carthage where they lay encamped a number of Weeks to the No. of 900, as far as I can gather until early in September they marched into Nauvoo. My two Sisters, [Mary Fielding] Smith and [Mercy] Thompson, and myself with our Families had just got over the River (Mississippi) with all our goods except two Boat Loads before they came in Contact with the Citizens. They came and encamped on the Farm that I had just left. They took this course to avoid any ambushment that might be laid for them. From there they sent Balls into the City, but before they came near the Temple they were met and repulsed, but I shall not attempt to record the whole of Scene of outrage. The poor Saints had to flee, sick or well. They hastened to River, but the Citizens judged it not best to let men leave when they were so much needed, but the Sick, the Women and Children got over as fast as they could. I went down to the Bank of the River, and found many of the Saints in distress. Some had left their goods and were destitute of Food and Clothing. Others had left their Husbands in the Battle.

The Cannons roared tremendously on both sides for several Days, but Mob as it seems to found themselves losers and Plan was got up to prevent their own destruction. A Committee came from Quincy, professing to be Friends to both Sides, and Proposed to put a stop to the fighting on terms which the Saints thought it best to accept, as the Mob increased daily, and they, the few Saints, (I suppose not more in number than 150) were almost forsaken of the new Citizens. The Number slain of the Mob is not well known, but it is probable that 150 fell in Battle, and altho their number was so great and that of the Saints so small, the former said to be not less than 1100, yet but three of the Saints were slain, Brother [William] Anderson and his Son [Augustus Leander] and a Brother Norris; this is truly surprising.

The terms of Peace were, of course, such as would suit the Mob, and as soon as the Saints had agreed to lay down their Arms, they had to flee, but many of their arms were taken from them. The Mob found themselves in Possession of the City, and they proceeded to capture, rob and plunder in the most fiend like and unlawful manner. They rendivouzed in the Temple. We had guarded it by Night and Day a long time, feeling unwilling to leave it in their Hands, but they now had it to themselves. They even Preached in it and cursed the Saints, but did no great Damage to it, thinking it would add to the Value of their Property. They treated the Saints with various kinds of indignity. Some they pushed over the River in haste; some they took and tried; some they baptised, etc., but in the midst of this some more humane from Quincy brout up a quantity of Clothing and Provision for the Poor as they got over the River, where the Poor Saints were in great numbers. Here also the Lord sent upon them, as it were, a Shower of Quails. They came in vast Flocks. Many came into the Houses were the Saints were, settled on the tables and the floor, and even on their Laps, so that they caught as many as they pleased. Thus the Lord was mindful of his people, and it was truly a Matter of astonishment that in all this Persecution, etc. only 3 of our Brethren lost their Lives.

The Trustees still stayed in the City, (viz) John T. Fulmer, Alman Babbit, and Joseph L. Heywood. As soon as this unlawful Proceeding was staid, we (my Sisters and myself) started on the Way to the Camp of the Saints, having 9 Waggons, 6 of them Sister Smith's, 1 Sister Thompson's, and 2 of my own. In Sis Smith's Family 6 Men, 5 Women, besides one Sister that came with her 4 Children; Sis Thompson, one little girl; in my Family 2 Men, 2 Women and 5 Children; and we had together besides our Teams, 21 loose Cattle, as Cows, etc., 43 Sheep, but the Sheep soon began to diminish. We found it difficult to keep them in Sight; some times we have had to seek them 2 or 3 Days, which hindered in traveling by so much

Much of the Road at the first was through the Woods and thick underbrush was on each Side of the Road, and it was difficult to drive our Cattle. Some of the Brethren lost a many on the Way, but with great care we did not lose any but a young Calf or 2. At Bonapart we bought Flour, etc., which was the last Market we found.

Soon after we left this Place, about 40 Miles on the Way, Brother E. Cliff, one of Sister Smith's Men, accidenally shot off his Thumb, and we had to send for a Doctor to take it off. Sis S. labored hard, and her Men were slothful. She might cook for and serve them, and then gather together the Cattle while they stood by the Fire, but J[ames]. Lawson was a blessing to her; he was very diligent.

But we got on our Way as well as could be expected, Sis Smith and Sis Thompson often several Miles a Day, driving the Cattle. My Women had each a young Child, and they in general managed the Team of Horses that they road with, before we got to journeys end the Weather became cold and the Nights frosty so

that the Grass was killed and as our Corn was spent our Horses
began to fail one of mine became lame in her Shoulder so as to
Disable [her] for Work, and it was so much the harder on the
Cattle and the other horse[s] we came within 10 or 12 Miles of
Garden Grove - the first Camp, passed through Pisgah the 2nd
Camp. It is by no means a handsome or a healthy Place many of
the Saints had died their and, the People there look pale and
sickly much of the Corn planted there was too late to ripen we
tried to buy some Corn but no one had any to sell but Brother
Charles C. Rich gave Sister Smith a Bushel or 2 of green Corn
and some Pumpkins of these we all shared Sister Th was very lib-
eral

as we came within about 20 M's of the Camp we found
Brethren who had settled in choice Spots for Water Wood and
feed for Cattle They generally tried to discourage us from coming on they said it was sickly by the Camp that there was no Wood
but what they fetched several Miles the Indians were killing the
Cattle, some said 2 some 7 and the last Report was 15 in a Day.
We found the fact was that many of these Men had some Property
and did not wish to go to the Camp, and of course were willing to
believe or raise an evil Report to justify themselves for not going
to the Camp some thought we had better go and find out the
Truth about it before we took our Stuff over but we felt no desire
to stop short of the Camp we had seen such things before We
crossed the River and came to the Camp on the [unfinished]

Brother H. C. Kimball kindly sent a young Man to drive up
the Cattle and had [them] put into his own yard, it was dark
before got to the Camp, the Light of the Camp of the Saints as
we saw the Lights at a Distance was very interesting, it reminded
us of Israel of old in the Wilderness this was not long after the
Saints removed to the River there ~~was~~ were but a few houses
nearly all were in their Tents upon about a square half Mile, we
were conducted to Brother Kimball's stopped by his house for
the Night and the next Day he took us to the Place reserved for us

where we also pitched our Tents and the next thing was to obtain Food for our Cattle our Horses especially had become feeble, and we were too late to cut Hay, the grass was killed by the Frost, & Sis. S was advised to send them to an Island some 8 Miles off the Camp and we took them all there but one which one strad [strayed] off a short distance and was found dead in a Creek where she had got mired, and when we went to see the others we found 2 of them in the same Case one of my Sisters and one of mine so we brought them home and bought Hay for them the main part of the Oxen and Cows we sent off about 20 Miles to feed on Rushes, etc reserving 2 Yoke at home to get Logs to build our Houses by Council we put the Sheep into the general Flock the 12 engaging to furnish half the Number over the Mountains, but as soon as the winter came on and it was no longer any use to take them onto the Prairy [prairie] and they had to live on Hay and some little Corn Flock, which numbered 1400 began to die and it was found that they could not be sustained and we were advised to take them home having lost 5 there but they still kept dying, so that before the Winter was over we had but 18 left of the 43 that we started with. I had on leaving Nauvoo 1 Pair of Horses and 2 yoke of Oxen but long ere the end of the Winter 1 Horse and 2 odd Oxen had died so I had an odd Horse and 2 odd Oxen, several of Sister Thompson's Cows and Oxen died not yet ascertained how many, Sister Smith also lost 2 good Mares, 1 young Colt and it [is] supposed 1 or more Oxen besides the Sheep which belonged to us all,

I had but little Provision to begin the Winter I labored hard to get Sis Smith a House built, we drew the logs about 1 1/2 miles first built a double House each end being 16 feet by 16, put on Clapboards and then laid Sods over them to keep out both the Cold and the Rain we also built [Sister] Thompson a Room by setting up Poles in a slanting form, and then cover[ing] them with Earth, and my own House of Logs 14 feet by 16 with Clapboards and Sods on the Roof the Fall of the Year was very fine and pleasant and it was a blessing for the Saints, as it was late before we got our houses up, I was much troubled with Diarea [diarrhea] which made me very weak and my work was a Burden to me and as my Sister's Men were not the most active we seemed to move slowly. I suppose [I] earned something of my Sister S but she as well as Sister T assisted me far more than what I had any Claim on her for She had some little Money and she let it go for Corn and Hay for the Cattle and Flour, etc. the Lord Reward her for her kindness, Brother T. Cotham who lives with us labored for Wages to help to supply our Family and is now in Missouri for that Purpose, but has been sick and lame most of the time he has been off, the Saints have been sustained here better than could have been expected The whole Camp is divided into Wards 22 and one over the River over each Ward is a Bishop with 2 Councilors. The Saints are tythed and the Tything is applied to the Relief of the Poor, by this Means the Poor have been furnished with Financing etc. and I suppose the Bishops have generally been faithful in taking care of the Poor I myself was made a Councillor to Bro. Rolf of the 13th Ward who judged that with my Family and my 2 widow'd Sisters with whom also were 3 other Widows, if we provided for ourselves we should be free from paying another tithing. I have had a great desire to earn something, but while there was Work to do at house-building etc I had enough to do for myself and my Sisters in building our Houses and in fencing in yards for the Cattle and fetching Hay etc and when I could have labored for Provision[s], there was nothing to do, but still I always have been strong and it is a fact that I always [have] been at work. I have lived bare, with my Family my Children have worn out their Clothes and the Prospect of getting more is bad, but we have had our Health in general and I have felt no disposition to complain, but think that all has been done for the best, we have the Kingdom of God among [us] and no one can take it from us we must take it to a Place where we can establish it and execute its Laws, which could not be done in the Midst of the Gentiles, and I suppose if we could have staid in peace in Nauvoo many of the Church would have remained there weather the Kingdom had been set up or not, as to hard times it is nothing strange for I said 2 years ago that I expected things would be as hard as we could bear them, we are now just stepping over the threshold into the Kingdom, the Gate is too strait for some and they turn back, it is indeed a time of trial to the Saints, if it were not so many would go into the Kingdom that are not fit for it So I feel satisfied, and say it is all right, about the beginning of Feb-47 President Brigham Young had a remarkable Dream, one Morning, he said [he] was taken sick and the Pains of Death seized him and as he told us he died and his Spirit left the Body, his Wife watched him for a While till he returned again to Life, she said that as he was returned to [life] he exclaimed "I have been with Joseph and Hyrum it is hard to come back to life again" the next Day he dreamed that he saw and talked with Joseph, he was sitting in a large Room, sitting by the Window. Bro. Y[oung] went to him shook Hands with [him] and kissed him many times, told him how anxious the People of the Church were to see him or to hear something from him particularly with respect to sealing Power Joseph began to preach to him told him to tell the Saints to give diligent heed to the Whispers of the good Spirit, he said they might know the good Spirit for it always produced Peace, Joy and Gladness, he said, tell them to get the Spirit this he said with great feeling and earnestness, tell the People to get the Spirit and not to rest without it, and to keep it, they should have their Hearts open to any Spirit, so that they might try them if they shut their hearts against what was presented to them they would be in danger of shutting out the good Spirit. if they received whatever was presented to them they would know the true Spirit by its fruits Brother Young [asked] if he might not come to him they had had many happy Days together and why could they not again, he said he could not come to him at Present but must go back for a Season, but it was all right, it was all right. this question and answer were repeated he told him he should come to him after a While but it was all just right, he talked for some time, and finally told him that as to the Sealing Power etc they should understand all about it he said they would stand just according to their original Organization before they took their Tabernacles shew'd him how they stood in regular Order, and they stand the same again in the End, and as Bro. Young left him he seemed to pass through some thick Darkness. Bro. Y[oung] told this at several times, he said he knew it was from the Lord through Joseph. I was much pleased at this it was very seasonable.

In April a Company of about 140 with Horse and Mule Teams [left] the Camp of Winter quarters, for the Mountains A journey of 1000 or 1100 Miles, this they performed in great Peace & union there were with them of the 12, B. Young, H. C. Kimball, O. Pratt, W. Woodruff, W. Richards, G. A. Smith, A. Lyman. they took but few Women, intending to return before the next Winter they went out like Abraham of old not knowing the Place of their Location but trusted in God to direct them, they were greatly blessed on their Way and on their return to the Camp in November not one of their Company had died, they got to the Place of Location on the [24th] of [July] and commenced at once to lay out a City etc planted about 100 Acres of Grain and left Corn several feet high about the middle of August to return to their Families they reached home on the of November they had been much hindered by having 49 of their Horses and Mules taken by the Sioux Indians this laid so heavy a Burden on the rest that they tired and for [a] great distance they had to lift them some of them up when they laid down, one or two came on and sent off a Company with Horses and Provision to meet them they traveled 250 Miles and were as they said as Angels of God to them they brought along all the Horses etc they had they lost none but what were stolen, but both horses and Men [were] weary and faint but there was great Joy in the Camp on their arrival.

In June, another Company left the Camp 566 Wagons 2600 Souls P. P. Pratt and John Taylor of the 12 being at the Head, my Sister Thompson and her little girl were among them, we felt great Anxiety for this Company it was great, the Weather hot, the Loads heavy and the Country full of Indians of whom it had been reported, credibly, that they had a little before robbed the Oregon Company and caused them much trouble and Loss, so great was my Anxiety that I could scarcely sleep some of the Brethren in the Camp also had the same [trouble] as Joseph Young and others and at one time it was proposed to send off Bro. Hosea Stout with a Company as many as could be spared to be as a guard[297] but it was overruled by the Idea that we at the Camp stood in as great [a] need of a Guard as they did, and we felt to leave them in the Hand of the Lord, daily bearing them up in prayer before him, but it was not many Weeks before we got Letters from them dated 400 Miles on the Way, which they had gone in 4 Weeks they had lost only one they had no Sickness and as little Difficulty as possibly could be, so our fears were laid aside and we praised the Lord for his Goodness and for his wonderful Works to the Children of Men we afterwards received other Letters containing the same good News all things went well with them excepting the Loss of some of Bro. J[edediah]. M. Grant's Company's Oxen, the Pioneer Company waited as long as they thought it prudent for fear of the Winter but they left the Valey before the others got in and met them Miles on this side but supposed they would get in before the Cold would become severe, so that co[n]sidering all the dealing of God with them all,

---

297. Hosea Stout was then serving at the head of a unit of men selected to protect the Missouri encampment against marauding Indians as well as to police it from internal infractions of camp rules.

we felt to give thanks to the Lord with all our Hearts, he has done all things well.

After the Return of the 12, it was determined that a number of the Elders should go out into the States and to England During the Summer we in the Camp have been diligent in cultivating the Ground, raising Corn. Buckwheat Potatoes etc, it was late in the Season before we began but the Lord greatly blest our Labors, so that we have I suppose plenty of Produce, with Hay for Man and Beast for the Winter and some to take us to the Mountains, ploughing up the Sod, fencing it in, having our Food to fetch from Missouri, the Hearding [herding] of our Cattle, and guarding the Camp from the Indians etc has kept us very strong. but I do not complain though some have done, I view all the Tribulation[s] of the Church and conclude that it is no more than might be expected in such a Conflict as is now going on between Satan and the Almighty, the World has to be redeemed out of the hands of the Wicked One and to be brought back to its proper and rightful Owner, he will not give it up without a mighty Struggle to hold it, and I expect it will cost a great amount of Labor, Pain, and even Blood to accomplish it, but the work is going on if it be slowly.

As to myself, I feel strong in the Faith, more and more so, and I have great Joy in the Lord I feel a Measure of his Spirit, I am a Subject of his Kingdom and I desire I think above all things to see and aid in the Rolling on of this great Work I still hold a Place in the Council of Fifty,[298] and have done from its first Organisation by Joseph Smith, and have resently been chosen one of the High Council, the Quorum of High Priests have lately been called together under the Presidency of Bishop N[ewel]. K. W[h]itney for the time being in the Place of Brother George

298. The Council of Fifty was formed in Nauvoo in 1844 by Joseph Smith. It functioned under the First Presidency and Council of the Twelve. Although its members were not required to be members of the Church, they were required to be God-fearing men and to seek to know God's will.

Miller, who has left us and is gone off I suppose [to] join Lyman Wite [Wight] in Texas,[299] the Church still hoping that he will see his Error and return to the Fold he was dear to me in the Office he held, he was indeed a fine Man, and I hope to see him again in our Midst. The 70's also meet often under the Guardian Care of Joseph Young,[300] who is a good Man. I believe the 12 are striving to act as Fathers to the Church as far as possible, but most of them have large Families to take Care of with their Sealed and adopted ones, I suppose they might lawfully claim their Support from the Tything of the People, but they do not seem to do it, their Boys as they call them [have] been farming together while they have been to the Mountains and the fruit of their Labor is their chief Support, President Brigham Young sets himself to magnify his Office and Calling, and to fill the Place of Joseph there are already I suppose near 3000 Souls in the Valey of the great Salt Lake and according to the last Reports, made by some of the Soldiers of the Saints arrived from California about a Week ago, it is likely they will suffer some for lack of Food before they can produce more, but there they are, shut in by the Mountains they cannot get out nor can any get into them, so they are in the hand of God, we hope that Game will come into the Valey in the Winter if not, they may have to kill their Cattle, I suppose they have near 3000 Head of them, Cows and Oxen no doubt Bro's P. P. Pratt and John Taylor will find it quite a Work to keep all thing[s] straight, may the Lord give them Wisdom, and let his Spirit rest upon all the People there.

The Soldiers who went to California and have returned have had a hard time of it, some had to eat their Mules, and even the rawhides, grass etc yet they have come from the Valey in less than

---

299. George Miller, baptized in 1839, was an active member of the Church until 1847 when he refused to follow Brigham Young, instead leaving the main body of the Saints to join Lyman Wight in Texas. He eventually became a member of the Strangite organization, a splinter group formed by James J. Strang shortly after the martyrdom of the Prophet Joseph Smith.

300. Joseph Young was the elder brother of Brigham Young.

2 Months they have brought us (me and my Sister) [news] that my Sister Thompson has got married to Bro. James Lawson this has been done without my council or consent and is against my Mind, but I shall be sorry if she should be a Loser by it to any amount.

It is now Christmas Day the 25th of December 1847 My Family consists of myself two Women and five Children, having buried two Male Infants in the Fall Hyrum T. on the 4 of August and John on the 16 of September[301] (i.e.) they died on those Days, they were buried in one Grave here at Winter Quarters.

My Work at Present is to get Wood for Fuel for my Family and Sister Smith's I do what I can to make my Family comfortable and if there were more Faith in them they might be so, but one has but little of the true Principle of Faith and at least questions some of the Doctrines of the Church, so that my Family are not one I feel a Need of more Wisdom, that I may act my Part aright, I wish not to lower the Priesthood, which I hold, and I am sorry to grieve my Wife my Daily prayer is that God may give me Wisdom to do right, and that he may forgive me if I err perhaps if I had perfect Peace at Home I should not be willing to leave it to go out into the World as I expect before long to be called to do, so I will try to bear it as a necessary Evil I have not heard from my Relations this long time, it seems of no use for me to write to them and I suppose they think the same on the other hand.[302]

We as a People have been preserved here in Peace through the last Summer, and by keeping Men on Guard constantly have not suffered from Indians to any great amount, but this has been much against the Minds of some, it is plain that nothing but the strictest Laws [must be] enforced with what some call rigor altogether considered by many in the Camp oppressive and has been

---

301. Hyrum Thomas was the son of Joseph Fielding's first wife, Hannah Greenwood, and John Hyrum was the son of his plural wife, Mary Ann Peake.

302. He and his sisters maintained a correspondence relationship with their siblings in England.

a Source of much Evil and hard feeling, yet if we had not had such Laws a great Part of our Corn etc. would have been destroyed. some of the Police would at times give way to Passion, and would swear like Blackguards and this would give to those that [did] it accution [accusation?] against them I have heard them call their Brethren, who held the sacred Priesthood, damned infernal Liars etc the Office of Policeman is no desirable one if there be any rough ones, they have to deal with them, and they are likely enough to be rough too the Captain of the Police is Hosea Stout he is a Man of Experience and as I think a good Man for his Place we have also had a daily Guard of from 5 to 10 Mounted Men to be on the watch against the Indians, and to see if the Cattle went astray

1849 Feb 4th It is now more than a year since I wrote any in my Journal, while in Winter Quarters I lost three Oxen out [of] Four, and one of two Horses, almost all my Sheep once I hurt my Toe so that I could not get my Shoe on for some Weeks once I was thrown down and my Side was hurt so that I could hardly attend to my Business and once I bruised my Finger and about the Month of February I had a severe Sickness, what is called Chil[ls] and Fever, and my Life seemed in danger but through the goodness of God and the great Faithfulness of my Family I was restored to Health in a few Weeks, at one time also while there I was nearly crippled with the Skurvy, a Complaint which prevailed much among the Saints there it appeared in small dark Specks on the lower Parts of the Body, and contracting the Sinews of the Legs, so that they could not be straightened,

At the close of the last Winter I commenced repairing my Sister's Waggons etc to prepare her for her Journey to the Valey, but as I saw no possibility of going myself I bought the Improvement of five Acres of Land, and sowed it with S [spring] Wheat, but still felt a desire to go if the Way should open, and as I was a Member of the Council I was advised by Bro. H. C. Kimball to try and make a Start, I sold my Claim, borrowed some Corn and did my best for Starting, but both my Sister and myself found it very difficult to get off A great Part of our Teams was made up [of] Cows and young Oxen that had not been broke and we were obliged to fix two Waggons together for lack of Leaders and Drivers, Bro. Terry, who had [been] engaged to drive a Team to the Valey and to bring one back to take his own Family, was quite discouraged, and said it was great Folly to attempt to go as we were fixt

We left Winter Quarters on Sunday the 4th of June being about the last. Bro. Kimball's Company was waiting for us at the Elk Horn River some 25 Miles when we had got about half the distance there we received from Bro. Egan 2 Yoke of Oxen through the Influence of Brother Kimball, and we joined the Company on Tuesday Evening and the next morning the Co. started, we seemed to improve in our traveling, and our Cattle improved in their Condition untill we crossed the Platte River, we overtook Bro. B. Young's Company at the Loup-Fork, and it was an interesting Sight when to behold in the Morning a String of Oxen reaching from one Side of the River to the other about a Mile, from Brigham's Co. coming to assist us in crossing, for the Waggons sunk into the Sand, and it was hard drawing for the Cattle so we put our Cattle to our Waggons and put an extra Team to each and got through well, it was indeed an interesting Sight, you might have taken us for two Armies encamped on either Side of the River waiting the Signal for Conflict but how different was the Case when we saw almost the Whole Strength of one, wading through the River from one to 3 feet in depth to help their Friends here we stayed over Sunday as I did not keep a Journal, I cannot now give any detail of the long and laborious Journey, Brother Young's Co. went ahead, so we in all formed two Companies each Co. being organised into 50 and 10 C[ornelius]. P. Lot was our Captain of 10, and John Park of 50, Henry Herriman of the 100, with Bro. Kimball at the Head, but when the Feed began to fail we were separated into Fifties and finally into tens, as the feed for our Cattle was very short and each 10 had to do the best they could, and we could travel but short journeys Per Day and some times it was judged necessary to rest our Cattle for several Days, we crossed the Platte River about __ Miles below Fort Laramie from which time we had but little good feed and the Road was much worse, it is wonderful to see the Buffalo and the Marks of them, for several hundred Miles the Prairie is covered with their Dung, from which one is sure there must be Thousands of them our Companies shot many of them we ate freely of the Flesh and also dried great quantities and brought [it] on to the Valey

[Over] a great Part of the Road the ground is partly covered with Salaratus or Salt-Petre which is very injurious to the Oxen as they eat it freely, owing to this many fine Oxen died in fact you cannot go far on the Road but you see the Carcase [carcass] or the Bones of Cattle, at one Place we came to large Beds of Salaratus where almost every Family gathered as much as they wished to carry I and my Family got from one to two Bushels in some Places the Road is sandy and is hard upon the Cattle especially when the Weather is hot and dry, we sometimes had to ascend Mountains of Sand, several times the Companies received fresh Cattle from the Valey which in our Situation was very acceptable we saw but few Indians, and they were quite friendly I never heard of them taking any of our Cattle

We cross[ed] the Loup Fork (but first the Elkhorn a small Stream), the Platte about a Mile across the Laramie Fork, and then the Platte again at the last Place it [is] quite narrow, we also had to ford several small [rivers] viez the Green River, the Bear River and the Weber River besides many Creeks great and Small. We found some frost in the Mornings early in September, but as we came near the Valey the Weather became warmer although the Snow lay on the Top of the Mountains, and in the Valley there had been no frost in the middle of October the last 40 or 50 Miles the Road is shocking bad, in short I wonder that so little Damage was sustained, it seems a Wonder that any Waggon can stand it, one Creek we have to cross 17 times, but after all, we came safely into the valley on the evening of the __ of October we found our Friends well, and the whole People here seemed to rejoice, but we had [been] about four Months on the Way this was in some Measure owing to the bad Feed and the sickliness of our Cattle, we did not find as much Grain here as we expected, they had generally planted rather late, and the Crickets had destroyed a great deal of the Corn, Wheat etc, but still the Saints here seemed to be generally in good Spirits believing that the Land here will produce plenty of Grain, etc though the last Season they labored hard for a little, they believed that they would know better how to manage the land here another Year as to watering, and also by having their farming Land more compact, they hoped to avoid the Crickets I was surprised to see the Work they had done in Ploughing, Planting and Fencing, and I thought that altho we did not find the Crops of Grain as good as had been represented, yet there would be enough for all that were here, but as the Corn was planted rather late, or, that which was planted early was cut off by the Frost the Summer was too short, so that the Corn did not ripen, many of the Beans also were killed before they got ripe, and much of the Buck Wheat came out very light, so that it was evident that there would be little enough for the Inhabitants, and the Price of Produce rose high, During the Fall many were busily employed in making Adobies, and in getting Timber to build on their City Lotts, and some few got their Houses built, but fewer of them got the Roofs on, for the Winter came on and caught them in all Stages of building. I could not make Adobies on account of a sore Finger which troubled me a long time but I got Logs from the Cannion gave one fourth for sawing and so got up the Walls of my House but could not get Boards sawed for the Roof, so I spread the Tent over the House and so passed the Winter, the Tent I had borrowed for a Week or two but we were compelled to keep it at least 4 Months, the Ground being covered with Snow about 12 Weeks, this length of Winter was very unexpected, and took us by Surprise and unprepared, and in fact it has been a time of much Suffering to the Saints in the Valey about the end of January the Council caused to be ascertained the Amount of Provision, (i.e.) what we call Bread Stuf, but it was more than was feared, nearly one Pound per Head till the 9th of July, I myself and my Family seem to have lived by Faith yet we have not suffered much for lack of Food and as my Lot of Land is mostly covered with Wood, we have not wanted for Firing so that we are truly thankful, we have had health and Peace and on the 7 of January [1849] A Daughter was born to me of Mary-Ann which we call Josephine all went well with Mother and Child and it was really pleasing to notice that no one could tell by the Conduct of the two Mothers which was its Mother but we have been much exposed to Cold and sometimes to Rain, I suppose it is owing to this that my Wife Hannah has for some Weeks been much troubled with Rheumatism but we live in hope of being better off our Children have gone barefoot almost entirely, through a long and severe Winter, and many times have I been grieved to see their naked Feet in the Snow, and many a Cry have they had, I have fetched [and] took my Bread Stuff in Corn chiefly on my Shoulder 2 Miles to Mill and in the latter part of the Winter I have had Corn of my Sister Mary Smith by the Bushel, but at this time it is likely I can have no more, we have also had a few Bus. of Wheat in the same way, which I intend to return to her with Interest.

It is now the 11th of March, and the Ground is covered with Snow, and Snow is falling. There is no sign of Spring. The Cows and the Cattle are poor, and many of the Saints find it very difficult to draw their Fuel with their Oxen. The Wolves have killed some few, but not so many as last year. The Indians have killed from 12 to 20 Cows and Oxen. Near 2 Weeks ago a Company of 25 of our Brethren were sent by the President of the Church to get back, if possible, some Horses and Cattle taken by the Indians of the Eutaw Valley. They found 13 Skins, and killed four of the Indians. This was [under] the Direction of the President. They had killed 17 of our Cattle last Year, making in all, 30 head.

2

"We'll
Find the
Place"

INTER HAD NOT BEEN KIND TO THE exiled Saints scattered from Garden Grove to Winter Quarters. Too little nourishing food, too little protection from the harsh weather, and too much disease and death held the refugee camps in a tight grip of misery and discouragement. "It is a growling, grumbling, devilish, sickly time with us now," Eliza R. Snow complained.[1] There were some who had had enough. Like Nauvoo, Winter Quarters and the difficult trail leading to it had proved to be places of sifting, a crossroads of faith in Brigham Young and in the mission of the Church. But Brother Brigham was not troubled. Those who would follow him were "under the influence of the spirit of gathering," like John Dart and his family, for whom "the counsel of church leaders had molded their lives."[2] Brigham Young

1. Eliza Roxcy Snow, Diary, 10 August 1846, in Maureen Ursenbach Beecher, ed., *The Personal Writings of Eliza Roxcy Snow* (Salt Lake City: University of Utah Press, 1995), 139.
2. "Sketch of the Life of Mary Dart Judd," typescript, 12, LDS Church Archives.

knew that only Saints with enough faith to face the hard times had the right spirit to build the new Zion.[3]

Once again he was looking to spring to move his people on, or in words of the time, "when the grass grows and the river runs." Nauvoo had not given him that choice, but now, a year later, the Mormons could make their plans in peace for the thousand-mile overland journey that yet awaited. They could wait until the grass grew.

Well before spring reached the Missouri and brought its warm and healing touch to the itinerant campers along its banks and surrounding bluffs, Brigham Young had conferred with his fellow apostles, his scouts, and the maps of the Rocky Mountain region; by late winter plans began to emerge.[4] An advance party would find the place to settle, plant crops, and prepare it for the Saints who would follow. Brigham Young wanted 144 men and 72 well-provisioned wagons.[5] Every useful skill was to be represented.[6] While many volunteers vied for a chance to be in the vanguard company of pioneers, some who were chosen felt woefully unprepared. Saddle maker and carpenter Levi Jackman worried that he had only one yoke of oxen and no wagon. His clothing was "old and scarce," and except for some breadstuffs to last the required eighteen months, he had only a few beans and a little pork "but no groceries." Nevertheless, he was willing to go, although, he wrote, "[to] where, we could not tell or what we

3. Advance scout Bishop George Miller, who spent the winter with a group of followers at a Ponca Indian village, and Apostle Lyman Wight, then in Texas with a handful of his followers, were among the spiritual casualties.

4. Richard Bennett discusses the preparations for moving west in "Finalizing Plans for the Trek West: Deliberations at Winter Quarters, 1846–1847," *Brigham Young University Studies* 24 (Summer 1984): 301–20.

5. The biblical number may well have been another Israelite parallel. The number dropped to 143 when one man returned to Winter Quarters. The number was augmented later in the journey when thirty Saints from Mississippi and a contingent of sick or disabled members of the Mormon Battalion and followers joined the group. Among the original number were three blacks and two non-Mormons.

6. According to Stanley B. Kimball in *Historical Resource Study: Mormon Pioneer National Historic Trail* (Washington, DC: United States Department of the Interior/National Park Service, 1991), 47–48, there were blacksmiths, wagon makers, hunters, teamsters, accountants, sailors, bricklayers, and many other tradesmen and artisans represented.

should have to contend with. We only knew that we must go and the Lord would attend to bringing out the results."[7] Sylvester Henry Earl, another of Brigham's advance company, was also hesitant about going. "It was hard for me to leave my little family sick among howling wolves and the roaming savages of the West," he wrote, "but the servants of the Lord said go and I felt as ever to leave all for the benefit of the Gospel or the salvation of the people."[8] Henry Earl and Levi Jackman were exactly the kind of men Brigham Young wanted in his company.

There is no record of how many women wanted to sign on, but three had the distinction of being part of the pioneer band. Harriet Decker Young, wife of Lorenzo Dow Young, Brigham's brother, was especially eager to go. Her asthma was growing worse in the humid climate of Winter Quarters, and she believed her only relief lay in the fresh mountain air of the Rockies. Lorenzo and Harriet also brought two sons.[9] To give Harriet female company, Brigham brought his wife Clara Decker, Harriet's daughter whom he had married in Nauvoo; and Ellen Sanders Kimball accompanied her husband Heber C. Kimball.[10] Neither Clara nor Ellen shared Harriet's initial enthusiasm.

None of the women kept a journal. Perhaps their tasks were too demanding or they deferred to record keepers such as Thomas Bullock and William Clayton. Maybe they saw so many of the company hunched by their candles or lanterns each night writing their own private records that they felt adding another chapter to what would be a well-recorded event was needless.

---

7. Autobiography of Levi Jackman, 29 March 1847, typescript, Utah State Historical Society, Salt Lake City, Utah.

8. Sylvester Henry Earl, Autobiographical Sketch, 10 April 1847, microfilm of typescript, LDS Church Archives.

9. One was Isaac Decker, age seven, Harriet's son by an earlier marriage, and the other was Lorenzo Sobieski Young, age six, Lorenzo's son of another wife.

10. Details of the three women's lives can be found in Kate B. Carter, *Our Pioneer Heritage*, 20 vols. (Salt Lake City: Daughters of Utah Pioneers, 1958–1977) 8:171–79. See also Mrs. Clara Decker Young, "A Woman's Experience with the Pioneer Band," (1884) typescript, LDS Church Archives, original in Bancroft Library.

Whatever the reason, their voices are silent except for a few brief sentences from Clara Young written forty years later. Clara noted that she "never felt as badly [sic] in her life as when she was actually starting on the uncertain pilgrimage." She was "relieved," however, and "really satisfied" when they finally reached their destination. The valley didn't look as dreary to her, she explained, as to the other women. "They were terribly disappointed because there were no trees, and to them there was such a sense of desolation and loneliness."[11] Harriet confessed her disappointment to her husband. "We have traveled fifteen hundred miles over prairies, deserts and mountains, but feeble as I am I would rather go a thousand miles farther than stay in such a desolated place."[12] Her first months in the Valley didn't do much to change Harriet's mind. Giving birth to a son just two months after arriving, she found her hopes again bitterly crushed when he died five months later. Ellen Kimball also lost a son within the first year of his life as well as twin sons born a few years later.

With the others left to winter in the Valley, the women lived in the hastily constructed fort, each occupying a room with a door and a wooden window, taken out for light during the day and nailed in at night. Within weeks, emigrants from Mississippi came into the Valley, and in September word came of the impending arrival of the second company of pioneers. For the lonely settlers, "the excitement was intense," Clara remembered. They were overjoyed to receive letters, though they arrived "without envelopes and tied with buckskin thongs wound around again and again." The news from Winter Quarters was good, and they were especially happy to learn that the company was bringing "plenty of food," including peas, "indeed a luxury."[13]

For the Saints, the trail west would be another test of Joseph

11. Mrs. Clara Decker Young, "A Woman's Experience with the Pioneer Band."
12. Carter, *Our Pioneer Heritage* 8:176.
13. Clara Decker Young, "A Woman's Experience with the Pioneer Band."

Smith's vision of a "holy nation," which blurred the boundaries between the secular and the sacred.[14] If the Saints were indeed a covenant people, he believed, they would be willing to be governed by spiritual laws. The law that would rule them as they journeyed westward was revealed to Brigham Young and given to the Church in January 1847. It was known as "The Word and Will of the Lord concerning the Camp of Israel in their journeyings to the West" (D&C 136:1), and it would be their constitution and guide. It outlined the preparations to be made and the organization of companies. It exhorted the Saints to righteousness and invoked the spirit of the Nauvoo covenant in admonishing them to look to the needs of others and prepare for the Saints who followed. Most important, it was a revelation from God to his people, assuring them of his continuing care and reminding the homeless Saints that they were on a holy errand. Even as they were counseled to "provide themselves with all the teams, wagons, provisions, clothing, and other necessaries for the journey" (v. 5), they were also counseled to "walk in all the ordinances of the Lord" (v. 4).

When the wagons started rolling out of the grand encampment on the Missouri in April 1847, it was an emotional time for the Saints. So much and so many depended on the success of this pioneer band. Fanny Young Murray, Brigham's sister, was deeply moved at their leaving. "The wagons went four abreast, and you can hardly imagine their appearance. Some that were there declared it the grandest sight their eyes were ever blest with. Their wagons were all neatly prepared with everything for their comfort that could be obtained, but yet they will suffer enough."[15]

14. Ronald Esplin describes this concept as a "sacred cosmos" and explains how Brigham Young committed himself to fulfilling this vision of the establishment of God's kingdom as he understood it from Joseph Smith. See Ronald K. Esplin, "Brigham Young's 'Social World': Sacred Cosmos in a Secular Age" in "Emergence of Brigham Young and the Twelve to Mormon Leadership, 1830–1841," (Ph.D. diss., Brigham Young University, 1981).

15. Fanny Young Murray to Gould and Laura Murray, Winter Quarters 5 July 1847, in Helen Mar Whitney Papers, LDS Church Archives; also in Helen Mar Whitney, "Scenes and Incidents at Winter Quarters," *Woman's Exponent* 14 (1 November 1885): 129.

That first band of pioneers did not suffer as much as Fanny feared. They encountered no Indian raids, no debilitating storms, no serious lack of provisions, and no deaths. They were as well prepared and carefully organized as any west-bound company could be. Iowa had been a useful training ground. Few other Mormon wagon trains have received more written attention than this pioneer band or produced so many diaries and journals. It was the quintessential trail experience which would be modified over the next twenty years by variations in the route, the makeup of the companies, and the mode of travel, but this company's one hundred and eleven days on the trail became a pattern for the companies that followed.[16]

The West attracted many emigrants in 1847. Besides the twenty-two hundred Mormons in the four companies to make the trek to Utah that year, forty-five hundred other westerners traveled to Oregon and California. Like the pioneer band, the three companies that followed from Winter Quarters that summer also reached the Salt Lake Valley with few of the problems that beset later groups. But even in their eagerness to be on their way, leaving brought mixed emotions. Preparing to go reminded Patty Sessions of an earlier difficult parting. "We start for the mountains or a resting place and leave Winter Quarters," she wrote on 5 June 1847. "[It is] Ten years ago today since we left our homes and friends in Maine. We are now leaving many good friends and I hope they will soon follow on to us."[17] Mary Jane Mount Tanner, just a girl when she left Winter Quarters, remembered the sight of the "little company of wanderers as they

---

16. Stanley B. Kimball and other trail historians have noted the variations: in the trails followed by different companies; in the varied staging centers, especially as the railroad moved west; in the disembarkation points for European emigrants; in the mode of travel, including the conveyances used (wagons, carriages, handcarts); and in the introduction of Church trains which made a round trip from the Salt Lake Valley to the staging places where they gathered the Saints, and took them to Utah, all in one season. It is interesting to contrast this journey of more than a thousand miles made in III days with the 300-mile crossing of Iowa by the vanguard company of Nauvoo exiles, which took almost as long, 109 days.

17. Diary of Patty Sessions, 5 June 1847, LDS Church Archives.

wound slowly along the long train of ox teams creeping as it were day by day." She recalled the long wait at the rendezvous point on the Elkhorn River, a few miles west of Winter Quarters, and the "undulating prairie that stretched as far as the eye could reach, covered with grass and flowers." She knew that her mother was "thinking of all she was leaving behind, and wondering what the future held in store for her."[18]

All who began the long western trek were required to take a basic store of supplies and gear. Some, on their own or with the help of friends, secured these provisions and teams in time to follow after the first band of pioneers. Charles C. Rich's family was one of them. "We were fitted up as comfortable as we could be, with wagons and teams and provisions, beside some cows and sheep and teamsters, and some to drive the stock, for all that had loose stock brought it along," wrote Sarah Rich. "The names of those two brethren that so kindly helped us to be able to come along with the first company were Zesabel Shoemaker and Aaron Cherry; they and we traveled together in the same company all the way to the Valley."[19]

Others took a year or more to acquire the teams, wagon, provisions, tools, and gear needed for the long journey. By 1853 most of the Saints had vacated not only Winter Quarters but also Kanesville, St. Louis, and the way stations in Iowa. The town of Florence, near the site of Winter Quarters, remained as an outfitting post for the thousands of emigrants from other parts of the United States and Europe yet to make the trek.[20]

The trail west was a journey of discovery. The region between the Missouri and the Great Salt Lake held many surprises for the

---

18. Margery W. Ward, ed., *A Fragment: The Autobiography of Mary Jane Mount Tanner* (Salt Lake City: Tanner Trust Fund, University of Utah Library, 1980), 42.

19. Reminiscences of Sarah DeArmon Pea Rich (1885–1893), LDS Church Archives.

20. The term "emigrant" or "emigrant company" was used to designate the companies that followed the original band of pioneers led by Brigham Young in April 1847. The terms were not necessarily restricted to European emigrants.

emigrants, especially those from Europe. From the broad, flat plains of Nebraska to the steep mountain ranges and narrow passes of Wyoming and Utah, travelers saw something of wonder on every side. The "broad, shallow, braided" Platte River was their main corridor to the West. They followed along its north bank for more than six hundred miles, some companies crossing it several times to find feed for their animals, which was often more plentiful along the southern bank.[21] Sophia Goodridge described the wide sweep of level grasslands of the Platte Valley as "one endless sea of grass, wavy and rolling like the waves of the sea, and now and then a tree."[22] Journal writers, like Sarah Mousley, searched for words to describe the scenes unfolding each day. "Oh how I wish mine were a painters pencil or a poets pen," she lamented. But on several occasions her pencil did justice to the view. A prairie scene caught her imagination: In the "midst of a wide spreading prairie . . . [be]decked with varied flowers a beautiful grove we thought it had been trained by a skillful hand to suit the taste of the possessor instead of being in the wild domein [sic] of nature my heart exclaimed how beautiful how wonderful thou art sweet earth."[23]

Another scene by the Platte River moved Sarah to declare it "the beautifulest scenery my eye's ever rested upon. The bluffs on each side the wild flowers beautiful to behold the air redolent with odor the calm still waters of beautiful lakes all, all serving alike to invoke an adoration to the God [by] whose word we have left the happy scene of childhood years to repair to the mountains with the saints of light."[24]

As the Saints moved farther west, the topography changed dramatically. The broad prairies gave way to the unusual and

---

21. Merrill J. Mattes examines the physical and social geography of the great Platte River in *The Great Platte River Road* (Lincoln: Univerity of Nebraska, 1969). These references are on page 6.

22. Diary of Sophia Lois Goodridge, 29 June 1850, Utah State Historical Society.

23. Diary of Sarah Mousley, 18 June 1857, Utah State Historical Society.

24. Ibid., 24 July 1857.

magnificent geological formations with names to match their
shapes: Ancient Ruins Bluff, Court House and Jail Rocks,
Devil's Gate, Witches Rock, and the remarkable natural curiosity
Chimney Rock. Distance seemed to evaporate as the clear air of
the high country magnified these spectacular landmarks and
made them seem closer to the traveler's eye than they actually
were. Emigrants were surprised to find they had to travel days,
not hours, to reach them after they were sighted.

Some journal writers found words to match these natural
wonders. The Ancient Ruins Bluff, named "Bluff Ruins" by
Willard Richards when he first saw them, reminded many travelers,
particularly European emigrants, of ancient castles and fortresses.
Seeing another range of bluffs farther along on the trail, British
convert Hannah Tapfield King caught the romantic images they
conveyed. "They are Sublime and Mysterious," she wrote. "There
is beauty and order in them - and it requires no fanciful stretch
of imagination to form Baronial buildings - 'keeps' - gateways, etc
etc - and Georgy [her daughter] even made [out] 'The Porter'
looking over the Gate!! They are very high - I should like to hear a
philosophical description of them - They please and interest me
more than I have language to express - There is much design in
them - yet they say they are solely the work of Nature - Well I must
leave them like all mysterious things."[25]

Of all the wonders, Chimney Rock seemed most to draw the
interest of the emigrants. It was described by one early adven-
turer as having a pyramid or cone-shaped base giving rise to a
gradually narrowing shaft, the whole formation reaching "up
from the prairie in solitary grandeur, like the limbless trunk of a
gigantic tree."[26] Britisher William Clayton was reminded of a

---

25. Diary of Hannah Tapfield King, 10 September 1853, LDS Church Archives.
26. This 1830 description was written by Warren A. Ferris of the American Fur Company, quoted
in Mattes, 383. Orson Pratt attempted to measure its height by use of instruments and arrived at the figure of 260 feet. Other calculations made by other means ranged from 300 to 500 feet. See Mattes,
398–99.

large factory chimney in England when he first saw it.[27] Other accounts also noted its tremendous size, which reduced wagon trains to ant colonies when they were viewed from the top of its conical base. Some emigrants were challenged to climb the hundred or so feet to the top of the base, but thousands more were content to leave their names on the monument, silent witnesses to its universal fascination.

Before leaving the Platte, the westerners were treated to another geological phenomenon known to them as Scott's Bluffs.[28] Frederick Piercy had talent enough to memorialize the scene with both brush and pen. When the Bluffs first came into view, he noticed that the shadows, which had played around the rocky formation throughout the day, were by evening "an intense blue, while the rock illuminated by the setting sun partook of its gold, making a beautiful harmony of colour. They present a very singular appearance," he wrote, "resembling ruined palaces, castellated towers, temples and monuments."[29] Independence Rock was another noted landmark. More easily scaled than Chimney Rock, it offered a pleasant hike to its rounded summit. Names of emigrants also covered its face. From its summit, Sophia Goodridge, an 1850 pioneer, declared the view "beautiful. The Sweetwater flows southwest at the base of the rock and winds around the foot of the mountains." She could see the "Saleratus Lake to the northwest and Devil's gate to the West while mountains are to be seen on all sides."[30]

Wilford Woodruff and John Brown of the first band of pioneers were probably the first Mormons to climb the rock—but

---

27. Ibid., 386.

28. Most pioneer journals referred to the bluffs in the plural, referring to the entire range of bluffs. They were so named because of the starvation death of an early trader, Hiram Scott, at the base of the bluffs in 1828. More information about Scott and the geographic and historical significance of the bluffs is in Mattes, 421–36.

29. Frederick Hawkins Piercy, *Route from Liverpool to the Great Salt Lake Valley* (Cambridge: The Belknap Press, Harvard University Press, 1962), 118–19.

30. Diary of Sophia Lois Goodridge, 8 September 1850, Utah State Historical Society.

for prayer, not pleasure. Ahead of the rest of the company, they climbed to the rock's highest point. There, Wilford Woodruff recorded, "we offered up our prayers according to the order of the priesthood. We prayed earnestly for the blessing of God to r[est] upon President Young & his brethren the Twelve & all of the Pioneer Camp & the whole Camp of Israel & House of Israel, our wives & children, & relatives the Mormon Battalion, all the Churches Abroad . . . And that the Lord would hasten the time . . . [for] the building up of Zion in the last days. . . . And while offering up our prayers the spirit of the Lord desended [sic] upon us and we truly felt to rejoice."[31]

John Lingren, a Scandinavian emigrant, was intrigued by the "wild weird romance about the country like some dream, some imaginary scene materialized." In the evenings, he wrote, "the sound of music in different parts of the camp seemed strangely harmonious with the almost deathlike silence of these uninhabited regions."[32] Unlike most of the other points of scenic interest, however, the first sighting of the western mountains and Laramie Peak seemed to elicit a more cautious response from the journalists. These mountains were not just part of the scenery; they were part of the trail. "I have seen the Rocky mountains for the first time today," Martha Spence Heywood declared to her diary. "They look stupendous in the dim opaque of the horizon and but a faint line marking their existence and altitude."[33] Though ominous at first sight, they would eventually frame the view of most interest to the pioneers—their valley home.

While others wrote of what they saw, Ingrid Christine Holestie, an 1866 pioneer child, wrote of what she heard.

31. 21 June 1847, in Scott G. Kenney, ed., *Wilford Woodruff's Journal, 1833–1898*, 9 vols. (Midvale, Utah: Signature Books, 1983) 3:211. This experience is also recounted in Joseph E. Brown, *The Mormon Trek West: The Journey of American Exiles* (Garden City, N.Y: Doubleday, 1980), 126.

32. "Autobiography of John Lingren" in Kate B. Carter, comp., *Treasures of Pioneer History*, 6 vols. (Salt Lake City: Daughters of Utah Pioneers, 1952–1957) 1:239.

33. Juanita Brooks, ed., *Not By Bread Alone: The Journal of Martha Spence Heywood, 1850–56* (Salt Lake City: Utah State Historical Society, 1978), 19.

Because she was sick throughout the trek, Ingrid experienced trail life from a wagon, hearing rather than seeing the activities of the wagon company as it moved westward. She noted the crying of children and babies and the sound of animals braying, snorting, and mewing. She heard the moans of women struggling over their stoves and campfires in the rain and sleet or in the pangs of birth. And she heard the songs of the camp when day had finished and night brought blessed relief.[34] Her account reminds us that the history of the trail is as much in its sounds as in its sights.

Adding to the wonder of this hauntingly beautiful land were its native inhabitants. Sometimes they stole horses and cattle, bargained for wives from among the young girls, set off stampedes, or kidnapped lost children. Others traded buffalo robes, moccasins, and other useful items for food and trinkets. At Fort Laramie, one Indian woman took special interest in Hannah Cornaby's young daughter. She "measured her foot, and next day returned with a very tastily embroidered pair of moccasins which she placed on her feet, refusing to take anything in payment," Hannah remembered.[35]

Diana Eldredge's company encountered a band of Sioux Indians at Chimney Rock. "There were about 100 braves in war paint and feathers headed by a chief," she wrote. "They thought we had come to take their land away from them, but when they were finally convinced that we did not want to molest them, they seemed quite friendly. We cooked them a dinner after which the 'peace pipe' was smoked by all men in both bands. A large fire was built and the pipe was passed around the circle. As we moved on they followed us for two or three days, but they offered no opposition to us."[36] Sara Alexander, an 1859 pioneer, was more intrigued than frightened by them. She often watched them rid-

---

34. Arvilla Rasmussen, "A Pioneer Child Speaks Out," typescript, 5, Utah State Historical Society.
35. Hannah Cornaby, *Autobiography and Poems* (Salt Lake City: J. C. Graham & Co., 1881; reprint, West Jordan, Utah, 198?), 35.
36. "History of Diana Eldredge Smoot," typescript copy in author's possession.

ing their horses "as far as the eye could reach over the vast plains" and found them "picturesque and magnificent in their own environment." When she later mused on her memories of those images, she wrote, "I shall always be glad I have seen the Indians in their primitive grandeur, in their own country where they were kings and where they dominated so royally. I pity their humiliation in compelling them to become civilized. So much has to be crushed in the march of improvement and in the making of a nation"[37]—an unusual sentiment in the nineteenth century.

Sharing dominion of this western land were the vast herds of buffalo that roamed at will across the prairies. In small numbers they seemed harmless, but often the animals suddenly appeared as a tiny spot far off in the distance, a small dust cloud steadily looming larger until it became a black, moving, thundering mass filling the horizon. The animals bore down so rapidly on the wagon trains that the pioneers hardly had time to take cover or hold to their oxen as the immense herd rushed toward them. Diana Eldredge remembered how "they surged down upon us on their way to water." "The men of the company," she wrote, "crowded all the wagons of the train into as close a bunch as possible and all the women and children into the wagons. They crowded the cattle into a line with their heads turned from the buffalo, and then stationed themselves at the head of their oxen with whips and no other weapons. . . . As the herd crowded closer to us, pawing the earth and tossing their heads, the men kept up an incessant shout and cracking of whips. Suddenly when they were just about upon us, the herd separated and one part went on one side of our camp and the other half circled the other side of our camp. Not one head of cattle was lost, nor one person injured."[38]

---

37. "A Little Story of the Experiences of Sara Alexander When Crossing the Plains in 1859," typescript, Utah State Historical Society.

38. "History of Diana Eldredge Smoot."

These sudden encounters often stampeded the oxen and livestock, and many loose cattle were caught up in the thundering rush of animals. When a wagon train and buffalo herd crossed paths, there was no question which had the right of way, especially, Eliza R. Snow recalled, "when crossing their watering paths in near proximity to a river, and we were compelled to make a break in a line of wagons, and wait for two or three thousand of those uncompromising animals to pass."[39] The travelers were delighted, however, when the hunters brought back fresh buffalo meat to divide among the camp.

The emigrants found more than the natural wonders of the new land to discover. They also found their journey to be one of self-discovery. The western odyssey not only challenged them with new modes of daily living; it also tested the strength of their coping abilities. Men who had never seen, let alone driven, a team of oxen, for instance, had little time to learn the "science of oxology," as Horace Whitney dubbed it.[40] British emigrant Duckworth Grimshaw stood helpless beside his newly acquired team of oxen until experienced driver John W. Young offered to instruct him on the fine points of "bullwhacking." According to Grimshaw, "he took the whip and brought it down on the ox leader then gave the nigh leader a prod in the ribs with the whip stock and this brought the cows up in good style. I thought, well they seem to understand that sort of driving, but when I tried it I found the lash around my own neck and decided [that] to become efficient in driving required practice like everything else." Christian Nielsen was also a novice teamster and struggled with his two teams. "In the beginning," he found, "it went slowly as the oxen were not acquainted with us and we not with them, as the way in which they drive them here is entirely different from the Danish way."[41]

---

39. "Sketch of My Life," in *The Personal Writings of Eliza Roxcy Snow*, 27.
40. In Helen Mar Whitney, "Our Travels Beyond the Mississippi," *Woman's Exponent* 12 (15 January 1884): 126.
41. In Carter, *Our Pioneer Heritage* 11:231–42.

Rounding up hundreds of wagons, hitching up teams, and finding a place in the line of travel overwhelmed some emigrants. Andrew Nielson would always remember the July afternoon in 1864 that he left Atchison, Kansas, with a Danish company for the West. The combination of "wild and ignorant teamsters," who couldn't speak English, captains who couldn't speak Danish, and the struggle "in getting those wild animals yoked up and hitched to the wagons" made an unforgettable scene. "For five miles all around the plains," he remembered, "you could see oxen, wagons, teamsters, and a dozen horsemen going at breakneck speed, and it was a miracle that no one was hurt, nor anything broken, but under these conditions I have seen strong men cry."[42]

Hannah Cornaby, mercifully exempt from the frustrating struggle, found the whole process humorous. "Imagine, if you can," she wrote, "the operation of starting over one hundred ox teams, chiefly by men who had never done anything of the kind before. . . . The oxen were wild, and getting them yoked was the most laughable sight I had ever witnessed; everybody giving orders, and nobody knowing how to carry them out. If the men had not been saints, there would doubtless have been much profane language used; but the oxen, not understanding 'English,' did just as well without it. But it did seem so truly comical to witness the bewildered look of some innocent brother, who, after having labored an hour or more to get 'Bright' secured to one end of the yoke, would hold the other end aloft, trying to persuade 'Buck' to come under, only to see 'Bright' careering across the country, the yoke lashing the air, and he not even giving a hint as to when he intended to stop."[43]

If driving oxen tried their strength, night guarding challenged their endurance. "This was not a pleasant task," young

42. "Andrew Christian Nielson, Pioneer," in Carter, *Our Pioneer Heritage* II:277.
43. Hannah Cornaby, *Autobiography and Poems*, 32.

Duckworth Grimshaw felt when his turn came round, "especially when the nights were dark and stormy."[44] Richard Warburton felt the same. "No one knows," he wrote, "unless they have had the same experience what a trial it was to drive team all day and guard at night. The loss of sleep was something fearful."[45] When they added hunting, wagon repairing, yoking and unyoking balky animals, and herding the livestock to their day's tasks, emigrant men discovered new dimensions to the meaning of *long-suffering.*

Women trudged alongside their men in long skirts and petticoats, which were never designed for the western trail.[46] Against all odds, they tried to maintain some domestic amenities in the routine of camp life. But cooking on open fires, washing clothes and bathing in cold streams, birthing while on the move, and living without privacy were strong deterrents. Nothing daunted, Bathsheba Smith was not going to be deprived of the womanly nuances of daily living. When she left for the Valley in 1849, she arranged her wagon to be as homelike as possible. Projections from each side and a wagon cover tall enough for her to stand upright inside the wagon gave it a roominess others lacked. Across the back she laid a corded frame that served as a bedstead. She carpeted the floor and hung a looking-glass, candlestick, pin-cushion and other necessaries from the bows. She even found room to place four chairs in the center of the wagon, where, she wrote, "we and our two children sat and rode as we chose."[47]

Few pioneers traveled in such Cadillac comfort. Margaret Watson DeWitt, a young single woman traveling with the family of Thomas Lyons, whose wife was an invalid, "cooked every bite that

---

44. "The Records of Duckworth Grimshaw," in Carter, *Our Pioneer Heritage* 12:245.

45. "British Immigrants," in Carter, *An Enduring Legacy* (Salt Lake City: Daughters of Utah Pioneers, 1987) 10:117–18.

46. Some westering women adopted the bloomer costume, so much maligned in the East but much more functional in the West than traditional long skirts.

47. In Edward W. Tullidge, *The Women of Mormondom* (New York, 1877; reprint, Salt Lake City, 1975), 342–43.

was eaten by our outfit of ten" and took care of the five Lyons children. A shared tent was her bedroom, and she pointedly noted that she was obliged to walk "all the way to the valley, carrying the Lyons baby most of the way."[48]

Order and efficiency were the mainstay of camp life. Whatever one's habits might be, everyone had to follow the group regimen. For Louisa Palmer's company, the day began at six o'clock, "and at eight they were on their way. At noon camp was made for lunch and at night camp was made for the night by water if possible. A corral was made of the wagons. The cattle were herded if there were no Indians in the vicinity. After supper there was usually a dance; the fiddle music was furnished by the teamsters. After the dance a meeting was held which was opened by song and prayer and the subject spoken upon was about the travel for the next day. The roll was called twice each day. At nine-thirty all were supposed to be in bed." Louisa's account is as orderly as her trail days must have been.[49]

To the tight schedule and unpredictable circumstances of their various camping places, women adapted their domestic tasks. They washed their clothes in the rivers and streams and dried them on the banks or by the campfires. They depended on buffalo chips for fuel when wood was scarce. Sarah Burbank knew just how to use them. She would dig a hole in the ground, put the skillet in the hole with a tight lid on it, and then lay the buffalo chips on the lid and ignite them. "It baked the bread just fine," she found.[50]

Sarah gave special care to her milk cow. A sick, lost, or dead cow was a severe blow to a family, especially one with small children. Not a drop of milk was wasted. Women put any unused milk or cream

---

48. "Autobiography of Margaret Miller Watson DeWitt," *Relief Society Magazine* 16 (July 1929): 380–85.

49. Louisa Harriett Mills Palmer in Carter, *Our Pioneer Heritage* 13:456.

50. "A Sketch of the Life of Sarah Burbank," 3, in *Pioneer Journals*, bound typescript, Special Collections, Harold B. Lee Library, Brigham Young University, Provo, Utah.

into tightly covered wooden churns and fastened them either inside or outside the wagon, where they would hang during the bumpy ride. By day's end there would be butter for supper. Bread dough, mixed in the morning, rose in the same fashion. By evening it was ready for baking in the large black kettle that most women used, or sometimes in a wayside rock oven built by previous travelers.

While many pioneers were reduced to a diet of dried bacon and biscuits by journey's end, supplemented by berries or a little beef or buffalo meat, others seemed to have a wide range of provisions that lasted the entire journey. Caroline Hopkins Clark, an 1866 pioneer, detailed her family's well-stocked larder. "We do not get any fresh meat or potatoes," she noted, "but we get plenty of flour and bacon. We have some sugar, a little tea, molasses, soap, carbonate of soda, and a few dried apples. We brought some peas. Oatmeal, rice, tea, and sugar, which we had left from the vessel [she was a European emigrant]. We bought a skillet to bake our bread in. Sometimes we make pancakes for a change. We also make cakes in the pan, and often bran dumplings with baking powder. We use cream of tartar and soda for our bread, sometimes sour dough. At times Roland goes to the river and catches fish and sometimes John shoots birds. We get wild currants and gooseberries to make puddings. All together we get along very well."[51]

Though Hannah King, a forty-five-year-old pioneer of 1853, thought it foolish for an expectant mother to undertake such a journey, that impending event deterred few women. Nor did it delay travel. Sarah Burbank remembered more births than deaths in her company, none of which "hindered the march as they would move on the next morning making quite a hardship for the women."[52]

Women developed close companionships on the trail as they

---

51. Diary of Caroline Hopkins Clark, 14 June 1866, *Our Pioneer Heritage* 10:48.
52. Burbank, 3.

assisted at times of birthing, illness, and the shared tasks of camp life. Those wives of the first company of pioneers who traveled in the next company drew support, both physical and spiritual, from one another as they journeyed west without their husbands. Eliza R. Snow, a plural wife of Brigham Young, seemed to function at the center of a web of social and family relationships in the company in which she traveled, continuing the social and spiritual gatherings and prayer meetings begun in Winter Quarters.[53]

Midwives such as Patty Sessions also filled a central place at the center of camp life, entering into a family circle at its most vulnerable times and linking families in their common needs.

Eliza Cheney willingly cast her lot with her sister Saints and told her family, back in the States, "I am willing to endure anything my sisters of the Church have to endure to help to build up this great and [latter-day] Kingdom that the way may be prepared for the judgment of God upon the earth."[54]

If learning new tasks or coping with old ones in a new setting were not exercise enough in self-discovery, dealing with simple annoyances on the trail, as well as hardships and tragedies, told the pioneers much about themselves. Dust, mud, rain, wind, and pesky mosquitoes and buffalo gnats challenged their patience. But losing an ox meant serious trouble. The teamsters kept a watchful eye on their well-being, corralling them for protection, hunting them when lost, and even blessing them when they sickened or grew sullen or tired. Peter Neilson, Sr., wrote, "[I] as well as other brethren have quietly gone between our oxen and blessed them and immediately they moved on, showing us that the Spirit of the Lord can subdue and make biddable the ox as well as man."[55] In their dependence on their oxen, families developed

53. Beecher, *The Personal Writings of Eliza R. Snow,* 176–204.

54. Eliza Cheney to Parents, Brothers, and Sisters, January 1848, in Historical Letters and Sketches, 1841–1919, Eliza Jane Rawson Collection, LDS Church Archives.

55. Biographical Sketch of Peter Neilson, Sr., typescript copy, 10, in author's possession, compliments of his descendant, Reed Neilson.

strong attachments to them. When the Adolphia Young family reached the Valley, they had to sell their team to buy a house. "This made the family very sad," Rhoda Young remembered. "It was like selling a cherished member of the household."[56]

Losing one's best ox or only milk cow was bad enough; stampedes, however, not only carried away cattle and livestock but also upset or destroyed wagons and injured or even killed people. A careless shaking of a robe in front of the corralled animals, a sudden shot, or the deliberate provoking of the animals by marauding Indians set the animals off in an instant. No one knew what startled the teams in Ole Jensen's camp one morning, just four miles along that day's travel. But suddenly "the frenzied animals broke into a wild run . . . simultaneously rushing across the Plains at utmost speed. Women and children were leaping from the flying wagons, men were applying whips or using reins in a vain attempt to check the terrified animals. Scattered and broken vehicles only added to the fright of the animals." When Ole tried to regain control of his animals, he slipped and fell beneath the wagon wheels. Somehow he managed to save the wagon but lost his life in doing so.[57]

Broken axles, wagon wheels, and yokes hindered travel more than birthing, sickness, or death and tried the patience of those who were ready to move on. River crossings also begged patience since all had to cross before the company could proceed. It took sheer grit to plunge into cold or muddy water when the pioneers knew that wet clothes would have to dry on their backs. Long skirts never proved more inappropriate for trail travel than at river crossings. Martha Patterson made a habit of tying her skirt over her shoulders, carrying her shoes in one hand, and driving her oxen across the river with the other.[58] Men double-teamed

---

56. Rhoda Byrne Jared Young, in Eleanor McAllister Hall, *The Book of Jared* (n.p., 1963), 34.
57. Karen Nielsen Jensen, in *An Enduring Legacy* 6:168.
58. Martha Fillmore Patterson, in *An Enduring Legacy* 5:247.

their oxen to pull the wagons across streams full of quicksand. In James Bryant's company, every crossing point was tested for depth. "There was always one of the men," wrote James, "ready to ride his saddle horse into the river[;] if his horse had to swim he would return as soon as possible, but if man and horse could wade all of the way across, the company was allowed to march on through. If he had to swim we then made camp, sometimes for ten days making rafts or floats to enable every thing to be taken over to the opposite side."[59]

One of the great fears of both young and old was getting lost or losing someone on the trail. When little Robert Olson didn't answer the dinner call, a posse immediately went back along the trail to find him. A three-day search failed to find the boy, so the wagon train moved on, his distraught parents with it. When Robert showed up in another company days later, the whole camp cheered. Roll call at least once or twice daily had untold value when the wagon teams were spread over miles of broad plains, and wooded mountain passes led to dozens of hidden dangers.

A great scourge of the trek was cholera. Diarrhea and dysentery were close rivals, but when the Asian cholera appeared on the plains in 1849, with periodic outbreaks for several years afterwards, few wagon trains escaped devastating losses.[60] Cholera caused a large share of the estimated six thousand deaths of Mormon emigrants during the pioneer period. It attacked European emigrants as soon as they arrived in New Orleans, following them up the Mississippi to the various staging camps. The commissary at Mormon Grove, outside Atchison, Kansas, noted that cholera attacked three hundred new emigrants and only three survived.[61] It pursued them along the western trail where

59. James Bryant in "John Murdock Company," in Carter, *Our Pioneer Heritage* 6:61.
60. Farley, 63. Details of the impact of this disease are in J. S. Holiday, *The World Rushed In* (New York: Simon and Schuster, 1981).
61. Emily Pauline Malan Farley, in Carter, *Treasures of Pioneer History* 5:63.

little could be done to avoid it. "You never knew when you got up in the morning whether you would live to see the sun go down or not," recalled Julia Sophia McKee.[62] Sarah Burbank recalled the fear that swept through the camp when the captain's wife succumbed. "All the women in the camp were afraid to prepare the body for burial for fear they would catch the cholera from her," she wrote. So Sarah and another young woman washed and dressed her for burial in "her underclothes and a nightgown, . . . We sewed her up in a sheet and a quilt. That was all that could be done for her burial. This young girl and I were not afraid to take care of the body. We were only sixteen years old but brave in the case."[63]

With no medical treatment available to stop the spread of the disease, prayer became both a remedy and a comfort. As more and more of Sophia Goodridge's company succumbed, the camp felt discouraged and helpless. "We felt like humbling ourselves before the Lord, and pray that He might turn from us the sickness and distress among us," she wrote. "We therefore met together, the speakers exhorting us to be diligent in our devotions and united. A vote was taken to that effect. They called upon the Lord in prayer that he would bless and preserve us on our journey to the Valley. We then started on our journey rejoicing."[64] Though cholera claimed more of the company until they reached higher country, their spirits had been rejuvenated and their coping skills measurably strengthened.

In our era of fast-moving vehicles, it is difficult to imagine anyone's being injured by an ox and wagon moving two miles an hour. But oxen were difficult to stop, and a misstep by a driver, a slip from the wagon tongue, or a fall from the wagon bed could suddenly throw a victim under a wagon's heavy wheels. Children

62. "Incidents of the Life of Julia Sophia McKee, written by Herself from Memory, November 30, 1892," 4, typescript copy in author's possession.
63. Burbank, 3.
64. Diary of Sophia Lois Goodridge, 1 July 1850.

were particularly vulnerable. They broke their arms or legs, and others died when a wagon wheel rolled over them. There were also drownings, falls over ravines, and gunshot wounds, as well as simple cuts, bruises, and snake and insect bites. Healing miracles, however, preserved the lives of many victims and gave evidence of the "efficiency of faith," as one woman observed.[65] Eliza R. Snow acknowledged the efficiency of faith in the healing of her friend Nancy Maria Love, who fell from the tongue of her wagon which contained "sixteen hundred freight." "To all appearance," Eliza noted, "she was crushed, but on being administered to by some of the elders she revived; and after having been anointed with consecrated oil, and having the ordinance of laying on of hands repeated she soon recovered, and on the fourth day after the accident, she milked her cow, as usual."[66]

Accidents and disease could decimate a family. Laura Swenson was only one of many children orphaned. Her father died after falling from their wagon, and her mother died a week later in premature childbirth. Rhoda Young was widowed when her husband Adolphia, a captain of ten, was stricken with cholera during their 1852 trek, and three days later her eldest son died of the same disease. Brother Rollins in Mary Dart's company lost twelve of the fifteen members of his family. William Jex lost his closest friend. They had endured a hard ocean voyage together, and an equally difficult western trek proved too much for William's friend. "He had given his life for this 'new faith,'" William wrote in a memorial to his friend, "and he had divided his inheritance with me, that I, too, might enjoy the blessings of the new world and the new faith."[67]

The long waiting in the Valley by children for parents or par-

65. Emily Pauline Malan Farley, in Carter, *Treasures of Pioneer History* 5:63–64.

66. Beecher, *The Personal Writings of Eliza R. Snow*, 27.

67. Laura Swenson Fowers, in Carter, *Our Pioneer Heritage* 12:95; Rhoda Byrne Jared Young in Hall, *The Book of Jared*, 34; William and Eliza Jex, in Carter, *Treasures of Pioneer History* 4:45.

ents for children coming in later wagon trains sometimes ended
sadly. Isaac Hunt had sent his parents laboriously saved money
to emigrate and anxiously awaited their coming. When the
expected company reached the Valley, Isaac looked for his parents but without success. "What is the matter that they didn't
come?" he inquired. "Yes, my boy," he was told, "they did come,
but both died on the trail."[68] The frequency of death did not
diminish the anguish that it brought to those who lost loved
ones, especially in leaving them in unmarked graves along the
trail. "There is a feeling, a loneliness connected with burying our
dead a long distance from human habitation," wrote Mary Dart
after the death of her mother, brother, and sister on the plains.[69]
The trail west, observed Martha Payne Thomas, was "paved with
the sons and daughters of Zion."[70] But their writings confirm
their acceptance of loss and their ability to endure "all the pinch-
ing times," as Alice Houghton Greenwood labeled them in her
journal.[71]

But all was not hardship and sorrow, and many wagon
trains traveled the long journey with little difficulty. In fact,
many of the diarists write of invigorated health, of good times,
of adventure, and the thrill of being in a new and challenging
region of the country. Each day held a new discovery, and
evening brought rest and recreation. Community prayers,
singing, dancing, storytelling, and games made up an evening's
activities. Despite her weariness the next day, one young girl
refused to miss the dancing each night. Mary Leatham particularly remembered the music in the evening gatherings around
the camp fire, probably because her musician father could play
many instruments and evidently brought several with him.

68. Autobiographical Sketch of Isaac Hunt, typescript, LDS Church Archives.
69. "Sketch of the Life of Mary Dart Judd," 16.
70. In *Daniel Stillwell Thomas Family History* (Salt Lake City: Kate Woodhouse Kirkham, 1927), 47.
71. Alice Houghton Greenwood, "Letter to my Grandchildren," typescript, LDS Church Archives.

"Come, Come, Ye Saints" found its way to many emigrant trains by way of Utah teamsters and captains, who taught the song by rote to the newcomers.[72] Romances bloomed on the trail. "Young lovers strayed in the moonlight not far from camp, and I suppose repeated the old, old, but ever new story," remembered Mary Jane Lyttle, whose future husband courted her on the trail. Even the 24th of July was celebrated on the trail. Caroline Hopkins Clark's company of 1866 traveled only half the day on the 24th and then circled the wagons for singing, dancing, and general merriment.[73]

A new method for bringing emigrants to Utah, begun in the 1860s, was known as the Church train.[74] Young men were called to serve as teamsters for the well provisioned wagons going back to the Missouri or the current jumping-off place, picking up the waiting emigrants and returning to the Valley in one season. This method of travel brought nearly seventeen thousand emigrants to the Valley before 1869. It was a summer adventure for the young men, delighted to have the first opportunity to meet the young convert women.

Nothing in the trail experience quite matched the moment of arrival. Brigham Young's words when he first gazed on the Valley are legendary: "This is the right place."[75] But not all who

---

72. Mary Williams Leatham, typescript, Utah State Historical Society.

73. Caroline Hopkins Clark, 25 July 1866, *Our Pioneer Heritage* 10:47.

74. Information on Church trains can be found in John K. Hulmston, "Mormon Immigration in the 1860s: The Story of the Church Trains," *Utah Historical Quarterly* 58 (Winter 1990): 32–48; Leonard J. Arrington, *Great Basin Kingdom* (Lincoln: University of Nebraska Press, 1958), 105–11; "Freighters and Freighting," *An Enduring Legacy* 2:272–74; William G. Hartley, "Down and Back Trains: Travelers on the Mormon Trail in 1861," *Overland Journal* 11, 4 (1993): 23–34.

75. Several accounts describe this event. The most familiar is Wilford Woodruff's description in a speech given at a 24th of July celebration in the tabernacle in Salt Lake City. He wrote, "On the 24th I drove my carriage, with President Young lying on a bed in it, into the open valley, the rest of the company following. When we came out of the canyon into full view of the valley, I turned the side of my carriage around, open to the west, and President Young arose from his bed and took a survey of the country. While gazing upon the scene before us, he was enwrapped in vision for several minutes. He had seen the valley before in vision, and upon this occasion he saw the future glory of Zion and of Israel, as they would be, planted in the valleys of these mountains. When the vision had passed, he said, 'It is enough. This is the right place. Drive on.'" (*Deseret Evening News*, 26 July 1880.)

followed him to the Valley were so sure it was. Sophia Goodridge deigned to write what many others may have only felt when they first viewed their new home. "It was rather a dreary homecoming," she wrote in October 1850. "It was very dry and dusty, and the wind was blowing the dust in clouds. Only a few little log and adobe houses to be seen, fenced in with rail and willow fences. A few shade trees were to be seen here and there. I thought at first: 'Have I got to spend the rest of my days here in this dreary looking place?' But I soon felt all right about it and loved my mountain home."[76] When Ann Ham Hickenlooper, a young single woman from England, first saw the desolate scene in 1856, she "cried out to the Lord, 'where shall I find me a home?'"[77] Eliza Lyman, who arrived in 1847, remarked, "I do not think our enemies need envy us this locality or ever come here to disturb us."[78]

But others saw beyond the unpromising terrain and infant city and felt the joy of coming home. "After our long desert travel Salt Lake city was beautiful to us, with its streams of crystal water murmuring along the streets," Mary Dart observed. "There were not many houses but there were enough to give an air of civilization and comfort."[79] When Hannah Cornaby reached the Valley in October 1853, she felt "more than repaid for the nine months of travel, and all the hardship [they] had endured." Hannah was delighted with the "peaceful loveliness" of the city: "The neat adobe houses with their trim gardens, the crystal streams coursing along the sidewalks, giving life to avenues of shade trees, all aglow with the lovely tints of autumn, presented a picture that is indelibly fixed upon our minds."[80]

Some viewed the Valley through spiritual eyes, little noting

76. Diary of Sophia Lois Goodridge, 14 October 1850.
77. Della H. Barker, "Life Sketch of Ann Ham Hickenlooper," typescript, LDS Church Archives.
78. Diary of Eliza Partridge Lyman, 17 October 1847, LDS Church Archives.
79. "Sketch of the Life of Mary Dart Judd," 18.
80. Hannah Cornaby, *Autobiography and Poems*, 36.

the landscape or the fledgling settlement. Despite the unending difficulties Ann Jarvis experienced in getting to the Valley, when she first "saw the valley where God's people were," she said she was willing "to endure a great deal more for the same privilege."[81] Levi Jackman was ecstatic when he saw the Valley in July 1847. "When we finally got through it [the steep canyon]," he wrote, "it seemed like bursting from the confines of prison walls into the beauties of a world of pleasure and freedom. . . . We felt to thank the Lord . . . we had found a good country of land where we thought our enemies could never find us and where we could worship God unmolested."[82] William Grant was similarly excited when he first viewed the Valley two decades later. "The Beautiful City of Salt Lake Burst in our View. Joy, Joy, here was to us a paradise indeed."[83]

It was a paradise for Wilford Woodruff, too. He saw only beauty as the Valley scene rose up in full view when he emerged from Emigration Canyon. Before him lay a "rich fertile valley . . . surrounded by a perfect chain of everlasting hills," their "fresh water springs rivlets creeks & Brooks & Rivers of various sizes . . . wending there way into the great Salt Lake . . . & mountains Covered with eternal snow with there innumerable peaks like Pyramids towering towards Heaven." But his spiritual eyes saw "the land of promise held in reserve by the hand of GOD for a resting place for the Saints upon which A portion of the Zion of GOD will be built."[84] The Saints had found their Zion, and there they would stay.

For many, this was also a time of reunion with friends and family. Mary Ellen Kimball, who arrived with the second company of 1847, like many others greeted her first view of the Valley with relief, delight, and thanksgiving. "I shall never forget the

81. Ann Prior Jarvis, Autobiographical Sketch, typescript, 17, LDS Church Archives.
82. Journal of Levi Jackman, 22, 23 July 1847, typescript, LDS Church Archives.
83. Autobiography and Diary of William Grant, photocopy of manuscript, LDS Church Archives.
84. 24 July 1847, Journals of Wilford Woodruff 3:233–34.

sensation it gave me to see that peaceful lake," she wrote. "It seemed that my heart jumped into my mouth, and tears in my eyes. I felt to thank my Heavenly Father that we are so near our place of destination." But she was even more heartened when she entered the Valley to see the welcome face of a beloved friend and sister wife, Ellen Sanders Kimball, who had come with the pioneer company. "How charming to walk in a house and sit down to a table once more," Mary Ellen wrote. "She told me of her travels and I told her of mine."[85] Is it possible to imagine what these two pioneer women said to one another as they sat together in that bare little room after their thousand-mile journey?

A poignant note in all the accounts is the new arrivals' efforts to "arrange our attire as best we could after so long a journey in expectation of meeting our friends," as one diarist wrote. They shook the outer layer of dust from their clothes, washed their faces, smoothed their hair, and cleaned up their children in anticipation. But the "neat, clean and fair appearance of the people [in the Valley]," Mary Lois Walker Morris found, was still quite a contrast to the "brown and grim" appearance of the new arrivals. Mary Lois had done her best to avoid the telltale signs of the trek. She had always washed her face each day and protected it with a bonnet, but the marks of three months of trail travel were hard to hide.[86] In time, however, the physical traces of their long trek would fade. The memories would linger much longer, enhanced perhaps by each telling of the experience and, for some, a lasting allegiance to the company and captains that brought them west. Looking back in his trail experience, George Washington Hill was pleased with the performance of the wagon company in which he traveled, one of the first to enter the Valley. "I believe today that notwithstanding we had to suffer so much for even the commonest necessities of life," he wrote, "that the

85. Diary of Mary Ellen Kimball, typescript, LDS Church Archives.
86. Mary Lois Walker Morris, in Carter, *Treasures of Pioneer History* 3:40–41.

first immigration were the best satisfied and grumbled the least of any immigration that has ever come to Utah. We were all poor alike, we were all hungry alike, and we were all naked alike and we could each sympathize with the other."[87]

Their journey over, the pioneers discovered that a new task awaited them as they took their part in fulfilling the Prophet Joseph's vision. The long trek west had been a preparatory school in developing the tools they would need: commitment, hard work, patience, obedience, self-reliance, cooperation, endurance, and, most of all, faith. Faith had sent them on the journey west, faith had brought them to their journey's end, and faith would help them build their Zion. When the journey was hard, many others besides Charles Smith[88] found strength in the words of the Lord to ancient Israel: "Gather my saints together unto me; those that have made a covenant with me by sacrifice."[89] The pioneers had met the terms of the covenant. They could now enjoy its blessings.

87. George Washington Hill, Autobiography, typescript, 32, LDS Church Archives.

88. See Reminiscences and Diary of Charles Smith, 1842 March–1905 June, photocopy of typescript, LDS Church Archives.

89. Psalms 50:5.

Levi Jackman joined the Church in 1831 and was fifty years old when he made the journey west in Brigham Young's pioneer company. He kept a daily journal of the trek and his first winter in the Valley. He was a keen observer and wrote an unofficial account of that first historic journey to Utah. He also provides insight into the lives of those who remained in the Valley after Brigham Young and other Church leaders returned to the Missouri.

LEVI JACKMAN[90]

MARCH 29, 1847. I left home in company with Liman Curtis[91] to join the camp of pioneers to find a home for the Saints somewhere in the Rocky Mountains. I had one yoke of oxen and a wagon. Lyman had one horse. We took breadstuff to last us eighteen months, some beans, a little pork, but we had no groceries for we were not able to get them. My clothing was old and scarce. In this condition we started to go—where, we could not tell or what we should have to contend with. We only knew that we must go and the Lord would attend to bringing out the results.

We arrived at Winter Quarters on the 31st and after finishing our arrangements we left April 3 and on the sixth we arrived at the

---

90. Autobiography of Levi Jackman, typescript, Utah State Historical Society, Salt Lake City, Utah.

91. Lyman Curtis and Levi Jackman traveled to the Salt Lake Valley together, sharing a wagon and provisions. Levi's wife, Angeline Myers, died in 1846 in Nauvoo. After the death of his wife, Levi married a widow, Sally Plumb; however, she did not undertake this particular journey with him. Lyman's wife and six small children stayed in Winter Quarters until he returned for them, bringing them to the Valley in 1850.

Elk Horn where we found four teams that had started before us. We crossed the creek on a raft and waited for the remainder of the camp.

Saturday, April 10. The main camp commenced crossing the river and finished the next day. The river was about ten rods wide. This place is in latitude 41–46 north and 1,330 miles from the mouth of Bear River where it empties into Salt Lake, according to Fremont's account.[92]

Monday, April 12. Brothers Brigham, Kimball and some others returned to hold a council with the remainder of the Twelve who had just returned from the East. The most of the camp of about sixty-three wagons moved on up the Platte about ten miles and awaited their return.

Thursday, April 15. Brothers Young and Kimball and others returned to our camp on the Platte. The next day, the 16th, the camp was organized and started and went a few miles and camped; when all together the camp was seventy-three wagons and 143 men. The weather was cold—ice three-fourths of an inch thick in the mornings—no grass for our teams; had to chop down cottonwood for browse. This day we traveled about seven miles and camped. It was a cold day.

Wednesday, April 21. Cold wind N. E. Signs of rain. About 10 a.m. we had got within a few miles of the Pawnee Indian winter quarters,[93] and some few came out and met us and seemed very friendly. A little after noon we stopped to rest our teams opposite their camp which was on the other side of Loup Fork. The chief and about thirty others soon gathered in. They appeared friendly and wanted presents. But when we did not give them as much powder, tobacco, etc., as they wanted, they went away. Some of them stole a few things, such as bridles, etc.

---

92. John Charles Fremont and his men explored and charted the Western American frontier, including the Great Plains, the Rocky Mountains, and the Salt Lake Valley. His reports were very popular and were used widely by western travelers.

93. The Pawnee village was located near the mouth of Loup Fork, near modern Columbus, Nebraska.

We went on about eight miles and camped. To prevent a surprise by the Indians in the night we had a hundred men on guard, fifty at a time. We had some wind and rain and cold. The Pawnees are much fairer complexioned than most other Indians. They had their heads shaved with the exception of a strip about two inches wide from a little back of their foreheads to the back of their necks that was about two inches long and stuck straight up, resembling a rooster's comb. Their dress was a breechclout and a buffalo skin or robe used as a blanket to throw over their shoulders. Some had leggings.

Thursday, April 22. Fine day. Followed up Loup Fork and a little after noon crossed Beaver Fork, a stream about three rods wide, two and one-half feet deep. The banks were high and steep. We had to attach ropes to the tongues of the wagons and men to the ropes to help the teams up. This is in latitude 41–25. A little before sunset we reached the old Pawnee Mission Station, but it was evacuated.[94] This is a fine situation.

Friday, April 23. We went up about seven miles and commenced making arrangements for crossing the river, which is about half a mile wide and about three feet deep in some places, with quicksand bottom. We spent the day in preparing for crossing. We had come up the Platte and Loup Fork about 130 miles through as fine a country as I ever saw for farming or grazing. The great difficulty was the lack of timber. We camped about three-fourths of a mile below the old Pawnee town. I went to see the place. It is situated on the north side of the river and on a beautiful plain which is about twenty feet above the river. The plain is about one-half mile wide. Back of that, the ground rises. The town stood on the bank of the river. It contained about 140 lodges.

Last winter, when the Pawnees were all gone on a hunt, the

---

94. The Pawnee Mission had been abandoned and burned the autumn before because of Sioux raids.

Sioux Indians came and burned the town, only leaving the chief's lodge which for some reason they left unhurt. The lodges had all been built alike. The one remaining was about forty-five feet on the inside and about fifteen feet high in the center. They were built round with a row of posts about seven feet high standing nearly straight up and down. On the top of these posts were plates to support the upper part. The timbers were put on these plates running quite steep to the top, leaving a hole in the center for the smoke to go out, the fire being in the center of the lodge. From the east side an entry was made running out about twenty feet and of good width.

The first covering to the lodge was poles running up and down. The next was small poles running round and lashed to the others. The next was long grass laying up and down. Then all was covered with turves of grass. The lodges were all made in that way. They had stables made with poles stuck in the ground, and others running around fastened with strips of rawhide or bark. The timber for all this work had to be brought a number of miles and must have cost a vast amount of hard labor. [. . .]

Tuesday, April 27. We left the Loup Fork and went south to strike the Platte. About 10 a.m. we came to where the old grass had been burned and the young grass began to make its appearance. Through all our journey thus far and still further, we had to feed our teams some of our breadstuff to keep them up. At this place we found the first signs of buffalo. Before we reached the Platte bottoms, the ground became so sandy that it looked like a barren desert. We stopped this night on a fine little creek, but found it difficult to find a few dry willows to make a little fire. One antelope was killed. This was the first game of any size that had been killed since we started. Just as we stopped, a gun was carelessly discharged and broke a horse's leg. This was the fourth horse that was lost since Friday. On that night a horse belonging to Brother B. Young got hung by it's halter. [. . .]

Saturday, May 1. Windy and cold. About nine a.m. we saw

about fifty buffalo. Our hunters went after them but got none. Soon after, we saw hundreds of them and we got five old ones and a number of calves. This day we passed through what is called a prairie dog town, which covers many acres. These rodents live in holes. We stopped a little before sunset and got in our buffalo meat, which was received with much joy. We had a fine feast that night. We camped on a creek which we called Buffalo Creek. We found some wood. Traveled that day about twelve miles. We have passed through a fine bottom country of good land for some days. The interior is too broken for cultivation.

Sunday, May 2. Our camp this morning had the appearance of a meat market. All hands were fixing their beef [buffalo] for cooking or drying and making ropes of the hides. The ice was near one-half inch thick this morning but soon came off warm and pleasant.

We have passed for some days a country of buffalo grass. It resembles blue grass in that it is fine and usually not more than four to six inches high. In many places the grass is fed down by the buffalo so that it has the appearance of an old pasture; only the fence is missing. We went on about three miles to good grass and camped on the bank of the Platte, a little above Grand Island and at the north of a creek that we called Bluff Creek. No wood, only willow brush.

The buffalo meat came good to us, for [Lyman] Curtis and myself had lived on cornmeal bread and water porridge for some time. If only we could get a little milk of John Brown[95] to put into it. When he could spare it, he would give us some. I shall never forget his kindness to us.

Monday, May 3. The camp stopped this day to do some blacksmith work and let the teams recruit a little, it being the best place of grass we had found. At the same time a company

---

95. John Brown was the captain of the thirteenth ten, of which Levi Jackman was a member. Brown was also one of the chief hunters of the company.

of twenty hunters went out to hunt and to see the situation of the country ahead of us. About three o'clock they returned and reported that they had discovered a large body of Indians who tried to surround them, but they made their escape. Much anxiety was felt for the hunters who had gone forth, and a company sent out for them. They all returned to safety. They killed two or three antelope and about as many buffalo calves. We saw smoke ahead and found that what little feed there was would soon be destroyed by fire, which would be hard for us.

Tuesday, May 4 [1847]. We started on but had not gone far before we found that our fears were too true. The Indians had set fire to the old grass which was among the new and all had been burned together, excepting here and there a small spot. The sight was gloomy indeed. At this time a small company of traders was passing down on the other side of the river. One of them came over and informed us that the grass was good on the other side, but after a short consultation we concluded not to cross but continue on the north side because it would be better for our brethren who would follow us. So, after writing a few letters to send back by them, we started on. We traveled about ten miles and camped on a creek which I called Clear Creek. We found grass at this place.

Wednesday, May 5. We found the land more moist and flat than before. The wheels cut in considerably in places. Most of the grass was burned. At about half past four we had to stop because of the smoke and fire ahead, and the wind had blown a furious gale all day from the south. We camped close to the river and put our teams on a small island where there was grass. This day the camp killed one buffalo and five calves. We had plenty of beef, veal and antelope, all first-rate meat. We traveled about ten miles and camped. [. . .]

Friday, May 7. We started late this morning that the teams might have a chance to fill themselves. The wind blew hard from the north and cold. The Indians have camped along the way in large bodies, and the sticks they left and a little driftwood and buffalo dung served for our fuel. The buffalo are so plentiful that it requires a strict watch to keep them and our cows from running together. We can kill all we wish but we kill only what we need to eat. We are in full view of hundreds of them all the time. This day we went about nine miles and camped near the river by a slough. [. . .]

Monday, May 24. It was so cold this morning that we could not keep warm with overcoats and mittens. It snowed a little. The road was quite sandy today. A little before night we discovered a party of Indians on the other side of the river coming up on horses. When they saw that we were going to camp they hoisted the American flag. We answered it with a white one. They then commenced crossing the river. There were about forty of them. They camped on the bank. We camped near about one-half mile back from the river. Some of them came to us and were very friendly. We traveled this day sixteen and one-half miles. (Before this time, Brother William Clayton had fixed a way of measuring the road with the wagon wheel [roadometer].)[96]

Tuesday, May 25. The most of the Indians and squaws came to our camp this morning and wanted to trade. Some of our camp traded some cornmeal and bread and got robes, etc. Some traded horses. They were fine-looking people; good behaved and a happy company. They were dressed neat and clean and were truly gentlemen and ladies. When we started they recrossed the river and went on their way. They were a band of the Sioux. Traveled twelve and one-half miles that warm day. [. . .]

---

96. Originally, Clayton determined distances by measuring the circumference of a wagon wheel, tying a piece of red flannel to a spoke near the wheel and counting the revolutions. Clayton and Orson Pratt upgraded his development by the setting of several wooden cogs in the wheel that measured miles and quarter miles. This final version of the roadometer was built by Appleton Harmon and was completed 12 May 1847. A useful study of the various devices assembled to measure distance on the western trails is Norman E. Wright, "Odometer: Distance Measurement on Western Emigrant Trails," *Overland Journal* 13 (1995), 14–24.

Saturday, May 29. Cold, wet morning. Did not start early. For some time past some of the brethren had indulged in many things that were leading them astray, such as dancing too much and playing cards, dice, etc., and using bad language. Brother Young, seeing the situation of the camp, improved an opportunity this morning after the rain had stopped to call the camp together. He reproved them sharply for their conduct and warned them of the distress that would come to them unless they repented and reformed. After much good instruction and admonition, he called on them to know whether they would reform. They covenanted that they would. He appointed the next day for a day of fasting and prayer, and for breaking bread. After noon we traveled eight and one-half miles. It rained smartly before we camped, but stopped before sunset.

Sunday, May 30. We attended to the duties of the day. A good spirit prevailed and many expressed their determination to do better. [. . .]

Wednesday, June 2, 1847. We spent the day making arrangements for crossing the river to the south side.

The traders had a flat boat at this place which we hired to cross our train and paid them fifteen dollars for the use of it. They were quite friendly to us. The leaves on the trees are about half grown.

Thursday, June 3. The trader fort stands in the fork between the Platte and the Laramie forks.[97] The Platte is about twenty rods wide at this place. We commenced crossing but were hindered by rain.

Friday, June 4. We finished crossing and I went out to the fort, which was about one and one-half miles from the Platte. The walls of the buildings are made of adobes with a door attached to the walls on the inside; one was two stories high. A

---

97. He is probably referring to Fort Laramie.

row of houses also runs through the center of the fort. About forty men belong to this station. Three of our company who had been members of the Mormon Battalion, whose families were left at Pueblo, left our company to go for their families, a distance of 180 miles. We were also joined by a small company of Saints with several wagons and one cart; they had wintered at Pueblo.[98]

A little timber stood along the riverbank and a little on the bluffs. I saw in this place a sample of the way the Indians deposit their dead. They roll them in a blanket or buffalo robe and lash them in the forks or to a limb of a tree, high up from the ground. [. . .]

Friday, June 11. Fine weather and mostly good roads. Killed plenty of antelope and some deer. By this time we had to diminish our allowance of bread and eat more meat, which came rather hard on me for fresh meat gave me the bowel complaint. This day we traveled seventeen miles and camped on the river bend. Here we overtook one of the Oregon trains that had passed us. They were crossing the river, but we went farther up to cross.

Saturday, June 12. I was quite unwell today. We had tolerably good roads. We went eleven miles and reached the main ford. The water was so high that we could not ford it. Our men, who went ahead to prepare for our crossing, had overtaken the first Oregon train and had taken their goods over in a leather boat which we had brought with us from Winter Quarters. They received a fair reward in provisions, which we much needed. The bluffs to the south some miles off were covered in spots with pine or balsam.

98. During the winter of 1846–47, three sick detachments consisting of 273 people were sent from the main body of the Mormon Battalion to Fort Pueblo in Colorado. These detachments included some soldiers and most of the families that had accompanied the battalion. The small company of Saints was from Mississippi and had hoped to rendezvous with the pioneers the year before but decided to winter in Pueblo, Colorado, when they learned the Saints were remaining at the Missouri during the winter of 1846–47. See Carter, *Our Pioneer Heritage*, 2:421–431.

Sunday, June 13. We had a meeting as usual. Brother B[righam]. Young, H[eber]. C. Kimball and O[rson]. Pratt gave good instructions. The provisions received, as before mentioned, were divided in the camp which gave each five and one-half pounds of flour, two of meal and of bacon, all of which was needed, as our provisions were scarce. We had fed so much to our teams to keep them alive. The Lord has, thus far, blessed and preserved us.

Monday, June 14. We made rafts of pine and fir poles that we had brought from the bluffs or mountains, on which we crossed the river with the wagons; we took the goods in the leather boats. In the afternoon we had a thundershower with heavy wind, which stopped us.

Wednesday, June 15. We crossed what we could but the water was high and rising. The river at this place is about one-fourth mile wide and ran so swift that we had to tow or pull our raft upstream more than a mile to land at the ferry on the opposite side. The Oregon companies were coming up to us. They wanted we should take them over. We finally concluded to leave a few men with the boat and raft for a few days.

Finally two canoes were made and fastened together, which did well for a ferryboat. After everything was arranged and we had all crossed—as well as some of the other companies—we got ready to start. We were detained at this place until Saturday. We left a company at the ferry to cross the Oregon companies that were continually coming upon us, and we went on. We traveled twenty-seven and one-half miles and camped in a place without much grass. All the wood that we could get through this section of the country was dead wild sage and green bush, a small sort of brush.

Sunday, June 20. For the want of grass for our teams we went on. We found some small patches of grass and some water in a number of places. We got to Willow Springs about noon which is a good campground for a small camp. We then rose a high hill and from the top we could see beds of snow away south on the mountains. Gravelly hills and a sandy bottom made it hard wheeling.

Monday, June 21. Some frost this morning near the creek. We passed this morning a number of what we then called salt ponds, but which proved to be saleratus ponds.[99] We have come south direct for about twelve miles. We reached Stillwater at Independence Rock at noon, and according to our measurement it is 174 1/2 miles from Laramie to Fort John. Some of the men went back at noon and got pails full of the saleratus which proved to be pure and good. [. . .]

Sunday, June 27. The morning is pleasant but cool and frosty. The mountains a little north of us, covered with snow, look a little odd at this season of the year. The scarcity of grass compelled us to go on. We met a company from Oregon, and one old mountaineer, who gave gloomy accounts of the country around Bear River and the Salt Lake. The day was warm and the land loose and gravelly.

Monday, June 28. Warm day, good roads, level. This afternoon we met Captain [James] Bridger of Fort Bridger. He gave us much information in regard to the Salt Lake country, which was not very favorable. We traveled about fifteen miles today and camped on the Little Sandy. It is about three rods wide and about two feet deep. [. . .]

Wednesday, June 30. We struck the Green River at noon; had come eight miles. It is skirted with bitter cottonwood of good size. We had to have rafts to cross on, which were made this afternoon. At this place Sam Brannan from California met us. He brought a good report from that country.[100]

Thursday, July 1. We commenced crossing the Green River

---

99. Saleratus is a bicarbonate or baking soda. It was used by westward travelers in baking.

100. A year after his six-month voyage to California from the East Coast, Samuel Brannan intercepted Brigham Young to urge him to continue on to California to settle.

which is about forty rods wide with a heavy current. It was a job to cross it.

Sunday, July 4. After crossing the river we traveled three miles down the river where we camped. From here we sent five men back to meet the camp that was coming after us, to take dispatches and to guide them on. The weather was warm and quite a number of our company had been taken sick with mountain fever within a few days past. They would generally get better in two or three days.

Wednesday, July 7. Crossed Black's Fork a number of times and camped near Fort Bridger. It consisted of three log rooms and a small yard enclosed with pickets. We came this day seventeen and one-fourth miles. On Monday last I was taken violently sick with the mountain fever. I do not know as I ever experienced such excruciating pain before in my life as I did through the night Monday. It was mostly in my back and hips. I am now getting better. There more or less are several taken sick almost every day. The stony ground that we have to travel on makes it very hard for those who have to ride in the wagons. [. . .]

Monday, July 12. Better roads. Crossed Deer Creek. The soil looks better. Some herbage on the hills. Found scattering flax for some days past. Brother B. Young was taken sick today where we stopped at noon. He stopped and a few wagons stopped with him. We came sixteen and one-half miles today. We began to find grass quite a plenty. My health remains quite poor so that I am hardly able to walk. It was thought best to send on a few teams and men to look out and fix the road, and the remainder, with most of the sick, to stop a day or two. Accordingly, twenty-three teams started a little after noon on Tuesday 13. We took the valley of Wells Fork and followed it down about twelve miles and camped. Our measuring wagon stayed, so we had to guess the distance.

Wednesday, July 14. We found scattered flax of good size. The valley was fertile but very narrow and the hills on both sides were several hundred feet high. In many places it was difficult passing. A little before night we struck the Weber Fork and camped. We came about fourteen miles today.

Thursday, July 15. We wound our way up the ravine to the top of the hill, which was very difficult to ascend, for about seven miles, and raised from four hundred to five hundred feet. We then descended another ravine, equally as bad, and camped after traveling about twelve miles. Curtis was taken sick this evening, and I was far from being well, which made things look rather gloomy. [. . .]

Tuesday, July 20. We left Kenyon Creek [Canyon Creek] this morning and struck up a ravine. Our journey for a number of days has been rather gloomy. The mountains on both sides have been so high and the ravines so crooked that we could see but a short distance ahead and it looked as though we were shut up in a gulch without any chance of escape. The ground was quite rising for about five miles. We found more timber today than we had had since before we left home, but much of it had been killed by fires. After we got to the top of the hill, we had a long, steep hill to go down. [. . .]

Thursday, July 22. This morning a part of the camp that we had left came up with us and others had to stop on account of sickness. Our move has been slow for it took all the able-bodied men from one-half to three-fourths of the time to make the road so we went about four miles. We had to pass through a canyon that was full of timber, mostly of small maple, and the bluffs came almost together at the bottom. When we finally got through it, it seemed like bursting from the confines of prison walls into the beauties of a world of pleasure and freedom.

We now had entered the valley and our vision could extend far and wide. We were filled with joy and rejoicing and thanksgiving. We could see to the west, about thirty miles distance, the Great Salt Lake stretched northwest to a distance unknown to us, and the valley extending far to the north and south. No timber was to be seen. We went on west about two miles and camped on a creek with plenty of grass and some brush for fire. Brother Pratt and others who went out in the morning to explore the country soon joined us. They reported that they found but little timber—only what was in the mountains.

Friday, July 23. We went a short distance north to a small grove on a little stream and camped. Brother Pratt called the camp together and dedicated this country to the Lord. We then commenced plowing to put in a little early corn, buckwheat, potatoes, peas, beans, etc.

The soil was good and before night we had put in seed. We felt to thank the Lord that we had been preserved on our journey; that no lives were lost; that we had found a good country of land where we thought our enemies could never find us and where we could worship God unmolested. According to our measure we are 1,040 miles from Winter Quarters.

Saturday, July 24, 1847. About noon Brother Young and company arrived and we had a time of rejoicing together without restraint. We had a meeting with much good instruction. Brother Young said that we should find a place for a permanent location. We should then have our lands set off to us and each one manage his own affairs and work for himself, etc. We had men out every day exploring the country and it was found that there was a large amount of timber in the mountains, though mostly hard to get at. The timber was mostly pine and balsam with some oak brush and ash. [. . .]

July 28, Tuesday. This is my fiftieth birthday. This evening Brother Young called the camp together and the men who had been exploring made their report. They had found no place that looked so well as this place. Many of the brethren expressed their feelings and all seemed to feel that this was the place to stop. Brother Young then said that he wanted to know how the brethren felt in regard to it; but he knew that this was the place for the city, for he had seen it before (in vision), and that we were now standing on the southeast corner of the temple block. He said many other things which did us good.

A vote was taken then on the subject and all voted that this be the place to stop. It was then advised that we build a fort to protect ourselves from the Indians. The plan was that it should be made of sun-dried brick, or adobes, enclosing forty squares of land. The wall to be ten feet high, which was to form the back side of the houses, and to have one large gate on each side of the square. I presume that a colony was never settled under so many disadvantages as this.

The appearance of the country was truly forbidding. The face of the earth had the appearance of a barren desert. No grass, only on the streams or on low land. Nothing green on the remainder. The mountaineers said that grain would not grow here for they had tried it and every appearance went to prove the fact. All we had was in our wagons. Our tools for farming, etc., our seed, our clothing, our provisions to last till we could raise some, if that ever was. In fact, our all. Out of the reach of commerce, and one thousand miles from any settlement to the East rendered the hope of assistance out of the question, no odds what our wants might be. We must depend on God and do the best we can, feeling, however, that the mobs would not be likely to disturb us for a few years at least. So we took courage and went to work, some at farming and some on the walls of the fort.

About this time a part of the Mormon Battalion arrived, which gave us joy. It was deemed advisable to send back as many teams to Winter Quarters as could be spared to help others the next spring.

Accordingly, as soon as they had time to recuperate a little, the ox teams started back. Curtis went with my team, which left me without any; and what was worse, I had not provisions to last me more than six or eight days. Brother Kimball advised me to stay, which I was willing to do, for to go back was like going to the land of sorrow and death. I felt sure that the Lord would preserve us in some way and that seemed to be the feeling of all of us.

About two weeks after the ox teams started, Brothers Young and Kimball and others started back with the horse teams. Taking out so many reduced our number to a few; but we drove business to the best advantage that we could, soon expecting a company of our brethren with their families to arrive. We expected there would be about one hundred families of them from Winter Quarters, and I was anxious for their arrival as I expected my son, Ammi, was with them.[101]

My provisions were soon gone. Brother [Shadrach] Roundy had gone back and left his flour with me. He said that if his family was not on the way he would go on, and in this case I could use his breadstuff. So when mine was gone I used some of his. He, however, met his family and came back.

About September 20, the camps began to arrive, but instead of one hundred families, there were about 660 wagons and many of the teams were driven by women and children, the men being either dead or in the army [Mormon Battalion]. The camp had lost many of their cattle by disease and starvation. Only two or three deaths had taken place among the people.

About the middle of September, we had a frost which killed some of our crops. Soon afterward they were all destroyed by the cattle, the land not being fenced. Now the cattle are guarded. But we had proved that the earth would produce grain, etc.

September 30. I went out about ten miles and met Ammi in a train. Our meeting was one of joy, being in a land far from our former home and under these peculiar circumstances with no other connections within one thousand miles. I had not seen him for more than two years.

In a few days all the camps got in, which made a large show.

---

101. At this time, Levi Jackman had five living children from his union with Angeline. Ammi Rumsey, the youngest, was about twenty-two years old.

Up to this time I had hoped that I should have received some help from my company of ten which I had belonged to in the East, but none; and every visible prospect for a living was cut off. Some of those who came had got plenty for themselves; while others had scarcely any left. It looked like a dark day, but I consoled myself by thinking that I was in the line of my duty, and that this was the work of the Lord and He would see us safely through. So I felt to resign myself into His hands.

We found now that our fort, which contained 160 rooms, would house only about one-fourth of the people. It being too late to make adobes the most of the people got some kind of timber for houses and enlarged the fort on the north and south, making from north to south 160 rods and forty east and west. Some of the brethren who had nothing to eat got a chance to work for some who had plenty, thus receiving board for their work, which was better than to starve.

I went to making door and window frames out of split timber and got some provisions for it and some work on my house, firewood, etc. I moved into my house or shop the latter part of November. I lived alone.

A high council was organized soon after the companies came in, and I had the honor of being chosen one of them. In the forepart of November, we sent a company to California to get some spring wheat and other seeds, and cows, and to make such trades as they thought best, in the name of the people. This undertaking was a very hazardous and hard enterprise—to start a journey of hundreds of miles at this late season of the year, through an untraveled mountain region, and none of them knowing the way.

About this time more of the Battalion arrived from California. They were destitute of means of subsistence, which made our case look much worse than it did before. Winter had come on and it must be a long time before we could raise our own bread, if ever.

A number of the Battalion started back to Winter Quarters to their families. Our main dependence for living was our cattle and many of them had been sent back. The remainder were very poor, which was rather slim picking. A few Indians came and camped near us for the winter. They lived mostly on seeds and roots and wolf meat. We found they eat the large thistle root. I went out to get some one day, but by the time I had got about a bushel the snow fell and covered the ground and I could find no more. I only regretted that I could not get enough of them; they tasted much like a parsnip. I have to eat very sparingly, and frequently do not know where the next bite is coming from; yet the Lord opens the way for my support and preservation.

January 1848. Being without a first presidency seemed to give the people a chance to show out what was in them. It having cost the people so much to fetch provisions so far, some appeared to be disposed to make the necessities of the destitute their opportunity, and sold things, I thought, rather high. I feared that such a principle, if not checked, might prove our destruction. I went to Father John Smith, who was then the president of the place,[102] and recommended that prices should be set by the council for labor, provisions, etc. The proposition was opposed, but it was finally carried into effect and the results were good. Some few were not pleased with the arrangements, but it changed the drift of things much for the better.

The most of the people were desirous to do right and were kind and did all they could to help the poor and the needy and to build up the kingdom of God on earth. I had expected that we had left the thieves behind, but in this I was disappointed for we found that they were in this place too. As fast as they were detected, they were dealt with according to law.

A spirit of dissatisfaction began to show itself as to the coun-

---

102. John Smith, uncle of the Prophet Joseph Smith and fifth patriarch of the Church, presided over the Great Salt Lake Valley from his arrival in September 1847 until October 1848.

try and against our leaders. Some wanted to go to California and were determined they would go at all hazards. The council took the subject into consideration.

Not knowing what influence they might use in that place, and for other reasons, we passed a law that none would be permitted to go until the presidency should return next season. Yet some did start and we sent the marshal and brought them back. They, however, got permission to go from somebody, and they started on again. I must acknowledge I thought it bad policy but it was not for me to judge. It seemed to give them power over the council, and others took license from it to do a little more as they pleased. I thought that we had better have no law than to have it trampled underfoot.

The winter has been very mild, with but little snow in the valley. Cattle have lived well by grazing. The large wolves have killed some of our oxen and cows, and the Indians near Utah Lake have driven off some stock which was truly a loss to us under our impoverished circumstances. But we hope for better times.

Notwithstanding the dissension and covetousness that was among us, take us as a whole we enjoyed ourselves and were as happy a people as could be found in any place.

On March 12, a company of seven men started for Winter Quarters with the mail. Ammi was one of them. It was a hard and hazardous undertaking; over one thousand miles to go at this season of the year without an inhabitant only at Bridger and Laramie; perhaps to lose their way in the mountains or on the plains, or to be killed by the Indians. But the mail must go. I felt bad for Ammi under such circumstances, but I believed the Lord would preserve them, although they might have to suffer much.

Both did take place. They narrowly escaped death by the Indians and by freezing and starvation; yet they got through alive and were joyfully received by the presidency and all the Saints. I felt rather lonely for awhile, not having any connections within one thousand miles. Yet in the main I enjoyed myself well.

*George Washington Hill left his home in Dallas County, Missouri, in 1846
after becoming converted to Mormonism through his associations with a
Mormon girl, Cynthia Utley Stewart. After marrying, they left Dallas County
with Cynthia's large family, which included her mother, her numerous siblings, and her uncle's family, determined, he wrote, to find "the Church of
Christ and identify myself with [it] and to cast my lot with theirs, come weal or
woe." Finding the Saints in Mount Pisgah, he moved to the Boyer River, where
he settled his family for the winter. He was baptized in June 1847 and traveled with his large family in the Abraham O. Smoot company, which left
Winter Quarters later that month. He was glad "to get away from that inhospitable place with life even," he wrote, "for we did not think we should have
had even that if we had remained much longer."*

GEORGE WASHINGTON HILL[103]

IN JUNE, 1846, [I] bade adieu to home
and friends by the ties of nature, and
launched forth into the wide world with
a large family to see to and very little
means to see to them with, but placing
my trust in God. Like Abraham of old,
I started forth to a strange land. I knew
not where, but determined to find the
Church of Christ and identify myself

103. Incidents in the Life of George Washington Hill (1878), LDS Church Archives.

with, to cast my lot with, theirs, come weal or woe. It did not matter with me if I knew I was right; I did not care what country I got to if I was able to find the Church.

We took our course for Warsaw [Missouri], thinking that by the time we had crossed the Osage River we should be able to learn the whereabouts of the Church. In this we were disappointed, for we could not learn anything definite about them, only that they had left Nauvoo for the wilderness. I knew that they were north of us somewhere, so I determined to steer north until we would strike their trail, and I knew that once on their trail we could follow them up so we turned our course for Boonville [Copper Co., Missouri], crossed the Missouri River at that place, still getting no tidings of the Mormons. We passed on up by the way of Keitsville [Keytesville, Chariton Co.]. Sometimes we would hear they were up in Davies County, sometimes that they were already out on the plains. Getting so many reports, and no two of them alike, we hardly knew what course to pursue.

I was musing on these different reports as we were traveling along in a big plain road when we came to where there was a dim road turned off to the right, like an old wood road that did not look like as though there had been a wagon on it for a year. But I did not want to travel the course we were going any longer, now we had got across Grand River. I felt all of a sudden as soon as we crossed the river that I wanted to go more to the right, and as soon as my eye caught sight of this old road, the spirit seemed to say, "Take that road." I turned my team into it and went right along without asking anybody where it went or how far it was to the end of it. After I had taken this road I was satisfied again with our course.

The same evening the little one-horse wagon my mother-in-law [Ruthinda Baker Stewart] rode in broke down, every spoke in one hind wheel breaking. We now seemed to be in a fix. There was no blacksmith nor wagon shop in twenty miles of us, as I knew of, but I thought there had to be a first time to do anything, and although I had never done anything of the kind I knew we could not stop there to hunt for somebody that knew how to do such work. So away I went to a field that happened to be in about half a mile and got a rail out of the fence and went to work with a dull axe, a dull hand saw and a dull drawing knife, which was all the tools we had, filled the wheel, put on the tire and started on in one day, thinking I had done very well in my first attempt at wagon making. Although I had seen nicer jobs done, still it answered our purpose very well. I had this job to do twice that summer, but after I had performed my first feat I did not mind it for I thought I was getting to be quite a wagon maker.

After following this old road some forty or fifty miles it brought us to Kelsey's Mills.[104] Here we got the first correct information that we had had at all about the Mormons. We learned that they had established a resting place about eighty miles from here that they called [Mount] Pisgah. We learned also that it was the council to exc[h]ange our horses for oxen as they would travel better on grass than horses. This suited me and seemed to be good council, so we stopped here one week trading our horses for cattle.

Here were the first Mormon elders that I had ever seen. Their names were Thomas Workman and Samuel Branon.[105] They went with me all around the country and were of good service to me, assisting me to trade. Resting here for a week was also of great benefit to my wife as her health had been very poor for some time.

After having finished our trading, resting one week, and obtaining supplies, we resumed our journey. A few days brought us to Pisgah. This was a place that President Young had prepared for a resting place for the poor that could not prosecute the journey. It was a nice-looking place situated on Grand River (probably Soldier River now). Here I rented a log house for a

104. If his mileage estimates are correct, Kelsey's Mills was probably located in northern Missouri. There is a possibility he is referring to Coulsons Mills located in Linn County, Missouri, north of Keyesville.

105. It is unclear to whom he is referring since the more familiar Samuel Brannan had set sail for California in February of the same year.

short time, but I did not feel satisfied. Here I found the heads of the Church had gone on to the Missouri River. I wanted to get near to where the heads of the Church were, thinking I would get more information than I could back in the rear, and then I did not like Grand River for winter.

Accordingly, in a few days I took James W. Stewart [his brother-in-law] with me and went on to the Missouri River. Here I found an uncle to my wife, William Stewart, with whom we stopped a day or two and then returned to Pisgah in time to be at the confinement of my wife on the twenty-second of August, 1846. My oldest son [George R.] was born at Mt. Pisgah, then Pottawattamie County in the State of Iowa.

In about two weeks after this event I took the teams and went back to Kelsey's Mills after provisions I had bought and left there as we came out. I was gone between two and three weeks on this trip. When I returned, I found my wife and child well, as well as the rest of the family. During my absence one of my neighbors had killed two of my cows, quite a loss to me as we were where I could not replace them. I brought him up before Charles C. Rich, who was left there to preside, but was told plainly that, as I did not belong to the Church, that my testimony could not be taken against one who did belong to the Church. This seemed rather hard for me to bear, as if I could not tell the truth before being baptised. Still, I passed over it as well as I could.

About the first of October, we hitched up and rolled out for the Missouri River and selected a place for wintering on the Booyou River on account of the joint rushes that grew there in abundance and keep green all winter; stock do well on joint rushes. Here I had my last cow stolen and had one mare and colt drowned in Booyou River.[106]

---

106. The main body of the Church decided against camping on the Boyer River in spite of the abundance of rushes because, according to an Indian report, the area was not suitable for winter camping. Boyer was given a French pronunciation, "Boyay," which accounts for Hill's curious spelling of it.

Here we had a very hard-winter and were very poorly prepared for it; we had a very hard time. I built a small log house
with a chimney, made of sods cut out with a space. We were very
poorly clad, poorly fed, poorly housed, and I think the most
severe winter I ever experienced. It seemed as if the adversary was
determined to leave no stone unturned that would discourage
me or that would hinder me in the prosecution of the journey
or the accomplishing of the purpose for which I had set out, but
I had endeavored to count the cost before starting and I had
determined to go through if I had to go alone and on foot with
nothing, realizing that the Saviour's words were just as true when
he said, "He that will not leave father and mother, houses and
lands, wives and children, is not worthy of me" [Matthew 10:37],
and also, "He that putteth his hand to the plow and looketh back
is not worthy of me" [Luke 9:62], as when he said, "He that
believeth and is baptized shall be saved" [Mark 16:16]. So that the
exertions of the adversary were all wasted on me; they never
served to discourage me in the least. They had but one effect on
me, and that was to make me weep when alone that circumstances
were so hard with me and that I could not provide any better for
those that were dependent on me during this winter.

We had a good many councils as to how we should provide
for the journey in the spring. We had neither money nor teams
and provisions suffucient for the journey, and how to obtain
them was the great consideration with us. My wife's mother had
an old negro woman slave she wanted the boys, some of them, to
take her off to Missouri and sell her, as she had become dissatisfied and did not want to go any farther, but they refused. It was
finally decided that I should do this job.

Finally I consented to take her and do the best I could with
her, so I got one of the boys to go with me as far as Council Point
where I sold her to Captain Whitehead for fifty dollars in cash,
two cows, two yoke of cattle and one wagon. The wagon, oxen and
cows I had to go to Missouri after. I sent every cent of the money

home with the boy that went with me lest I should be obliged to spend some of it for something to eat. And away I went after the cows and oxen, and this was quite a severe job, as I had two cows to drive loose and the oxen and wagon, this giving me plenty of exercise. In fact, it kept me running nearly all the time. The snow was pretty deep and the wind came howling down the Missouri Bottoms, driving the snow in my face for four of the coldest successive days that I had ever experienced.

I finally arrived home with my cows, oxen and wagon without injury except that I had frozen my ears, but I thought I got off well at that. My wife's mother was well pleased with what I had done and promised me one of the cows, but I never realized the promise.

We remained in this place until about the middle of February when I concluded to move over into Winter Quarters and get to work preparing [for] the journey the following summer. We were now busy fitting up the pioneers. I now tried to get my oldest brother-in-law [James Wesley Stewart] to remain and bring on his mother and brothers and sisters and let me go on with the pioneers, but he absolutely refused, said he would have nothing to do with bringing that great family of children into the wilderness to starve to death, but offered to go with the pioneers himself if I would remain and bring on the family. To this I finally gave my consent and went to work and fitted my own team and wagon. In company with my wife's uncle, William Stewart, we got our team and outfit fitted up according to requirement and started them off with the pioneers about the middle of April, 1847.

I now turned my attention to getting ready for following with the families. This involved another trip to Missouri, a distance of one hundred and twenty-five miles and back, making some two hundred and fifty miles. With ox teams that had to travel over one thousand miles with heavy loads and without roads to travel on, there was only one thing that made the venture to start from the Missouri River in 1847, and that was the health of my wife. She had taken the scurvy in the winter superinduced by our living as we did without vegetables. And as soon as the weather began to get warmer in the spring, she got worse instead of better and came very near dying. In fact, I had no hopes for her but to get on the road traveling as soon as possible, thinking a change of scenery, a change of air, and a change of water might be beneficial to her. I was determined to try it, let the consequences be what they might. I knew that we did not have money enough to get a decent outfit to go with, but I would have preferred to have started with my gun only and to have taken my chance as an Indian rather than to have remained in that inhospitable region with the scurvy taking the people off by the hundreds as it was doing.

Accordingly, I took what money we had, and taking G. R. Stewart [his brother-in-law] with me to drive one of the teams, away we went to Missouri to get an outfit which consisted of three hundred and fifty pounds of corn to each one in the family. This was to do us some eighteen months and would leave us at least one thousand miles from where we could procure fresh supplies in case we did not raise anything the next year. You may think this was a very hazardous undertaking; well, we thought so too, but the stakes were terrible we had to play.

Shortly after my return I was baptized by Br. Benjamin S. Clapp at Winter Quarters, now Florence; this was in the fore part of June. We now hastened our departure from winter quarters, glad to get away from that inhospitable place with life even, for we did not think we should have had even that if we had remained much longer. We made our way as best we could to the Elkhorn River to the place where we could be organized for the journey. Here we had to make a raft of logs to ferry ourselves over the river. I assissted to ferry the whole of the companies, consisting of some five hundred and sixty wagons, over this river on a log raft, accomplishing this feat without accident of any note.

We were here organized into A[braham]. O. Smoot's hundred, Major [Samuel] Russel's fifty, and Samuel Turnbow's ten.

I had now got fairly started on the journey. It was amusing to see us with our oxen, cows and two-year-olds all yoked up, and in some instances the yearlings, as we thought that even yearlings could pull something, following the tracks the pioneers had made through the illimitable prarie, going we knew not where, but determined to seek an asylum where Christian charity would never come, notwithstanding our destitute condition. We left, indeed, without a regret. For some five hundred miles we traveled in one body as much as possible for protection against Indians that swarmed in thousands over the plains. As soon as we had got fairly under way I was appointed hunter for the company. This increased my labors a great deal, for whenever we were in camp I was off with my gun trying to obtain meat for the fifty. And sometimes while traveling I would leave my wife, although she was hardly able to set up, to drive the team of four yoke of cattle, and take my gun and travel for miles away from the track to procure meat. In this way I have killed deer and hung them on my shoulders and carried them for as much as four miles without laying them down. And always, as soon as camp was formed in the evening, in the place of resting myself from the labors of the day, I would take my gun and go and try for meat. In this way I managed to keep meat for the family all the way and for the company the most of the time.

I well remember the day that I saw the first antelope and the first buffalo. We had just got started when the wagon G. R. Stewart was driving broke and the company had to stop and put the blacksmith shop to repair it. The Captain came to me and said we would not get started any more that day and wanted me to go hunting. There were several that wanted to go, as we expected to go a good ways. It was decided that we should go horseback; I rode a mule belonging to my wife's uncle, William Stewart. Well, when we had got a good ways out we found an antelope, and some of the boys, having heard that to raise a red handkerchief that they would come to you, accordingly Albert Dewey pulled out his ramrod and tied his handkerchief on it and went riding around on the smooth prairie trying to coax the antelope up to him, when in reality if he had seen the antelope before it saw him and had secreted himself where the antelope could not have seen him and then have hoisted something, the antelope might have come nigh enough to him to see what it was to enable him to have shot it, but as it was, his riding around on the smooth prairie in plain sight, only made the antelope run so much the faster away from him. But as he ran from Br. Dewey, he did not notice well enough where I was, for he came running by me at full speed within about one hundred and fifty yards of me. Now this was entirely too nigh me for an animal to attempt to pass me in safety. I brought up my gun and knocked him down at once.

Just at this time we saw two buffalos come over a hill some two miles away with General Charles C. Rich and Doctor Richardson[107] in full chase after them. So I hastened and reloaded my gun and left my antelope lying where he fell and joined in the chase after the buffalos, but my mule would not run worth a cent. I continued to urge him, and it seemed like the more I urged him the farther I got behind. We had taken up a small hollow, thinking to intercept the buffalos at the crossing of this hollow, as their course was quartering towards us. Well, in about one mile running I was left at least one hundred yards behind. I had begun to think that mules were not much on the run, but as the buffalos were crossing the hollow, the foremost of the horsemen were within about one hundred yards of them and when the mule saw the buffalo come bounding down the hill

---

107. Charles C. Rich's company arrived in the Salt Lake Valley 2 October 1847, about a week after Abraham O. Smoot's company. Doctor Darwin Richardson traveled in the Daniel Spencer company, which reached the Valley at the same time as Smoot's company.

he became wonderfully excited, and now it was that he showed us what a mule could do at running, and although he had fell so much behind while I was whipping and spurring him with all my might, when he saw the buffalo he let out at such a rate that I do not think we went more than two hundred yards until he brought me alongside of the horses, jumping it seemed to me as high as my head, every jump, and so stiff-legged that just as I was passing the first horseman, one stirrup broke. This bothered me considerably, but just as I was nearing Doctor Richardson he fired on the buffalo. His horse fetched a skip to one side and he lit flat on his back. Seeing the Doctor shoot and fall almost by his side excited him still the more, and he jumped so furiously that my other stirrup strap broke. This almost unhorsed me, and seeing where my stirrup fell I thought to stop and get it, but he carried me so far before I could get him stopped that I could not find it, so I straddled him and joined in the chase. But I had hindered so much time looking for my stirrup that they had both of the buffalos down before I got to them. The boys loaded their horses with the meat of the buffalo, but I preferred antelope, so I went back to where I had killed the antelope and put him on my mule and started for camp. I also killed the largest and fattest badger that I almost ever saw and carried him to camp, thinking that he was good to eat. Now we had got so far from camp that it was just midnight when we got to camp. This was my first day with buffalo and antelope and the first badger I had ever seen.

In about two or three more days' travel we got into the buffalo country where we could see them by the thousands. We would now see them all around us as far as the eye could reach, as thick as you would generally see a cow herd. We had now to guard against their stampeding our stock.

We continued our journey in this way on the north side of Platte River until we got opposite what is now called Ofalon's [O'Fallon's] Bluffs on South Platte. Here Jedediah Grant's cattle got stampeded and he lost about sixty head. We stopped here a few days trying to find his stock. I went over to South Platte in company with A. O. Smoot, Samuel Turnbow, George B. Wallace and Peter Nebeker, hunting for the stock belonging to Br. Grant's company.

In running the buffalo along the South Platte there was a buffalo cow, in jumping down the bank broke one of her forelegs. This crippled her, so that we concluded to drive her to camp and butcher her, but when we went into the river to drive her out she only drove at us. We continued driving until she drove us clear across the river which was about two miles wide, but when she got to the bank she refused to go up, so we threw two lariats on her and undertook to pull her up, but she was too good at holding back. I then went into the river and took my butcher knife and would prod her in the rump, thinking to make her go up that way, but it was no go. Finally, Br. Smoot took a bit of a run and jumped straddle of her, thinking to ride her up the bank, but she kicked so when I was prodding her that she was just as wet as water would make her, which made her so slick he never made any stop on her, but landed head foremost in the river. But she concluded that she had rather go up the bank alone than to be rode up, so up she went charging.

The boys now spread apart with their lariats and held her while I came up the bank and got my gun and shot her as a beef. While we were dressing her, there came the most singular looking animal that we had seen. Bro. Smoot requested me to kill it. I took my gun and just as it came to the river and commenced to drink, I shot him. When he dropped dead into the river he sank like a rock, and with all the hunting we could do we could not find him, so that we never knew what he was. He looked like a wolf with long, shaggy hair and was white, but what he was we never knew.

While some of the boys were dressing our buffalo, the rest of us were chasing the buffalo and found a steer that had been left by the Oregon emigrants, I suppose on account of lameness, as he was quite lame. But we drove him to camp with us and brought him to the valley with us, but we got none of the lost cattle. After searching for the stampeded stock until it was considered in vain to search longer, we continued our journey.

We arrived opposite Scott's Bluffs (now Scottsbluff) on Saturday night, and as we always laid by on Sunday to let our animals rest, some of us boys concluded to cross the river and ascent the bluffs. Accordingly several of us went over and ascended them to the top and rambled all over the top, finding some mountain sheep on the top of the bluffs. We chased them, thinking that we could make them jump off of the cliffs and kill themselves, but we found out that they could ascent or descend precipitous rocks better than we could. In fact, they would skip up and down cliffs that seemed to be almost perpendicular.

On coming down off of these bluffs, I was coming skipping along from one projection to another. I came suddenly on Parley P. Pratt paralyzed on a cliff. While ascending this precipice, he had happened to look down, and seeing the distance so great below him, he became ex[c]ited and had stuck his fingers in a crack of the rock and held on for dear life, continuing to look below him. He could not control his nerves, but was trembling like an aspen leaf when I got to him. And seeing the condition he was in, I took him in my arms and carried him by force to a place of safety, thus saving him from falling several hundred feet and dashing himself to peices. I then remained with him until he arrived safely at the bottom of the bluffs.

We continued our journey on the north side of the river until we came to the mouth of Laramie, for here we crossed over on the south side near old Fort John, near where Fort Laramie now stands. About five miles above here at a grove of white ash, we camped and laid by for about a week to burn tar, there being plenty of pitch pine here. We also needed rest. From here we went on to Horse Shoe, about forty miles. Here we laid by one day for the women to wash.

We were now fairly well into the Black Hills and in full view of Laramie Peak.[108] This was such a novel sight to me that I proposed to Captain [Samuel] Turnbow that we should go to the top of the peak and kill some mountain sheep, which were supposed to abound there. He accepted the proposal, and away we went, supposing it to be about ten or twelve miles when in reality it was about forty miles.[109] We went about twelve miles and the peak looked just as far off as it did. We got discouraged about going to it and returned the same day as we thought when we started.

Here we came across an old buffalo bull, and Turnbow proposed that I should crawl as close to him as I could and shoot, and we would load ourselves with meat and return. So I crawled up within about three rods of him, as he was feeding away from me, but he would not turn around so as to give me a fair shot at him. So I peeled away at his flank, ranging forward. At the crack of the gun he jumped and kicked and ran; in a short distance he entered the brush out of sight. Turnbow come up laughing and we followed his track a little ways in the brush when I saw him walking along with his head down, very sick, so I shot him again. He ran off a very little ways and stopped and laid down, too sick to go farther.

Turnbow now proposed to shoot him in the head, saying he had heard it said that a bullet would not penetrate a buffalo bull's head, and he was going to try it and see for himself. So he went up within about one rod of the old bull, as he was lying there with his tongue out, and raised his gun, when the old bull began to struggle to get up. Turnbow thought he was gone sure; he jerked off his had [hat] and ran as hard as I ever saw a man run until he got to some cottonwood trees about forty yards off before he looked behind him, thinking the old bull was right at his heels,

---

108. Not to be confused with the Black Hills of South Dakota, the "Black Hills" observed by the pioneers west of Fort Laramie are now known as the Laramie Mountains. Laramie Peak is their highest peak.

109. This was a common illusion experienced by the pioneers.

while I was laughing almost fit to split my sides to see him run, as there was no danger, for the old bull hardly got to his feet when he fell dead, before Turnbow was half way to the trees. When he saw the old bull was dead he came back laughing, saying he was going to have his shot anyhow. So he went up about to where he was before and peeled away, the bullet going into his head just the same as any other beef.

We now went to work and skinned a part of him and cut off about one hundred and fifty pounds of the meat. I objected to taking so much, telling him he would give out and we would have to leave it after carrying it a good way, but he declared he knew he could carry it to camp. So we strung it on a pole between us and started for camp, but he soon got tired and we would have to lay it down and rest, then we would start on again with the whole of it in place of throwing a part of it away so as to make it light enough so that we could carry it. In this way we continued carrying and resting until we got about half-way to camp when he declared he could not carry it any farther. So he proposed we should hang it up in a tree and go to camp and come after it in the morning with horses. Finally I agreed, so I climbed a tree and hung it up and we went to camp.

That night the Indians stole every horse in camp but seven head. We knew it was folly to pursue them on foot, so we gave them up and proceeded on our journey. Having had experience enough the day before in carrying on foot, we left our meat to hang and dry and did not go for it so that we had our tramp to Laramie Peak for nothing.

In this way we traveled until we had come down out of the hills onto the Platte again. As we were coming along one evening just before camping time we saw three bears on the other side of the river near by a thicket of brush. Smoot, the captain, called to me to get ready and go with him and kill them. Accordingly I got my gun which was empty and loaded it with a double charge, as I knew it would stand it, and took my pistol - a single barrel -

in case I got into a close fight, and went with him. By the time we got started there were three more boys who had got ready also and went with us. Their names were Charles Chipman, George Peacock, and Lorin Roundy.

Well, by the time we got across the river the bear had gone into the brush so that we could not see them, but we had three large dogs with us which we put on their tracks and into the brush they ran, but when they got to the bear they were so astonished they would not even bark at them. When we got pretty well up to the brush, Smoot charged right up, thinking, I suppose, to get the first shot, but when he saw the bear he was about like the dogs. He was so excited he forgot he had any gun but hollowed, "Here she is boys, come and shoot her quick" Accordingly we ran as fast as we could right up to the brush, but when we got there the brush was high enough that we could not see them on foot. Just at this time the old bear noticed Smoot on his horse and she paid no more attention to the dogs, but came from them to us with a vengeance. This excited Smoot the more, and he hollowed, "Take care, boys, run - here she comes. She is a fifteen hundreder," and turning his horse he laid whip and away he went with a vengeance.

This so alarmed the boys that they all turned and ran as fast as they could, leaving the bear and me to settle our little difficulties as best we could. In the moment of their running by me and leaving me to fight it out alone, I thought of Daniel Boone's companions running and leaving him alone in like circumstances when attacked by a panther. But I thought I was equal to the emergency and knowing my gun and myself also, I brought my gun to my face and ran backwards from the brush to try and get far enough from the brush to give me a chance to shoot. The old bear, in the meantime was not fooling away her time, for I had not got more than twenty feet from the brush until she made her appearance. When she saw me she was filled with rage and she came for me with all the vengeance that she had in her, blowing and whistling so that you might have heard her a half a mile at least. But there was no time to lose, so quick as thought I brought my gun on her and fired, striking her in the sticking place and coming out through her kidney, knocking her a complete somersault with her head from me.

I immediately reloaded, turning the powder into my gun out of the powder horn while I was getting a bullet out of my mouth where I had placed them to be ready to load quick, for I expected to fight. I had not started from camp after them calculating to run from them when I saw them.

After I had killed this one, which proved to be an old she-grizzly with her teeth all worn off, I looked to see what had become of my companions. They were just turning around some large trees about fifty yards from me; when they saw the bear down and that I was master of the field they came running back about as fast as they had run away, but I was reloaded and ready for another before they got back to me.

We then got the dogs after the young ones; the dogs would fight these. They all three turned loose on one but they could not stop him. He would travel along as fast as a man could walk with all three dogs doing their best on him. I went up to him while the dogs and he were fighting and ran my knife through him, killing him instantly. The other one fled and got across the river and almost the whole company ran after him. Of all the dogs in camp there was but one that would fight him, and he could not do much with him. Then a man by the name of Armstrong got to him and putting his gun close to the bear's head, he fired, missing him. He then turned the butt of his gun and struck the bear over the head, breaking his gun into two pieces but not hurting the bear any. This brought him to his senses. There was another fellow that ran up to the bear and did the same way and missed him. Not taking time to bring any ammunition with them and not having any more guns, they had no other res[c]ource but to throw rocks at him. Finally Mayor

Russel, the captain of the fifty, hit him on the nose with a rock and knocked him down and he laid there until he ran up and cut his throat. Thus ended the first bear fight I was ever in.

We now proceeded slowly. Our teams were getting worn out with heavy loads and no roads. We traveled slowly until we got to the Pacific Springs. Here we met the First Presidency returning from Salt Lake Valley. Here our hearts were made glad by their rehearsing to us that they had found a good country at Salt Lake Valley, counselled us on our arrival in Salt Lake Valley to weigh out our provisions and ration ourselves so as to make it hold out until time for harvest.

From here to Fort Bridger game was scarce; but little could be got while traveling. At the Springs, six miles west of Bridger, I left the wagons and went on foot and alone to Bear River to try and kill some meat to do us into the valley. I made Bear River a little after dark, and the next morning started on a hunt in the hills, hoping to kill several antelope that day, as I expected the wagons to get there that night. I soon had a very fat antelope down and another large buck came running up to see what noise that was. I blazed away at him, thinking I had him sure, but the tube and cylinder blew out of my gun and I do not suppose the bullet went half way to him. My hunt was now played out. After my leaving my wife to drive two days, I got but one antelope. Still, I thought I would not give it up, so I took another gun to try it the next day while the train was on the move.

I started out in the morning, but I had not gone more than two or three miles before I came on a mule and mare that had been left there by the Battallion boys a couple of months before. They were as wild as if they had never seen anybody in their lives. I tried a good while to get the better of them, to catch them, but finding my efforts unavailing, I undertook to craze the mare, thinking by so doing I should get both of them. So I blazed away and down came the mare. I ran up to her and slipped a bridle on her, taking the bridle off the horse I was riding and letting it go on the prarie. The one I rode ran off with the wild mule. I gave the bridle to Br. Chipman who was with me to hold, telling him to get something and stop up the bullet hole so as to stop up the blood while I went after the one that had run away. It took me a good while to catch my horse; I was gone over an hour. In the meantime, Chipman thought the mare bled so fast that she would bleed to death anyhow, so he took the bridle off her and turned her loose. She got up and went off down by the train just as I was getting back and fell down dead. I then gave up the mule and came ahead.

When we got over into Echo Canyon we met James W. Stewart with my oxen that I had sent out with the pioneers to help us over the mountains. This was timely help, and it enabled us to cross the mountains a great deal easier than we could otherwise have done.

In East Canyon I came very near having an accident that would have been quite serious. My oxen refused to take the crossing straight; they crowded me onto the haw side and ran the wagon up on the bank so far they came very near upsetting my wagon. I was obliged to run around to the off side and take the wagon on my back and hold it until we could drive down into the creek. My wagon was loaded with provisions which, if it had tipped over in the creek, would almost have ruined us, but we got over safely and arrived where Salt Lake City now stands, on the eighteenth day of September, 1847.

We had now got to our journey's end. As soon as we could after we had got to our camping ground so that we could do it, we went to work and weighed out our provisions. We found that we had a little over three-fourths of a pound of corn a day to the head.

Having accomplished all I had agreed to do, and that was to see my wife's mother to her journey's end in safety, we now separated and each went to ourselves. It had occupied my time and had caused me a great deal of hard work in taking the oversight of her family and bringing them through, but once having given my word I was determined to accomplish it and although I was as tough as men ever get to be, I was well nigh worn out. In fact, I had been judged to be forty-five years old before I got to the valley, although I was but twenty-five.

I now went to work and got out logs and built a log house in the fort and prepared for winter. During this winter the Indians stole a great deal of our stock. They got the last I had, which set me entirely afoot. Neither was there any chance to get a new supply for work. We were all poor together. The first winter was very light; in fact, there was ploughing and sowing done all winter. In the spring of 1848 I went out on Mill Creek six miles south. Here I managed to get in about ten acres of corn, but just as my corn was up nicely, the crickets came down in swarms from the mountains and in one days' time destroyed my whole crop, and where they ate it never grew again. They would suck all the virtue out of the roots.

I then took ten acres to attend on shares, but the nights were so cold it would not grow worth a cent and there was not any that ripened fit to eat. Still, we had to eat it, soft, mushy, half-rotten as it was.

In the fall I got to work for Van Cott and got about twenty bushels of him, but it was all of a piece—no sound corn in it. In fact, I almost came to the conclusion that we would have to import our seed corn; it seemed that we never could get any ripe enough for seed. It rained but very little, not enough to spoil the salt in the Lake, so but what it could be got all winter, but to say that we passed the first two years in destitute circumstances does not express our situation. But I believe today that notwithstanding we had to suffer so much for even the commonest necessities of life, that the first immigration were the best satisfied and grumbled the least of any immigration that has ever come to Utah. We were all poor alike, we were all hungry alike, and we were all naked alike and we could each sympathize with the other.

Sarah Pea Rich is a familiar traveler to the reader by now. Her reminiscence continues here with the remainder of her journey across the plains and through the Rocky Mountains. Like the other companies that came in 1847, the John Taylor company, with which Sarah traveled, experienced fewer of the difficulties of travel than later companies. They were spared the dreaded cholera and had no serious mishaps along the way. Being one of the first companies to go west in such large numbers, they were still a curiosity to the Native Americans, as the Indians were to the white travelers. Since Sarah Rich's whole reminiscence is a testimonial of her faith in the mission of the Church, this part, like the earlier section, includes a statement of her conviction that struggle and sacrifice are symbols of faith.

SARAH DeARMON PEA RICH[110]

[*PLAINS—1847*]

So on Monday June the 14th, [1847] we started from Winter Quarters with all our family together with our teamsters, numbering in all seventeen persons; we traveled out about 3 miles that day and camped and the next day [we] traveled on about 15 miles and overtook Brother [John] Taylor's company, and on the 16th we reached Elkhorn River and overtook the main camp

---

110. Reminiscences of Sarah DeArmon Pea Rich, (1885–1893), holograph, LDS Church Archives.

crossing the river. It took a long time to cross over, so maney waggons and stock here. We had to stop a few days to organise the different companys. And heare the brethern held a council, and it was desided that a part of the company should start on, and our company was to waite untill others came up; and that night about dark Bishop [Newel K.] Whitney and Father [Alpheus] Cutler arived bringing with them Jacob Wetherby,[III] who had started back to Winter Quarters in the mourning on buisness, in company with 2 other men and 2 wimen, and while passing through some tall grass 3 naked indians sprung up out of the grass, and Jacob and another man tried to get them to let the team pass which they had stoped; and while the[y] wore laboring with the 2 indians that had stoped the team, the 3rd indian shot Brother Wetherby, and then the 3 indians runt and disapeard. Soon after Bishop Whitney and Cutler came up and brought the wounded young man to our tent. We all [could] see that he could not live, so we fixed him a bed in our tint and done all we could to ease his pain. He suffered awfuly pain all through the night; and the next mourning, it being Sunday, about 9 o'clock, his suffering ended in death. He was conchious untill a few minits before his death; then he droped off like one going to sleep. So as the company wore nearly all gone on they had to burry Brother Wetherby that night. Our folks [the second company of pioneers] had raised a Liberty pole; and he was laid to rest with a few words from C[harles]. C. Rich, and prayr by him. He was burried just at dark as we wore in fear of Indians, and had to keep out guards all night. Here we had to waite untill the brethern would arive that had gone back to Winter Quarters to bring on the cannon and amonishion and guns that were left, for the indians wore reported to be hostile. So it was thought best that

---

III. Jacob Weatherby traveled in the fourth hundred of the 1847 companies (Abraham O. Smoot, captain). He traveled in the first fifty (George B. Wallace, captain) and the first ten (James Smith, captain). He was born 25 July 1826 in Chihager, Ohio.

this company should bring on the Artilery thare was allso a skift
or a boat fitted up on wheels, and the cannon placed on that and
drawn by a strong yoak of oxins. So earley the next morning, on
Monday the 21st, the big cannon was fired off; and after brakfast we again took up the line of march to overtake the companeys
that had gone ahead. We traveled about 12 miles and reached the
main camp; here they had to arainge to put on 2 yoak of cattle
onto the cannon, and furnish a driver for the same, as we had
not a driver to spare in our company; and it was desided that Mr.
Rich should have charge of the cannons as there was two cannons
to be taken West in case of aney attack by indians. So the boat and
one cannon and the big [Temple] bell was in our company. Mr.
Rich had charge of the company. After all was arainged we started
in travling through this country. We had to place out strong
guards at night so you can judge the feeling of wimon and children traviling through an indian country, not knowing what
moment we might be attacted by the wild savages, and not verry
strong in number of men, for there was more wimon and children than men in our camp. So we realised that we must be
humble and prayrful and put our trust in the Lord. And it was
through His mercy and kind care that saved the people on this
daingerous jeorney; for we praid to the Lord in faith, and he
answerd our prayrs; for He will hear those that trust in Him and
obey his laws as given through his prophets. We continued our
jeorney on, traveld ten or twelve miles a day untill we reached the
platt river. Some times it was thought best to travil in five companyes abreast for safety. One night there was an indian arrow
shot into one of our cows in our company. We now had to correll
[corral] our stock at night by making a correll of our waggons,
and keep a guard at night; then in the morning, at daylight the
big bell would be rung for the men to drive out the stock to git
what feed they could git before time for starting. The bell was so
arainged over the boat and cannon, that it could be rung by
pulling a roap. It soon was found not nessary to travil so maney a

brest and then we would travil faster. We wore detained a good
deal by having to repair bridges that the pioneers that had left
ahead of us in the spring, had made for President Young and
some of the Apostles and others wore gone ahead to look out a
location for our final stopping place; and we now wore following
up there trail in travling up the plat river. Timber sometimes was
verry scarce and hard to git, but we maniage to do our cooking
with what little we could gether up while in camp. One morning
my husband was trying to hitch up an unruly ox, and the ox
jumped over the waggon tonge and fell on my little son Joseph,
and came verry near killing him. We wore all verry much frightend about but he soon got over his hurt and we travel on, but
with some little fear of trouble with the indians as we were near
the Pawnee agency, and had met some men from the station that
had told our men that there was a war partty prowling through
the country that might give us some trouble, but our companyes
would generly camp clost together, and when we would stop to
camp would sometimes fior off the cannon, as those indians
wore verry fraid of the big gun, as they called it and as we wore
frequently meeting traders they would keep us posted as to the
movements of the indians, and when in camp a strong picket
guard would be placed out, and by using great care and wisdom,
we wore permitted through the mercies of our heavenly father to
travel among the savages, tribe of indians, unmolested, alltho us
nurves [nervous] wimon wore often verry much frightend for
fear of an atact of the indians, and I do know it was throug the
protecting hand of god that we made the long jearney across the
planes from Illinois to Great Salt Lake Valley, when we wore but
few in number. At one time an arrow shot into a calf, which
showd to us that indians were prowling around near our camp,
and several time men out garding the stock at night would see
indians lurking around which would cause our men to drive the
stock into our waggon correll for safty. Along about this time we
passed through several indian viliages, looked over by white

Agency; they seamed verry friendly, but seeing so maney waggons passing seamed a suprise to them. It truley was a daingerous trip; and had we not been convinced by the power of the Lord to know that we wore preparing to help lay the foundation for the building up of the kingdom of our heavenly father on this earth according to his holy commandment to his Prophet Joseph Smith, we never could have undertaken such a jearney. It was our faith and our knowledge that the Lord had set his hand the second time to establish his work on the earth in order to prepare a people to be worthy to receive him at his Second Coming, which we as a people know is near at hand, and that this, the work of the latter days will never stop, nor be stoped untill he makes his appearence the Second time to redeem his chosen people. The day is now near at hand, and the rising generation that will read this book will maney of them live to see that day. So my dear children and grand children and great grand children, and maney others of my young readers, let me beg of you to lay aside all folly and foolishness, and humble yourselves before the Lord, and seak a knowledge of this the work of the Lord in this the latter day, and be prepared to help in this great work for as shure as you live and read my testamony to the truth of this Latter day work; it is true, for I have seen the prophet of god; I have set under the sound of his voice; I have heard him prophecy, and live to see the fulfillment of his prophecies, and I do know for myself that he was a true Prophet; and that the work that the Lord brought forth through him and the foundation he has laid for his followers to build upon will last throughout time and all eternity; and no earthly power can hinder the same. The Heavens are preparing for the fulfillment of all the words utterd by our prophet Joseph Smith; He is allso thare to work in behalf of this work, and will be with the Savior at his coming. So the wicked may stop there efforts against this people for there works will fall to the ground to thare shame and disgrace.

We jearneyed on up the platt river, came into the buffalow

country, saw maney large heards of buffalow. Brother Lewis Robison was the first one in our company to kill a buffalow; he killed one that would weigh over a thousand pounds, now we all stoped and had a feast all through our camp. We stoped a few days to wash, iron and cook, while the men folks repaird up there waggons and let there teames rest and recrute up as we wore in good feed; and when all the companeys would all come up we would start on again. But while passing through the buffalow country we did not travel verry fast, for all the men folks seamed to want to kill a buffalow, so they would travel a few miles and camp, and go hunting, for that was new sport for them. So Mr. Rich got after a large herd—him and several of our company, the[y] wore a [on] horse-back; he killed three, the first one he wounded, it was a verry large one, and it turned upon him and came verry near killing the horse he was riding, but he shot again and killed him. So on the next day he killed two more, and they dressed them and divided out the meet in the company and the men folks fixed up scaffels out of willows and spread out the meet cut up in thin slices, and made fiars underneath, and as one side of the meet would git dry they would turn it over, and by so doing it became dry. They called it "Jerk" meet.[112] We put it into sacks, and we had enough to last us all the jearney through, and it was the sweetest meet I ever tasted. The children grew fat on it. We allso tried out the tallow, for we needed grease in our cooking. Every other company allso suplied themselves with "jearked" meet. We wore severl days travling through the buffalow country. Some days we could see herds of thousans together, and several times the[y] would come in large herds crossing just ahead of our teams as hard as they could go, and in such large numbers that the roaring of them would frighten our teams, so that the drivers had all they could do to prevent a stampead among our cattle.

---

112. The common name was *jerky*.

It was verry daingerous in travling throw this country, but we wore presearved from aney searious accident while on this trip. It was a grand sight to see those herds of wild animals, thousands in a gang, raicing across the prairies; for the sight of our waggons seamed to frighten them, and it caused us to fear they might attack us in there flight. Well, after we got through with the buffalows, we came into a land alive with what is called praria dogs— the [w]hole country was alive with them. They lived in holes in the ground, and would make the hills sound with there barking all night long. They are about the size of small puppys, and as cunning as they can bee. They would set near there holes by hundreds and bark and yelp untill the boys would git allmost up to them and then dodge back in there dens and stick there heads out and bark. Some of the men shot some of them and they are hansom little dogs with more fur than hair on them. If we could have caught them alive we would have tried to tame them just because they wore so small and pretty. Some of our company named that place dog town. From Mr. Rich's jeornal, he sais he believes he saw at one time ten thousand head of buffalow feeding together while passing through the buffalow country.

On the 29th of July we camped in sight of what is called Chimney Rock, and on August 1st we camped at the foot of Chimney Rock. This is a large mound with a rock sticking up in the center like a chimney about two hundred and fifty feet high here manye of our camp went to the top of the mound, and found the names of some of the pioneers that was ahead of us, for they had pass there some time before; here my husband [w]rote his name on the rock with red keal,[113] allso my name, and the names of his other wives[114] that was with us, and our children's

---

113. Keel is a red ocher used for marking something such as lumber or sheep; a colored marking chalk or crayon used by engineers or surveyors.

114. Wives of Charles C. Rich who traveled with Sarah were Eliza Ann Graves (md. 2 January 1845), Mary Ann Phelps (md. 6 January 1845), Sarah Jane Peck (md. 9 January 1845), Emeline Grover (md. 2 February 1846), and Harriet Sargent (md. 28 March 1847 at Winter Quarters).

names. We left and traveld on, and came in sight of Larama [Laramie] Peak. We then began to cheer up thinking we ware gitting nearer our jearney's end. For we had word from President Young and Kimball telling us to cheer up, and it would not be long before we would find a resting place.[115]

On the 5th of August [1847] we camped on a site—Larama Fort, crossed over the river and traveld on the west side and on the tenth we struck the Black Hills: and on the 12th we camped on horse Shoe creek; found a nice coald spring of good watter; it was named by the pioneers that was ahead of us and called Kimball's Springs. About this time we ware having verry warm wether, so much so that we wimon got verry much ware sunburnd. We had sand and dust, rocks and hills to pass over, and some times ware worn out and verry tired, but not so much so as our brethern that had to walk most of the time, and drive teams, and stand guard at night. O what a time we all had crossing the plains from Nauvoo to Salt Lake City[!] When I now see those brethern and sisters come to these valleys riding in cars in the shade, and that too, in one-third shorter time than we wore coming, and when they git here have somthing nice to eat and plenty in the land, and then hear them complain of hard times, I think they ought to have at least about 2 weeks of expearence, such as the brethern and sisters had when we came; then, perhaps they would feel more thankfull and would not feel to complain, as I have heard maney do. For when we came there was no one to welcom us with potatoes, fat beefs, honey, butter and all the good things that the country could produce. No, we could have nothing of the kind, but yet we felt to thank the Lord for proticting us to where we could rest in peace. About the 25th. we came to the Saleratus Lake. This was a beautifull lake, as white as snow, and was pure saleratus, which we could cut out in large

---

115. Messages were left in prominent rocks and even buffalo skulls by the members of the first company of pioneers, noting distances and features of the terrain.

cakes. We gethered sacks full and brought with us to the Valley, which lasted us a long time to make bread with. Here we camped at independence rock, where we again left our names on the high rock; this was quite a plesent camping ground. From this place we traveld on passed another saleratus lake and camped on the sweet watter [Sweetwater River]; and from that [time] on maney of our cattle wore sick, and a number died which caused a delay in our travels; for our teams by this time wore verry weak.[116] But we still mooved on a few miles a day and sometimes lay by a few days to repare waggons and wash and bake and let the teams rest. And on Monday the 30th, [we] camped between the mountains; we then traveld a few miles and camped on Sweet Watter. As we traveld along the Sweet Watter river September the 1st. we traveld over bad roads of sand, mud and rocks. So bad was the roads that we could not make much headway.

On the 2nd of September, [1847] we met about 30 waggons of pionears that had been with President Young and company, to look out a stopping place for the Saints, among them was brother William Clayton and John Pack, they wore returning to Winter Quarters to bring on there familys. Hear it blew up coald and rained, and was verry disagreable; but we bid adieu to those brethern and traveld on, knowing we soon should meet President Young, Kimball and the rest of the Twelve. And on Sunday the 5th, [1847] we reached the pacific springs, having traveld through the South Pass. Here we met President Young and all the ballence of the Twelve and pionears. This was a time of rejoicing[!] Here the two companeys lay by 2 days to hold meeting and hold council with the brethern, and talk over what was best to be done. And on the 7th the pionears started on there return trip and our company started on our jearney towards our resting place in the Valley of the great Salt Lake. About this time

---

116. Some of the water in this area was alkali which poisoned the cattle. It was common for many companies to lose cattle on that portion of the trail.

my mother-in-law, my husband's mother [Nancy O'Neal Rich], was taken verry sick and about the same time her youngest daughter [Nancy Rich Porter], the wife of Brother John Porter, who was allso in Mr. Rich's company, was confined in her waggon and had a fine son. So alltogether we had to travel verry slow, and on the day we parted with the company of pioneers it commenced snowing and snowed all day. This was the 7th. of September; it was a sudden chainge from the hot wether of the month of August. We traveld 9 miles and camped on the dry Sandy. Here one of our oxen died. We still continued our jearney untill the 11th., when we crossed the green river, and traveld 4 miles down the river and camped, and on Sunday the 12[th,] lay by to rest our teames and from there traveld on and camped on black fork, and from there traveld on untill the 17th. we camped on the muddy; and on the 20th we crossed bear river and for a few days severl of our company was unfortunate in braken there wagons, which would detain the [w]hole company for a while. So after fixing up the wagons we started on; and on the 27th traveld up the canyon five miles and companeys camped all together; and on the 30th cross[ed] over the big mountain and then down the canyon had a verry bad road one of our companey a brother Cheery overturned one of his waggons but not much damiage done we got all rited up again and passed over another mountain and camped.

On the 1st of October [1847] we camped in the edge of the Valley; here mother Rich was verry sick; and on Saturday October 2nd, we traveld six miles and landed in what is now Salt Lake City; camped at a deep spring near the Old Fort. Great was our joy to think we had reached a resting place that we could call our home in the mountains.

The following letter, written by Harriet Decker Hanks in 1914, contains a brief but detailed reminiscent account of her travels west in 1847. Harriet's mother, also named Harriet, and her sister Clara Young, were two of the three women in the first company of pioneers. Harriet Hanks traveled to Utah in the second company of Saints under Jedediah M. Grant's leadership. She was a widow, since her husband died in Iowa in March 1846. In 1848 she married Ephraim Hanks, mentioned earlier in this volume as the horseback-riding teacher of Louisa Barnes Pratt and who figures prominently in the story of the rescue of the handcart companies.

HARRIET DECKER HANKS[117]

I WAS BORN MARCH 13TH, 1826 in the State of New York, town of Phelps, married to Edwin S[obieski] Little at the age of 16 years[118]–in the City of Nauvoo, Illinois–Residing there– until 1846–when the Saints were expelled from the the State– in 1946 [1846]. My Husband was a Nephew of President B. Youngs[119]–and they were intimate and congenial to each other—consequently he was called by his Uncle to drive His Family carriage when they were ready to cross the Mississippi River—we started at night on

---

117. "A Sketch of My Pioneer Life Written for My Dear Grand Daughter Madie E. Hatch," in Golden Leone and Teton Hanks Jackman, comp., *Descendants of Ephraim Knowlton Hanks and his Wives* (Provo: n.p.), Library, Church of Jesus Christ of Latter-day Saints, Salt Lake City, Utah.

118. Harriet and Edwin were married in Nauvoo 22 March 1842. Edwin was twenty-six years old at the time.

119. Edwin's mother, Susannah Young, was an elder sister of Brigham Young.

the 12th of Feb crossed the River on the Ice—made our first camp at Sugar Creek Iowa—the last Wagon crossing the river Broke through the ice—My Husband in helping to get the wagon from the river got very wet and took a violent cold that settled on his lungs from which he never recovered—He died six weeks later and was burried by the roadside between two large trees to mark his resting place[120]—I was then 20 years old-a widow- a baby boy a few months old[121]—Left to get along the best I could—I had been tenderly cared for 4 years of my married life—but was—inexperienced in this and many things I was called to go through—and you that have lost a kind loving husband and protector—even when surrounded with home comforts know the sorrow and loneliness of heart—but homeless and traveling I knew not where I felt desolate indeed—I was not friendless there were many to sympathize with me—but except their circumstances were not much better than mine—I cannot dwell longer on the unhappy scenes I had to pass through—It was a horrid nightmare from that time until we arrived at Council Bluffs now called Omaha—We spent the Winter there and in April 1847, The original company of Pioneers consisting of one hundred and forty-three men and three women and two children-my Mother [Harriet Page Wheeler Decker Young]—My Sister Mrs Clara D. Young, Wife of Brigham Young Mrs. Ellen Saunders Kimbal and my youngest brother [Isaac Perry, age 6] left Omaha for the Promised Home of the Saints—arriving here on the 24th of July of the same year— On the 13th day of June of the same year a company of one hundred persons of which my self and baby were numbered left our Winter quarters to cross the plains-Jedediah M. Grant was captain of the company—I was given the honorable position of driving an ox team—My wagon was loaded with mill irons that was

---

120. Edwin Little died 18 March 1846 at Richardson's Point, fifty-five miles from Nauvoo. He was buried near present-day Keosauqua, Iowa.
121. Harriet's boy, George Edwin, was born 6 August 1844 in Nauvoo.

put into the first mill erected in Utah[122]—the walls of the old mill still stand as a land mark-in our beautiful Park.[123] My little boy and myself slept on those irones for 5 months-there has been a vast improvement in bed springs since that time—We had a long tiresome journey-but we had some very pleasant evenings after our wearisome day was over we would have songs and prayer and thank our Heavenly Father that our lives had been spared from the cruel Indian and wild beasts that were often seen on our way— But we had all we could endure both men and women as well as the poor cattle—I drove my oxen through the day—milked 5 cows at night and morning—Baked the bread for fifteen persons eleven of them men—done everything that came to me to do but yoke my oxen—I was asked to do that by the Captain of the ten I was traveling in—But I drew the line at that request—and on mea-suring the yoke with me the odds was in my favor—I could not lift the yoke—my weight at that time was 80 pounds-But with all our hardships we were blessed with good health and looked on the cheerful side and the months passed away and we were nearing the valley as it was called—Theres one more—incident that occurs to my mind—I had never heard of a cloud burst—but I was called to witness one that nearly cost myself and baby our lives—We had camped in Emigration canyon for noon lunch—I started with my little boy for a walk—I had not got far from the wagon when I heard a very unusual sound-and looking back across the canyon the mountain seemed to be coming down into the road—and the roar was deafening. In less time than it takes to describe it—the water was-upon me—I started for my wagon—but the water came to my waist—I had my babe in my arms—I found my strength leaving me—I could not stand—I was near a stump—I placed my

---

122. Credited with being the first mill in Utah was Charles Crismon's gristmill, built in 1848 at the mouth of City Creek Canyon. The Chase Mill, built by Isaac Chase, was also constructed then but not completed until 1852. It was located in what is now Liberty Park in Salt Lake City.

123. Memory Grove Park, dedicated in 1924, is presently located on the original site of the mill on City Creek Canyon Road. Harriet is possibly referring to the early beginnings of this park.

baby on the stump and held him and myself from being swept away in the current—until an old gentleman seeing my danger came to me—I took baby in my arms and he took us both to our wagon—by this time the water was running into my wagon box and logs, stones and other debris were hurled in every direction—but the blessed mill irons saved the day—they anchored the wagon and kept it from oversetting—But the End was not yet—after the flood had passed—we had no road left—we had to stay on two days until the road was made safe we had on the evening of the 5th of October 1847 we arrived in Salt Lake Valley and camped in what was called the North Fort-the place that was to be my abiding place for the next year——

Now my dear Madie I hope this will not be tiresome to you or your friends—But it has been 67 years since these events took place—and I am near my 89th birthday so you will excuse all poor writing and composition

Mrs. H.A.Hanks

Another 1847 pioneer was Ann Agatha Walker Pratt, a plural wife of Parley P. Pratt, whom she married at Winter Quarters in April 1847. She was born in England and traveled to America in 1847 just months before moving west in her husband's company. The only extant copy of her reminiscence is a published account in a March 1893 issue of the Woman's Exponent *entitled "Personal Reminiscences." It is a polished account, clearly written for a wide audience, informative and lively.*

ANN AGATHA WALKER PRATT[124]

EDITOR WOMAN'S EXPONENT:

DEAR Old Friend:—My Exponent had not come for some time, and I had began to feel hungry for, and wonder why it had not reached me. When yesterday I heard a dump on the doorstep and there was a parcel of four numbers truly a feast of fat things. As I read the beautiful inspiration, "The Christmas of the Pioneers," by our gifted sister, Augusta Joyce Crocheron, my mind went back to the spring of 47, when I, a young girl of seventeen, had just arrived at Winter Quarters from my home in England. Notwithstanding the dire poverty, and much sickness which prevailed, most of the people were preparing to follow in the wake of the Pioneers who had just started on their journey. My husband [Parley P. Pratt], with others was busy mending wagons, looking up yoke-bows, making bow-keys, or pins to hold the bows in the yokes, hunting up the cattle, mating them, finding chains, especially lock-chains, for, bear in mind there were no "breaks" to hold wagons back going down steep hills in those days.

These and a hundred other things occupied their time. While we were busy making and mending wagon covers, making crackers, and in every way aiding and assisting to prepare for the long and toilsome journey. At last we started and got as far as the Elk Horn River, where we camped about a month, waiting for the rest to arrive, so as to organize into companies of hundreds, fifties and tens.

The brethren made a large and substantial raft, on which to

---

124. "Personal Reminiscences," *Woman's Exponent* 21 (15 March 1893): 139.

ferry us across, for the river was swift and deep, and every wagon and person had to cross in that way. The cattle were made to swim over. I forgot to say that our family being numerous and help scarce, two of we women rather thought we could manage with the oversight of my husband to drive our own team, which consisted of a yoke of cattle, for, though just coming from a large city, and not being used to this kind of a life—never having seen cattle yoked together, still I thought, well- what any other woman can do, I can, so, shouldering my whip, I drove out of Winter Quarters, and soon learned to manage my team first class.

I learned to put on the lock-chain instantly at the top of a steep hill, and would jump out quickly while the cattle were going, to take it off, so that the impetus afforded by the end of the descent would aid them in starting up the other side, for we often passed through deep gullies. On one occasion I was jumping out while the cattle were going, and my skirt caught on the tongue bolt, and threw me down, and before I could extricate myself the nigh front wheel passed over my leg just above the ankle. I scrambled into the wagon the best way I could, I turned down my stocking expecting to see a bad bruise for it was very painful, but lo! and behold there was no bruise there. I was much astonished but very thankful. The pain soon passed away and I drove my team as usual. I must relate another remarkable incident that happened. While toiling through the quick-sand of the Black hills—the "reaches" had been shortened, teams doubled, and, while they were toiling slowly up the hills all but the driver pushing behind, one of our dear little ones, a boy fifteen months old, being asleep was left in the wagon. It being a hot day, the sides of the cover had been tied up. The child on awaking, finding himself alone, looked out at the side and fell right between the wheels, the hind one passing over his limbs before he could be rescued. His father picked him up—I durst not look up for I expected to see his tender limbs severed from his body, but strange to say—owing to the soft sand, and the great mercy of God, all the hurt was a red mark made by the iron tire across his limbs. His father administered to him, and in a little while he was holding the whip apparently as well as ever. The first part of the journey I enjoyed much, being young, and having good health. I did not mind the driving and the labor incidental to such a journey, cooking, washing, and etc. At night, when we drove into camp the wagons formed in the shape of a horseshoe, the first two with the front ends pretty close together, the next drove close enough for the tongue to lie out-side of the wheels of the first one, and so on until the fifty were in place. The enclosure forming a corral for the cattle through the night. Each driver unyoked his cattle (I frequently unyoked mine) then those whose turn it was, herded them till dark. The rest of the men would gather material for fires, often nothing but dried grass or Buffalo chips as they were called.

As we neared our destination, our journey became wearisome and full of toil. Grass became scarce, cattle began to give out, often, when an ox gave out, a cow was put in its place. The roads were rough, wagons had to be pitched up, till sometimes you would wonder how they could go at all. One of my calamities was my lock-chain giving out, and in going down a hill I had to hold the nigh ox by the horn and tap the off one over the face and keep saying, "Whoa, Back; Whoa, Back," and nearly hold my breath till I got down to the bottom, then stop, draw a breath of relief, see that all was right, then on again, for others were right on our heels and we had to get out of their way, (you can just imagine what a condition our skirts were in.) I never shall forget the last day we traveled, and arrived in the Valley. It happened to be my turn to drive that day Sept. 28th. The reach of our wagon was broken and tied together after a fashion, and the way the front wheels wabbled about was a sight to behold. I kept expecting every minute to see the poor old concern draw apart and come to grief, but it held together and when my eyes rested on the beautiful entrancing sight—the Valley; Oh! how my heart swelled within me, I could have laughed and cried, such a comingling of emotions I cannot describe. My soul was filled with thankfulness to God for bringing us to a place of rest and safety—a home. No doubt our valley looks astonishingly beautiful to the strangers who come here now, but it cannot evoke the same emotions as it did to us, poor weary tired, worn out, ragged travelers. When I drove into camp, unyoked my cattle, and sat down on the wagon tongue, and began to realize that, in the morning I would not have to hitch up and toil through another day, such a feeling of rest—blessed rest permeated my whole being that is impossible to describe, and cannot be realized except by those who have passed through similar scenes.

After a day or two my husband with others began to explore Emigration and other canyons, made a road to the timber and in a very short time a log room was up, a rough fireplace was built, what few chairs we had brought with us, our trunks and boxes were brought in, and a few rough seats were improvised, enough for us to assemble around the fire with a semblance of a roof over our heads (we did not wait for it to be finished) that was an evening never to be forgotten. The first one of the kind in more than three months.

We spent the evening in singing prayer and praise to that kind Being who had brought and guided us to this haven of peace and safety. Soon more rooms were added, and made as comfortable as possible, we slept in our wagons far into the winter, after our breath would be frozen and our pillows. But those of us who were well did not mind it very much, we were contented and happy. I accompanied my husband into the canyons, cooking and making things as comfortable as I could, for him and the men with him. I well remember the first night I slept on the ground with the star bedecked firmament over head.

My husband cut a large heap of tender twigs, placed them evenly, then placed a Buffalo robe over them which, with plenty of covering made a comfortable bed. The fresh air, laden with the odor of the pines, the gentle swaying of the trees was all novel and delightful to me and while the rest of the camp slumbered restfully, my mind wandered away to my home, far across the seas, and to the loved ones there, but joy and thankfulness mingled lovingly with the sadness. Not then, or ever since, have I regretted the ties I had found which were so different from the majority of mankind.

Though very brief, Hannah Blakeslee Morley's account is one of the relatively few diaries of women on the trail. Hannah was married to Isaac Morley, the founder of Morley's Settlement, a few miles south of Nauvoo. She was a plural wife along with Leonora Snow Morley, the sister of Eliza R. Snow, and traveled in the Lorenzo Snow company to the West in 1848. "Father Morley," as Isaac was fondly called, took his family south after reaching the Valley, founding a settlement in Sanpete County.

HANNAH BLAKESLEE FINCH MERRIAM MORLEY[125]

[MAY 1848—ELKHORN RIVER]

Sunday 28th—remained all day at the Horn [Elkhorn River], very rainy and muddy, all in good health. Monday 29th remained again at the Horn all day, washed having good place and good water and plenty of wood. Bro. Brighams teams crossed the river. Father Morley took a ride with Bro. Brigham on the 31st, assisted in organizing a company to go on. Two ladies

125. "Partial Diary of Hannah Blakeslee Finch Merriam Morley," in Morely Family Histories, typescript copy, LDS Church Archives.

 belonging to Bro. Kays[126] company went out after gooseberries, got lost, stayed out all night, they were found the next morning about 3 miles from camp.

Thursday June 1st—about one oclock a company of 100 left for the Platte, Lorenzo Snow, (captain). Bro. [Heber C.] Kimbal[127] arrived at the Horn with company and some of them crossed the river. A child of Bro. [Samuel] Gully's[128] was buried today on the West side of the river. Friday June 2nd the remainder of Bro. Kimbal's company crossed the river. Bro. [Orson] Hyde and [Wilford] Woodruff came to visit us also a Mr. Mudge and Stootsman—this day we have attended a funeral of a sister [Martha] Taylor [age 45] from the State of New York, she died of the measels, also a pair of twins were born and died and were buried today. Saturday June 3rd all well nothing particular to mention except a very heavy thunder shower in the midst of which two of our oxen stayed away, but were found 2 miles off. June 4th Sunday—went to meeting in the forenoon, washed in the afternoon (good soft water) singing in the evening. Monday June 5th—7 oclock took our departure from the Horn, quite cold, uncomfortable riding, about 9 oclock a sister [Lucy] Grove[s] fell from ~~ch~~ her wagon and one wheel passed over her body, another over her leg, broke the bone but the company was detained but a short time. [. . .]

We arrived near the Platte about 3oclock in the afternoon, very pleasant place to camp, singing and prayers at Bro. [William W.] Majors[129] wagon in the evening.

---

126. Brother Kay is possibly William Kay, a captain of ten in the Third Division of 1848, headed by Willard Richards. William Kay was also listed on Brigham Young's First Division roster—the division in which Hannah traveled.

127. Heber C. Kimball headed the Second Division of wagons in 1848.

128. The infant son of Edward M. Smith Gully died 31 May 1848.

129. William W. Majors served as captain of fifty in the First Division.

Tuesday June 6th—journed 13 miles, camped beside the Platte, pleasant place, all well except father Morley, his side very sore.

Wednesday June 7th—proceeded onward traveled 10 miles to Shell Creek encamped about 2oclock had quite a heavy shower, after the shower some of the men went hunting, Bro. Potter[130] killed an Antelope and plenty of fresh clams in the creek also fish one of the brethren caught one that weighed 10 pounds, singing and prayers at father Morley's wagon in the evening.

Thursday June 8th—very rainy and cold in forenoon, cleared in afternoon some of the brethren went hunting, brought in another Antelope, singing and prayers at Bro. [Thomas] Bullock's[131] wagon, peace and harmony prevailing in our midst.

Friday, June 9th—left Shell Creek, traveled 15 miles encamped beside another creek, pleasant place and pleasant day, a boy broke his leg, the wagon run over it. Found plenty of sweet flag,[132] singing and prayers at father Morley's wagon, peace and harmony prevailing.

Saturday June 10th—traveled 13 miles very warm day, Bro. Bullocks oxen gave out so camped by a lake which abounded in fish. Amasa [Lyman] caught 6 in a short time, good clear water and plenty of good dry wood, all well, singing and prayers at father Morley's wagon. Sunday June 11th held meeting, instructions from Bro. Young, very warm day, Evening services at father Morley's

Monday June 12th—quite cool, traveled ₂ 16 miles crossed Beaver River, and encamped at Rumb [Plumb] Creek.

Wednesday July 26th (1848), cool in morning, warm in middle of day, traveled about 14 miles, camped in a hollow where we had a little better feed, no water or wood except pine.

---

130. This is probably Gardner Godfrey Potter who traveled with the First Division.
131. Thomas Bullock served as scribe in the First Division.
132. Sweet flag (*Acorus calamus*) has long, sword-shaped leaves and a pungent, aromatic rootstock. It is also known as sweet calamus.

Commenced raining about sundown, rained all night, had a good road all day with exceptions of hills and cobblestones.

Theresa[133] appears a little better but tired. Passed Bro. Kimbals camp in the morning, health generally good. Currants and cherries in abundance all along the road.

Thursday July 27th, rainy and cold in morning, broke away and grew warmer in afternoon, traveled 4 miles and camped at Heber Springs, thick timber underbrush a little grass, choke cherries, currants and gooseberries in abundance, poor chance for cattle.

565 miles from Winter Quarters, met some brethern from San Francisco who brought papers published by our brethern at the Bay,[134] dated April 1st.

Wrote some letters to send to our friends in Iowa State, a very severe thunder storm in the night. Friday July 28th—cloudy and very wet and muddy in the morning cleared at noon, mud dried up some, we went on 43 [?] miles, camped for the night, found various kinds of currants and first ~~serv~~ sarvice [service] berries we have seen. Saturday July 29th cloudy and cold all day, uncomfortable riding, traveled 13 miles over hills and hollows, camped at LaBone river, a small stream of red looking water, our cattle had to pick bushes for a living. One of Bro. Bullocks oxen found dead in morning.

Sunday July 30th traveled about 6 miles, found good feed, woods inhabited by buffalo. Saturday, August 26th, unloaded one of our wagons and father Morley with others went back to assist Bro. Kimbals company shower in afternoon, wrote letter to send to folks in Iowa. Sunday Aug. 27th the teams started back to Iowa in the afternoon, also some more of the teams from the

---

133. The daughter of Isaac Morley's first wife, Lucy, who died 3 January 1847 in Winter Quarters leaving seven children.

134. Probably issues of the *California Star*, published by Sam Brannan.

valley arrived here. Bro. Brigham went back to meet Bro. Kimbal. Weather windy and disagreeable.

Monday August 28th—cold in morning very white frost and ice quite thick, but pleasant in middle of day, done our washing, plenty of good water and wood, Williams company left here for the valley. Father Morley came back from Bro. Kimbal's camp. Tuesday 29th - cold and windy rain and hail in afternoon, some of Bro. Kimbals company arrived. Wed. August 30th more mild and pleasant. Isaac went back to assist Bro. Billings[135] with a team, 46 wagons arrived from the valley, Bro. [Tarleton] Lewis came with them. Bro. Brigham returned from Bro. Kimbals camp quite sick.

Thursday August 31st very cold in the morning, ice over an inch thick on the wash dish, Isaac returned from the other camp.

Friday Sept. 1st rain in forenoon cleared in afternoon, Bro. Brighams company left the camp in the afternoon. Bro. Bullock went with him, Bro. Kimbals company arrived at the Sweet Water, camped 1 mile below us, Helen[136] very sick, a sister in the mississippi company, buried a short distance from the place, also a child of Bro. [Sylvester] Earl. Saturday Sept. 2nd - very rainy and cold all day and night. Mother [Abigail Schaffer] Woolsey died in the night left at Sweet Water. Sunday Sept. 3rd—very cold traveled [?] miles, camped on Pacific Creek, weather moderated some.

Another British immigrant who traveled to Nauvoo in 1842 entirely on her own was twenty-one-year-old Mary Pugh, who married John Scott as a plural wife two years later. "I felt perfectly at home with the Saints," she wrote,

---

135. This is probably Titus B. Billings.
136. Helen Mar Kimball Whitney was the daughter of Heber C. Kimball and Vilate Murray Kimball. Before leaving Nauvoo, she married Horace K. Whitney.

"and whenever I was sick I was always cared for and comforted." She traveled with John and two of his other wives from Nauvoo in March 1846 and on to Salt Lake City in the Heber C. Kimball company in 1848. Her account is full of the daily routine of trail travel. "Dismayed by the very immensity of the view," when she first saw the Valley, she declared herself willing to make a "good home in this new wilderness."

MARY PUGH SCOTT[137]

WHILE WAITING TO LEAVE for Zion, I washed and ironed the Temple Clothes in the basement of The Nauvoo Temple. John Scott was a very prominent man in Military affairs in the early days. He held the rank of Colonel in the First Regiment of the Nauvoo Legion. He was also a body guard of the Prophet Joseph Smith and he was one of his best loyal and true friends. He was so dependable and when the Prophet Joseph and Hyrum were Martyred John went with others to bring thier bodies back to Nauvoo.

The Mob Thought that now they had put an end to the Mormons by killing thier leaders but little did they know that there was in reserve another Man of God to continue the work and build up the kingdom that will endure forever. At the public burial only sand was in the caskets as they were deposited in the grave.[138] Later John helped when they were laid to rest at the

137. "Life Story of Mary Pugh [Scott]," (1848), typescript copy, Utah State Historical Society, Salt Lake City, Utah.

138. The fear of grave robbers seeking the reward offered for Joseph Smith's head led to the secret burial of Joseph's and Hyrum's bodies. The caskets, filled with sand, were buried separately.

rear of the home where Joseph Smith had Lived. I, Mary Scott heard and saw the sham trial of [the murderers of] Joseph and Hyrum Smith. I saw some of the guilty men pointed out.

Some of them were trying to whittle sticks, but thier hands trembled so much that they made little progress. The reason that I was there, I accompanied the young woman who gave her testimony against the murderers.[139] She lived in Warsaw[140] at the time at the Hotel and saw the mob that had tried to wash the black off thier faces there, then ate thier supper at the Hotel. So she got a look at them, and was able to point them out. But the Guilty were not brought to Justice. Thier crimes were just winked at.[141]

They were allowed to rob us of our homes and Widows and Children were turned out of thier homes sick and shaking with the ague. They were driven to the banks of the River to starve and die. They had no mercy on Young or old. After The Prophet Joseph's death there was great worry and confusion about who should be the President of the Church. John, Elizabeth, Sarah [plural wives] and I went to the Meeting. It was held in the Bowery[142] to decide this. We all bore testimonies of the Transfiguration of Brigham Young.

While he was speaking he seemed to have the voice of the Prophet Joseph Smith. We also saw the form of Joseph Smith before us. So there was no doubt in our hearts and minds from

---

139. Eliza Jane Graham, the lone female witness for the prosecution in the trial of the Smith brothers' murderers, was a thirty-three-year-old Mormon from Nauvoo. She was a waitress at the Warsaw House, where she reportedly served dinner to the participants in the martyrdom as they returned from Carthage and overheard their conversation concerning the events.

140. The city of Warsaw, located less than twenty miles from Nauvoo, was the site of anti-Mormon meetings prior to the martyrdom.

141. The trial resulted in a "not guilty" verdict. Attorney, author, and former Secretary of State, John Hay, stated in *The Atlantic Monthly:* "There was not a man on the jury, in the court, in the county, that did not know the defendants had done the murder. But it was not proven, and the verdict of NOT GUILTY was right in law." (John Hay, "The Mormon Prophet's Tragedy," *Atlantic Monthly* 24 [December 1869]: 669–79.)

142. In Nauvoo, Sunday meetings and other large gatherings of the Saints were held, weather permitting, in the grove, an outdoor area near the temple. It was the site where many people claimed Brigham Young assumed the voice and countenance of Joseph Smith. The bowery was a man-made shelter of brush and boughs.

then on. as to who should be our leader. The Scott Family knew unitedly that Brigham Young was the right man in the right place. In 1846 the companies were being organized to start for the Rocky Mountains. March the first we were told to be rea[dy] to start at noon. We reached the Missouri River about the middle of June.

Then they called for six hundred men to go to Mexico to fight. They thought that by taking all those men the Mormons would be wiped out of existance. Men were selected and by the middle of July the Mormon Battalian march began. All plans were now abandoned to leave this year.

We went into Winter Quarters, now called Florence. John was called on a special mission to stay one more year and help prepare all for the trip. Finally May 30 1848 John Scott and Family started in Heber Kimballs Co. John was Captain over 10 wagons His company included 662 People- 266 wagons- 150 loose cattle- 25 Mules- 737 Oxen- 57 horses- 299 chickens- 96 pigs- 52 dogs- 17 cats- 3 hives of bees- 3 doves- 1 squirrel

Rules of a camp: Each had a Captain, A captain of the Guard, a chaplin and clerk.

All names were enrolled. 1. Noise and confusion will not be allowed after 8 p.m.

2. Camp will be called by trumpet for Prayer meeting morning and night.

3. Arise at 4:30 a.m. Assembly for prayers 5:30 a.m. Card playing will not be allowed.

5. Dogs must be tied up at night. 6. Profane language will not be tolerated.

7. Each man will help driving the cattle 8. Rate of travel for Oxen 3 miles an hour. (The corral made by wagons will not be broken until all of the cattle have been yoked.)

John's responsibility for ten wagons made it difficult at times to help his own Families. Elizabeth in one wagon had sons 4 [John William]- 6 [Ephraim]- and 11 [Isaac], Daughters 8

[Louisa]-10 [Matilda] and a new baby [Elizabeth] too Mary had a son [Hyrum] 22 months old and Sarah 23 years old had a son [Joseph L.] 11 months old in her arms Yet here we two who have been raised in luxury, are bravely trying to drive a Mule Team across the plains, holding our Babies. We take turns driving. You can just imagine we three women climbing in and out over wagon wheels to cook on the camp fire and wash clothes.

We sleep in our Camp wagons or on the Ground along the swampy river bottoms. John helped a lot before leaving going among Non Mormons and asking for clothes, bedding and money for those who had every thing in the world taken from them. He also Converted three people to our Gospel. I am now 27 years old and trying hard to be a good wife. We cook in a camp kettle, it is an iron pot with three legs

It had a heavy lid and could be set right on the beds of coals and biscuits corn bread or cake could be put in, then a shovel full of coals was put on top to bake them. Some who had no kettles cooked on hot rocks to do thier baking. Some of our meals were just broiled meat and bread. Other times all we had to eat was water gruel (a very thin mush) One Wedding dinner on the plains consisted of fresh bread baked in a skillet, fresh butter and a piece of meat.

Milk and cream could be placed in a churn in the morning and by night you could have a pat of butter by the jolting wagon over rough trails. An English Emmigrant whose sense of smell had left him due to age, was one day hungryly out looking for food, found a strange animal and killed it. (it was furry and black and white) He skinned it and proudly brought it to camp. "a skunk" and to his amazement everyone fled as he approached and for some days he was an outcast.

Our daily exertions made hunger a constant companion. The quanity of food was limited and meals were usually scant. At other times fish was caught in streams and ducks, geese, turkeys and prairie chickens were shot. The men hunted for buffalo elk and deer and these added to our daily diet. Pig weeds,[143] thistles and other greens were gathered at times and cooked to add variety. And some times if several [Buffalo] were shot the Saints woud stop over for a day or two and we cut the meat in strips.

This we dried for future meals. Some places an abundance of wild red and black currants and sometimes gooseberries were gratefully gleaned. Some of the Children while walking wore a bag and picked up buffalo chips and sticks to make fires for the evening meals. As soon as we camped everyone tried to share in the labors. Some carried water and gathered wood for fires. Big high sagebrush was used and in timber country we burned wood. But all was not desolation on the long journey.

We enjoyed the smell of the pretty wild roses. At some places beautiful wild flowers of all hues could be seen and we enjoyed the singing of the birds. Young girls tended weary babies until they could be fed and put to sleep After prayers the camp retired for the night, with camp fires burning and the lights of lanterns in the wagons. The looing of the cattle, bleating of the sheep mingled with the neighing of the horses in the corrals of wagons.

The howling of coyotes and wolves on distant hills and prairies mingled with the Half Hour Cry of the Faithful Guards, "All is well" "All is Well." Right.

There was always the dread of crossing dangerous streams and rivers. Yet many plucky women gathered up thier skirts and waded right through them. Some times large herds of Buffaloo crossed our path, so many that at times we had to wait one hour or two while they clumsily lumbered by. And there was always the danger of meeting Indians, some friendly and others hostile and dangerous and they almost always demanded some of our scant food supply. One day we nearly lost our lives.

One day due to a delay, our Family Wagons got separated

---

143. Pigweed, found wild on the prairie, can be cooked and eaten like spinach.

from the main body of the Saints. Suddenly we were completely surrounded by a big band of wild Indains who enjoyed scalping people just for the fun of it. We sat terrified and motionless with fear praying silently that we would some way be spared a tragic end. Yelling and shouting wildly they rode around us. We shook with fear not daring to move or speak. They came closer and closer. Then they Gathered in a big group.

They held a big "Pow-Wow" minutes seemed like hours as we tried to keep our children quiet. They gestured and yelled louder and we grew more frightened as our fate seemed so hopeless. Again I breathed a prayer, Father I am so young, will I have to die here on the plains with my Family, now we are so near the end of our journey? Will I never see Zion after I have given my all for my religion? Then some of the Indians slid off their ponies and as they came nearer we saw a young white man.

He had been captured by them and forced to live with them— but he had recognized John Scott as a boy he had gone to school with in Canada. He begged and pleaded with the Indians to spare our lives and he finally persuaded them to go away. It was a miracle from God we always thought after, and today we owe all of our lives to that brave young man's pleadings and to our kind Heavenly Father. Once during the journey the authorities gave John ten gallons of whiskey to pacify the Indians

They were on the war path at the time. At last we near the end of the long, long journey, as we enter the Valley of the Mountains and look out over the vast land of Zion. I am dismayed by the very immensity of the view. The boundless Silence and I see miles of sage brush every where. Behind us now are the heart aches and many thousands of silent tears, that fell on the long unknown trail. I remember my dear home in England, of the flowers and trees and beautiful surroundings at that safe place.

And I am home sick for my Dear Mother and Father. But just as I have covered those endless hundreds of miles, so now I will begin work with renewed Faith, begin the task of building a good home in this new wilderness.

Nancy Naomi Alexander Tracy and her husband were in the East when they heard the news of the Prophet Joseph Smith's death in Carthage. They imme-diately returned to Nauvoo. Once prosperous farmers in New York, the Tracys lost most of their belongings and savings as they followed the Church to Ohio, Missouri, and then Nauvoo. They were never again to know the comfort and security they had enjoyed before joining the Church. An intensely spiritual woman, Nancy Tracy used the hardships she encountered and the sacrifices she made as instruments of faith and died vowing she would do it all over again to be counted among the community of Saints. She and her family traveled west in 1849.

NANCY NAOMI ALEXANDER TRACY[144]

AS SOON AS WE ARRIVED [from our visit to our relatives in the East], we went right home and prepared to go to meet-ing for that day was appointed for us to choose a first presidency to lead the Church. The saints convened in a grove. Sidney Rigdon and his followers were on hand to contest their right to

---

144. "Life History of Nancy Naomi Alexander Tracy Written by Herself," (1895), typescript copy, Special Collections, Harold B. Lee Library, Brigham Young University, Provo, Utah.

be the leaders of the Saints. At one time he was one of Brother Joseph's councilors, but he was not righteous, and Joseph shook him off saying that he had carried him long enough and he would carry him no longer. Therefore, it was out of the question to have such a man lead the people.

Brigham Young was the man chosen and sustained by unanimous vote to be the mouthpiece of God to the Saints. I can testify that the mantle of Joseph fell upon Brigham that day as that of Elijah did fall upon Elisha, for it seemed that his voice, his gestures, and all were Joseph. It seemed that we had him again with us. He was sustained by the voice of the people to be the prophet, seer, and revelator.

Soon after this, my youngest child was taken sick and died in two weeks. His name was Theodore Franklin and he was two years and two months old. Now I had two little boys laid side by side in the burying ground, their little graves the same size.[145]

Well, the Temple was so far completed that fall that the Lord accepted it at the hands of the Saints, and it was dedicated. The Saints began to receive their blessings. Therein we had our endowments in that house.

The evil one saw that the Saints were getting power from on high. Of course, he raged and stirred up the feeling of enmity against us, and the people again determined to drive us from our homes. So during the winter months preparations were made and some had already left their comfortable homes and crossed the river on the ice to go into the wilderness beyond civilization we know not where only as the hand of the Lord shall lead us. O liberty! thou precious boon that our Fathers shed their blood to gain, whither hast thou fled? But the hand of the Lord is over us, and so we shall find a resting place.

---

145. Her son William Frances Tracy died February 1842.

On the 15th of March, 1845 [probably 1846], my sixth son [Austin Walter Tracy] was born.

About the last of May [1846], previous to our departure from Nauvoo, I was aroused from my slumbers on [at] night, hearing such heavenly music as I had never heard before. Everything was so still and quiet when it burst upon my ear that I could not imagine where it came from. I got up and looked out of the window. The moon shone bright as I looked over at the Temple from whence the sound came. There on the roof of the building heavenly bands of music had congregated and were playing most beautifully. The music was exquisite! And we had to leave all this; the Temple, our homes, and the pleasant surroundings and bid farewell. It was to your tents, O Israel.

At another time, fire caught in the roof of the Temple. How it caught, I never knew, but for awhile it seemed that the house would be destroyed. Men, women, and children came out and formed a bucket brigade. The wells were drained and finally they went with wagons and barrels to the river for water and at last succeeded in putting out the flames. The damage was considerable. It seemed that if the evil powers could not harass the people one way, they would do it in another.

But now the time had come for us to take up the line and march, this time far away to the west where white man's foot had never trod. We were going to find a resting place among the red men of the forest. Our journey had been delayed some time on account of my confinement, but as soon as I was able to travel we started out. So farewell to beautiful Nauvoo. May the Lord have mercy on our enemies' souls for their cruelty and wickedness to an innocent and law abiding people. But we are to be a tried people and to be made perfect through suffering. We took with us what effects we could with one strong yoke of cattle. We crossed the river, went over the bluffs, and camped until a company got together so it would be safe to travel. The companies were small. For the present, nothing occurred. The travel was slow. I think

there were about ten families of us. We had not as yet an organized camp, but we went on until we neared Council Bluffs and
camped one afternoon on what was called Mosquito Creek. Our
second son [Laconius Moroni Tracy], eleven years old, took his
fish hook and line as he always did when we camped on a stream
and went to the creek. He caught quite a string of fish and came
up to the wagon and gave them to his older brother. Then he
came to me and said, "Oh, mother, my head aches so it seems all
on fire." It was about the middle of July and whether it was a sun
stroke or brain fever, we could not tell. Of course, we could not
travel on. We did everything we could under the circumstances,
but he died on the third of August [1846]. This was indeed a trying ordeal to have to bury our dear boy here in the wilderness.
There were four families who stayed with us. It was night when
the boy died, and we were alone in the wagon except my husband's cousin, Orlin Colvin. I happened to have some fine
bleached cloth, and I made his clothes and dressed him. Brother
Blodget[146] took the side boards of our wagon and made him a
decent coffin. We had funeral services, and he was laid in the
silent grave on a little hill not far from where he caught his last
fish. There was one other little grave there where someone had
buried a child but the grave was not marked.

We were ten miles from the Missouri river and where the
Pottawatamie Indians with some French and half breeds and
some Indian traders lived. This was the time when Uncle Sam
followed us up to get 500 able-bodied men from the Mormon
camps to go and help to fight Mexico. How was this when and
after they could not let us have a place amongst them and we were
already on the march for the wilderness. Did not this look like
they were determined to follow us and harass us to demand all
the able-bodied men and thus leave aged and feeble men,

---

146. Probably Newman Greenleaf Blodgett. He and his family traveled to the Salt Lake Valley in
1850.

women, and children to travel through an Indian country unprotected. Who ever heard of such a thing? But our brethren complied with this demand and the 500 volunteered and went, leaving their wives and little ones to travel on as best they could.

We now came to the conclusion to stay here at Council Bluffs until the next spring; so a few families of us built log cabins and prepared for winter. That fall there were many families that had made a late start stopped here for the winter. They build little cabins and finally a log schoolhouse and opened a school and held meetings there. There were at last about 35 or 40 families stopped here for the winter. The place named Carterville because there were so many families by that name there. There was another stopping place three miles farther on called Kanesville where the Saints that were late stopped for the winter and built up quite a place. They had a store, etc.

Still farther on, there was another place called Winter Quarters. In fact, the Saints had to stop all along to recruit. Of course, it was hard times and much sickness and suffering prevailed, especially at Winter Quarters. In the early part of winter, my husband's old employer, Amos Davis, came along through our settlement with a load of goods from his store in Nauvoo. He stopped with us for a day. When he left, he gave us some tea, sugar, and coffee, which was highly appreciated and was a luxury in those hard times. So, taking it all together, we got along very well. Wood was plentiful and also good water. We rested and took comfort in our religion. We were not conquered.

Well, the winter passed on, and where were we going? Should we take up the march? No, this was decided against this spring. We stayed and put in a crop and got better fitted out for that long journey, for now we knew that we were going to the Rocky Mountains, a long way off, and we must have better outfits to take us there. Others did the same and stayed for over a year or two that they might better their condition. But little did we think when we stopped here with our sick boy that we should prolong our stay as we did, but the hand of the Lord is over his people.

The gold fever had taken hold of the people in the states, for the news had gone like wildfire that gold had been discovered in California. Emigration went through thick and fast and we had a chance to trade a good deal with the people as they passed through. They paid for food and vegetables and things we could spare. It was surely a great help to us. So we stayed on for three years more and enjoyed ourselves for we had meetings. We felt free for no one molested us. We could go down on the river bottom in the fall of the year and gather bushels of grapes to make wine, and we gathered walnuts and hickory nuts and there was no one to ask why we did so.

The second winter here, on the 25th of February, 1849, my seventh son was born. We called him Helon Henry, a name to be long remembered, but now he is dead and gone before me and has left a large family. In the fall before the birth of this child, there was a circumstance that cast gloom over our settlement. William Carter married a young and beautiful girl by the name of Meekham [Roxena Mecham]. One afternoon she went home one mile to see her mother. She did not return the next day, and so they went over to her mother's where they discovered that she had not even been the day before. Therefore they instituted a search. There was a stream of water to cross on the way she should have gone. Above the bridge a short distance, they found her shawl and bonnet on the bank, and in the stream they found her dead body, drowned. No one ever knew why she committed this deed, for she seemed all right when she left. My husband helped to take her body out of the water, and she was buried by the side of my boy.

Diminicus Carter also buried a wife there,[147] and before we left this place there was quite a little burying ground.

---

147. Sophronia Babcock Carter died 26 August 1847 near Council Bluffs, Iowa.

As I said, we stayed in this place for three years. The third year we began to make preparations to go on our journey. My husband had had three of his brothers come on from the east and two of them were going with us. We had been able to get in better condition to travel this time. We could put two yoke of cattle and one of cows on the wagon and were pretty well fixed for the journey.

There was a widow lady by the name of Brocket who wanted to go with us. We thought she could help me, and so concluded to take her along, but she was very sickly although a very good woman. And then there was the widow Lamb that Amos Davis had fitted out with wagon and a yoke of cattle and a yoke of large cows. He wanted my husband to find a driver to take charge of this family and team. There were two little children in this family.

So all being ready, we started out, crossed the Missouri River, and went into camp to wait for the company to be organized. One brother [Benjamin] Hawkins was chosen to be captain over 100 wagons, and then a captain was chosen over each of the two fifties' and one over each 10 wagons. Thomas Johnston was over our fifty and my husband [Moses Tracy] was captain over the second ten they organized. In this manner we rolled out. There had been a general rally this year for the great Salt Lake.

We traveled on in this way for days and all went well. We had a good rest while at Council Bluffs. We enjoyed ourselves around the camp fire at night when the moon shone. After supper was over and the work done for the night, they would clear away a place and go forth in the dance for we had plenty of music in camp.

Finally we got as far as the Platte River. Here they thought it was best to divide the camp into two companies and travel separately in order to travel faster.

The Indians were generally peaceable although sometimes

they were a little troublesome, begging around. However, they did not commit any depredations in particular. Once a large band of Sioux came up to where we camped and came inside the corral of wagons. One of the young bucks picked up a sack of crackers and ran off with it. The chief was informed of this, and he soon brought him back with the crackers and gave him a tremendous whipping over his naked head and shoulders.

While we were traveling along the Platte River, the men thought they would stop and give the cattle a rest and have a buffalo hunt for the buffalo were quite numerous. In the meantime, the women could do their washing and baking. We camped in a little skirt of timber. The next morning the men started out to hunt. It was a very hot day, but the men came in at night loaded with meat. However, there was a young man, Charley Jonson, the widow Lamb's teamster, who, when he came in was so thirsty and hungry that he could not wait for supper, and so cut a piece of raw buffalo meat and ate it. The poor fellow, that night he was taken with cholera and died next morning. The brethren worked all night with him but could not save him. His groans were heart-rending to hear. They dug a deep grave, rolled him up in blankets, and buried him there. They could do no better under the circumstances.

When we made ready to move on, we discovered that one of the widow Lamb's cows was missing. They hunted for her but could not find her and finally came to the conclusion that Indians had driven her off. So we had to go on without her and had to leave poor Charley in his lonely grave. My oldest son [Eli Alexander Tracy, 16 years old] then had to drive the widow's team. The large wolves followed us that morning for they were very numerous.

We went on without further incident till we passed Fort Larimie when one evening there came two deserting soldiers into camp. They began to travel with us, saying that they could stand it no longer at the fort. They traveled two days with us, and then were overtaken by officers from the fort. Poor fellows! they might easily have been protected, but there was a reward up for them and our captain delivered them up. They were strapped to horses and taken back to receive their punishment. My husband and our captain had quite an argument about it. It was indeed cruel, but a little money was tempting for it was scarce.

There began to be considerable sickness in camp and some deaths. Peter Shirts, captain of the first ten, had to bury his wife by the wayside.[148] Abram Durphy [Abraham Durfey] buried one of his children, and there were others who died.

There were two emigrants traveling with us bound for California. One of them came down with small pox and died, but there were such precautions taken that no one else took it. However, the whole camp was vaccinated, and some were quite sick. I was, myself.

Well, those were very long and toilsome days. Still we plodded on until they had to stop for rest. The cattle were giving out and becoming footsore and had to be shod. So we stopped in the country of the black hills for twelve days. There was water and plenty of timber, but previously to this, they sometimes had to tie up the cattle at night without feed or water. But here there was good feed and water and the poor animals surely needed it for they were about worn out. My two cows had given milk all the way and worked in the yoke besides, and so when there was no other alternative, we could drink their milk. But they were failing in this now. So we camped and overhauled and cleaned up generally while the men were busy shoeing the cattle and making tar out of the fat pines for the wagons for pine trees were abundant. When they got through with all this, they spent the time hunting until we were ready to move on. They killed elk and deer; so we had meat. But O the wolves! At night they made the air hideous with

---

148. Margaret Cameron Shirts died in 1849 near the Platte River in Nebraska.

their howling. Of course, we always kept a guard at night ever since we started, and this was telling on the men. Many a time when my husband was on guard along the Platte River, I have gone out with some nourishment even if it were nothing but a hot potato.

There was one circumstance I forgot to mention in its proper place. We had to cross over one fork of the Platte River. It was one quarter of a mile wide. We had to pile everything as high as we could in the wagon and then sit on top. The water was shallow at first but grew deeper as we got into the stream. Of course, the men had to go in the water to guide the teams and hold on to the ox bows. The water came up to their shoulders and was very chilly. But we got across safely and unloaded the fifty wagons and crossed back to bring a herd of sheep over. That meant that the men had to cross the ugly stream three different times. Then we had to stop over one day in order to dry the things. I was glad we saw the last of that river as I also was when we rolled out of our camping ground in the Black Hills, although we had a good rest there.

We were now on the last half of our journey and began to feel anxious to get to our final stopping place. My husband was beginning to feel the wear of the trip severely.

Memory fails to think of anything worthy of note as we traveled on, although there was one place I remember well. The wagons had to be let down an embankment into a stream and had to travel on some distance in the stream before they could climb the bank to the road again. The men in letting the wagons down the bank into the stream had to tie strong ropes to the back of the wagons and several of them had to pull back on the ropes so as to let the wagons down easily. It took some time and was slow work but was accomplished. I often think how different the mode of travel is now to what it was at that time in 1850, and it is now 1895.

The travel became slower and more fatiguing. At last we got

to the crossing of the Green River. The river ran on very swift and looked angry and deep. The first ten drove in. There was one Brother Gifford[149] who held on to his ox bows till he lost his hold and went down. He could not swim but one of the brethren went to his rescue and brought him out more dead than alive but he was brought around after a while. The rest got across safely and moved on toward the mountains that we were now approaching. In a few days, we began to raise the heights of the big mountain and reached the summit. When we did reach the top, we were struck with amazement as we gazed at the valley below, the long sought for place of rest. O how beautiful and grand the valley, dotted with dwellings and with the Great Salt Lake sparkling in the sunlight, appeared. We feasted our eyes upon the scene. It looked like paradise after three months of toil through the hot summer. We were about to reap the reward of our labors. We had found a place of rest far away from our enemies and those that had persecuted us and shed the blood of the Saints and prophets of the most high. Here we could live and worship God and keep his commandments. Will they let us alone now or will they follow us? Time alone will tell.

On the 12th day of September, 1850, we came down into Salt Lake City. We went to the west of the city and camped for a few days and looked around. But as feed for the teams was scarce, we moved on north to a place called Session Settlement [Bountiful] where some people by that name had settled.[150]

We stayed in this place for three weeks. My husband and son went into the mountains and got wood and took it to Salt Lake and sold it for provisions for we were out. The times were pretty hard for the crickets had made such havoc with the crops. But we got enough together to last awhile, and learning that a good many people had gone up north about the Ogden river to settle, we

---

149. Probably Samuel Kendell Gifford, who also traveled in Johnson's fifty.
150. Peregrine Sessions and his family settled Bountiful, originally known as "Sessions Settlement."

concluded to follow on and settle there. Sister Brocket was still with us but she could get a place in Salt Lake to live, and as her health was poor, she decided to stop. It was now the middle of October and would be sometime before we could build and have a shelter; so we bid her good-bye and started north.

We came to the Ogden river and found a few log houses there. We crossed over at this point about one mile and camped at Farr's Fort where there were a few families. It was getting to be cold, and the wind from the canyon blew all the time. Timber was plentiful; so we had a cabin thrown up as soon as we could, and under shelter, the next thing was to secure something to live on through the winter. We sold a yoke of cattle for one large beef ox, and this we sold for twelve bushels of wheat, which was scarce and hard to get at any cost. We had a little corn meal, and the cows still gave a little milk. There were six of us in our family. I would cut the children a slice of bread, make some cruit coffee with a little milk in it, and tell them to thank the Lord for it, and they were satisfied.

In 1833 Warren Foote "professed" his belief in Mormons and associated himself with the Church in 1837 when he moved to Kirtland to teach school. He followed the Church to Missouri and then on to Nauvoo, where he was finally baptized in 1842. He left that city in May 1846 and situated himself and his family in Kanesville, Iowa, where he stayed until going west in 1850. He is one of many who recorded special promptings of the Spirit in connection with their departure for the Salt Lake Valley. He evidently kept a daily journal and drew from it to write an account of his 1850 stewardship as captain of a hundred.

WARREN FOOTE[151]

I WILL MAKE SOME EXTRACTS from my private Journal in order to show my situation in the spring of 1850, and the dealings of the Lord with me, in causing me to seriously consider the advisability of going to Salt Lake Valley this year.

My nephew, Franklin Allen, and myself had purchased the little gristmill at Kanesville of Jacob Myers, our fatherin-law,[152] and was running it ourselves. There was a heavy emigration of California Gold Diggers, (as they were called) and grain was scarce and very dear. Corn $2.00 per bus. Wheat $2.25. We made considerable money and made some payments on the mill. About the first of May I took a severe cold, and was not able to do anything. I hired a brother, who had just come to Kanesville from Scotland, (a miller by occupation) to run the mill my half of the time. His name is David Adamson.

My health being so poor, I began to reflect upon my situation and about going to the Valley of Salt Lake. I felt that my health would never be much better here in this changeable climate. One day, being greatly impressed by the spirit, I repaired to the top of the bluff north of the mill, not far from the burying ground, and there earnestly poured forth my soul in prayer to the Lord, asking Him to make known His will to me, - What He would have me do; and if it was his will that I should move to the Valley this season to open up the way, that I might sell my share of the mill, and obtain a fitout for that purpose. While I was thus engaged in prayer, the Spirit of God rested upon me,

151. Journal of Warren Foote (1850), holograph, LDS Church Archives.

152. Both Warren Foote and his nephew Franklin Allen married daughters of Jacob Myers. Warren married Artemisia Sidnie, and Franklin married her sister Rebecca.

and impressed me by a still small voice which thrilled my whole body; saying: "The way shall be opened before you, and notwithstanding your ill health, inasmuch as you put your trust in me, I will preserve your life, and not one of your family shall fall by the way, but I will bring you safely to the valley of Salt Lake." This filled my soul with joy, and I returned to my house with a full determination to set about preparing to go.

While the California Emigrants were passing through, I had a light wagon at Bro. Obanion's shop,[153] for which he was making a box. One of the emigrants seeing it, wanted to trade a heavier one for it. I told bro. Obanion to trade with him, I gave a little chopfeed to boot, and thus got a good strong new wagon - strong enough to haul 4000 lbs to the Valley. This was before I had any idea of going to Salt Lake this year. But I am satisfied that the Lord was then preparing the way for me.

About the last of May I sold my half of the mill back to father Myers, and obtained a comfortable outfit.

Two weeks from the time I sold out I was ready to start with one wagon, two yoke of oxen, and three cows. Two of the cows I worked between the oxen. George Kent, whose brother is in the Valley is going to drive my team for the privilege of going with me, and board. I will say here, that brother Otis L. Terry, who had been following blacksmithing in Kanesville, and with whom I had become intimately acquainted, was preparing to go to the Valley this season. We agreed to go together in the same Company. On the 10th of June, we started from Kanesville in company with brother Terry's father, and his brother Charles A. Terry. The Saints are crossing the Missouri river 18 miles below Kanesville this year, and going up the south side of the Platte

---

153. This is probably Evan or Evans Obanion, born in Kentucky in 1799. He lived in Nauvoo after joining the Church and was still in Kanesville in 1849, just a year before Warren Foote had the box made for his wagon..

river. We drove down to Musquito [Mosquito] Creek bridge and camped.

12th We moved on down to within a mile and an half of the Ferry and unhitched our teams just in time to attend the meeting for organizing the Company. Elder [Orson] Hyde soon arrived and proceeded to organize the hundred. There was quite a congregation present but many who were going had not yet arrived.

Brother Hyde arose and after looking over the congregation, said, "I nominate bro Warren Foote for captain of hundred." This was so unexpected to me, I must confess that I was completely dumfounded. It was voted unanimously. Then brother Hyde nominated Otis L. Terry Captain of first fifty. Voted unanimously. He was as much taken by surprise as I was. Elder Hyde then asked for some one to nominate a Captain of the second fifty, and some one nominated William Wall. It was voted unanimously. Elder Hyde then said that the captain of the hundred and the captains of fifties, would organize the fifties into tens. This we accomplished during the afternoon.

As has been stated, brother Otis L. Terry and I had agreed to travel together across the plains, but little did we think then that we would be associated togather as leaders of the Company. Elder Hyde asked if the brethren were generally supplied with firearms. Upon inquiry we found that there were several families who had none. He said there were muskets belonging to the Nauvoo Legion stored at Kanesville and that we could have them on conditions that we would deliver them to the Authorities of the Church in Salt Lake City. It was decided that I should return to Kanesville and get the muskets. Accordingly I returned on horseback and selected 15 that were in shooting order, and got a man who was going down to the ferry to take them along. I returned to camp the next day, (June 16th.) The second fifty commenced crossing on the 13th. I had my family ferried over the 14th and camped with the second fifty a short distance from the river. On the 16th the first fifty were all ferried over and all camped by a creek three miles from the Ferry. As brother Terry <and I> had agreed to travel togather. I concluded to travel with the first Fifty, and <it> was decided that my wagon should take the lead or head of the Company which place I occupied throughout the journey.

I have written the foregoing as a kind of preliminary to bro Mulliner's Journal.[154]

The succeeding pages contains my Review of the Journey.

I will briefly review our Journey.

As I have previously stated, ~~my health~~ my health was not very good before I left Kanesville.

After starting from the Missouri river I made it a practice towards camping-time, to get on a horse and ride ahead of the company and select a camping place. After we had been traveling about a week as I was about five miles ahead of the company looking for a camping place, there came up a thunder shower, and I was completely drenched. I took a terrible cold which settled on my lungs which caused the illness spoke of in the Journal. I was not so but what I could get around a little, but my lungs were so weak, that I could scarcely speak above a whisper. When we were along about Plum Creek, the atmosphere was so close and heavy, that it seemed to me that I would have to give up breathing altogather.

I remembered the promises of the Lord that were made to me before I sold my share of the mill; and humbly asked the Lord to fullfil the same. I was impressed to be baptized for my health; and requested brother Mulliner to perform the ordinance; which he did; and was then administered to by the brethren.[155] After this I began to recover slowly. When we arrived at Scotts' Bluffs I was able to walk short distances. From this place

154. Samuel Mulliner was the clerk of the Warren Foote company. Warren Foote also kept a journal of the trek. This is a summary.

155. Several journals note that rebaptisms were performed for health reasons, a common practice in early days.

onward the atmosphere became lighter, and dryer, and my health improved very fast; and I was able to again take a more active part in the management of Company.

It was a very serious time while the Cholera was raging in the company, but after it abated, we enjoyed our travels, and as a general thing, a good spirit. In places where feed was very scarce, there was some who murmured about our camping where there was so little grass, but the next morning as we traveled along, they would acknowledge that our camping place was as good or better than it was a "little ahead." They would say on camping, that there was a better place a "little ahead."

Although there was some murmuring occasionaly, yet I think that we crossed the Plains with as little difficulty as any company that has crossed them. I am certain that a journey through a desert country of a thousand miles, with five hundred souls will try the patience of any man, or set of men who are appointed to preside over them as leaders, especially so, when the company consists of different nationalities, having different customs, and some without experience in driving ox teams and taking care of them.

I am thankful to be able to say that, the Lord blessed me with patience to such a degree, that one Captain of ten said in one of our council meetings that I was certainly one of the most patient men that he ever saw. I do not think that he said this as a compliment to me, but it was because I would not agree to a tyranical proposition that he was proposing. I was determined that every person in the Company should have their rights respected, and I am pleased to say that Captain O. L. Terry stood firmly by me, in fact we were one in all our councils.

Bro. Mulliner has omitted to state that at the foot of the last mountain, where we camped for the <last> time before we entered the Valley, the first fifty were called together for the purpose of settling all difficulties, if any existed, and ask each others forgiveness; so that we could enter the Valley free from any hard feelings towards any of our brothers or sisters. A good spirit prevailed; and all expressed a desire to forgive and be forgiven.

The second Fifty arrived in the Valley a few days before the first Fifty. When we stopped to rest a few days, and hunt, a little east of the Devil's Gate, the second fifty was Camped about a mile ahead. Captain Wall came to see me, and get some instructions. I told him that they had better push on to the Valley as fast as their teams were able to travel, and not wait for the first Fifty, as it was getting pretty well along in the season. I also charged him in particular to take the muskets, (10 in number) belonging to the Nauvoo Legion, that were in his fifty and deliver them to the Authorities in Salt Lake and take their receipts for them. This he never done. He did not even go to Salt Lake City, but as soon as he got into the Valley he took a road running south and went direct to Provo. As the second fifty were all dispersed before we got to Salt Lake City, I never recovered them. I got those that were in the first fifty and delivered them to the President's Clerk and took his receipt. I spoke to him about those that were in the second fifty. He said that they were all in the valley any way, and he seemed to think that it did not make much difference whether they were delivered or not. In fact they were not of much use to any one. The first Fifty passed through Salt Lake City in the afternoon of the 26th of Sept. and camped on the Jordon bottom west of the City. Many of the brethren were anxious to get some counsel, where they had better locate. On the morning of the 27th, Captain Terry and I went up in to the City and found Elder Hide [Hyde] at Bro. H[eber]. C. Kimballs residence and reported our arrival, and told him that some of the brethren wanted to know where would be the best place to locate. He said that they had been up north looking for locations for the saints to settle, and among other places he mentioned Ogden, and said that place would suit him best. On our return to Camp we reported what bro. Hyde said to us, and many of the brethren resolved to go north. Some located in Salt Lake City, and a few went south to Little Cottonwood.

Warren Foote,
Captain of One Hundred

One of the first settlers in Cache Valley, Utah, Mary Ann Weston Maughan joined the Church in England, where she and her husband entertained the missionaries and opened their home for preaching. When the missionaries were attacked by mobs at one of their meetings, her husband, John Davis, was severely injured and later died of his wounds. Mary Ann decided to emigrate to Nauvoo to be with the Saints there. Soon after her arrival in 1841, she married Peter Maughan, a widower, and took on the care of his five children. After receiving their endowments in 1846, the Maughans moved to New Diggings, Wisconsin, near the lead mines in order to earn money for the trip west. In 1850 they traveled to Kanesville and joined the Warren Foote company that year for the journey to Utah. Mary Ann Maughan kept a journal for most of her life. Her narrative is an anecdotal, observant, and sensitive record of her impressions of her trail experience.

MARY ANN WESTON MAUGHAN[156]

IN THE SPRING [1850], Mr. Maughan went out in the country and bought our teams. We had 2 good wagons with double covers and projections on the sides. We had 3 yoke of cattle and 1 yoke of cows to each wagon. This took some of our money, so we did not have more than we could take care of after this. My babe was nearly 3 weeks old when we left our log cabins [in New Diggings] on the 17th of April, 1850. I have been out in some cold storms since then, but I do not think I ever experienced a colder morning in my life. The wind blew down from the North so pearcing cold that our covers were fastened down, so I could not shake hands with my friends, when they came to the wagon to bid me good-bye when we passed through New Diggings. We had a cold stormy time till we reached the Mississippi river on the 22d. That night I attended Sister Kind (?) in her confinement of a daughter. The weather was very cold but she was taken good care of, and done well.

Some more teams met us here, and Mr. Maughan was appointed Captain of the company. We traveled in mud and rain through Iowa, the road leading through many creeks, filled with water by the heavy rains, and had many bad storms. Sometimes it seemed that our covers would be torn off and wagons blown away, but my babe required my care, also my large family of 8 to cook for. I had no time for writing, so could not keep my journal.[157]

We arrived in Kanesville in May, near the end of the month. All well. Staid there one week to wash and to rest our cattle. Here

---

156. "Autobiography of Mary Ann Weston Maughan" (1894–1898), typescript copy, LDS Church Archives.

157. Her experience was that of many faithful journalists who found the demands of the trail left no time or energy for writing.

we found some friends of Mr. Maughan's from the North of England. We were organized into Captain William Wall's Company of 50 and Captain [Warren] Foote Company of 100. Mr. Maughan was appointed captain of first 10.

June 6, 1850. We started early this morning. At noon came up with Captains Bear [John Bair] and [Warren] Smith.[158] Traveled behind them till near sundown, then turned off the road. Found a good camping ground on Black's fork. Plenty feed. We met Bro. Call from the Valley.

7th. We remained in camp till noon, then started. Found Captains Wall, [Chester] Loveland, and [Gilbert Belnap] Belknap. Camped on Hams Fork. Concluded to wait here in hopes Mr. Ebley will come up. Traveled 5 miles.

14th. Today our 10 have crossed the river. We are camped on the bank. We had a shower of rain this afternoon but the weather is still very warm.

17th. We started about noon today. We have been waiting for some muskets which Captain Foote went back to Kanesville after, as there was a deficiency in our arms. We traveled 3 miles. Camped on 3 mile creek. Had some bad roads but no bad accident happened.

19th. This morning we had a powerful rain; comenced at breakfast time and continued till near noon. Started in the afternoon. On the way passed the grave of Bro. Warren, who died of cholera. This is the 1st grave we have seen. Traveled 8 miles. Camped on a small stream.

21st. We were called to bury 2 of our company who died of cholera this morning, a man named Brown and a child. There are more sick in camp. Have been in sight of the Platte river all day. Traveled 15 miles, camped on Salt Creek. Soon some of our company came up with another child dead. They buried it at twi-

---

158. Captains of their own independent of 1850 companies.

light on the bank of the creek. There are more sick. It makes us feel sad thus to bury our friends by the way.[159] Weather very hot.

22nd. This morning before starting we were called to bury 3 more children. They all belonged to one family. We started late and before all had crossed the creek it comenced to rain very hard. We were detained till noon. Traveled 9 miles, camped on the Paria [probably prairie] without wood or water, or some that is very poor. This is the worst time we have had since we crossed the Missouri river. Every thing wet and several sick in camp. Very little fire.

23rd. We buried 3 more this evening. Traveled 8 miles.

24th. This morning is wet and uncomfortable. It was thought best to remain in camp. Some are washing and baking, all were busy. About noon it cleared up and we had a public meeting in camp. Some fasted and humbled themselves before the Lord and prayed that He would remove disease from us. Brother Crandall[160] said in four days five of his family had been taken from their midst and requested the Brethren to pray that the other members of his family might be spared.

25th. The mother of the three children spoke of yesterday died this afternoon. She will be buried this evening. We are camped on a creek which we call Pleasant Point. Here we buried Sister [Martha Stiles] Spafford, the mother of nine children. There are no more sick in camp and we hope the worst is over. Traveled 10 miles.

27th. There has been wagons in sight before us; we think they are the Snow company [William Snow/Joseph Young sixth company], a part of which crossed the Missouri River when we left it. About noon we met the mail from the valley. They said

---

159. The cholera was capricious, devastating some companies during specific years and hardly touching others.

160. This was likely Myron Nathan Crandall and his family (including his brother who was unmarried on the trek).

there was some sickness ahead, but not much, and that we must travel faster or we would be caught in the mountains.

29th. At noon the last wagon came up with a corpse, a Sister [Ann Deacon] Beal. I heard that she had been sick for sometime. They buried her on the bank of the creek called Clear Water and baptized more for their health. That evening some Elders camped with us. They were missionarys on their way to England. Sister Grover,[161] one of our Nauvoo neighbours, is traveling with them. I wrote a letter and sent it to mother. They brought the emigrants mail.

30th. We were called upon to bury another of our company, Sister Crandall. She died in childbed. This makes seven out of a family of 15.

July 1st. Started at the usual time this morning. We kept near the bank of the river, then left it and passed through Indian Town. There were about 200 wigwams, some of them large. They are neatly woven into wicker work with stick and dried grass. They belong to the Pawnees, who are gone farther down the river, as the imigrants' teams destroyed their crops. We passed 4 graves. Traveled 12 miles. Are camped on the river bank. This water is so high we have to wade for wood and the water is very mudy. Weather pleasant.

July 4th. This morning we found one of our oxen a little lame and sent him into the herd, and it was thought best for the last 2 tens to go a mile around to avoid crossing a slough. At noon we found the herd[s]man had left our ox on the road and our 10 immediately camped, and 3 men went back after him. Soon Bro. [Lester] Russell went by, going after his cow that was also left. The herdsmen are thought very careless to leave our cattle behind when they know we are not on the same road

---

161. In 1850 Thomas Grover and his family left Salt Lake City and went to Missouri to purchase cattle. His wife Hannah or his wife Laduska could possibly be this Sister Grover.

behind them. We heard the guns at the Fort Kearney. To day it is the 4th of July. Traveled 9 miles.

5th. About noon today the men returned without our ox. Brother Russell found his cow. Captain Maughan called a council to decide if we should go on, or go back again and try to find him. All agreed it was best to go back and 2 of our Brethren volunteered to go with him. They returned at night without finding him. We all feel sorry to leave a good ox on the prairie, not knowing what had become of him. We heard afterwards that a company traveling close behind us killed him for beef. Some Brethren that knew the ox saw his head.

6th. Started early this morning, traveled 18 miles over a beautiful country, but no timber except on the river bank. At 11 o'clock found a letter left by Captain Wall. They had waited till 10 the day before for us to come up, said they would go on slowly and for us to travel with all possible speed. We have passed 9 graves to day, mostly children. Are camped on the prairie in sight of Fort Kearney.

8th. This morning 26 government teams passed our camp. Bro. Wood's cow and one of our oxen are lame. They had to dress their feet, which made us late in starting.

10th. We had a shower of rain last night which makes it feel cool and refreshing this morning. Traveled 16 miles, passed 11 graves, and camped on the prairie without water or wood, at a place I call Mosquito Plain, in honour of the vast numbers of that tormenting little fly. There is a good bed and stove lieing near our camp ground.[162]

12th. About noon as we were traveling along on a good plain road, my little Peter, about 3 years old, was sitting in the front of the wagon between his brother Charles and his sister Mary

---

162. Discarded possessions along with dead oxen, broken wagons, and tools littered the western trails as thousands of westering migrants to California, Oregon, and Utah turned it into a major thoroughfare with traffic going both east and west.

Ann. They were looking at a cow that had lost one horn. He
leaned forward, lost his balance, and fell before the wheels. The
first passed over him and he tried to escape the other one. But
alas the wagon stoped just as the hind wheel stood on his dear
little back. The Brethren from behind ran up and lifted the
wheel and took him from under it. He was bruised internaly so
that it was impossible for him to live long. We done all that was
possible for him, but no earthly power could save him. He did
not suffer much pain, only twice for a very little time. The people
left their wagons and gathered around mine, and all wept for the
dear little boy that we knew must soon leave us. I had talked to
him many times to be careful and not fall out of the wagon, or
he might be hurt very bad. He only spoke twice. I said to him,
"Pete, did you fall?" and he said, "Yes," and seemed to know that
his father had fainted for the Brethren stood to hide him from
my sight. On my asking for him, they said he would come soon.
As soon as he was able he came to the wagon, covered with dust.
But his little boy could not speak to him. He opened his eyes and
looked so lovingly at us, then gently closed them and passed
peacefully away, and left us weeping around his dear little bruised
body. Then loving hands tenderly dressed him in a suit of his
own white linen clothes. He looked so lovely. I emptied a dry
goods box and Bro. Wood made him a nice coffin; and it even
was a mournfull satisfaction, for we had seen our brothers and
sisters bury their dear ones without a coffin to lay them in. We
buried him on a little hill on the North side of the road. The
grave was consecrated and then they laid him to rest. Some one
had made a nice headboard, with his name printed on, also his
age and date of death. This was all we could do, and many prayers
were offered to our heavenly Father, that he might rest in peace
and not be disturbed by wolves. We turned away in sorrow and
grief. A few days after, we heard that his grave had not been
touched, but another little one made beside it, and afterwards
some more were buried by them. This was a great satisfaction to

us, to know that he remained as we left him. Our dear one's name was Peter Weston Maughan, born in New Diggings, Wisconsin Territory, May 20th, 1847.

13th. Started early this morning and overtook the company that passed us while stopping yesterday. Passed on 3 miles further to Ash Creek. Here we all camped to wash and bake. Traveled over a beautiful country today, timber in sight all day. Passed 12 graves, mostly grown people. We have a fine place to camp; plenty of wood and water, also grass. Weather cool and pleasant.

14th. We are obliged to wash and bake today to last 1 week. Formerly emigrants have found food on the river but there is none this year on account of high water in the spring. The rain has also injured the buffalo chips. We had meeting this afternoon in camp, and several were baptized for their health.

15th. We are again permitted to renew our journey, which lies through the buffalo country. They are seen by thousands, and this country seems made for them, being high bluffs and deep ravines. In the ravine there is plenty of cedar and water. We can see the Bluffs as far as the eye can reach. At night we came up with our company. All are well. While traveling through this country, the road was near some hills on our left, and the river some distance to the right, our company saw a moving mass on the bottom near the river. We could not tell what it was, whether Indians or not, but they came rapidly towards the hills; and our train, being a long one, was standing right before them. We soon saw that it was a large drove of buffalo, that had been to the river for water and were returning to the hills. The Brethren stood by their teams, as there was great danger of our oxen stampeding and running away. Mr. Maughan stood in front of our oxen, and the boys by theirs. My wagon being the first one was in the most danger. The large drove came bounding on until the leaders saw their way blocked; then they hesitated a moment and then swerved to the right, and all galloped by in front of my wagon, so we had a good view of the noble creatures.

16th. We took our places in the company this morning, and it seems like home. Traveled 18 miles today over very sandy country. The soil is sand mostly. Met 3 wagons from Fort Laramie. There is plenty of game through here, such as buffalo, deer, elk, and antelope, also the largest kind of wolves. Passed 3 graves, and camped in one of the pretty places on the river bank. All well.

19th. Started early this morning and traveled as fast as possible in order to reach the south ford at noon. Found about 30 wagons already there, and our fifty made 80 wagons; but we all crossed safely in half a day. We camped on the bank. Weather pleasant.

21st. We are again pursuing our tedious journey. The first 3 miles were up hill, then we came on a ridge; this extended to Ash Hollow. When we came in sight of the Hollow, we saw steep precipice and deep ravines; among the rocks are growing Ash and red Cedar. This is a very romantic looking place. When we came to the bottom of this hollow we found a good road and a fine spring of cold water, plenty timber, and some grass. The hollow is 3 miles long. We camped at the mouth in a pretty place. Passed 6 graves.

22nd. We stopped to wash and bake here. Must take wood to the sandy hills that are ahead of us. We are now in a very different looking country, have high sand hills on the left. We are now in the Sioux Indian country.

25th. Since we left Ash Hollow we have traveled in small companys, and find it better where there is but little grass. This afternoon we passed Ancient Ruins Bluffs on the north side of the road. We could see them; they look like Castles and fortifications gone to decay.[163] Traveled 22 miles. Passed 11 graves. Crossed a beautiful stream.

---

163. Some diaries claim that the Ancient Ruins Bluffs were named by Mormon pioneers from England who thought the large, eroded formations resembled the ruined castles of their homeland.

29th. This morning started early, as we had to travel 20 miles without water for our cattle. About 5 o'clock found good place to camp. A fine spring of water, and plenty of dry wood. Found Bro. [Chester] Loveland's Company camped here. Bros. [Gilbert Belnap] Belknap and [Abraham] Coon arrived afterwards. This made up our company of fifty wagons. We held meeting at night, and many spoke of the joy it gave them to meet their Brethren and sisters again in camp. Wall said he felt to rejoice in his heart that we were all met together again. Also spoke in the highest praise of the good conduct of his company, and prayed for the blessing of God to rest upon us. Some Indians came to see us in the evening; these are the first we have seen since we crossed the Missouri River. We have Scott's Bluff on one side and the river at a distance on the other. Traveled 20 miles.

31st. Today we found a letter on the road left for us by Bro. Belknap, stating that a old Indian had died with the smallpox. The Indians left a little boy with the corpse. We think they fled to avoid getting the disease in their camp. We saw a kind of platform made by driving four stakes in the ground and covering it over with sticks and about 4 feet high. This was covered with a buffalo robe, under which we suppose the man was. The little boy was standing by its side. Close by was a dog hung by the neck, and a wigwam made of boughs.

August 1, 1850. Today the weather is very warm. We have crossed the Laramie River, a fine swift stream 100 yards wide. Passed 8 graves; one was empty and we think wolves had dug up the corpse, as a man's suit was lying by it. We camped on the bank of the river Platte, 1 miles from the fort, which is in full view of the camp. As I am writing in my wagon, have fine view of the fort. Its stars and stripes are waving over the Battlements. There are several buildings there.

7th. We rose at 4 o'clock this morning. Started early as we want to go with Bro. Belknap's company who camped by us last night. We found a good spring of cold water at noon, which greatly refreshed us all. Mrs. Ebley found a good side-saddle in some bushes. She took the saddle with her. I was with her when she saw it first.

8th. I was very sick this morning with the Mountain fever. As I lay in my wagon today I thought the wheels went over every rock there was in the road. Camped in the Black Hills. After camping, Mr. Maughan laid my bed in the shade of the wagon. On the outside, chains were fastened across the wheels to keep some sheep in. Thinking my bed would stop them, my wagon wheels were not chained. Seeing an open place, the sheep darted through and every one sprang over me. I clasped my baby close to me, lay still and was not hurt, not even touched by one of them. I think the sheep were worse frightened than I was.

10th. Today we came up with [David] Bennett's Company. They have the whooping cough among them. We drove off the road while they passed.[164]

September 8, 1850. Today we heard from Captain [Ute] Perkins. He is 40 miles back. Two wagons from his company have come up. Captain Foote is 60 miles back.

12th. We were delayed this morning by some of our Brethren going to the tar springs to gather tar. Started at 11 o'clock. Crossed some big hills. Camped at Yellow Creek at the foot of Rocky Bluffs.

13th. This morning it comenced raining before breakfast, continued about 2 hours, then dried up, and we started. Passed Loveland and Belknap in camp, met a white man and Indian woman dressed in man's costume. We think she was his wife. At noon Bros. Belknap and Loveland came up and stated that Bros. [Lewis] Nellie had broken his wagon wheel. In consequence of the accident they camped, but we drove on till near sundown.

---

164. The common contagious diseases were often fatal, and precautions were taken, when possible, to avoid contact with them.

Passed Cache Cave.[165] I had a fine view of it from my home on wheels, but did not go to it. This is at the head of Echo Creek. We now travel down a narrow ravine between high Mountains. Camped alone on Echo Creek.

14th. We rose at day break. The U. S. Mail passed before we started. A part of the road is on the side of the hill, which makes it dangerous for if great care is not taken a wagon is very easily tiped over into the creek.[166] From my wagon I had a fine veiw of the high ruged mountains with small cedar growing on the sides. We think the road today the worse we have had yet. Camped on the Weber river. 2 miles on the new road.

17th. This morning we entered the canyon and traveled on the most dreadful road imaginable. Some places we had to make the road before we could pass. Passed the toll gate and paid for passing over the road we had made. We had a view of the Valley, and it delighted me much to think I was near my long journey's end. The road today has been the worst we ever saw, but we came safely through without any accident. Camped at dusk I mile past the toll house. Here is no food or wood.

18th. We rose at day break and all are happy because our long journey is so near done. When we came near the city we met Bro. [William] Blackhurst, a friend of Mr. Maughan's. On arriving in the city we soon found many kind friends. We camped in the street in front of Bro. [Jacob] Peart's house. I think this is destined to be a great place. There are stores and houses going up in all directions. We staid in Salt Lake City one week and enjoyed the Society of our friends. Then we were counciled to settle in Tooele, 35 miles west of Salt Lake City. This Valley was then being settled. Here I found 2 old friends from England, Bro. and Sister [John and Hannah Eliza] Rowberry, and some of our friends from

---

165. Cache Cave is so named because mountain men first cached supplies there. Later westering wagon companies used it for the same purpose.

166. Many diarists refer to the difficulty of this passage.

Nauvoo. Here we camped in tent and wagon on our city lot untill we built a nice large double log house. We moved into our house in the middle of November, 1850. I had not eat or slept in a house since we left our own home in New Diggings, Wisconsin Territory.

A prominent lawyer, judge, and newspaper man in Utah, Elias Smith, after being taught the gospel by Joseph and Hyrum Smith, was baptized by Hyrum in 1835. (He was born in Royalton, Windsor County, New York, near Joseph Smith's birthplace.) He lived in Kirtland and Missouri and then settled in Nashville, Iowa, when the Saints moved to Nauvoo. While there he worked as business manager of the Times and Seasons and Nauvoo Neighbor. When he went west in 1846, he settled in Iowaville, Iowa, remaining there for five years while he farmed the land. Finally, in 1851 he moved to Kanesville, arriving in July in time to join the John Brown company headed for Utah. His is an excellent journal for trail buffs since he notes distances, road conditions, and camping sites with great precision.

ELIAS SMITH[167]

JULY - 1851

Tues, 1 - Samuel [P. Hoyt][168] and I went to Kaneville, at which place as well as at other places this side of the Nishnabottany

---

167. "Elias Smith's Journal," vol. 1, comp. Sarah C. Thomas, typescript, Library, Church of Jesus Christ of Latter-day Saints, Salt Lake City, Utah.

168. Both Elias Smith and Samuel P. Hoyt served as officers in the John Brown company of 1851.

[Nishnabotna] we saw many of the brethren with whom I was acquainted. Most of them advised us to go ahead, as we were ready, and the companies not all gone from the ferry on the Missouri.

Wed, 2 - We got our cattle across Muskets [Mosquito] Creek to brother Silas's[169] and I made arrangements to have an axel tree fixed as one of mine had got badly sprung. We went over to Silas's to supper and then to our wagons to sleep on the bank of the creek.

Thurs, 3 - Silas went and took my axeltree and two wheels to a smith shop and I got the tire set, axeltree ironed, and some chains mended which took all day. Weather warm.

Fri, 4 - We went to Kaneville and did some trading after waiting for a shower or two in the morning. On our return we got our wagons over the creek in a shower, the citizens having built a bridge and finished it today whilst we were in town.

Sat, 5 - I wrote two or three letters in the morning. We then packed up our wagons again, and about two o'clock we left brother Silas' house and came to Kaneville. He and Hiram [Bennett][170] accompanied us. We did some more trading, laid in our supplies and at night camped near the town. Hiram and Silas returned after bidding us farewell.

Sun, 6 - We started early, but before we got out of town we met with brother Silas again. The road to the ferry near Winter Quarters across the Missouri for the first 6 miles was very hilly and the last six was low and muddy, and in some places the water was two feet deep. We arrived at the ferry just at dark and met a company of Oregon emigrants recrossing the river, having lost

---

169. Silas Smith was Elias's brother who lived near Kanesville in 1851.
170. Hiram Bell Bennett married Elias' sister Martha in 1845. They lived near Silas Smith and his family in a campsite near Kanesville.

so many of their cattle in a stampede that they had not enough to proceed with; so they returned after getting out one hundred miles or more.

Mon, 7 – We crossed the river and came ten miles over a hilly road. At the ferry I made a bargain with Mr. William Janes [Jaynes] to drive one of my wagons to the Valley on condition of taking him a ways with us. He is one of the returning emigrants who had lost his cattle in the stampede on Beaver River. Showery in the morning and warm all day.

Tues, 8 – We started early this morning as we were anxious to overtake a company of emigrants under Captain [John] Brown which we ascertained from the returning emigrants would be at Elk Horn on Monday (yesterday) evening. Having concluded to go that way instead of taking the new route round Elk Horn, which most of the emigrants have taken this year owing to the high waters.[171] We arrived at the ferry at three o'clock and found the company crossing over. We had come near overtaking the rest of the train at the Pappea [Creek] eight miles from where we camped and nine from Elk Horn. The roads were good and the weather being cool we travelled fast. We stopped an hour at Pappea as we saw the train and knew that we could overtake them before they would get to the ferry. We camped on the bank of the river as we could not get over that night.

Wed, 9 – A shower in the morning after which we went to the ferry, crossed our wagons, swam the cattle, and came two miles and ferried a creek and then camped. Before we left the river, Robert McCoy, a man who was driving a team for a Mr. [Thomas] Judkins, an Oregon emigrant whom I had seen near Kaneville, came up and wanted some to wait at the creek and help them to get over when they came up, which we did, and got them

---

171. Because of unusually heavy rains, the Elkhorn River widened to four miles, making crossing impossible. The new route traveled in a northwesterly direction for about 400 miles and came to the old traveled road near Ft. Kearney on the north side of the Platte River.

over the river and creek and camped there together, the balance of the train having gone ahead to a better camping ground.

Thurs, 10 - About three o'clock we came up with the main camp at the Platte River, thirty-nine miles from Winter Quarters, consisting of fifty-four wagons and a buggy or two and some sixty men.

Fri, 11 - Travelled thirteen miles over rather heavy road and camped on the bank of the Platte.

Sat, 12 - The roads better today. Travelled sixteen miles. The weather fine the last three days and everything about looks prosperous. Camped on the prairie.

Sun, 13 - I sent a few lines by some men who were looking after cattle, to brother Silas, to let him know how we were getting along. We travelled some six or seven miles to get to a camping place, crossing two or three bad sloughs. The weather warm.

Mon, 14 - The roads good today. Came twenty miles and camped on the banks of a small lake near the Loup Fork, having travelled up that stream all day.

Tues, 15 - Crossed Looking Glass Creek, Beaver River, and camped on Plumb Creek near the old Pawnee Mission Station, having travelled some over sixteen miles. West of Beaver the Bluffs near the road were covered in place with scrubby looking oaks. The roads generally good, and the weather warm.

Wed, 16 - Started late, having to fix a bridge over the creek and get some wagon timber in the morning. We stopped at the lower ford and examined it. Thought it too deep, and concluded to go the upper ford on Loup Fork to cross. In the afternoon crossed Cedar River and camped on the high prairie. Distance today, 7 miles. A pleasant shower in the evening after we camped.

Thurs, 17 - The road not so good as it might be. Crossed deep ravines, some of them muddy after the shower yesterday. We passed an old Pawnee Village, and another today. At one half mile from the old village we came to a muddy creek which was hard to cross and one company of the train did not get over, but remained on the east side of the creek. That company was ours. Distance, about ten miles.

Fri, 18 - Last night soon after we went to bed it commenced raining and we experienced one of the most tremendous showers ever seen accompanied with wind and hail. Fortunately it lasted but a short time. In the morning the creek was out of its banks, and we had a bridge to make before we could get over, which took till late in the day. The train swerved on to the upper ford of the Loup Fork, six miles, where we encamped. The country beautiful on the banks of the river extending back two or three miles to the bluffs. The soil of the best quality.

Sat, 19 - On examining the river this morning it was found unfordable. I went with two or three others to examine an old mountaineer ford, four or five miles higher up the river, but the water was too deep. Captain Brown concluded to wait till Monday, by which time he thought the river might be forded, as the water was falling.

Sun, 20 - Rested today. Had public service in the afternoon. A woman, Mrs. [Erthur] Kimpton, late from London, died and was buried late in the evening.

Mon, 21 - Forded the river without difficulty in the forenoon, travelled four and 3/4 miles and camped, as we cross here to go nineteen miles before fording water. A gentle shower about noon today.

Tues, 22 - Travelled nineteen miles, most of the way over sandy bluffs. Camped on the south side of Prairie Creek. Got wet in a shower before we travelled.

Wed, 23 - Came 11 3/4 miles to Wood River, and about one mile above a wagon broke down after one upsetting, and we stopped to have it mended. Very warm.

Thurs, 24 - The weather very warm. We travelled about 15 miles. One ox in Capt. [Edwin] Rushton's company died, and one in Capt. [Alex] Robbins' was left behind no better than dead. The road the very best. In the evening I wrote a letter to Lucy's [his wife] friends in England. Camped on the Platte.

Fri, 25 - The road today over rather flat land, and in a wet time would be bad enough. We have even got along very well. Wrote a letter to Mr. Turman and finished one to brother Silas. Capt. Brown is going over to Fort Kearney to mail letters, so I improve the opportunity. Camped on the Platte south of road. Travelled about 13 miles only, being hindered some by Capt. [George D.] Watt's company, the fourth ten in the course of the day.

Sat, 26 - Capt. [Preston] Thomas's, the first ten went ahead today, it being their turn. Travelled twenty miles. The roads excellent. Camped on Dry Creek, so-called, tho there was plenty of water. 217 3/4 miles from Winter Quarters. Came 84 miles this week, 65 3/4 last week, and 80 (from Kaneville) the week before.

Sun, 27 - Lay in camp and rested, tho some of the company had to fix their wagons, as the dry warm weather during the last few days had loosened the tires on many of them.

Mon, 28 - There were some twelve or fourteen tires set this morning before the company started. Crossed Elm and Buffalo Creeks and camped near a slough on the south of the road, having travelled about 13 miles. About noon, and at Elm Creek, we first came in sight of buffalo, the plains being covered with them for miles and miles as far as the eye could reach, and before night we passed thousands and tens of thousands of them on the hills and plains on both sides of the river. Several were killed by the hunters before night, and we had any amount of fresh meat, which was a great luxury to some.

Tues, 29 - Had to wait this morning to have a wheel mended which was broken down carelessly yesterday evening by a raw teamster from the Old Bay State, named Riggs. Started late; the weather warm, the road dusty. Came 13 miles and camped near the Platte opposite an island. Saw thousands of buffalo. In the afternoon met Samuel Newcomb, a brother Bateman (an apostate, as afterwards ascertained), and some others eight days from Salt Lake City. From them we learned that Elder [Orson] Hyde, Judge Brookers,[172] and those with them who left Kaneville one week before we did and went around the Elk Horn (the new route)[173] had been robbed by the Pawnees. They had come into our road some five or six miles back, and were ahead of us, but Elder [Orson] Pratt[174] and company, and several other companies were yet behind on that route which was represented as being very hilly and bad.

Wed, 30 - Some time in the night after all were in bed but the watchman, there was a tremendous shower of rain and hail, and the wind blew a hurricane. This morning the air is some cooler. Travelled eighteen miles. The road excellent. Turned off the road and camped one and a fourth miles west of Deep Dry Creek.

This evening from our encampment we saw a company ahead of us encamped on the prairie which proved to be Captain [Luman A.] Shurtliff's company, the first fifty of Capt. [Easton] Kelsey's company, which went the new route round the Elk Horn; and before dark another company, Capt. Morris Phelps' came in just ahead of us, and before morning the company from Garden Grove, Capt. [Harry] Walton, came in, most of the companies having taken a route farther west than the one mentioned by the company we met from the Lake on Tuesday last. We also learned that Elder Hyde came in on the upper route. These companies, or some of them, had lost some of their cattle and one company, Captain Shurtliff's, were in some confusion and had left one company of ten behind some thirty miles look-

172. Judge Perry E. Brocchus of Alabama was appointed by President Millard Fillmore to serve as associate justice in Utah's territorial government. He traveled to Utah in 1851, arriving in early September.
173. Elder Hyde and his company were the first to travel this new route.
174. Elder Orson Pratt, in company with his family, was just returning from presiding over the British Mission.

ing after their cattle. They report two other companies near by and think Elder O. Pratt some days behind. He is with the last fifty of his company. They confirm the report of Elder Hyde being robbed, and the bad roads by the new route, which is some 200 miles farther. That we found incorrect, as it was some twenty or twenty-five miles ahead to where they started the old road. In the course of the day we passed vast herds of buffalo, and about ten thousand in one herd came running past our train, and about fifty ran through between my wagon and Samuel's, which were a little distance apart, but as fortune favored us, our cattle were not frightened.

Thurs, 31 - Travelled nineteen miles, part of the way over a very sandy road, especially at the sandy bluffs. Camped on Skunk Creek. A fine shower in the evening after we retired to our wagons to sleep. The companies which came in from the north went on ahead of us with the exception of the one from Garden Grove which stopped to look after some cattle which they had lost in a stampede some days ago.

AUGUST - 1851

Fri, 1 - The road today has been very sandy and the weather warm. Passed a beautiful cold spring at the upper end of the Pawnee Swamp. Travelled fifteen miles and camped on Carrion Creek.

Sat, 2 - This morning our company passed Capt. Phelps' company in their camp, and also Capt. Shurtliff's, both of which came on and passed us at noon. The last went ahead, and the first camped soon after they passed us at noon, opposite some willow islands, intending to stay there till Monday as the two hundred mile stretch without timber is now before us. After gathering a little wood, consisting of willows only, we came ahead, again passing Capt. Phelps and company, and encamped for the Sabbath on the banks of the Platte near a small creek 317 1/4 miles from Winter Quarters, having travelled 99 1/2 miles during the week.

Sun, 3 - Lay in our encampment. Very cold in the morning. Had a meeting in the afternoon and had a goodly session together.

Mon, 4 - Came to North Bluff Fork three and a half miles from our encampment, which we crossed without difficulty. At the east foot of the sandy bluffs Brother Samuel and I came up the bed of the river with our teams to save coming over the bluffs. The balance of the train came over. We got into the road of the west foot of the bluffs about one hour before the others came up. Crossed the second sandy bluffs and camped near Bluff Creek, having travelled fifteen miles. Road very sandy.

Tues, 5 - Our road today has generally been sandy and hard on teams. Crossed the third Sandy Bluffs and several small streams, such as Petite, Piccanninni, Goose, and Duck Weed Creeks. After we crossed the latter the road was excellent. Camped on a beautiful prairie near the river two miles below Rattlesnake Creek, having travelled some eighteen miles. At noon Lisbon Lamb came up and reported Capt. Smith's ten, which were left behind by Capt. Shurtliff,[175] were close upon us; also Capt. Phelps and company, and several others were within ten miles. Before night we learned that the Garden Grove company had had another stampede and lost some more of their cattle.

Wed, 6 - We travelled nineteen miles today, mostly over a good road, crossed Rattlesnake Camp and several other small creeks. Met a company of men returning by way of Salt Lake from Oregon and California, twelve in number, with pack animals. They left the Lake the 15th July and report all well there at that time. Camped on Wolf Creek at an early hour. After we camped [met] two more men belonging to the same company we met in the forenoon. They had been left in consequence of los-

---

175. This could possibly be Lewis A. Shurtliff, who headed the third fifty in the John G. Smith company.

ing their horses, and having found them were pursuing to over-take the company.

Thurs, 7 - Came some over nineteen miles. Mostly a good road after crossing the bluff at Wolf Creek, which was very bad. Captain Phelps overtook us before we all got over. That company is only a few miles behind us tonight. James Monroe was over to our camp this evening from the other side. His company [Captain Homer's company] left the frontier a week or ten days before ours, and are now only fifteen miles ahead.

Fri, 8 - Today we travelled twenty and a half miles. Road first rate. Camped on Crab Creek. Saw a train on the other side the river going down. Some one of our company was over. It proved to be a merchant train, Phelf's [?] 20 days from Salt Lake with mule teams and no load. In the forenoon I went out on a hunt-ing excursion with Bros. Brown and Thomas. One antelope was the fruit of our labor, which was rather dearly bought.

Sat, 9 - Crossed Cobble Hills and passed the "Ancient Bluff Ruins," west of which about six and a half miles we encamped, having travelled about sixteen miles; and one hundred and eight and a quarter miles during the week. In the forenoon saw another train going down on the south side (ten or eleven wag-ons) supposed to be a government train from Laramie. Went out a-hunting in the afternoon with brother Thomas. We caught no game, but saw a fine grove and good water in a valley in the bluffs (unobserved before by the emigrants as far as we know) about five miles west of the Ancient Bluff Ruins. There is an abundance of cherries and currants there to be found by going up the ravine a short distance.

Sun, 10 - The Garden Grove company passed us today, and one ten of Capt. Shurtliff's company which had been left behind to look after their lost cattle. They travel on Sunday's, but we think it best to rest. We had a pretty shower in the evening.

Mon, 11 - The road in the forenoon some sandy. After crossing a sandy hill the land in wet weather I should think was rather wet, tho the road is excellent now. Turned off the road some distance to camp, as the road from the bluffs below to Scott's bluffs does not run very near the river. Came about nineteen miles.

Tues, 12 - The road excellent but very dusty. The air in the morning was very cool. Passed "Chimney Rocks" and camped about eleven miles west, having travelled about twenty miles. Capt. Phelps' company keep about two miles behind us, and have, since overtaking us last week.

Wed, 13 - Passed Scotts Bluffs today. Road first best. Very warm in the middle of the day. Morning and evening cool. Came 17 miles. Turned off the road a little and camped on a creek some earlier than common as one ten, Capt. [Joseph] Chatterly's, had to stop to set some tires in the morning and have been far behind all day.

Thurs, 14 - Travelled eighteen miles or thereabouts. One of my oxen has been lame two or three days. There was a fine shower last night, and it has been good travelling. Saw an Indian for the first time on the road. Several were seen by others ahead of the train.

Fri, 15 - Came about fifteen miles. Road most of the way sandy. Passed Raw Hide Creek (now dry) and camped about six miles below Laramie. Passed many Indian encampments along the river and saw many of the Lamanites of the Sioux tribe. They were thick about our train all day and after we camped. A span of horses took fright at them and ran, which started several of the ox teams, and in the confusion one woman, Sister Sandifor,[176] was run over and hurt, tho not very bad.

Sat, 16 - This morning some of the cattle were missing and were not all found in time to start till noon. Six of them went on ahead to another camp in the night. We tied up all our cattle

---

176. Probably Eliza B. Sandifer, wife of John Norman Clark. She traveled in Captain Harry Walton's company (the Garden Grove company).

every night till within a few days, but the grass is getting shorter and we have thought best to let them be loose that they might have a better chance to graze, and we have never had any stray away till this morning. After starting we came past the camp of the last ten (so called) belonging to Shurtliff's company. They were laying by to buy some cattle, if possible. At Laramie Fort we passed Capt. Phelps' company again, as they had started before us in the morning before finding our cattle. Capt. Brown did not think best to cross the river at Fort Laramie, so we kept up on the north side about four miles and encamped, having travelled about one hundred and a half miles during the week. Capt. Phelps' company went on a little further and camped in a very poor place. Ours was bad enough, as the grass was very short. There are so many Indians all along the river that the bottoms are covered with their mules and ponies, and in the neighborhood of Fort Laramie the animals belonging to the Government would keep down the grass if the Indians were not about. I did not go over to the Fort, but some did. I sent over two letters to be mailed, one to A. B. Fuller and the other to brother Silas.

Sun, 17 - The grass was so short that Capt. Brown thought best to move on a piece in order to find better feed for our cattle, so we started on at a late hour. Came about two miles and crossed over the river to the south side. Soon after we got over we passed Capt. Phelps' company once more, they having stopped in the place we expected to in order to spend the sabbath. After passing them about four miles we passed the Garden Grove company, also encamped for the sabbath, which they do not often do. We found little feed till we came to the point where the road leaves the river 12 1/2 miles from Laramie, and then had to turn our cattle over the river. Distance travelled today eight and half miles.

Mon, 18 - The company did not get started till late, and before we all got on the road the Garden Grove company, Capt. Walton, came up and kept close to our train all day. Capt.

Phelps' company was close in the rear of Capt. Walton's, and as we wound over the hills all together we made quite a splendid show. Soon after leaving our encampment, Capt. Brown took the river road, so-called, which was very good but some hilly. We travelled till late to get where there was feed and water, and camped by two excellent springs of water. The season has been very dry and feed is scarce, tho there is water enough in places. Before we stopped we passed Capt. Thomas' company (which came up the south side of the Platte) in their encampment, some off the road. Came about twenty-three miles. Two wagons' wheels broke, and a part of Capt. Chatterly's company did not reach camp tonight.

Tues, 19 - This morning whilst waiting for Bro. Chatterly, Capt. Homer's company passed us. In the company I found several of my old acquaintances, among whom were: Brother Alfred Bell and family, D. Porter, Capt. Homer and others. The two companies that were behind us yesterday also went past us in the course of the forenoon. It was so late when Bro. Chatterly came up that it was thought advisable to remain where we were during the day and repair wagons, wash, etc. At night the cattle were taken two or three miles ahead to some excellent feed on Horn Creek, and a few took their wagons to the creek, among whom were Samuel and myself. The place was beautiful and the evening delightful. Plenty of currants and cherries and we enjoyed ourselves first rate.

Wed, 20 - It was late before the cattle could be taken back to the camp and the company get up to where we were, so I wrote, or commenced writing a letter to Silas and Hiram. Lucy and other gathered cherries and currants till the company came up. Mr. Judkins stopped to wait for his son who had gone back in search of a cow. There was a child born in the camp today. Sister [Emma] Sharkey, wife of Robert Sharkey had a fine little girl born in the forenoon. We came about nine miles to the Platte River, where we stopped at noon. Then the road took into the bluffs again as the river just above where we came to it runs thro a deep cut in the rocky bluffs which the road had to wind into the bottom above. We came to the river again at night. Travelled in all some eighteen miles.

Thurs, 21 - Crossed the river to the north side and came about twenty miles and recrossed it, and camped on the south side again. The road today some sandy in places. Passed several dry creeks and several bad places being rough and crooked. The ford where we crossed in the morning very good, much better than where we forded at night. Overtook Capt. Phelps' company and camped with them on the same ground. One wagon broken only, which was good luck considering the road and the teamsters.

Fri, 22 - The road today some crooked and rough. Came about thirteen miles. Mr. Lytle,[177] an Oregon emigrant, had his oxen run away and his wife got hurt badly. Camped on the banks of the Platte, as usual, for there is no feed only on the river or near it and on the small streams, most of which are now dry.

Sat, 23 - It was late when we got ready to start. The morning was cool, but as soon as the sun began to shine it became very warm. At about eight miles we came into the road that crosses the Black Hills. From thence we came to Deer Creek, five miles, where we expected to find plenty of feed. But the season has been very dry in this region, and the grass was so short even there where it was supposed to be good that Capt. Brown thought best to go on further. We came about seven miles further and camped at a late hour. About ten o'clock Mr. Judkins, who had stopped behind on Wednesday to look after a cow, came up and joined us again. We have made about the same distance as last week, one hundred and three fourths of a mile allowing the road we came to be the same distance as the road over the Black Hills.

---

177. Thomas and Mary R. Litell and their family were Oregon emigrants who traveled in John Brown's company.

Sun, 24 - We lay in our encampment all day and Elder Thomas preached a sermon on the first principles of the Gospel in the evening.

Mon, 25 - We started early and came eight miles and encamped where there was good grass on the south side of the river for the purpose of setting some wagon tires and repairing wagons. Soon after we stopped two men from the Lake, Brother James Ferguson, and Mr. Holman, son of the Indian agent [Jacob H. Holman], rode up. They were on their way to Fort Laramie after some soldiers to guard the Snake Indians who are between here and the South Pass on their way to Laramie to attend the Great Council of the tribes there the first of September next, as they are afraid of the Shyens [Cheyennes?] with whom they have been at war. In the evening I went out to the mountains with a party from the camp on a hunting expedition and camped out there all night.

Tues, 26 - Got in from our hunting excursion in the afternoon, the company having killed four or five buffaloes and some other game, very tired and weary indeed.

Wed, 27 - At a late hour this morning we got started and travelled about twelve miles and encamped a little below the Upper Platte Ford. There was a woman died about noon today. She had been confined a day or two since, and had not been well for many weeks before. Her name, I believe was Henderson,[178] or perhaps Henry.

Thurs, 28 - Crossed the Platte and then took the road up the river which was some hilly, but not bad, only in a few places. Came twelve or thirteen miles and camped on a small creek where there was plenty of grass a short way up from the river. There was a light shower about noon, the first rain we have had for about three weeks. Met a company of Snake Indians going to

---

178. Probably Mary Henderson, who traveled in Captain Watt's ten in the John Brown company.

the treaty at Laramie, being the chiefs of the tribe and part of those mentioned above, being afraid of the Chyans. Mr. Holman, the Agent was with them, a subagent or two together with a small company of returning gold diggers, Mr. [Stephen B.] Rose, subagent, and Joshua Terry and B. Wood, mountaineers.

Fri, 29 - We travelled today some twenty five miles. Road very good. Passed the Alkali Swamps and Willow Springs and camped at a late hour on a small creek south of the road some four hundred yards where there was grass and plenty of water. Four mountaineers from Green River camped with us at night on their way to the states. Frost and ice this morning.

Sat, 30 - Crossed Greasewood Creek, a fine stream, and then left the old road and followed the creek down to the Sweet Water River. This road is some farther than the old one, but the sand is not so bad and we could reach grass on the river nearer than the other way. Came about ten or twelve miles and camped on the river near the saleratus lakes.

Sun, 31 - We lay in camp today and rested our cattle. Lucy went with me and some others to the Saleratus Lakes and got some saleratus to take to the Valley. We travelled last week only sixty-seven miles, according to the Guide, but we came some further in consequence of taking other roads in order to find feed for our cattle.

SEPTEMBER - 1851

Mon, 1 - Started at a late hour and came fifteen miles, passing Independence Rock, crossing river, and camped about seven miles above "Devil's Gate" on the south side of the Sweetwater, where there was excellent grass.

Tues, 2 - Camped at night near the Gravelly Bluff. Came seventeen miles. Road sandy enough, tho we kept the river road. Several oxen sick this evening.

Wed, 3 - Came seventeen miles. Crossed the river three times and camped just below "ford No. four." A little shower in the evening. Some cool, but fine. We overtook Capt. Phelps' company and are camped near them tonight.

Thurs, 4 - Before we got started this morning Capt. Walton's company hove in sight. They having been off the road a short distance west of the "Devil's Gate" to repair wagons, and recruit their teams a few days, and we have passed them on Monday last. Capt. Phelps went on ahead of our company, and Capt. Walton was close in our rear all day till we turned off the road to camp about three miles below Ford "no. Five." Came about fifteen miles besides going off the road to a good camping ground some two miles further. One wagon broke down (br. Margetts)[179] and several oxen gave out. The road most of the way very sandy.

Fri, 5 - Capt. Brown thought best to lay by today and let our cattle rest, as there was excellent feed for them and some of the wagons wanted fixing a little. I spent the forenoon in fixing mine and bringing water to wash with, and in the afternoon went and caught some fish in company with Capt. Brown, Thomas, and others.

Sat, 6 - This is an anniversary of my birth day,[180] and the semi-annual conference of the Church will commence in Salt Lake City. I should have been happy to have been there, but I am glad that I am as near and am with the prospect of being in the Valley in a few weeks. We came twelve miles today and camped before night as we could not reach grass if we went on till after dark. This week we have made seventy-five and three fourths miles.

Sun, 7 - We lay in camp in the forenoon, and as Capt. Brown thought best to move from where we now are in consequence of poor feed, we started on and camped on a branch of

179. Probably Lorenzo Erastus Margetts, who traveled in Captain Watt's ten in the John Brown company.
180. He turned forty-seven years old.

the Sweetwater, which took us till late in the evening. There we found water, but little grass. Distance thirteen miles.

Mon, 8 - We could not find all the cattle till late, and as I had mine I came over to the Sweetwater with Samuel's team ahead of the train and others followed as fast as possible after finding their cattle. Some however did not get off till afternoon. A heavy frost this morning. Before starting this morning the mail from Salt Lake came past, and Doctor [John Milton] Bernhisel was along on his way to Washington, having been elected Delegate from Utah Territory to Congress at the August election.[181]

Tues, 9 - This morning I set the tire on one of my wagons, having prepared for it yesterday afternoon whilst laying by, as we could not find grass after leaving the Sweetwater short of twelve or fifteen miles. We started early, crossed the Sweetwater for the last time, came through the Pass and camped on Pacific Creek about one mile below the crossing. Came nearly eighteen miles. Frost in the morning. Two wagons belonging to Capt. Robbins were broke down and his ten did not get in till late at night.

Wed, 10 - Stopped all day to mend wagons. The day remarkably fine tho frosty in the morning.

Thurs, 11 - Some frost in the morning. The country we travelled today was very barren. Came down the Pacific creek about sixteen miles and turned off the road to camp a mile or more.

Fri, 12 - Came to Big Sandy and crossed over and camped about five miles below the old ford. Distance about fifteen miles. Country level, barren, and sandy.

Sat, 13 - Started late. At about two miles from camp we came to the old road which we had left near Pacific Creek. After we struck the old road we came to the point where it leaves Big Sandy for Green River, and camped to spend the sabbath a little off the road near the creek or river. Came seventeen miles, and 87 dur-

---

181. He was Utah's first delegate to Congress, having been elected 4 August 1851. He was re-elected three times, serving Utah Territory for eight years as a delegate.

ing the week. In the morning Capt. Robbins and his drivers had a little difficulty, and six of them left him, which made him late in starting, and he did not get in till late. The difficulty arose about their provisions. The men came on ahead but stopped and camped with us at night.

Sun, 14 - We rested today. Some teams from the Lake passed us with provisions for the companies. The difficulty between Capt. Robbins and his teamsters was settled. Elder Brown preached to us in the afternoon, and we had an excellent meeting.

Mon, 15 - Came to Green River, a beautiful stream, forded it, and then went down it some three miles below to where the Guide road leaves it, in order to find grass. Camped in a beautiful cotton wood grove on the banks of the river, and turned our cattle over it to graze.

Tues, 16 - A light shower last night, and this morning everything around looks smiling. Started early; that is a mistake—we meant to start early, but did not. Came sixteen miles and camped on Black's Fork. Road sandy, rough, and in some places crooked. Land extremely barren.

Wed, 17 - We came fifteen miles or thereabouts. Crossed Ham's Fork about two miles from where we camped and Black's Fork soon after and camped on it just below the ford, and about seventeen miles from Fort Bridger. A little rain fell in showers and it thundered a little.

Thurs, 18 - Last night after supper I went back some distance to help Capt. Robbins' men get a broken wagon. He is himself sick with mountain fever, started late, and only came about eleven miles. Turned off the road some distance and camped near Black's Fork once more.

Fri, 19 - Passed Fort Bridger at noon. The road some rough and stoney, especially toward night. Came down one very steep hill and camped on a creek ten miles from Bridger. Distance made during the day 16 miles.

Sat, 20 - We came about eleven miles, part of the way on the Guide Road and part not, and camped on a high ridge and drove our cattle down into ravines on each side of the ridge. We are now about ninety miles from the city of the Great Salt Lake, and have travelled eighty-five miles during the week. Mr. Litell, an Oregon emigrant, with two wagons, left us this morning and went ahead. A man named Riggs also went with him.

Sun, 21 - At about eleven o'clock we started on our way as we were encamped in an uncomfortable place, and Capt. Brown thought we had better do so. It rained all night, tho not so very hard, and the road is some slippery. Two miles from where we camped we reached the top of the east rim of the Great Basin and began to descend the ridge that divides the waters of the Colorado from those of the Salt Lake. The descent is lengthy and some steep. We crossed Sulphur Creek and arrived on Bear River about four o'clock, where we encamped on the west bank. One of my oxen died suddenly on the road about one mile before arriving on Bear River. Several have died in the same manner lately. Cause unknown.

Mon, 22 - We came about nine and a half miles to Yellow Creek. The road first rate. Some of the cattle could not be found and Capt. Chatterly's ten did not start till late and did not come up at night. Two children have been born in the camp within two days, Brother [Zacarias] Derrick's wife [Mary] had a daughter [Ursula Shepherd] born Sunday morning, and Walter Baker's a son last evening. Near where we camped there was a grave made a day or two before, I think on the 20th, purporting to be that of James Monroe. He was with Homer's train and was taking thro a large quantity of goods to the Lake.

Tues, 23 - We came over a high hill and down a valley to Cache Cave five and a half miles and camped for Capt. Chatterly's company to come up. The day beautiful and fine in the extreme for this season of the year.

Wed, 24 - Before we started this morning two men came by

from the Valley after the body of James Monroe. He was shot by Howard Egan, who came from the Valley and met him where we saw his grave and shot him with a pistol for some interference with his family during his absence in the gold mines of California. We came seventeen miles and camped on Echo Creek at a place surrounded by high hills some—about five miles east of the Weber River.

Thurs, 25 - We came to Weber River, at which place we met Elder Hyde on his return to Kaneville, and some other going to the states. From Weber River came about three miles and camped at an early hour. Came about twelve miles today. Several men from other companies behind us passed us during the day.

Fri, 26 - Early this morning we met several more brethren on their way to different parts of the world, among whom were Elder E[zra]. T. Benson, J[edediah]. M. Grant going to Kaneville,[182] and A[braham]. O. Smoot, Willard Snow, and Samuel Richards on their way to England. Came to Kanyon Creek seven miles, and at night camped about two miles below where the road leaves the creek to ascend the mountain, having come about thirteen miles.

Sat, 27 - After leaving Kanyon Creek we ascended a high mountain and thence descended to Brown's Creek, on which we camped at night twelve miles from the city. Two or three wagons were broken, and Capt. Rushton did not reach camp, and Capt. Robbins' ten did not get far down the mountain before they stopped for the night. We had not gone far in the morning before we overtook five or six wagons belonging to Capt. Phelps' company which had been left behind, and before we camped we passed Capt. Homer's company camped and waiting for some of his wagons to be mended which were broken coming down the mountains.

---

182. Elders Grant and Benson were called to serve in Pottawattomie County to superintend the 1852 migrations.

Sun, 28 - We came over the Last mountain and down the Last creek to the mouth of the kanyon where most of us camped, tho some went down to the city. Those behind us did not come up at night as we expected. Capt. Brown left us after we stopped and went to the City, and thence to his family from which he had been absent about one year. Several brethren from the city came out to our camp as soon as they heard of our arrival, and among them we had the satisfaction of seeing John L. Smith, Joseph Cain, A[ndrew]. Lamoreaux, and other of our friends and old neighbors from Iowa who had preceded us to this beautiful valley of the mountains.

Mon, 29 - I got up my cattle as soon as I could and came down to the City of the Great Salt Lake in company with Samuel P. [Hoyt] There we had the pleasure of meeting with many of the old Saints from Nauvoo and other places with whom I had passed thro many scenes of pleasure and sorrow in years gone by, who greeted us joyfully and bid us welcome to the city. We drove through the city to the Council House, where we met with President Young, George A. Smith, D[aniel] H. Wells, [. . .] Morly [Isaac Morley], [David] Pettigrew, and many others who received us with every expression of joy and friendship, and my heart was made glad once more after being separated from the Saints during five years and upwards at seeing the faces of so many of my old brethren and friends once more in the land of the living. We left our wagons in the street near Uncle John Smith's, and George A.'s and took our cattle to a pasture over the Jordan to stay a few days till we determined what we should do and where we should go. We had a joyful meeting with Uncle John Smith and family, and with our cousins George A. [Smith] and John L[yman]. [Smith] and their families,[183] and there was only the absence of our own dear father and mother in the world

---

183. His father, Asahel Smith, was the brother of Joseph Smith, Sr., and of John Smith, the father of George A. Smith and John Lyman Smith.

of spirits that caused our hearts to weep at meeting with our kindred in the distant valley when we had fondly hoped on leaving Nauvoo in 1846 we should all live to greet each other once more this side of the grave. We were highly pleased with the general appearance of the city, which in point of improvement far exceeded our anticipations. Many elegant houses built of adobes, or unburnt bricks, presented themselves in all of the city, and the hammer of the builders were heard on every hand; and all appeared to be busily engaged in preparing for the winter and prosecuting every branch of agricultural and mechanical business necessary for the subsistence and comfort of the Saints in this new and far-off valley of the mountains.

Ruth Page of New Jersey joined the Church in 1843. She traveled with her father's family to Kanesville, arriving in 1850. Unable to secure enough provisions for the entire family to travel together, the Page family split up for the journey west. Ruth's parents and sisters traveled together in one company, but Ruth and her brothers traveled in another, where Ruth hired herself out as a cook and washerwoman in exchange for their fare.[184] They traveled with the Harmon Cutler company in 1852. A year after reaching the Valley, Ruth married the man who had baptized her, Samuel Hollister Rogers, and they settled in southern Utah and later, Arizona. Her diary is a brief overview of her travels.

---

184. Occasionally families were separated when they could not secure sufficient provisions and wagons to accommodate all members. Daughters, like Ruth Page, assisted with the domestic tasks in exchange for their travel, and sons hired on as teamsters.

RUTH PAGE ROGERS[185]

JULY 12, 1887 When I commenced to write I done it for my own satisfaction and amusement, not thinking of writing to have it preserved for others, knowing I am a humble person, one that has lived in a humble condition all my life, my worley goods are few from my writings this can be learned but as the Lord has been mindful of me and blessed me in this life and by the spirit has whispered to me that I should have my writings preserved. [. . .]

May 21st, 1852 I made arrangements with Wallace Raymond and wife to go with them to Great Salt Lake. My father [Daniel Page], mother [Mary Sockwell Page] and sisters[186] were all getting ready to go. June 1st, father started on the way left me and daniel [her brother, age 23] and Joseph [her brother, age 22] we expect to travel in our company I am sorry that mother and my sisters were seperated from me and going such a hard journey I knew it would be hard for mother and the distance great they were traveling with ox teams

The agreement was, that I was to do the washing ironing and cooking for six persons and nurse his wife in her confinement

June 14th I commenced the journey this day we travel three miles stayed three days near Musquito [Mosquito] Creek

18th traveled to the Bluffs near the Missouri River Stayed there and done our washing and cooking

20th <at night> Camped in a canyon hard rain thunder and lightning

21st I went to a Welsh meeting John Taylor preached

---

185. "Autobiography and Journal of Ruth Page Rogers," holograph, LDS Church Archives.
186. Ruth's sisters included Lucy Ann (20), Mary Ellen (17), and Lorane (8).

25th Crossed the Missouri River near Winter Quarters

Sunday 27th Stayed at six mile grove this day the People were Organized into company and called the Springville company Harmon Cutler the head captain of the company Thomas Jenkins captain of the first ten I traveled in his ten fifty wagons in the company a captain to every ten

29th Crossed the Elk Horn July 2nd Abner Brooks died of Cholera

3rd Camped at Shell Creek on account of sickness in the company 4th same place held meeting three Children baptized the sixth very stormy thunder and hail the largest I had ever seen we crossed the Lope [Loup] Fork very dark when we camped and raining water on the ground shoe top deep

July 7th three deaths of Cholera and a storm of hail July 21st Mrs [Almira Cutler] Raymond gave birth to a son, raining all night 23rd where we camped there was neither wood nor water Aug 3rd Came to Ash Hollow Aug 9th the Cattle and people very thirsty about noon we came to a spring the captains had cautioned their companies about drinking too much water a young woman by the name of Mary Moss died from drinking too much she was <Dead> in one hour after drinking

10th Passed Chimney Rock 11th our oxen stampeded about one O clock five wagons to mend which took the most of the night Aug 12th I was sick all day unable to work the Rattle snakes were very numerous and fears were entertained that the Cattle would be bitten we came to an Indian village the Indians came to us on their horses with their Bows and Arrows told our Captain we should not pass until we gave them flour hard Bread Sugar Tea and Coffee they wanted a big heap we could not help ourselves they spread down their Blankets to put it in we were stopped about two hours it was stated they numbered about three hundred they were Siou[x] Indians we traveled the most of the night we were afraid if we camped they would steal our cattle they run off one ox.

16th Crossed the Platte River near fort Laramie the water came into the wagons the next day we camped took the things out of the wagons to dry 23rd we camped on Wood river next morning my brother Joseph[,] Wallace Raymond and James Newel went to hunt Buffalo when night came they did not return which made us very uneasy about them there was some poles fixed to the wagons and lighted lanterns hung upon them we were afraid they were lost we did not know what direction to go to find them at eleven O clock at night my brother came to camp his first words were give me some water and stretched himself upon the ground I gave him some water and he wanted more I told him he must not drink so much he said they had not had any water since they left the camp in the morning he said Wallace and James Newel were bringing a buffalo hiefer they had killed and they had not tasted water to day had been riding hard all day and nothing to eat he did not think they could get into camp unless some water was taken to them [he] told where to find them and some men took a keg of water and went to them they saw two Indians while chasing the buffalo

25th divided the meat when we were almost done eating our breakfast Captain [Harmon] Cutler got on to his wagon to see if his horses were feeding which were staked out a short distance from camp and to his astonishment there was not one to be seen nearly all the men started immediately to find them saw their tracks where they went into the river and mogasin [moccasin] tracks they were gone the most part of the day and came back without the horses my brother Daniel went with them he got thirsty and drank bad water the number of horses stolen was seven only one left in the company they have never been seen or heard tell of since by their owners at night my brother Daniel had a severe attack of Cholera I with others were waiting on him most of the night 31st crossed Rattle Snake Creek

September 10th rained all day 17th my brother Daniel very

sick camped at Green River Snowing I was up with Daniel all night nursing him

18th very cold forded the River 21st came to Fort Bridger

28th crossed Weber River 29th a girl seven years old was killed by a wagon upsetting and a large chest of tools falling on her when she had been dead two days her cheeks were red.

October 1st Snowing the roads very bad Mrs Raymond and I had to walk all day the cattles feet were sore three wagons upset to day

Oct 4th 1852. I arrived at Salt Lake City in good health Wallace Raymond and his wife treated me well they were very kind to me and my brothers we did not have one disagreement she was as kind to me as a sister could be under the circumstances.

Bishop David Pettigrew came out and invited Captain Cutler and those in the ten with him to his house the day before we got into the City we went to his house he had a good dinner prepared for us we enjoyed it very much he took a good deal of pains to make us welcome he invited me and my brothers to stay a week at his house and attend conference which invitation we accepted

5th his Daughter Caroline and I washed clothes all day Oct 6th Conference commenced Daniel was sick I done what I could for him and attended Conference part of the time my father and the rest of his family excepting my sister Ellen had gone as far South as Provo,

(distance from Winter Quarters to Salt Lake one thousand thirty miles)

For Augusta Dorius (Stevens), "crossing the plains" meant a journey of more than eight months that began in Copenhagen, Denmark. She was the first of her family to emigrate, traveling, as a girl of fifteen, with eighteen other Danish converts under Erastus Snow's leadership in 1852. They all traveled west in the Eli B. Kelsey company. She wrote, "I wondered how I received courage to leave my family and go to a strange land and then too, when I did not know how far we should have to travel to get to Zion, and I could not speak the language." From her reminiscence, one would not guess her to be a Danish emigrant; her responses to the events of the trek, and language to express them, resemble those of her American traveling companions.

AUGUSTA DORIUS STEVENS[187]

AUGUSTA DORIUS STEVENS, daughter of Nicholi and Sophia Christopherson Dorius, was born October 29th, 1837 in Copenhagen, Denmark. When I was two years of age I lost one of my eyes through an accident. I had many minor accidents but got through them all right. I attended school until I was about thirteen years of age. About that time the Mormon Elders came to Copenhagen with the Gospel of Jesus Christ of Latter-Day-Saints. My father embraced the Gospel ~~of~~ and was baptised November 14, 1850. For this reason I had to quit school on account of the immediate persecution waged against me in school on account of joining this then unpopular religion. We lived in the same house where the L.D.S. meetings were held; we lived down stairs and the meetings were held upstairs. One night the mob came up to the hall and broke down the door. They wanted to get Brother Erastus Snow and subject him to bodily punishment. We had to

187. Autobiography of Augusta Dorius Stevens (1922), typescript, Augusta Stevens Papers, LDS Church Archives.

break up the meeting and Brother Snow walked out with the crowd of saints and the mob did not get him. My mother could not see that our church was any better than her Lutheran Church, and so she did not join until 1862 when my two brothers Carl and John left Utah for a mission to Norway. While there the boys went to Copenhagen, Denmark, and took Mother with them to Norway to the city of Christiania where they made their headquarters, and where she was baptized. Mother did not come to Utah until 1874. I was accordingly away from my mother for twenty-two years.

I did not know how many persons had joined the church when I left for Utah. But at that time the spirit of gathering becam[e] an important item among the Saints in Copenhagen and there were twenty-eight persons who got ready to emigrate with Elder Erastus Snow when he returned from his first mission to Scandinavia and I was one of this number. I had assisted a family by the name of Ravens as a girl in their home at general domestic work. Mr. [Christian Hildur] Ravens was a sea Captain; the family was quite well off. They had joined the church and took quite a liking to me for the work I was doing for them and inasmuch as I had also joined the church, they offered me the opportunity to join them in coming to Utah and they paid my way. My father thought it would be a good thing for one of the family to go to Zion and the rest of the family would come later. So it was arranged for me to go. I thought this was a fine plan and I was happy to think I was the first of the family to go to Zion.

The day came for us to start; it was the fourth day of March, 1852. I had great faith in the gospel I had embraced, so I fle felt all would be well for me. But when I said farewell to my parents and brothers and sisters, and seeing the steam boat sail out and my folks begin to fade out of sight, I felt alone, and I surely felt badly and wept as I then realized for the first time that I was alone to face the world and that too on foreign soil. If I had known or realized how far that journey would have been, I certainly should have felt worse, but traveling was something new to me and there were many interesting sights for me to see which were interesting and entertaining and I wonder sometimes how I received courage to leave my family and go to a strange land and then too, when I did not know how far we should have to travel to get to Zion, and I could not speak the language. But it was the gospel I had received and the Spirit of Lord that helped me. I was ignorant of the world and did not understand it as I came to know later. When I think of one of my daughters starting out at that age, going into my fifteenth year, I wonder how it would go for her. But if she ha[d] the same faith I had I think it would be alright for her, too. But there were few who have strong faith as those who came from the old country in those days. I have never regretted that I came when I did, but am thankful to the Lord that I was thus permitted to come to Zion.

As the steam ship on which I left Copenhagen reached Liverpool, England, we transferred to a sail ship by the name of Ital[y] and the ship propelled by the wind on the sails took nine weeks in which to cross the Atlantic ocean, and we landed at New Orlea[ns.] The Mississippi River at its mouth was quite shallow and sometimes the wind unfavorable and our larger sail ship was tugged up the river by two small steam boats—one pulling on each side of the sail ship Italy. Thus the ship was pulled up to the city of New Orleans. From this city we completed the balance of our river journey by steam boat to the city of Kanesville on the Missouri River. This unloading point is on the east side of the river, and we remained there a month to prepare for crossin[g] the Plains; getting the Oxen, wagons, and equipment ready for the journey. At this point I experienced a new phenomimon. There came a day the worst wind and thunder storm that I could ever ~~in~~ imagine and an experience I had ever known of in Denmark or on the journey so far. The appointed time came for the great journey across the Plains into the almost unknown

West. The wagons and equipment and members of the emigrating party were taken over the Missouri River by ferries and the oxen, cows and horses had to swim across as there was then no accommodations for ferrying animals across the Missouri.

There were representatives of several nationalities including Americans but in our particular division of the emigrant train which included fifty wagons, there were twenty-eight from Copenhagen and in our company of ten wagons there were included quite a number of Americans. Our Company was presided over by John Butler who was the Captain over our Company which occupied ten wagons. The entire fifty wagons with occupants was presided over by a head captain in the person of E[li B.] Kelsey, and the whol[e] emigrant train is known as Kelsey's Company. There were then five companies with ten wagons to each company. Each presided over by a captain; a chief captain to preside over the entire train of fifty wagons. The women generally rode in the wagons and always slept in the wagons. Personally I thought the emigra[nt] wagons most remarkable vehicles as I had never seen anything of the kind before starting on this journey. Upon nearing the Rocky Mountains, the oxen became somewhat worn out and then it was necessary for many women to walk while traveling. Upon camping at night the wagons were driven in a circle and the camp fires were made inside the circle. Being young and in my fifteenth year, this being the year 1852, it became a part of my regular duty to gather buffalo chips which served as part of the fuel for the camp fires. During the first part of the journey across the plains, the novelty of travel was new and the evenings across this trip we felt to enjoy the company of the members and the friends we had made. One member had a fiddle as we then knew it and all joined in the evening dances around the camp fires within the big circle. Prayers and hymns were part of the daily morning and evening program. After walking a good deal during the days, I felt so tired I could often have been glad to have gone to bed without supper but I always had to help with the dishes and help with camp duties including the preparing of the beds.

Occasionally I walked with some of the other girls in head of the train; as far as we dared to go on account of the Indians and then wait for the wagons. My thought would go back to my parents in Denmark feeling sure that I should never see them again because the journey into the wild west seemed so long and hard and uninviting that it seemed I could never hope to have them join me in the distance place somewhere far in the west known as Zion. Surely my elderly parents at least when I had left in the Old Country could not endure the hardships of such a journey. I had my sobs and cries and pangs of sorrow. What comfort it would have been to me if I could even have been able to speak or understand the American language in this to me the New Land of American.

One of the singular incidents that happened enroute was the occasion of a stampede of a herd of buffalo which came direct to ward our wagon train. The stampede ran providentially just in head of the train with the fierceness of the rush and tramp and as it appeared almost a cyclone of dust. This caused a great commotion and almost stampeded among the oxen and horses of the train. The few rifles available were used and fortunately enough for the emigrants, a few buffalo fell which were prepared and this gave us extra provisions on the long journey in head of us. Upon another occasion nearly a dozen Indians came on their horses and approached the emigrant train. A great deal of apprehension was caused among the emigrants as they felt sure an impending disaster was before them. They thought this was the first contingent of hordes of Indians that lurked in the ravines near the trail. The daily prayers were answered and we were assured that Heavenly Father was mindful of the needs and protection of his Saints. The Indians spread their blankets by the side of the trail and each wagon was required to give its toll of food to the Indians as it passed.

Most unusual treatment and care was given me by the family

of Ravens who stood the expenses of my journey. Especially did I appreciate the kindness of Sister [Maren Marie] Ravens as she cared for me as her own child. I assisted them all I could on the journey to at least partly pay for their unusual kindness to me.

When we had advanced to the Green River Station, now Green River, Wyoming, the supply of flour had been exhausted. The fall snows commenced bringing the cold blizzard and wintery blast all of which added to the perils of the journey. It became necessar[y] to send a man with the best and fastest equipment on to Salt Lake City to get flour and rush back to Green River which was only sufficient enough to sustain the party in the train for the balanc[e] of the trip.

On into the mountains we went along the already broken trail which had now been traveled over by the emigrant trains of for five years. We arrived in Salt Lake City October 16, 1852, after eight months and twelve days of journeying since I had waved my last farewell to my parents and friends from the deck of the ship that sailed away from the port port of Copenhagen.

Elder Erastus Snow had come by horse conveyance across the Plains and had not stopped the month at Kanesville. Upon entering Salt Lake Valley, Elder Snow met the train and invited our original twenty-eight Scandinavians to his house for dinner at which we were served salt, rice and bread (raisin). I must here remark that I have never tasted a cake that to me tasted as good as that bread after this prolonged and tedious journey of hardships.

I remained in Salt Lake City one year until October 1853. During this time I worked for an American family by the name of Warner[188] that came in our company across the plains. Of course this was of great assistance to me to learn to speak the English language. In the fall of 1853 there came a large company of Scandinavians from the old country and there were several from

---

188. This family was probably the Charles Warner family, which traveled to Utah in Kelsey's company.

my home city of Copenhagen. I was so happy to see them and they seemed almost like my own folks from home. Only those who have been through a similar experience of breaking away from all family ties and going on a similar pilgrimage journey can appreciate my real inward feelings.

Gustave Louis Edward Henriod, one of the earliest French converts to Mormonism, left a detailed narrative of his early life and travel to the Salt Lake Valley in 1853. Clearly meant either for publication or for future readers, his account is polished and highly readable. It shows his mastery and sometimes extravagant use of the English language. Appointed clerk to Joseph Heywood, the territorial marshal, and clerk of his ward, he also assisted George D. Watt in developing the Deseret alphabet. He had quickly demonstrated a facility with the English language and pleasing writing skills. His encounter with an Indian tribe, which he graphically describes, may be somewhat embellished in the telling, but other accounts confirm the lack of hostility among most of the Indians the pioneers met during their travels.

GUSTAVE LOUIS HENRIOD[189]

J, *GUSTAVE LOUIS EDWARD HENRIOD*, son of Jean Louis Henriod and Domitile Deligne, was born August 25th, 1835, at Havre, Seine Inferieura, France. My father was a descendant of "Halvetia," and supposed to be of the Celtic

---

189. "Gustave Louis Henriod" (1893) in Carter, *Our Pioneer Heritage* II:316–32.

original race of people,[190] while Mother was a thorough descendant of the old Britons who inhabited the country called anciently, Brittany, whom the Roman Emperor Julius Caesar found difficult to subdue or conquer in his magnificent conquests of 56 years B.C.

Father's childhood and his first recollection of infancy will refer the reader to the beautiful and quiet lake called "Leman"[191] in Switzerland where his father owned vineyards, farms and stock. He took much pride in some of his pleasant and happy conversations by telling his hearers that his father had in the family archives, numerous genealogies of our ancestors, that could be traced back to Henry the Fourth, King of France. Mother's recollection of her childhood days seemed different. Her mother died and left her young in years in care of an aunt and her own father who was then captain of a French man-of-war. He was killed in a naval engagement some years after. Mother drew the pension of her father even when she lived in the United States until the day of her death. She died in France at about the age of sixty-eight. Father's occupation was shipping and consignment business, nearly the whole forwarding being for the United States ports. Havre, our home, stood as one of the largest, finest seaports and harbors in the world.

After my years of schooling were over and my father had examined my scholastic qualifications, he had me placed in the office of a maritime insurance company, named Fortune, doing a large insurance business on ships going to all parts of the world. The age of sixteen found me at the desk occupied at a salary of sixty francs per month with the promise of an increase every year after. The privileges of making friends and acquaintances among hundreds of leading merchants and business men was equal to a

190. Helvetians were descendants of the ancient Helvetii, an early Celtic people of western Switzerland in the time of Julius Caesar.

191. Lake Léman, otherwise known as Geneva Lake, lies on the Swiss/French border near the city of Geneva.

good salary also. On the first day of each month my welcome salary was received promptly and I was very proud to place it into my father's hands. If I was in need of pocket change he would provide me with the same, otherwise I never had any claim nor disposition to use any part of my salary.

My brothers were Auguste, Henri, Eugene and Samuel. My sisters were Henriette, Clementine, and Lea. Auguste, the oldest, graduated at the age of twenty-one in the Geneva College and went to England as a professor. The sudden change of climate from the mountains pure and light air to the damp and foggy atmosphere of Great Britain caused him to be taken with consumption. He returned home and in a few days ended his earthly career. A young, robust, intelligent gentleman and scholar, hardly in the prime of life, with a bright future before him, passed away without a murmur, except saying to Mother, "It seems too bad to die so young."

In June of 1850, Mormon missionaries came to France from the United States. They were John Taylor, an apostle, Curtis E. Bolton and John D. Pack and others.[192] Bolton came to Havre and directed his steps to my father's house, not knowing us from anyone else. They were traveling without purse or scrip. Father told Bolton that as he had no home, he might stay with us until he could do better. He lost no time in telling us of his mission to the world; that the gospel had been restored to the earth together with the authority and priesthood of God; that baptism for the remission of sins was again, as of old, a part of the gospel; that the Church of Jesus Christ had been again established on earth and the fullness of the gospel had been revealed to Joseph Smith, Jr. in America. My father was a Protestant and a man very well versed in the Scriptures. A regular church attendant, and very

---

192. Elders Piercy, Arthur Stayner, and William Howell were added to John Taylor's missionary group in addition to Elders Bolton and Pack to proselyte and raise branches of the Church in France.

strict with his family concerning religious and moral training, he proved a powerful antagonist to Bolton in quoting the Bible.

My mother had been a Roman Catholic from her youth, but had modified her religion from natural consequences after her marriage to a member of the Protestant Church.

Our parents had somewhat used an influence over their children, each from the doctrine and training that early had been planted within their conscience so that when we came to years of maturity and of understanding, we had naturally wondered and studied over the situation and were very undecided as to what course to pursue or which religion to adopt; for our future lives and the salvation of our souls were at stake, and depended much upon the selection or choice we should make. It was about that critical period that the preachers of Mormonism entered my father's house in a moment when we were undecided and knew not where to look or apply for information so much desired.

The keen and quick judgment of Bolton soon had us located in our proper or unproper situation. He opened the Bible to us many times and read verse after verse, bearing upon the subject, and so simplified the scriptures that it was almost impossible for any of us to contradict with success. Our school and college education was very little assistance in battling with this interpreter of the Sacred Writ.

The result was, in brief, that the family, one after another, were baptized, except Father, and joined The Church of Jesus Christ of Latter-day Saints. With few exceptions, I believe that we were the first Mormons of the French Mission. I was baptized on the second day of November, 1851, in a beautiful stream of clear water near Havre. It had been raining incessantly for several days, but as we were entering the stream for baptism, the sun came out brightly and a magnificent rainbow arched over our heads, lasting until the ceremony had terminated. It seemed that the heavens were smiling upon us and it occurred to those present that even the angels were rejoicing for the repentance and obedience manifested, and also for the establishment of the everlasting Gospel in a new country.

In a few days, a branch of the church was organized in Havre, and an English elder, John Hyde, was sent as our president, and was succeeded by another one, James Hart, a few months later. I was ordained a deacon, December 14th, 1851; teacher, February 29th, 1852; and priest, April 16, 1852. I was never called to preach the Gospel, but usually at all meetings, bore my testimony to the truth of the principles which I had honestly embraced, not only before the Saints, but also to others who were not converted to our faith.

Gathering to the Valleys of the Mountains was then advocated and preached by the elders in conformity with the passage of Scriptures "Come out of Babylon, O! Ye my people, "[193] or something near those words. My father having observed a great change in the every day deportment, the honest, sincere and moral life of his children and also their love and strong adherence to the Gospel of the ancient days as now again revealed, first favored and then advised us to gather to Utah with the Saints and devote our lives and abilities to the faith and church which had so re-generated and ameliorated the conduct and spiritual improvement of his children; being willing to admit to John Taylor that there must be something wonderful in Mormonism according to its influence and workings upon the heart and minds of the believers, although to himself it had not been given to see and understand the principles as we all did, claiming also, that he had, as required and advised by the elders, tried to seek vigilantly for a testimony of the truth by fervent prayer, after all of which the testimony never came. Undaunted in his researches, his last words to us before leaving him, were that he would still seriously investigate our principles and try to obtain the knowledge that

---

193. See Revelation 18:4 (2–4).

Mormonism was of Divine origin, the sequel of which is that he, just before his last days on earth, asserted that his labors had all been in vain.

He cheerfully furnished the necessary means to send my sister Henriette and myself, (respectively past eighteen and sixteen years of age) to the United States of America, that we might gather with the Saints in the pleasant vales of Utah Territory, and more strictly and fully devote ourselves to the preparation of meeting the great unknown hereafter. On the 1st day of January, 1853, we embarked at Havre on the steamship Commodor, Captain Little, then plying regularly between said port and Liverpool, England. My vivid impression at our parting scene, was that I never should again look upon my father's face in this world. My mother's last advice was, "Gustave, always keep company with those who are better, not worse, than you are." Father's admonition still lingers in memory, "Gustave, be true to your friends." The first advice, I might have adhered to more closely; the last, I have strictly endeavored to keep. If my conscience must be the judge, then my decision on this subject is final. Sister, having acquired a good English education spoke the language fluently. I had badly neglected that necessary part and was just a thoroughbred French boy. The first half day I mastered "yes" and "no."

That voyage was terrific for me, although born and brought up near the Atlantic Ocean, in fact on its very shore, the crossing of the Irish Channel completely upset what there was of me. Father had very thoughtfully and generously provided us with oranges, lemons, claret, brandy, but the sailors, between Havre and New Orleans could tell more about what became of their distribution than I can. The only mementos left us were the empty cases on our arrival at New Orleans. We had good friends among the crew while traversing the Atlantic, for we made them such.

A day or two later found us upon the James Toy a steamer

ploughing through the muddy and mighty Mississippi River on our way to St. Louis, Missouri. Staying in that city two weeks, we were overtaken by my brother Eugene and some ladies from the French mission, Julia Leroy, Ernestine Nichols and Mary Mallet, the wife of Eugene. Another trip on the Missouri River conveyed us to Keokuk, Iowa, where we camped for several weeks, waiting for our wagons, and cattle to take us over interminable plains over a thousand miles in length with but two oases in the desert; namely, Fort Laramie and Fort Bridger.

Life on the plains cannot be very well described with such a pen as mine nor imagined or appreciated by a stoic. You, my kind reader, will never know the sports and vicissitudes, joys and fears, gladness and disappointment, grief and delight, cravings and satisfactions, hope and despair, anxiety and contentment, pains and pleasures, all of which are familiar associates, or rather were in the year 1853 between Omaha and Salt Lake City. Yoking up half wild oxen every morning, staking down the tent every night, picking up buffalo chips to cook the food, loading and unloading boxes and bedding mornings and evenings, in the saddle or on foot guarding the stock every night and driving loose cattle in the day, digging trenches around the tents to keep from being drowned by the torrents, singing the songs of Zion, mending a broken wagon, carrying on your back across some deep stream about 140 lbs. of female avoirdupois without losing your feet on the rocky bottom of a river, washing your clothes - everybody forgot a clothes line.

Some nights in a dangerous part of the prairies, we formed our sixty wagons into a round corral, putting the stock inside for safety and guarding outside for protection from Indians, for if the cattle are stampeded how will you reach either Omaha or Salt Lake? And if your scalp is lifted, where are you going? When there was danger on the plains from either fire or Indians, it was similar to the dangers of the sea, when you are threatened with fire or water; if you escape the one, the other gets you. One is the sea of water, the other a sea of earth. One is drowning, while the other is starvation. If there is a choice, then you certainly can take it. Being unfortunate by having a spare saddle-horse, Captain Cyrus H. Wheelock often detailed me as a pilot, being often several miles ahead of the traveling Caravan on the Great Sahara, so as to select a good grazing noon stopping place and another for our night camp of about 600 souls.

Upon one occasion, having lost track of the road, I traveled for miles alone until late in the shades of evening, approaching a small stream running into a deep ravine surrounded by a beautiful cluster of lovely shady trees. Suddenly descending the banks of the creek, what was my terrible surprise in stumbling in the midst of a band of Sioux Indians who were busily engaged in jerking buffalo meat, they having just concluded a big hunt. What could I do? Hungry and tired, lost and alone, a youth sixteen years old, standing before about one hundred stalwart, ferocious powerful sombre kings of the prairies, ready to sacrifice human lives and torture a defenseless being, and that for the sport of having a living target and of placidly studying the dying expression of a human being while in the agonies of death. One hundred pairs of dark and devilish eyes were fixed on that youth, who but a few weeks before, was sitting quietly on his tripod, figuring percentage on some maritime policy in one of those offices pleasantly located among the largest thoroughfares of a large city in the commercial world.

There was a quick commotion among the moccasins, bows and arrows, the young bucks smacking their lips for the feast, while I the victim instead of quickly preparing for the sacrifice, had the cowardice of unmounting my pony and making of the poor frightened steed a fortress, such as it was, to protect the also frightened rider from a shower of arrows. They never came. It must have been the transmission of that original and native Celtic blood into my arteries which gave the impulse of accelerated pulsation to my heart, that lighted up the spark of bravery

473

in me at that critical moment. I carelessly fastened my horse to a young sapling then quietly stepped in the midst of the tepees and singling out one of the big Tycoons offered to shake hands with the great warrior who in return gave me a very unmusical grunt; having had a fair musical education my ear was not slow to catch the vibration of his dissatisfied growl. I pointed with a smile to the tempting broiling buffalo steaks, having a fear in my heart that I might be an unwelcome and uninvited guest, intruding among the Royal blood of princes and princesses of the forest.

No signs of approval from anyone. I helped myself to a good size chunk of half fried meat, this must have been a settler for my dark friends, they interpreted it as an act of great courage and bravery on my part and no one interfered with me while I partook of one of those lunches that would perhaps have caused Delmonico's chef de cuisine to blush as well as to my epicurean proclivities.[194] They were all amazed. I managed by gestures and signs to make my red friends understand that I had lost my way. They pointed to me where to find the wagon road, and starting out in that direction about twilight, I reached our camp just before the break of day, my friends keeping up fires all night around the camping ground, so as to attract my attention in case I was still alive.

Every day of travel westward brings us nearer our destination and also finds our teams weaker and our weary immigrants nearly worn out with fatigue. The travel of the last few days is no longer on the plains, but through rocky mountains and rugged canyons. Now our bull-whackers have almost become experts and he must be a very dull student who cannot drive his wagon over every rock and stump on the road. [. . .]

The year 1853 was noted for its large amount of immigrant and freighting wagons from the East to the West. They could have

---

194. He is evidently happy to show his fluency in English, as this sentence demonstrates.

been counted by the hundreds; it would have been an interesting sight to an aeronaut speeding through the ethereal blue above us, to look down upon the plains that summer and photograph the long stretches of living masses wending their way towards the sunset as they were moving onward towards the shades of the evening; or when majestic Sol first began to shed his piercing flash upon the camps of the travelers either when resting, or rustling for the day's journey.

The many little columns of smoke, curling upwards and forming themselves into clouds hovering over the camping grounds long after the tenants had moved away, was a well fitted companion for the silence and the vast stillness of the plains after the departure of a train.

It was some little pleasure for me, when ahead of our company looking for a nooning place, to find written upon some buffaloes' bleached skulls, a silent but encouraging message left as follows: "Capt. Duncan's Company of fifty wagons camped here last night, August 20th, 1853, all well." It was like a letter coming from home or some friend, it assisted in breaking the monotony of the quietness upon the plains. The reader cheerfully consoled himself in knowing that he was not alone in the desert, for others' footsteps were not very far before him. Such news was soon distributed throughout the train and everyone must read or see the welcome message.

At last we came rolling down Emigration Canyon and out into Great Salt Lake Valley. It was on the 6th day of October, 1853, the weather was beautiful and every heart seemed joyful, giving a sigh of relief and contentment in beholding in the near distance the "City of the Saints," the destined home and headquarters of the Mormons. It was a city, an embryo, not many houses, and those well scattered from each other. They were built of sundried adobes and with two or three exceptions one story high, but very few with more than two rooms. Shade trees had been planted on either side of some of the most important streets which gave the aspect of comfort and civilization to the tout ensemble[195] of the picturesque scenery.

Arriving that day on the "public square," the wagons were driven into a line, the cattle taken away by herders, and people soon arrived looking for friends or relatives among the immigrants from many parts of the world; those who were fortunate to have such, were taken to their homes, while the rest or mostly all, were questioned by some bishops or leading men as to their occupations, wants, and intentions for the future, their prospects of finding positions or labor in the city. In a few days, all had been located, especially the girls, in town or in some settlement and thus were provided for. It happened to be my lot to find occupation and a home in the house of Joseph L. Heywood, who was then Bishop of the 17th Ward, and also United States Marshal for the Territory of Utah, besides which he was president of a late organized settlement called Nephi, in Juab County, Utah. These offices necessarily required him to employ a clerk. Being well satisfied with my style of writing and other needful requirements for such a position, he readily engaged me and I soon became as one of the family. The reader will easily perceive that I claim rightfully the title and honor of having been the first clerk of the first United States Marshal in and for the Territory of Utah in the year 1853 and after a position now (1893) that is much sought for, and difficult to obtain. I was also clerk of the 17th Ward. These two offices required but little of my time that winter so that I made myself very useful in and around the house, until I became a favorite with the family and in the 17th and other surrounding wards. There was but one large store in Salt Lake City, and the proprietors, Mes. Livingston and Kinkead[196] were boarders at our house.

---

195. In French, literally "all together."
196. Livingston and Kinkead operated a successful non-Mormon firm in Salt Lake City from 1849 to 1858, providing Salt Lake citizens with much-needed and desired commercial products.

I had a good opportunity of making acquaintance of, and being introduced to the leading and influential men of Salt Lake City, among whom were besides the above named, Brigham Young, Heber C. Kimball, Jedediah M. Grant, Orson Hyde, D. Bernhisel, Albert Carrington, John Taylor and many others. My youth barred me from being intimate with such men, besides my timidity and the rules of French etiquette which had taught me to be reserved, unassuming, nor too free with other persons than I, so that I cheerfully endeavored always to keep myself almost unnoticed while in the presence of company, never addressing myself to dignitaries or men in high station except when necessary.

I slowly introduced in my schools of music and dancing classes the customs and etiquette of the French, which should never be called aristocratic refinement, for it is the every day, unaffected and usual practice of the nation in general. My young scholars, in a few weeks, were singled out in parties and sociables, their deportment becoming more refined and agreeable in their social intercourse and less awkward. The reader must bear in mind that I was a fresh arrival from France and brought with me the manners and customs of a nation of etiquette, fashion and refinement.

One of Mormondom's most gifted poets and writers, Hannah Tapfield King joined the Church in 1850 and was baptized with her children in the River Camm, which runs through the city of Cambridge, England. Her husband did not join the Church but was willing to emigrate to America with her and their children: Georgiana (twenty-two), Louise (twenty), Bertha (nineteen), and Thomas Owen (thirteen). Georgiana was the wife of the captain of their ten, Claudius Spencer, with whom Hannah had a troubled relationship. The Kings bought a large, commodious carriage in which to travel and carried with them many purchases from New Orleans for their future home. Ann, a young hired girl, traveled with them to assist Hannah with the family's needs. Hannah's diary often mentions the friendship she developed with a young man traveling with them, referred to as S.N. (Samuel Neslen). He was particularly kind to her and became a companion and confidante. Until the last few weeks of travel, Hannah found camp life interesting. "There is something in this life that suits me," she wrote, "a sort of Eastern Oriental life, suits my taste and fancy." But in time she became impatient with the tedious travel. Like the other Saints who traveled those thousand miles by cart, wagon, and carriage, she found that the closer she came to the end of the journey, the more obsessive she became about reaching the Valley. Her diary begins near Sugar Creek, Iowa.

HANNAH DORCAS TAPFIELD KING[197]

[MAY] 20TH [1853] [IOWA] Lovely morning—Oh! this is a sweet spot—the same party breakfasted with us—at Eleven I made them Eggs beaten up with wine and Brandy—They dined with us—I then went & sat in my carriage as usual Br [Horace] Eldredge came & Talked with us—In the course of our talk, it came out he

197. Autobiography and Diary of Hannah Tapfield King (1864–1872), holograph, LDS Church Archives.

had 2 wives! He was the first man that ever confessed that to me I exclaimed Oh! Br Eldredge! he is a good man—I liked him as soon as I saw him There is a chaste look about him—

Saturday 21st Lovely day In the Evening I went for a walk alone—I shall long remember this lovely location—I do so much enjoy it—Saturday night & Sunday morning Violent thunder storm and poured with rain which continued until Sunday 22 I had my break fast & dinner in my carriage We all felt triste—Had it been fine we should have had much company. Went to bed early—in the night was awoke by some one touching the Carriage. looked out of the window & saw S[amuel] N[eslen] sitting over a fire he was on watch—felt rather poetical about it but have not yet Embodied my thoughts—

May 25 left our late Locality and went up the Hill Here we have been till this morning

May 27th My first daughter's birthday—She would have been 24 or 5—but she has gone to her Father in Heaven[198] Walked alone in the Evening down to our late Location enjoyed it—a meeting in the Evening to organize the company—Mrs [Eunice] Neslen [mother of 21-year-old Samuel] complained to me and seemed in a bad spirit—27th Left again & came into our present Location—a lovely spot! Oh! how I enjoy these Exquisite places— They are my delight! and I feel I have nothing to regret "The lines have fallen to me in pleasant places" literally and I Bless God for all things would that all were as happy as I am—S. N. is often my companion—always my friend & confident

28 Left Sugar Creek at 8 A M and journied to the prarie a distance of about 15 miles where we camped—We passed thro' Farmington and over the Mississippi [Des Moines], Just before we reached our destination we nearly had a serious accident— Going down a steep short hill with a muddy place at the foot of it

---

198. Her daughter Margaret was born 27 May 1827 and died 23 July 1828.

our Horses sank in up to the middle & could not extricate themselves or the Carriage—They got them out and then Br
[Christopher] Arthur brought his horses & fastened them to the
back of the Carriage and drew it out—The brethren pushing at
the wheels One of our Horses in the morning had been very gay
and had broken the whipple tree—which we had stopped to get
mended. had he been in it might have been serious affair—but
every thing proves daily—hourly to me that "Whatever is—is right"
when applied to the people of God! I feel thro' all things, to
rejoice and to Thank Him always, for indeed He has been very
good to me from the beginning of my life even to the present
moment—and I daily experience "Not more than others I
deserve—yet God hath given me more"—

Sunday May 29th Had a good night and awoke refreshed—
being very tired last night I wish Mr Shores could have come
again to take me out for a drive once more—he certainly was very
kind, and kindness in a foreign Land is doubly valuable—how it
calls out the heart with it's noblest and best affections—

Monday arose early, and started. had to pass a terrible
place—but Claudius went forward & they laid down trees &
bushes & we got over pretty well—had nearly had an accident with
the carriage, but our Guardian Angels were around us, & it all
passed off with a little fright!—Camped soon after we passed
"Dog Town—" walked at the back of the Camp in the Evening,
& fell in with a Scotchman—he had been in America some
Years—Mr [Thomas Owen] King [her husband] bought a Yoke
of Oxen of him—he brought them up next morning and drove
me over a bridge & places that I was afraid to pass—we talked
much during the Time, and he seemed pleased—and said he
hoped we should meet again—also a friend of his a nice man who
had been in England—I drove over some horrid places, which
made me very nervous for long after—Often when coming to a
dangerous place I have stopped the Horses & prayed the Lord to
give His Angels charge of us—Ive got over—Sometimes I would

call Anne[199] when no man could be got & she would head the Horses or perhaps drive them thro'—At last we camped near String Town—a thunder storm came on us as soon as the Tent was put up—I had not felt well for some days & this Evening I feared was going to have an attack of erysiplas[200]—I had worn my English bonnet this day and the Sun scorched my face—it felt on fire—Mr Shores took particular pains to caution us against getting our complexions spoilt—even Anne he talked to about covering her arms—he said he hated to see a Woman's fine skin burned up—Mr Shores! Thou wert a Man!! Went to bed Early & had a tolerable night—Was awake with the men greasing my carriage wheels wherein I was sleeping I found my face & eyes swollen lips parched & tongue white—I have been excited by driving over these awful places—however I eat 2 or 3 mouthfuls & mounted my post i e to drive the Horses—They are pets [unreadable word]—but plenty of spirit and such frightful places! I feel sure few women (English) dare drive over where I have gone—and it has shaken my nerves into a muddle—at 1/2 past 2 a Thunder storm came on—Could do nothing but sit still and wait—it poured down in torrents At last we got some tea—I did not get out of the Carriage—Anne brought it to me and I enjoyed it as well or better than I ever did in my drawing room—I then made part of the bosom of a shirt for Tom Owen and made up my Journal so far—Thank God for all things—I rejoice ever more and am grateful that I feel well to night—Bertha not very well—The rest quite well—

Wednesday 8th, June Anniversary of Margaret's wedding day, 20 years ago! It is some days since I journalized—Much has transpired of small matters but which at this time seem all importance—True it is that "trifles make the sum of human things"

---

199. This may be Ann Newling, a member of Hannah King's household in England. She introduced the Kings to Mormonism.
200. Erysipelas is a disease characterized by inflammation of the skin or mucous membranes.

The 1st of June Bertha has taken poorly & has continued up till the present time—I believe it is the Lords plan to punish her for a complaining disobedient Spirit to which she has forever given way to and had not been produced by this Journey or anything attendant to it—it seems inherant in her had she only given way to it I should have thought the present circumstances were too trying for her but such is not the case For when surrounded by all that mortal Girl could wish she was discontented as at the present time and that complaining—unhappy spirit has attended her every step of our voyage & journey—& my heart tells me it is necessary that she should be afflicted that she may be brought to know herself—I have prayed much a bout her, and give her entirely into the hands of the Lord to do as He pleases with her for I have long felt she was more than I could manage!—

June 6th a baby died—Oh! by the bye on Sunday we camped on a beautiful hill & had afternoon service and all seemed to enjoy it much. The sacrament was administered—a few strangers were present who expressed themselves much pleased & Edified Friday morning we came down the steepest & most frightful hill I ever saw—Tho' we had passed thro' a splendid Country before we came to it—Monday Sister How's baby died & was buried the next morning before we started—we then travelled on thro' the new Town of Chariton [Iowa]—

June 7th Went to a Store and bought a few things that we needed and we then came on to our camping place this morning—

June 8th We started at 8 oc but it came on rain and we were obliged to Camp at 12 oc—All very wet. I brought Bertha in the carriage—but she complained of cramped limbs & fatigue so she might as well have been in the wagon—here we are all wet & uncomfortable externally but with a tolerable degree of peace and equanimity for myself I feel happy all the day, and only wish that all surrounding spirits were as happy & peaceful as my own—I have been blest with good health except sea sickness & debility in consequence ever since I left England—and I am a marvel to myself, for truly I have had many trials—but then God has blest me every day—and raised up friends that have been kind & good to me even in a foreign land—I have ever found friends or at any rate one friend to go where I might that has stuck closer to me than a brother!—

Saturday June 12th started at 1/4 to nine in the morning reached Pisgah about 4—and our Camping place about 5 oc Had tea & went to bed soon—Anne washed some things for us—

Bertha still ill and very trouble some—she is a strange unaccountable girl! I feel she did not enter this Church with the right spirit of the Church—& has not progressed in it Yet she came in of her own will & pleasure

Here I take a breathing pause.—it seems hardly worth while to write every days journal for they consist all the time of thunder storms—mud holes making bridges—getting wet thro' beds and all I note down some of these, and then add how I enjoy my Carriage bed & how thankful I am for my many blessings &c &c

June 24th—53. Yesterday morning very busy packing in the waggons—re-arranging the things—luggage &c &c In the afternoon Mr King Saml Neslen and I went to the Bluff City [Kanesville] to see Sister Merrill—She was quite overjoyed at seeing us—She had letters for me from Br Johnson,[201] Wallace,[202] and Larkin[203] as also one from Mr Barber—but Oh! That ugly little word—They were in a box that had not yet arrived—and indeed she almost feared was lost!!! Heighho! how trying are such things But 'tis vain to repine—disappointment in such matters appears to be my lot—or rather I seem in my present dearth to be unable to lose any thing—The Bluff City is most beautifully situated it is a

---

201. Joseph W. Johnson was the Mormon elder who baptized her in England.

202. George Wallace was a missionary in England who was influential in converting her. He also spoke at her funeral in 1886.

203. Elijah and Sara Parfey Larkin were friends of the Kings in Cambridgeshire. They followed the Kings to the Valley in 1863.

spot marvelous for its beauty—but the Houses are poor—and the people look queer and uncultivated—S. N. and I richly enjoyed ourselves—We had some delicious coffee with Sister [Mary Ann] Crawley—where Sister Merrill is staying We also called on Sister Bray—then came home rather late—Mr King being very nervous on acc of the bad road—However at last we got into Camp safely and to bed—Claudius sent me a glass of port wine, enjoyed it much.—S. N. came to bid me good night. I anticipate that "Good night God Bless You" as the Ultimatum of the good things I experience thro' the day—He has been ever kind—gentle and respectful to me—and in the dearth and the wild of this Journey such are to be blessings that I cannot over look I acknowledge the kindness of the Lord in sending him to me—in my present circumstances for whom can I make a friend of?—I dare not tell Mr King much that has troubled me and does still—he came out for the love of his family and for the cause of God & the love I bare him I wish to make his path as smooth as I can—My son is a child—I cannot tell him & Claudius I have not full confidence in—and he holds me aloof and is often unkind to me—and inconsiderate of my feelings but Samuel is wise & kind, & withal my friend and I can trust him with my life if need be—and all that is dear to me—Oh! my Father! give Thine angels charge concerning them—for in my present dearth all things are Valuable! that is, of love & kindness Mr King and Claudius gone off to buy a waggon and cattle—Mr K. to give him 43—10S and he will buy them and bring on our Luggage but the waggon & cattle are to be his all the time! I don't understand this logic! Well I am in a school, and if I receive the lessons aright, I shall be improved by them if not, they will do me harm—Oh! my Father! hold me and bless me or how shall I proceed? Last day of peace—encamped on the banks of the Missouri River—I feel weary today and my Spirit flags—drove thro' the water up to the axel of the carriage—few women would have cared to have done it—I went behind Claudius—Met two brethren in the water—One turned and walked by my Carriage till I was out of the "deep waters" it was very kind of him & I will not forget it I must learn his name! I know his face well I wish I could get my letters—but it is a satisfaction to know they have written—Bless the Lord for the kind friends that I have—it is in answer to B [Elijah] Larkins' prayer & his words Certainly no woman had ever had more disinterested Love & Kindness offered to her than I have ever had bestowed on me! & thank God, for it is better to me than Gold or Silver—Here follow a few petty disagreeables—Tho' not petty at the time to those who were made to feel them—but I will not write them down—let them go!—A few weeks more and I shall enter that renowned place, "The Valley" I feel I cannot analyze my feelings at the present time—They are so complicated—and I see thro. a glass very darkly. There is a strong Vein of pleasure and happiness and then there are uncertainties—but my Father, Thou Knowest—I have given all my affairs into Thy Keeping—& I know in whom I have trusted—This night a dreadful thunderstorm & other annoyances—here follow some more remarks which I throw into my Oblivious Reservoir—and I finish by blessing the Lord for his goodness!

July 3rd—Sunday.—Lovely morning—No prayers I feel starved spiritually—but soon we will hear the prophets voice—S. N., Lizzie[204] & I walked to the top of one of the beautiful hills that surround this spot—Sat on the top, Lizzie gathered some "fat hen"[205] for dinner—descended & returned home—put my Carriage in order read in the bible & wrote—The sun is now setting on those beautiful hills—The Cattle are feeding as tho' they knew it was their supper time—and all around looking beautiful The girls are in the Tent talking—Anne washing the supper things—Mr King sitting at the side of the Tent & Claudius with him—talking! S. N. walking around our circle—he ever appears

---

204. Lizzie is most likely Elizabeth Burgess Neslen, eighteen-year-old sister of Samuel Neslen.

205. Any of several succulent or fleshy-leaved plants, especially of the genus *Chenopodium*. Examples include lamb's quarters, ground ivy, buckwheat, shepherd's purse, and mugwort.

to be happy to be near us—& I feel he is my friend & does me good—How I wish I could hear from my dear parents it would comfort me and be a delight—Here follow a pouring out of sorrowful feelings—always winding up with Thankfulness for my great blessings—seven oc same day—Claudius gave me a glass of port wine being the 4th of July!! and asked me for a Toast for my adopted Country! This filled up my heart which was full before—I got out of the Tent and walked to the top of one of these beautiful Hills—where I sat down & prayed & thought. Then returned;—Georgey came & sat in my carriage also Br Robert[206]—Then he went and Sam[207] came The fire flies are beautiful here They are like diamond dust over every thing at night.

7th Better this morning—Anne brought me, with her accustomed attention, some tea & toast, enjoyed it much, felt better—at 7 oc started on our way—[unreadable word.] have felt better to day as S. N. said I should last night—got safe into camp & to bed. Anne has been very attentive to me and her duties generally and this is something on the plains Started at 7 oc—nice morning—a flat road—high grass road not very good—camped for an hour to water the cattle—We also got some Refreshments Started again & got to our Camping place about 4 oc—a tolerable nice place—had tea &c—felt better as S. N. said I should he came & sat with me a short time at luncheon hour—mosquitoes troublesome—but all things considered all is well My heart rejoices that every day we are approaching nearer the Valley. I long for my letters—dreamt last night that Louise & Mr Barber were married in secret saw him very plainly—I know all about it

9th Started at 4 oc in the morning—got to a camping place at 9—had breakfast—On again—crossed the Platte River—last night we had a syllabub.[208] S. and R. Neslen with us—A tempest in

206. This could be Samuel Neslen's brother, Robert.
207. This is probably Samuel Neslen.
208. A whipped milk dish often laced with wine or cider.

the night—Alarm from the Watch at 3 oc that the Cattle were gone astray? false report—made partly a sun bonnet to day—Went to bed—slept nicely—

10th Rose at 1/2 6—got ready to start at 7—Went 10 miles to Loup Fork Ferry ferried over by 5 oc PM set the wagon & tent—washed & had tea I wrote this much of my Journal and here I feel to thank Thee Oh My Father for Thy Great and boundless Goodness to me & mine and to the Camp generally for His Great Kindness to us on this long Journey—truly His Hand has been displayed almost palpably to us His frail & erring people!—This is the 7th Sunday after Trinity[209] I recall how often we have sung that beautiful collect[210] and its no less beautiful accompaniment—and a 1000 recollections crowd upon me—S. & R. Neslen came into our tent in the evening—We sang—a beautiful moonlight night—soon all went to bed S. N. & I walked thro' the Camp last thing—then bade good night at the Carriage door—

11th. Woke in the morning with the cry that the Cattle were all gone astray!! All the men called up! false alarm!!—at 6 oc S. N. put two lovely Tiger Lillies thro' the curtains of my Carriage—The offering pleasd me—every kind act however small seems a blessing in the dearth of the present time—He is ever kind to me—God sent him to me!—We went off to a pretty Camping place late—but a regular mosquitoe bottom—

12th Wet morning set off—went on till the Evening Camped again—S. N. not well—came and sat in the Carriage with me—had some nice conversation—as we always do when we talk at all bid him "Good night" and to bed—at 9 or before.

13th Slept feverish and awoke unrefreshed—Thundered in the night—off at 9—not good roads—slight mud holes—& no good water—got to a place at 4 oc where there was some tolerable good

---

209. Trinity Sunday is the Sunday after Pentecost. It is observed as a festival in honor of the Trinity.
210. A "collect" is a prayer used in liturgical services, spoken or sung. She was referring to the collect for the Seventh Sunday after Trinity included in the 1839 edition of the Anglican Church's *Book of Common Prayer*.

water long grass & hosts of snakes! which destroy my happiness—
Got into the Carriage and finished my sunbonnet for Georgey
Carried it into the Tent when I went to tea—had nice tea & toast
bacon—pudding & rice—enjoyed it much Felt grateful for all
things & happy—Mr King was in a grumbling spirit which marred
it as he often does—finding fault with every thing—This is his way
at times—he would do it were he surrounded with all he wished—
so I do not feel so bad over it—I detest a grumbling spirit—I had
washed him and brushed his hair & did what I could for him—S.
N. a little better—This morning before starting I gave him a glass
of new Milk with some brandy in it—I love to do good—& he says
I always do him good I have not much Scope now—but I do all I
can and that the Lord will accept—

14th A long day's travel all weary and worn—I felt used up—
All things looked dark—The dark things darker—and the bright
things clouded—much that I have suffered crowds upon my
mind—the harshness I have suffered the changes—the privations—
all—all crowded upon me and steeped my soul in the waters of
Marah![211] Oh! how I wept! for I felt how changed were all things
around me—& what was far more trying to me how changed were
those who were so lately all to me! but there has been an influence at work, ever since I have been on this Journey trying to
withdraw my influence from those dear to me—Can this be
right?—I cannot think it is!—felt low and nervous—but slept tolerably—

15th St Swithen[212]—did not rise till 7 oc got some breakfast—
felt shaken and triste—Set off to walk.—having declared I would
not drive the Horses again—as I had been made to do—Having
had an accident yesterday—poor Tom having run his waggon
against the carriage as we were waiting at a horrible mud hole—I

---

211. See Exodus 15:23. "And when they came to Marah, they could not drink of the waters of Marah,
for they were bitter; therefore the name of it was called Marah."
212. St. Swithen's Day is 15 July, viewed superstitiously as a day that, whatever its weather, will be
followed by forty consecutive days of similar weather.

have often been spoken to severely when an accident has happened—so I came to the decision—I would drive them no more—
and poor Tom—a mere child—has been made to drive a
waggon—when of course he knows nothing about ox teaming—
Proposed Mr Spencer to drive it—But Mr King would not hear
of any thing but that I must drive it as before,—So I walked on
leaving them to settle it: Anne was started off with it and overtook me—I soon rode, still feeling queer—On we went Louie
looking gloomy, I have done what I could to comfort and cheer
her on this Journey—I think also that I have done much to keep
up faith and good feeling & love—but I have failed in most cases—
however, I feel to leave all tho' my heart often suffers—Oh! for
the Valley—Last night I had a few words with Claudius he has
taken a curious Course with us, & me in particular—he does not
seem to me to have the element of happiness within him self &
therefore he cannot confer happiness. We crossed "Prarie Creek"
a wicked creek as C. calls it. They threw in grass and brush—wood
& earth & so filled it up enough for the waggons to cross—all are
by this time nearly over—Sam & Robt. Neslen came & chatted
with us—these young men cause ennui often to disappear from
my Orbit—They are always on hand to do us good where they
can—

Sunday July 17th We again crossed this wicked Creek twice—
and then went on to Wood River which was a bad place to cross,
but all got over safely—Camped by the side of it—In the Evening
about 11 oc a dreadful Tempest—yea, awful—I think I never in
England witnessed such a one—I thought it would have blown the
Carriage over—I prayed earnestly & felt my prayers were heard—
Mr King dead asleep the whole time at last after about an hour
it abated—The Watch were indefatigable & the Cattle were all
safe—our bed got very wet—at last got some sleep—dreamed I got
my letters—but I thought they had been opened & were briefer
than usual—This I do not believe would be the case—at any rate
I wish I had the trial—In the morning felt tired and prostrated as

I often do after a tempest—Walked some of the way with Bertha
& Br Samuel—sang two hymns with Anne & him—then came into
my Carriage & wrote this much of my Journal I feel happy &
cheerful but by no means elated—had meeting in the afternoon.
Br [John Joseph] Hayes, [Samuel] Neslen [probably Senior],
[Henry] Walker, and [Daniel] Spencer spoke—A Baby blest by
the name of Samuel, My Brother's & Grandfather's name—May
all the blessings spoken over it be ratified in the Courts above
Some Californian Emigrants passed while we were in meeting—

Monday 18th felt tolerably—Sister [Harriet Coman] Dye
confined last night with a son—These Mormon Women I think I
should have been left in my grave in similar case—but truly God
fits the back to the burden—This we realize daily and I think in
nothing more than in such cases—She went on with the Train and
reported "all right" at night "Going on well" "Beautiful boy" &c
&c Long drive to day got in late—had a deal of trouble to find a
Camping place—at last Br Spencer selected a spot in the midst of
the wild Prairie Our carriage was set close by a g[rea]t hole, which
we all thought was a grave! Had the Carriage & waggons moved
on a little—Went to bed at dark—after I got in smell a very
unpleasant smell. Thought it came from the old grave! The
thought of it made me feel ill—and I could not sleep—at last fell
asleep—soon awoke feeling ill—all next day felt unwell—Was it
fancy?—it was not fancy that I felt ill, but the cause I leave in
doubt the idea was enough

Tuesday 19th Drove to wood river. crossed a deep ravine and
then on 2 miles—Camped close by some Californians with a large
flock of sheep.—Slept well—

Wednesday 20 Started early—Claudius drove the Horses
attached to the Carriage. Georgey I and Lizzie rode with him—
also Louie—Had some agreeable & edifying talk upon plurity—
the first wife being head or Queen Lizzie said she would be first
wife or never be married and Br Spencer tried to convince her
it was a mistaken idea—but it seems to be in corporated in her

system the idea of being great according to her notions of great-ness—perhaps she'll learn better in time—we are all more or less biased by such feelings—Crossd several creeks & above all Elm Creek, where Br Spencer was driving the horses over. it was an awful bridge where few but "Mormons" would think of crossing a large piece of wood stuck up at which the brown mare shied & Lo! she pushed over the other Horse right into the water!—but by dint of real presence of mind & management we saved the Carriage from being dragged in—The Californians came to our assistance, & we got the horses landed without a buckle being broken!—After this wonderful feat (Br Spencer jumped into the water to his Knees) He helped over the 48 waggons! One of the Californians killed a buffalo—We had a large portion of it Had some fried for dinner—got into camp late—had tea & to bed—did not sleep the first watch! S. N. on watch till 12 oc—saw them thro' the window of the Carriage—Then composed myself & went to sleep—dreamed an uncomfortable dream about my Mother—

21st Rose early—breakfast & then off we were. Claudius drove us—Louie & Georgey & Lizzie rode with us—had more talk upon plurality—but it never seems a happy theme—arrived at Buffalo Creek.—Found a letter stuck in a stick from Br Atchinson[213] say-ing they were all well, i e his company and had left some Buffalo meat for us I had the tongue to pickle—Got safe over the creek. as Sister Chambers came up her Son told us his Father was dead![214]— He had been ill a long time They asked me to go & look at him which I did He looked like a statue so thin & wasted—Death is ever aweful! and it made me feel low & triste at last they all came up & got safely over—we then went to Sister C. and asked her if we could do any thing for her—she gave me some domestic to make a shroud or wrapper for the corpse—which I did. Then sent her some wine—

---

213. William Atkinson was a captain in the Jesse W. Crosby company that reached the Valley about two weeks before the Spencer company.

214. Joseph Chambers died 21 July 1853 and was buried near Buffalo Creek. He left a wife (Mary Ann) and four children.

for herself and the women who laid him out—dined & Br Spencer decided he would not go on till to morrow so we prepared to wash some clothing—at 1/4 to 3 the grave was completed & Br Spencer told us he wished to attend the funeral of Br Chambers to the grave—We did so—it was a nice dug grave They laid leaves at the bottom & then lowered the Corpse into it some boughs over him & then was filled up Br Samuel assisted all thro' Br Neslen made ahead board—on which was "Joseph Chambers—Native of England aged 53—Anno—53—We can only say "Resquiescat"

22nd—Last night a very heavy tempest—Br Spencer says the heaviest we have yet had—And we have had many—Our bed was very wet indeed—we got but little sleep—had breakfast and started at 10 A M—passed thro' a very wet road—saw many Buffaloes & a Rattle Snake—at 1 oc arrived at a deep creek—water too deep for us to cross—Obliged to Camp got our Biscuit wet—had some fried for dinner and Bacon & boiled beef—fine day and a nice healthy Air—Claudius—Georgey—Louie & Lizzie rode in the Carriage—wrote a few of my Thoughts to S. N. not being able to have a word with him and wanting to do so—Oh! how I long to be in the Valley! to behold the Servant of the Lord! and those that have been so good & kind to me in past days—& whose society I have so much Enjoyed in England—I feel when I attempt to realize it it will be almost Happiness too much—and that I shall almost feel like Israel of old "Let me die since I have seen thy face"—it is Enough—

26th of July—Days have passed & I have not Journalized Today rose early and started on our Journey—after Camping near the Platte river—had a good night Walked on—after a time got into the Carriage alone with Claudius—We got into an agreable chat—He asked me who Susanna was engaged to?!!—as I had told him I Knew—I at once said, "May I speak plain?" he said Yes—I said to you!!![215] This led to an excitable conversation—for cer-

---

215. Claudius Spencer married Susannah Neslen (sister to Samuel and Robert Neslen) 9 October 1853, the same day he wedded Louisa King.

tainly I did not think he had treated well very often—and we then
got up to the Girls & feeling quite unfit for conversation or
Company—I got out walked alone—and at last rode in the waggon Staid & had some refreshments at 1 oc—in the afternoon
rode again with Georgey—Louie & Lizzie—at last I suggested we
staid, as I was afraid of Indians—C. said there was but one Lady to
take—being Miss Stayner[216]—as I and G. were married & Louie
engaged!—Louie started and said—It was more than she knew!—
The conversation then went on in a diamond cut diamond fashion—strain between C. & me—at last he said I should either do
an immense deal of good—or an immense deal of Evil!!! I felt
this to be a most cutting remark—God knows how I desire to do
right—and as I told Him I will have no other faith than that I shall
do an immense deal of Good—In my past life I have had the
power to do so & I believe that God will love and nurture that
which He alone has sown & fostered—I will believe that the past
will be guarantee for the future but I thought it unkind &
unmanly to attack me in that rude manner, for we can not but
Know how great are my trials & how I do try to be brave.[217]

27th. Claudius brought me a note this morning in answer
to one I wrote him last evening after his cutting remarks. It was
good, but somehow he does not comfort my heart—is the fault
in me? not all certainly—I think we lack that confidence in each
other which makes advice acceptable—I drove the Horses a good
part of the day—C. being with his team—staid in midday nearly
one hour—Saw a company of people upon the hills opposite—Set
off again A tempest gathering—Got to the camping place at 5 oc—
a sharpish tempest Sat all the evening in my Carriage—Read
Brigham's Sermon & other things in Deseret News S. N. came

---

216. T. S. Elizabeth Stayner is listed singly in the company roster without husband or other family
members.

217. The difficulty between Hannah King and her son-in-law seems to relate primarily to the practice of plural marriage, publicly announced just the year before (1852). Hannah was evidently not yet
comfortable with the principle.

for a few moments but no talk—It appears we can seldom talk now—it seems there is an influence at work trying to destroy our friendship or at any rate the Life & beauty of it—went to bed at 8 oc—

Sunday July 25th, 1853 MCIII Set off in the morning having been detained a day on acct of the Creek being so swollen Got over safe—Br Walker taken ill and died almost instantly—On we went—came in sight of a company & found it was the Elders that we expected—and Oh! Joy! As soon as I got [to the] creek, Br Spencer being first with Georgey Louie Miss Staynes & Lizzie with Mr King—Louie held up a letter found it was one from Br Johnson sent to me by the Elders—This was an unexpected plea-sure and I Enjoyed it much—tho' it was a brief affair—but all's right—it was a letter! and thats some thing as times go—In the afternoon we had a meeting Several spoke—among them Bros Ross & [William Warner] Major Br M. brought my Letters, and I gave him some to carry to England—and 1/2 a Sovereign for a present Gave Captain [Philemon] Merril a Sovereign for the Company Mr King gave him one also, ditto—ditto A party of them took supper in our Tent—and we did what we could for them. Baked some cakes for them & gave them sugar & tea &c—They stood on the opposite side of the creek & prayed & blest us as a company, and said we should be blest We then bid farewell & on we went on our Respective Journeys.

July 28. Had a good night wind very high—feared the Carriage would be capsized—started in the morning at 7—soon reached a mud hole—flies & mosquitoes very troublesome it was a horrid place—Claudius drove me over—the girls went in the waggons Some wheels were broken—had to wait for them to be mended—'tis very troublesome but words are Vain in such a case—Deeds, not words is indeed the motto of this Journey—if not of the Church itself.—I feel weakened & my Spirit Caged by stopping—

Last of July Sunday—Rose—breakfasted & started at 8 oc—

Lovely morning.—drove over mudholes—creeks—&c till we arrived at an immense bluff, which we ascended & found ourselves on a high Eminence—soon Camped, at 3 oc—Poor water—but otherwise pleasant We had some wood with us & found Buffalo chips I have no Sunday feelings while travelling on Sunday Yet I desire to go forward—Yesterday we had a long day's travel & camped near the Platte River S. N. came for a few minutes Said he felt sad—we had a little talk—but said nothing tho' both inferred that something made us feel triste—we seemed truly to understand each other—

[July 29] Friday Evening—he drank tea with us but there did not seem to be a happy spirit with in the Tent—The fact is C. V. feels—towards tho' I Know for what reason—we all parted and said good night. Louie & Lizzie stood by their waggons for a moment, & I stood by my Carriage when some one came behind me—it was S. N. came to bid me good night Valley fashion! he is ever good & kind to me & in this dearth I can but love him—may God bless him for his goodness

August 1st Another day nearer the Valley—We have come about 19 miles today,—good road a few creeks & no mudholes and no accident. I hear S. N. singing—I am glad for he has seemed low of late—We all feel tired and somewhat used up but we shall be immortal till our work is done Oh! my Father my heart is full but I do not feel to make it all palpable but to Thee Work for me and by the whisperings of The Spirit, lead me right—remove far from me those that stand in my path to Salvation!

2nd Lovely morning. This day 20 years ago—Mr King Sen[ior] died—We started at 8 oc—we went on very cherily—at last met an Indian on horseback He told us 300 were a head He seemed very friendly—rode by the side shaking hands, &c, Br Spencer made a few arrangements—and soon we met the whole body of them—a party of Horsemen came forward to meet us— Br Spencer advanced with his gun—& made a sort of Military

Salute or pass—which they responded to very gracefully—descending from their Horses & kneeling or rather squatting in their not ungraceful Indian fashion Br S. then went up & shook hands with the Chief who presented a paper recommending them to white men they might meet—The name of the Chief was "Shell"—He came forward to the Carriage with Br S. who introduced him to us & to Georgey as his Squaw!! he shook hands with all of us—Br S. gave him some whiskey & water which he seemed to Enjoy after he had tasted it—but he seemed to fear to taste it till Br Spencer had done so. We i e the Camp all contributed some sugar, coffee—biscuit &c &c for them and we then bid them adieu—they drawing off on one side to allow our train to pass on—did not camp till 2 oc—by accident I got a long way off—but still in sight—Enjoyed my silent position as I ever do enjoy solitude at last gathered the Cattle and off we went—had not gone far when a thunder storm came—had to "put up"—When it ceased on we went and are now Encamped 2 miles from Crab Creek.—

3rd Rose & breakfasted & started passed Crab Creek—Camped at 1 oc after passing the Bluff ruins—They are very beautiful—I should like to have an explanation about them—but I suppose none know their history—They stand out in bold relief with a silent eloquence that speaks trumpet-tongued to every thinking mind—There they are looking eternally silent—walked as I often do after dinner or rather Supper The Mosquitoes dreadful! Had a talk with Sister Smith of Northampton She said she quite enjoyed it We have had the Platte river by us for the past week it is very pretty—full of little islands—Oh! I can write no more the mosquitoes drive me mad! Oh for an end to this Journey! truly we pass over "The bridge of sighs" to the Valley of the Free!

August 5th A long day's travel! this day these Sublime Bluffs in view all day!—They plainly speak a designer—tho' ages must have rolled along since that design was carried out—I felt extremely ill & prostrated last night & this morning I revived again—on we went without water all day till 8 oc in the Evening when we camped—I went to bed at once and Anne brought me my tea in bed S. N. came to bid me good night—Br Spencer also came and we had a long talk in the Carriage—enjoyed both!!

August 6th Arose & set off at 8 oc got into Camp at 3 oc— Cleaned out the Carriage & other jobs—got tea—

Sunday, 7th Fine morning—Got into Camp about 3 oc—Just as tea was ready two indians came & put us about a little & frightened us some a strong Guard was put on at night. I dreamed several things, among other things that I returned to England and to D. D![218] and all looked so changed & I felt so wretched that I had been so foolish as to return, I will not go into particulars— suffice that when I awoke & found it to be a dream, I did not Know how to feel Thankful enough—and I feel sure such would exactly be my feeling—All is well

Monday Louie very poorly—nervous and weakened. Claudius laid hands upon her—& advised her going into his wagon with Georgey.—so she went all day & seemed very happy & to enjoy themselves well—I have had some conversation lately with C. & G. They told me their minds a little—but I do not feel to write— Yea, I don't feel to analize my own feelings—but somehow they do not feel happy and comfortable when I think about it— Whether my feelings are right I do not Know—but I wish to do right, & to be right—I must leave it where I leave all I possess—in the Hands of Him who is my Father as He is the Father of All! Some American Gentlemen came from the Fort & talked with us—One is going on to the Salt Lake & offers to take letters for me—I sent one to Br Johnson by him

August 9th—Tom Owen not very well to day

11th Dull weather this morning—rose & drest—had breakfast in the Carriage—then got out and arranged my bed &c—and then

---

218. Thomas and Hannah King's homestead near Cambridge, England, was named Derford Dale.

went into the Tent a Gentleman soon came, who staid nearly all
the morning had quite a chat—I then went to the Carriage &
found S. N. sitting there—he remained a bout an hour reading to
me—but there is no rest—They came to grease the Carriage! Soon
Tom came feeling ill—wanted me to wash him—I did so and he
felt better—

12th Finer day—Louie's birthday We had a plum pudding—
some Gentlemen came & dined with us—Mr. MacDonald—
Fleming Stewart & [Hector C.] Haight[219] had a meeting in the
afternoon enjoyed it pretty well—but I feel saddened—All seems
changed & somehow against me!—

13th Left our encampment near Fort Laramie Journeyed on
to a place near a Creek—where we found Brs Haight & Stewart
already camped—felt low—mournful & worn down—I see the
determined attention Claudius keeps to Louie, and it takes away
my Soul—drinks up my Spirit. I feel too that it affects Georgey!
Surely he might wait till he gets to the Valley.—it seems to me that
such a girl as Georgey ought to content a man for a proper time
at any rate—I cannot reconcile myself to this new doctrine coming in such a form—I feel that it works upon Georgey's feelings
also—Oh! my Father—help me & give me not up to my own dark
thoughts—Tom Owen very unwell—Went to bed unhappy and
dejected

14th Tom awoke us this morning about 2 oc—having got up
in a delireum. Came to our Carriage calling to us that some of
the Carriages were gone ahead We took him into our Carriage
bed for an hour to soothe & comfort him—& then Mr King took
him back to his own bed He rose again early—we had breakfast &
started at 7 oc—T.O. in the Carriage with me—he was drowsy &
quite delirious all day—Oh! how unhappy I have felt this day!
Claudius is so very odd & unkind to me—God knows I desire to

---

219. Hector C. Haight, in company with Horace Eldredge, had been serving in Keokuk, Iowa, aiding immigrants traveling to the Valley.

do right—& to please him as far as is consistent but it appears I have not the power.—

15th T. O. very ill—which makes all look dark with me—Br Neslen & Claudius administered to him at noon as he lay in the Carriage—I felt wretched but hope at the bottom of all—Claudius asked him before he laid his hands upon him—if he knew what he must do to get well—he said, have faith in God! He then clasped his hands & went off into a beautiful little prayer which startled us all—Claudius thought it was one he had learned—but not so it was spontaneous it broke up the deep fountains of my heart & all seem affected—They then laid hands upon him and we all felt he had received a blessing The disease Mountain fever seemed arrested from that time—tho' he still continued very ill—Claudius slept with him that night

16th T. O. still very ill—delirious—travelled all night till 1 oc "under the moon" my thoughts were "Legion" & have been for some days past—but when is it they are not?—Thought with me is a Kingdom—Got into Camp & had some tea & went to bed at day break.—Tom slept with me in the Carriage Rose Early—

17th Rose & washed him all over with Saleratus Water—got him into the Tent and soon again into the Carriage which was set in a shady place—Sat with him all day—he was calmer seemed Exhausted—S. N. came & sat with me in the afternoon—

18th T. O. still very ill—had him administered to by Br Arthur & Claudius he being all unconscious Yet I felt more happy and hopeful.

19th Set off at 8 a m T. O. no worse—a beautiful morning lovely air—Got into Camp at 1 oc John Tom ran against one of our other waggons & smashed the wheel! Consequently we could not go on—Sat in the Carriage all the afternoon with T. O. he no worse—I hope better—S. N. went on "Doctor" to our Late Camping place to find one of their Lost Oxen Slept in the Carriage with T. O.—

20th Lovely morning—beautiful pure air quite ambrosial! I

hope Tom is better—but still nothing very decided about him—I washed him all over in vinegar and water—changed his bed & put him on all clean Linen—he looked comfortable and comforted my poor wounded heart.—I feel still hopeful—I cannot think the Lord will take him from me—in this embryo stage of his temporal & spiritual Existence! Surely He will remember mercy seeing the integrity of my heart all my life Long for 'tho conscious of my imperfections—Yet thro' all one strong pervading bias has run thro' all I did & said, i e the Love of my God & the desire to do His Will—I have also sacrificed as few women have the strength to sacrifice—I stepped out of my beautiful happy Home & from all I held dear for the Gospel's Sake—His Gospel—& will He forget all this? And is not this dear boy one who promises well to be good & useful—& have I not already buried 4![220]—and have I not again & again dedicated him to the Lord? and if he will restore him I will religiously carry out my determination and my Vow!— He will be faithful to His promise that those who trust in Him shall not be confounded and I believe & therefore will I speak— therefore will I hope—therefore will I contend asking all only and entirely of Jesus Xt—Amen.—

[Aug. 21] 4 oc P M Sunday We are now camped at Deer Creek, a beautiful place for such wild surroundings Trees & water and a patch of green grass make it an Arcadian Paradise after our weary toil for so long over such an arid soil—After we got in T. O. appeared worse—he had a paraoxysm that quite alarmed me— it appeared anger when I at tempted to wash him—he is now calm & lies peacefully Oh! My Father! Grant that the destroyer may have no power over him—forgive me if I have done any thing to bring this up on myself for God Knows I value his life & would not for the world lose him Oh! set a watch up on my mouth &

---

220. At this point, she had lost four sons: Owen (1831–1840), Peter Tapfield (1837–1838), Andrew Cookson (1841–1842), and an unnamed boy who was born and died about 1825. She had also buried two daughters.

Keep the door of my lips—Oh! spare this child to me Oh! God
my Father 4 weeks more & we shall be in the Valley or very near
it, if we have good fortune—is it possible that this Long Looked
for and anticipated—much sought after—much talked of—prayed
for—worked for and suffered for Event—This Consumation,
devoutly wished for is really so near at hand!!! I cannot realize
it—Am I to realize also Thy afflictive Hand?—Oh! spare me my
Father this one more dreaded event I ask it only in the name of
Jesus Xt—

Monday 22nd I have been too much engaged & my mind too
feeble & full & too unhappy to journalize—T. O. has been very
ill—I feel nothing but faith has saved him But today he is decid-
edly better—and my heart rejoices—Yes I am right Thankful to
my Heavenly Father, to His Servants and to my beloved friends
for the blessing of his restoration—I ever felt our faith & prayers
& exertions would Keep his life on the Earth—Bless the Lord
Oh! my Soul, & forget not all His benefits for indeed he has
been gracious to me He raised up Bertha who was nearly as sick as
T. O.—yet I never saw Death around her but I did around him
every day—but she is healed & I feel he is saved & for all this my
heart swells with gratitude—We are now about 380 miles from the
Valley—Can it be possible? Oh! how sad it seemed to me travelling all night last Thursday & he delirious all the time—but his
voice was weak & pretty of 5 or 6 & he talked innocently but not
outrageously—Once he called out "Mama—Grandfather has been
here & Eddie!"—Oh! how Kind is my Father in Heaven!! how
gently He chastises me, & warns me of the frail tenure of all
Earthly possessions! Oh! may these Gentle Lessons be never forgotten by me but may I apply them to the bettering of my
Nature—for I desire to be right & to do right—The scene around
is wild & dreary Oh! for the beautiful Valley—where my heart has
long been—Upper Platte River—

28th August—Sunday—I have not journalized for some days—
Much has transpired & I have intended every day to write—but

something has always prevented me or we have been late in Camp.—Thought as usual has been busy with me & I have felt weary & worn both in body & mind—Tom O. has been exceedingly ill—but faith has saved him—and he is better Thank God!—I have many thoughts about many things but God is all-sufficient & will leave all my affairs in His Hands—Who knows what is best for me—Oh! may His will be revealed to me—and may I be obedient to it—We have been for some days passing the "Rocky Mountains" they are rather more wonderful than beautiful—yet they are certainly Sublime—it seems something marvellous & mysterious that our Cavalcade should pass along breaking the Eternal Silence of these wild places—my feelings are undefinable but there is a degree of awe & sadness about them to me Yesterday we passed "The Devil's Gate" but I did not see it—Louie went & Lizzie—and others went but I staid in the Carriage with the invalid—S. N. rode a little while in the Carriage with me—We are now only 300 and a few miles from the Valley Marvellous! wonderful! I rejoice & yet I dread I hardly Know why Either—Lord Charles Fitzwilliam[221] came by invitation from Claudius into our Tent and took wine & some refreshment with us—he seemed to Enjoy it—he spent a few hours with us he is returning from California—he was Entirely clothed in buckskin from head & feet—like a Mountaineer—I told him I should like to see him walk into some of the splendid drawing rooms of London—how the ladies would stare—Memo, first saw a Splendid bearded Comet on the 22nd of August—1853—A death in Camp—Vincent T. O. very poorly—I in low spirits—thinking him worse—This death makes me feel gloomy—All were to be off as soon as a wheel was mended The funeral had taken place We set off—T. O. improved as we went along, and before Evening I saw a decided change for

---

221. Charles William Wentworth Fitzwilliam was the son of Earl Fitzwilliam, a member of the English Parliament. Like Hannah King, Lord Fitzwilliam was originally from Cambridgeshire. He was traveling to Fort Laramie.

the better Sister Neslen brought him some broth which did him good—All were Kind he has lost his Voice & cannot articulate a word—thro' excessive talking while delirious—Bertha lost her hearing in her attack—both mountain fever—To day we passed the splendid Rocky Mountains Truly, they are "the everlasting hills"—they are immensely high & look as if piled up by Giants and some huge stones thrown down—We passed Green River 3 times & saw several Indians—an Indian Village and a multitude of Horses—One of the sisters strayed off & lost her way & fell in with them They took her money & looked for earrings & jewels—but when the Chief heard of it he whipped them, and made them restore all they had taken & then saw her home himself to our Camp!—Good for him—had a duck for dinner at 6 oc or later—chatted around the Camp fire then to bed—but my rest was troubled—heard the wolves howling close to us—had a watch to guard.—

30th Rose & got off Early T. O. mending Thank God! Sandy road saw some graves—S. N. came & drove for me a little while—he is ever kind Claudius & I by no means happy together—why I hardly Know—but I do not feel that he fills the place of one Son to me yet & he desired two—to which I am not yet reconciled—Oh! may the Lord reveal His will to me—Mr King is better—he is Kind & Good in many ways—tho' no Mormon—How often I think of my own dear Parents—and their Love for me!!

31st Rose after a good night which is something as times go—Felt happy & refreshed—Temperance in all things sweetens Life!—set off on our daily trip—the wind blowing a perfect hurricane Crossed Green River 3 times before 12 oc!! What a serpentine affair it is!—Camped—I hope not for the night—One of the Sisters is ill so we wait for her—how foolish of women to be in that way on Such a Journey as this! but some people consider nothing but their own appetites Bah!! T. O. better Thank God! Most heartily do I thank Him—Saw several graves this morning.

1st Sept. Thomas Robinson's birthday I wish he was here with all my heart—he would be a great Comfort to us all—This has been a long day's travel to us—camped at Sweet Water Creek—in a perfect basin—Got in late—and then off to bed feeling cold & the carriage not placed nicely or comfortably—but these things are trifles—Which by the by "Make the Sum of human-things"—Came over mountains high & ridgey—They are truly named "Rocky Mountains" for they were nothing but rocks piled up. T. O. mending but still slowly—very weak. The Saints are all Kind—The Children i e the girls assemble round my carriage every morning Just before I start to ask how he is—and to bring him flowers &c—Kind little things! Only 240 miles from the Valley!! 'Tis wonderful! I seem I cannot realize it—

Sept 2nd Rose after a tolerable night—T. O. somewhat better—The Cattle all tired out—Set off in the morning & come on 7 miles & here we are camped at Willow Creek.—We wait to day Yesterday Sister Jones[222] was confined with a daughter amid Thunder & Lightening—I should think something of it were it my case—We often get wild ducks & hares & other game which I like very much but I pine for the Valley—

Sept 7th Lovely morning—We are Camped in a nice place.—We are just going off—I have not Journalized for some days—perhaps it's as well—for my mind has been shook up into a muddle by what I see going on around me, but I hope all will be well—& that the Lord will reveal His Will to me, & then I shall be able to obey We have seen such a number of dead oxen it makes me sad We have lost one thro' carelessness perhaps before we get to the Valley we shall be taught the folly of such neglect

Sept 8th Just going to start this morning when came that Sister Sutton was shot in the arm accidently of course—Br Spencer went to administer to her & Sister Neslen to bind up the wound—We travelled late & met Br Decker with the Mail from

---

222. A Jones family is listed in the company roster. The mother's name is either Emma or Mary Ann.

the Valley—Claudius gave them some wine coming to ask me for it nearly a week has passed & I have not bidden S. N. good night! I suppose it could not be—but I miss his kind "bless you" which ever does me good—The road pretty good the last few days prospect wild were it not for the Lovely Skies and pure atmosphere it would be bleak indeed but they are something Heavenly!—different to any thing we ever saw in England— Reminds me of Byron's exclamation, "So cloudless clear, & purely beautiful, that God alone was to be seen in Heaven"![223] T. O. mending fast tho' he cannot speak! he has been very very ill!—I had a dream this morning that I was pulling out one of his teeth that was horribly decayed—Which I don't like—

Sept 10th Yesterday we travelled till quite late & passed some splendid bluffs ruins—These Bluffs are something I cannot describe They are Sublime & Mysterious—There is beauty and order in them—and it requires no very fanciful stretch of imagination to form Baronial buildings—"Keeps"—gateways, &c &c— & Georgey even made "The Porter" looking over the Gate!! They are very high—I should like to hear a philosophical discription of them—They please and interest me more than I have language to express—There is much design in them—yet they say they are solely the work of Nature—Well I must leave them like all mysterious things—T. O. mending up to last night when he had an attack of diarhea Could my dream portend this?—I trust he will do well yet—but he is very delicate tho' he has an immense appetite for Eating—Last evening S. F. N. came & had a nice chat with me which I enjoyed much—This morning we started at 9 oc & went only 2 miles—Camped to feed the Oxen here being some food & water—Black's Fork being the name—We now are going on for Fort Bridger—We saw the smoke from it last night—The air here is so pure and rarified and the sky lovely

---

223. From Byron's poem "The Dream."

Louie not very well—I expect her mind is bothered about what she shall do and I expect C. V. is always after her either by a "dumb expression" or otherwise and she "halts between two opinions"—Well I shall leave it but as I now feel I shall never give her to him—if it must be it will only be to Georgey that I can ever give her—& she is a gem of the first water, and she is worthy of all I can do for her, or her husband either—I only hope he appreciates her!—he ought to—here is another Saturday [September 10]—how fast time flies!

Sept 17th I have not had a moment to Journalize the past week—I would fain recall a few things We have passed beautiful & sublime scenery, Echo Canyon especially—that surpasses every thing I have yet seen before—and some spots yesterday I felt I could live and die in! but here we have truly "no continuing city"

Sept 15th Last Thursday was a day of days! The iron belonging to the whipple tree of the Carriage broke—I called to Anthony[224] to come and assist me & Mr King went on—Br Spencer then detained him to help mend the road—Soon Claudius & I went on—When we soon saw one of our waggons overturned! The very one T. O. was in on acct of his enfeebled health Oh! the agony I suffered till we got up to it & found he was safe & well—Darling Georgey, with her every prompt kindness came towards the Carriage leading him gently along to let me see he was safe blessed children!! how dear they were to my poor heart!—even then the Excess of Joy was as hard to bear—but suffice 'twas a moment of agony that I shall long remember We soon got the waggon over & all right again and we camped close by—S. N. came back as they were sent forward in the Evening!—he ever does me good by his Manly comfort—days passed over after this—beautiful Bluffs—beautiful Kanyons & some things that were any thing but beautiful—sorrows & troubles & tears! &c

---

224. Possibly Anthony L. Anthony, a member of the company.

&c were mixed up with the beauties of nature Our Carriage Horses gave out—perfectly worn down We had oxen put to our Carriage—but on Sunday the two Brs Cahoon[225] met us & put to our Carriage their horses & at last on Monday 19th of Sept 1853 we entered the Valley of the Great Salt Lake!!! the goal for which we had so long panted—and were set down at Br Daniel Spencer's [the father of Claudius Spencer]—found her pleasant and kind— she provided for us a delicious supper and was very hospitable— felt tired—worn & exhausted—Dear Georgey has been ill some days very ill to day[226] The company did not come in with us Lost therefore our kind friends & fellow travellers, the Neslens—and I ever miss kind friends—They are scarce!

Louise Graehl's story of coming west began in Geneva, Switzerland, where she and her husband ran a confectionary shop. She claimed to have been the first woman in Geneva to join the Church when she was baptized in 1853. She and her husband and their three young daughters traveled the next year to the United States and continued on to Utah in the Robert Campbell company. Her account is brief but shows the interdependence of women on the trail and their self-reliance in the face of adversity.

---

225. Probably two of the elder sons of Reynolds Cahoon.
226. Georgiana ("Georgey") died 26 September 1853, just a week after reaching the Valley.

LOUISE CHARLOTTE LEUBA GRAEHL[227]

I *WAS BORN IN GENEVA, SWITZERLAND* on the 15th of September, 1822. Both my parents died when I was quite young and I went to live with her [my mother's?] dear old friend, Mrs. Maurice, "Aunty," as I called her. I was married to George L. Graehl on the 31st of August, 1844. We kept a confectionery store. Ten years had passed since our marriage when we lost a sweet little girl, Emma, just fifteen months old. At the funeral I had a visit from the minister of the ward [Church] in which we lived and another minister of the Christian Church, who came to comfort us, but they could not tell me if my sweet baby was saved, for they said there was no provision in the Bible for the salvation of children, but that we may hope that the Lord would take care of them. This time I felt indignant at their speech for in my heart I was sure that my little angel was all right and that those ministers knew nothing.

Sometime after this Mr. Roulst, one of our acquaintances, came and spoke to me about a new religion that he had just embraced. He seemed to be full of joy and said many things about the great light he had received; but I must confess that I paid very little attention to all that he said for I had known him only as a man of the world and I thought it very funny to have him speak that way about religion. At that time I did not care for any religion anyhow. However, he continued to talk and one day he brought me some pamphlets to read. They were on the first principles of the Gospel, and I was astonished in reading them, for they threw a new light on the Scriptures that I had read so often, but not understood before.

I was baptized into the Latter-day Saint Church on the 7th of June, 1853, being the first woman in Geneva to join the

---

227. "Story of Louise Graehl," in Carter, *Treasures of Pioneer History* 4:56–59.

church, and my husband was baptized one month later. It was arranged that the first emigration of the Switzerland saints should start for Utah on the 7th day of February, 1854, so we sold our business, with considerable loss, and got ourselves ready for the long journey. On that memorable day we got up early for we had to start at eight o'clock in the morning. Our three little girls, Eliza, Fanny and Adeline who had expected to take their pretty dolls along, at the last moment had to kiss them a tearful goodbye, for it was found impossible to make room for them. At the station we found a few very dear friends who had come that cold morning to bid us goodbye. My heart was sad for I was leaving forever the city of my birth.

On the 12th of March we boarded the John M. Wood which was to take us across the Atlantic. We were seven and a half weeks on the sea. We were very glad to arrive in New Orleans where we parted with some of our fellow travelers. Without even getting a look at the beautiful city, we were ushered on a steamboat that was to transport us to St. Louis. We were twelve days on that boat. After eight days in St. Louis we took another steamboat for Kansas where we were to begin our camping life. This was indeed something new for us. The fixing of tents under the trees in the wood, the building of a campfire, the baking of our bread in baking kettles, the washing of our clothes, and the tending of our baby boy just learning to walk were sometimes trying to one who had hardly ever cooked a meal, mixed bread or washed clothes. But, though some of the work was hard and many were the privations that we were beginning to feel, we still felt happy.

Eliza, my oldest girl and constant companion, died and was buried in a lonely grave in the wilderness. They made a fine coffin of black walnut and six young ladies of our company carried my lost treasure to her final resting place. Not even a flower was found to put on her bier, but we made a wreath of wild grape leaves.

Little Fanny was very sick with the dread disease[228] and we were very much afraid that we were going to have to part with her, too; and as we were going to move our camp, we asked the brethren to come and anoint her and pray that if she was to die, we would rather have her buried with her sister. The next morning she was better and, though it took quite a long time to get her restored to health, still she lived to come to Utah and is living at the time of this writing.

It was the beginning of July that our tiresome journey across the plains begun. We found out when we were ready to start that we lacked many things that would be needed on the road and that it would be difficult to procure them. Father had met some people who had discouraged him, and one fine afternoon, taking his trunk and his gun, he started for the village, where he had not been able to coax me to remain. I was afraid of the country, for there were many apostates around, and I had not left my beautiful country to make my home anywhere outside of Zion.

That afternoon was a sad one for me, for I felt bad for my husband and didn't know how I could manage to travel alone with my children. The sisters came and comforted me promising that I would certainly be helped. But, in the evening, my husband came back having met a good brother who promised him that he would procure the desired articles and so we resumed our journey.

We had been traveling a few days. I was in the wagon with my three little ones, when all at once we had a stampede. Our team composed of two yokes of oxen and another one, started running in the grass that at that place was about five feet high. Sometimes the wagons came near wrecking each other, then again the animals ran in different directions not seeming to feel any trouble at pulling their heavy loads. At last they stopped, our

---

228. Probably cholera, which was rampant that year.

companion losing one yoke of oxen that could not be found again. After such a scare we were glad to walk to camp, but it was not so easy for me for I had to carry a little girl in one arm and a baby in the other and to find my way through the high grass. I was very much afraid that I would trample on a rattlesnake.

We arrived in camp at last—it was past dinnertime. The good sisters came to welcome us and gave us some dinner. But the next day and for quite a long time I could not persuade the children to ride in the wagon, and as for myself, I had to help father drive. I tell you it was a pretty hard job to help drive through the long summer day with a baby in my arms and another at my side crying to be carried but after a time we had no more runaways and the children rode in the wagon.

Well, we had many adventures in crossing the plains; they would fill a volume if we could write them all. My husband had not been well since we left the old country and now he became worse and had to keep to his bed in the wagon so I had to drive. That was all right for some of the sisters helped, but what made it hard for me was that we had a yoke for the oxen that was not strong enough. It was tied with buckskin strings that would wear out and break at any time causing me much trouble. Once, for instance, it was dusk and we were a little behind the company when our yoke broke and our oxen ran away to camp about two miles off. There we were right in the road, obliged to stay alone until some good brother, by chance meeting our oxen, had the kindness to come to our rescue. I could not light a fire for I had no materials so I sat in the front seat holding my axe in my hands ready to try to defend myself and dear ones from the wolves who were howling all around. So I waited until midnight when some brothers came for me. They made a fire to scare the wolves away and we slept, by turn, until morning.

Another time there was a river to cross, and again it was toward evening and we were the last of the company. There was no one to help us as our captain was absent. "What are you going to do?" called dear father from his bed. "I am going to drive right over and the Lord will help us," I answered, and we did it all right. At camp, in the evening, the captain went around to find out who had helped Sister Graehl. Well, it was the last night before we reached Salt Lake City. It had been snowing and it was dark before we stopped for the night. That night I could not get any wood to light a fire nor could I bake bread. The next day we mixed sugar with flour and ate it raw. The same night a little child was born in the camp. The next day we arrived in Salt Lake. It was with a sad heart that I parted with many of our traveling companions who had been so kind and obliging to me in my trouble.

It was October, 1854, that we arrived and we immediately started in search of rooms in which to live. After much trouble we found two small rooms—then we had to buy a stove. We had to pay twenty-two dollars in gold for a little sheet iron stove and nine dollars for about five feet of pipe. We had no wood to burn and wood was very expensive. Some one had taken charge of our oxen out in the country for the winter or else I could have rented them to some party that would have brought me plenty of wood to burn and money besides. I only found that out too late, and as I had only a little money left, I did not like to spend it for wood. I had noticed how many people seemed to be careless about picking up their chips, so I took a gunny sack early every morning and filled it and that lasted us all day. But by and by, when the chips got frozen under the snow, I could not pick them up anymore, but I found a way of getting wood by renting our wagon.

Isaiah Moses Coombs, a second-generation Mormon (his parents joined the Church before his birth in 1834), poignantly describes the emotional turmoil of leaving his young wife a year after their marriage in order to join the Saints in Utah. Married in 1854 when he was just twenty, Isaiah, a new school-teacher, felt the pull of the gathering and consulted with apostle Erasmus Snow in St. Louis about emigrating to Utah. His wife, Sarah Turk Coombs, pregnant with their first child, would not convert and refused to leave their home in Columbia, Illinois. Isaiah was appointed company clerk in Isaac Allred's company. He eventually remarried and became a teacher. He also supervised the tithing office for seventeen years. His diary is introspective and emotional, revealing the compelling draw of the gospel.

ISAIAH MOSES COOMBS[229]

AFTER A NIGHT'S REFLECTION on the subject, sleeping none, praying much, I decided to go with the emigration to Utah, be the final decision of my wife what it might. "Very well," said Bro. [Erastus] Snow, "that is as I would have decided myself. It is the best thing you can do." Accordingly, on my return home [to Columbia] I represented to Sarah how my affairs stood. I told her that the only course left for me to pursue was to go among the people whose cause I had espoused and cast my lot with theirs and that I had resolved to go that spring, and to start in a very few days. Said I, "You are my wife and as such your place is by my side. I shall expect you to accompany me." She wept long and bitterly, calling on me to renounce Mormonism

---

229. This account is a summary of his journal (microfilm of holograph, LDS Church Archives) and was published as "From the Journal and Diary of Isaiah Moses Coombs," in Carter, *Our Pioneer Heritage* 1:321–408.

and stay with her. "Your school," said she, "will soon be full
again when the people learn that you are no longer a Mormon,
and beside this there are many positions of honor and profit
open to you if you will but identify yourself with the people." At
the close of our interview I felt more desolate than ever for I
knew that there was but one course for me to pursue and it
seemed more evident than ever that in pursuing that course I
should have to sever myself from the dearest object of my affections. What made me feel worse than anything else was the
knowledge that in a few months my wife would become a mother,
and that during the most trying and critical period of a woman's
life she would be without a husband's sustaining arm and tender
care. But I thought of all of this before I made up my mind. I
had counted the cost and I was ready for the sacrifice. I dismissed
my little school and in sadness and silence prepared for my long
and lonely journey.

At length the day arrived, the hour when the parting hand
must be taken. Father, brothers and sisters bade me good-bye but
they looked forward to a joyous meeting, distant perhaps, but
sure, when they should follow me to the gathering place of the
Saints, and this thought was an anchor to the soul; but when I
came to part with my wife, my heart sank like lead within me.
Henceforth, we were to see each other no more in this life. Such
was the thoughts of my anguished soul as I pressed her to my
aching heart. That ordeal was passed in silence. No word was spoken. Hurrying away I entered the wagon that was waiting, buried
my face in my hands, and looked not up again until Columbia
and all its near and dear associations were left far behind. If I had
not turned to a pillar of salt or ice, the sight of my beloved wife
standing in the door would have melted my heart within me and
I should have returned, and thereby braved the displeasure of the
Almighty and perhaps have yielded little by little to the voice of
the tempter until I, with her, should have been eternally lost and
shut out from the presence of God and the holy Angels. The

responsibilities resting upon me were too great. My father, brothers, and sisters tied hand and foot in Babylon with the iron chain of poverty, looked to me as a deliverer; they expected me to go ahead and open the way for them to come. A long line of ancestors who had died without the gospel in the ages past were calling to me with their spirit voices and bidding me go up and assist in rearing a temple wherein to officiate for them that they might come up and receive blessings equally with the living. And last, though not least was the consideration that I was obeying the voice of God and that I was taking a course that would secure my own glory and exaltation and that would eventually either in this life or that which is to come enable me to bind my wife to me in bands that could not be broken. She was blind then but the day would come when she would see.

The thirteen miles that intervened between Columbia and St. Louis were soon travelled over. I went immediately to Pres. E. Snow's[230] office on the corner of Washington Avenue and Fourth Street and was received by him with open arms.

I was informed that a company of Saints would start up the river in a few days and that I could go with it. But the few days lengthened out to two weeks before we started. I spent the time writing in the office, visiting among the Saints and walking about the city with my brother Hyrum who was learning the printer's trade in the office of "The Luminary," a weekly paper published by Bro. Snow. Here I counted my money and valued my clothing and found myself worth just one hundred dollars. Ten dollars of that I handed over to the church clerk as a commencement of my tithing, the receipt of which is carefully kept among my papers.

Finally on Tuesday the 8th day of May, I embarked with a large company of Saints on board the Golden State bound for Atchison, Kansas, the outfitting point for the overland journey

---

230. Apostle Erastus Snow presided over the Church in the Midwest from 1854 to 1856. During this time he published the *St. Louis Luminary* for a year and established Mormon Grove, Kansas, in 1855.

to Salt Lake. Nothing worthy of record occurred on this trip. We were just eight days in making it. We found many large camps of Saints scattered on the prairie near Atchison, outfitting for their journey across the plains. Far as the eye could reach in every direction were to be seen the tents of Israel with their vast herds of cattle grazing on the rolling prairie. The largest of these encampments was out about twelve miles from the river at what was known as "Mormon Grove." All the camps finally centered around this point near which a large tract of land was taken up by the church which the emigrants fenced and cultivated, but which was soon afterwards jumped by some rascally gentiles. I soon found employment, first as a herdsman, then as cook for the returning elders of the Church, and finally as clerk and collecting agent for the Superintendents of the Emigration, Elders Daniel Spencer, R[ichard]. Ballantyne and Erastus Snow. In these several capacities I labored and toiled heart-sick and weary for over two long months. I think during all that time I received but one letter from my wife. In the performance of my duties as collecting agent, I had to make frequent trips to Atchison. These trips were nearly always performed on foot and frequently when I could scarcely stand for bodily weakness. But I did not complain and no one suspected how much I suffered.

One hot afternoon I was sitting in the tent humped up over my writing suffering from a severe attack of cholera morbus. My suffering was excruciating. While I sat thus Elder Daniel Spencer came to the tent door leading a horse by its bridle. "Here Bro. Coombs" said he. "I wish you would mount this horse and take a ride about twelve miles out to the little Grasshopper where Bro. [Jacob] Seicrist's[231] company will camp tonight and borrow some money for Bro. Snow." I answered that I could not possibly—that

---

231. Brother Jacob F. Secrist had just returned home from a mission to Europe and was made captain of the second company heading west that year (1855). He contracted cholera and died 2 July 1855 on Little Blue River, near Ft. Kearney (now in Nebraska).

I was racked with pain and had made up my mind to die that night. "Oh, no," replied Bro. Spencer. "You shall not die—you will have a pleasant canter over the prairie and I promise you in the name of the Lord that you shall return feeling much better and that you shall be sick no more till you get home."

With that promise I allowed him to help me into the saddle, and after receiving my instructions proceeded slowly and wearily to wend my way through the encampment till I reached the highway on the prairie. Here I gave my horse the rein and just as the sun was sinking beyond the western horizon I started off on a keen gallop for the distant Grasshopper. The first few jumps of my steed occasioned me great pain, but I hung on to the pommel of the saddle determined that that ride should either cure or kill me. I had not gone far before all pain left me. Thereupon a wild, reckless spirit took possession of me and putting spurs to my horse I dashed along the road at headlong speed, whooping and yelling as I went. But I continued not in that mood a great while. On reaching a grove of timber I dismounted and on my knees returned thanks to God for this manifestation of His loving kindness to me. I there promised if He would forgive the luke-warm service I had hitherto rendered him that I would in future give Him my whole heart. I arose feeling that I stood on holy ground, remounted my horse and pursued my journey. I came up with Capt. Seicrist's company just as they were camping for the night. I spent the night in the captain's tent, formed a pleasant acquaintance with him. Next morning I transacted the business with which I was intrusted and started on my return just as the company was striking their tents. I never saw Captain Seicrist again as he died of overwork on the journey and was buried by the wayside.

At last what was known as the Church train was being fitted out for the journey and I was to accompany it. One of the Salt Lake missionaries, a Bro. Gregory, had died at the Grove on his return home from the Eastern States where he had been to get some means that had been left him by some relative, and his body was to be taken to his family in a metallic coffin. A light wagon was selected for this purpose and two yoke of young half broken cattle were purchased to draw the same. This wagon and team with Bro. Gregory's body and effects were placed in my care with instructions to take them to the family of the deceased in the far off city of Salt Lake. Bro. Snow helped me yoke my wild team and hitch them to the wagon and as I was a new hand entirely with an ox team, never having before handled one, he condescended to drive out half a mile for me on the road. The train had got the start of me and were at least two miles ahead. I had taken the precaution to tie a rope to the horns of my near leader and was taking hold of this when Bro. Snow bade me goodbye. Away I started July 28, 1855, an independent teamster bound for Utah. I went on gloriously for a time, but alas! the chain that connected my leaders with the tongue of the wagon broke. I managed to stop my team but in trying to toggle my chain together one of the oxen took a notion to kick up its heels and have a run, and as I was in the way I received one hoof in my stomach which sent me to the grass breathless, perfectly hors du combat,[232] and away the leaders ran in the direction of the train that was now about a mile ahead and in plain sight followed by the other yoke with the wagon. As soon as I could recover my breath I started in pursuit as fast as possible. It did not take us long at this rate to overtake the train and some of the brethren soon helped me recover my refractory team. Fortunately they had kept the road and as it lay over a level prairie no harm had been done.

That evening we camped on the Big Grasshopper and next day returned to the Grove with our teams to draw out some more wagons and this we did also the next day. We had not more than one third enough teams to draw the wagons that had been

---

232. *Hors du combat*, properly written, is *hors de combat*. The translation is "disabled" (French).

assigned us but we had been promised some more in a few days. But we got no more teams and at the end of two weeks dragging through the mud we had to leave ten wagons by the side of the road. Even then we were too heavy loaded, and after breaking one wagon down in a mud hole, we left three more. The wagons then left were all loaded with church property: books, clothing, steam engine, etc. Even after this we dragged along but slowly. I have often wondered how Bro. Snow could have had the heart to start out a train so late in the season and so illy provided with teams. A thousand miles of weary travel lay before us. We labored under another disadvantage which proved to be a serious one before we got through. We were the last train on the road. Scores of large emigrant and merchant trains had traversed the road before us and their teams had eaten out the grass so thoroughly on the line of travel that our poor oxen had hard fare indeed. In many localities the ground was full of alkali and as the grass was short many of our cattle got alkalied and were left behind to die. Of the four oxen that I started with not one lived to reach Salt Lake. Our company numbered 61 souls including the women and children. Out of this number two died. One, an old man, died and was buried on the banks of the Little Blue. The other, quite a young man, Joseph Redfern, fell off his wagon tongue and was run over, which caused his death in two or three hours. This was as we were crossing Scotts Bluff, and we buried him that night on Horseshoe Creek.

Isaac Allred, a returning missionary, was Captain of our company, James Pace was his counsellor and Jas. C. Sly was captain of the guard. The last two named were also returning missionaries and all three were fine men. We dragged slowly and wearily along. We at last got into the mountains and found better feed for our poor animals in the shape of bunch grass, but as it grows high upon the sides of the mountains, it was hard work for them to get at it. The scenery was now more diversified and grand and travelling actually seemed less laborious than when we traversed the unbroken plain. At last we reached and crossed Green River. Here we found ourselves compelled to call a halt, and send on to the valleys for assistance. Capt. Allred, myself and eight others of the brethren remained with ten wagons and all the worn out cattle while the rest pushed on for Salt Lake. We grubbed willows out of the midst of a dense thicket and here we had a picturesque camp where we spent two long and tedious weeks. During that time our provisions ran out entirely, but were again replenished from the camp of a trapper in the vicinity whom Capt. Allred accidentally found one morning while hunting for game. At length on the evening of the fourteenth day a solitary horseman was seen approaching our camp at a swift gallop from away toward the west. It proved to be the eldest son of our Captain with the news that Bishop Abraham O. Smoot was at hand with plenty of cattle and provisions.

It was a joyous meeting of father and son after a separation of over three years, and we, who had never before seen the boy, was scarcely less glad to meet him for the news he brought us. We were now, of course, in the midst of the Rocky mountains, those grand, old rock ribbed hills I had read of as a boy and my heart throbbed with wild joy as I trod their lofty summits or walked in the deep vales and canyons between them. Old winter was coming on apace. It was late in October that we abandoned our friendly willow camp and set our faces once more homeward. It was a cold, windy, snowy day. Mountains were already shrouded in snow half way to their base and the wind that came sweeping down from those dizzy heights was piercing cold. I was placed in charge of about ten yoke of our worn out cattle that could but just creep along and with a sick man placed in my wagon was appointed to bring up the rear. Long before night I found myself in the rear and my cattle almost ready to lie down in the road with fatigue. With the helpless man in my wagon I felt far more lonely than if I had been entirely solitary. I tried to grope my way but the road was so completely covered with the drifting sand that

I was completely baffled. I accordingly let the oxen take their own course and plodded on by their side bewildered and anxious not knowing whether I was travelling east or west. At last, I observed a light in the distance which proved to be the camp fires of my friends and soon I heard the friendly shouts of brethren who had been sent back to help me on.

And thus we toiled on through snow and sand drifts, threading canyon after canyon, climbing mountain after mountain for eleven weary days. Fort Bridger was left in the distance, and at last standing on the dizzy top of Big Mountain we caught a glimpse of the distant valley of the Great Salt Lake, the home of the Saints. Our hearts swelled with joy at the sight and we gave vent to our feelings in three hearty cheers. That was the last night that we spent in the mountains. When I arose next morning I threw from my blankets at least six inches of snow. By noon we had gained the bench land that overlooks the lovely city of the Saints with the lake from which it derives its name sleeping in the distance. Date Nov. 2, 1855.

With so much to tell, Christian Nielsen somehow condenses in a single letter to his family in Denmark a compelling story of his travels to Utah and the life he made for himself and family as converts to the Church. Such letters had to bridge time and distance to keep together families that the gospel had separated. Only a portion of the letter follows. A model of comprehensive and informative correspondence, it continues on for many pages offering a detailed description of the Sanpete Valley where the Nielsens settled, the Indians of that area, and his experiences establishing a home and farm in Manti, Utah.

CHRISTIAN NIELSEN[233]

MANTI CITY, Sanpete Valley, Utah Territory,

April 27, 1856.

To Fisherman Carl Nielsen,

Dear Brother-in-law, brothers and sisters, brother, son, family, friends, old neighbors and acquaintances and everyone who might be interested in hearing from us. We greet you all with loving and friendly greetings in the name of our Lord and Saviour Jesus Christ. Amen.

We don't know if you have had any news from us since we left Denmark. In the summer of 1854 we wrote a letter to a man who lived close to Vejle,[234] but he was on his way to this country before the letter could reach its destination, so we don't know if the letter has come to his successor or not. In the future—as long as it is the will of God that we shall live and He will grant us His grace— we shall write a letter once or twice a year to our family, but not to everyone each time. First of all, we want to tell you how we are. You probably believe that we are dead, but we are, thanks be to God, alive and are living well; we are all healthy, bodily and spiritually; we own our own home and land, cattle and tools to till the soil; for the time we have five head of cattle, besides calves etc., about 27 acres of land, and two lots of about 3 acres which we use as a garden. We have a deed to this. In the city in which we live, we have a lot for our houses, room for our cattle and grain and a small flower garden. On this lot we have up till now built five houses, and this coming summer we expect to build two

---

233. "A Pioneer Writes Homes," in Carter, *Our Pioneer Heritage* 11:231–42. The original, written in Danish, is in the LDS Church Archives.

234. Christian Nielsen's birthplace and home of many of his relatives.

more. The house which faces the street, and which will be at least
two stories high we cannot manage to do. I hope that my son
Niels Emanuel will come and help me build it, and with the help
of God I shall keep him to build two. Fritz is our farm hand and
a little girl whom we had with us from home is with us most of
the time. Our daughter Sophie is not with us here, but remained
in the capitol—Salt Lake City—when passing through there. It is
150 miles north of us, where she was married January 13, 1855,
to a young man, Jacob Knudsen, from the island of Funen.[235] I
expect that they will settle here this coming summer. In this town
there are about 300 Danish families, and 7 miles to the north
are almost just as many.

We have hundreds of things to tell you, but space does not
permit us. First of all we wish to tell you that the journey to the
valley was a very good one for us. We left Liverpool January 16,
1855, dropped the anchor at the mouth of the Mississippi March
7, and we stayed here until the 14th as the ship on which we were
went too deep; 1400 sacks of salt were thrown overboard; two
steamships tried to pull it out, but to no avail, and the ship was
grounded, and we had to stay there during the night. In the
morning the water had risen, and the steamers hauled us for
about 4 miles, where we anchored, and stayed there until sunset, when a steamer came with another frigate, and took our ship
along, one on each side, and we arrived in New Orleans on
March 17th, 100 miles. On the 19th we went aboard a steamship
which was to take us to St. Louis, 1200 miles, and we arrived
there on the 29th. Our travel on the Mississippi was very interesting, varying with forest, beautiful houses, gardens and lovely
cities. The houses were surrounded with flowers and fruit trees in
the most beautiful bloom; oranges and lemons were hanging on
the trees in the plantations where Negroes worked and plowed

---

235. A large island in Denmark off the eastern coast of the mainland.

and the Negro women drove the plows. The birds were singing, and in each place we sailed by women and children, well dressed, greeted us with white handkerchiefs; there was only arable land where the forest was destroyed by fire, and in several places the forest was on fire. We stayed about a month in St. Louis. Towards evening on April 30 we boarded a steamer which took us 200 miles further up the Mississippi to Keokuk [Iowa] where we arrived in the evening of May 1st. Here was a very large camp of English, Welsh, Americans and Danes etc. and here were also many hundreds of wagons and tents.

Here we received wagons, tents, and oxen. Every day companies came and left; it was very lively and the surroundings lovely. The forests, for the most part oak and all kinds of fruit trees and vines were blooming. We now had to live in our wagons which were covered with canvas, and tents where we slept as well as in a house. We were given four oxen, one wagon and a tent. On the 21st we started on our journey. In the beginning it went slowly as the oxen were not acquainted with us, and we not with them, as the way in which they drive them here is entirely different from the Danish way. They pull with a yoke of trees which is placed on the neck of them in which there is an iron brace to put the wagon ring in; there are four oxen, the first ones pull in an iron chain. It can be removed in a minute. They are steered with a whip and some very definite words which the oxen know, and in this way from eight to ten pair of oxen are steered by one driver. This form of transportation is common in North America. Our wagon is of excellent quality and solid and is far superior to the Danish. We traveled through the state of Iowa to Kanesville at the Missouri River, and arrived there on June 25th, about 360 miles. The country through which we traveled was sparsely settled; a few towns and houses, many miles apart, but boundless grass fields of the very best kind. Our oxen became fat, fields and forests were full of fruit. The roads were very poor. Here we received supplies for the remainder of the journey, and were ferried across the river. It took us to July 12th before we were ready to travel further. We were now in the State of Nebraska. The country was unsettled. We traveled for a couple of days and came to a river called Loop [Loup] Fork, across which we were ferried. On August 2nd we came to a place where there were buffaloes and the very biggest. In the afternoon of the 5th I went hunting for buffaloes together with some other men, but the time was too short. The camp broke up, and we had to return. We went up into the mountains where we could see a great plain, full of buffaloes. There were several thousands of them besides deer, antelopes, wolves, etc. We camped for the first time on August 4th on the banks of the La Platte River, viz. on the north side. We traveled along it for about 500 miles to Fort Laramie where we crossed the river to the southern bank; in this fort there were soldiers to protect the emigrants against attacks from the Indians. Lately we had previously been visited by the Indians who are always begging and stealing. We often came across gold diggers returning from California, mostly riding, driving mules before them. On July 31st we met among others a man from Kiel Germany; he had been a soldier in Copenhagen, but during the Schleswig War he had joined the insurgents. Until the middle of August we had fine grass for our cattle, but now it began to become less fine, and sometimes we had to travel for two or three days before the oxen could graze. We lost one of our oxen and had to drive with three. Once in a while the road was sandy; oxen and cows lay dead by the thousands at the roadside. The road and the country were strewn with carriage fittings—the wood was burned—bedding, clothing, kitchen ware, guns etc. I wish to say here, that before us 12,000 emigrants had traveled to California. They are the ones who burn the wagons when their cattle die, to join the others, as otherwise they will have to stay. The Mormons do not burn their wagons, they help each other; does a person lose his oxen, the others come to his rescue; is anything broken, the whole company will have to wait until it is repaired; generally speaking there are blacksmiths and other craftsmen in the company. The blacksmiths set up their workshop, and in a short while everything is fixed. Nothing is thrown away unless the wagons are overloaded which is often the case, and they have to "throw it overboard." One would think that we could become rich by picking things up in the desert; this is not the case; there might be some who are greedy and cannot stand to see all that iron and clothing lying there; to begin with they pick up everything they see and are running around in the camps to find more. They load it on their wagons and let their oxen drag it along; sometimes they take it along for several hundred miles. More and more is thrown along the road; they can't take it along, and it breaks their hearts; here they see a fine wheel, there a brass kettle, here a pan and there a kitchen range, etc. They have to drive past it; they are stuck in every hole they pass over; the others must help them all the time; at last they get tired of it and leave them behind, as it is generally that kind of people who constantly ask for help, but will help no one else. Here they are sitting now. First of all they try to give the oxen a sound thrashing, but they are overloaded and cannot do it. It irritates them; they take off what they can, and finally they get the wagon out. They load it again; they cannot leave the things behind, they have brought it so far. They now drive on for a distance of a gunshot or two; they are stuck again; they do as before; but they overstrain themselves, the pulse beats intensely, they must leave some of the things behind to their dismay. Thus they are stuck several times, until they have nothing but the empty wagon; the oxen are tired and can neither get food nor water; they cannot be saved and are at once attacked by wolves to which they fall a prey. It is most comical with those who have preceded them, and who are greedy; in the morning they load their backs and are ready to give the whole thing up in the afternoon, as they have to leave it; the next morning they again find something which they feel they must take with them, it is a good piece which they can use for many purposes, sell it at a good price, they make big calculations, until it goes like the day before, and thus it continues every day in such a way that when they arrive in the valleys, they have nothing.

On September 20th we came to a fort called Bridger; here were soldiers from the valleys to protect the emigrants against the Indians; we heard that a war was being fought with them in the valleys and that they had stolen a couple of hundred cattle. We now got up in the mountains where sometimes we journeyed upwards for a couple of days and then downwards, tearing along. In some places the wagon was lowered with ropes. At last we reached the valleys on September 30th; at 8 o'clock in the evening we entered Great Salt Lake City. From Kanesville we had traveled 1,031 miles. One would think that we didn't like to travel any further; no, we at once made up our minds together with several others to proceed to this valley (Sanpete Valley), 150 miles south of here. On October 4th we started on our new journey. We traveled through many settlements; the people were very good to us; they gave us all kinds of things. In Provo a fat cow was killed for us, but the farther south we got the more warlike it looked; all were armed. In Nephi we camped in a place where eight Indians were shot a few days before. From there we traveled through a mountain pass to this valley where we at once came across two wagons, from which the boxes were thrown off, and beside was a trunk that had been broken open, some wheat, several percussion caps, etc. which we gathered and picked up. Here the Indians had killed four of the brethren from this town. The fort in which we were to live was the one from which the Indians had stolen the many head of cattle, and the settlers had left there to go to other places. It was a miserable fort, the walls were poorly made, the houses in uninhabitable condition, and we had to be armed constantly; there were good pastures which could have become wonderful fields, but we were too weak to resist the Indians. My family and I didn't stay very long there. A new mill had to be built in the city and I was recommended to build it as a millwright, and traveled to this place on November 10th. I took the job to build the mill, which by the help of God went very well; it is built Danish style. I made more than $300.00; a dollar is 2 "daler" and 2 "skilling" in Danish money.

The whole journey is in no way dull. Everyone had his special duty. The voyage across the Atlantic Ocean was as pleasant as one could wish. We sailed along the West Indian Islands, between Cuba and Jamaica. At the latter island we stayed on February 24th; it was dead calm. The ship was turning around; it was quite a sight for us to see the sky-high mountains; it was extremely hot, and we perspired extremely.

The journey across the country isn't dull either. In the morning we are busy preparing breakfast and make ourselves ready to go as soon as the horn is blown. At noon we generally camp for about an hour if we can get close to water and grass. Now they are busy preparing dinner, get wood and water; the same thing in the evening. We have to walk most of the way, for our loads are big; is the road good the children and the women ride. I had a widow with two children from the island of Bornholm in my wagon, so I had to walk almost all the way. To economize on my boots I walked barefooted for about 200 Danish miles, or about 800 English miles, and let my beard grow for a long time. Many of us looked awful with sunburnt faces and long beards; my beard was so long that it hung way down on my chest. I was afraid to look in a mirror. The Indians stared at me; they don't have any beard. The weather during Nebraska until we reached Fort Laramie in the middle of the desert was warm with much thundering. In Iowa it was terrible; it is almost impossible to imagine it unless you have seen and heard it yourself; it was lightning constantly day and night, about every other night or day we had thunderstorms the like of which is never heard in Denmark; as a rule it comes and begins with a terrible storm and a whirlwind. The thunder is approaching with awful booms and bangs, the air is one big blaze; the rain is pouring down and fills the tents with water, and many of the tents are blown down. In Nebraska we drove behind the company for a little while when a thunderstorm hit us; the lightning hit us. My wife felt a pressure on her head, my daughter in her chest, and Anders Nielsen who was the driver one on his right arm; those in front fell to the ground; I walked around among them and saw the lightning among us, but didn't feel anything. In the wagon were two children; we opened it very fast; they were lying well and safe. God had protected us.

One of the more colorful individuals who traveled west was Sara Alexander, a young woman of twenty who accompanied her mother, Sarah B. Alexander, her sister, Mary Ada, and brother-in-law, James Finlayson, in the Horace Eldridge company in 1859. Sara became an actress and dancer, performing in the Salt Lake Theatre and later in New York and San Francisco. She also taught dance to the daughters of Brigham Young. Her flair for the artistic is evident in her reminiscent account of the trek west.

SARA ALEXANDER[236]

In June 1859 a very large company of "Saints" started for Utah.

My Mother, my sister and I were among them, my Mother having become in-terested enough to "gather to Zion." We went from Louisville Ky. to St. Louis and from there to a place now

---

236. "A Little Story of the Experiences of Sara Alexander When Crossing the Plains in 1859," (n.d.), typescript copy, Utah State Historical Society.

called Florence in Nebraska. Then it was a barren plain. It was the starting point for the trip across the Great American Desert and was called "Winter Quarters." It looked like a good sized city with all the people assembled for a trip of 500 miles which took three months to accomplish. Each family provided themselves with at least one large canvas covered wagon—some had more according to size of family and funds—and a pair of oxen and a tent. The wagon carried the tent, food, bedding and all necessary belongings for such a journey. *People* had to walk,—at least for a time, until food supplies diminished sufficiently to lighten weight. Then the older people and children could take turns in resting, for the oxen must be cared for. If anything happened to them we would have been in sore straits. The dear, faithful, patient, dumb things slowly plodding along. I preferred to walk rather than burden them with my extra 80! pounds. I look back upon it as a great and not unpleasant experience, traveling across the country in that primitive manner. After the day's journey we halted for the night (they knew just where to stop as previous pathfinders had located the distance so as to camp near a stream of water) the wagons were corralled making a large space inside in the form of a ring with a small opening at each end. This protected the people from Indians.

Guards assigned each night to see that the camp was not surprised by them and that they did not stampede the cattle, which was a trick of the Indians to disable the train from moving on the next day and so be at their mercy. Everything was ordered and carried out with military precision.

Tents were pitched, preparations for the evening meal commenced and every one was busy. My business among the rest of the youngsters was to gather sage brush and "buffalo chips" for fires. Each family prepared its own meals and attended to its own affairs. Each being like a neighbor to the other, just like a town or city, but of course more closely associated. Everything was managed with perfect system. No friction, no interference from each other. It was a perfectly harmonious journey. If any other conditions existed it did not reach my understanding. Of course there were many happenings of which I had no knowledge: everything and everybody, then, was lovely to me. Each wagon or tent represented a family in their own house with their own interests and belongings. It was an interesting sight, the camp making in the evenings. With the country's advancement these picturesque scenes have passed away. When we saw the noted landmark, Chimney Rock, it told us that half our journey was completed. We forded a stream called Laurence Creek, and that too meant we were leaving the greater part of our journey behind us.

We were inspired with renewed energy and spirits, feeling the end was nearer in sight.

Our party of nearly one hundred families was most fortunate in making the long journey without any serious mishaps. No loss of cattle to delay us.

Our marches were promptly made each day. In fact no casualties of any kind. A remarkable trip for there were other trains that experienced many sad happenings.

I was at an age when everything was interesting and beautiful—sufficient to lighten the privations and hardships.

I think at times all humans turn to primitive life and take pleasure in roughing it and that is why men love to emigrate and build up new countries. It is free from responsibilities and conventions.

Of course the leaders had much responsibility in caring for and watching over so many people who had faith in their judgment and ability to guide them to the "Promised Land."

I did not even take in the sense of danger that menaced us

day and night from Indians who were in sight almost all of the time. It was most interest-ing to see them riding like the wind, without saddle or bridle, clinging to their horses and looking as if a part of them. I have watched with wonder and delight, as far as the eye could reach over the vast plains, seeing them disappear in the horizon. It is one of the grandest sights my memory recalls.

The Indians are picturesque and magnificent only in their primitive habitant: in their own environment: civilization and Indians seem out of harmony.

Their wonderful faces and commanding attitude gave them an appearance of superiority. Those real "tommyhawk" savages of those pioneer days were my admiration and fear, and yet I sort of envied them their free and untrammeled life. I shall always be glad I have seen the Indians in their primitive grandeur, in their own country where they were kings and where they dominated so royally. I pity their humiliation in compelling them to become civilized. So much has to be crushed in the march of improvement and in the making of a nation.

To return to the evening meal. I don't think anything ever tasted so delicious and appetizing as those sage-brush cooked meals, in the cool of the evenings and the setting sun was heavenly.

All had an iron oven, a flat bottomed pot with a lid. It held a good sized loaf of bread which was eaten warm with bacon or ham and potatoes, coffee and tea if desired. Mormons did not believe in these two last mentioned expensive luxuries and advised against them. To abstain, was adopted by the majority of the members. It showed faith and a desire to "obey council" which was, "living their religion" and to eliminate tea and coffee is called "the Word of Wisdom." Many did without and many had it with them.

I felt like an old Irish woman who did washing for my mother, who one day said to her, it being Friday and she ate meat, "Why do you eat meat on Friday being a Catholic" she replied "I eat onything I can git, any day and thank the Lord oive got it to eat" and I think there was a good deal of wisdom in that too. There were cows in the party too and we sometimes got a little milk for *our* coffee as a great favor. Canned foods were not then in the market, had they been, how luxuriously we would have fared.

Sometimes a Buffalo would be killed and then we had fresh meat.

We often saw large herds of them. I have seen a whole herd stampede and rush into a stream of water and swim for their lives. They are timid and afraid of the human animal. It was a beautiful sight to see those immense and clumsy looking creatures plunging into the water so many of them at once and swimming with such grace and stateliness. Poor things, they too have been quite banished in the march of civilization across the continent.

After the suppers were over and everything was cleared away as spick and span as army quarters and a long evening before us, the camp fires giving light and warmth, there would be prayers and discourses by the Elders and Teachers, singing with the accompaniments of guitars, violins, cornets and such musical instruments. Those evenings recall memories of the most spiritual and soul-inspiring religious sentiments I EVER experienced.

The vast, open surroundings, our camp which looked like a little dot on the face of the earth, our insignificance and helplessness without Supreme protection, was forced upon the consciousness: the stillness, the vastness, the night with the moon and stars shining over us, (at times when there were moon and stars), was all so overwhelming in its beauty and greatness that a heathen must have been impressed with the presence of a God.

When the night came the beds would be prepared in tents and wagons and all but the watchers had retired for the night and quiet reigned, then was the time that the supremecy of One All Ruling Power was the greatest and grandest. Alone in the stillness with the Supreme Ruler over all, in that apparently boundless space. THOSE were the SERMONS that impressed *me*.

Our sleep was sound, sweet, and refreshing and all were ready in the morning to strike tents and start anew the journey.

Horace S. Eldridge, one of the prominent men in the Church, was the leader of our company.

The road I WALKED over I have since traveled several times in luxurious Pullman trains.[237] I looked at the road and could picture myself as I first traveled it, and with tender recollections.

The railroad company laid their tracks over the same path (the Read & Donner trail)[238] so many weary feet had trod and where hundreds were left on the way.

The sufferings of many of the pioneers who crossed the plains were great. Some frozen to death, some arrived at their destination only to have their limbs amputated because of their being frozen. One hand-cart expedition had sufferings too horrible to repeat. Through mistaken instruction from the emigration agent, they started too late to reach Salt Lake City before the very cold weather set in and that fearful history has been told in the Salt Lake Deseret News.

A hand-cart company left Florence some days before *we* started,[239] and I never saw such enthusiasm and religious ferver as those people displayed, men, women and children. They started with song and almost dancing. Women pushing their carts containing food supplies; they could scarcely hold much besides.

---

237. Named after George Mortimer Pullman, nineteenth-century inventor and railroad car designer, Pullman trains were characterized by their elegance and distinctive features such as sleeping cars, dining cars, and parlor cars.

238. Until 1850, the Mormon pioneers followed the trail of the ill-fated Donner-Reed party of 1846 from Fort Bridger to Salt Lake City. In the fall of 1850 freighters and emigrant companies opted for the route through Parley's Canyon, although some continued to pass through Emigration Canyon.

239. George Rowley's eighth handcart company left Florence, Nebraska, 9 June 1859, five days before James Brown's company.

They were from many foreign nations, the women were used to hard physical labor but I did not like to see it not being used to seeing women doing laborious work, but they were joyously happy, had arrived in America but a short time before and were going to "Zion" the home of the "Saints."

We overtook them on the way and poor things, they were not so hilarious and they looked fagged and worn already but filled with Faith and Hope.

I don't know how they managed about sleeping, their small carts did not look large enough to hold anything sufficient for comfortable rest at night.

It was a company like this that nearly all perished on the way, from the snows and exposures to the severe cold weather. Word got to Salt Lake before they were half way and people with wagons, provisions and warm coverings were sent to meet them.

One incident in particular remains in my memory.

Being tired and perhaps a little rebellious, I sat down on the ground to rest and watched the long train go by and as it finally passed me (the people kept well ahead with the train, especially the women and children) it was a sort of weird sight to see it moving along, the only sounds intruding on the silence were "gee" and "haw" meaning right and left, which the oxen understood and promptly acted upon. I sat there until the last wagon passed.

I thought I would be missed and they would feel sorry for me being so tired and let me ride a little way. I must have looked a forlorn speck sitting there. As the last wagon looked a little distant and left me there alone I felt as if I were in an empty world, and looking off in the distance I saw some Indians rapidly riding in my direction, the first emotion of fear took possession of me, and I made a good run to catch up with my family.

I HAD NOT EVEN BEEN MISSED. WHAT A BLOW. Every one that was able took care of themselves and we were warned to keep close to the train: aside from that little diversion, things went on in the same monotonous way each day.

We heard of a very sad occurrence that happened to one of the companies in crossing. When coming to a stream of water there were trees and wild flowers, it was hard to keep the young girls from wandering too far from the camp, and they, not realizing the dangers, were fearless.

Two young girls wandered off in this fashion when five Indians sprang from some bushes and carried one of them off. The other being further behind was saved from the same fate. The train stopped over several days hoping to rescue her, but they had at last to move on and she was lost to them forever.

We traveled through the homes of noted tribes of Indian warriors. They sometimes came to our camping grounds (every Mormon company had an Indian interpreter) they appeared friendly. They tried to barter for the women and girls, wanted to trade them for ponies.

The Platte river stayed in my memory, we followed it for days, crossed it many times sometimes wading thru if shallow enough: the oxen forded the deeper streams and the men improvised rafts to take the women over: children were placed in the wagons, some of the men wading or swimming over.

How refreshing after a long hot day's journey to come to a cooling stream.

If we did not reach water in time to camp in the evening we would travel into the night: could not stop until there was water.

When nearing the end of the trip expectation was great and enthusiasm ran high.

We entered Salt Lake City by way of Emigration Canyon and the sight of the city in the valley with its white adobe houses and beautiful streams of water, and green trees was indeed a grateful picture.

We had left Florence Neb. in June and we arrived in Salt Lake City Aug. 29, 1859.

So ended the long and weary wandering across the plains.

For thirty-year-old Ulrich Loosli, Zion was not only a spiritual haven but also a material blessing, a place where he could enjoy "the richness that nature affords." He traveled with his wife and two children in the James D. Ross company. In a letter to loved ones in Switzerland, he described the new land in farming terms, noting its productivity and potential commercial value. He also reaffirmed his decision to leave his native land to gather with the Saints in Zion. His letter shows that by 1860 both traveling west and making a home in Utah were easier than a decade earlier.

ULRICH LOOSLI[240]

DEAR BELOVED MOTHER [Barbra Kahser Loosli], Brothers and Sisters in our Lord Jesus Christ:

Once again I take my pen to write to you to give you further information concerning my travels over the plains of America, concerning which you hear so much of in Europe. Also the hardships and inconveniences of the travelers. So I thought I would write some of my own experiences as I found them.

It is 1030 English miles from Florence to Salt Lake Valley. I had a real good wagon, three yoke of oxen, two cows and one calf, which I bought in Florence. Our company consisting of thirty-six wagons left Florence on June 14th, 1860. Our company's captain's name was Br. [James D.] Ross, who was first counselor of

---

240. "A Famous Letter," in Carter, *Our Pioneer Heritage* 11:248–51. This letter also appeared in *Stern*, no. 8 (February 1861).

the European Mission. This company was divided in four sections and each one had a leader. I was appointed captain of the Swiss Company, which consisted of ten wagons. We bought our provisions in Florence, which consisted of flour, ham, bacon, butter, onions, sugar, dried fruit and many other things. We took many cows with us; therefore we had an abundance of milk. During the first five hundred miles the feed for the cattle was plentiful, but as we traveled further the grass became scarce, and so naturally by the time we reached Salt Lake City the cows were nearly dry.

As a rule we traveled fifteen to twenty miles a day. We started at six o'clock in the morning and stopped an hour for lunch at noon. We pitched camp early in the evening, after which each man took care of his oxen, which didn't take very long. The men then gathered wood while the women prepared the evening meal. Everything was done in order. The wagons were drawn in a circle, the tents were placed within the circle and outside of the tents the women did the cooking. The cattle were guarded day and night as a protection against the Indians and to prevent them from straying. Each morning I blew the horn to call the company to prayer.

The English gathered on one side while the Germans gathered on the other side, after which we all had breakfast. I blew the horn again as a signal to hitch up the oxen. After everything was in readiness I blew the horn as a signal for the company to start. In the evening I blew the horn for prayer, after which we retired. The signal for us to rise was given by the guards, or by those who watched the cattle during the night. In the beginning the oxen were hard to catch and hitch, but they soon became tame. Many people in Switzerland think that this kind of travel is hard, but I can truthfully tell you that during the last twenty years I've worked harder than I did on this journey even though I was the leader of the company and had to do more than the rest.

I had to take care of my company; each day I had to blow the horn eight times for all four companies. Whenever we came to a bad place in the road I had to stop and wait until every wagon had passed safely. My brothers Hans Kaspar and [Jacob] Fuhriman often say this journey was only a joke for them. We had good times, spending our evenings in songs, speeches, and in encouraging entertainments of all kinds. I had my wagon at the head of the company all during the trip. Notwithstanding we had many bad places in the road to pass, our trip was better than we had expected. For hours and hours we traveled on a road which was wide and level. It was a beautiful sight to see, these thirty-six wagons traveling along the level road. I had a brother from Thurgau[241] who drove my oxen, but many times I had to take the whip and drive them myself. When I was four hundred miles from Florence I purchased another yoke of oxen. I then had four yoke of oxen on my wagon and with them I was able to drive safely under any conditions. It took knowledge, alertness and skill to drive over the bad roads, but on good roads the driver could ride if he understood the driving of the oxen.

In Switzerland you should be amazed to see from four to six oxen on one wagon without a line or halter or rope of any kind to drive them. It also made me open my eyes. On the more unruly oxen we placed ropes on their horns so we could guide them. Many times when the oxen became unruly I had to drive them for the other drivers. On our trip we lost a few oxen. The English and the Americans admired us and marveled at our strength and many times we helped them out of their troubles. On the 1st of September we camped ten miles from Salt Lake City and on the 2nd, four Apostles[242] came to our camp and preached to us; on the 3rd we entered Salt Lake City. The same

---

241. A canton or territorial district in northeastern Switzerland.

242. George A. Smith, Lorenzo Snow, and Franklin D. Richards were three of the apostles who met the company.

day, Brigham Young and Brother [Daniel H.] Wells, his second counselor, and many others came to our camp to give us any advice we wanted.

Let us take one more glance back over our trip. I have often wondered at the success of our journey for we were always so happy and blessed. The people in Salt Lake City marveled at our appearance. Some men made the remark that we were in better condition at our arrival than any other company they had seen. We had but one death in our company; a man from Switzerland. There were no accidents to the wagons or oxen throughout the whole journey. Everything went well and successful; we sang and prayed together like the children of a good family. Many times during the journey we went hunting and caught rabbits, sage hens and ducks. We also killed one deer and a bear. It was a great joy for me to travel over the great plains. As we traveled we passed many houses, also some stores where we could buy anything we wished, such as: coffee, sugar, vinegar, brandy, ham, bacon, butter, soap, whips, rope, etc. but we paid a very high price for these things.

As far as the Indians were concerned, we had no complaint to make. During the first six hundred miles, several Indians visited our camp and wanted something to eat. We gave them some flour. I saw the Indian town of Genoa[243] of about 5,000 inhabitants, the most Indians I have seen in one place.

I am at present living in Salt Lake City; most all the other Swiss emigrants have gone to other places. Hans Kaspar went with other emigrants to Cache Valley, which is about 80 miles from here, on the 7th month. There are many valleys where new

---

243. The settlement of Genoa, located near the Platte River, was established as a Mormon way-station in 1857. One hundred Mormon families from St. Louis, Florence, and Alton, Illinois, settled in Genoa and erected a steam-powered mill. In 1859 the settlement became part of the newly-formed Pawnee Indian Reservation, and the Saints were forced to abandon the colony. Genoa served as the Pawnee Indian Agency until 1876, at which time the Pawnee were removed to Indian Territory and reservation lands were sold.

settlers are going to make their homes. The city of Salt Lake is larger and more beautiful than I thought it was. I think it is about one-half hour broad and one-half hour long. There are quite a few houses, several manufacturing establishments, and stores where one can buy anything necessary to live on. The city is so nicely built and laid out, that many of the unbelievers wonder at it all. There are several cities in other valleys some distance from here. I am working at present on a new road, 17 miles from the city of Salt Lake and receive one dollar and one-half per day or 1 Fr. 7, or 87 Centimes.

Bro. Kaspar had an occasion to send me a letter, and reported that he and Bro. Fuhriman are well and are working for a man at a sawmill. They intend to build themselves each a small house in the near future. I am looking around in different localities and wherever I like it best I will settle next spring.

There were lots of grain and good large potatoes raised this year. I have heard nothing about sickness. I have been inquiring about the fruitfulness of the land and this week I heard from an Englishman that he sowed 1 1/2 bushels of wheat and harvested 75 bushels, each bushel weighing 60 lbs. I inquired many times of English and Americans about different things and they have always been very kind and courteous to me. They have invited me to their homes and to meetings, and they have helped in every way possible. The food and drink the people have here is as good as any gentleman has in Switzerland. The land is very easy to work and the harvests are good. I have seen brethren here who came four, five or six years ago without money or a wagon or oxen and some of them in debt, and now they possess a farm, house, cows, oxen, horses or mules, pigs, a number of chickens and ducks, and all paid for. The people have plenty to eat and they live like lords. The land is irrigated wherever possible, and it yields abundantly. It only rained five times last year, but we hope next year it will rain more.

The Latter-day Saints are not going to Zion to find riches

and be selfish, but instead, to be blessed by the God of Israel with the richness that nature affords; the fresh mountain air, and the pure water which flows through the land. I don't wish myself back in Switzerland one moment, because I feel happy and thank God that He has led me here. Not until now did I realize how poor the Swiss people are, and how nice they could have it if they would obey the call of the Servants of God and keep the commandments of the Lord.

William Wood, Sr., a British convert, was baptized in 1855 and then joined the Royal Navy as a butcher, sailing to Peru, China, Japan, and Ceylon. Returning home in 1860, he resumed his association with the Church and eventually made up his mind "to gather." He and his fiancée, Elizabeth Gentry, left England together but traveled with different companies to Utah, William in the David P. Kimball freight train and Elizabeth in the John S. Brown independent company. His concern for her flows throughout his account. He arrived in the Salt Lake Valley in October 1862 and married Elizabeth the following month.

WILLIAM WOOD, SR.[244]

I WAS BORN AT OSTEND, near Burnham, Essex, England, on May first, 1837. My parents were members of the Church of England;

---

244. William Wood left two reminiscences, one written in 1906 and another in 1915. This is the 1915 account. Typescript copies are in LDS Church Archives. A published version based on the 1915 account is in Carter, *Our Pioneer Heritage* 13:254–300.

thus I was christened in the old Burnham Church. My parents moved from Ostend to Heybridge in 1847. I attended the school of those times; also the Sunday School of the Church of England. My father moved from Heybridge to Queensborough, Isle of Sheppy, Kent, in 1852. At this time I obtained a situation at the town of Whitham with Mr. Charles Barwell, a butcher, for 2s. 6d. per week and board. I lodged with a Mr. Philip Wood, no relation of mine, but a very religious man. He would preach and persuade me to join the Independents.[245] This unsettled my religious views very much; however, I continued to observe my mother's advice on our parting, so I always attended the Whitham parish Church at Chipping Hill every Sunday afternoon. I often delivered meat to the Roman Catholic Monastery in Whitham during the week and the Sisters often talked to me and would advise me to attend the services in their chapel on Sunday mornings. I often attended and always felt much interest in their devoted service, and especially in the beautiful singing. The Sisters gave me much encouragement.

Just at this time Mr. Barwell closed his business through advanced age and he secured me a position with Mr. John Walford at the same wages (2s. 6d per week with board and lodging). When I had been with Mr. Walford for a few months he closed his business; however he got a position for me with his cousin, Mr. Robert Blaxall, a butcher of Maldon, Essex. By this time I had become very much unsettled in mind as to which church was right and which were wrong; however, by invitation from Mr. Blaxall, I attended the parish church with his family,

---

245. Otherwise known as Congregationalists, Independents believe that the local church contains the fullness of the kingdom of God and therefore should be independent from any superior ecclesiastical or civil authority.

having the privilege of sitting in their pew. I had now reached my 17th birthday. There was a school fellow of mine, John W. Bridge, serving his apprenticeship to a harness-maker, only a few doors from Mr. Blaxall. After closing in the evening Mr. Bridge often came to talk with me. Just at this time I was very much concerned as to how I could escape the damnation of the wicked. I had a most terrible fear of death, received through a sermon which was most impressively preached by the Reverend Harwood upon the damnation of the wicked. I told Mr. Bridge how I felt in regard to this sermon.

It happened about that time that he became a Latter-day Saint, and there was to be a conference held in Maldon, in the Cromwell Lecture Hall attended by some of the prominent Elders of the Latter-day Saint's Church, from America, Mr. Dunbar and others; also some local Elders, among whom was Charles W. Penrose. The latter preached a sermon upon the Godhead, and it upset all my very confused ideas of the God represented by the Church of England Prayer Book wherein the Deity is described as being without body, parts, or passions. I learned from Mr. Penrose' sermon that the true and living God was a God with a body, and parts, and passions, and that his attributes were developed to perfection. After reflecting sincerely and candidly upon the attributes of the Deity, as explained by Mr. Penrose, I found that through faith, I could lay a sure foundation for life and salvation. This idea removed the fear that I had suffered through Reverend Harwood's sermon concerning the damnation of the wicked.

By this time Mr. Bridge discerned that I was gradually learning the truth. Thus a full explanation of the precept and example of Jesus Christ followed. And it dawned upon my mind that my mother's church was not the Church of Jesus Christ, from the fact that it ignored the vital principles introduced by our Saviour, and thus the organization was by an uninspired man, and I found the Lord had nothing to do with it. I had prayed often and fervently to my Heavenly Father that I might be correctly impressed as to what was right for me to do, and Mr. Bridge urged me to yield obedience to the teachings of our Lord and His apostles of which I had read in the New Testament promising that I should receive a testimony that God had revealed to Joseph Smith the Primitive Gospel and divinely authorized him to declare it in the name of Jesus Christ to all nations, kindreds, tongues and peoples.

I was now almost eighteen years old, and was baptized in the River Blackwater, Maldon, Essex by Joseph Silver, who with Henry Squires confirmed me, after which I was ordained a Priest. At my baptism I received a strong testimony and that a very peculiar one. In coming to the surface from the immersion I looked down the ebbing tide and saw a very large bundle of sticks, and, as I looked, the band broke and the sticks all floated rapidly down stream. It was to me the promised testimony in evidence of my obedience to the principle of baptism for the remission of sins; and no man on earth could persuade me otherwise, and now that sixty years have passed it is as unchanged in my mind as at the moment it appeared to me. It was soon reported that I had become a Mormon; and I was jeered at and called old Joe Smith and old Brigham Young, and many things were charged to them as well as to myself. However, all this only caused me to cling with a stronger tenacity to the principles of truth and to defy their charges. [. . .]

[In 1860] After having been home about 2 weeks [from a four-year stint in the Royal Navy], I made ready to go to our meeting at Sheerness. My sister thought I was going to see my sweetheart so I told her to come along and she did. The meeting was held in a little upstairs room in a dirty back alley. On going into the room, President George Wager gave me a hearty reception, and the Saints who knew me did the same. In a few moments the meeting opened and I was invited to speak and I related briefly some of my travels, and offered a testimony to the truth of the Gospel. You can imagine the surprise of my sister at finding me still a Mormon and hearing me preach, as she called it. My desire to come to Utah had increased. I secured a position with a Mr. Bilby, a butcher in Sheerness, and after having worked for him for two months I received a letter from my old employer Mr. Blaxall asking me if I would return and work for him. This offer I accepted and went to Maldon, whence I found many of the old Saints had emigrated. I had placed my money in a bank and was adding to it all I could save.

I was now twenty-four years of age and began to think of selecting me a wife. I became quite intimate with Mrs. Blaxall's sister, a Miss Gipp. She was not a member of my church, however I used to influence her as much as possible but as her relatives were all against it I could not accomplish much. Mr. Blaxall called me in and talked the matter over with me. He said "Why do you want to go to such a bad place as Salt Lake City?" He said he had a proposition to make to me if I would relinquish that detestable Mormonism and stay in Maldon. He said that if I would stay and marry Lucy he would start me in a good business. I told him that I never could do that, because I knew Mormonism was true, and that I would never marry a non-member of the church.

It was now 1862. Brother Francis M. Lyman and Brother Geo. Taylor were traveling Elders in Essex Conference. So I thought no more of Miss Gipp, and formed an acquaintance with Elizabeth Gentry. Brother [Edward Samuel] Gentry was president of the Maldon Branch, and all the family belonged to the church. I had now made up my mind to gather and to bring my young lady, to whom I was now betrothed, with me to Zion. I had enough money to pay all expenses to the frontiers, so I gave Mr. Blaxall a month's notice, after which I stayed at Father Gentry's and made preparation to leave for the Valley by May 13th in the old sailing ship William Tapscott. Brother F. M. Lyman had counselled me in everything, and particularly as to the journey. Miss Gentry accompanied me in visiting my father and mother and all our kindred. They all treated us very kindly, but expressed their sorrow that we were led away by such a disreputable people as the Mormons.

After our visit we returned to Maldon and took farewell of Father Gentry and all our Maldon friends, gathered up all our baggage and proceeded to London, meeting the Saints to start for Liverpool. When we arrived we boarded the William Tapscott. It was an interesting sight to see the Saints boarding the ship with all kinds of tin utensils tied in bunches and some were carrying their straw mattresses on their heads, while others were loaded down with all kinds of parcels and lunch baskets. Some had old pieces of furniture, such as a tea-caddy or teapot or some old picture of great-grandparents.

After the English Saints were on board, several hundred Danish and Swedish Saints embarked, making a total number of eight hundred. There was a little confusion until after the doctor's inspection; however, it was remarkable how quickly the people settled down to the requirements of those who were selected as bishops over the respective wards. I do not think the same number of non-Mormons would have settled down to such order. Nothing but the Spirit of the Lord would produce such harmony. Songs of Zion were being sung, such as: Ye Saints Who Dwell on Europe's Shore; Come, Come, Ye Saints; Oh Babylon, Oh Babylon, We Bid Thee Farewell; I Long to Breath the Mountain Air, and others and a very divine influence seemed to prevail.

We sailed from Liverpool May 13th, 1862, and the eight hundred people were organized into wards, and space with bunks allotted to each ward with a presiding officer. Brother Lyman had charge of the company. He was returning from his first mission, and because I had been on a British warship for five years, he requested me to look after the following persons: Sister Filer and her daughter from Braintree, Essex; Sister Coalbear and son

David from Mundon, Essex; Sister Rose Livermore from Maldon, Sister Elizabeth Gentry from Mundon and an aged Brother Perkins from Essex. I was to look after the above by way of getting their rations; also to see their food cooked and to render them any assistance that they needed. I was also appointed by Brother Ebenezer Farnes to assist in the serving out of the provisions. After the ship had got fairly out to sea the people were lying in all directions with seasickness. It was a severe trial to them, being so closely confined. However, they tried to bear up in a marvelous manner and called upon the Elders to administer to them in the name of the Lord Jesus Christ. Brother William Gibson and a Brother John Clark rendered great assistance in regard to the governing of the company. We had head winds and double reef topsail breezes often, thus the good ship labored very heavily. We encountered a violent gale of wind on Whit Sunday which affected the people badly, and which they never forgot. Poor Brother Lyman was very sick.

After forty-two days we arrived in New York and were quickly hustled into Castle Garden[246] and passed the inspection, after which we took train for St. Louis. On account of the Civil War we were routed and changed about a number of times. At one place we were hustled on board of a freight train. The cars had been loaded with hogs and they had not been swept or cleaned out, thus we were choked with the dust and we could taste it for days afterward. We arrived at St. Joseph on the Missouri River on the 4th of July. We camped in a large barn waiting for a steamboat. Everyone in the town was celebrating the 4th, and there was much excitement, as reports came that the Confederate Army was making toward the Missouri. We were hurried onto a

---

246. Castle Gardens is a circular building at the southernmost point of Manhattan. It was the site of a seventeenth-century Dutch fort and was later turned into Castle Clinton for harbor defense during the War of 1812. In 1845 it opened as a popular theater, and in 1855 it served as an immigrant receiving station until the immigrant receiving station on Ellis Island was established. The old fort, Castle Clinton, became a national monument in 1950.

small steamboat, the crew of which consisted of Negroes who were very rough. On arriving opposite Council Bluffs on a very dark night, the boat ran alongside of the river bank and landed the gangplank in a big bunch of willows and then pitched our baggage all into the willows. It was midnight and we laid about as best we could on the bags and bedding till daybreak when there was a hunt for baggage. I found mine easily enough as they were sailor's black bags with my name on them.

By eight A.M. Brother Joseph W. Young, who was our Church emigration agent that year, called a meeting and explained the circumstances, telling us that teams would be sent down to the river to haul up our luggage to a camping ground and provisions would be served out to all who needed it; and that tents also would be given to every ten or twelve persons. Thus we were again organized into tens, fifties, and hundreds. I was appointed Captain of the Guard.

The teams began to haul up our baggage and when about half of it was hauled onto the camping ground, a fearful tornado started with heavy rain and the most vivid lightning, just like those encountered in the tropics. It scared the cattle and they stampeded, doing great damage and running over Brother Young and nearly killing him. Those who were already on the camp grounds were almost drowned by the cloudburst. The volume of water washed gullies ten feet deep and in some instances washed away boxes and bags and buried them in the sand, some of which were never found. Three persons were struck dead by the vivid lightning, one being a teamster from the Valley and the other two were from the London Conference. Several others were badly injured. One sister was confined in the midst of it. I was Captain of the Guard so rendered her all the assistance I could by covering her with the tent that had blown down. Mother and babe both pulled through very well, and the dear woman settled in Bountiful, Davis County, Utah, and was always a fast friend. The boy grew up and traded with me for many years. A group of men was organized to assist all the women and children and old folks to the Church store. In two or three days we recovered from the terrible experience, but some never found their bags.

We returned to camp and put up our tents and prepared for the long wearisome journey across the Great American Plains. While here in camp all who had the means bought wagons and cattle as they had to be broken to the yoke. The young tenderfoot men from the big cities were not much in it, and were generally out of the way when most needed. As my sea experience fitted me for the job, I was engaged by a man by the name of Cooper to break his cattle to the yoke and get everything shipshape, and to drive a team to Salt Lake City for the hauling of my young lady and her baggage. We had got nearly to a stream called, I think, Loup Fork when Mr. Cooper said, "Brother Wood you are a young man and can do well to take up a farm at Wood River where I am going to stop, and I want you to stop with me." I said, "No Sir, I am bound for the valley of the Saints." "Well," said he, "if you will not agree to stop with me I shall turn you and your girl right out here." I said, "Sir, I will never agree to stop with you." So he went back to my wagon and pitched out my baggage and told my girl to get out, and he drove on and left us without bread or water. My dear girl wept bitterly, but I did not feel like weeping but rather like meeting the peculiar circumstances.

Cooper drove on about half a mile and camped at a small stream. I remembered that Cooper had a fifty-foot rope that belonged to me, and I made up my mind that I would have that rope and so told Elizabeth that I was going to get it. She begged me not to, but I thought I would be a coward to let him get away with that rope so I started to the camp with a full determination to get it at any cost. As I approached the wagon Cooper said, "I thought you would change your mind." I told him that my mind was still unchanged and that I had come to get my rope that he had staked his cow out with. He said that if I touched that rope he would shoot me. I replied that he could shoot but I was going to have that rope. He went into his wagon and drew a beeline on me with his old Yorker. I went straight for the cow and pulling her up hand over hand as near to me as I could. I cut the rope and away went the cow. I coiled the rope and returned to the wagon and Cooper did not shoot. I laid down the rope and said, "Mr. Cooper I am going to lay off my religion and give you a licking so that you won't forget me." So I went for him and gave him a good boxing. By this time my young lady was on the ground praying me not to hurt him.

I left him and we returned to our baggage. While we were reflecting on our condition, we observed a big dust in the west coming rapidly toward us. In a short time it came up to us and proved to be Elder Lyman and Apostle C. C. Rich. We were both overjoyed at the sudden and unexpected change in affairs. Brother Rich sat down and comforted us, telling us to be faithful and the Lord would bless us. While talking, we noticed a dust coming from the east. It proved to be a family [the Wardell family] that had crossed the sea with us. The result was that my young lady was to continue on with them to Salt Lake City and I was to pay forty dollars for her fare, and I was to go to Florence with Brothers Lyman and Rich.

I think this was the greatest trial I ever underwent—to leave my betrothed and go back. However, I submitted and kissed my girl goodbye and gave her a half sovereign, all the money I had in the world, and jumped into the buckboard and off we went, I with a sorrowful heart and a mind full of reflections as to the outcome of it all. Brother Rich found I was in tears and told me to cheer up and have faith and all would be well.

On our arrival at Florence all was excitement. I was introduced to a number of young men fitting out a freight train, some of whom had crossed the sea with me and some who had come from the mountains who were dressed in buckskins fringed and tasseled, (rough looking Saints they seemed to me). In the evening they all gathered into the tent and D[avid]. P. Kimball called all to order. He called on one of those rough looking buckskin-clad fellows to offer prayer, which was done in very appropriate manner and words. During all this time my mind was rambling over many things, especially as to when I should meet my dear girl again. As the shades of night closed down upon us and we were all in the tent, the talk was principally about breaking steers, putting up wagons, and selections made as to duties required of each one. I was appointed grease boss and was to drive four yoke of cattle and stand guard half of every night until our arrival in the Valley. I was asked if I accepted of these conditions at $30.00 per month. It was explained to me that through my peculiar experience, Brother Rich had used his influence on my behalf[,] and as I had agreed to, through his counsel, pay to Brother Wardell the usual fare paid by emigrants for crossing the plains[,] I was to receive the amount mentioned above, I being the only one of the tenderfeet to receive pay. The others had to work for their passage only.

After this business, we began to turn in. I had occasion to go to my bag for some clothes and in taking out what I expected to be white duck sailor overalls and holding them up and examining them they turned out to be some sort of ladies' unmentionables trimmed and adorned with lace. The eyes of the crowd caught onto it, and in all the long years that have passed, in meeting any of the old friends and comrades who were there that night, this circumstance would be rehearsed and has caused many a good laugh. I had made a mistake and got my sweetheart's bag instead of my own. Of course you can imagine the remarks that followed. Some claimed that they had a full rigged lady aboard. Everybody was now turning in and someone asked me where I was going to sleep. I told him I was provided with an outfit. I had rolled up into quite a small parcel a hammock and blanket of my own manufacture. The others who all slept on the ground came out to

see me sling my hammock and get into it. This was the way I slept
for three months; when it stormed I would just throw a canvas
over me. I fastened my hammock from wagon wheel to wheel.

In a few days we rolled out. My duty as grease boss was to see
that every wagon in the train was greased every sixty miles. Our
little troubles began soon, especially with the young men who
were indeed tenderfeet and inexperienced. Their ropes and
chains would often break and they could not toggle a chain nor
splice a rope, and it was a week or two before they could manage
their teams. They got into the queerest predicaments that you
can imagine. Our first trouble was a terrible thunderstorm, then
in guarding the cattle at night some of the men would doze and
the cattle would get away. It was some time before they could realize the responsibility of watching, as well as praying, which latter
was attended to night and morning. Our first great difficulty was
when we came to a swollen stream and no bridge. The water was
deep and the banks abrupt and we had thirty wagons, a very small
train, but they were loaded to their full capacity, four thousand
pounds. Of course they were the old-fashioned kind, built
expressly for cattle. D. P. Kimball was an experienced pioneer.
He ordered all hands to fell timber. Some had never taken an
axe in hand; however, enough timber was felled to build a raft.
The next thing was to cut down the banks of the stream so that
the wagons could be run down onto the raft. In this way we succeeded fairly well and ferried all the wagons over, then the cattle
and a few horses were forded.

By this time we had become inured to the great change in our
circumstances, and as we drew further west day by day the scenery
and weary travel became very tiresome. We often saw antelope
and black-tailed deer and occasionally a few buffalo. Brother
Kimball sometimes went with two or three other mountain men
on a hunt and never failed to bring in meat or game of some sort
which always came in very acceptable, especially as our ham and
bacon were becoming low. The rations of our camp life were

good. We laid over on the Sabbath and sometimes a day to wash clothes or repair wagons and shoe cattle. As we approached what is called the Chimney Rock our cattle became affected with murrain, and day after day we sustained losses which curtailed our travel, and shorter drives were the result, which tended to lengthen out our journey, and we missed reaching a cache of flour and thus were on half rations.

About this time, on account of strong saleratus bread, I was taken with bloody flux, and the worry about my young lass all had a bad effect upon me, although I stood my ground and never gave up. By this time we had reached a locality where the plains were strewn with dead carcasses and the bleached bones of horses, cattle and mules. Upon these bones much writing was left by the trains, and information given as to the health and success and ofttimes a few words from some lover would be written on the rib of an ox and stuck in the ground alongside of the trail telling the oncoming lover or friends of the incidents of travel, and much interesting matter. However, not a word from my lass did I find, although I had learned that she had not forgotten me. Of course it was a kind of lottery business whether the identical bone would be found by the right person. Something like this would be picked up: "Miller's train, July 24th, Mr. John Ford is to be married to Miss Sue Brown on arriving at Plum Creek," and on another, "Miss J. Jones has made love to Simon Hicks." I began to be afraid that someone would pick up a rib with "Miss E. Gentry has made love to someone or married someone or is to be married to someone."

1862 was the year that the telegraph poles were erected from the frontiers. One day we came across a stranded played-out cow. The poor brute had been left to perish. She had just the power to wink her eyes. I butchered her very quickly and hoisted her to a pole. She was almost a skeleton. However, as we had been on half rations then a number of days, we thought it a Godsend, so we feasted, with the result that a number were very sick. We were by this time nearing the south pass. Our oxen were continually dropping down until I had only three left out of my eight, and so we doubled up, leaving some of the wagons, and would then lay over and go back the next day and pull them to the main camp. Of course in the midst of this, many incidents occurred; such as wagons breaking down, tongues getting broken, tires coming off, and we had to be our own blacksmiths and set them. We had an emigrant train overtake us more than once. It was then that we would have dances, and sometimes good sermons were preached encouraging us to bear all the trials and Zion would soon be reached. These spurred us on, as we believed that our Father in Heaven was ruler over all these circumstances and that our promises and blessings were sure. And thus we journeyed on in the faith that we were obeying the principle of the Latter-day Israel and felt we were going up to the House of the Lord God of Jacob to learn of His ways and to walk in His paths. For we believed as Isaiah says, I think in his 2nd Chapter, that the work of God should go forth out of Zion and the law of the Lord from Jerusalem. These circumstances were happening to almost everyone. I remember Mr. Turner who was driving the next team in the rear of mine fell from the tongue of his wagon. I saw him fall, and both wheels of the wagon pass over his head, and to my astonishment he got up without help and shook the sand out of his curly hair. No injury was sustained, probably due to the fact that it occurred in a sandy place. It was to me a marvelous escape. He came to Utah and raised a family.

By this time we were reaching Ham's Fork and we had to send a horseman to report that we could travel no further without assistance. So we laid in camp till aid came from the Valley in the form of four-span mule teams laden with the fruits of the promised land and with meats and cakes and pies like those from home, also blankets, overalls, wagonsheets and every imaginable thing to comfort the tired and weary pilgrims. They came with mules enough to take in half of the train; we then had cattle enough to double up and take the remainder. We were now getting into the mountainous part of the west. Fort Bridger and Bear River were passed and in a few days the noted Echo Canyon was reached where just a handful of Mormons held back the army of General Johnston and kept them at Bridger all winter to pick bones of many a starved mule. There are prominent bluffs or rocks that project into the canyon around which the Mormon boys made trails in sight of the Army's reconnoitering parties and the boys kept circling the rocks at these points until the soldiers concluded that there were thousands and tens of thousands of the Mormon army in the canyon, when in fact only forty or fifty men were there. The canyon is a nearly impregnable pass and well adapted for a stronghold or a defense.

Passing this formidable place, we emerged on the Weber River where we were in the fastness of the Rocky Mountains proper. There had just been new dugways and roads opened that year which, however, in many places were left unfinished, so that it was dangerous, especially to inexperienced drivers and teamsters, and we had quite a time pulling through. While going up Silver Creek a rock bluff projected so that it formed a corner or bend in the creek, and in rounding this I did not keep in and hold the cattle enough and the result was that my wagon stalled against the rock. Nothing was broken, however, and when the boss missed me he came back and through his skill as a teamster I soon got out of the difficulty.

We passed through all kinds of barriers while going through Parley's Park, a place of high altitude and among big timber. We were now within twenty-five miles of the Valley of Salt Lake and it was down hill all the way. Passing through Parley's Canyon we emerged into the graceful and enchanting valley with the Great Salt Lake in the distance, and the many homes of the Saints in the foreground, the City, with its wide streets laid out by the points of the compass. Imagine if it is possible, our feelings of joy and thanksgiving to God whom we acknowledged as the means of our safe arrival to the haven of our hopes.

It was on Saturday evening and the sky was illumined in many colors by the setting sun which to me was sublime, indeed I have not the language to express the gratitude of a thankful heart to the Almighty.

Another British convert was Henry Stokes, who emigrated from Staffordshire, England, in 1860, worked in New York for two years, and then went west in Henry W. Miller's Church train. He married Elizabeth Jane Hale and settled in Cache County. He was appointed to keep a journal for the company, and that account follows.

HENRY STOKES[247]

WE LEFT NEW YORK CITY about the 17th of June, 1862, in an emigrant train of cars bound for St. Joseph, Missouri. [. . .] We arrived at St. Joseph and remained there one night. The next day we went on board a boat and started for Florence on the Missouri River. We landed on the shore of the river at midnight, and the next day were formed into a camp on the east side of the river under supervision of Joseph W. Young.

247. A journal of his life in England before emigrating is in the LDS Church Archives. The account of his traveling west is "Henry Stokes," in Carter, *Our Pioneer Heritage* 6:54–60.

Here we remained in camp for six weeks waiting for the church team to come from Utah. The reason for their non-arrival was caused by high water in all the rivers and streams between Salt Lake City and the Missouri River. The company built bridges or made fords at every river and stream before it could cross. While camped here we had a fearful storm of wind, thunder, lightning and rain. One man was killed instantly by lightning and another so badly injured that he died in the night, after the storm had passed. It was found that nearly every tent in the camp had been blown down and everybody was wet through to the skin and terror struck the hearts of all. Such a storm as this was never before experienced by any of us. While camped here, we were advised by Elder Joseph W. Young, our president, to make out lists of burned luggage against the railway company and demand damages. This was done, and damages were paid by the railroad company. I was one of those chosen to do this business and was up town at the office with the other brethren when this terrible storm began and it was with great difficulty that we found our way down to our camp and our families.

About the end of July the emigrant teams from Utah arrived under the charge of Henry W. Miller of Farmington. As the season for emigration to Utah was already late, all the necessary preparations were made with all possible haste and no time was lost in crossing over the river and arranging the train in readiness for the start on August 5, 1862. About one o'clock in the afternoon, we made a start and traveled a few miles through a pleasant hilly country and passed by a long house on the way, and for a short distance a line of telegraph was by the side of the road.[248] We walked by the side of the train and as we looked forward or

---

248. A national telegraph line had been completed the year before. Edward Creighton supervised a line built from the terminus of the Missouri and Western Telegraph line at Julesburg, Nebraska, to Fort Laramie, thence through South Pass and over the Mormon Trail to Salt Lake City. This line was begun the spring of 1861 and completed to Salt Lake City 24 October 1861.

backward, we thought it was a grand sight to behold such a train
of people and teams all bound for Zion.

August 6th. Pursued our journey to the Elkhorn River where
we arrived early in the afternoon. I was very much fatigued, so
much so that I was not able to assist in pitching the tent. I had to
sit down and rest myself for about two hours. Our camp ground
was on the north side of the river. We remained here three days
waiting for the provisions wagons to arrive. We found this to be a
pleasant place to camp. The river abounded with fish and we
found a variety of wild fruit, such as gooseberries, currants, and
wild grapes. The men and boys indulged in bathing and fishing;
the women and girls in gathering fruit. One boy caught a fish
which weighed eighteen pounds and he could not pull it out of
the water. One of the men got a gun and shot it for the boy. A
boy named Peter Barker had a narrow escape from being
drowned in the river. He went to bathe and could not swim and
got into deep water, but he was seen by a man, after going down
the third time. The man rescued him.

7th. The family all well, except me. I was lame in my foot. Eliza
Olivia [his oldest daughter, age nine] went out and picked some
wild grapes with which my wife [Elizabeth Jane Hale Stokes] made
a nice roller pudding. In the afternoon I went with our teamster
and some other brethren down to the river and had a good bath.
We found it to be a good place for bathing. It was a clear, swift current with a good, sandy bottom. In the late afternoon I went with
Eliza Olivia into the woods and got some firewood.

August 8th. Eliza Olivia and some other girls went into the
woods to pick grapes but they soon came back as they were scared
by Indians. Some of the Indians came into camp. One of them
represented himself to be the Chief of the Omahas. He wanted
to beg a pair of boots or some money to buy them.

9th. Captain H[enry]. W. Miller came into camp. Five teamsters were sent from our camp to assist the church train.

11th. Arose early and prepared for an early start. I rode in the wagon this morning because I had a sore foot. After eating my dinner, I went to see Captain H. W. Miller. Found him sick and laying down in his wagon. He requested me to see him at night or tomorrow morning.

14th. I arose at the sound of the horn. Left camp about half past six. Before leaving camp, I had to write out a list of strayed oxen which were lost while camping at Florence. Arrived at Loup Fork about noon. The train crossed without accident. After crossing the river, we passed through some woods where we found some wild currants with which my wife made a pudding for supper. A sister in brother [James] Perk's tent was taken very sick and thought she would die. The elders administered to her and she seemed to revive a little, but remained very ill all night. Captain [Hector D.] Haight's train crossed the river and camped on the west side of the fork. Wrote a letter for Captain Miller to brother J. W. Young at Florence, informing him of our where-abouts and of the health of the camp in general.

18th. We started out of camp about eight. Passed several houses. Eliza Olivia got half a pound of butter for five steel pens and had a little milk given her. It was quite a treat to us. We passed by a telegraph office at Shoemaker Point. The captain inquired if there were any messages for him but there were none.

23rd. After prayers the guard went out to bring in the cattle, but some of the cattle had strayed away (around fifty yoke.) The guard succeeded in finding them and brought them into camp.

24th. Captain Miller addressed the people on their duties while traveling over the plains. Obtained the names of the different camping places and the distance traveled each day from Captain Miller to be entered in the journal I had to keep of the journey.

26th. Elders Amasa Lyman and Charles C. Rich and com-pany[249] arrived in camp this morning, just as our camp was start-

---

249. At this time Apostles Amasa Lyman and Charles C. Rich were returning from a mission to Europe and were traveling with their sons.

ing out. They stopped with us a short time and had breakfast, and then started out on their journey, leaving us behind.

28th. Provisions were dealt out to one part of the camp. Brother [David P.] Kimball's train was at the Fork and waited for us to cross over. Also Brother [Cyrus W.] Bates' train was there.[250] All crossed without accident. Two births occurred at night, one of them died. Sister Miller in Tim Parkinson's wagon gave birth to twins. The roads had a variety of beautiful flowers on the side. Distance traveled was eleven miles.

30th. Eliza Olivia and I traveled by the side of the Platte River a long way and in coming to a nice shallow creek which we had to cross, we pulled off our shoes and stockings and washed our feet and drank freely of the water.

Sept. 3rd. Started out at seven and just as train began to move out Kimball's train passed along and was a great hindrance to us because they did not move as quickly as we wanted. Captain Miller appeared to be angry. After traveling about seven or eight miles, we stopped for noon on the Platte River. Soon as we stopped our train, Kimball's train stopped. In the afternoon we again started out on our journey. As soon as our train began to move out, Kimball's began to move. But we were successful in gaining the road first. We traveled eight miles and camped for the night on the Platte River.[251]

5th. Here we had great difficulty in cooking supper and breakfast because the rainstorm had wet the buffalo chips and we sat up until a late hour trying to cook some beans, but we could not succeed. We hoped the buffalo chips would be dry in the morning.

---

250. David P. Kimball was the captain of a freight train (of which William Wood, Sr., was a member), and Cyrus W. Bates was the captain of an independent company.

251. The large number of wagon trains traveling west often competed for camping grounds and grass and feed for their livestock. Members generally showed a strong loyalty to their own traveling companies but sometimes exhibited impatience when compelled to wait for wagon repair, lost oxen, or other problems encountered by their traveling companions. Non-Mormon companies had less reason to stay together and often formed new companies several times in a single season's crossing.

8th. Felt sick and was not able to perform my usual duties. My wife and Eliza Olivia had to attend to them. Stopped for noon at the Platte River. In the afternoon we pursued our journey about five miles east of Scotts Bluffs where we camped for the night.

15th. Wet, miserable morning. Had rained nearly all night and whole camp ground was flooded. Many had to dig trenches around the tents to draw off the water. Did not start out of camp until one P.M., on account of bad roads and some of the oxen had strayed. Pursued journey about four miles and camped in the hills. Had plenty of wood but no water. Large fires were made around the camp and it was quite an illumination. It looked as though we were holding a celebration for some important event.

16th. My wife was sick this morning and couldn't cook breakfast or bake bread so Eliza Olivia had to do it. We started out of camp about seven.

18th. Continued journey on to the LaRounty bottoms and arrived at a creek where we camped for noon. We found some very nice plums along the creek. Many of the people and I gathered all we could pick. Wrote out some receipts for Captain Miller for flour which he had lent to Kimball's company.

21st. Some of the oxen had strayed and we did not start from camp until about eleven. Took the children down to the river and caught four fish which made us a nice supper. Came to a trading station. Captain and several others made some purchases and exchanges for buffalo robes.

23rd. Captain took up some flour which he left when passing down. Camped for night at small vacant station near Platte River, abundance of buffalo berries.[252]

27th. After dinner, I struck down towards river and succeeded in finding some fine mushrooms which I gathered, and

252. Buffalo berries, or *Shepherdia argentea*, are found in prairie valleys, banks of streams, and steep, eroded, dry hillsides. The fruits are tart but pleasant with a fairly large seed that is easily chewed.

we had them fried for supper. It made us a nice, delicious dish. We thought it was the best meal we had had since leaving New York City.

28th. Today Brother William Fuller and Emma Happen were married. Brother Wm. F. Critchlow officiated. Brother Critchlow sang two love songs and played some lively tunes on the fiddle. Afterward we sang two hymns. Brother Darton conducted the singing.

October 1. When we passed over the rocky ridge, we could see the Wind River range of mountains which were covered with snow and on the left hand we could see the mountains on the other side of the pass.

10th. Scenery pleasant to look at while traveling. There were fir trees growing, and it looked more encouraging to us. We found grass growing and trees were more abundant. Just before we stopped for noon, sister Alice Barker was taken in labor. We had to stop for about two hours, pitch the tent and attend to all necessary services. Elizabeth and the children went on with the train but I stopped behind with the wagon. While the sisters were attending to sister Barker, we brethren made a fire and cooked some bacon and made some nice pancakes. Sat down by the fire and ate freely. After sister Barker and her baby son were safe and all right, we pursued our journey and traveled over the mountains. It was a steep descent and rather dangerous in the dark. The sun set when we were about half way over the hills, and the moon did not shine upon us until we were near the camp ground. Camp was located about five miles east of Bear River. I found my wife and children safe.

12th. It was a fine morning and all nature seemed to smile upon us. The mountains seemed to smile at the thought of us soon arriving in Salt Lake City for we were now only about seventy miles from it. We passed a large new station where some Mormons were supposed to be living. One of the teamsters went and shook hands with one of them. Arrived at Echo Canyon,

563

passed Cache Cave and continued down the canyon. In the afternoon we passed by a station where by order of Captain Miller I left a letter for Brother Haight's Company. Continued down the canyon. Met a small train of four wagons loaded with grain for one of the stations east of the canyon. Our captain wanted them to wait while our train descended down the hill but they would not, so we had to wait while they ascended the hill. The horn was blown for a meeting at the usual time after we camped. Captain Miller and the chaplain spoke to us about the journey which we had nearly completed and said this may be the last Sunday we should all be together.

13th. Scenery was varied and changeable. Many curious looking rocks of different shapes and forms were seen on the right hand side, and on the left side were to be seen mountains covered with brush and grass while the rocks were adorned with pine trees growing in abundance in all kinds of places where a person would be supposed to think there would be no nourishment. The creek ran down the middle of the canyon and in some places it made the road very narrow. On both sides of the creek, willows grew in abundance. Their leaves now indicated the season of the year. They were turned to a beautiful orange yellow color. After dinner we passed through the mouth of the canyon and turned to the left, around a great mountain by the side of Weber River and close by the river was a small settlement. The captain and some of the people stopped there for a short time. We came to a little settlement which reminded us of civilization. The houses were one story high and about square and at regular distances from each other. All of them were built a few yards from the traveled road and all were fenced. Trees were growing by the side of the foot path and everything appeared neat and pleasant. After passing the settlement, we camped for the night. Name of the place was Chalk Creek.

14th. Continued on through Silver Creek Canyon. We found it difficult to pass through it. Many of the passengers had to walk, even many small children. It was very wearisome and dangerous. Brethren walked by side of wagons on the upper side and held on to the side of the wagon to prevent it from capsizing or tipping over. We passed through the canyon about two or three miles and had to stop a long time being hindered by Kimball's team and Haight's trains. In many places we had to lock the wheels of wagons and put on brakes. It was steep and rocky. The creek ran through the canyon in its wild, rushing manner and ran first to one side and then on the other. Camped for night at Parley's Park. Went around camp and procured report of births and deaths which had occurred since leaving Florence. There had been eight births and twenty-eight deaths. Some of the brethren engaged to work at Hoyt's mills near Silver Creek.

17th. I went in advance of the train until I came in sight of the famous and most beautiful city in the whole world, Salt Lake City. I thought it was the most beautiful sight I had ever seen. Before entering the city I sat down and wrote a brief letter of the journey from Florence to Salt Lake City for publication in the Deseret News. When I had nearly completed it, the captain came up and passed on slowly. I hastened after him and gave him the letter. He took me up into his wagon and drove into the city near the public square where we met the captain's brother, Daniel Miller, and his son. After stopping a short time, we continued through to the public square where we camped. Many of the people took their baggage out of the wagons and soon met friends and acquaintances with whom they had been familiar. Among others we saw Walter Huish, and Mrs. Everett, gave her a letter from her Aunt Sanford of New York. Went to the post office and received a letter, but I was much disappointed because it was not from any of our family or relatives. Met Brother Thomas Tame who lent me a three cent piece to pay for a letter. I saw Brother Chadd, who invited us to go and stay with him for a few days, but I concluded to go with the team which had brought us to Salt Lake City. We started out with the teams which had come from Mendon, Cache Valley. Brother Thomas Tame accompanied us through the city and we stopped a short time and looked at the theatre and also at the temple. There were several men working on the temple and we thought by looking at the foundation it would be a fine structure when it was completed. We also saw the Court House and the President's house and passed up the main street and also saw the Literary Institute of the Ninth Ward, and I was struck with admiration of the plan of the city. I thought I had never seen such a beautiful city in my life.

It took William and Amelia Slade many years to raise the money to take their young family to the United States and eventually to Utah. William emigrated first and settled in Philadelphia; the others followed three years later. When William died unexpectedly, Amelia Eliza, their oldest daughter, remembered her mother's determination to "go home" to Zion, although it seemed impossible at the time because of her large family and their lack of means. With help from the Church, however, the family was able to begin the long journey west. Amelia Eliza Slade Bennion, who recounts the trip of her mother's family, was just ten, but as the eldest child in the family, she had adult responsibilities and her recollections are vivid, especially when she remembers the strength and determination of her mother. Though Amelia Eliza wrote that "'Going home' meant unsurmountable difficulties," the Slades met and overcame them all.

AMELIA ELIZA SLADE BENNION[253]

THERE WAS A BRANCH of the Mormon Church in Philadelphia at this time [1864], to which Father and Mother had been able to go occasionally as it had meant a long ride on the cars for them. The children, rather than receive no religious training, had attended a Presbyterian Sunday School. Mother had said with firm conviction, "I'm going home."[254] But as far as human eye could see "going home" meant unsurmountable difficulties. Once more "man's extremity proved God's opportunity." While Mother sat in the Sunday meeting the president of the branch arose and announced that on the following Wednesday a company of immigrants were leaving for Utah and that means had been provided for Sister Slade and her children to go with them. Mother's prayer had received its answer. Orson Pratt and Hyrum Clawson were the speakers, and after the meeting was over they both came to Mother. Orson Pratt placed $2.50 in her hand saying, "I'm on my way to England. I have enough money to get me there, and I am sure you need this worse than I do." Brother Clawson gave her $5.00. They shook hands with her and spoke words of encouragement and cheer. Some of the sisters, Sister Ware and Sister Fenton, especially, were willing and anxious to help.

There was much hurried preparation to be ready in time.

---

253. "Amelia Eliza Slade Bennion, A Pioneer Mother," in Carter, *Our Pioneer Heritage* 2:216–27.

254. After her husband died, leaving her in financial straits, Amelia's mother was encouraged by her husband's employer, William Sellars, to "bind out" her older children so she would not be financially responsible for them. She refused, and Amelia's diary relates the following incident. "Mr. Sellars tried to get her to change her mind, and became almost exasperated when she steadily refused. 'What are you going to do?' Mother thought of Utah and all it meant to her, and raising her head with a certain conviction she answered him, 'I'm going home.' He said no more."

Mrs. Bancroft[255] cried when Mother came for me. "She is so dependable," she told Mother, "that I can trust her implicitly in all things." This was a splendid compliment to live up to. Then I came in contact with some bitterness that existed against the Church in those days. When Mr. Sellars[256] saw our arrangements for leaving, and came to tell Mother good-bye, he said, "Well, I'm glad you are going back to England instead of with those Mormons; had you decided to go with them, I certainly would have taken steps to have these children taken away from you." Mother did not tell him that home meant Utah. She was soon on her way to New York. We each had a bundle to look after. Mother found it quite difficult to keep track of all of us—Rhoda, Martha, Willie, Eliza, Eddie and baby Charlie—to say nothing of the bundles.[257] Here we took the train for the little town of Wyoming,[258] on the banks of the muddy Missouri River, where we were to wait until a company of emigrants from England joined us before proceeding west by ox-teams.

How vividly I remember the little town of Wyoming on the Missouri just one thousand miles from Utah. What a change from the green woods and meadows of Pennsylvania. So desolate and wild. The Missouri, just one big river of mud, flowing out of somewhere, sluggishly past, and on to nowhere. "How ever can we wash our clothing in this?" was my uppermost thought and I was greatly relieved when I found that all the washing was to be done at a spring pleasantly located in a group of trees near the camp.

---

255. Rather than permanently "bind out" her children, Mrs. Slade had sent Amelia to live with Mrs. Bancroft, a married daughter of William Sellars, and Amelia's brothers and sisters to other homes. Amelia assisted with the household work at the Bancrofts.

256. William Sellars, a Quaker, employed Amelia's father, William Slade, on his estate in Philadelphia from Slade's arrival in America until Slade's death.

257. During the summer of 1864, when the Slade family started on their journey, Rhoda was eleven years old, Amelia (also referred to by her middle name, Eliza) was ten, Martha was eight, William Alfred (Willie) was three, Edward (Eddie) was almost two, and Charles was a few months old, having been born the previous May.

258. Wyoming, Nebraska, is on the west bank of the Missouri River, about forty miles south of Omaha.

Here, also, we had our first experience at sleeping in the
great out-of-doors, a rather terrifying one till we got used to it.
Every single night, it seemed to me, it stormed. The inky darkness would be broken by sudden, blinding flashes of lightning,
and the steady howl of the storm by roars of rolling thunder. The
seven of us huddled even closer together, but not even tent walls
and bed clothes could shut out the blinding flashes of lightning,
nor deaden, but very little, the terrific claps of thunder. Then
one awful night, the tent blew down, the pole falling across
Mother's neck in such a way that she was left utterly powerless,
either to call for help or to assist herself. She must have soon
died had not Rhoda, sensing her peril, managed to move the
heavy pole in such a way that her neck was freed. Supplies were
issued from a storehouse centrally located. We did our cooking
over bonfires. We lived like this about a month or six weeks; then
we were joined by a company of Saints who were emigrating from
England.[259]

One day came the glad shout, "The ox-teams are coming!"
"The ox-teams are coming!" Everybody turned out to give them
welcome as they lumbered slowly into camp, a long train of covered wagons, each drawn by yokes of oxen. This was the train that
was to take us to Utah, each outfit being furnished by the men
who had been called on a mission by President Young to meet
the emigrants and bring them to Utah.[260] We were all anxious to
get started on our way, little sensing, any of us, what a long,
tedious journey it was to be, and little sensing the trials and
hardships we were to encounter, but bravely ready for whatever
fate held in store for us. The train was in charge of Brother
Warren Snow.[261] Our outfit was in charge of Brother Frank

---

259. These English Saints had traveled to America aboard the *Hudson*, which, under the direction
of Captain Pratt, had a late start and a long passage. The *Hudson* was the last ship of the season.

260. The company was part of the "down and back" teams that made the round trip from Utah.

261. Warren S. Snow had just returned from serving a mission in Europe that he began in 1861.
On his way back to Salt Lake Valley, he supervised this last train of the season.

Cundick. Besides our seven, there was a feeble old lady, sick and ailing, who was assigned to ride with us. Baby Charlie was assigned to Rhoda's care, and little Eddie to mine. They were both beautiful children, rosy and healthy, giving every promise of growing to strong and sturdy manhood.

After what seemed many days in August 1864, we bade Wyoming good-bye and turned our faces westward. Conditions were too crowded for us all to ride at the same time, so those who were able, took turns walking. We would fill our aprons with dry buffalo chips as we walked, or with anything that would burn and could be used to make our campfires. Then, one day, Mother discovered that the bundle containing Rhoda's clothing and shoes had been left behind, with other luggage belonging to the train. Poor Rhoda, her feet grew sore and blistered and cracked. One day I heard her scream, and running to her, found that she had stepped upon a prickly pear. The blood was falling in drops from her wounded foot, but she would not let me pull the thorns out. I helped her all I could and finally we hobbled into camp. Her foot was growing more painful. "That cactus must come out," I thought, and then aloud, I cried, "Oh, look, Rhoda, Indians, quick!" and as she turned her head to look, I jerked the cactus out of her foot, before she had even time to say "ouch." My fingers were filled with thorns, but we soon got them out, then found Mother. We cooked our meals over the campfire and went to bed. In spite of the strange cries of prowling beasts and birds, we slept soundly through the cool, sweet night. The next morning we were up at sunrise, fresh and ready for the long day's march. Rhoda's foot was still somewhat sore. "Do you know," said Mother, "I dreamed last night that your shoes were coming and that they will be here today. I am sure they will." To our great joy they did come, along with the rest of the missing luggage, save some that had been stolen. Mother's dreams often came true. Our money, fifty or sixty dollars, all we had in the world, was missing. Then one night Mother dreamed that she saw it sewed up in a feather bed. When she awoke she arose and looked for it, and found it just as her dream had told her.

One day the old lady with us died, the first of our band who didn't finish the journey through. They made her a grave at the side of the trail. Then watering places grew scarce and we were obliged to buy our drinking water at twenty-five cents per keg. It was not always good water at that, for dysentery broke out among us. The woman in the wagon ahead of us died. Mother was very ill and so were two of the children. Brother John Kay, a young man returning from a mission, was stricken and died. A side was taken from a wagon to make him a coffin. For little Charlie there was not a thing that could be utilized to make him even a rude coffin. Mother tore a shawl in half, and we left him sleeping by the long trail. Later, the other half was used for little Eddie. Sick, disheartened, and weary, we had to carry on.

I remember one cold wet day in particular. We kept huddled up for warmth in the wagon all day long, while the rain beat its monotonous tattoo on our canvas roof. When we stopped for the night, fires were out of the question. We were hungry and went to bed crying for something to eat. Next morning Mother climbed out of the wagon. Through the drizzling rain and mist she saw a little old shack with smoke pushing its way out of the chimney. She made her way to it and as the door opened to her knock, there greeted her a rush of warm air, fragrant with the odor of frying meat. "Will you sell me some bread?" she asked of the woman who answered the door. "We haven't any to spare," replied the woman, but seeing how sick and weak Mother looked, she said, "We are just going to have a bite, come in and eat with us." "I cannot eat, my children are hungry." "You shall eat," she insisted, "and you shall have bread for your little ones even if we have to go without." When Mother came back, we were all out on the wagon tongue. She broke the bread in chunks and handed each of us a piece.

Eddie died as we were nearing Green River. This final stroke proved too much for Mother, and she became very, very ill. One day as Rhoda and I came near the wagon, we heard voices. "Yes, Sister Slade, your children will be cared for." The wild fears that arose in my breast seemed to smother me. Baby Charles and Eddie, and now Mother! Taking my sister by the hand we ran off some distance into the sagebrush and kneeling down we prayed in all our childish anguish, "Please, Heavenly Father, don't let Mother die. Please make her better, in the name of Jesus, Amen." We felt sure then she would get well. Next morning she was much better, and after some days she was trying again to take her share of the burdens.

One day we passed large, white saleratus beds. Mother had read of saleratus biscuits, and, as we were nearing our journey's end, food supplies were running low. Mother decided we were going to have hot biscuits, so with a zeal not backed up by knowledge, she made them. We ate them, for the bitter flavor was entirely outdone by their delectable rich orange coloring.

The last day of our journey our food gave out and we became really hungry. Towards evening we entered Emigration Canyon. As we came into the valley, we could see in the distance the glow of a big bonfire that had been lighted to welcome us. About ten o'clock we stopped at the square where the City and County building now stands. Such laughing and crying, such hugs and kisses! Soon we were seated around the big fire, while willing hands, backed by warm hearts, served us with everything that the little settlement could afford in the way of delicious hot food. There were mashed potatoes and gravy, chicken and vegetables, pie and cake. Then, when we just couldn't cram another delicious morsel, I noticed by the light of the fire, a tempting green slope. "Come on," I said to the girls, "let's roll down here," and roll we did, to our hearts content, entirely unreproved by the older folks. They were "Home" at last and too happy to notice it.

It was a long trip by sea and land for Johanna Larsen Winters to reach Utah from her native Denmark in 1867, just two years before the end of the pioneer period. Once in America, seventeen-year-old Johanna and her family traveled by train to North Platte, Nebraska, where they joined Leonard Rice's company for the remainder of the long journey to Zion. Though they were later emigrants, traveling when the trail was well defined and conditions easier, they still met unforeseen difficulties and were not too happy to hear a recitation of the Eliza R. Snow poem, "Think not when you gather to Zion, your trials and troubles are through. . . ." "It gave us food for thought," Johanna remarked.

JOHANNA KIRSTEN LARSEN WINTERS[262]

I N THE YEAR OF 1867, on the 5th day of May, I left my native city Aalborg [Denmark], on board a steamer to take us to Copenhagen, and there to meet with other emigrants from different parts of the country. That little sea is always rough and I was the first to turn sick. However, we landed the next day about noon and were met by a number of missionaries who took us around to see the city. The same afternoon the emigrants from other parts had arrived, and we were ordered to board a large steamer to take us across the North Sea to England.

So we, the Mormon emigrants, were loaded on one end of the deck with our belongings, and two hundred cows on the other end to be shipped to England—and the poor cows were just as sick as

---

262. "Johanna Larsen Winters," in Carter, *Our Pioneer Heritage* 11:60–64.

we were. We landed at Hull, England, and went from there by railroad to Liverpool, where we had to wait about ten days while the steamer Manhattan was under repair. This ship was to take us across the Atlantic Ocean. When at last completed, we were taken on board and all were happy and thankful to get started. At about midsea a heavy storm arose and for three days and nights it seemed as though the steamer might capsize at any minute. The captain told some of the missionaries that he never had met with bad luck yet when he had Mormons on board. He said, "There is something peculiar about you Mormons, anyway." The storm abated and we landed in New York Harbor on July 4th, but were not allowed to go ashore until the 5th, when we marched up to Castle Gardens for official inspection; from there we traveled through the states partly on steamboat and on the railroad. We crossed the Niagara River on the hanging bridge, which, of course was a great wonder. I had read about it being completed, but never expected to see it; and about half a mile or so after crossing, all our belongings were dumped in the wilderness, there to await another train from the opposite direction to come and pick us up. We wandered around for several hours looking at the falls and the barren waste. As far as the eye could see, there was not a spear of grass or weeds or anything that showed sign of life.

At last we could see the train at a distance, it soon reached our camp and we began to load up as fast as possible. Apparently it was an old work train, but we were glad to get aboard. I was feeling somewhat ill before the train started. I had evidently been exposed to something during our travels, and in a few minutes developed a high temperature and begged for water. There was ice water in the car, but the brethren said not to give it to me and I said, "Mother, for your sake do give me a drink, I am dying." She did not say a word but brought me a drink of ice water in a large tin cup. I drank that and asked for another and she gave it to me. I then went to sleep—I don't know how long I slept—my mother woke me and told me I had had a long sleep. She said that we would soon be at

North Platte.[263] I was then completely covered with measles and very weak when the train stopped. Our belongings were all dumped off as usual and everybody began finding their own. My father [Niels Larsen] put up the tent and Mother [Signe Jensen Larsen] made a bed for me and it seemed such a relief to lie down on something besides a hard board seat. I felt like "now I can die and be happy." But, oh, such a disappointment. Mother just came in and said, "Now, Father has gone to get some of the brethren to administer to you and you will soon feel better." I turned my head to the wall of the tent and cried, for I was sure if they administered to me I would recover and equally sure if they didn't I should die. I felt that it was too hard to try to live again.

The brethren came; they promised me health and strength, said I would be able to do my part while crossing the plains and reach Zion safely. I had a good night's rest and felt better although very weak. There was little food in camp and nowhere we could buy any. By this time all the younger children in the company were sick and it began to look as if we should all perish. Means had been provided by the heads of every family to cover all expenses from the time we left our old homes until we should reach Salt Lake, as there would be no Church teams to meet the emigrants that year. The money was forwarded and men sent from Salt Lake to make the purchases, one man to buy the provisions and another to buy the oxen and wagons and a few cows. All were supposed to be at the Platte Station at the time of our arrival. There was nothing, not even a message.

Brigham Young, Jr. was with the company, returning from his mission to England; he was such a kind, fatherly man. His brother, Joseph A. Young, and wife came to North Platte to meet him and with them our wonderful Captain [Leonard G.] Rice who was to lead us across the plains. A meeting of the brethren had

---

263. Terminal of the railroad at that time.

been called and each man according to the number in his family put up enough to buy a few sacks of flour from the nearest point, which was divided every morning, a pint cupful for each adult in the family. Two children had already died and a number more were not expected to live. It was train time, again everybody waiting and watching, and sure enough it was loaded with wagons, oxen and a few milk cows. Everybody got busy unloading and putting the wagons together with Captain Rice there to help them. But no provisions, nor a word from the man in charge had come. Brigham Young, Jr. had sent several telegrams to different parts of the State of Maine where he was ordered to make the purchase, but no reply. The situation was becoming alarming—children sick and dying. The oxen were numbered and corresponding numbers were drawn by the brethren, so each man had three teams. The cows were sold to anybody who had the money. My father paid $90.00 for the best one, the others were sold for less, and all were anxious and willing to help feed the sick. It was now towards night and a message to Brigham Young, Jr. came from "Mr. Man" from the east. (I shall not mention his name.) The message said that when he got there he saw a large stock of bankrupt goods advertised for sale at a bargain, so he bought the goods with the money belonging to the company on the strength of getting the same amount that he had coming to him in the adjoining state, but failed to get it and said he dared not come back without the provisions. Brigham Young, Jr. called a meeting of all the returned missionaries so each would know what had happened.

My father said the suspense for a few moments was terrible. At last, Brigham Young, Jr. asked the returning missionaries if they knew of any in the company who had any surplus means. A Brother Neilson from Sanpete said, "Yes, there is one man, but I doubt whether he will let it go now." Brother Young told him to call the man and talk to him. They told him what Brother Young wanted to see him about and he said, "Yes, I have a little more money left, there are seven of us in my family, besides I paid the emigration for twenty-one poor persons, including teams and provisions until we reach Salt Lake. I have money left, but not one dollar more for that man to handle."

Brother Young then said, "Will you lend it to me?" He said, "Yes, provided you promise to purchase the provisions yourself," which he did. Brother Young and another man left the same night for the east and returned on the third day with the provisions which were distributed according to numbers in each family. Captain Rice ordered all to pack up and hook on to the wagons. He said, "We must pull out of this death hole if it is only half a mile." Ten children had already died and were buried there, besides an old lady eighty-two years of age. We had been waiting there three weeks—it did seem good to get into fresh air and to obtain a drink of fresh water. Captain Rice was a wonderful man—he seemed to know every inch of the road between North Platte and Salt Lake. We had to walk; few were allowed to ride. He said the oxen had all they could do to pull the load. The feed was beginning to dry up.

The captain said we must cover at least thirty miles a day in order to reach Salt Lake by October Conference, which must be done. A certain number of the younger brethren were to take turns herding the oxen at night, and before starting in the morning the hymn, "Come, Come Ye Saints" was sung and prayers were offered by one of the brethren. Then we started out to walk ahead of the teams. We were not allowed to walk behind because of Indians. We made aprons of burlap sacks and picked up fuel as we went along, mostly buffalo chips or anything that would burn. If there were streams to cross, the captain would pick us up, one in front of him on his horse and another behind him and keep on going back and forth until all were across. Every day was about the same only the farther we got, the more rough and rocky the roads seemed to be; sometimes we would find some old Indian sandals and tie them under our shoes to ease our feet a little. At times some of the returning missionaries would walk along with us telling some of their experiences.

One of the brethren asked us one day if we ever sang, "Think not when you gather to Zion your troubles and trials are through. That nothing but comfort and pleasure are waiting in Zion for you." I think he had a purpose in doing it—we looked up the hymn and at least it gave us food for thought and study. [264] Things went along as usual. The days getting a little shorter and the nights colder and longer. It seemed like we were traveling up hill all the time. We got up one morning and found the ground completely covered with crickets. They would hop into our pans and kettles over the fire as fast as we could flip them out with a fork. We traveled in crickets for two days. They would crush under the wheels like so much sand or gravel. Once in a while we would see a deer or an antelope.

It was within the next day or two we were camped on a large open flat, the oxen were brought to camp as usual and yoked up ready to start and prayer was offered by Brigham Young, Jr. Just then we all noticed at a distance something like a small campfire in the direction which we were traveling. There was no sign of anything else to be seen, the fire increasing in size and the wing bearing right toward us. The captain ordered the oxen unyoked. The oxen were driven in an opposite direction for fear of a stampede. The fire was now coming close and the heat from it could be felt. Brother Young stepped upon the highest part of the wagon tongue, raised his hand and said, "Brethren and Sisters, stand still, we are not here to be destroyed." He still stood there. All at once

---

264. The hymn text was written by Eliza R. Snow as a poem entitled "A Word to the Saints Who Are Gathering" and set to music. It seemed to be well known and provided an accurate assessment of what awaited the early Saints when they entered the Valley. The words follow.

> "Think not when you gather to Zion
> Your trials and troubles are through
> That nothing but comfort and pleasure
> Are awaiting in Zion for you
> No, no, 'tis designed as a furnace
> All substance, all textures to try,
> To burn all the wood, hay, and stubble;
> The good from the dross purify."

he pointed to a little cloud not much larger than a man's hand and said, "There is our deliverance." At the same moment a terrific peal of thunder was heard and a flash of lightning seen and then the rain poured down. We then thanked the Lord for our deliverance, and went on our way rejoicing. We traveled on as usual making over thirty miles a day. All went well until it commenced to rain. It rained steadily for four days. It was difficult to find anything to make a fire with. Then it turned to snow, which was worse. For three days the ground was covered with snow, the poor oxen could find nothing to eat except the tops of dry bushes and a few branches on the side hills, but still we had to travel. The nights were cold and the days grew shorter. A few cases of mountain fever developed, my father was one of them. There was not much left at this time that the sick could relish, only milk, and everyone who had any were willing to divide. Brother Young was handy with his gun; he would kill a deer once in awhile and divide it among the sick for stew or broth which was a great help to them.

We now traveled on until we reached Green River. At this point Brother Lewis Robison from Salt Lake was running a ferry boat. It was then arranged that the few small rigs drawn by horses or mules should be taken across first on the boat, then the women and children. The oxteams had to cross the stream and the driver with them. The water was high and swift. The oxen had to swim and pull the load. The captain on his horse followed each wagon across to steady it and keep it from turning over. There were fifty wagons, two yoke of oxen on each wagon.

I do not remember how long it took us from there to Salt Lake. We traveled late and early. We reached the old camping ground on October 5th at 11 o'clock at night. But oh, how strange the next morning after the captain had gone! Brigham Young, Jr. had gone, and Joseph A. had gone—we all felt like a flock of sheep without a leader. About 10 o'clock the next day Brigham Young, Jr. and others came to camp to pay Brother Jensen the money which saved us all from perishing while crossing the plains.

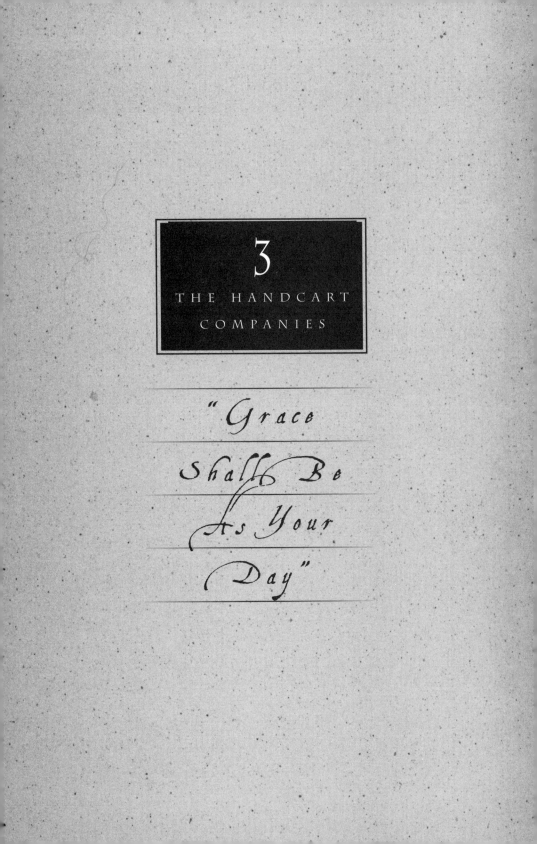

3

THE HANDCART
COMPANIES

"Grace
Shall Be
As Your
Day"

T EARLIER CROSSINGS OF THE Sweetwater, this Wyoming river had appeared "beautiful to the eye as it rolled over its rocky bed as clear as crystal," one handcart pioneer remembered.[1] But in the grey light of November, it no longer held any beauty or charm for the sick, weary and desperate people of the Martin handcart company. By the time they reached the last crossing of the Sweetwater near Devil's Gate, what they saw was a wide, menacing stream, numbing cold and thick with ice floes. All were dismayed when they reached the river, remembering the devastating crossing of the Platte before any rescue teams had reached them, but one fatigued and weakened man gave in to his despair. "Oh, dear! I

---

1. From T. B. H. Stenhouse, *The Rocky Mountain Saints: A Full and Complete History of the Mormons* (New York: D. Appleton and Company, 1873), 312–32. The pioneers were obliged to cross the Sweetwater at least four or five times as they proceeded westward.

can't go through that," he exclaimed as he dissolved in tears. At once his solicitous wife replied, "Don't cry, Jimmy, I'll pull the handcart for you."[2] With that tender exchange, James and Elizabeth Bleak entered history, their words permanently inscribed on the historical record of the ill-starred Martin handcart company. James was just twenty-six years old, his wife Elizabeth, twenty-seven, among the youngest and hardiest adults of the company at the outset. Traveling with their four children and five hundred seventy-six other converts from England, the Bleaks relied on a blessing promising that they would "not fall by the way" to see them through this uncertain venture.[3] As it turned out, Elizabeth did not have to pull the handcart for her husband. The small rescue party that had shepherded the destitute company sixty-five miles from Red Bluffs to this crossing of the Sweetwater would pull the handcarts across the stream and ferry women, children, and the disabled on their backs. Among the rescuers were three teenage boys whose youth came to symbolize the heroism of all who joined in the rescue effort, many of whom received no individual public commendation. Though "some writers have endeavored to make individual heroes of some of our company," wrote Daniel Jones years later, "I have

---

2. This story is a familiar one from the handcart accounts and appears in several publications. It was originally recorded by John Jacques, a member of the Martin handcart company, in "Some Reminiscences by John Jacques," *Daily Herald*, 30 November 1878–18 January 1879, quoted in Stella Jacques Bell, *Life History and Writings of John Jacques* (Rexburg, Id.: Ricks College Press, 1978), 160–61; see also Orson F. Whitney, *The History of Utah*, 4 vols. (Salt Lake City: George Q. Cannon & Sons Co., Publishers, 1892), 562–63; Rebecca Cornwall (Bartholomew) and Leonard J. Arrington, *Rescue of the 1856 Handcart Companies* (Provo, Utah: Charles Redd Center for Western Studies, 1982), 23.

3. James Bleak endured illness throughout the trek and was often compelled to ride in a handcart because of weakness. He was thus less physically able than some of the other men to make the treacherous crossing. Lynne Watkins Jorgensen focuses on the London members of the Martin company, including the Bleak family, in a well-researched article, "The Martin Handcart Disaster: The London Participants," *Journal of Mormon History* 21 (Fall 1995): 171–200. Of the fifty-eight Londoners who joined the company, seven died and one was born during the trek. This promise to James Bleak was recounted by Bleak in Scribo (his pseudonym), "An Item of Handcart Experience," *Juvenile Instructor* 37 (15 June 1902): 365–67 and quoted in Jorgensen, "The Martin Handcart Disaster," 192. Reference to it is also made in Caroline Addy, "James Godson Bleak: Pioneer Historian of Southern Utah" (master's thesis, Brigham Young University, 1953), 11.

no remembrance of any one shirking his duty. Each and everyone did all they possibly could."[4]

Nothing else quite captures the drama of the handcart migration more than the heroic rescue of the two belated companies of 1856. This incident at the Sweetwater also demonstrates that the gathering to Zion was an organized cooperative undertaking, and swift action followed if the system faltered for any reason. A chain of responsibility linked Church headquarters with every company on the emigrant trail from Europe to the Salt Lake Valley throughout the period of the gathering.

The Willie and Martin companies have become historic signatures of the entire handcart migration. The tragic circumstances that engulfed them and the heroic rescue mission that saved them are extraordinary incidents in the history of the western trail. Some have concluded that this plan to bring the "poor saints from Europe" was ill advised and reckless considering the tragedy that befell these two companies. Their suffering was indeed acute and their death toll enormously high, numbering more than two hundred, but it is also remarkable that nearly eight hundred of their number survived the same extremities of cold, hunger, and privation.[5]

The genesis of the handcart migration is found in Brigham Young's commitment to bring thousands of Latter-day Saint converts in the States and Europe to Utah as inexpensively as

---

4. Daniel W. Jones, *Forty Years Among the Indians* (Salt Lake City: Juvenile Instructor's Office, 1890), 68. The three teenagers were David P. Kimball (eighteen), George W. Grant (eighteen), the son of George D. Grant, captain of the rescue mission, and C. Allen Huntington (eighteen). Solomon Kimball, in his account of this event, quotes Brigham Young as declaring that act of compassion ensured the young men "an everlasting salvation in the Celestial Kingdom of God, worlds without end." *Improvement Era* 17 (February 1914): 288. Only their youth singled them out for such commendation.

5. Statistics vary on the number of individuals in the two companies and the number of deaths. According to LeRoy R. Hafen and Ann W. Hafen in *Handcarts to Zion: The Story of a Unique Western Migration, 1856–1869* (Glendale, Calif.: The Arthur H. Clark Company, 1960), there were 1,076 members of the two companies with between 202 and 215 deaths. Stanley B. Kimball, in *Historic Resource Study: Mormon Pioneer National Historic Trail* (Washington, D.C.: United States Department of the Interior/National Park Service, 1991), 68, suggests a total of 980 persons with 222 deaths in the two companies. Figures from individual diaries further confuse the estimate.

possible. Many emigrants had funds to provide their own transportation, but many more did not. In 1849 as many as ten thousand Mormons still waited at the Missouri for the means to move on to the Great Salt Lake Valley, and many thousands more waited in Europe. The solution was a revolving fund, known as the Perpetual Emigrating Fund, to which the Salt Lake Valley Saints contributed five thousand dollars to launch the enterprise.[6] The fund first brought the emigrants from the States, but in 1852, when Kanesville (now Council Bluffs, Iowa) was finally vacated by Church members, European Saints were targeted for assistance. Over the forty years of its existence, the PEF, nearly always in debt and the subject of constant appeals for support, managed to bring twenty-six thousand gathering Saints to Zion.[7]

With stirring epistles from Brigham Young, appeals in the *Millennial Star* (the Church's British publication), and the impassioned urging of missionaries, European converts, who made up the ten handcart companies, could hardly resist the "spirit of gathering."[8] As early as December 1847, Brigham Young counseled them to "come home speedily,"[9] now that the resting place for Israel had been established in the West. He continually warned the Saints of impending catastrophes and counseled them to "listen to the call of the Good Shepherd." There would be "safety in Zion," he promised, "the land of God's appointing—the home of the Saints." All, he urged, "who can procure a bit of bread, and one garment on their back . . . come

6. Both American and European Saints were encouraged to contribute to the fund as well as contribute monies to support missionaries, build and furnish chapels, assist the poor, and support other Church-related concerns. All who emigrated by means of the PEF were expected and continually exhorted to repay their loan in order to keep the program in force.

7. Richard L. Jensen and William G. Hartley, "Immigration and Emigration," in Daniel H. Ludlow, ed., *Encyclopedia of Mormonism*, 4 vols. (New York: Macmillan, 1992) 2:674.

8. Numerous passages in the Doctrine and Covenants express the Lord's will that a place should be established to which "the righteous shall be gathered from among all nations." See, for example, 29:7,8; 33:6; 38:31; 42:36; 45:71.

9. General Epistle from the Council of the Twelve Apostles, 23 December 1847, *Millennial Star* 10 (15 March 1848): 81–88.

next year to the place of gathering."[10] The Church was ready to help. Cutting the cost of emigrating was clearly the answer to bringing all of the "faithful poor" to Zion.

Wagon travel was expensive and lengthy. Buying and outfitting a large wagon with enough teams to pull it was beyond the reach of most European emigrants, who had the expense of a long ocean voyage and land travel over half a continent to consider. Bearing the cost of transporting Saints to Zion this way took a heavy toll on the PEF and on contributing Church members. By 1856 only one of twenty who wanted to come to Zion had benefited from the fund.[11] A simpler and cheaper way had to be found to spread the funds among more people. As early as 1851 Church leaders had considered using handcarts as a possibly faster, less cumbersome, and much less expensive way to travel. Finally, in 1855, with the PEF deeply in debt and a devastating grasshopper plague curtailing surplus resources in Utah, the time had come to try this new idea for western travel.

It would be a test of faith, Brigham Young declared, for if the Saints "have not faith enough to undertake this job, and accomplish it too, they have not faith sufficient to endure with the Saints in Zion the celestial law which leads to exaltation and eternal lives."[12] In 1856 the Saints in England read in the *Millennial Star* that the Church was providing money for emigration that year only if they were willing to "walk and draw their carts across the plains." Have them "gird up their loins and come

---

10. Seventh General Epistle of the First Presidency, 18 April 1854, *Millennial Star* 14 (17 July 1852): 325. See also Doctrine and Covenants 45:66.

11. These figures are taken from Hafen and Hafen, *Handcarts to Zion*, 27–28. This book still stands as one of the most complete studies of the handcart story although studies of individual companies have been done in recent years. See Howard W. Christy, "Handcart Companies," *Encyclopedia of Mormonism* 2:571–73. Kate B. Carter also discusses details of this unique travel experiment in various of her volumes. For an overview, see especially *Heart Throbs of the West*, 12 vols. (Salt Lake City: Daughters of Utah Pioneers, 1939–51) 1:72–87. Forthcoming from the University of Utah Press is a study of the Martin company by Lyndia McDowell Carter entitled *One Long Funeral March*, intended to be one of a four-volume series on the handcart pioneers.

12. Thirteenth General Epistle of the First Presidency, 29 October 1855, *Millennial Star* 18 (26 January 1856): 49–55.

while the way is open," Brigham Young advised mission president Franklin D. Richards. This the Saints did, in large numbers, showing their faith in this untried means of reaching Zion.

Among the first to answer the call were 130 Welsh Saints who sailed on the *Caravan,* leaving the British Isles in February 1856. Most of them traveled in the third handcart company under Captain Edward Bunker. Nearly three thousand more Saints set sail from Liverpool between March and May of 1856: the *Enoch Train* carried 534 LDS passengers followed by the *Samuel Curling* in April with 707 Welsh emigrants.[13] Not until May did the *Thornton* leave with 764 passengers, and the *Horizon* with 856 passengers. Of these emigrants, a thousand either stayed in the States or traveled in wagon trains that year, financing their own transportation.[14] Nearly two-thirds, or 1,891 of them, however, accepted the offer to travel to Utah that year by handcart. Not all of them could be considered "poor Saints." Some who might have bought teams and wagons nonetheless elected to travel by handcart to stay with friends and family. Others, like James Bleak, were branch presidents who felt obliged to travel with their congregations.[15] At the outset, people like Archer Walters and his family left their homes "rejoicing in going to help the building up of the Lord's kingdom in the valleys of the Rocky Mountains."[16] They

13. *Millennial Star* 18 (23 February 1856): 121–25; 18 (5 April 1856): 217; 18 (3 May 1856): 282–83; 18 (24 May 1856): 330. It is estimated that the PEF assisted between 26,000 and 30,000 Europeans to emigrate by 1887. Some priority was applied to the recipients of the fund besides their financial status. Those with needed skills, those whose relatives or friends had donated to the fund, and those who had been faithful Church members for ten years or longer received first consideration.

14. In 1856 three wagon companies preceded the handcart companies to the Valley: Philemon Merrill's with 200 people; Knud (Canute) Peterson's with 250; and John Banks' with almost 350. Two wagon companies followed the handcarters and fared only a little better: William B. Hodgett's with 150 people and John A. Hunt's with 240 people. (Andrew Jenson, "Church Emigration," *The Contributor* 14 (December 1892): 66; 14 (February 1893): 157–61.

15. Jorgensen makes this point in her analysis of the six London branch presidents who were reluctant to emigrate at that time, and especially by the proposed means of travel, but felt the obligation to stay with their branch members who overwhelmingly desired to take advantage of the offer (Jorgensen, "Martin Handcart Disaster").

16. Journal of Archer Walters, Pioneer, Enroute from England to Utah, U.S.A., March 18, 1856 to September 5th, 1856," typescript, LDS Church Archives.

were filled with the spirit of gathering, a compelling call that promised both spiritual and material reward. The promises were fulfilled for many, but at a heavy cost for some.

Like the tragic tale of the Donner party of 1846, the drama of the Willie and Martin handcart companies a decade later has tended to eclipse the rest of the handcart story. But eight other companies with double the number of travelers also walked their way to Utah with fewer than forty deaths among them. All ten companies that traveled west between 1856 and 1860 experienced the misery of food shortages, unrelieved exhaustion, the vagaries of weather, and the usual claims of disease and accidents. But eight of them escaped the tragic toll that an early winter exacted of the two late-starting companies of 1856. It was not the mode of travel that created disaster for these two companies, but a late start, hasty and inadequate preparations, and an early change of weather.[17]

Iowa in 1856 was not nearly as hazardous as it had been for the Nauvoo refugees a decade earlier. Traveling on what locals called "river to river" roads and on a more northerly route than the 1846 refugees took (though it was just as dusty and muddy despite being more clearly defined and passable), the handcart pioneers also encountered more villages and towns along the way. A major challenge was conditioning themselves to push and pull their heavy loaded handcarts across the three-hundred-mile Iowa stretch while coping with sudden summer storms, hot and humid Iowa weather, and the novelty, for most them, of camping out every night. For some, the occasional stares and taunts of the villagers and other western travelers may have been equally daunting. "Saw quite a novel sight," wrote one California-bound traveler, "58 hand carts with 3 or 4 women and a man to most

---

17. Handcart travel went in both directions for a brief period. From April to June, 1857, seventy-one missionaries enroute to service in the United States and Europe traveled by handcart from Utah to Florence, Nebraska.

of them. The poor deluded creatures are Mormons bound for Salt Lake City. . . . Some of them poor old gray-headed men looked as though they ought to know better."[18]

Most of the handcart emigrants embarked on their long walking journey from Iowa City, a town in eastern Iowa that had become the terminus of the Chicago and Rock Island Railroad late in 1855. There each trainload of emigrants encamped for several weeks getting properly outfitted for their walking journey. Out of heavy cotton cloth called drill or drilling, women made cart covers and tents large enough to sleep twenty. Some of the handcarters, particularly those in the Willie and Martin companies, had to build their own handcarts, often from unseasoned wood without the iron supports to strengthen them for the heavy use ahead. The shafts, about five or six feet long, were connected at the front by a heavy cross bar on which to lean or push the handcart.[19] For most of the European emigrants, the stay in Iowa City was their first experience living outdoors, cooking over open fires, washing in streams, and sleeping on the ground with only a tent for protection or privacy. They had much to learn.

The organization required to coordinate sea, train, river, and overland travel for thousands of emigrants took masterful planning, especially in the days before the telegraph. LDS emigration agents in Liverpool, New York, Iowa City, and Florence, Nebraska Territory (the former Winter Quarters and final outfitting post), many of whom were Church leaders and returning missionaries, carried a tremendous responsibility for chartering

18. Diary of Eva Morse, Special Collections, Harold B. Lee Library, Brigham Young University, Provo, Utah.

19. For all but the Willie and Martin companies, handcarts and supplies were generally ready. The insufficient number of handcarts for these two companies was due in part to the unexpected number of people who decided to go west in 1856, despite the delays they had encountered. Outfitters, however, tried to accommodate all of them, which necessarily delayed their departure even more and required many of the emigrants to assist in making their own handcarts. John Chislett provides a detailed description of how the handcarts were made in "Mr. Chislett's Narrative," in Stenhouse, *The Rocky Mountain Saints*, 314. See also *Millennial Star* 18 (February 1856): 127–28.

ships, purchasing railroad tickets, preparing schedules, meeting emigrants at arrival and departure points, buying and distributing equipment and supplies, and keeping financial records in order. Ideally the ocean crossing would be timed to bring the Saints to Iowa by May or June at the latest, so that after the three- to four-week trek across Iowa, they could leave Florence, Nebraska, no later than sometime in July. All connections clicked for the emigrants on board the *Caravan,* the *Enoch Train,* and the *Samuel Curling* the summer of 1856. While not all of their number went on to Utah that year, those who did had only a brief layover in Iowa City to collect their handcarts and another brief period in Florence to make final preparations for the main stretch of the trail.

Following the policy of organizing each wagon company, the handcart Saints organized into companies, a captain of hundred supervising five tent groups. Four or five people were assigned to each cart and twenty people to a tent. Each person was allowed seventeen pounds of luggage, carried on the carts along with bedding, utensils, and some food. Two or three large supply wagons accompanied each group carrying the main store of provisions, tents, tools, and other gear. Milk and beef cattle completed the caravan.

Starting out with light hearts and utopian dreams, these European Saints knew little about the American West and a physical environment so different from their own. The prairie heat and mountain cold, the swift rivers and sandy plains, the mountain passes and sudden bursts of wind and storm left them struggling to adjust. Thunder and lightning over the broad, treeless western plains alarmed those not used to such celestial fireworks. While walking to reach a destination was not unusual for most of them, pushing a loaded handcart thirteen hundred miles was a Herculean task, especially for the elderly. Their excitement at finally being on the road to Zion was their saving grace. Only when their energies were totally spent did they fail to sing the familiar hymn of the handcarts: "Some must push and some must pull, / As we go marching up the hill, / As merrily on the way we go, / Until we reach the Valley, oh!"[20] If the captains of the companies seemed to keep them moving at an often exhausting pace, as one handcarter complained, it was only because they knew that timing was crucial, something not yet fully appreciated by these novice frontiersmen and women.[21]

The vast reaches of the American West never failed to surprise European emigrants, and the drudgery of primitive travel over such a wide expanse set in quickly. The unrelenting labor of pushing and pulling the carts, their need of constant repair, the changeable weather, and diminishing food supplies gnawed at the enthusiasm and goodwill of the handcart travelers. C. C. A. Christensen, the well-known Mormon artist, and his wife Elise honeymooned their way west as part of Christian Christiansen's 1857 handcart company. He noted that "our hats, or what might once have been called hats, assumed the most grotesque shapes, seeing that the sun, wind, and rain had the superior force. The ladies' skirts and men's trousers hung in irregular trimmings, and the foot coverings proportional to the rest, with or without bottoms. Our faces were gray from the dust, which sometimes prevented us from seeing the vanguard; our noses with the skin hanging in patches, especially on those who had as much nose as I have; and almost every lower lip covered with a piece of cloth or paper because of its chapped condition, which made it difficult to speak and particularly to smile or laugh."[22] Disease often hovered near; even the hardiest had no defense against the dev-

20. The song was written by J. D. T. McAllister, a British missionary who served in Iowa City for a period as an agent for the handcart pioneers. One old Scottish lady in Captain McArthur's company sang her own song, a one-liner she loved to repeat, "Huree for the handkerts!" Even a rattlesnake bite didn't slow her down for long, and she made it to the Valley, singing all the way. (In Kate B. Carter, comp., "Records of the Handcart Pioneers," *Our Pioneer Heritage*, 20 vols. [Salt Lake City: Daughters of Utah Pioneers, 1958–1977], 14:297.)

21. Journal of Archer Walters, 24 June 1856.

22. "By Handcart to Utah: The Account of C. C. A. Christensen," *Nebraska History* 66 (Winter 1985): 342. Translated from Danish by Richard L. Jensen.

astating sweeps of cholera and dysentery. When she started the journey, Priscilla Evans enthusiastically wrote, "This is a glorious way to come to Zion," but in time the unrelenting squeal of ungreased cart wheels began to wear on her bright optimism, and sharing a tent with her one-legged husband, two blind men, a one-armed man, and a widow with five children did little to lighten her load or lift her spirits. Besides these incursions on her good nature, she bemoaned her inability to converse with her fellow travelers. Though she was Welsh by descent and traveling with three hundred other Welsh men and women, she had lived only in England and did not speak Welsh; there were only a few in the company besides the captain, her husband, and the widow and her children with whom she could converse.[23]

The first three handcart companies, under the guidance of Captains Edmund Ellsworth, Daniel McArthur, and Edward Bunker, left Florence, near the site of Winter Quarters, before the end of July in 1856, and all arrived in the Salt Lake Valley to tumultuous welcomes.[24] Though they had subsisted for weeks on the emigrant diet of salty bacon and flour (made into gravy, biscuits, or gruel), occasionally enjoying a taste of berries picked along the way or a little buffalo meat or beef, even these items disappeared well before the end of their journey. They were overjoyed when relief wagons met them with bread, melons, potatoes, onions, and other fresh vegetables, which they had not enjoyed for months. Brigham Young and his counselor Heber C. Kimball were among the welcoming party that traveled as far as Big Mountain, twelve miles east of Salt Lake City, to meet the weary travelers, relieved and heartened that they had arrived safely. Bands played, people cheered, and a veritable parade

---

23. Autobiography of Priscilla Merriman Evans, in Carter, *Our Pioneer Heritage* 14:279–92; also printed in Cathy Luchetti, *Women of the West* (St. George, Ut: Antelope Island Press, 1982), 163–71, esp. 164–65. Evans admired Captain Edward Bunker very much for his help and compassionate oversight of the company.

24. The Ellsworth and McArthur companies arrived the same day, 26 September; the Bunker company arrived a few days later on 2 October 1856.

escorted them into the Valley to the homes of the Saints, where the travelers were immediately given rest and food.[25] Of the 815 emigrants who traveled in these first three companies from Florence to the Salt Lake Valley, twenty-seven died, a reasonable number considering the hazards of such travel and the number of elderly in the groups.

The success of the first three companies in reaching the Valley with relatively little trouble proved the system was workable. Edmund Ellsworth, the thirty-seven-year-old captain of the first company, was a veteran of the original 1847 pioneer band. Completing a mission to England in 1856, he had shepherded the passengers of the *Enoch Train* across the Atlantic and all the way to Iowa City. There he was appointed captain of a handcart company with 274 people, fifty-two handcarts, and five supply wagons. Among the group was Mary Ann Jones, a pretty nineteen-year-old girl traveling on her own. During months of travel, Mary Ann slipped easily into the warmth, camaraderie, and security of her traveling community. Captain Ellsworth kept a watchful eye on her throughout the trip and evidently decided to make such scrutiny permanent, with which she was agreeable, and the two were married soon after they reached the Valley. All accounts indicate that age and family situation made a marked difference in the kind of experience a traveler had. A young girl without family responsibilities, like Mary Ann Jones, usually fared very well.

25. Details of this celebration can be found in Jenson, "Church Emigration," *The Contributor* 14 (December 1892): 67.

MARY ANN JONES[26]

ON THE 21ST OF MARCH 1856 a company of Latter Day Saints, 534 in number left the shores of England on the ship Enock[h]. Train arrived in Boston May 1st. Went to Iowa to wait for the hand carts to be got ready for the start across the plains. Left Iowa [City] on the 9th of June. Traveled to Florence, left Florence July 16th, went 4 miles then stopped to have hand carts fixed up they were made so flimsy they were continuly breaking down. Started again on the 20th of July and began our long march across the plains we had on leaving 274 persons in the company, had only 7 deaths on the journey which I think remarkable as we had a number of aged people & lots of children. We had 4 wagons 3 of them drawn by oxen and one 4 horse team.[27] We traveled 1400 miles in nine weeks. We were alloted 1 tent to 20 persons & 4 hand carts to each tent. We traveled as high as 28 miles a day & always got to camp long before the wagons. We were allowed 17 lbs. of baggage each, that meant clothes beding cooking utensils etc. When the brethern came to weigh our things some wanted to take more than alowed so put on extra clothes so that some that wore [were] real thin soon became stout so as soon as the weighing was over put the extra clothes in the hand cart again but that did not last long for in a few days we were called upon to have all weighed again & quite a few were found with more than alowed. One old Sister carried a teapot & calendar on her apron strings all the way to Salt Lake. Another Sister carried a hat box full of things but she died on the way. The LORD was with us by His spirit for all-though tired

---

26. Diary of Mary Ann Jones (age 19) on her trip across the plains," 1910, typescript copy, LDS Church Archives.
27. The official account indicates five wagons accompanied the first two companies.

& foot sore we could sing the songs of zion as we went along. Some stomacks may recoil at a supper cooked with the water dug in a buffalo wallow & cooked with buffalo chips but it tasted good to us. We came to an emence herd of buffalo. It seemed as if the whole prairie was moving we waited for over an hour for them to cross the road so we could go on. We were stopped on the Platt[e] river by a large band of Indians who demanded food. They were painted in war paint & very hostile. Captain Edmund Ellsworth talked to them & told the brethern to pray while he talked, he gave them some beads and they let us go on our way, for which we felt very thankful. A very remarkable thing happened on the Platt river. One of the oxen died & Bro. Ellsworth was asking the Brethern what could be done. Could they put a cow in the team so we could go on. When one of the men said look Bro. Ellsworth at that steer on the hill for There stood a big fat steer looking at us. Bro. Ellsworth said the Lord has sent him to help us in to the valley, go & get him so we can move on. They did so & he worked as good as the others. When we got within 2 days travel of Salt Lake we met some teams sent out from the valley with provisions & to help us in the next morning when the boys went to round up the cattle to start that steer was gone. They hunted for hours but we never saw him again he went as misteriously as he came. Bro. Ellsworth said the Lord lent him to us as long as we needed him. We were met in Emegration Canyon by the first Presidency & a brass band & hundreds of people in carriages on horseback & on foot, it was a day never to be forgotten. We had reached the goal & on foot all the way. I never left my handcart for a day & only rode over 2 rivers. We waded streams, crossed high mountains & pulled through heavy sands, leaving comfortable homes, fathers, mother, brothers & sisters & what for? To be where we could hear a prophets voice and live with the Saints of God. I have never seen the day I regretted my trip – We arrived in Salt Lake the 26 day of September 1856.[28]

---

28. Mary Ann Jones became the wife of Captain Ellsworth on 10 October 1856.

At age twelve ("almost thirteen"), Mary Powell, another young member of Captain Ellsworth's company, was old enough to recognize the hazards of the journey on which she and her family had embarked but young enough for time to soften her memory of its harsh edges by the time she retold her experiences. Traveling with her father, John (age forty-three); her mother, Elizabeth (thirty-five); her elder brother William (fifteen); and four younger siblings (Margaret, eight; Elizabeth, six; Hanna Susan, four; and David, an infant), she brings to life a twelve-year-old's impressions. Upon reaching Deer Creek Valley, for instance, she recorded that it was "charmingly sylvan with little groves here and there and a bright clear creek lined with timber. Said I to Father," she recalled, "'let's build a little log house and stay in this place always.' 'What shall we do for food?' asked father. 'Do as we're doing now,' said I. 'Go without.'"

MARY POWELL SABIN[29]

WE REACHED IOWA CITY late at night. We walked four miles from Iowa city out to the camping place of the saints. Mother [Sarah Elizabeth Harris Powell] rode, not being strong enough to walk. A missionary, Brother [Philemon Christopher] Merrill,[30] whom Mother had entertained in Wales, helped her to alight from the carriage.

29. Autobiography of Mary Powell Sabin (1926), LDS Church Archives.

30. Philemon Christopher Merrill served a mission to Europe, 1853 to 1856, and took charge of a company of emigrants on his way back to the Valley.

Said he, "Sister Powell, it affords me great pleasure to welcome you to this blessed land of America."

We remained in Iowa six weeks. All the men were busy making handcarts. Our bake kettle which Father had ordered had not come. We had to fry our dough in a pan over the campfire. A lady seeing me do it said, "come into my tent and use my stove." This lady was not a member of the company. She lived in a tent nearby and owned a nice stove with a good oven which she allowed me to use. In the course of my acquaintance I learned that she was a relative of the Joseph F. Smith family.

Each day I took pains to watch the women bake bread in their bake-kettles. I was taking lessons from them. I knew that I should have to do the baking when our own kettle came and I was anxious to learn the best way to do it.

It became necessary for Mother to dispose of some of our things. She sold a little flat iron that I had taken care to carry with me. How I cried when it was sold. I think this was the only time I cried on the whole long journey. I felt worried and said, "Whatever will we do for something with which to smooth out our clothes when we get to Salt Lake City."

At last the handcarts were all made. There were two handcarts for our family. My brother [William] pulled one of them all the way from Iowa City to Utah. I and father took turns pulling the other one. When I was not pulling father's handcart I was helping to pull someone else's. I walked every step of the way. I was light hearted and glad and had not self-pity.

Being almost thirteen years old I felt quite responsible for my younger sisters. Sometimes when father or mother took sick I worried, as I did not want them to die by the way side.

We hadn't been long on the march when Brother [John] Kettle died. [He left a wife and 6 children.] We took the last lumber in the company and made him a coffin. We buried him beside a mulberry grove.

While the company halted, I took a walk in the woods to get

away from it all. There were wild grapes, persimmons, hickory nuts, black berries, walnuts and hazel nuts by the score. Here I learned to know a peach. There were many fruits new to me also. I was surprised at the variety I found there.

I went into the woods every possible chance. How I enjoyed swaying in the grapevine swings. The moss was velvety green, the wild flowers beautiful. Ah! but the time flew by so very quickly.

I was never lost in the woods. Some folks thought it remarkable how I could find my way out without the least bit of trouble.

The journey was very hard on Mother. Picture a lady with dark blue eyes, black hair and a face very very pale from exhaustion. She is bearing the trials of the journey without complaint. That is my mother.

On the road to Council Bluffs, we met a man, woman and child driving in a white topped rig. They seemed to become alarmed on seeing Mother's weakened condition. The man poured out a stimulant for Mother to drink. The woman gave me a slice of corn bread mixed with white flour for Mother to eat. They pitied her very much.

At Council Bluffs we had the pleasure of meeting an old lady who clapped her hands in delight to see us. She took Mother into her neat little log house and made her lie down on the bed. It was snowy white and the room was spotless. While Mother slept the woman hurried and churned. When Mother woke she gave us buttermilk. Mother said she could never forget it.

We dreaded to leave this cosy little house. It stood propped on blocks alone in this little grove. It was the only house we saw that day.

From the Bluffs we went up the river to Florence, Nebraska. At Florence we remained two weeks fixing handcarts and wagons. There were two buildings at this place—a large store house and a mill.

We had been in Florence a little over a week when our bake kettle came. I was overjoyed. Now Mother should have light bread. I took the kettle and went off about a block. In this quiet place I built me a fire, took dough and made twenty four beautiful brown biscuits. I was glad as glad could be. I took the biscuits to camp and surprised Mother. All the women had to come and get a peek into our bake-kettle.

While in Florence, Nebraska, a gentleman came in our camp. Said he to the captain, "Is there a man here from Wales by the name of John Powell? That's the man I want," said he. "I've been on the look out for him for the last five years. My wife wants to see Bro. Powell. She thinks the world of him. He gave her a home in the old country."

This man offered Father eighty acres of land if he would settle in Nebraska. He also was willing to help erect a house for us.

While we were encamped at Florence father secured work. He laid the foundation, also dressed the corner-stone for the first court-house in Omaha. He received eight dollars per day.[31] He needed this money for said he, "I cannot let my children go bare-footed across the plains."

Father bought me a pair of shoes, the ugliest I've ever seen in all my life. It was the best he could get.

From Florence, Nebraska, began our real journey across the plains. All our other experiences had not been a foretaste of what lay ahead of us. There were two hundred and seven souls in our company.

Our first day's march commenced about noon. We went through acres of hazel brush covered with hazel nuts in the mill. I began gathering nuts, other[s] joined me, and we ate a good many.

That night we camped by a stream. The next day we traveled out into the prairies and didn't see any houses at all. One afternoon Father noticed Bro. [Daniel] Jones pull away and halt by the side of the road. "What is the matter, Bro. Jones?" asked Father.

---

31. This amount seems inordinately high for the time and place. Her memory may have faltered at this point.

"I see danger ahead," said Brother Jones, "I promised Ann's [his wife's] father [I] wouldn't lead her into suffering. I see danger ahead."

Bro Jones and his wife remained behind in Omaha. Bro. Jones being a butcher by trade, likely secured good work. Father said we should give him due credit for keeping his word to Ann's father.

Now we halted preparing the crossing of a stream on a ferry. The dark green forest was all around us. I grabbed a bucket and ran into the woods and picked it full of black berries. I took some little girls with me. Someone in camp began worrying about us. Bro. [John] Oakley said, "Don't worry, she'll come back, she always does."

When I came out with my blackberries they all cheered. As often as I could I ran into the woods. I loved the hills, woods, moss, and hanging grape vines and wild flowers. There were so many birds. Their joy notes swelling in the woods brought a flood of rapture into my soul.

The fifth day out we reached a little trading post. The men here sold tobacco to the Indians, also trinkets of various kinds.

Each morning at day break the bugle sounded. Up we rose and assembled for prayer. We then ate a scanty breakfast of dough cakes fried in the frying pan. Once in a while we had a few stewed apples. Then we were ready for our march. At ten o'clock we rested one half hour. Then we traveled until we came to water. At the next meal we would eat what was left over from breakfast. At night we often went to bed without supper. There was very little food to cook and we were too tired to cook it.

There were twenty one persons in Father's big round tent which we pitched every night. We spread down quilts and blankets and went to sleep.

One day three men went out to shoot a buffalo. The buffalo attacked a horse and ripped its sides. We didn't get any meat that day. Later a crowd of boys went out and shot a steer. That day we had beef.

Our bake kettle now came in handy. We put twenty pieces of meat (each piece about fifty cents worth of beef) into our bake kettle. In this way we cooked for about twenty families. There being no wood we gathered buffalo chips and built a hot fire under the kettle.

One night a brother made us a present of a piece of steak. The hour was real late, but Mother was anxious to get it partly baked in order that it might not spoil. I undertook to do the baking all by myself. The fire was quite a distance from the tent. I sat by it watching the kettle until I fell fast asleep. The night guard came and tapped me on the shoulder.

"Are you Bro. Powell's girl?"

"Yes."

"You go to bed, I'll finish your meat for you," he said.

"But I've promised Mother to do it. I cannot break my word." said I.

"You are too tired little girl." said he. "Run along, I'll bake your meat."

"But there are a couple of dogs in camp. I'm afraid they'll get it after it is baked." I said.

"Never worry, I'll put it in a safe enough place," said he. "Don't worry, go to bed."

Trusting his promise I crept inside of Father's tent. I must have gone to sleep the moment I touched the pillow.

In the morning I was awakened by Father's heavy laughter. Bro Card's[32] wagon tongue was propped into a perpendicular position. On the end of the wagon tongue hung our bake-kettle. The sight of it way up in the air made a great round of laughter as we came outside the tent to take the morning air.

---

32. Cyrus Williams Card and his family accompanied the first handcart company with two yoke of oxen and a wagon.

It was my habit to get up early and sit outside of Father's tent to drink in the cool morning breeze. It rested me for the remainder of the day.

Some days we traveled more than thirty miles to reach water. Often we would come to a place where the springs had dried down. It might be near midnight. Then little children would form a circle of eager watchers while the men dug down several feet to water. At last when they saw the chunks of wet mud they would lay it on their face and hands. Some of them would suck the water from the mud. When the water burst forth it was usually very thick. The children drank heartily, straining it through their teeth. The next morning it looked quite clear.

We saw water for miles and miles before we reached the Platte river. The distance was very deceiving. The water seemed much nearer to me than it really was. Mother was getting faint with thirst. There was a selfish old man in camp that did not offer her a swallow from the water in his canteen. It made me quite vexed. That day I walked more than ten miles extra to get Mother a drink. I ran part of the way but secured drinking water for her.

Traveling in the Platte Valley was very pleasing. My little sister, [Annie] aged four, usually walked beside the Captain. "Come my little partner." said he, "let us begin our journey." Some days she walked eighteen miles.

During those days the thought upper most in the minds of every man, woman and child was "Oh! to reach the Platte." We could see the milky looking waters far in the distance. How long it took before we reached it.

One day we saw a speck like a cloud of dust miles behind us. The cloud kept moving toward us and increasing. Within two hours an immense herd of buffalo passed us. They did not seem to notice us in the least but moved right along solid and dumb in one great mass. They passed us with a steady trot and not one soul was harmed.

The next night we saw a few buffalo off alone. The men went out and killed one, again we had meat.

At last we reached the Platte. There was a trading post near by. Our captain asked the men at the post how much they would charge to ferry us across. The price they asked was more money than we had in camp.

The river was between two and three blocks wide. First the men took the handcarts across, then the women and girls followed wading. The water kept getting deeper and deeper. In the middle of the river it was under my chin. When we reached the opposite side we went right on in our wet clothes. We traveled thirteen miles more that day.

We crossed the Platte in several places. At Fort Laramie it was over my head.[33] I started down stream. Bro. Oakley pulled me back. At Fort Laramie there was an encampment of sixteen thousand Indians, they were holding a treaty [council]. They were camped for a distance of thirty miles up the river. We camped near the river that night but without a fire.

The next morning we met five hundred Indians on the road. They were on their way to the treaty. Father presented some of them with beautiful peacock feathers. This pleased them very much. They stopped and looked at our handcarts. "Little wagons, little wagons." said they. How the squaws laughed.

When we struck the mountain region the paths became more rugged to our feet. I picked up pretty little rocks and put them in my apron. By the time my pocket was filled I found other rocks still prettier. I threw away these and took them instead. I wish I could have saved some of the pretty rocks I gathered.

I was captivated by the place called "Deer Creek's" beauty. It was so charmingly sylvan with little groves here and there and a

---

33. By the time the handcart companies encountered Fort Laramie, it had become a military fort, much more extensive than the old fort that the first pioneers had passed.

bright clear creek lined with timber. Said I to Father, "Let's build a little log house and stay in this place always."

"What would we do for food?" asked Father.

"Do as we're doing now," said I, "Go without."

A little farther on I wanted to go down into a certain green cove. The captain forbade and called me back. Just then three bears came out and ascended the flat.

In the mountains we lost an old man. He had lain himself down and fallen asleep. We had to stop four days to find him. The delay alarmed our captain. He was anxious to keep ahead of the McArthur company.

Once in a while we stopped half a day to wash clothes. While the clothes were drying the men mended handcarts.

One night the McArthur company overtook us in the mountains. However, they had to wait for some cause or other. We therefore continued to move on ahead.

It was easy to make our way over Green River for the crossing had already been prepared. It did us good to view Green River valley. It was almost like taking a rest.

At Fort Bridger we stopped all night. The men killed a beef. This was our first meat since leaving the buffalo on the prairies. At Fort Bridger we met Bro. Parley P. Pratt. He was then starting on his last mission.

When within one day's journey of Salt Lake City we ran out of provisions. Two men who had joined us at the fort were on their way to Salt Lake City.

"What word shall we take from you?" said they to the Captain.

"Tell them we haven't a bite of food left in camp," said Captain Ellsworth.

A relief party met us with food before we arrived in Salt Lake City. How enchanting it was to enter Echo Canyon to call and have the echo answer.

The night we were encamped on Little Mountain the

McArthur company again overtook us. There was general rejoicing in all hearts. Early the next morning bread, beef and coffee arrived from Salt Lake City.

That very morning we passed a wagon company that had said goodbye to us in Iowa. I had acquaintances in this company who had said "We will beat you into Salt Lake City." I now had the pleasure of passing them. The men took off their hats and cheered.

There was a lazy man in camp who had a wife and a baby. For the sake of the wife and child, I had often helped pull his cart. Now we were nearing our journeys end and I made up my mind to let him do his own pulling. We were passing down a slope, he was on the bottom so I simply let his cart go rolling down the slope. "Catch it! Catch it!" I cried. He sprang forward and caught it in the nick of time. Everybody laughed.

That afternoon the same man climbed into a wagon of soap to ride awhile. We had been better provided with soap than food it seems. Coming down a rough place the wagon partly tipped over. Our friend was almost buried in soap to the amusement of the rest of us.

When we arrived in Immigration canyon we were met by Pres. Young and several members of the quorum of the twelve apostles. They arrived in wagons drawn by oxen and mules. We halted, they served us melons. Pres. Young told us to eat moderately of the mellon, to eat the pink, not to eat into the green. Father said he was quite sensible.

My little sister, Annie, age four, had been promised a big piece of bread and butter when she should reach the valley. Just as we were lined up to hear a few words from Bro. Brigham Young, a lady held up a large piece of bread. Annie ran toward her. "That's my piece of bread and butter," she cried joyously. At the sight of this Pres. Young wept, "God bless the child," said he. There were tears in the eyes of the people from the valley but there were only dry eyes among us who had just arrived. Pres. Young said he could defer his remarks until a little later.

That afternoon we went down into Salt Lake Valley. We camped on the square in the sixteenth ward, remaining there from Friday night until Monday morning. Bro. Brigham Young came and spoke to us. He told us that we had fulfilled a prophecy. He also said that although we had endured privations and hunger on the plains we should never again feel the pangs of starvation if we would do right and live right.

On monday morning a man came to the camp grounds, said he, "I've a little one room log house down in the Fifteenth Ward. I was going to move it away for a stable but if you wish to use it you may."

"What will be the rent?" asked father.

"One dollar and a half a month." said he.

We moved into this place. Bro. Nelson Empey loaned us three chairs. Bro. Thomas loaned us a chair and table. Bro. Grenic[34] loaned us a bedstead.

I did not remain at home. I went to work for some people from London, situated between the Gardo House and the Theater.[35] The man was known as Clive the Tailor. I worked for these people for five weeks. They did not pay me one cent. On pretext of being afraid food might harm me (due to my scanty living on the plains) they did not let me have half enough to eat.

Father took his tools and put in a days work on the Temple. Thus the promise made to him by the L.D.S. Elders in Wales, that he should go to Utah and work on the Temple, was fulfilled.

Exactly two weeks after our arrival in Salt Lake City, Father died. I had been home to see him but once during these two weeks. He died Friday afternoon and was buried about noon Saturday.

---

34. This man is probably Daniel Grenig, a baker and grocer who resided in the Fifteenth Ward.

35. Writing this account as a reminiscence, she is describing a location identified by these later-constructed buildings. Brigham Young had begun construction on the Gardo House in 1873. His wife Amelia Folsom was the first person to occupy the home. In December 1881 it became the residence of John Taylor and his family. It was located on the southwest corner of South Temple and State Street in Salt Lake City. The Salt Lake Theatre, constructed in 1861–62, was located on the northwest corner of State Street and First South.

As the father of five children, Archer Walters, a skilled carpenter and convert from Birmingham, found his experience with the Ellsworth company less care-free than either of the young Marys. With two sons and three daughters ranging in age from six to eighteen, Walters keenly felt a father's anxiety for his family. Concern over the fast pace of travel that Captain Ellsworth held them to and the ever-decreasing rations of food fill many lines in his diary. "My children cry with hunger and it grieves me and makes me cross," he wrote on the first of July after their food supply was almost depleted. Giving his portion to his children, he found his own strength waning as day followed day with nothing to ease the hunger pangs or lessen the exhausting labor with the handcarts. After writing almost daily from Iowa City, he ceased to write just days before the company was joyously greeted by Brigham Young and others from the Valley.

ARCHER WALTERS[36]

MONDAY MAY 19TH [1856] Went into the city of Iowa. Short of lumber. Saw a chapel or church burnt down. They say they were preaching against us yesterday but perhaps they will learn better by this purifying by fire. Had some whiskey and water which took all my strength for it was so hot. Got to camp about 1/2 past 8 o'clock.

---

36. Journal of Archer Walters, "Pioneer, Enroute from England to Utah, U.S.A., March 18, 1856 to September 5th, 1856," LDS Church Archives.

20th Went to work to make hand carts. Was not very well. Worked 10 hours. Harriet[37] very poorly.

Wednesday 21st Went work. Harriet not so well. Very hot. All very well considering the heat and change of diet.

Thursday 22nd Harriet worse with what we are told is the American Fever. Sometimes like the Ague. Sarah [his oldest daughter, age eighteen] went to Lindley's Farm to work and sent poor Harriet some milk and crust of bread.

Friday 23rd Harriet still very ill. I went to work. Still very hot to me. All the rest very well and I thank my Heavenly Father.

24th Harriet still very ill. Still at work at the carts. Rations served out and got more sugar.

Sunday 25th Morning meeting. Bro. [John] Godsall,[38] from Birmingham, addressed the meeting. Meeting 1/2 past 2. Brother [Chauncey G.] Webb[39] spoke and someone had been speaking against us. He roared out like a lion and would of slain them with a look of his eyes and if any was honest in heart and had been guilty they must have trembled for he spared none.

Monday 26th Went to work. Harriet still very bad. Lightened [lightning] very bad; began about 8 o'clock until 11 o'clock. Never saw it so in my life and it rained hard and our beds began to swim. I was wet on my side as I laid until I found it out.

27th Went to work at hand carts. Shift tent on a hill and was scolded for it.

Wednesday 28th At work.

29th Thursday at work. Harriet still very bad.

30th A child born in our tent 1/2 past one A.M.

1856 Saturday May 31st Martha [his daughter, age twelve] began to be ill. Still at work at the hand carts. a meeting at night and we are to prepare for off.

---

37. Archer Walters married Harriet Cross in 1837. She was forty-seven during this journey.

38. John Godsall had previously been called to preside over the Birmingham Conference. He came to Salt Lake City in the fall of 1856 in W. B. Hodgett's wagon company.

39. Chauncey G. Webb superintended cart-making at Iowa City.

Sunday JUNE 1st Meeting 1/2 past 10. Bro. _____ spoke and Bro. Webb. Sarah still at the farm, -Mr. Linley's. Henry [his son, age sixteen] went on watch to the cattle. The band played several tunes after the meeting.

Meeting 1/2 past two. Many people here.

2nd Harriet very ill. Still working at the hand carts.

Tuesday 3rd All well but Harriet.

Wednesday 4th Martha poorly. Made a coffin for a child dead in camp.

Thursday 5th All expect to go with our hand carts. I was liberated from working and my tools to go with us to do repairs on the road.

Friday 6th Made another child's coffin and a rough table for the Elders to eat upon. Bro. [Daniel] Spencer[40] said as I had been working my extra luggage should go through.

Saturday 7th 8th Started about 60 yards. Camped for the night and remained Sunday, June the 8th, and meetings held as usual. Harriet dreamed about eating fish and Henry went and catched one and she eat it all. I road Harriet in the hand cart round the camp. Very bad night owing to camping so late, the dew being on the grass.

Sunday 8th Meetings as usual. Went to bid Mr. Lindley good-bye. We journeyed 3 miles. Lost the cattle at night. Camped amongst bush and did not rest well. Harriet very ill. Found cattle Tuesday night at the old camp ground.

Wednesday 11th Journeyed 7 miles. Very dusty. All tired and smoothered with dust and camped in the dust or where the dust blowed. Was Captain over my tent of 18 in number but they were a family of Welch and our spirits were not united.[41] Had a tent

40. Daniel Spencer was dispatched from England early in the spring of 1856 to serve as the Church emigration agent at Iowa City.

41. The English and Welsh were traditionally begrudging neighbors in the British Isles and carried their rivalries with them.

but Elder Ellsworth would not let me use it and had to leave my tent poles behind me.

Thursday 12th Journeyed 12 miles. Went very fast with our hand carts. Harriet still ill.

Friday 13th Journeyed 7 miles. A pleasant road but journeyed so fast.

Saturday 14th Journeyed 7 miles. Pleasant.

Sunday 15th Got up about 4 o'clock to make a coffin for my brother, John Lee's son named William Lee, aged 12 years.[42] Meetings as usual, and at the same time had to make another coffin for Sister [Mary] Prator's[43] child. Was tired with repairing hand carts the last week. Went and buried them by moonlight at Bear Creek.

Monday 16th Harriet very ill. Travelled 19 miles and after pitching tent mended carts.

Tuesday 17th Travelled about 17 miles; pitched tent. Made a little coffin for Bro. Job Welling's son[44] and mended a hand cart wheel.

Wednesday 18th Rose before sun rise; travelled about 10 miles. Very hot; and camped for the day. Harriet still very ill but hope she will soon be better if it please my Heavenly Father.

Thursday 19th Travelled about 13 miles. Camped Bear Creek.

Friday 20th Travelled about 14 miles.

Saturday 21st Travelled about 13 miles. Camped at Indian Creek. Bro. [James] Bower died about 6 o'clock; from Birmingham Conference. Went to buy the wood to make the coffin but the kind farmer gave me the wood and nails. It had been a very hot day and I was never more tired, but God has said

---

42. John Lee (thirty-three) was traveling with his wife Sarah and their six children.
43. Lora Pratter, age three, died of whooping cough.
44. Job Welling was one and a half years old when he died of canker or inflammation of the bowels.

as my day my strength shall be. For this I rejoice that I have good health and strength according to my day. Indian Camp Creek.

Sunday 22nd Got up at day break and made the coffin for Bro. James Bowers by 9 o'clock and he was buried at 11 o'clock. Aged 44 years, 5 months, 2 days. His relatives[45] cried very much after I lifted him in the coffin and waiting to screw him down. 11 o'clock, washed in the creek and felt very much refreshed. Meeting 2 o'clock until seven. Bro. [Daniel D. McArthur] MacCarter spoke about being driven and he did walk into the Gentiles first rate and told them that they did not mean to be driven again and not to be excited by the priests to come against us as a people again for they would find them a terrible people.

Monday 23rd Rose early and travelled 10 miles; then repaired the hand carts. Harriet a little better.

Tuesday 24th Travelled 18 miles. Very hot. Bro. Ellsworth being always with a family from Birmingham named Brown and always that tent going first and walking so fast and some fainted by the way.[46] Bro. [Edward] Frost worn out by going so fast and not resting and many more.

Wednesday 25th Travelled about 13 miles. Sold some files to a Carpenter; repaired some hand carts.

Thursday 26th Travelled about 1 mile. Very faint for the (lack) of food. We are only allowed about 3/4 of lb. of flour a head each day and about 3 oz. of sugar each a week. Tea good and plenty; about a 1/4 of a lb. of bacon each a week; which makes those that have no money very weak. Made a child's coffin for Sister Sheen - Emma Sheen aged 2–1/2 years.

Friday 27th Got up before sun rise. Cut a tomb stone on wood and bury the child before starting from camp. Travelled about 10 miles. Repaired hand carts and quite tired and slept without rocking.

45. James Bowers left a wife and six children.
46. Edmund Ellsworth had just returned from serving a mission in Birmingham, England.

Saturday 28th We think Harriet a little better. Rose soon after 4 o'clock. Started with high wind. Short of water and I was never more tired. Rested a bit after we camped then came on a thunder storm, and rain blowed our tent down. Split the canvas and wet our clothes and we had to lay on the wet clothes and ground. I thought of going through needful tribulation but it made me cross. I took poor Harriet into a tent and fixed the tent up again as well I could at Bear Creek Station.

Sunday 29th Rather stiff in joints when we rose and thought, As thy day thy strength shall be, was fulfilled upon us for which I feel thankful to my Heavenly Father. Busy all day. My wife and Sarah mending. Short of provisions. Children crying for their dinner. Got the tent up and slept comfortable.

Monday 30th Rose in good health, except Harriet, and started with our hand carts with but a little breakfast as only 3–1/2 lbs. of flour was served out over night, but never travelled 17 miles more easily. Got 5 lbs. of flour and bacon about 1–1/4 lb. 3/4 rice, sugar 3/4 lb. and was refreshed after satisfying nature. Sleep very well after prayers in tent.

Tuesday JULY 1st Rose soon. It looked very cloudy and began to rain. Travelled about 15 miles. Walked very fast, - nearly 4 miles an hour. Brother Brown's family and some young sisters with Bro. Ellsworth always going first which causes many of the brothers to have hard feeling. I have heard them call them and Bro. Ellsworth as well, as he always walks with them and looks after them, being in the same tent. 1/2 lb. of flour each; 2 oz. of rice; which is very little and my children cry with hunger and it grieves me and makes me cross. I can live upon green herbs or anything and do go nearly all day without any and am strengthened with a morsel. Repaired hand carts. A storm came on about 11 o'clock and lasted 1 hour 1/2. Split the tent and not a dry thread on us.

Wednesday 2nd Rose about 5 o'clock after sleeping in wet clothes, and made a coffin for Bro. [Cyrus William] Card belonging to the Independent Company but travels with us, for his daughter named Polly Caroline Card, aged 14. 5 miles from Indian town. Brother [Robert] Parker's boy [Arthur], from Preston, England, aged 6 years, lost. 2 miles, gone after him which makes us stop today and we hope the brothers will find him. Not found; travelled about 14 or 15 miles.

Thursday 3rd Ever to be remembered. Bro Card gave me 1/2 dollar for making his daughter's coffin. Start with my cart before the camp as others had done but was told not and had to suffer for it. Went the wrong way; about 30 of the brothers and sisters and went 10–1/2 miles wrong way. We put our three hand carts together and made beds with all the clothes we had and all layed down about 1/2 past 10 o'clock. 11 o'clock Bro. [William] Butler, who had charge of the mule teams, came with the mules and wagon to fetch us. Got to camp when they were getting up. Laid down about an hour and started with the camp.

Friday 4th About 20 miles. Tired out. Tied my cart behind the wagon and we got in, after 3 nights. 1st night, thunder, lightning and rain and our tent splitting and blowing over. All wet to the skin. 2nd night: wind blowing; had hard work to hold the tent up and this last night no sleep. Went to bed; sleep never better and rose refreshed.

Saturday 5th A deer or helk[47] served out to camp. Brother Parker brings into the camp his little boy that had been lost. Great joy right through the camp. The mother's joy I cannot describe. Expect we are going to rest. Washing, etc. today, Jordan Creek. Make a pair of sashes for the old farmer. Indian meal; no flour. Slept well.

Sunday 6th Made 2 doors for the farmer, - 3 dollars and boarded with the farmer.[48]

---

47. His British pronunciation may have prompted him to put the letter "H" before a variety of words.

48. Provisions could be replenished by working during stopovers in the various Iowa villages and farm communities.

Monday 7th Harriet better. Lydia poorly. [his daugther, age six] Travelled about 20 miles.

Tuesday 8th Travelled around-about road about 20 miles. Crossed the river Missouri and camped at the City of Florence. Very tired; glad to rest. Slept well. Lydia better and Harriet. All in good spirits. Expect to stop some time. Old Winter Quarters.

Wed. 9th Rested. Florence City.

Thur. 10th Repairing hand carts. Could of got 3 or 4 dollars per day had I not engaged with Brother Spencer to repair the carts. Harriet better.

Friday 11th Repairing carts.

Saturday 12th Ditto.

Sunday (13th) Wrote to England and rested.

Monday (14th) Worked all day at carts.

Tuesday (15th) Ditto. Harriet still very ill.

Wednesday (16th) Ditto.

Thursday (17th) Left Florence City and we travelled about 3 miles. Went to _____ to seek work to buy a pair of shoes for Sarah but got no work for want of tools. Stopped there all night; slept in a stable. Came back to camp Friday morning, 17th. (18).

Friday (18th) Harriet very ill. Bought her some little niceties but she could not eat the pickles. Had a piece of buffalo beef given to me.

Saturday (19) Repairing carts all day.

Sunday (20) Preparing to start; travelled about 7 miles.

Monday (21) Travelled about 18 miles. Harriet better.

Tuesday (22) Passed of[f] the ferry at Helk Horn [Elkhorn]. Travelled about 12 miles. Thunder storm.

Wednesday (23) Very hot day. Travelled about 14 miles. Harriet much better.

Thursday (24) Very hot. Went about 18 miles. Harriet still better.

Friday (25) Travelled about 18 1/2 miles.

Saturday (26) Passed over the Ferry -Luke [Loup] Fort.

Travelled about 6 miles. Has soon has we crossed it looked very heavy and black. We had [not] got far and it began to lightning and so on the thunders roared and about the middle of the train of hand carts the lightning struck a brother and he fell to rise no more in that body, - by the name of Henry Walker, from Carlisle Conference; aged 58 years. Left a wife and children. One boy burnt a little, named James Studard [Stoddard]; we thought he would die but he recovered and was able to walk and Brother William Studard, father of the boy was knocked to the ground and a sister, Betsy Taylor, was terribly shook but recovered. All wet through. This happened about 2 miles from the Ferry and we then went 2 miles to camp. I put the body, with the help of others, on the hand cart and pulled him to camp and buried him without coffin for there was no boards to be had.

Sunday 27th The next morning, Sunday 27th, 1856, four miles west of Luke [Loup] Fort Ferry. Rose about 4 o'clock. Put a new axle tree to a cart that was broke yesterday. Travelled about 2 miles to a better camping ground.

Monday 28th Travelled about 18 miles. Harriet much better; for such we feel thankful.

Tuesday 29th Travelled about 15 miles. Met a Company coming from California. A child born in camp. Sister [Ann] Doney. *My birthday.*[49]

Wednesday 30th Travelled 22 miles.

Thursday 31st Travelled 18 miles. Heavy thunderstorm.

AUGUST 1856 Friday 1st Travelled 16 miles and camped at Prairie Creek.

Sat. 2nd Crossed over 2 creeks, - forded them. Stopt [for] dinner. Camped by Wood River. We saw many buffalo. Travelled about 18 miles.

Sunday 3rd Rested but mended hand carts. Got shell fish out

---

49. His forty-seventh.

of the creek for we was very hungry. Only 3/4 of lb. of flour; 1–1/2 oz. of sugar; a few apples; tea plenty.

Monday 4th Travelled 18 miles. Camped by Platte River.

Tuesday 5th Travelled 16 miles.

Wednesday 6th Saw thousands of buffalo. 4 was killed. So thick together that they covered 4 miles at once. Camped by Buffalo Creek. Travelled 10 miles.

Thursday 7th Thousands of buffalo. Travelled 25 miles. Camped late at night. Had to dig for water and it was very thick. Our hungry appetites satisfied by the buffalo. Got up soon to repair hand carts.

Friday 8th Rose soon to repair carts. Travelled about 15 miles. Camped by the side of Flat River. Repaired hand carts. Harriet getting round nicely and I feel truly thankful. My wife very ill tempered at times. An old brother lost named [Walter] Sanderson.[50] Many went in all directions but could not find him.

Saturday 9th Found the old brother Sanderson on a hill about 6 o'clock. Brought him into camp on a mule. Travelled about 15 miles after repairing hand carts until 12 o'clock.

Sunday 10th Travelled 14 miles. All, or most of the people had with the diarrhoea or purging,- whether it was the buffalo or the muddy river water.

Monday 11th Travelled about 17 miles. 4 men sent to shoot Buffalo. Harriet much better; very weak myself. I expect it is the short rations: 3/4 of a lb. of flour per day. It is but little but it is as much as the oxen teams that we have could draw from St. Florence. Forded over 2 creeks. Met a man coming from California by himself; going to the States. One of our cows died. Buffalo killed.

Tuesday 12th Rested while some of the brethren with Captain Ellsworth went and shot 2 more Buffalo and we dried the meat.

---

50. Captain Ellsworth records this man's name as Walter Sanders.

Wednesday 13th Travelled 12 miles; forded a large creek.

Thursday 14th Travelled 18 miles. Crossed three creeks. Last herd of Buffalo seen.

Friday 15th Forded over 5 creeks; camped at Snake Creek. Travelled 19 miles; from Florence 352 miles. Harriet much better and walked all the way.

Saturday 16th Forded over 5 or 6 creeks. Travelled 17 miles. Camped by Wolf Creek.

Sunday 17th Crossed over some creeks. Camped over the Platte River. Travelled 12 miles. Brother Missel Rossin, Italian, found dead by the side of the road.

Monday 18th Travelled 20 miles. Camped by the Platte River.

Tuesday 19th Travelled 19 miles. Camped by the Platte River. A nice camping ground. Buffalo chips to burn.

Wednesday 20th Travelled 19 miles. Camped by River Platte.

Thursday 21st Travelled 18 miles. Camped 4 miles past Chimney Rock, Platte River. Sandy Road the last 3 or 4 days.

Friday 22nd Good road. Travelled 24 miles. Camped by Platte River.

Saturday 23rd Travelled 16 miles. Camped by Platte River. Harriet getting well, thank God, and not been in the wagons to ride. Our allowance of flour tonight was 1 lb. a head. For this I was thankful for I never was so hungry in my life. Captain Ellsworth shot a cow. Very thankfully received.

Sunday 24th Rested from travels but had to repair hand carts. Meeting at night. Received the Sacrament. Spoke at the meeting. Bro. Ellsworth spoke some time and said we had made great improvement; that the last week there had been less quarreling and those that had robbed the hand carts, or wagons, unless they repent their flesh would rot from their bones and go to Hell.

Monday 25th Travelled about 19 miles. Saw many Indians. Camped about 19 miles from Fort Laramie. Hand Cart axle tree broke on the road. Plenty of wood. Quite a treat after burning so many Buffalo chips.

Tuesday 26th Travelled about 19 miles. Camped 3 miles from Fort Laramie. Trucked [traded] away a dagger for a piece of bacon and salt and sold one for 1 dollar 1/4. Bought bacon and meal and Henry and me began to eat it raw we was so hungry. Forded the river. Sister Watts got hurt by the wagon. My wife thinks she would of fell when half way over the river. Bro. John Lee came to her assistance.

Wednesday 27th Travelled about 18 miles. Had bacon and meal porridge for supper; the best supper for many weeks. A camp of Indians passed us.

Thursday 28th Travelled about 15 miles. Mended hand carts good and had road hilley. Camped at a nice place called Horse Shoe Creek. Mother and Sarah washed clothes.

Friday 29th Travelled 25 miles. Camped Platte River. Met some Californians.

Saturday 30th Travelled 22 miles. Met some Californians and they told us the wagons was waiting at Deer Creek for us.

Sunday 31st Very poorly, faint and hungry. Travelled to Deer Creek, 22 miles. Brother R. Stoddard from Carlisle Conference, about 54 years old, died in the wagon on road.[51] More provisions given out.

SEPTEMBER Monday 1st Rested from travels. I mended carts. Meeting about flour and paying for extra that was brought in the wagons. Harriet getting quite well and walks all the way. 18 cents per lb.

Tuesday 2nd Platte River. Travelled 19 miles. Walter Sanderson, aged 56, died.

Wednesday 3rd Met 4 wagons: Henshaw from Nottingham; John Barns from Sheffield. Travelled 15 miles.

51. He left a wife and three children.

Thursday 4th Travelled 10 miles.

Friday 5th Rested. Rained all day.

Saturday 6th Lost cattle.

Sunday 7th Travelled 26 miles. Bro. Nipras [George Nappriss, age 23] died. Left on road.

Monday 8th 11 miles. Had dinner at Devil's Gate.

Wed. 10th

T. 11th

F. 12th Sarah very poorly. Harriet quite well.

Saturday 13th Travelled 28 miles. Camped at Paciffick Springs. Trucked a blanket with a brother from the Valley who came from Rotherham, named Goldsmith, part of Bro. Bankses Wagon Co.[52]

Sunday 14th Traveled 3 miles. Camped to mend hand carts and women to wash. Sister Mayer died. [Mary Mayo, 65, a widow traveling alone.]

[Diary ends here. Company arrived in Salt Lake Valley, September 26, 1856. Archer Walters died two weeks later.]

The successful crossing of the prairies and plains by the first three companies, despite the hardships they faced, encouraged Church leaders, and the way seemed clear to continue this kind of travel.

But such sanguine hopes were starkly shaken by the next two companies to start out that same year. The plan that had worked so well for three of the companies faltered at crucial points for the next two. Even before the following two shiploads of more than a thousand emigrants and returning mission-

---

52. John Banks's company, known as the St. Louis company, consisted mainly of British Saints who had stopped temporarily in St. Louis to raise money and supplies to continue their journey. They left Florence the middle of June and arrived in the Valley on 1 and 2 October 1856.

aries left Liverpool, there were signs of potential trouble. Their late departure from England in May was surely cautionary to those who knew how crucial timing was to each step of the way from Liverpool to the Valley. But the emigrants eagerly left England, largely unaware of the impact of this first misstep. They were responding to the call to gather, and many of them had left their jobs, sold their farms or shops, and collected their savings and belongings, and they had no alternative but to emigrate that year.

Another weakened link in the chain of organization was communication; the Iowa agents did not expect such a large contingent of emigrants who planned to go west that year and did not have sufficient equipment and supplies for them when they reached Iowa City. While fewer than 800 people made up the first three handcart companies earlier that spring, more than a thousand emigrants and returning missionaries arrived in Iowa City in late June, determined to make it to the Valley that year. They might well have wintered in Iowa City since available work seemed likely in the thriving railroad town, but few were interested in staying. Instead, they spent more crucial weeks making their own carts and acquiring provisions.

Finally on their way in late July, they spent another month crossing Iowa. That trek helped condition them for the longer and more difficult segment of the journey that lay before them, though it was like "only a mile" to what they yet faced, as one pioneer remembered.[53] Florence might also have been a stopping place for the winter, but it offered little opportunity

---

53. Emma James in Laleta Dixon, "History of Her Ancestor, William James of the Willey [sic] Handcart Co., 1856," typescript copy, LDS Church Archives.

for work, and few of the emigrants had enough supplies to see them through another year before completing their journey to Zion. But to go on was hazardous. Levi Savage, a returning missionary, was well acquainted with the peculiarities of the trail and the power of the weather on its travelers. His apparently lone voice urged caution. Several diarists recorded his dissenting words as he pled with the Saints to wait until spring. "Some of the strong may get through in case of bad weather, but the bones of the weak and old," he predicted, "will strew the way." Savage knew that a thousand inexperienced men, women, and children could easily flounder under the best of circumstances, and the timing of their journey had already put them in jeopardy.[54]

But the "determined look" that Emma James saw on her mother's face appeared on nearly a thousand others, and the warning was overruled. "We must put our trust in the Lord as we have always done," Jane James exclaimed. Her response was understandable. The eagerness of the Saints to reach the Valley that year and the longing of the missionaries to return to their homes easily superseded any anxieties they might have felt. The straitened circumstances of many of them also offset any enticement to wait another season. The encouraging words of British mission president Franklin D. Richards, who arrived in Florence with several missionaries shortly before the Martin company left the outfitting post, seemed to be the final endorsement of the plan to

---

54. Emma James notes that a meeting was held in Iowa City to decide their course of action, but it was more likely held at the Missouri, as recorded in John Chislett's narrative. Despite his worries at leaving so late, Levi Savage pledged to stay with the Saints, whatever their decision, willing to "work, rest, suffer, and if necessary die with them." Levi Savage Journal, as quoted in "The Handcart Migration," Kate B. Carter, comp., *An Enduring Legacy* (Salt Lake City: Daughters of Utah Pioneers, 1981) 4:213.

push on.[55] Only a hundred were persuaded to stay over. And so it was that late in August the fourth handcart company, under James G. Willie, and the fifth of the season, under Edward Martin, both returning missionaries, left the Missouri with nearly a thousand eager handcart pioneers. Both companies had supply wagons carrying their provisions, as well as cattle for milk and beef. The 385 emigrants who could afford to travel in wagons followed behind in either W. B. Hodgett's company of thirty-three wagons or John A. Hunt's company of fifty wagons.

The earliest problems besetting the handcarters, such as broken carts, sudden rainstorms, Indian harassment, and swollen feet, were mere inconveniences next to those that befell them as the journey wore on. The loss of their cattle early in the journey, the sudden sweeps of diarrhea and dysentery, the crossing of rivers in freezing temperatures that left them wet and exposed to the cold, and the rapidly diminishing food supply taxed their patience, strength, and spirit.

But the real trial for both companies came with an early frost in September, which led to brief periods of snow, culminating, on 19 October, with a heavy, continuing, and devastating snowfall. It brought all travel to a halt. The Willie company had reached the fifth crossing of the Sweetwater,

---

55. Although there is no record of any specific words spoken to the Saints at Florence by Franklin D. Richards, who orchestrated the emigration of three thousand Saints before he left England, he likely encouraged them in the decision they had already made. Richards did, however, write a letter to Brother Little on 3 September, published in the *Millennial Star*, in which he expressed his concern over the last two companies that year. "From the beginning," he wrote, "we have done all in our power to hasten matters pertaining to emigration, therefore we confidently look for the blessing of God to crown our humble efforts with success, and for the safe arrival of our brethren the poor Saints in Utah, though they may experience some cold." (In *Millennial Star* 18 [25 October 1856]: 682.)

and the Martin company was several days behind at Red Bluffs, sixty-five miles east of Devil's Gate. To these companies, already weakened and demoralized, this storm was brutal. The clothing in their small bundles was no match for a Rocky Mountain snowstorm of such magnitude. Many had dropped heavy clothing and bedding along the way to lighten their load as their strength waned. How much they wished for them now! With their food nearly exhausted, their clothes thin and worn, and tents and handcarts their only shelter, both the Willie and Martin companies found themselves helplessly stranded in the Wyoming mountains.

Eighteen-year-old Sarah James and her seventeen-year-old sister Emma, who were traveling with their father and mother, William and Jane James, and their younger brothers and sisters, had no trouble graphically recalling their family's experience with the Willie company.

EMMA JAMES[56]

WE WERE CALLED TOGETHER in a meeting one evening and there was quite a bit of guessing as to the reason for it. It was a large group who gathered circling the leader. The meeting was called to order, one of the brethren offered prayer, then we were told the reason for the council meet-

56. From Laleta Dixon, "History of My Ancestor, William James of the Willey [sic] Handcart Co., 1856," typescript copy, LDS Church Archives.

ing. We were told that it was 300 miles to [Council Bluff] which was the actual place for starting the trek and that was just a mile to what we had to go to reach the valley. We would have carts such as they were, but the season was late and bad weather could prove dangerous to us if we were in the mountains. Even if we had no trouble we would be late getting to Utah. There had been much talk of these dangers by experienced men in the camp, but I think that the thing which I will remember for the rest of my life and wish that we had heeded was said by a Brother Savage. With tears streaming down his cheeks he pleaded with the people, "Brothers and sisters, wait until spring to make this journey. Some of the strong may get through in case of bad weather, but the bones of the weak and old will strew the way." I can remember that when he finished there was a long time of silence. I was frightened. Father looked pale and sick. I turned to mother to see what she was thinking, and all I saw was her old determined look. She was ready to go on tomorrow. There were many others like her. We really didn't have much choice. There was no work here for us to keep ourselves through the winter, and our family had to live. "We must put our trust in the Lord as we have always done" said mother, and that was that.

There was nearly 100 people of the companies who decided to winter over and come on in the spring. The majority voted to go on as soon as everything was ready. July 15 our company, under the direction of Captain Willie, with 500 people, 120 carts and four or five wagons left Camp Iowa and headed for our outfitting station at Council Bluff. It was great fun pulling empty carts and imitating the wagon drivers with a "gee" and "haw." We got away ahead of the slow wagons and had to wait for them. We had plenty of time to see the country we were passing through—to run here and there and to explore this and that. There were many things to catch the eye in this strange land. [. . .]

When we started out on the trail each morning [after leaving Florence, Nebraska] there was always something new to see.

Maybe it was a bird running along the road which we chased but never did catch. There were always flowers and pretty rocks to pick. This land was so different from the one in England that it kept us interested. We were constantly being warned not to go too far away from the trail, but I can't remember that we heeded the warning until we had one or two experiences which made us more careful.

One day as we were skipping along beside the carts and singing, for we were always happy as I remember it, a group of Indians on horse back rode up and followed along with us for a while. We didn't know the redman well enough to be too friendly, so we quieted down and stayed close to our parents. One of the Indians seemed fascinated by the contraptions being pulling along by people. Finally his curiosity got the best of him. He leaped off his horse, ran over to one of the carts which was being pulled by a woman and her daughter and gave it such a hard push that it nearly ran over them. The woman and girl screamed and got out of the shafts as fast as they could. The Indians pushed the cart for a little ways, and then, apparently sat-isfied, he jumped on his horse and rode off. He, with some of his friends, came back later to beg for food. We gave it to them because we were told that the Indians were our brethren and that we should treat them so. We never did have any trouble with them except that they never seemed to learn that it was stealing to take something which didn't belong to them. [. . .]

One evening as we prepared to stop for the night, a large herd of buffalo came thundering toward us. It sounded like thunder at first, then the big black animals came straight for our carts. We were so scared that we were rooted to the ground. One of the captains, seeing what was going on, ran for the carts which were still coming in, jerked out some of the carts to make a path for the steady stream of animals and let them go through. They went passed us like a train roaring along. I'm sure that but for the quick thinking of these men, many of us would have been trampled to death. The animals acted as if they were crazy the way they ran. We hoped that we wouldn't meet such a large herd soon again. After they had gone somebody called out that the cattle had gone with them. This was our only supply of meat, so the men started right out after them. The men on foot soon lost the sight of the herd. Those of us who were left made preparation for the night hoping the men would be back with our cattle by dark. As the sun went down, a terrible storm came up. A strong wind tore the tents out of our hands and sent everything flying in all directions. The thunder and lightening was like nothing we had ever seen before. We had all we could do to keep track of each other. The noise terrified the children so that they ran for any shelter that they could find. Soon we all did for the rain came down in torrents, and in a matter of minutes we were soaked to the skin. The men came in from the hunt empty handed but in time to help gather up our belongings and get ready for our meal. We all went to bed wet and cold.

The loss of cattle so early on the trek proved to be disastrous. Using their milk cows to pull the wagons, the handcarters soon found their milk supply diminished as well as their beef, which curtailed the rations earlier and more drastically than they had anticipated. The lack of food denied them the strength to combat the other difficulties they encountered, expecially as the weaterh changed from fall to winter. Sarah James remembered them well.

SARAH JAMES[57]

WE WERE COLD ALL THE TIME. It was either rain or snow or wind. Even when you wrapped up in a blanket your teeth chattered. Father told us one night that the flour was gone and that the word was that we might not get help for some time. Father was white and drawn. I knew that mother was worried about him, for he was getting weaker all the time and seemed to feel that there was no use in all the struggle. Mother had taken as much of the load off his shoulders as she could in pulling the cart. We girls and Reuben [her brother, 13 yrs old] did most of the work so that father could rest a lot. Mother didn't have much to say, and I wondered if she remembered that council meeting in Camp Iowa and wished that we had taken the advice of more experienced people. I'm sure that many of us had those thoughts.

We were grateful one morning when we heard that the captain had ordered all the animals in the company killed so that we could have fresh meat. We were so hungry that we didn't stop to think what it would do for our wagons. How good the soup tasted made from the bones of those cows although there wasn't any fat on them. The hides we used to roast after taking all the hair off of them. I even decided to cook the tatters of my shoes and make soup of them. It brought a smile to my father's sad face when I made the suggestion, but mother was a bit impatient with me and told me that I'd have to eat the muddy things myself.

It snowed day after day, and we managed to get a few miles each day. We were sort of dizzy and sleepy a lot of the time, so I

57. From Laleta Dixon, "History of My Ancestor, William James of the Willey [sic] Handcart Co., 1856," typescript copy, LDS Church Archives.

can't remember too well just what did happen all of the time. Sometimes when we felt that we just had to rest for a time, a captain would come up and help us pull our cart along for a time. I'm sure that we would have laid down and died if it hadn't been for their help and encouragement. Sometimes they had to get cross with some people. I can remember the time when one of the men who was pulling a cart just ahead of us laid down in his shafts and started to cry. We all wanted to cry with him. One of the captains, I don't remember just who, came up to him and just slapped him in the face. It made the man so mad that he jumped right up and started to run with his cart. I remember that it was a mean way to treat the poor fellow but now that it saved his life.

The day we reached the last crossing of the Sweetwater river I will never forget as long as I live. It was a bitter cold morning in October as we broke camp. As usual there were dead to be buried before we could go on. Father and Reuben were with the burial detail. Mother, who was helping to pull the heaviest cart, had stayed behind until they could finish their sad work. After a short service, we, with light cart, went ahead to catch the rest of the company, and mother and Rueben started to follow. Father collapsed and fell in the snow. He tried two or three times to get up with mother's help, then finally he asked her to go on and when he felt rested he would come on with Rueben. Mother knew in her heart that he had given out, but perhaps she said in a few minutes with some rest he could come on. She took the cart and hurried to follow us.

She found us on the river bank. We were too frightened and tired to cross alone. We had forded this river before many times, but it had never seemed so far across. It was about 40 feet I guess to the other bank. Mother soon had us on our way. The water was icy, and soon our clothing was frozen to our bodies. Our feet were frozen numb. Cold and miserable we reached the other bank, put on dry clothing and joined the rest of the company.

When we stopped for the night, we made inquiries about our people, but nothing had been heard of them. Since there were some who had been a few hours behind us, we felt that they would come with the next group. All night we waited for word. Toward morning some of the captains who had gone out to gather up the stragglers came into camp bearing the dead body of my father and the badly frozen body of my brother Rueben. His injuries were so bad that he would suffer from them for the rest of his life. When morning came, father's body, along with others who had died during the night, were buried in a deep hole. Brush was thrown in and then dirt. A fire was built over the grave to kill the scent to keep the wolves from digging up the remains.

I can see my mother's face as she sat looking at the partly conscious Rueben. Her eyes looked so dead that I was afraid. She didn't sit long, however, for my mother was never one to cry. When it was time to move out, mother had her family ready to go. She put her invalid son in the cart with her baby, and we joined the train. Our mother was a strong woman, and she would see us through anything.

The time came when we were all too tired to move, so we huddled in our covers, close to each other for warmth. It was snowing, and we were so tired. Suddenly we heard a shout, and through the swirling snow we saw men, wagons and mules coming toward us. Slowly we realized that help had come. The wagons brought food and clothing. They hauled in wood for us, and as we gathered around the huge fire and ate the delicious morsels of food, we came alive enough to thank the Lord for his mercy to us. [. . .]

Now that we had food and warmth for our bodies, we realized that we would have to move on for the weather was getting worse as the days went on. It was decided that we would leave everything except some extra clothing, utensils to cook in and many of our carts which would be guarded until they could be brought on in the spring. Those who couldn't walk would ride in the wagons, and we would travel as fast as we could to the valley.

I remember the rest of the journey as being terrible with the cold and snow, but we did have food and some hope of getting to Zion.

We arrived in Salt Lake City 9th of November having been on the plains for nearly five months. The Saints took us in and were very kind to us. Bishop [Aaron] Johnson of Springville sent word that he could take one family into his home for the winter, so we were sent South. We older children found work in the homes of the good people in the town, and mother moved into an unfurnished shack where she kept her younger children alive until spring with what work she could find. We stayed in Springville for a year and then moved back to Salt Lake City. Mother's children were marrying and making homes for themselves, so when Mary Ann [her sister] moved to Provo she came with her. Here she spent her last years, and at the time of her death at the age of 96, August 14, 1911, she left a great posterity to revere her memory and give thanks that she had had the determination to come to Zion.

A member of the Willie company, Susanna Stone Lloyd, at age twenty-six, traveled alone to Utah, the only one of her family to join the Church. Writing her memoirs late in life softened her memory of some of the cruelties of that journey, but her reliance on "the hand of Providence" is evident throughout her brief story. In a small display of personal pride, Susanna wanted to make herself presentable before meeting friends whose companies had preceded hers to the Valley. She had sold her looking glass to an Indian for some buffalo meat long before, so seeing herself in a borrowed mirror proved startling. As she feared, some of those friends did not recognize her, despite her efforts, because she was "so weatherbeaten and tanned."

SUSANNA STONE LLOYD[58]

MY PARENTS, RELATIVES, AND FRIENDS did all in their power to keep me from coming to America, but I had the spirit of gathering and the Lord opened the way and I came to Utah in 1856 with a handcart company. Brother Willey was our captain, Millen Atwood was his counselor. We traveled through sunflowers and sagebrush for many miles.

The first part of our journey was pleasant, the weather being good. We left Liverpool in May on the sailing vessel Thornton, landing in New York the latter part of June. While crossing the Atlantic, the people's galley took fire and burned, which caused great excitement, but through the blessings of the Lord we were saved. After we landed, we came up the Hudson River in steamboats and continued by railroad cars until we came to the Iowa campgrounds. We stayed there several weeks while our handcarts and tents were being finished. Oxen drew the wagons which brought our provisions and tents. Our clothing to last the journey, which was over one thousand miles, was brought on our handcarts. The rest was brought the next season by the Walker Brothers.[59]

After we had proceeded quite a distance on our journey, we lost a number of cattle that drew the provision wagons. Some supposed that the animals were stampeded by Indians or buffalo. We met several tribes of Indians going east to war. It was in the year 1856 when Colonel Almon W. Babbitt had been doing business with the United States Government. Babbitt and his team-

---

58. Susanna Stone Lloyd, in "Information on Thomas and Susanna Lloyd" (1915), microfilm of typescript, LDS Church Archives.

59. The Walker Brothers were Mormon emigrants from Great Britain who established a successful mercantile business in Salt Lake City but later left the Church.

sters were massacred. They were a day or two ahead of us with a train of goods which was seized by the Indians. We met a tribe of Indians with an interpreter, who told us all about the circumstances, but we were not discouraged. We traveled on, feeling that the Lord would protect his Saints, and so he did; although we passed through many trying scenes, his protecting care was over us.

After leaving Iowa [City], we traveled about one hundred [300] miles and came to Florence. By this time we had grown accustomed to traveling and made better headway, but through losing our cattle and having to camp on the Plains for several weeks, it threw us late in the season and made our provisions short for the latter part of our journey. We left England May 2, and arrived in Salt Lake Valley November 5, 1856. I am thankful that I was counted worthy to be a pioneer and a handcart girl. It prepared me to endure hard times in my future life. I often think of the songs we sang to encourage us on our toilsome journey. It was hard to endure, but the Lord gave us strength and courage.

After we had traveled about seven hundred miles our provisions being short, our captain bought up all the biscuits and flour that he could get in Laramie. We had to live on short rations and it became very cold. A number of our older people died. Sixteen were buried at one time. Traveling as we were with scant clothing and lack of sufficient food, we suffered greatly from the severe cold and snow. On account of the loss of cattle, it became necessary for each hand cart to take additional load, but each taking a share of the provisions that were left.

We waded through the cold streams many times but we murmured not for our faith in God and our testimony of His work were supreme. And in the blizzards and falling snow we sat under our hand carts and sang, 'Come, come, ye saints, no toil nor labor fear, but with joy wend your way. Though hard to you this journey may appear, grace shall be as your day,' etc. Only once did my courage fail. One cold dreary afternoon, my feet having been frosted, I felt I could go no further, and withdrew from the little company and sat down to wait the end, being somewhat in a stupor. After a time I was aroused by a voice, which seemed as audible as anything could be, and which spoke to my very soul of the promises and blessings I had received, and which should surely be fulfilled and that I had a mission to perform in Zion. I received strength and was filled with the Spirit of the Lord and arose and traveled on with a light heart. As I reached camp I found a searching party ready to go back to find me, dead or alive. I had no relatives but many dear and devoted friends and we did all we could to aid and encourage each other. My frosted feet gave me considerable trouble for many years but this was forgotten in the contemplation of the many blessings the Gospel has brought to me and mine. A young man whom I had kept company with in England but would not promise to marry, as I wanted to be free, died enroute and was buried on the plains with many others. When we were within about a hundred miles from Salt Lake our captain had a dream that a company was coming from Salt Lake to meet us. Brigham Young got a lot of our brethren to come and meet us with provisions, buffalo robes and blankets. You may guess the joy that was in camp the day they arrived. We were near Fort Bridger when they met us, and we rode in the wagons the rest of the way, but we had walked over one thousand miles. When we got near the City, we tried to make ourselves as presentable as we could to meet our friends. I had sold my little looking glass to the Indians for buffalo meat, so I borrowed one and I shall never forget how I looked. Some of my old friends did not know me. We were so weather beaten and tanned. When we got near Salt Lake Valley, President Young with a company of our brethren and sisters came out to meet us, and bade us welcome and when we got into the city we were made very comfortable until we met our friends and relatives. There were many things that would be interesting if I could remember them in their proper order. While we were traveling thru the United

States the people tried to discourage us by telling us there was famine in Utah, that the grasshoppers had eaten up everything and that there had been a grass-hopper war, etc., but we traveled on, trusting in God.

George Cunningham was a fifteen-year-old English youth when he traveled across the plains with the Willie company. Emigrating with his parents and three sisters, he, like Susannah Lloyd, left a brief, episodic reminiscence that lacks some of the emotion of firsthand diaries but highlights vividly-remembered incidents. In one dramatic phrase he captured the "dull and benumbed" senses of the desperate travelers. "No one feared death now," he wrote, "nearly everybody seemed indifferent or stupefied."

GEORGE CUNNINGHAM[60]

MY PARENTS [George Cunningham and Elizabeth Nelson Cunningham] were the first to embrace the Gospel around our district[61] but later nearly half of the citizens joined, probably twenty or thirty families. I was raised in the strictest sense of the word 'Mormon.' In the spring of 1856 the chance opened up for us to emigrate to this country, for which we were truly

---

60. George Cunningham in "The Handcart Pioneers," in Kate B. Carter, comp., *Treasures of Pioneer History*, 6 vols. (Salt Lake City, Daughters of Utah Pioneers, 1956) 5:252–56.
61. George was born in Dysart, Fifeshire, Scotland.

thankful. We sold our small effects and bade our friends farewell, took a train for Glasgow and from there by steamboat to Liverpool. On the 4th of May we embarked on the ship Thornton bound for New York.

How well I remember the first step that I took on American soil! How thrilled I was to be in the land of the free—the land of promise! I had been taught to believe it was the land of promise blessed above all other lands, and although only a boy of fifteen years, I felt like thanking God for the blessing I then enjoyed.

After a few days in New York we sailed up the river to Albany then by railroad about three hundred miles, by ship on the Great Lakes and then again by railroad to Iowa arriving the latter part of June. We went to the Mormon campground just outside the city [Iowa City] and stayed there for five or six weeks. At length we were appointed to continue our journey with Captain James Willie's handcart company. This meant a three-hundred mile trip through the state of Iowa before reaching a permanent starting place at Winter Quarters or Florence, where we arrived after several weeks of pulling, hauling and praying. People sneered at us and laughed crying out "Gee-haw" but this did not discourage us in the least. We knew that we were on the right track and that was enough.

I can remember being at a meeting when Brother Levi Savage, a returned missionary, spoke. He counseled the old and sickly to remain until another spring. The tears rolled down his cheeks as he prophesied that if such took the journey at that late season of the year, their bones would strew the way. At length we started, but the number was greatly reduced, about one hundred remaining. I must state here that there was not one of our hundred remained for which we received great praise. The wagons were heavily loaded and we were delayed much by having to wait on them. When we arrived at Wood River we came across a large camp of Omaha Indians who invited us to camp with them for the night. We did so and they were very friendly. We resumed our journey the next morning.

One night after a long and tiresome day's journey we turned out the oxen and the cows to feed and a large herd of buffalo came running towards them. The oxen ran off with the buffalo and although we hunted the country over for miles we never found them—not one of our cows left with the herd. As soon as we had formed camp one of the terrible prairie storms blew up. It was dark as pitch and all hands had to hold on to the tents to keep them from going up like balloons. The heavy rain soon flooded the prairie, accompanied by the deafening roar of thunder and vivid flashes of lightning which seemed to electrify everything. When morning came all the able bodied men and boys turned out again to look for the cattle. We scoured the country but not even their footprints could be seen because of the heavy rain. The search was kept up for a week and often when we thought we could see old Brin and Nig or Buck and Bright they would invariably take to their heels and prove to be nothing but an old buffalo. I have heard the song, "Through the Wildwood I'll Wander and Chase the Buffalo," but I never expected to experience it in this shape.

At length the command came to 'Move On.' Provisions were getting very short and with a six or seven hundred mile journey before us, we knew that we must do so or perish in the mountain snows. We transferred our provisions from the wagons to the handcarts and hitched the thirty milch cows to the wagons to haul the sick and the children who were not able to walk. We plodded on through the mud with all the courage we could muster. We traveled along slowly and after a few weeks arrived at Fort Laramie. As our provisions were very nearly exhausted our captain went into Fort Laramie and bought a ton or two of flour for which he had to pay $20.00 per hundred pounds.

After leaving here we met a company of missionaries going to the states. Elder Parley Pratt came and talked to us trying to encourage us. The nights now began to get very cold and feed was poor, also our provisions were running out fast. Starvation looked us in the face. We were put on rations of six ounces of flour each per day and nothing else. The old and the weak began to die for want of proper food, and a great many of the young and strong ones soon followed suit. I, myself, have helped to bury ten to fifteen in a single day. We who could stand it were barely kept alive and after several weeks of this ration it was reduced to half this amount. I, however, stirred my three ounces with some water and gulped it down. To make things worse we were caught in a heavy snowstorm on the Sweetwater. It was extremely cold and the last of our flour was gone. Nothing was left but a scant supply of crackers reserved for the sick and small children. The captain ordered that every critter in the train be killed as needed but they were nearly as poor as we were. However, we used to boil the bones and drink the soup. Every particle that could be used was taken, even the hide was rationed and after scorching the hair off, we would roast it a little over the coals and cut it in small pieces and it made what we considered a delicious supper. Towards the last the weather was so cold that all but five or six men in camp had been severely frozen, and let me add right here is where the great test came—some would sacrifice by giving their food and clothing to their friends, relatives and children while others seemed to be devoid of natural affection and would let their family members die off merely for the sake of getting their few mouthfuls of food or perhaps an old blanket that covered them.

In these trying times with eighteen inches of snow and very cold weather, I remember how we built large fires with willows which were abundant at this place. Everybody stood around the fire with gloomy faces, as if in a death trap, when all at once flashed into my mind my dream of the previous night as follows: 'That a number of wagons loaded with provisions were soon to meet us.' How joyfully I related my last night's dream in detail.

My mother told them that she knew it would come true, as I was promised that gift in my blessing. And to our great pleasure every word was literally fulfilled. I can recollect that I was in the lead of the crowd, feeling quite inspired by my dream. At their approach I roared out, 'See! See them coming over that hill!' We soon met the wagons with provisions and were very kindly treated and all felt to thank God.

Now the great difficulty was by eating too much. The feelings and senses of our people were dull and benumbed. No one feared death now. Nearly everybody seemed indifferent or stupefied.

Our Captain showed us a noble example. He was furnished a mule to ride on but he said, 'I will never get on its back. I will set the example—you follow it.' And thus our captains set the example. They would crowd ahead and be the first in the streams to help others across and they were the last out. They waded every stream, I might say, a dozen times between Iowa City and Green River with the exception of the Missouri River. Their feet were worn and bleeding, they became exhausted and had to be hauled the balance of the way, some of them not being able to stand. Among these heroic leaders were: James Willie, our captain; Milan [Millen] Atwood, Levi Savage, William Woodard [Woodward] and another Danish brother whose name I have forgotten.

At our arrival at Salt Lake City our company was kindly cared for and when we had rested up a bit we were sent to various settlements. We were sent to American Fork where my home has been ever since. Here we met with many old acquaintances and soon made friends with others who helped us. 'Ere long I found employment and thus we were removed from our very straightened circumstances.

639

Samuel Openshaw of Lancashire, the eldest of William and Ann Openshaw's children, traveled to Utah with his parents and five siblings in Edward Martin's company. Samuel, age twenty-two, kept a daily diary of his journey, especially through Iowa, noting the settlements they passed, rivers crossed, and mileage covered each day. The latter part of his account was evidently written some time afterwards. At the end of the journey, he had to give more attention to surviving the trip than to writing about it.

SAMUEL OPENSHAW[62]

JULY 11 [1856]. We started for Iowa City at five o'clock A.M.; found that the rest had gone to the camp ground. There was a thunderstorm in this city last night, but I heard nothing of it. In Davenport [Iowa] We continued on the camp ground until the 25th, when we made a short move just down the hill, more for our health than anything else.

July 26. Sunday. We moved none today. We had a meeting in the afternoon, partook of the sacrament and heard addresses from the Captains of Hundreds.

July 27. We made another short move across the river (creek).

July 28. We still remained here; perhaps on account of some of the cattle being lost.

---

62. Diary of Samuel Openshaw (May–November 1856), typescript copy, LDS Church Archives.

July 29. Still on this place; about three miles from the City of Iowa.

July 30. We made a hunt for the cattle (eight), over the plains (prairies) but found none.

July 31. We made another hunt for the cattle, but could not find them. We started at 12 o'clock with our handcarts and traveled about seven miles, pitched our tents at seven o'clock p.m.

August 1. At ten o'clock A.M. made another start. The roads were all sandy. At seven o'clock P.M., pitched our tents on the top of a hill from whence we could look as far as the eye could carry, but the water was not good.

August 2. Orders were given to start at seven o'clock this morning, but a thunderstorm came which delayed us until 12 o'clock. We traveled until eight o'clock when we pitched our tents in the midst of a wood called Bullrun. We kindled a great fire and set round to warm ourselves as night air is cold, and then began to talk about our friends in the old country and compared their situation with ours.

August 3. Sunday. On account of the unhealthiness of the place, we made a start today and traveled about seven miles. When we had traveled about a quarter of a mile we beheld a ball of fire brighter than the sun before us in the air and came within about three yards of the ground and then drew out in the form of a spear and vanished out of our sight. We pitched our tents two miles from Marengo.

August 4. Still beautiful; and hot day. We did not move until four o'clock P.M. Traveled about seven miles and pitched our tents in the midst of a wood.

August 5. We started about eight this morning, but the road through the wood was full of the stumps of trees. We had not got out of the wood before we ran our handcart against a stump and broke the wheel off. We took our luggage and placed them upon the ox teams. We then tied our cart up with ropes and overtook the rest about two o'clock there they were camped for dinner. We got a new axletree on, and traveled about two miles farther where we camped for the night.

August 6. We were told we should start at seven o'clock this morning but a thunderstorm delayed us until 12 o'clock. I was so weak that I was unable to pull the handcart, therefore I went to drive the team for Father [William Openshaw]. We traveled about ten miles, part by the light of the moon, pitched our tents about ten o'clock among the prairie grass.

August 7. We started about seven o'clock this morning and traveled through a beautiful country where we could stand and gaze upon the prairies as far as the eye could carry, even until the prairies themselves seemed to meet the sky on all sides, without being able to see a house. Thought how many thousands of people are there in England who have scarce room to breathe and not enough to eat. Yet, all this good land lying dormant, except for the prairie grass to grow and decay, which if men would spread themselves and obey the commandment of God to replenish the earth, instead of thronging together in cities and towns and causing the air to be tainted with stinks and giving rise to disease, what a blessing it would be for men (people). We traveled about 15 miles and pitched our tent about two o'clock P.M.

August 8. We traveled about 18 miles up hill and down. In fact, it has been so all the way. We started at seven o'clock this morning, passed through the town of Newton, which contains 1200 inhabitants, traveled about two miles farther and pitched our tents at 8 o'clock in a valley by the side of a wood through which the creek runs.

August 9. We started about 10 o'clock and traveled through woods and across creeks. We stopped for dinner about two o'clock at the edge of a wood where we found plenty of ripe grapes. We started again at three o'clock. We had not gone far before a thunderstorm came upon us and we got a little drenched in the rain. We pitched our tents about six o'clock close by a creek.

August 10. Sunday. We traveled none today. We washed ourselves in the River Skark [Skunk] which is beautiful water running as clear as crystal upon a sandy bottom, which appeared like
the waters of Silon.[63] Eliza [his twenty-one-year-old sister] began
to be very badly. We had a meeting in the afternoon, and partook of the sacrament. Elder Tyler addressed us.

August 11. A brother and a child were buried this morning,
which delayed the camp until half past ten o'clock. We had to wait
until the coffin was made. We traveled about 14 miles and pitched
our tents about four o'clock.

August 12. We should have started at seven o'clock this
morning, but for two of the mules ran away. We found them and
started at 9 o'clock and arrived at camp ground at twenty minutes to six and camped upon the prairie grass not far from the
wood, but water was not so fluent.

August 13. We were delayed again at nine o'clock on account
of the mule teams having to turn back a little for some flour. We
traveled about 20 miles and arrived at the camp ground about
six o'clock. We passed through Fort Des Moines which is quite a
new settled place. Lots of brick buildings which form a new styl-
ish town.

August 14. We started about eight o'clock this morning and
crossed over the North Coon [North Raccoon] with our handcarts in the water which is about knee deep. Close by is the town
of Adel which is the county of Edeby [Dallas]. We found Robert
Thirkman. He had stopped behind from Haven Company last
Saturday night and was cut off from the Church. We took him
along with us and crossed over another river, which is also about
knee deep. The women and children crossed over the river on a
small bridge. We camped close by the river about five o'clock.

August 15. A child was buried this morning. The coffin had

63. He might have been referring to the pools of Siloam just outside the city of Jerusalem, described
as clear and beautiful.

to be made which delayed us until about eight o'clock. We traveled about 13 miles and pitched our tents about half-past twelve o'clock which gave us a chance to wash a little. James Ferguson, [J.D.T.] McAllister and Dan Jones came up with their carriage and stayed all night with us.[64]

August 16. We started about seven o'clock and traveled about four hours before we saw a house or any water to drink. We took but little water with us and all of it was finished up long before we got to any house. The day being hot we felt the want of water. We traveled about 17 miles and pitched our tents about two o'clock.

August 17. Sunday. We started about seven o'clock this morning and traveled all day without seeing a house or even a tree except a few at a distance. Nothing but prairie grass to be seen. We traveled about 18 miles and pitched our tents about two o'clock. As soon as we had put our tents up a thunderstorm came. In our travels today we found a well by having a pole set up with a flag upon it having wrote on it, "The Devil in the well below the spring." Eliza is a little better. We camped at Morrison Grove.

August 18. We started from Morrison Grove at eight o'clock and traveled until eleven when we stopped two hours for dinner; started again; traveled 21 miles and pitched our tents at six close by the Misslebetley River.[65]

August 19. We started at twenty minutes to eight o'clock, passed through Indian Town, which at the time the Saints were driven from Nauvoo they passed through this place. It was settled with Indians and was an Indian village. We passed over the Indian River; we stopped three hours for dinner, started again and traveled 21 miles that day. Camped at seven o'clock at Jordan Creek.

---

64. Missionaries returning to Salt Lake City from England.
65. He probably means the Nishnabotna River.

August 20. We started at eight o'clock from the Jordan Creek, passed through Russing Botany [West Nishnabotna] and over the Silver Creek, stopped one hour for dinner at Mud Creek. We started again at one o'clock, traveled 21 miles and pitched our tents at five o'clock at Keg Creek.

August 21. We started at eight o'clock from Keg Creek, traveled 9 miles and stopped for dinner at the big Mosquito Creek upon the same spot of town where the Saints were who were driven from Nauvoo in the depth of winter without food or house or anything to shelter them from the inclemency of the weather, when the Americans demanded from the Saints five hundred men to enlist in the American cause for the Mexican War. It is from Council Bluffs about three miles. We started again at one o'clock, passed through Council Bluffs; about 7 miles and camped about seven o'clock where we found a beautiful spring.

August 22. We started at eight o'clock and traveled about 4 miles when we arrived at the Missouri River where we were ferried across to Florence. We went to the top of a hill where we could view the country all round and the Missouri River to a great distance. Every place we came through we were admired by the people very much.[66] Some looked upon us as if we were deceived; others who were old apostates came with all the subtlety of the devil, and all the cunning they have gained by their own experience, trying to turn the Saints to the right hand or to the left, but thanks be to God, but few or none adhered to their advice.

August 23. Rested here.

August 24. Sunday. A cow was killed today, and was divided among us—one-half pound each. A meeting at eleven o'clock

---

66. The *Council Bluffs Bugle* expressed this admiration in its August 26, 1856, issue: "This is enthusiasm—this is heroism indeed. Though we cannot coincide with them in their belief, it is impossible to restrain our admiration of their self-sacrificing devotion to the principles of their faith." As quoted in Hafen and Hafen, 95.

and four o'clock. Elder [Cyrus H.] Whelock [Wheelock] and others addressed us.

August 25. About one P.M. we moved about three miles and passed over the spot of land where so many Saints died and were buried, after being driven from Nauvoo in the depth of winter—men, women and children—and driven on these plains to die from starvation. Their bodies are now moldering in the dust while their spirits are gone to await the day of recompense and reward. Camped in sight of the Missouri River.

August 26. We moved none today.

August 27. Another cow was killed today and we had our dinner of it. About three o'clock we started and traveled about six miles; camped at five o'clock at the Little Paprio [Papillion].

August 28. We started at eight o'clock; stopped at the Big Paprio [Papillion] for dinner, a distance of three miles. Started again at one o'clock. Traveled today 15 miles; six o'clock camped at the Elk Horn.

August 29. Began to ferry at eight o'clock across the Elk Horn, and had all ferried across about twelve o'clock—132 handcarts, 180 head of cattle, 8 wagons. We had our dinner and started about two o'clock; traveled three miles, mostly through a sandy road, arrived at the Raw Hide Creek where we camped for the night.

August 30. Started about eight o'clock and traveled until about one o'clock when we camped for the day upon the banks of the Platte River.

August 31. Sunday. We started today about seven o'clock and left the river a little on our left, but being nigh to the banks of the river, the road was very sandy, which made it hard pulling. We camped again about two o'clock upon the banks of the Platte River.

September 1. Started about seven o'clock. The road was not so sandy as yesterday. Traveled until one o'clock when we stopped for dinner at the Shell Creek. Started again at two o'clock and

traveled until seven; the sun had set below the horizon, therefore, we were obliged to stop on the prairies before we got to the
river. There is no wood upon the prairies, only at rivers and
creeks, and having nothing cooked we were obliged to lie down
without supper. Traveled about 20 miles; we were a little tired.

September 2. We started about half-past five o'clock this
morning; traveled about four miles when we arrived again at the
Platte River; stopped to breakfast about two hours, started again
at ten o'clock for the Loup Fork Ferry, where we arrived; about
thirty in one part were ferried across the Platte today.

September 3. We commenced to ferry this morning about
seven o'clock and finished about sunset.

September 4. We started about eight o'clock and traveled
about 9 miles; stopped for dinner again, and traveled 14 miles
today; camped at four o'clock, killed a cow and it was divided.

September 5. We were notified to start at seven o'clock this
morning, but a thunderstorm came which delayed us until half
past two o'clock. In the meantime another cow was killed and
divided among us—one-half pound each. We started and traveled until five o'clock; camped again at the Platte River. We put
our tents up and then a rainstorm came upon us.

September 6. Started about eight o'clock this morning. We
met a large party of Indians—men, women and children with
their horses and mules all loaded with skins going to Missouri to
trade with the whites. They are the first party of Indians that we
have seen. Camped (Stopped) about twelve o'clock for dinner.
We then went to the top of the hill and camped for the day.

September 7. Started about half past eight o'clock. Eleanor
[his sister, age fourteen] has the ague and diree [diarrhea] and
is so badly that we had to pull her in the handcart. Eliza also is
yet so weak that we had to pull her also in the handcart which
made it just as much as we could pull. We camped again near the
Platte. About five o'clock Franklin D. Richards, D[aniel].

Spencer, [Cyrus H.] Wheelock and others came up with their carriages.[67] We found a good spring here.

September 8. We started about eight o'clock this morning; traveled until one o'clock; stopped for dinner one hour, started again and traveled until ten o'clock at night on account of not being able to find any water or wood. Traveled about 24 miles and found some (little) water in holes that had been dug in the sand. We pulled Eliza on the handcart all day.

September 9. We started this morning about eight o'clock and traveled through a very hard, sandy, uphill and down road; halted for dinner about two o'clock but there was no water, but an old mud pit; started again at six o'clock. It thundered and lightened awfully, and rain at a distance, but as if to give everyone their share it rolled over and gave us a good soaking in the rain. Rolled on until it died away at a distance. We were almost worried with mosquitos. Traveled until eleven o'clock when we camped at the Prairie Creek, which is very good water. We have traveled two days without water except mud water and that only twice.

September 10. Started about nine o'clock from the Prairie Creek. We went about 3 miles and then crossed it, traveled until one o'clock when we stopped for dinner one hour, traveled until six o'clock and camped again at the Prairie where we found a little wood which is the first wood that we have seen since Monday morning; we had to cook with buffalo chips.

September 11. We started about nine o'clock again this morning, traveled until one o'clock, stopped for dinner, started again and traveled until six, camped again at the Prairie Creek.

September 12. Started about eight o'clock, traveled about 4 miles when we came to the Wood River which we crossed on a small bridge yankee; continued down the side of it, stopped for

---

67. Missionaries returning to Salt Lake City from Europe. Franklin D. Richards had just been released as mission president.

dinner at twelve o'clock. For ought we knew, but a cripple, a young man who walked with crutches, had been left behind. We sent four men back to search for him, which caused us to move none today. About sunset they brought him into the camp.

September 13. Started about half-past eight o'clock this morning, traveled until one o'clock when we stopped for dinner nearly opposite Fort Kearney where the soldiers are stationed, started again and traveled until five o'clock when we camped at the Platte River. A man fell down dead. The Indians are very hostile about here. They have attacked some of the immigrants who have passed through this season and rumor says that some have been murdered, but they have kept out of our way for we have seen none since the sixth, not even so much as one.[68]

September 14. We started about nine o'clock and traveled until twelve noon when we stopped for dinner, started again and traveled until five o'clock when we camped for the night. Eliza is a little better, but is so weak that we have yet to pull her on the handcart.

September 15. Started at eight o'clock and traveled until two o'clock when we stopped for dinner at Buffalo Creek, started again and traveled until seven o'clock; saw several droves of buffalo but could not get no nigher to them than three or four miles. Camped at Buffalo Creek.

September 16. Started at half past eight o'clock. The weather is extremely hot which makes it hard traveling. Stopped at one o'clock, but moved no farther today. It would truly be an amusing and interesting scene if the people of the old country could have a bird's eye view of us when in camp; to see everyone busy—some fetching water, others gathering buffalo chips, some cooking and so forth upon these wild prairies where the air is not

---

68. Col. Almon W. Babbitt and some of his wagon train returning from Fort Kearney to Utah were attacked and killed by a band of Cheyennes who were retaliating for the killing of ten of their warriors by U.S. soldiers. Thomas Margetts and James Cowdy and their families were also murdered that same year.

tainted with the smoke of cities or factories, but is quiet here. One may see a creek at a distance and start and travel one hour towards it, yet seem no nigher than you did when you started.

September 17. An old sister died this morning, which delayed us until ten o'clock. When we started out it was a very hard, sandy road and the wind was extremely cold, as if we had come into a different climate all at once. Stopped for dinner at one o'clock, started again, and traveled until six o'clock when we camped for the night.

September 18. Started at seven o'clock this morning, traveled until one o'clock when we stopped for dinner at the Platte River. Old Sister Greegry [either Ann (63) or Mary (59) Gregory] from Chew Moore died and was buried on the banks of the Platte River. Started again and traveled over the sandy bluffs and camped again at the Platte River.

September 19. Started at eight o'clock and traveled until twelve when we stopped for dinner, started again at one o'clock and still continued to travel over the sandy bluffs which is hard pulling. Eliza continues in a lingering state so that we have to haul her on the handcart. We camped at half-past seven o'clock.

September 20. We started and left the sandy bluffs on our right, went about three miles and then crossed a creek about knee deep; the weather being cold, it felt disagreeable to go into the water. Went about 8 miles and came to the Platte River where we stopped for dinner, started again, continued down the side of the Platte. Measly rain. Camped on the Platte about six o'clock.

September 21. Small measly rain which delayed us until two o'clock. In the meantime another cow was killed. Eliza, on account of being exposed to the weather, is considerably worse. Traveled until seven o'clock when we camped, but being not nigh to any wood and the buffalo chips being wet we were unable to [do any] cooking.

September 22. Started at eight o'clock this morning, traveled until twelve when we stopped for dinner at the Platte; started again, went about three miles, came to the north fork of the Platte which is ten rods wide and two feet deep; crossed over with our handcarts. It was a sandy bottom. Camped as soon as we had crossed, being about six o'clock.

September 23. Started half past seven o'clock, crossed over sandy bluffs and sandy roads, stopped for dinner at twelve, started again, continued over the sandy bluffs until six o'clock when we came to the Sandy Bluff Creek where we camped for the night. Traveled 11 3/4 miles today, and it is, I think, the hardest day we have had on account of deep sands. We had to pull Eliza all through them. Saw [Almon] Babbit[t]'s buggy burnt.

September 24. Started at eight o'clock this morning, stopped for dinner at twelve o'clock, started again, saw the blood-stained garments of Thomas Margett's wife and child who had been murdered by the Indians. They are committing depredations behind and before. In fort they made an open attack in daylight upon Fort Kearney. On the twenty-second of August, the soldiers killed a great number of them, which has stirred them up against the white man, but they keep out of our way. Camped at the Platte.

September 25. Started at eight o'clock. Still continued over the sandy bluffs. Saw several Indians on horseback, which are the first that we have seen since the above mentioned. Stopped for dinner at twelve o'clock at the Platte River. Started again, the road is rather better, camped near the Platte at six o'clock.

September 26. Started at eight o'clock, continued until twelve when we stopped for dinner. For several days we have crossed through a great many creeks and forks of the Platte which gave us plenty of opportunities to wash our feet.

October 3. Passed Chimney Rock, which is a rock that rises in the form of a monument or chimney and can be seen at a distance. We continued our journey as quick as we possibly could. The cold increasing upon us. It is severe nights and mornings. Our provisions are running out very fast so that our rations are reduced to 12 ounces of flour per day. Our common allowance has been one pound per day. The snow now came upon us and being so cold and the oxen wore out many of them were now froze to death, which rendered almost impossible for us to travel; we also being pretty nigh wore out with fatigue and hunger; a great many died. I have seen several buried in one grave. The cattle that were froze and died were eagerly ate up by us. We [are] now seeing the storms increasing upon us in the midst of an inclement and howling desert far away from an[y] human succor and having only a few days rations in the camp, summoned all our strength and efforts to make another move, but our oxen having died off and our strength being very much reduced—the snow, cold, the blasting winds, it seemed impossible for us to travel, in fact, we were traveling all day, cold, hungry and fatigued and only traveled about 5 miles. We put up our tents and then shoveled out the snow and put it around the bottom of the tent in order to keep out the winds and to make ourselves somewhat comfortable. We continued here for several days; our rations were now reduced to eight ounces per day. After camping here several days, and all the flour in the camp nearly used up and were not able to move and about 370 miles from Y. S. City [S. L. City], and it being by far the nearest to look for succor. Yet, we did not despair. We looked forward for support with gleaming hope upon our countenances.

In the midst of all this uncertainty and doubt our hopes were realized, for lo and behold, Joseph A. Young and two others with him came riding into the camp; voices from all parts of the camp, "Help for the camp." We all rushed together to hear the news. He told us that there were about ten wagons loaded with flour and sent out from the valley for our relief and was about fifty miles ahead of us at a place called Devil's Gate. After they had learned our circumstances, they started back again in order to have them come out and to meet us. In the morning, we summoned all our efforts and strength, impulsed with the prospect of deliverance, we again started on our journey. After traveling about two or three days, and they traveling towards us, we met. The last flour was all ate before we met them. We now had one pound of flour per day, which in a measure began to recruit our strength so that we were able to perform the journey before us. The brethren who came out to meet us did administer every comfort and help that was within their power to the sick and the infirm. We continued our journey until we arrived at the Devil's Gate. Here we were obliged to stop, the snow being about fourteen inches deep on the level, and not withstanding the teams that had come out to help us, there was not sufficient help to move the aged, sick and the women and children along, so that we again stopped several days.

A council was held in which it was decided that we should leave all our clothing and cooking utensils (except what was absolutely necessary, such as a blanket to wrap ourselves in and the clothing we stood in) to be left at Devil's Gate and that a number of the brethren who had come out to meet us should stay to take care of them until spring should open (when they would be sent for from the valley) and that we leave all our handcarts, except one to each tent in order to carry our cooking utensils only. Our blankets were put in the wagons that came out to meet us. Also it was decided that Joseph A. Young should go on an express to the valley in order to start out more help. We now began to gather together all the cattle that we could find, and pulled down our tents and made another start in the snow.

We traveled about two miles, crossed over the Sweetwater; some on the ice and others waded through, which was about three and one-half feet deep. James Lord and myself pulled the handcart across the creek. The women and children were all carried across by some of the brethren who had come from the valley. We then went into a canyon [Martin's Cove] where we camped for about three weeks. In a few days after we arrived here our rations were reduced to four ounces of flour per day. This happened on account of a number of the brethren having to stay at Devil's Gate until spring to guard the effects that the company had left.[69] Having to leave all the flour that it was thought we could do without until we should meet a fresh supply from the valley; we now realized that such low rations and our bodily strength having been so much reduced by our former privations and being such cold and inclement weather, a great many died. However, we made another start, some with bundles on their backs, a number of others would join together and put them on a handcart. Some would be crying, others singing, and thus went trudging along as best we could. We traveled in this manner for a few days, when we began to meet wagons every day. Our rations now were one pound of flour per day. We continued to meet wagons nearly every day so that more of the sick, women, children and the aged could ride and were enabled to travel a little more every day. We now arrived at the South Pass, which is about 320 miles from the valley. The wagons that had come out to meet us were now increased to about fifty or sixty so that we were now all able to ride, which did increase our speed of march, for we traveled about twenty to thirty miles per day. We continued to travel in this way, attended with various circumstances, until we arrived in the valley, which was on the 30th of November, 1856.

_____

Elizabeth Horrocks Jackson Kingsford wrote a brief reminiscence of her life in order that her children "may read what their ancestors were willing to suffer, and did suffer patiently for the Gospel's sake." Elizabeth's parents and her ten

_____

69. Head of the rescue effort, George D. Grant, had a room in the old fort at Devil's Gate cleared out to store their belongings along with forty loads of baggage carried by the Hunt and Hodgett wagons, following the handcarts. Assigned to guard the goods throughout the winter were Daniel W. Jones, Thomas Alexander, and Ben Hampton. They were sustained at first by provisions left with them but soon resorted to the hide taken from dead cattle. Practice taught them how to prepare and cook it to make it palatable.

siblings joined the Church in England, as did her husband, with whom she emigrated, along with their three children. They all traveled west with the Martin company. She sometimes borrows details from other accounts to augment her own memory, but the experience was harrowing enough for her to remember with clarity many incidents herself. The lesson that she hoped her posterity would learn from her experience was "to stand firm and faithful to the truth, and be willing to suffer, and sacrifice all things they may be required to pass thru for the kingdom of God's sake."

ELIZABETH HORROCKS JACKSON KINGSFORD[70]

ON THE 27TH OF AUG. we made a final start from Cutlers' Fork,[71] on our long tedious journey across the vast plains of a thousand miles to our future home. We continued our toil day after day, pulling our hand-carts with our provisions or rations, our little children, etc., through deep sands, rocky roads, or fording streams. It was a dreary journey. Many miles each day were traveled ere, with tired limbs we reached camp, cooked supper, ate and retired for the night to rest, to pursue our monotonous course the following day.

On the 7th of Sept., near Loup Fork, we were overtaken and

---

70. Excerpt from *Leaves From the Life of Elizabeth Horrocks Jackson Kingsford* (Ogden, Utah, 1908), Library, Church of Jesus Christ of Latter-day Saints, Salt Lake City, Utah.

71. She probably means Cutler's Park encampment, about two and a half miles west of Florence.

passed by Apostle F. D. Richards, C. H. Wheelock and other returning missionaries from Europe. About the middle of this month we learned that A. W. Babbitt had been killed by some hostile Indians.

After toilsome and fatiguing travel, we reached Laramie on the 8th day of October. Here we rested for a short time. Our provisions by this time had become very scant, and many of the company went to the Fort and sold their watches and other articles of jewelry. With the proceeds they purchased corn meal, flour, beans, bacon, etc., with which to replenish their stores of food which had become very scant. Hitherto, although a ration of a pound of flour had been served out daily to each person, it was found insufficient to satisfy the cravings of hunger; but the weary pilgrims were then about to experience more deprivations in this direction. We rested a couple of days and then resumed our toilsome march. Shortly after leaving Fort Laramie it became necessary to shorten our rations that they might hold out, and that the company be not reduced to starvation. The reduction was repeated several times. First, the pound of flour was reduced to three-fourths of a pound, then to a half of a pound, and afterward to still less per day. However, we pushed ahead. The trip was full of adventures, hair breadth escapes, exposure to attacks from Indians, wolves and other wild beasts. When we reached the Black Hills, we had a rough experience. The roads were rocky, broken and difficult to travel. Frequently carts were broken down and much delay was caused by the needed repairs.

During the time of leaving Laramie and reaching the Platte, my husband [Aaron Jackson] had been taken sick. He was afflicted with mountain fever. His appetite was good and he could eat more than his rations. But his ambition was gone. All attempts to arouse him to energy or much active exertion were futile. On the 19th of Oct. the last crossing of the Platte River was reached; but when we went into camp that noon day my husband was not there. Two of the company went back to look for him. They found him sitting by the roadside, resting. He was very weak. They assisted him into camp. When we resumed our journey he was put into a wagon, and rode a few miles to the bank of the river, when it was discovered that the teams had become so weak they were unable to haul the freight across the stream, so my husband was compelled to alight.

"The river" says Elder John Jaques, "was wide, the current was strong, the water was exceedingly cold and up to the wagon bed in the deepest parts, and the bed of the river was covered with cobble stones."[72] Some of the men carried some of the women on their backs or in their arms, but others of the women tied up their skirts and waded through, like the heroines that they were, and as they had gone thru many other rivers and creeks. My husband attempted to ford the stream. He had only gone a short distance when he reached a sand bar in the river on which he sank down through weakness and exhaustion. My sister, Mary Horrocks Leavitt, waded through the water to his assistance. She raised him up to his feet. Shortly afterward, a man came along on horseback and conveyed him to the other side of the river, placed him on the bank and left him there. My sister then helped me to pull my cart with my three children and other matters on it. We had scarcely crossed the river when we were visited with a tremendous storm of snow, hail, sand and fierce winds. It was a terrible storm from which both the people and teams suffered. After crossing the river, my husband was put on a hand cart and hauled into camp; and indeed after that time he was unable to walk, and consequently provision had to be made for him to ride in a wagon. As soon as we reached camp, I prepared him some refreshment and placed him to rest for the night. From this time my worst experience commenced. The company had now become greatly reduced in strength, the teams as well as the

---

72. This quote is in Stella Jacques Bell, *Life History and Writings of John Jacques*, 144.

people. The teams had become so weak that the luggage was reduced to ten pounds per head for adults, and five pounds for children under eight years. And although the weather was severe, a great deal of bedding and clothing had to be destroyed—burned—as it could not be carried along. This occurrence very much increased the suffering of the company, men, women and children alike.

On the 20th of Oct. we traveled, or almost wallowed, for about ten miles through the snow. At night, weary and worn out, we camped near the Platte River, where we soon left it for the Sweetwater. We were visited with three days more snow. The animals and immigrants were almost completely exhausted. We remained in camp several days to gain strength. About the 25th of Oct., I think it was—I cannot remember the exact date—we reached camp about sundown. My husband had for several days previous been much worse. He was still sinking, and his condition now became more serious. As soon as possible after reaching camp I prepared a little of such scant articles of food as we then had. He tried to eat but failed. He had not the strength to swallow. I put him to bed as quickly as I could. He seemed to rest easy and fell asleep. About nine o'clock I retired. Bedding had become very scarce, so I did not disrobe. I slept until, as it appeared to me, about midnight. I was extremely cold. The weather was bitter. I listened to hear if my husband breathed—he lay so still. I could not hear him. I became alarmed. I put my hand on his body, when to my horror I discovered that my worst fears were confirmed. My husband was dead. He was cold and stiff—rigid in the arms of death. It was a bitter freezing night and the elements had sealed up his mortal frame. I called for help to the other inmates of the tent. They could render me no aid; and there was no alternative but to remain alone by the side of the corpse till morning. The night was enveloped in almost Egyptian darkness. There was nothing with which to produce a light or kindle a fire. Of course I could not sleep. I could only watch, wait, and pray for the dawn. But oh, how these dreary hours drew their tedious length along. When daylight came, some of the male part of the company prepared the body for burial. And oh, such a burial and funeral service. They did not remove his clothing—he had but little. They wrapped him in a blanket and placed him in a pile with thirteen others who had died, and then covered him up in the snow. The ground was frozen so hard that they could not dig a grave. He was left there to sleep in peace until the trump of the Lord shall sound, and the dead in Christ shall awake and come forth in the morning of the first resurrection. We shall then again unite our hearts and lives, and eternity will furnish us with life forever more.

I will not attempt to describe my feelings at finding myself thus left a widow with three children,[73] under such excruciating circumstances. I cannot do it. But I believe the Recording Angel has inscribed in the archives above, and that my sufferings for the Gospel's sake will be sanctified unto me for my good. My sister Mary was the only relative I had to whom I could look for assistance in this trying ordeal, and she was sick. So severe was her affliction that she became deranged in her mind, and for several days she ate nothing but hard frozen snow. I could therefore appeal to the Lord alone; He who had promised to be a husband to the widow, and a father to the fatherless. I appealed to him and he came to my aid.

A few days after the death of my husband, the male members of the company had become reduced in number by death; and those who remained were so weak and emaciated by sickness, that on reaching the camping place at night, there were not sufficient men with strength enough to raise the poles and pitch the tents. The result was that we camped out with nothing but the vault of Heaven for a roof, and the stars for companions. The snow lay

73. At this time, Elizabeth was left with Martha, age seven; Mary E., age four; and Aaron, age two.

several inches deep upon the ground. The night was bitterly cold. I sat down on a rock with one child in my lap and one on each side of me. In that condition I remained until morning. My sick sister, the first part of the night, climbed up hill to the place where some men had built a fire. She remained there until the people made down their beds and retired, to sleep, if they could. She then climbed or slid down the hill on the snow, to where there was another fire which was kept alive by some persons who were watching the body of a man who had died that night. There she remained until daylight.

It will be readily perceived that under such adverse circumstances I had become despondent. I was six or seven thousand miles from my native land, in a wild, rocky, mountain country, in a destitute condition, the ground covered with snow, the waters covered with ice, and I with three fatherless children with scarcely nothing to protect them from the merciless storms. When I retired to bed that night, being the 27th of Oct., I had a stunning revelation. In my dream, my husband stood by me and said—"Cheer up, Elizabeth, deliverance is at hand." The dream was fulfilled.

"The 28th of October," says John Jaques in his history of this journey, "was red letter day to this hand cart expedition. On that memorable day, Joseph A. Young, Daniel Jones, and Abel Garr galloped unexpectedly into camp amid tears and cheers and smiles and laughter of the emigrants. Those three men being the express from the most advanced relief company from Salt Lake, brought the glad word that assistance, provisions and clothing were near, that ten wagons were waiting at the Devil's Gate."[74] Thus you see, my dream and my husband's prediction were fulfilled.

The next day we left the Platte and started for the Sweetwater

---

74. Stella Jacques Bell, *Life Hitory and Writings of John Jacques*, 148–49.

country. On the 31st of Oct. another grand surprise met us. On
reaching Greecewood [Greasewood] Creek, we met Geo. D.
Grant, R. T. Burton, Charles Decker, Chauncey G. Webb, and
some others, with six wagons of flour, etc., sent from Salt Lake.
On the 1st of Nov. we arrived at the Sweetwater bridge, some five
miles from Devil's Gate. We arrived there about dusk in the
evening. We camped in about a foot and a half of snow. It was a
busy evening before bed time in clearing away the snow. For this
purpose many used cooking utensils, plates and other things.
The ground was hard and almost impenetrable; and it was with
the greatest difficulty that the tents could be erected. It became
a question that night, whether we should camp there for the winter or go forward to Salt Lake Valley. It was decided to go on. At
Devil's Gate the freight was left, as the teams were too weak to
haul it. It was left in charge of Daniel W. Jones, Thomas M.
Alexander and Ben Hampton, with seventeen emigrants to guard
it through the winter.

It was several days after that—I do not remember the exact
date—that we made the last crossing of the Sweetwater. In speaking of that memorable event, Elder John Jaques says:—"It was a
severe operation to many of the company. It was the last ford the
company waded over. The water was not less than two feet deep,
perhaps a little more in the deepest parts, but it was intensely cold.
The ice was three or four inches thick and the bottom of the river
muddy and sandy. The stream seemed to be about forty yards wide.
Before the crossing was completed, the shades of evening were
closing around, and this, as everyone knows, is the coldest hour
of the twenty-four, especially at a frosty time. When the hard carts
arrived at the bank of the river one poor fellow who was greatly
worn down with travel exclaimed: "Have we got to cross here?'
Being answered 'yes' he again exclaimed: Oh dear, I can't go
through that!' His heart sank within him and he burst into tears.
But his heroic wife came to his aid, and in a sympathetic tone said:
'Don't cry, Jimmie, I'll pull the hand cart for you.' In crossing the

river the shins and limbs of the waders came in contact with sharp cakes of ice which inflicted wounds on them which did not heal until long after they arrived in this valley. And some of them are alive, some of them bear the marks of them to this day."[75]

After this crossing we camped for several days in a deep gulch called "Martin's Ravine." It was a fearful time and place. It was so cold that some of the company came near freezing to death. The sufferings of the people were fearful, and nothing but the power of a merciful God kept them from perishing. The storms continued unabated for some days. Said E[phraim]. K. Hank[s] in speaking of it:—"The storms during the three days were simply awful. In all my travels in the Rocky Mountains, just before and afterwards, I have seen nothing like it—nothing worse." When the snow at length ceased falling, it lay thick on the ground, and so deep that for many days it was impossible to move the wagons through. I and my children with hundreds of others were locked up in those fearful weather-bound mountains. [. . .]

I will not continue this narrative much longer, but will hasten to convey us to our destination. We came by easy stages the remainder of the journey, and finally reached Salt Lake City at mid-day on Sunday, Nov. the 30th. Thus ended the ever memorable overland voyage from the Missouri River to the Capital of Utah, in the eventful year of 1856. The company furnished me transportation to the residence of my brother, Samuel Horrocks, in Ogden City. Here my children and I rested and recruited, and here we have remained ever since. And the Lord has blessed me, and rewarded me with abundance of this world's goods, for all my sufferings, and has also blessed me with the highest blessings of a spiritual nature that can be conferred upon man or woman, in His Holy Temple, in Mortality. I have a happy home for which I thank my Father in Heaven.

---

75. Stella Jacques Bell, *Life History and Writings of John Jacques,* 160–61.

The faith that had sustained these emigrants during the fearsome days before rescue was not unavailing. While they suffered the consequences of unnecessary risk and overzealousness, the Lord did not leave his people to perish. By the time Franklin D. Richards arrived in the Salt Lake Valley the first of October, well ahead of the debilitating storm, he knew the handcarters needed help.[76] Stunned when told that a thousand people were still far out on the trail, Brigham Young deliberated with the returning missionaries and other Church leaders to determine the needs of the companies and resolved to make their relief the primary topic of the general conference, convening the next day.[77] If he felt any recrimination toward those allowing the groups to leave so late, he reserved it for a later time and met the crisis head on, initiating a relief effort considered to be one of the great rescue missions in western American history.[78]

When the conference convened, Brigham Young told the audience of the plight of the handcart pioneers and announced to the thousands assembled that the text of his speech was "to get them here." "Go and bring in those people now on the plains," he commanded, asking for wagons, teams, food, clothing, bedding, and men. The response was swift. Volunteers announced their readiness, and supplies came from all over the territory. Some didn't even

---

76. President Richards and a group of returning missionaries traveled by carriage to Utah, easily arriving weeks before the Willie and Martin companies, though leaving Florence about the same time.

77. Three wagon companies, primarily carrying freight, were also still on the trail but very near to arrival.

78. An early detailed account is Solomon F. Kimball, "Belated Emigrants of 1856," *Improvement Era* 17 (November 1913): 2–15; (December 1913): 106–17; (January 1914): 200–211; (February 1914): 286–309. Hafen and Hafen also recount the rescue effort in *Handcarts to Zion*, 119–41, as does Stegner, *The Gathering of Zion* (New York: McGraw-Hill, 1964), 221–59. A more recent account is Rebecca Cornwall (Bartholomew) and Leonard J. Arrington, *Rescue of the 1856 Handcart Companies.*

wait to leave the Tabernacle. Upon hearing President Young's appeal, women in the audience tore off their petticoats and other unnecessary clothing and collected more articles at home to send to their sister Saints stranded on the trail.[79]

The advance team of twenty-seven men, with sixteen wagons loaded with supplies, elected George D. Grant as captain and William H. Kimball and Robert T. Burton as assistants. Five of this team were missionaries, home only two days but eager to rescue the people they had helped bring to America. Many of them were experienced scouts or trail riders. Most were members of local militias or of a younger group of "Minute Men." Caching supplies at Fort Bridger, they were alarmed when they found no sign of either of the companies a week after leaving the Valley. By the time they reached South Pass, they too had to wait out the storm that had stranded the travelers miles to the east. There they learned the plight of the Willie company when the haggard and frozen Captain Willie and his companion, Joseph Elder, staggered into their camp. They told the rescuers of the critical condition of the handcarters, holed up near the Sweetwater. Even as Captain Willie reached the main rescue party, an advance or "express" team located the stranded members of his company. The team had little to give the waiting company besides a few pounds of flour and hope for more to come. Then the team moved on to search for the Martin group. But their appearance had stirred the benumbed and discouraged Willie company to move forward

---

79. "Original Historical Narrative of Lucy Meserve Smith," (1888–89), microfilm of holograph, LDS Church Archives.

the next day. When the main rescue party finally met up with the Willie company, the rescuers knew immediately more help than they could give was needed, and they sent a rider to the Valley for more provisions. Though struggling to meet their own winter needs, the Valley Saints managed to round up two hundred wagons and teams, enough to bring all the surviving handcarters into the Valley.

Some of the sixteen wagons of the original relief party accompanied the Willie company to the Valley, joined at points along the way by the additional wagons. At Fort Bridger, all the handcarts still in use were left, the Saints now sufficiently supplied with fifty wagons to take them to the Valley. They "rolled into the city" on November 9, a sunny winter day.

Other wagon teams pushed on to find the Martin company. Well behind the Willie company, members were dying daily, and others were close to death from starvation and exposure. When the express team finally found them, they, like the Willie company, were roused to move on toward Devil's Gate, where they would find food and provisions and shelter in an old stockade. But they had to wait for more wagons to help them reach the Valley, and for five days the marooned emigrants waited, huddled in the stockade and sheltered caves nearby. At one point, a lone rescuer, Ephraim Hanks, appeared, bringing a little buffalo meat, a healing hand, and hope, once again.[80]

80. Hanks described a vision he had about the peril of the handcart pioneers even before the announcement made in conference. Following the vision, he had pledged himself to go to their rescue. In the record he made of this experience, he describes resuscitating a man pronounced dead. Bathing him all over with warm water, he then administered to him, and the man immediately came to life. Hanks notes similar healings under his hands among the sickly company. Accounts of his part in the rescue mission can be found in Solomon Kimball, "Belated Immigrants of 1856," Improvement Era 17 (February 1914): 290–94, and Andrew Jenson, "Church Emigration," The Contributor 14 (January 1893): 201–5.

Eventually, emigrants and rescuers came together, and on November 30 a hundred wagons plodded their way through heavy canyon snow and into the Valley, bringing home the survivors of the Martin company, nearly two months after the rescue effort began.

The Hodgett and Hunt wagon trains trailed behind the Martin company. They too had long since exhausted their food, and though they were not as helpless as the handcarters against the biting cold, they were just as handicapped by the heavy snow and just as dependent on the rescuers to find their way out of the mountains. They finally arrived 10 and 11 December. For the stranded Saints, their first sight of the rescuers in the Wyoming mountains was faith redeemed. They knew then that they just might make it. Their trials were far from over, however, and after reaching the Valley, many would forever bear the scars of lost or frostbitten limbs and disturbing memories of their struggle to reach Zion.

A counterpoint to all the deaths that struck these ill-favored bands of pioneers was one birth as the Martin company reached Echo Canyon, near the end of their incredible journey. Twenty-eight-year-old Sarah Squires gave birth to her fifth child on 27 November, three days before the company finally made their way into the Valley. She named her new daughter Echo in remembrance of her place of birth.

The men's strength had shown throughout the ordeal, but the handcart experience was also a proving ground of women's endurance. Jane Griffiths, who lost her father and two brothers, expressed what recent studies have theorized when she observed, "It seems strange that more men and boys died than women and girls."[81] As in the Donner party, more women than men survived the struggle, three times as many in the Willie company. But all suffered to the extreme. Handcart survivor John Jacques aptly expressed their sentiments in writing of his own misadventures with the Martin company: "[I] traveled one of the hardest journeys across the plains by handcart, nearly worked to death, starved to death, and froze to death."[82] Survival for anyone was little short of a miracle.

No bands played or parades greeted the survivors of this ill-fated journey. It had been a sobering experience, not only for those who had endured it but also for those who could only wait and pray. The valley Saints offered food and shelter to the homeless emigrants, their families often divided among several homes since few houses in those early days of settlement had many spare beds or extra chairs at the table. Moreover, Brigham Young did not want the emigrants housed by themselves, where there would be no provisions or comforts or someone to tend to their needs or recharge their spirits. After surviving the arduous ten-thousand-mile journey across water and land, they may well have shared young Peter McBride's doubtful query when they viewed the fledgling village in the stark grip of winter: "Mother," he said, "is this Zion?"[83]

The wrenching story of the Willie and Martin handcart companies was

---

81. Jane Griffiths Fullmer in Ella Campbell, "Reminiscences," typescript, LDS Church Archives. An article published in the June 1996 issue of *Journal of Anthropological Research* indicates that women, protected by body fat and toughened by childbearing, do better than men in famines and cold. Anthropologist Donald Grayson studied the Willie handcart company and found that the mortality rate among men was almost three times that of women, and for men older than forty it was ten times higher. (From a review of the article by Susan Gilmore of the *Seattle Times*, reprinted in the *Salt Lake Tribune*, 29 May 1996.) Men, however, bore the heavier physical burden of pushing the handcarts, and many relinquished their food rations to their families. These factors alone could well account for their higher mortality rate.

82. From Stella Jacques Bell, *Life History and Writings of John Jacques*, 277.

83. Peter Howard McBride, in Carter, *Our Pioneer Heritage* 13:361–63.

little discussed publicly or written about until years afterward because of its bitter effects, not only on Church leaders, who had invested so much in its success, and on emigration agents who were responsible for the emigrants, but also on those still waiting to come to Zion for whom no other form of travel seemed feasible. It is not surprising that some who endured or who were in some other way connected to the misfortunes of these two companies became estranged from the Church.[84] *Most, however, like Elizabeth Kingsford, counted it as a sacrifice they were obliged to make for the gospel's sake. And some, like Francis Webster, may have found a pearl of great price in their suffering. That experience had brought him, he said, "the absolute knowledge that God lives," for he "had become acquainted with him in our extremities."*[85]

The disastrous experience of these two companies slowed but did not halt the parade of handcarts across the Mormon trail. Five later companies carried more than a thousand more European emigrants across the plains, the last two leaving Florence in 1860. Only twelve known deaths occurred in all five companies.[86] *Though little help was available in 1857 through the Perpetual Emigrating Fund, two handcart companies and five wagon trains (one pri-*

---

84. Jorgensen enumerates some of the "fall-out" from the handcart disaster among British Saints who were not part of the handcart companies. See "The Martin Handcart Disaster," 194–97.

85. As quoted by President Gordon B. Hinckley in a general conference address, 6 October 1991, printed in *Conference Reports*, 5–6 October 1991, 77.

86. These occurred only from Florence to Utah. Other deaths occurred during the trek across Iowa. Hafen, *Handcarts to Zion*, 93. About two thousand European Saints emigrated in 1857, most of them either staying in the States until another season or coming in the wagon trains that crossed the plains that year. When the first shipload of Saints arrived in the East earlier than expected that year, emigration agent James Little was hard-pressed to have handcarts, wagons, teams, tents, and other provisions ready for them in Iowa City to avoid any more late starts. But he did, one day before their arrival in Iowa City. (Jenson, "Church Emigration," *The Contributor* 14 [May 1893], 343.)

marily carrying freight) made their way to Salt Lake City that year, carrying both European and American Saints, nearly thirteen hundred of them.

Israel Evans led the first handcart company out of Iowa City in 1857. No deaths were recorded among the 149 pioneers in his group, but they endured all the privations attendant to that kind of travel. Israel Evans performed his duties splendidly, according to one young traveler, "taking the best care of the immigrants, laboring faithfully from early morning until late at night; always selecting the best camping places and caring constantly for the health and comfort of his company." He even put the young handcart pioneer on his own mule during one difficult mountain crossing to ease the pain of a very sore foot, a gesture she never forgot.[87]

Nearly three weeks after the Evans company left Florence, Nebraska, the seventh handcart company followed. Made up of Scandinavian emigrants, the company was led by Christian Christiansen, a native of Denmark, who was just completing a mission in the United States. Comprised of strong, able-bodied "walkers," the company traveled fast enough to reach the Valley only a day after the Evans company. They had benefited by meeting Johnston's Army, commissioned by President Buchanan to accompany the newly appointed governor to Utah. Pitying the hungry travelers, one of the officers offered them a lame ox, which "seemed like a miracle" to the handcarters. They butchered the animal and carefully husbanded the meat to make it last until supplies came from the Valley to see them through the remainder of the

---

87. Margaret Simmons Bennett Beck, in Carter, *Heart Throbs of the West* 9:386.

trip.[88] The Deseret News *reported in a brief sentence the arrival of the two companies: "All in excellent spirits, time, and condition."[89]*

Kersten Benson, a young Danish convert, traveled in the Christiansen handcart company. While her account relates the physical strains of the journey, it was relatively free from unanticipated hardships. With 330 people in the company pushing sixty-eight handcarts, only three supply wagons accompanied them, and they made very good time.

KERSTEN ERICKSEN BENSON[90]

I LEFT COPENHAGEN, April 18, 1857 with my father, mother and grandmother. I was 20 years of age and unmarried. We stopped two days at Liverpool, and on April 25 left [at] three on the sailing ship Westmoreland under Mathias Cowley, President with 544 saints. We arrived at Philadelphia, May 31, having been five weeks on the sea. We were eleven days going from Philadelphia to Iowa City by rail and while on this journey I got separated from the company and was left behind and lost, a young girl in a strange land with no friends, and unable to speak the English language or to make my wants known.

---

88. Anna S. D. Johnson, "The Seventh Handcart Company," *Relief Society Magazine* 35 (July 1948): 451, 501.

89. As quoted in Hafen and Hafen, 164.

90. "Autobiographical Sketch of Kersten Ericksen Benson" (c. 1900), typescript copy, LDS Church Archives.

I was telegraphed for, and was found by the description of the clothing I wore, and made to understand, by the hands of a watch, that I could go to my company train at 6:30 that night.

At Iowa City we were organized as a hand-cart company under Captain C. Christiansen. There were about 100 [sic] hand-carts, with three ox teams to help the sick and weak and carry some supplies and the tents. We were allowed to take only fifteen pounds of clothing to each person, and our new clothing and even bedclothing had to be left lying on the ground as we left our camping place, for no one would buy them from us. This was a great trial to me, having brought good clothing from Denmark to leave on the ground for strangers to take. We then started for Florence, Nebraska. Each hand-cart had six persons, but I was assigned to a cart having only four persons, an old couple, a sickly girl and myself. We were heavily loaded with provisions, and myself and the old gentlemen were the pulling team. We traveled through a settled part of Iowa for three weeks, burying by the wayside, some of the aged, and young who died through the exposure and hardships of the journey. We arrived at Florence in the latter part of June, and laid over one week to rest. This three weeks hardships had proven that my father, mother and grandmother, who was 75 years old, could not stand the journey, and it was decided that they stay in Omaha. I came to the conclusion that I could not leave my aged parents in a strange country, and so made up my mind to stay with them. The captain of the company, C. Christiansen, came to me however, and advised me to leave my parents, and promised me if I would do so that God would bless them and me, and preserve us. This was a very sore trial to me, but I put my trust in God and promises of his Priesthood, and He has brought them to pass. On the 15th day of June 1857, we started our journey on the plains, a day never to be forgotten, full of sorrow in parting from my parents. About the fifth day out, I was worn out pulling over the rough roads, up hills and through the sand and was discouraged because I did not believe I could stand the journey, and I came to the conclusion that I might as well die there as suffer longer, and I was lonely for I had no relations in the company. So I purposely stayed behind while the company was traveling and laid down on the grass, expecting to die there, believing there was no one behind me and I would not be found. Soon after the captain came along and promised me that when we came to a hill or sand he would come and help me pull. And he kept his promise and helped me and soon after this the old couple who were with my hand-cart died, and I was changed to another cart that had six pullers and my task was easier than before. It was now July and August and very hot on the plains. My shoes were worn out and we had to get raw hide from the dead cattle along the road and make shoes for ourselves so as to be able to pull. Crossing the creeks and rivers would make the raw hide soft and the hot sun and roads would make them hard, and our feet were nearly all the time sore and bleeding. I being alone and having no bed clothes I had to sleep in an old shawl in the tent. Coming through the mountains the nights were cold and freezing, and having to get up in my turn in the night to bake my bread, I was often too warm on one side and much too cold on the other. When about 200 miles from Salt Lake City, we were overtaken by the U. S. Army under General Johnston, going to Utah to war with our people, but they treated us kindly, and the army was a blessing to our people in Utah. About two weeks journey from Salt Lake City, the relief teams came to our help and oh, how thankful I was to be able to walk and not have to pull the cart, for I was sick and worn out with the journey. We arrived in Salt Lake City, September 13, having been five months on the journey and when I saw how poor the people were in clothing, for they were ragged, I could not help thinking of the good clothing we had left behind. When I arrived at Lehi, I was so weak and sick that I was not expected to live. And B. Hyde (Bishop Hyde of Hyde Park) and Bro Rigby were called in to administer to me but I could not understand a word they said. Bro Benson being there interpreted it for me. I found kind friends who cared for and nursed me until well. The next year my Father and Mother and Grand Mother came into the Valley safe and well. And so were fulfilled the promise of our Captain C. Christensen made to me when I left my parents in Omaha. And so also have been the promises of Bro Hyde when administering to me in Lehi. And I realize that I have been blessed of the Lord and preserved for my obediance [sic] to the counsel of His Priesthood.

Because of the threat of a war in Utah in 1858, occasioned by the appearance of Johnston's Army the year before, only returning missionaries called home by Brigham Young and a few emigrants, no more than two hundred all together, crossed the ocean or the plains that year. While only 809 converts emigrated from Europe the next year, nearly 2,000 Saints crossed the plains, 235 of them in Captain Rowley's handcart company. The 1859 travelers escaped the long march across Iowa. Emigration agents had initiated a new plan that took the emigrants from the East Coast by train to St. Joseph, Missouri. From there they traveled by steamboat up the Missouri River to Florence. This route saved more than three hundred miles of foot travel.

Like the other handcart companies, Captain Rowley's ran short of provisions, but this group benefited from a generous impulse of some Colorado gold rushers. The party of prospectors, according to William Atkin, pushed on ahead of the handcart company and were successful in killing a buffalo. "They took one quarter of it and covered the three quarters carefully with the hide and put up a notice that read, 'This is for the handcarts,'" Atkin remembered. It was a lifesaver for the hungry company, since they did not have horses to hunt for themselves.[91] Like the first of the handcart pioneers in 1856, Captain Rowley's company arrived to a grand celebration with several bands and a parade of citizens to accompany them to Union Square in the heart of the city[92] This company suffered just five deaths in its three-month journey from Florence.

Sarah Hancock Beesley, a young bride, and her new husband, Ebeneezer, honeymooned their way across the plains in Captain Rowley's handcart company. In later years she refused to talk about her experiences traveling west, but the persistence of an unnamed interviewer drew forth this brief but emotional recollection of those long months of travel.

SARAH HANCOCK BEESLEY[93]

DON'T ASK ME ANYTHING about that [handcart experience]. You should go and talk to Mrs. [Hannah] Lapish. She can tell you all about it. Oh, she is full of life and very enthusiastic about it but I am not. Those are dreadful stories and I don't see why we shouldn't try to forget them. I say 'Bury them with the dead who died on the plains.' My children have often tried to get me to write my handcart story but I will not.

91. *An Enduring Legacy* 6:211.
92. Jenson, "Church Emigration," *The Contributor* 14 (July 1893): 439.
93. Mrs. Ebenezer E. (Sarah Hancock) Beesley," in "Handcart Stories," 28–34, typescript, LDS Church Archives.

(And so it was only by cautious suggestions that step by step her conversation was led back to the handcart stories.)

Indeed I did walk all the way. Neither my husband nor I were twenty when we were married in March and we left England in April [1859] for the Valley. We got our handcarts in a place called Omaha, I believe, at a town called Florence. I don't remember exactly when we left but we were thirteen weeks crossing the plains and it was September when we got here. I remember it was a Sunday afternoon and the people were just coming out of the old Bowery where the Assembly Hall now stands. I never shall forget how clean they looked. Oh, they all looked so fresh and clean and nice. The women were all dressed in calico dresses and wore sun bonnets. It was a different sight from what you see now-a-days but Oh! it was so good! I never shall forget it. Our company was the company of '59 and Mr. [George] Ro[w]ley was our leader. We didn't have nearly enough to eat and oh, the suffering! (Here her mind seemed to revert back and she tried to think of something else to talk about. It was rather difficult to lead her back to her story again. Finally she said), "We didn't have nearly enough food to begin with. There was 200 lbs. of flour to each handcart and four people to a handcart. Long before it gave out entirely we didn't have nearly enough bread. When we reached Green River, there wasn't a pound of flour in the company. When we started, we had eighteen team of oxen and not one of them reached the Valley. They didn't seem to be able to stand the trip as well as we did. When they were worn out and about ready to die, the men would kill them and we would sit up all night watching for a little piece of meat. Did you notice that wild rose bush in my garden near the gate? I've had it there ever since I lived here. You know there wasn't anything growing along the whole way that we could put in our mouths until we discovered these wild rose berries.[94]

---

94. The fruit (also known as berries or rose hips) of the wild rose (*Rosa arkansana*) can be used raw, stewed, or made into jelly. It is indigenous to the Great Plains, and the prairie Indians used it as an emergency food source. It is a good source of vitamin C.

When we would come to a bush we would pick just as many as we could and then eat them. Many a time they saved my life I know. They are rather soft and fluffy inside and didn't taste very good but we could chew on them for a long time. They were shaped like a pear only ever so much smaller, you know.

Yes, Mr. Beesley carried his violin with him and we used to gather around the fire at nights and sing and listen to the music.[95] The popular song was the handcart song. "For some must push and some must pull." Of course after a while we all got so hungry that we couldn't have good times any more. Lots of the men and women could not get out of their beds. There were about 250 or 300 people in the company and we only had eight tents. Once or twice we tried to sleep in the tents but that was dreadful, Yes that was dreadful. Everyone was in everyone else's way. We didn't like that a bit so we used to just sleep on the ground. We would draw our handcarts up in a circle and someone would guard us all night. If it rained we would sometimes sleep under the handcarts.

Of course we didn't suffer with cold but we did with heat. The sun was so hot that sometimes it seemed as if we could stand it no longer. Or sometimes the wind would blow the sand and dirt all over us. They told us in England that everyone had to eat a peck of dirt before he died. I had more than my peck while I was crossing the plains but it didn't take the place of food. One day I remember before we got to Green River we were all literally on the verge of dying of starvation. Some of the people could go no further and we were in the heights of despair when we met some rough mountaineers. They felt very sorry for us and told us if we would come over to their camp they would give us some breakfast. I never tasted anything better in my life and it was cooked by squaws too. They seemed to be living there with those

---

95. Ebeneezer Beesley was a composer and musician and served as conductor of the Mormon Tabernacle Choir from 1881 to 1890.

men. The first thing they gave us was milk and whiskey and we had to drink it out of gourds. Yes, I remember that so well. Then they gave us a sort of bread or cake that they cooked in kettles over the fire. Oh, it was all so good and there was plenty of it. Then when we were through, we carried some back to the one's who were too sick to come with us. I remember one Scotch girl stayed there with them. One of the mountaineers offered her a home and her legs were in such a condition she could travel no farther so she stayed. Yes, she never did get to Salt Lake and she left Scotland to come to Zion too. She wasn't the only one who never reached the Valley.

No, we didn't have any trouble with the Indians. They told us before we left England that we must be good to them and if we had any trinkets we could give them to bring them along. They did so like trinkets. At first we were a little annoyed at so many of them begging but we always treated them nice and they never hurt us. In fact they saved our lives at various times, such as when they gave us food.

Our handcarts had handles on the front and the back too, for some must push and some must pull, you know. The wheels were high so that they could be used for wagon wheels after we got here. It may sound funny to say that it was hard to push them down the hills but it was. Often the wheels were in sand up to the hubs and it was very hard to get them down hill. We had to ford a great many rivers and sometimes some of the carts were simply washed down stream. I remember when we had to ford the Platte River for the first time. We were in water above our waists and the current was strong. We couldn't cross it single file. Ten or twelve of us had to lock arms in order to get across. As long as we had flour the men had to carry it on their shoulders. Of course our clothes had to dry on us. It was very disagreeable and of course impaired our health. Our Captain had the only horse in the company and he had to ride in head in order to find a place where we could get water. We had to get water. I think we walked about 25 miles a day and sometimes [more], Oh it was so hard. The captain's wife and children were in the company.

Companies were sent out from Salt Lake to meet us and bring us food. They saved our lives and gave us courage to come on, for we were at Green River, 300 miles away then. The band came up Emigration canyon to meet us and escorted us to the City. We went down on the old High School square and there our luggage was dropped out and the handcarts taken away.[96] We slept out on the ground that night. We were used to it. The next day we carted what little bedding and luggage we had into some woman's house and dumped them on the floor. It was soon after our arrival, I remember, that Mr. Beesley heard a man playing on a tin whistle. He said to me, "If that man can play a tune on a tin whistle, he can play a flute" so he went and got acquainted wiht him. I think he was later the leader of the Military Band.

There is one woman, who whenever I meet her always says, "Now lassie, do your share." She was in our company and they put her to pull on a handcart with an old man. Very often he would say to her, "Lassie, now do your share," and she has never forgotten it. I also remember another poor woman whose baby was born on the plains and died a few hours later. There was no stop made. She was put in one of the handcarts and joggled along. I don't remember whether she ever lived to get here or not.

Yes when we moved up here on the hill, ours was the only house. We only had two adobe rooms but the adobe was poor and all washed away. We then built a little room in the rear until we built this house. Gradually we added on room after room as the children grew up and needed them. It seemed as if we almost lived in wood and mortar and now all the children are married and I am here in this house alone in nine great big rooms like this.

---

96. This was the 19th Ward square bordered by 2nd and 3rd West and 1st and 2nd North in Salt Lake City.

After we got here I wrote to my mother and told her what a dreadful time we had had and that she must wait until some other means was devised. She answered that they would come if they only had knapsacks. They came by ox team a few years later, and mother was carried into my little home. She only lived eight weeks. The journey was too much for her.

There were lots of dreadful things happened that I won't talk about because I'm sure those poor people would not like them talked about. I think we were not so badly off as the people who came in the cold weather. The man who built this house told me that he had seen men, women and children frozen to death while they were sitting up-right. We met a few wagons on their way to and from California and these companies certainly were strange sights to them. They often pitied us and gave us food. Yes, I crossed the plains with a handcart once but I am thankful I have never had to again. I couldn't do it. One such experience is quite enough.[97]

The final two handcart companies under Captains Daniel Robison (often mistakenly transcribed Robinson) and Oscar Stoddard left in 1860 as part of a migration that included nearly two thousand pioneers that year. While there was but one known death in the companies, both experienced the general afflictions of handcart travel. Running short of food made them all vulnerable to exhaustion and many forms of ill health. When Lydia Seamons, traveling with a wagon company, encountered some handcarters, she was appalled at their sorry con-

---

97. A detailed account of the Rowley handcart company is in Sterling E. Beesley, *Kind Words, The Beginnings of Mormon Melody: Ebeneezer Beesley, Utah Pioneer Musician* (Salt Lake City: Sterling Ebeneezer, 1980)

dition. *"They would have starved,"* she remembered, *"had it not been for our company helping them. My mother gave bacon and flour from our supplies."*[98]

Both Daniel Robison and Oscar Stoddard left brief reports of their journey west, somewhat minimizing the troubles recorded in other accounts but otherwise portraying the details of difficult but comparatively routine trips.

DANIEL ROBISON[99]

THE 7TH OF MAY 1860 we left all this [a cozy house, a beautiful orchard and a garden][100] and started west to Zion where we could be free to live our religion, for which we had sacrificed so much, unmolested. As we were nearing Niagara Falls, just across the line in Canada we were heartbroken again,[101] another little daughter [Agnes Ellen] was taken by death. This child was eight years of age, which only deepened the sorrow because of having had her with us longer. As we were traveling under contract the train in which we were riding was not allowed to stop; so our little daughter was carried away by a negro porter and buried we know not where.

We traveled by rail and water 2000 miles, landing in Florence, Nebraska. Here we camped for two weeks while arrange-

98. Life Sketch of Lydia Seamons Crowther, 1841–1917, LDS Church Archives.

99. Journal of Daniel Robison, in Carter, *Treasures of Pioneer History* 5:287–90.

100. Daniel Robison left his home in Pennsylvania (probably Quincy, Franklin County) to travel west.

101. While living in Pennsylvania, Daniel and his wife Rachel lost their two-year-old daughter, Anna.

ments were being made for the company; which was one of the last of the hand-cart companies to cross the plains. The companies to follow came with ox teams and horses, which made traveling a little easier. It was while we waited here in Florence that death called again. This time we lost our third child, a son, Johnny, age three. When we were called to team up six teams were put to lead, the carts were in the rear. The people pushed the carts. The boxes and carts were painted beautifully, and had bows over the top. These bows were covered with heavy canvas. The tongues of the carts had a crosspiece 2 1/2 feet long fastened to the end. Against this crosspiece two persons would lean their weight, this they called pushing instead of pulling. It was very common to see young girls between the ages of 16 and 20 with a harness on their shoulders in the shape of a halter, a small chain fastened to that, and then fastened to the cart. There were some four or five to a cart, some pushing, some pulling all day long through the hot, dry sand, with hardly enough to eat to keep life in their bodies.

I was appointed Captain of the company, and although it was one of the last companies it was one of the most successful in its journey.[102] I tried very hard to avoid any trouble which might arise, and was very much respected by all the people in the company. Provisions were weighed out to each family once a week; at one time we were rationed one-half pound of flour a day. Water at times was very scarce and on some occasions the only water to be had was in boggy places. Shovels were used and after digging three or four feet we would strike water, which was very yellow and resembled rain water which had stood for a long time. This was caused from the alkali in the soil. When we camped at night the carts were placed in a circle leaving an open space of about ten feet. This circle was used as a corral for the oxen. The oxen were

---

102. *Deseret News*, 29 August 1860, states that one child and one ox were lost during the trek of the ninth handcart company. It stated that they had come along "as well as any company that ever crossed the Plains. Their appearance on entering the city was indeed, if anything, more favourable than that of any previous handcart company."

unyoked inside the circle and then driven perhaps one-half mile away to feed for the night. Here they were guarded until midnight by two of the men and then they were relieved by others. When morning came the oxen were brought in, each man yoking up his own oxen. As soon as breakfast was over we were lined up for another hot day. The carts were loaded with bedding and cooking utensils, and sometimes little children were put in the carts if their feet had gotten too tired to walk any farther. Most of the mothers were seen trudging along on the scorching ground bare-footed, leading their barefooted little tots by the hand, pausing now and then, trying to do something to relieve the pain in their blistered feet. When we camped for the night we always had prayer and songs. We seemed very happy, we were putting our trust in God and were not deceived, for our journey was a peaceful one. Several bands of Indians passed our camp but we were not molested. At one time our food failed to reach camp. I swam the Platte River and made arrangements for provisions to be sent.

Arriving at the Sweetwater River we found the bottom of the river covered with fish. Everyone had all they could eat, which was a treat after having to eat salty bacon from the time we started until now. We had no meat of any kind, except the salty bacon, because we could not keep it, and we did not see any animals which we might kill. We had to cross the Green River on ferry boats, all except the oxen, who had to swim. We ran very low of provisions at this point and we became weak from hunger. We, however, did not get discouraged or lose our faith. We had pledged ourselves with the Lord, and so we would not permit ourselves to think of anything other than the Lord would pro-vide. As we were struggling on our way fighting against despair and hunger, a wagon drove up—we know not from where—loaded with provisions. This proved to us that we had not put ourselves in the care of the Lord in vain. He will always provide if we put our faith and trust in Him.

We camped at the mouth of Echo Canyon on the Weber

River, at a small town, Henefer, which was named after the only people living there at that time. Mr. Henefer donated five bushels of potatoes if we would dig them. The fishing was good in the Weber River, and so after the potatoes were dug and the fish caught and cooked, of course, everyone had a treat. We reached Salt Lake Valley on the 27th of August, 1860. It took us nearly eleven weeks to make the journey.

I came north as far as Farmington and here I made my home for three years. While living in Farmington, I helped lay rock for the old rock meetinghouse which is still standing. In 1863, I moved from Farmington to North Morgan. Here we built our first cabins with logs cut from the mountains of North Morgan. The roofs were made with small poles and wild wheat grass, the chimneys were built of rock, there was one small window without glass, no door just a quilt or carpet hung in place of a door. We passed through all the hardships of early pioneer days, losing four more children, making seven of our twelve children having passed away. The Union Pacific Railroad was built in 1868–69, money was now more plentiful.

OSCAR ORLONDO STODDARD[103]

A FEW INCIDENTS OF TRAVEL that took place on the plains the summer of 1860 in the last handcart company [to cross the plains] of which I had been appointed Captain by George Q. Cannon, Emigration agent for that year. Although not fully equipped, we went into camp with the handcarts on

---

103. "Oscar Orlondo Stoddard, Excerpt from Autobiography and Family Records" (1883), typescript copy, LDS Church Archives.

the evening of the Fourth of July and never camped two nights on the same ground from that time till we did it on the 8th Ward ground in Salt Lake City. It was three days before we fairly got all together wagons, teams and handcarts[;] there were 21 Hand carts and 7 wagons with three yokes of oxen to each wagon and there were also with us, traveling with their own team, Stephen Taylor and family; also, a brother Paul and family from South Africa, [who] followed us up and joined us about the third day out and by the advice of Brother Cannon, Brother Paul was chosen chaplain over the English speaking portion of the company. Brother Christian Christiansen having been chosen chaplain of the Scandinavian and Swiss portion.

Owing to the minutes of the journey being taken at the time with a lead pencil, they became illegible before I had an opportunity of copying them, so I am writing from memory. I cannot remember the number of souls who were in the company at the start [124], but Brother Cannon told them at the start if they would [be] humble and faithful, not one of them should die on the road to the Valley; which was literally fulfilled as everyone who started from Florence with us came into Salt Lake City with us, except a Swedish girl whom her parents left with Bro[ther] Myers at Bear River. We also picked up others on the road. A Brother Chapman and family with wagon and team joined us at Genoa [Nebraska]. A sister, left by some former company, was taken up by us at Wood River and brought to the Valley, also a family named Cherrington,[104] whom we found at Green River, who had had much sickness and had lost three children by death and another, a daughter, then sick unto death, but they were so anxious to come to the Valley that we took them in and brought them along. The sick daughter died in East Canyon a few miles below the foot of Big Mountain and was buried there.

---

104. Probably the John and Sarah Cherrington family.

Now, I will mention a few incidents wherein the Lord blessed us in a special manner. First, just after leaving the Wood River and reaching the Platte, while camped at noon, Elizabeth Taylor, daughter of the Brother Taylor spoken of as traveling with us with his family, while sitting on some bedclothes spread in the shade of a wagon, not feeling very well, was seized with spasms and severe jerking and twitching till it seemed as though she was going to die. I was called by a Sister Rogers[105] who was by her to administer to her and seeing her condition was wondering what could be the matter and felt fearful she was going to leave us immediately and with a humble and diffident feeling, I laid my hands upon her head and almost mechanically rebuked the evil spirits and in the name of Jesus Christ commanded them to depart and leave her system when immediately her paroxysm ceased and she spoke to us and asked why we did not let her go[,] why we called her back to this world of trouble. She had got past all pain and was going off [to Heaven] in a nice four-horse carriage finely caparisoned[.][106] During her convalescence she informed Sister Rogers (the sister who was with her) that while at Council Bluffs spiritualism was quite common and that in the family where she resided they often had sittings or circles headed by the circuit preacher and after awhile they induced her to sit at the table with them. When it was discovered she was the strongest medium among them and astonished them at the manifestation given through her, they obtained such a hold over her that she began to feel and fear their influence and resolved to break away from them when some of the spirits prominent among them, an Indian doctor, informed her as she was intending to go to Salt Lake City, she would not live to get there, for they would come and get her when she got to the Platte River. The result of their attempting to carry her off we have seen but the sequel is yet to

---

105. Probably the wife of George Rogers, who was the clerk of the company.
106. Ornamented or adorned.

be told. When Sister Rogers told me the foregoing, I immediately told sister Elizabeth she should go to Salt Lake City, but she
would have to go there through the Platte River[;] she would have
to be baptized in the Platte so on the 25th of July we camped on
the Platte and held a celebration and looked up a place to baptize
in and the weather was nice and clear but as we repaired to the
riverside to perform the ordinance of baptism, the sky became
suddenly overcast with clouds and a severe wind arose raising the
waves in the river till they looked fearful and almost discouraging
us from doing our work especially as to all appearance it looked
like keeping up for the day but a calm feeling came over me and
I mildly said, 'Brothers and Sisters, let us proceed with our
preparations, sing, pray and get ready and if your faith is sufficient, we will yet be able to do our work.' We kept on getting
ready and when we had finished the weather was clear and serene,
and the water was without a ripple and we finished our work
unmolested. That evening Brother G. Q. Cannon, H[orace].
L. [S.] Eldredge, N. H. [William H.] Hooper and others passed
our camp on the road to the Valley. As for sister Elizabeth she
came into the Valley, got married and became the mother of five
daughters and three sons all of whom except one daughter are
now living and call me father[107] and she has never been troubled
with those spirits since.

The next incident I will mention is the crossing the Platte
River at Laramie. Having traveled down the Platte on the north
side and found it to be a rough, hilly road and bad for handcarts
between Laramie and the upper crossing, I thought I would try
and cross the North Platte at Laramie and travel up the south side
of it and as there were some in the company who were timid
about crossing with the handcarts. I was in a quandary what to do
about it. We camped about four miles below Laramie, and dur-

---

107. Oscar Stoddard and Elizabeth Taylor were married 2 October 1860.

ing the night I dreamed I saw ourselves camped on the other side of the river and when I told my dream it seemed to allay all fears; so we started at sunrise and moved camp up the river till opposite Laramie Then the sisters did their washing while we overhauled our provisions, issued rations increasing the rations of flour from a lb per head per day which had been issued up till that time, up to 1 1/4 lbs per head per day and hunted up a ford and prepared to cross. We hitched up when ready and drove one wagon over[,] unloaded it, came back and took in the loads of the handcarts and then went over with them leaving the empty carts to haul over by hand, I helped to haul over the first one over myself. None but the men hauled the carts over the river[,] the women & children being hauled over in the wagons and we were over and in camp 2 miles up the river at sundown.

The next incident a [of] moment [occurred] at Independence Rock on the Sweetwater River. I got a letter from Brother Cannon informing me that there was 14 sacks of flour for me at the three crossings of the Sweetwater river. When I arrived at the three crossings, I found a man there with the flour, which we took into the wagon and from that raised our rations of flour to 1 1/2 lbs pr head, pr day, which we kept up till we arrived in Salt Lake City. At the first camp this the west side of Quaking Asp[en] ridge, a few teams from the valley passed us and camped a short distance east of [us] and they came back and spent the evening with us and enjoying themselves, as young folks will, till between 10 & 11 o'clock when they started for their camp and feeling jolly hurrahed, fired off pistols, and shouted and the Danish Saints, having gone to bed in a tent and all asleep suddenly aroused by the uproar were frightened and someone shouting 'Indians' it created a panic and a rush was made for the tent door to get outside. Bro Christian Christiansen, their Chaplain, a small man lying at the tent door started to go with the rest, but the rush was too soon and powerful for him and he was trampled underfoot till the tent was cleared when he found himself free but with a shoulder out of joint with the knuckle below the socket. The next morning one of the brethren by using his heel as a fulcrum tried to pull his arm out and pry the shoulder in place. After three or four unsuccessful attempts, he begged him to stop as he could stand the pulling no longer I was then informed of the circumstance and went to him and found him with his arm in a sling, but able to be around. We managed to get him on the camp pony and let him ride along the road as the camp moved along till we camped at night hoping to find some chance to send him forward in to the city but did not and in the evening just after prayers and we were preparing for bed he sent for me to come and administer to him. I complied and anointed his shoulder, as well as his head, with consecrated oil and in confirming the annointing with my hands upon his head I prayed for the muscles and sinews to relax that the joint might have room to get to its place and after I got through administering I said 'Brother Christiansen, go to bed and to sleep and if you will have faith, you shall wake up in the morning with your shoulder in its place.' and he said, I believe you Captain after which I went to bed. The first thing I heard in the morning the Danish interpreter called me and said, 'Captain, Christiansen's shoulder is in its place as you told him last night it would be.' and so it was and did not trouble him any more to my knowledge though I have never seen him since he left the camp ground in Salt Lake City.

One more incident and I will close this narration. When we got to the mouth of Echo Canyon, we stopped at noon and turned out our cattle near a mail station and when we hitched up for the afternoon start, Bro[ther] Paul, our chaplain, missed a cow of his[;] as the train started he went back to look [for] it and found it shut up in a pen and on going to let her out, he was accosted by the stage driver, who was also stopping for noon, who demanded him to desist and drew out a pocket knife and stabbed him in the back near the shoulder blade[;] he came on after the train[;] on his coming up word was brought forward to me, and I went back to the station on horseback and among the passengers on the incoming stage was a district judge for Utah. He told me the case should be looked into and for me to take the cow and as soon as he arrived in the city, he would have the case put into the hands of the prosecuting attorney and attended to. I came on with the cow and that is the last I ever heard of the scape [scrape?] but when we were coming up the big mountain we met the driver going down with the outgoing stage having changed teams with the driver of the same when they met and I have never seen him to know him since. The judge came in but did not stay long[;] he left with Governor Dawson[;] his name I think was Crosby

We landed on the 8th ward square in Salt Lake City on the 24th day of September 1860, having just dealt out one weeks rations and also meeting on the square persons under the direction of the bishopric with vegetables, molasses[,] provisions which were distributed among them as needed or required so they were well received[.] I must say according to the best of my understanding and knowledge that this[,] the last handcart Co.[,] came across the plains in as good condition as any one of them all.

There was one circumstance happened that I regretted and it caused me some anxiety at the time but I soon gained the ascendency over the difficulty it was this[.] Bro Geo. Q. Cannon in selecting teamsters to drive the teams with the wagons taking the provisions and extra freight of the company chose a couple that had came down from the valey that season with Joseph W. Young on a trial trip to try the feasibility of oxen making the trip from the valley to the Missouri river and back in one season and it proved a success and thus there was no more need for handcarts[.] one of these teamsters was danish and was to act as interpreter for me to communicate with the danish saints and the other as having a little experience was to have charge of the teams when it was necessary for me to be absent from them[.] with the handcarts I trusted him and at his request nominated him before the company as wagon master in my absence and it soon turned out that he got it into his head that he had sole charge of the wagons and had a right to sit in judgment upon the members of the company who were traveling with their own wagons[.] accordingly he cited Bro Paul our chaplain to appear before the council of his teamsters to answer to certain charges and when Bro Paul asked the privilege of bringing witnesses[,] he was refused[.] I thought it time for me to interfere and I told Bro Paul that he need not answer the summons if he was refused witnesses upon which the wagon master asserted his claim as independent master of the wagons whether I was present or absent[.] I gave him to understand that when the wagons and handcarts were together they were all under my charge and he was supposed to be included with them as I was captaining the company[.] if he had his will it was his intention to rule over the people like a tyrant but meeting with a determined check [,] he subsided and threatened me with a High council trial when we got to the city and took notes of my actions from that time on but his charges were not noticed and I never heard from them again[.] this was the most unpleasant incident of the journey and I send you the foregoing communication as Bro Palmer thought you would like it when I informed him I led in the last company of hand carts

Yours truly in the gospel of Jesus Christ
Oscar O. Stoddard
To Junius H. Wells
Editor of the contributor

The final account is by Hannah Settle Lapish, who traveled west in Daniel Robison's company. Her brief remembrance offers some interesting personal incidents and reveals a resourceful and optimistic traveler.

HANNAH SETTLE LAPISH[108]

EMIGRATING TO AMERICA (from England) we embarked May 30, 1857 on the ship 'Tuscarora' at Liverpool and arrived in Philadelphia July 3, 1857. This being the year of the great panic,[109] my husband [Joseph Lapish], together with others, went to Richmond, Virginia, to obtain employment and in the meantime I took in sewing from a knitting factory which proved quite providential at the time as I was left with a three months old babe. After the elapse of three months I joined my husband in Richmond where we resided about three years. During our residence at that place the so-called Harper Ferry raid occurred,[110] and during the excitement we received a letter from Geo. Q. Cannon counseling us (according to instructions which he had received from President Brigham Young), to leave for the West, as war in the East seemed inevitable. We were told to leave by hook or crook and I have always claimed that we left by the latter. We joined a number of the other Saints at Philadelphia and traveled to Florence, Nebr. where we joined Captain Daniel Robinson's [Robison's] handcart company and started on our journey to Utah on June 7, 1860. I had two children at the time, one about two and one half years old [Laura J.] and the other but six months [Emily V.]. Try to imagine if you can a mother with a babe at her breast undertaking a journey of hundreds of miles on foot. But even that babe seemed to understand something of the life going on about her. Why, do you know that if she wer [sic] in the middle of enjoying

---

108. Mrs. Hannah Settle Lapish in "Handcart Stories," 37–39, typescript, LDS Church Archives.
109. She may be referring to a sharp recession that was then plaguing the country.
110. This was the 1859 raid on a federal arsenal at Harper's Ferry, Virginia, by John Brown and eighteen followers, hoping to incite a slave uprising.

her dinner and she heard that bugle blow, she would stop, for she knew she must be put into the cart. I couldn't carry her—indeed no, and she certainly knew it.

Of course it was a dreadfully hard journey and like the other companies we suffered from lack of food. One day on the journey there was a great deal of suffering owing to the scarcity of provisions and as we were near a trading post, I decided to see what I could do. I left the rest of the company and went to a store where I offered the proprietors my jewelry in exchange for a little flour which at that time and place was $10.00 per hundred. I soon observed that he was not going to make the exchange and as I turned around I saw a very tall man, perhaps a trapper or a miner, dressed in beaded buckskin suit standing in the store. He eyed the jewelry which I had in my hand and finally said, 'What do you want for that thing (meaning the jewelry)? For a moment I hesitated and then the answer seemed to come to me by inspiration. "700 pounds of flour, Sir," I answered. He took the jewelry and sent the flour to the camp. I gave it to the commissary of the handcart company who dealt it out judiciously to the hungry travelors, the last measure, half a pint for a person, being distributed on the day we crossed Green River. While we were being ferried across that stream a shout of joy went up from our company as the word was passed that a relief train sent by the Church authorities had just arrived with provisions for us. With this relief our main troubles were over and we arrived safely in Salt Lake City August 27, 1860. Our company was one of the last companies to make the journey in that pathetic way—pushing handcarts across the western prairies and mountains. We are the crusaders of the 19th century. [. . .] We handcart people will never outlive the memory of those experiences.

By 1860 the handcart experiment had reached an end. The well-traveled western trail now made it possible for wagon trains to leave the Salt Lake Valley in the spring and make a return trip with emigrants the same season. A new program was inaugurated making use of this round-trip travel. Before the transcontinental railroad reached Utah nine years later, this new system, the "down and back" trains, brought more than eighteen thousand Saints to Utah. But no other phase of the Mormon pioneer story has caught the imagination quite like the handcart experiment. It was truly unique in western travel, and "the experience of these people," Church historian Andrew Jenson wrote in 1893, "will never have its equal in the history of the Church."[111] As far as we know, he was right.

The experiment did not really need vindicating. It brought nearly three thousand Saints to the Valley, most of whom could not have come any other way. Their zeal for Zion was no less fervent than the desire for gold that pulled thousands of others to California in makeshift conveyances. Though the hand-carters could not have known the magnitude of the challenges of such a journey to Zion, common sense told them something of what lay ahead. They were nonetheless willing to take the risk and endure the consequences. Their faith outweighed their fear. But when the journey was over, the handcarts, which must have seemed like an extension of their own bodies as they situated themselves each morning between the cart and its U-shaped handle, no longer held any value to them, real or sentimental. Probably most of them, had they dared,

---

III. "Emigration of 1860," *The Contributor* 14 (September 1893): 549.

would have joined the young woman who, upon reaching the summit of the last hill before entering the Valley and "tired of the long push, gathered up the few things remaining in her cart, and let it slide down the ravine into the canyon, glad to see the last of it."[112]

Brigham Young, who bore ultimate blame for the disasters as well as credit for the success of the handcart experiment, characterized the spirit that animated these intrepid travelers. "They only had faith and power for the day," he said, "and on the morrow it seemed as though they certainly had to stop. But when to-morrow came they had faith and power to perform the journey of that day, and so they have been prompted day by day, to this point. God is at the helm."[113]

And so ended a remarkable chapter in the pioneer history of the Church and of the West. The handcart pioneers were willing to push and pull their handcarts to Zion because of the magnetic power of the gathering. They were latter-day exemplars of "the poor of this world rich in faith" (James 2:5), a courageous band of westering Saints who tested the endurance of the Nauvoo Covenant as they proved their steadfastness in making their way to Zion.

---

112. Carter, "Handcart Pioneers of Utah," *Heart Throbs of the West* 1:83.
113. Brigham Young, "The Emigrating Saints were prompted by the Spirit of God," in *Journal of Discourses*, 26 vols. (Liverpool: F. D. Richards, 1855–1886; reprint, Salt Lake City, 1967) 4:111.

APPENDIX

Biographical Sketches

SARA ALEXANDER

A successful dancer and actress, Sara Alexander was born in 1839 in West Virginia. She traveled to Salt Lake City in 1859 with her sister, Mary Ada; her sister's husband, James Finlayson; and her mother, Sarah B. Alexander. In 1862, she moved to Payson, where she performed in local theatricals. Later, she returned to Salt Lake City, where she lived in the Lion House and taught dancing to Brigham Young's daughters. Sara danced in the first performance of the Salt Lake Theatre in 1862 and continued as an actress of the theater. She directed a Salt Lake City ballet group that included some of Brigham Young's daughters, and she performed as a leading dancer in the Deseret Dramatic Association. She left Utah in 1868 to dance with E. L. Davenport, a touring actor from the East, and earned a national reputation. Trained in solo dancing and comic acting, she played in stock companies on both the east and west coasts and also acted in several motion pictures. Sara never married, often saying she had seen "too much of marriage." She died in 1926 on Long Island, New York.

SARAH HANCOCK BEESLEY

Sarah Hancock Beesley was born 14 January 1840 at Wooburn
Moor, Buckinghamshire, England, to Henry Hancock and Sarah
Ayres. As a young girl, Sarah assisted her father in his shoemaking shop. Both Henry Hancock and Ebenezer Beesley, Sarah's
husband-to-be, were shoemakers. She was baptized 4 January
1851 and thereafter Church leaders in Wooburn held meetings
in the Hancock home. After her baptism, Sarah wanted to gather
with the Saints in America, and Ebenezer Beesley proposed that
she travel with him. Her parents tried to dissuade her from
going, but Sarah was persistent. She and Ebenezer were married
in the Parish Church of Wooburn 26 March 1859 and sailed
from Liverpool aboard the *William Tapscott* the next month.
Sarah took her wedding gown to America, hoping to wear it as
they traveled west, but handcart travel hardly allowed her the
opportunity. Traveling with the George Rowley handcart company, Sarah and Ebenezer reached the Valley September 1859
and moved to Tooele City shortly after their arrival. They
returned to Salt Lake City in 1861 when Ebenezer was appointed
conductor of the Tabernacle Choir. Sarah Beesley died 25 May
1921 in Salt Lake City. She was the mother of ten children, all of
whom lived to adulthood.

AMELIA ELIZA SLADE BENNION

Amelia Eliza Slade Bennion was born 10 October 1854 in
Crewkerne, Sommersetshire, England, the daughter of William
E. Slade and Amelia Lacey. Three years after her father's emigration to America, Amelia, her mother, and her brothers and
sisters also emigrated. They made their home in Philadelphia,
where Amelia briefly attended school before her father's death.
Afterward, she worked for some neighbors to relieve the financial

strain on her mother. In 1864, when she was ten, her family traveled to the Salt Lake Valley with the Warren S. Snow company. On 24 August 1882 Amelia married Alfred Bennion. They lived in Taylorsville, Utah, for most of her life. She died 20 October 1936 in Salt Lake City.

Kersten Ericksen Benson

Kersten Ericksen Benson was born in Denmark in 1837. In 1857, when she was twenty, she left Copenhagen with her parents and grandmother to join the Saints in Utah. They arrived in Philadelphia on 31 May and then traveled to Iowa City by rail. They continued their journey to Utah with the Christian Christiansen handcart company of 1857. On 29 November of that year she married Jens Peter Benson who was also born in Denmark and who had previously married her sister Mathie Christine Ericksen. The marriage was performed by Brigham Young. Kersten Benson died in Newton, Cache County, Utah.

Isaiah Moses Coombs

Isaiah Moses Coombs was born 21 March 1834 in Columbia, Monroe County, Illinois. His parents, Mark Anthony Coombs and Maria Morgan, were members of the Church when Isaiah was born. He studied to become a schoolteacher and then married Sarah A. Turk, a nonmember, on 30 November 1854. The young couple separated a year later when Isaiah desired to gather with the Saints in Utah and Sarah refused to move away from home. Isaiah was appointed clerk of that season's emigration under the direction of Erastus Snow. He traveled to the Valley in Isaac Allred's company, arriving 2 November 1855. Shortly after his arrival he resumed teaching school. The next spring he also taught a Book of Mormon class in the Fourteenth Ward Sunday School and within a year was made superintendent of the school. He served a mission to the States with Parley P. Pratt during late 1856 and 1857, spending most of his time in Illinois and Arkansas. On 28 July 1858 Isaiah married Fanny McLean (or McClean). They were the parents of seven boys and seven girls. Continuing his teaching, he moved to Parowan in Iron County during the winters of 1858 to 1861. In 1861 he settled in Payson and taught school until 1869. In addition to his teaching Isaiah Coombs also supervised the tithing office for seventeen years, served as assistant superintendent of the Utah Stake Sunday School, and served a mission to Great Britain. He took a second wife, Augusta Hardy, in 1875, and added six children to his family. In his later years he compiled a history of Payson, Utah, where he died 20 May 1886.

GEORGE CUNNINGHAM

George Cunningham was born 17 August 1840 in Dysart, Fifeshire, Scotland, son of James Cunningham and Elizabeth Nelson. Having been raised in the Church, he was encouraged to gather with the Saints. Therefore, he left England for New York 4 May 1856 aboard the *Thornton* and traveled to the Valley in James Willie's handcart company. After reaching the Valley he moved to American Fork. He was an alderman in American Fork from 1883 to 1886 and served as mayor from 1891 to 1892. He was also the city justice of American Fork from 1908 to 1911. He served as a counselor to Bishop George Halliday of the American Fork Ward from June 1889 until 28 January 1894. As a member of the state legislature he earned a reputation as a forceful debater. The story is told of a road-builder who had plans for a road that infringed on George Cunningham's property. Rather than confront him, the road-builder altered the plans, resulting in a crooked road that jogged sharply around the Cunningham property. In 1863 George married Grace Mary Wrigley in Salt Lake City.He died 15 March 1913 in American Fork, Utah.

BARBARA ANN EWELL EVANS

Barbara Ann Ewell Evans was born 16 May 1821 in Albermarle County, Virginia, to Pleasant Ewell and Barbara Fauber. The family moved to Tennessee when Barbara was nine years old, and then to Ray County, Missouri, in 1833. Barbara was baptized 10 June 1837 by David Evans whom she married on 23 November 1841. After leaving Nauvoo, Barbara and her family worked hard to outfit themselves for the journey west and were finally able to join a company in 1850, arriving in the Valley on 15 September. She lived in the Salt Lake Valley until 1851, when the family moved to Lehi, where she lived until her death in 1898. She was the mother of fifteen children.

JOSEPH FIELDING

Joseph Fielding was born 26 March 1797 in Honeydon, England, near Bedford, Bedfordshire, to John and Rachel Fielding. In 1832 he and his sister Mercy emigrated to upper Canada, followed two years later by his sister Mary. There he, with his sisters, was converted to Mormonism through the missionary efforts of Parley P. Pratt, who baptized him 21 May 1836 at Chesleton Settlement in Black Creek near Toronto, Canada. He was subsequently ordained a priest and moved to Kirtland, Ohio, in May of 1837. He helped open the British mission in 1837 with Heber C. Kimball and Orson Hyde. In the spring of

1838 Joseph Fielding was called to preside over the British Mission having been previously ordained an elder and high priest. While in Preston, England, he married Hannah Greenwood on 11 June 1838. He left Great Britain in 1841, taking charge of a company of Saints emigrating to America. Following his return to Nauvoo, he married Mary Ann Peak. Joseph left Nauvoo in late summer of 1846 with his family and his widowed sisters, Mary Smith and Mercy Rachel Thompson and their families, and traveled to Winter Quarters. He continued to assist Mary while at the Missouri, and they traveled together in the same wagon company to Utah in the fall of 1848, settling in Mill Creek, Salt Lake County. That remained his home until his death on 19 December 1863. Joseph's plural wives also included Mary Duff and Mary Farras.

WARREN FOOTE

Warren Foote was born 10 August 1817 in Dryden, Thompkins County, New York, the son of David Foote and Irene Lane. He moved to Greenwood, Steuben County, New York, in March 1832. Following a visit to the Kirtland area in May 1837, he settled there in October of the same year, teaching school during the winter of 1837 and 1838 in the western part of Kirtland township. In May 1838 he moved to Shoal Creek in Missouri, fleeing to Quincy, Illinois, the next year with the Mormon exodus. While there he taught school and drove a stage. Although he professed a belief in Mormonism as early as 1833, he was not baptized until 24 March 1842. On 8 June 1843 he married Artemisia S. Myers at Adams County, Illinois. He moved to Hancock County during the spring of 1845 and lived at Montebello, twelve miles south of Nauvoo, where he was elected adjutant of the Nauvoo Legion. On 4 May 1846 he left Nauvoo, locating at Kanesville for four years. In 1850 he traveled to the

Salt Lake Valley as the head of a company, arriving in September. He settled in the Little Cottonwood Ward, where he ran a mill. He served as justice of the peace for three terms and later as postmaster. He also served in the Cottonwood and Willow Creek Military District as first sergeant, second lieutenant, and major. In 1856 he married Eliza Maria Ivie. He moved to Round Valley in 1863, locating on the townsite of Scipio. He volunteered to help settle the Muddy Valley in Arizona (now Nevada) organizing the town of St. Joseph and serving as branch president. He later served in the presidency of the Muddy Mission. He eventually moved to Glendale, Kane County, Utah, where he was appointed a patriarch. He died in Glendale on 23 July 1903.

ROBERT GARDNER, JR.

Robert Gardner, Jr., was born 12 October 1819 in Kilsyth, Stirling, Scotland, the son of Robert Gardner and Margaret Calender. In 1821, the Gardner family moved to Dalhousie Township, Banthrest District, Upper Canada, where Robert attended school for six weeks. The family then moved to Warwick Township, Kent County, Western District (Canada). On 17 March 1842, Robert married Jane McKeown. Three years later he was converted and baptized. In late 1845 Warren visited Nauvoo for two weeks and decided to move there, arriving on 6 April 1846, when the Saints were already beginning to vacate the city. Almost immediately afterward the Gardners left Nauvoo, and in 1847 they traveled to Utah with a group known as the "Canada Company," a part of the Edward Hunter/Joseph Horne/John Taylor company. Robert moved to Mill Creek and there married his second wife, Cynthia Lovenia (Lovina) Berry. He moved to Jordan River to run a sawmill for two years, after which he returned to Mill Creek, where he married his third wife, Mary Ann Carr, 20 July 1856. He served a mission to

Canada in 1857 and 1858. After his return, he moved his family to Cottonwood and then back to Mill Creek in 1860. The next year he was called to settle Southern Utah. He served as bishop of the Saints in St. George, Shoal Creek, Meadows, Pinto, and Pine Valley in Southern Utah and was elected mayor of St. George in 1872, serving two four-year terms. He also married a fourth wife, Leonora Cannon. Robert was nominated president of the United Order in St. George. From 1884 to 1887 he served as a temple worker with his wife Cynthia. He died 3 February 1906.

LOUISE CHARLOTTE LEUBA GRAEHL

Louise Charlotte Leuba Graehl was born in Geneva, Switzerland, on 15 September 1822 to Henry Francois Leuba and Audrienne Elizabeth Elger. When she was still very young, both of her parents died, and she became the ward of a Mrs. Maurice. In 1844 she married George Louis Graehl in Geneva. Together they operated a confectionery store. She was baptized 7 June 1853, the first woman in Geneva to join the Church. In 1854 Louise and George sold the business and traveled to the Salt Lake Valley, arriving in October with the Robert L. Campbell company. Louise died in October 1904. She was the mother of twelve children, some of whom died in infancy.

HARRIET DECKER HANKS

Harriet Decker Hanks was born on 13 March 1826 in Phelps, Ontario County, New York, to Harriet Page Wheeler and Isaac Decker. Her family became close friends with Joseph Smith, Brigham Young, and Lorenzo Dow Young, Brigham Young's brother. She joined the Church in Portage, Ohio, when she was nine years old. Following their conversion and baptism, she and her family moved to Missouri and then to Illinois with the Saints. At Winchester, Illinois, Harriet met Edwin Sobieski Little and married him on 22 March 1842. Her mother married Lorenzo Dow Young and her two sisters, Clara and Lucy Ann, married Brigham Young. On 18 March 1846, just weeks after leaving Illinois with the exodus, Edwin died from exposure near Richardson's Point, 55 miles from Nauvoo. Harriet stayed at Winter Quarters during the winter and traveled to the Salt Lake Valley with the Jedediah M. Grant company the following year, arriving in October 1847. On 22 September 1848 she married Ephraim Hanks, a well-known scouter and freighter and former member of the Mormon Battalion. Harriet died 30 May 1917 in Salt Lake City, the mother of seven children.

URSULIA HASTINGS HASCALL

Ursulia Hastings Hascall (sometimes Haskell) was born 12 May 1799 to Consider and Phebe Hastings. She married Ashbel Green Hascall 3 March 1822 and settled in North New Salem, Franklin County, Massachusetts. To help the family's financial situation during the panic of 1837, Ursulia provided meals in their home for the numerous mill hands who worked in the vicinity. Ursulia and her family were converted to Mormonism and in 1845 Ursulia traveled to Nauvoo with her son Thales, leaving her husband behind to take care of business affairs. Ursulia and Thales sailed from Boston to New Orleans aboard the *Gloucester* with a company of Saints under George B. Wallace, then traveled by steamboat, *The Pride of the West,* up the Mississippi River to St. Louis, and on a riverboat, the *Tempest,* to Nauvoo. There they were reunited with Ursulia's daughter Irene and her husband, Francis Pomeroy. In February of 1846 the family (which included Ursulia, Thales, Irene, and Francis and their daughter) was driven from Nauvoo with the rest of the Saints. At the same time, Ursulia's husband left Boston on the *Brooklyn,* planning to rejoin his family in the West. Ursulia and her children spent the winter in Winter Quarters and traveled to the Salt Lake Valley in 1847, arriving the latter part of September. There they learned of the death of Ashbel after reaching California. The family lived first in Mill Creek and then moved south to Salem, Utah. They returned to their Salt Lake home in the fall of 1858. After Irene's untimely death in 1860, Ursulia cared for Irene's two-year-old twins. When the twins were almost teens, Ursulia took them to join their father in Bear Lake Valley. Ursulia lived in Paris, Idaho, in Bear Lake Valley, until her own death on 5 August 1875.

GUSTAVE LOUIS HENRIOD

Gustave Louis Henriod was born 25 August 1835 at Havre, Seine Inferieure, France. As a boy he worked for L. J. M. Daguerre, who developed the first camera. Louis was obliged to sit stone-still while Daguerre worked to get an image of him. In 1851 he joined the Church and secured work with a maritime insurance company, remaining with it for two years. In 1853 he emigrated to America aboard the *Commodor.* He traveled to Salt Lake City with the Cyrus E. Wheelock company, arriving in October 1853. He was befriended by Bishop Joseph Heywood and served as his clerk in the Salt Lake Seventeenth Ward and also clerk to Bishop Heywood in his position as territorial marshal. A literate and artistic man, he taught dancing and music lessons and also helped George D. Watt inaugurate the Deseret Alphabet, teaching it in Nephi, Utah, where he settled in 1855. He died there on 10 October 1904.

GEORGE WASHINGTON HILL

George Washington Hill was born 5 March 1822 in Amesville, Athens County, Ohio, the son of Richard Hill and Sarah Strait. The family moved often when George was a boy, eventually locating in Dallas County, Missouri. On 18 September 1845 George married Cynthia Utley Stewart. Through Cynthia he was introduced to the Mormon Church and decided to join the Saints. With the Stewart family, George and Cynthia reached the settlement near Kanesville. There George was baptized on 5 June 1847. The family traveled to the Valley in the Abraham O. Smoot/George B. Wallace company, arriving in September 1847. In 1849 and again in 1864 he helped bring emigrants to Utah. An Indian interpreter, he was called to serve a mission in 1873 to teach agriculture to the Indians in Box Elder County, Utah. He also worked with the Indians of the Malad River Valley. In the spring of 1855 he was called to the Salmon River Mission in Idaho and served there three years, baptizing more than a hundred Indians. He died 21 February 1891 in Salt Lake City, a high priest and patriarch.

WILLIAM HUNTINGTON

A direct descendant of Puritan immigrant Simon Huntington, William Huntington was born 28 March 1784 in Grantham, Cheshire County, New Hampshire, the son of William Huntington and Prescindia Lathrop. In 1804 the Huntington family moved to Watertown, Jefferson County, New York. Young William returned to New Hampshire, where he married Zina Baker on 28 December 1806. Then he took her to Watertown, which became their home until 1811. An earnest seeker of truth, William first joined the Presbyterian Church before accepting Mormonism in 1835. His home then became a meeting place for the Saints. In 1836 the Huntington family moved to Kirtland, where he was ordained to the offices of high priest and high councilor. The family moved to Far West, Missouri, in 1838 and later to Adam-ondi-Ahman. William assisted the Saints, particularly the poor, in leaving Missouri after the extermination order, and he eventually reached Nauvoo himself in May 1839. His wife died the following July, and in 1840 William married Lydia Clisbee Partridge, the widow of Bishop Edward Partridge. He also married Dorcas Baker. William worked on the Nauvoo Temple, having helped lay the cornerstone in April 1841. He was commissary general for the Nauvoo Legion and helped bury the bodies of Joseph and Hyrum Smith after the martyrdom. The Huntington family left Nauvoo 9 February 1846, traveling in Amasa Lyman's pioneer company as a captain of a hundred. He was chosen to preside over the Mount Pisgah settlement, where he died 19 August 1846.

LEVI JACKMAN

The son of Moses French Jackman and Elizabeth Carr, Levi Jackman was born 28 July 1797 in Corinth, Orange County, Vermont. In 1810 he moved to Batavia, New York, and on 13 November 1817 he married Anjaline Myers. In 1830 they moved to Portage County, Ohio, where they were converted and baptized the next year. In 1832 Levi moved to Missouri, where he was elected justice of the peace. In Nauvoo he worked on the temple and in 1844 served a mission. After the death of his wife in 1846, he married Sally Plumb, a widow. He traveled to the Salt Lake Valley with Brigham Young's vanguard pioneer company, arriving 22 July 1847. He married Lucinda Harmon in Salt Lake City 18 November 1849. His other wives included Mary Vale Morse, Delia Byam, Elizabeth Davies, Caroline Christiansen, and Ruth Rodgers. He moved to Salem, Utah, when he was sixty-seven years old and died there on 23 July 1876. Levi was a saddletree maker and a farmer by trade. He served as a member of the high council, as a first counselor to Bishop Roundy of the Salt Lake Sixteenth Ward, and as a patriarch.

Emma James

Emma James was born 8 June 1839 in England, the daughter of William James and Jane Haynes (or Haines). She joined the Church with her family, and when she was eighteen the family left England to gather with the Saints in Utah. They set sail from Liverpool with 764 other converts aboard the *Thornton* in May 1856. At Winter Quarters she and her family joined the Willie handcart company and traveled to the Valley, arriving 19 November 1856, suffering intensely with the other members of that beleaguered company. She married Lorenzo Johnson in March 1857 in Salt Lake City. After his death she married John Rowley in 1873 in Colonia Pacheco, Chihuahua, Mexico. She died 27 March 1926 in Nephi, Juab County, Utah.

Sarah James

Emma's sister, Sarah James, was born 13 August 1837 in Moore, Worcestershire, England. With her family, she joined the Church and traveled to the Salt Lake Valley in the Willie handcart company. During the overland journey Sarah helped her own and other families, carrying the younger children on her back when crossing the Platte River, which meant making several trips back and forth across the river. After arriving in the Valley 19 November 1856 she moved to Springville and married Aaron Johnson (Lorenzo Johnson's brother) on 1 March 1857. She was the last of Aaron Johnson's ten wives. They ran the crowded household by a well-organized division of labor and rotation of chores every two weeks. The forty-member family sat at a long dinner table with a track running down the center. A specially designed cart carried the food to family members down the length of the long table. Sarah had five children, three of whom lived to adulthood. After Aaron Johnson's death, Sarah took in washing for a living until she married Samuel Carter, two years later, in 1879. She had one child with him. He died in 1887. Sarah lived as a widow for thirty-five years, dying on 22 June 1922.

MARY ANN JONES

Mary Ann Jones was born 9 May 1836 in Starpourt, Shropshire, England, the daughter of Thomas Jones and Hannah Paine. She was baptized on 7 March 1854. She left England 21 March 1856 in company with 534 members of the Church aboard the *Enoch Train,* arriving in Boston 1 May 1856. She traveled to Iowa City by train and left Iowa City 9 June for Florence, where she joined the Edmund Ellsworth handcart company, one of the first to make the long trek on foot. Before reaching the Valley on 26 September 1856, the company was met in Emigration Canyon by the First Presidency, a brass band, and hundreds of people. Mary Ann married Edmund Ellsworth as a plural wife a little more than a week after arriving in Salt Lake City. She lived in West Weber, Utah, and Show Low, Arizona. She died 26 April 1925 in Fort Apache, Arizona.

HANNAH DORCAS TAPFIELD KING

Hannah Dorcas Tapfield King was born in Sawston, Cambridge-shire, England, 16 March 1807, the daughter of Peter Tapfield and Mary Lawson. She married Thomas Owen King on 6 April 1824 at age seventeen. She became the mother of ten children, only four of whom lived to adulthood. She was converted to Mormonism through her dressmaker in 1849 and was baptized 4 November 1850 in the Camm River. In 1853 she left England with her husband and her children aboard the *Golconda*. Her husband had not converted to Mormonism, but he supported her in her decision and traveled with the family. They reached New Orleans 24 March 1853 and traveled on to Salt Lake City with the company led by Claudius V. Spencer, her son-in-law. Hannah King was a regular writer for the *Woman's Exponent* and conducted a school in her home for two years. She also participated in the Polysophical Society in Salt Lake City. Before leaving England she wrote two books, *The Toilet*, for her girls, and *Three Eras*, for her boys. In 1878 she published *The Women of the Scriptures* followed by *Songs of the Heart*, a book of poetry published in 1879. She presided over the Young Ladies Mutual Improvement Association of the Seventeenth Ward for one year and also served as first counselor to Marinda Hyde of the Relief Society of the Seventeenth Ward. She died in 1886 in Salt Lake City.

ELIZABETH HORROCKS JACKSON KINGSFORD

Elizabeth Horrocks Jackson Kingsford was born 5 August 1826 in Macclesfield, Cheshire, England, to Edward Horrocks and Alice Houghton, the eldest of eleven children. When she was just seven she began work in a silk factory. She attended the Sunday School of the Wesleyan Methodists as a girl, but in 1841 she was baptized into the LDS Church by James Gallay. Seven years later she married Aaron Jackson, also a convert, with whom she had three children. In 1856 the family left England aboard the

Horizon and traveled to the Valley with the Martin handcart company, reaching Salt Lake City 30 November 1856. The extreme hardships suffered by the company took the life of Aaron Jackson a month before the company reached the Valley. The next year Elizabeth married William R. Kingsford. They made their home in Ogden, Utah, where she was active in the Relief Society. She died in Ogden on 17 October 1908.

HANNAH SETTLE LAPISH

Hannah Lapish was born 2 November 1834 in Beeston, Leeds, Yorkshire, England, to William Settle and Hannah Strickland, both of whom died during her infancy. She was baptized 29 February 1852 and married Joseph Lapish 3 July 1853. They had nine children, five of whom lived beyond childhood. In 1857 the young family emigrated to America aboard the *Tuscarora*, arriving in Philadelphia 3 July 1857. Without funds to continue their way west, Joseph traveled to Richmond, Virginia, to find work while Hannah remained in Philadelphia where she took in sewing from a knitting factory. After three months she joined her husband in Richmond where they remained for three years. Hannah worked in a factory until they returned, in 1860, to Philadelphia. There they joined a group of Saints traveling to Florence and on to Salt Lake City with Daniel Robison's handcart company. Hannah and her family lived in Lehi until 1868, when they moved to Salt Lake City. Four years later they moved to West Jordan, where Hannah kept a boarding and rooming house for Galena Smelters, with whom her husband was employed. When she heard that a railroad was to be built to Bingham Canyon, she invested in land on the line of what became the Utah Southern Railroad with money earned from selling sewing machines. She built a boarding house known as the Junction House and two cottages on her property. The Bingham Canyon Railroad

Company built a depot and machine shop, also on her property, but without her permission. She sued the railroad, and in 1881 "the court quieted my title and awarded me damages against the company," she wrote. The next year she moved to American Fork, where she lived until 1898. She became very active in civic affairs, serving as president of the Suffrage Association of American Fork from 1892 to 1898, organizing a Ladies' Civil Government Class during the spring of 1892, and acting as chair of the county committee for the Chicago World's Fair in 1892 and 1893. She was chosen to represent her county suffrage association in observing the proceedings of the Constitutional Convention in Salt Lake City, held in March 1895. In 1898 Hannah moved to Salt Lake City, where she served as secretary of the Twentieth Ward Relief Society for seven years. She was treasurer of the Utah Council of Women for many years and was elected by that council as a delegate to the national and international suffrage convention held in Washington, D.C., in 1902. She was founder general and president of the Utah Handcart Pioneers, organized on 14 April 1901 at her home in Salt Lake City. She died 9 April 1927 in Salt Lake City.

SUSANNA STONE LLOYD

Susanna Stone Lloyd was born 24 December 1830 in Bristol, England, the daughter of William Stone and Diana Grant. She was an avid scripture reader and attended a Wesleyan Sunday School. Her desire to "live in the days of apostles and prophets" was realized when she joined the Church in 1849. She emigrated to America in 1856 despite the pleas of her parents, relatives, and friends, arriving in the Valley 5 November of that year with the James G. Willie handcart company. She married Thomas Lloyd one day after reaching the Valley. They moved to Farmington, Davis County, and later to Wellsville, in Cache County. After her husband died, Susanna moved to Logan, where she died 23 January 1920. She was the mother of fourteen children, twelve of whom lived to adulthood.

ULRICH LOOSLI

Ulrich Loosli was born 22 April 1830 in Durrenroth, Bern, Switzerland, the son of Andrew (or Andreas) Loosli and Barbra Kahser (or Kaeser). On 21 February 1851 he married Magdalena Aeschemann in Hindelbank, Bern, Switzerland. They were the parents of three children. Ulrich and his wife joined the Church 31 May 1857 in Switzerland and emigrated to Utah 3 September 1860 with the James D. Ross company. They settled in Providence, Utah, where they lived for nine years. For the next few years they helped settle various places, including Newton and Trenton, Utah, and Marysville, Idaho, where Ulrich acquired large land holdings. He served a mission to Switzerland in 1868. Upon his return in 1869, he married Elizabeth Eggimann in the Endowment House in Salt Lake City. They became the parents of seven children. Their family home was in Marysville, Idaho. Ulrich Loosli died 30 March 1918.

ELIZA MARIA PARTRIDGE LYMAN

Eliza Maria Partridge Lyman was born 20 April 1820 in Painesville, Geauga County, Ohio, the eldest daughter of Edward Partridge and Lydia Clisbee. After her baptism in 1831, she moved with her family to Independence, Missouri, and two years later to Caldwell County, suffering all of the mob violence that occurred during the Saints' sojourn in Missouri. After being driven out of Missouri, the family moved to Quincy, Illinois, then to Pittsfield, and finally to Nauvoo. Eliza taught school for a period in Lima, about twenty-five miles from Nauvoo, and also worked as a tailor. She and her sister Emily briefly lived with Joseph Smith's family. Both sisters were taught the principle of plural marriage and were sealed to the Prophet in 1843. After Joseph's death, Eliza and her sister Caroline married Amasa Lyman. Eliza left Nauvoo with the Lyman family on 9 February 1846, arriving at Winter Quarters in August. She traveled to the Salt Lake Valley with the Willard Richards/Amasa Lyman company, arriving 17 October 1848. Her husband, an apostle, was called to preside over Church affairs in Fillmore, Utah, where Eliza joined him in 1863. During 1868 she taught school there. After Elder Lyman's death in 1877, Eliza lived with her son Platte Lyman at Oak Creek, Leamington, and Bluff, Utah. She died at Oak Creek 2 March 1886.

MARY ANN WESTON MAUGHAN

Mary Ann Weston Maughan was born 10 March 1817 at Corse Lawn, Gloucestershire, England, the daughter of Thomas Weston and Elizabeth Thackwell. From 1839 to 1840 she lived at Leigh, where she learned the milliner's trade. She also became a Sunday School teacher. In 1840 she was converted to the Church and in December of that year she married John Davis, also a convert. He died the next year from wounds suffered while trying to protect missionaries from an anti-Mormon mob that interrupted a Church meeting in the Davis home. Mary Ann decided to emigrate, and she sailed from Bristol on 12 May 1841, reaching Nauvoo via Canada 17 October 1841. On 2 November 1841 she married Peter Maughan, a widower, and assumed the care of his children. They went to Wisconsin when the Saints were forced to leave Nauvoo and did not travel west until 1850, when they joined the Warren Foote company and settled in Tooele. Willard

Richards of the Council of Health appointed Mary Ann to be midwife for the community, a service she continued to perform for forty years. She also organized the first Sunday School in Tooele. In 1856 the Maughans were called to settle Cache Valley. They built their first home there at Maughan's Fort (now Wellsville) and then lived in several locations in the Cache Valley, which remained their home until their deaths. Mary Ann was appointed president of the Relief Society in Cache County in 1869. She also served as an agent for the *Woman's Exponent* during the years 1872 to 1895. A beloved figure in Cache Valley, Mary Ann Maughan died 15 February 1901.

HANNAH BLAKESLEE FINCH MORLEY

Hannah Blakeslee Finch Morley was born 12 March 1811 in Woodbridge, New Haven County, Connecticut, the daughter of Daniel Finch and Mary Blakeslee. She married Edwin Parker Merriam on 6 November 1831 in Watertown, Litchfield County, Connecticut. After Edwin's death, she became the second wife of Isaac Morley in Nauvoo, Illinois. The Morleys left Nauvoo in 1846. After reaching the Salt Lake Valley, Hannah, Isaac, and his three other wives became some of Manti, Utah's, first settlers. Manti remained her home until her death on 16 March 1874.

CHRISTIAN NIELSEN

Christian Nielsen was born 24 May 1804 in Hover, Vejle, Denmark and was christened in the Engum Parish. On 13 May 1830 he married Anne Margrethe Madsen in Denmark. Christian became a member of the Church 8 April 1852 and emigrated to Utah, settling with other Danish emigrants in

Manti. Records show that he married Maren Hansen (also recorded as Maren Petersen) on 23 February 1849 and Maria Petersen 4 June 1864. Christian Nielsen died 13 April 1887 in Manti, San Pete County, Utah.

SAMUEL OPENSHAW

Samuel Openshaw was born 1 November 1833 in Brightmet, Lancashire, England, to William Openshaw and Ann Walmsley Greenhalgh. He was baptized a member of the Church on 24 April 1847. In May 1856, at the age of twenty-two, he sailed for America aboard the *Horizon* with his father, mother, and siblings, including Eliza (twenty-one), Levi (nineteen), Mary (fifteen), Eleanor (fourteen), and Mary Ann (ten). They traveled to the Valley with the Martin handcart company in 1856. When Samuel arrived, Church leaders sent him to Santaquin, where he began farming. After marrying Esther Meleta Johnson on 25 September 1863 in Springlake, Utah, he returned to Santaquin. He married Sarah Elizabeth Spainhower (Spainhour) on 26 September 1872 in Salt Lake City. Moving several times more, he lived in Springville, Utah, before settling for a period in the Salt River Valley in Arizona, making his home in Tempe. When the railroad bought his property he moved again, this time to Nephi, Arizona, serving from 1888 to 1900 as bishop of the Nephi Ward in the Maricopa Stake. He died 2 January 1904 in Mesa, Arizona.

IRENE HASCALL POMEROY

The daughter of Ashbel Green Hascall and Ursulia Billings Hastings, Irene Hascall Pomeroy was born 1 November 1825 in New Salem, Franklin County, Massachusetts. She attended the academy at New Salem, enjoying an education unusual for her day. Irene was introduced to Mormonism through her school friend, "Emmie" Woodward, later known as Emmeline B. Wells, and she began attending Mormon meetings with Emmie. Irene and Emmeline were baptized 1 March 1842. Irene helped her mother prepare meals for factory workers in North New Salem, where she met Francis Martin Pomeroy, also a member of the Church. They married in 1844 and moved to Nauvoo the same year. Their first baby, Francelle, was born shortly before leaving Nauvoo in February 1846. Francis joined the Mormon Battalion 6 April 1847, and Irene traveled with her mother, brother, and daughter in the George B. Wallace company to the Valley, arriving in late September 1847. After their arrival, Irene and her family settled in Salt Lake City, moving to Salem, Utah County, in the spring of 1858. They returned to the Salt Lake Valley in the fall of that same year, and not long afterward Irene suffered a severe burn on her hand, requiring amputation of her arm. She died soon thereafter, in June 1860, of pneumonia, while visiting in the home of her childhood friend, Emmeline B. Wells. She was the mother of eight children.

ANN AGATHA WALKER PRATT

Ann Agatha Walker Pratt, the eldest child of William Gibson Walker and Mary Godwin, was born 11 January 1829 in Leith, Staffordshire, England. She was converted to Mormonism through the missionary efforts of Parley P. Pratt and John Taylor and was baptized 18 July 1843. Emigrating to America when she was seventeen, she became the wife of Parley P. Pratt 28 April 1847 at Winter Quarters. She traveled to the Salt Lake Valley in Parley P. Pratt's company, driving an ox team the entire distance, arriving 28 September 1847. She was the first milliner in Utah. After her husband's death, she married Joseph Harris Ridges on

4 March 1860. Agatha was president of the Relief Society of the Nineteenth Ward in Salt Lake City and secretary of the First Ward Relief Society in Ogden. She was active in the Retrenchment Society during the 1870s and also became a member of the Tabernacle Choir. She died in Ogden 25 June 1908.

LOUISA BARNES PRATT

Louisa Barnes Pratt was born in 1802 in Norwich, Franklin County, Massachusetts, daughter of Willard and Dolly Stephens Barnes. She moved with her family to Dunham, Lower Canada, about 1810, and in 1820 she left home and moved to Vermont to be a seamstress and also a schoolteacher. She attended the Female Academy at Winchester, New Hampshire, in 1827. In April 1831 she married Addison Pratt in Dunham, Canada, and settled in Buffalo, New York. The couple thereafter moved to Chautauqua County, where both were baptized in June 1837. They left New York in 1838, intending to join the Saints in Missouri, but because of the difficulties there they stayed in Indiana until 1840, when they moved to Nauvoo. Louisa taught school to support her four daughters while Addison served a mission to Tahiti. She left Nauvoo in May 1846 for the West and traveled to the Salt Lake Valley in 1848. In 1850 she joined her husband on another of his missions to Tahiti, being set apart to aid him in teaching the gospel. She lived on the island of Tobuai, teaching English to the natives until 1852. Louisa returned to San Bernardino, California, in May of 1852 and lived there until 1858, when she moved back to Utah, settling first in Cedar City and then Beaver. In 1873 she helped organize the Female Relief Society in Beaver and served as secretary and counselor. An articulate and resourceful woman, Louisa Pratt died in 1880.

EMELINE GROVER RICH

Emeline Grover Rich was born 30 July 1831 in Freedom, Cattaraugus County, New York. Emeline's father joined the Church and moved to Nauvoo with his family, where he became a bodyguard to Joseph Smith. Emeline did housework to help support the family. In February 1846 she married Charles C. Rich (who later became an apostle) as a plural wife and traveled west with the Rich company, driving an ox team much of the way. She moved to San Bernardino, California, when Elder Rich was called to preside over the area in 1851, returning to Centerville, Utah, in the fall of 1854. In 1864 she moved to Bear Lake, where she served as a midwife for many years. She attended the Medical College of Utah at Morgan in 1881, studying obstetrics. Emeline worked in Logan for eight winters, beginning in 1890, living with her sons George and Heber, after which she moved to Paris, Idaho. She died on 14 May 1917.

SARAH DeARMON PEA RICH

Sarah DeArmon Pea Rich was born 23 September 1814 in St. Clair County, Illinois. She moved with her family to Tennessee in 1824 and later returned to Illinois. In the summer of 1835 the Mormon missionaries visited the family and made a singular impression on Sarah. She spent most of the evening following the missionaries' visit reading the Book of Mormon. Six weeks after the elders left, Sarah dreamed she would see them again, although her family was skeptical. On 15 December 1835, to her delight, they returned and baptized first Sarah and then Sarah's parents and sister. Friends who knew both Sarah and Charles C. Rich, who lived in Kirtland, Ohio, recommended Sarah to Charles, and the two commenced a correspondence. They finally met when the Pea family moved to Kirtland. They knew each other at first sight and were married 11 February 1838. The couple moved to Missouri and followed the Church to Nauvoo after its expulsion from that state. After learning the law of plural marriage, Sarah consented to the principle and helped choose her husband's other wives. She traveled to the Salt Lake Valley with the Rich company and settled in Centerville. Sarah remained in Centerville when Elder Rich was called to San Bernardino in 1851. She moved to Bear Lake in 1864 with other members of the Rich family but soon returned to Salt Lake City. In later years she moved with her son Benjamin to Ogden where she died 12 September 1893.

JANE SNYDER RICHARDS

Jane Snyder Richards was born 31 January 1823 at Palmelia (now Watertown), Jefferson County, New York, a daughter of Isaac Snyder and Lovisa Comstock. In 1831 she moved with her family to Canada, and after their conversion to Mormonism they moved to Indiana. Jane was not baptized until January 1840, when the family was living in Lake LaPorte, Indiana. The next year they moved to Nauvoo. On 18 December 1842, at Job Creek, Illinois, Jane married Franklin Dewey Richards, whom she had met when her family entertained him in Indiana on his way east some years earlier. Jane and her sister wife Elizabeth left Nauvoo on 11 June 1846 and traveled to Winter Quarters on their own while their husband served a mission in England. Elizabeth died in Winter Quarters, and Jane traveled to the Salt Lake Valley with the Willard Richards/Amasa Lyman company, arriving 19 October 1848. In 1869 the Richards family moved to Ogden, where Jane was appointed president of the Ogden Relief Society in 1872. As president she organized the young ladies of Ogden into a branch of the retrenchment society, promoting economy in dress and other material things as well as moral, mental, and spiritual improvement. On 19 July 1877 she became president of the Weber Stake Relief Society, the first stake Relief Society president in the Church. In October of 1888 she became first counselor to General Relief Society President Zina D. H. Young and served in this capacity for twelve years. In 1891 Jane attended the National Council of Women in Washington, D.C., as a representative from Utah and became acquainted with such prominent figures as Susan B. Anthony, Elizabeth Cady Stanton, and Belva A. Lockwood. She was appointed vice-president of the Utah Board of Lady Managers of the World's Fair in 1892. She died 17 November 1912 at the home of her daughter, Josephine R. West, in Ogden.

DANIEL ROBISON

Daniel Robison was born 21 March 1831 in Quincy, Franklin County, Pennsylvania, to Alexander Robison and Nancy Ellen Wagoman. He married Rachel Smith 5 August 1852 in Quincy. Seven of their twelve children died before reaching adulthood. Daniel and Rachel were converted to Mormonism by Angus M. Cannon in 1854, but it was six years before they and their family were able to leave Pennsylvania to join the Saints in Utah. When they reached Florence, Nebraska, Daniel was appointed captain of the ninth handcart company. It met with relatively few problems and arrived in the Salt Lake Valley without serious incident 27 August 1860. Daniel served as captain of additional companies for several years thereafter. He settled first in Farmington, Utah, and then moved to North Morgan in the fall of 1863. He was first counselor to Bishop Oluff B. Anderson in the North Morgan Ward, Morgan Stake. His wife, Rachel, was the president of the ward Primary for sixteen years and a counselor in the stake Primary presidency for twenty-four years. Daniel also served as the superintendent of the Sunday School. He died 25 March 1907 in Morgan.

RUTH PAGE ROGERS

Ruth Page Rogers was born in Fairfield, Essex County, New Jersey, on 1 May 1823, the eldest of the eight children of Daniel Page and Mary Sockwell. At age three she suffered severe burns to her face and arm, the scars on her face healing but those on her arm remaining visible. She spent much of her youth at the home of her grandmother. When she was just fifteen her father left the family to go west, taking the two eldest boys with him. Ruth and her mother went to Pennsylvania to work in a cotton factory, the Wagners Mille, for $2.25 per week. While there, Ruth joined the Methodist Church. In 1842 her father returned and persuaded Ruth's mother to move the family to Newport, New Jersey, with him. While in Illinois, Ruth's father and one of her brothers had converted to Mormonism, and when two missionaries, Samuel Hollister Rogers and James Flanagan, passed through Newport in 1843, the two stayed at the Page's home while preaching at the Newport schoolhouse. Ruth was baptized 29 October 1843 by Elder Flanagan and confirmed by Elder Rogers. She then moved to Bridgeton and worked seven years to help the family earn suffcient means to gather with the Saints in the West. In 1850 they were ready to leave and traveled by riverboat to St. Louis, where they met Wilford Woodruff, who advised them to continue on to Council Bluffs, Iowa. They stayed in a settlement near Kanesville for almost two years. In order to pay her expenses to Utah, Ruth hired on as a cook and washerwoman for the Harmon Cutler company, which traveled to Utah in 1852. The next year Ruth married Samuel Hollister Rogers. She lived first in Lehi and then joined her husband at Parowan on his mission to Iron County in 1856, living there until 1874. She was an active worker in the Relief Society and in the St. George Temple. In 1882 she moved to Snowflake, Apache County, Arizona, where she served as president of the East

Arizona Stake Primary Association. She died 20 May 1907 at Roosevelt, Wasatch County, Utah.

MARY POWELL SABIN

Mary Powell Sabin was born 6 November 1842 in Lanover, Wales, the daughter of John Powell and Sarah Elizabeth Harris. Her family converted to the gospel through efforts of their neighbors, the Huish family, who had recently joined the Church. Mary's parents were baptized in 1850 and Mary on 3 March 1851. In 1856 the family left Wales to gather with the Saints, sailing from Liverpool on the *Enoch Train*. They traveled by train from Boston to Iowa, where they joined Edmund Ellsworth's handcart company, which left Florence on July 20. During the trek Mary did most of the camp work, such as cooking and washing, since her mother was ill throughout the journey. She was twelve years old at the time. Her father died two weeks after reaching the Valley, and her mother moved the family to Payson. Mary married David Dorwart Sabin on 30 January 1864 in Payson. Together, the couple operated a co-op store in Payson. Mary died 8 January 1929 in Salem, Utah.

MARY PUGH SCOTT

Mary Pugh Scott was born 10 November 1821 at Dilwyn Commons, Leominster, Hereford, England, the twin daughter of Mary Bailey and Edward Pugh. Her twin sister died shortly after birth. Mary attended school at Dilwyn Commons, at Earldisland School, and at Haven Dilwyn, a private school. Her conversion to the Church greatly displeased her parents, but she decided to emigrate to America to be with the Saints, reaching

Nauvoo in 1842. She married John Scott as a plural wife on 2 March 1845 in Nauvoo. She left Nauvoo in March 1846 and traveled west with the Heber C. Kimball company, reaching the Salt Lake Valley 24 September 1848. Mary died 5 January 1905 in Salt Lake City.

CHARLES SMITH

The son of John Smith and Ann Varley, Charles Smith was born 10 June 1819 in Ipstone, Staffordshire, England, where he was apprenticed to a watchmaker. Charles was converted to the gospel in December of 1840, and in 1842 he emigrated to Nauvoo, becoming a member of the Nauvoo Brass Band. On 3 January 1843 he married Sarah Price. He traveled west in the Heber C. Kimball company in 1848, arriving in the Salt Lake Valley in October of that year. From 1852 to 1855 he served a mission to England, and upon his return to Salt Lake City he married Eliza Mathews. In 1862 he was called to settle St. George, Utah, where he was a farmer and a watchmaker. He had the care of the clock in the St. George Tabernacle. In 1866 he returned to Salt Lake City and continued his trade as a watchmaker. Another move took him back to St. George, where he joined a musical ensemble organized in 1885 that played for dances and theater entertainments in St. George and in the Social Hall in Salt Lake City. He died in St. George on 28 November 1905, having served as a counselor in the high priests quorum, a high councilman, a home missionary, and a temple worker.

ELIAS SMITH

Elias Smith was born 6 September 1804 in Royalton, Windsor County, Vermont, the oldest child of Ashel (Asahel) Smith and

Betsy Schellenger. He was a cousin to Joseph Smith and was introduced to the gospel by Joseph Smith, Sr., and Don Carlos Smith in Stockholm, Vermont. After his baptism on 27 August 1835 by Hyrum Smith, he moved with his family to Kirtland, where he taught school during 1837 and 1838. He was one of the captains of the Kirtland Camp, with which he traveled to Far West and Adam-ondi-Ahman. Selected to aid the fleeing Saints from Missouri, he was one of the last to leave in April 1839. In Illinois he settled in Nashville, Lee County, four miles from Nauvoo. While there he became business manager of the *Times and Seasons* and the *Nauvoo Neighbor*. He married Lucy Brown 6 August 1845 in Nauvoo. After leaving Nauvoo in 1846, he remained in Iowaville until 1851. That year he emigrated to Salt Lake City with the John Brown company and in 1856 married Amy Jane King. He was appointed a probate judge in Salt Lake City in 1852, serving until 1882. Along with his legal work he served as business manager and later the editor of the *Deseret News*. During the years 1854 to 1858 he was also postmaster. In 1862 he served as a member of the Constitutional Convention. He served as president of the high priests quorum in the Salt Lake Stake from 1877 to 1888. He died in Salt Lake City 24 June 1888, a father of eight sons and eight daughters.

LUCY MESERVE SMITH

Lucy Meserve Smith was born 9 February 1817 in Newry, Oxford County, Maine, to Josiah and Lucy M. Bean Meserve Smith. She was baptized in 1837, and in 1844 she moved to Nauvoo, where she hired out as a spinner and weaver. She married apostle George A. Smith 29 November 1844 as a plural wife. After leaving Nauvoo in 1846, she attended school at Kanesville, Iowa, and was later sent to Bellevue to teach at the Pawnee mission school.

She traveled to Salt Lake City in 1849 with the George A. Smith company and settled in Provo along with her sister wife Hannah. She lived there for seventeen years. Childless after the death of her only son, Lucy, along with Hannah, raised the infant son of their sister wife Sarah when she unexpectedly died. In Provo she also taught school and served as president of the Relief Society. Lucy died in Salt Lake City in 1892.

Augusta Dorius Stevens

Augusta Dorius Stevens was born in Copenhagen, Denmark, on 29 October 1837, the daughter of Nicholi Dorius and Anne Sophie Christopherson. An accident as a young girl cost her the sight of one eye. When she joined the Church at age thirteen, she was obliged to discontinue her schooling because of Mormonism's unpopularity. Church meetings were held in her family's home, where missionary Erastus Snow and others encountered mob violence. When the Ravens family, an LDS family for whom she did domestic work, decided to emigrate to Utah, Augusta's parents arranged to have Augusta travel with them. They sailed for Liverpool, England, with Erastus Snow and eighteen other emigrating Saints from Copenhagen on 4 March 1852, and from England to the United States, arriving at New Orleans 10 May 1852. They traveled up the Mississippi and Missouri Rivers to Kanesville, Iowa, where they joined the Eli B. Kelsey company for the journey to Utah. Shortly after arriving in the Salt Lake Valley, the Scandinavian Saints were instructed by Brigham Young to move to San Pete County to strengthen the area against Indian attacks. Augusta found a place to live in a settlement called Spring Town, where she was called to be the interpreter for the Scandinavians and the English-speaking settlers. When Indian attacks threatened the safety of the community, the colony moved to Manti. On 25 July 1854 Augusta married

Henry Stevens in Salt Lake City as his second wife. In 1859 they moved back to Spring Town with the other settlers, all of them living in wagons and tents until they could afford to build houses. In 1862 the Stevens family was called to help settle Dixie. After living there for thirteen years, they returned to San Pete County. After her husband died in 1899, Augusta had a home built in Ephraim, Utah, where she lived for nine years before moving to Salt Lake City. Throughout her adult life she served as a midwife. She died 28 July 1926 in Salt Lake City.

OSCAR ORLONDO STODDARD

Oscar Orlondo Stoddard was born 30 December 1821 in Elbridge, Onondaga County, New York, the son of Oren Stoddard and Harriet M. Cook. On 30 November 1847 he married Polly Serafina Ferguson. He was baptized 13 January 1856 by Elder Samuel Snyder in the Jordan River near Salt Lake City. Three months later he was called as a missionary to Michigan, returning to Salt Lake City 12 July 1858. Eleven months after his return, he left for a second mission to Michigan. On his return trip in 1860, he led the tenth and last handcart company to the Valley. He arrived with the company 24 September 1860. He married Elizabeth Taylor 2 October 1860. On 23 April 1861 he again left Utah to help bring Saints to the Valley as a captain for one of the first "down and back" companies, which made the round-trip to the Missouri in a single season. He crossed the plains seven times before the railroad was built, helping to bring emigrants to the Valley. In the fall of 1863 he moved to Rush Valley, and in the fall of the next year he moved to Tooele, Utah. In the summer of 1869 he moved to Porterville, Morgan County. He died 9 September 1896.

Henry Stokes

Henry Stokes was born 7 May 1829 in West Bromwich, Staffordshire, England, the son of Joseph Stokes and Alice Clark. At age eleven he started a job in glassworks and then worked in a brewery. He was baptized 15 August 1841 but did not emigrate until 1860, working in New York until June 1862. He obtained employment in a glass factory for six weeks and then in a military equipment factory. In 1862 he left to gather to Zion. He was appointed to keep the journal for the Henry W. Miller Church Train of 1862, which arrived in Salt Lake City on 17 October. He married Elizabeth Jane Hale and became the father of eleven children. For twenty years he made Cache County his home and then spent another twenty helping to settle the Snake River Valley. He died 8 May 1913 in Logan, Utah.

Leonora Cannon Taylor

Leonora Cannon Taylor was born 6 October 1796 in Peel, Isle of Man, off the coast of Great Britain. She was a daughter of Captain George Cannon and Leonora Callister. Leonora's father, a sea captain, died 19 July 1811 at sea, leaving the family on the brink of poverty. Therefore, Leonora moved to London where she lived with and worked for a wealthy lady of rank. On the basis of her employment in London and the lady's recommendation, when Leonora returned to the Isle of Man she was able to find employment with the family of the governor. These positions allowed her to meet many prominent persons, including a Mr. Mason who had been invited to assist the newly appointed governor of Canada, Lord Aylmer. His daughter insisted that Leonora join the Mason family in their move to Canada. Reluctantly leaving her family, Leonora traveled to Canada in 1832. She was at that time a devout Methodist and

727

distributed Bibles and tracts aboard the ship. After arriving in Toronto, Canada, Leonora attended the Methodist Church and met John Taylor, who was the class leader. The two were married a few months later on 28 January 1833 in Toronto. After the birth of their first two children, George John in 1834 and Mary Ann in 1836, the Taylors were converted to Mormonism by Parley P. Pratt. They were baptized in May of 1836. The Taylors joined the Saints in Missouri and moved with them to Illinois in 1839. That same year John was called on a mission to Great Britain, leaving Leonora and her children in straitened circumstances. They lived in a deserted army barracks in Montrose during his absence and experienced extreme hardship. Leonora also endured the uncertainty of his survival after being wounded in the Carthage jail when the Prophet Joseph and his brother Hyrum were murdered. The Taylors, numbering four children besides the parents, left Nauvoo in 1846 with the Church and reached the Salt Lake Valley in 1847. Leonora died there on 9 December 1868.

NANCY NAOMI ALEXANDER TRACY

Nancy Naomi Alexander Tracy was born 14 May 1816 at Henderson, Jefferson County, New York, the daughter of Aaron Alexander and Betsy Jones. Her father died when she was about four years old, and she was sent to live with her grandparents in Herkimer County. She rejoined her mother eleven years later. On 15 July 1832 in Ellisburg, Jefferson County, New York, Nancy married Moses Tracy. The next year she converted to Mormonism through the preaching of David W. Patten and was baptized the following year on May 10. She moved to Kirtland in 1835; to Far West in 1836; to Adams County, Illinois, in 1839; and finally, in 1840, to Nauvoo, where she joined the Relief Society after its organization in 1842. Nancy accompanied her husband on a mission to New York in 1844. The Tracys left Nauvoo in 1846 and traveled to Winter Quarters, staying at the Missouri until 1850. That year they traveled with the Benjamin Hawkins company to the Valley and settled at Mound Fort on the Ogden River. After a long debilitating illness her husband died in 1858. Two years later she married his brother, Silas Horace Tracy, who helped her raise the youngest of her eleven children. She died 11 March 1902 in Ogden, Utah.

Archer Walters

Archer Walters was born 29 July 1809 in Cambridge, Cambridgeshire, England, the son of Henry and Sarah Walters. He left Cambridge as a young man in pursuit of a trade. He met Harriet Cross, a factory girl, and married her on 28 August 1837. His parents, more affluent than Harriet's, were so unhappy with his marriage that they disinherited him. He then became a carpenter (joiner). His shop's sign read, "From the cradle to the grave," announcing his skill at both cradle and coffin making. Archer joined the Church on 3 September 1848, baptized by an Elder Sylvester. He left England with his wife and five children aboard the *Enoch Train* in 1856 and traveled in the Edmund Ellsworth company to Utah. He helped build the hand-carts for the company and also made coffins when necessary. He died two weeks after reaching the Valley (14 October 1856) as a result of the privations he suffered on the journey.

George Whitaker

George Whitaker was born 18 March 1820 in Blakedown, Worcestershire, England, the fifth child of Thomas Whitaker and Sophia Turner. He became curious about religion and the idea of heaven and hell when he was twenty-one years of age, about the time his sister Sophia joined the Church. She taught him the gospel and he "fell in love" with its principles. He was baptized in England in 1841 by Thomas Tyson and was ordained a priest and then an elder. He set sail for America four years later, arriving in Nauvoo 27 March 1845. He left Nauvoo on 9 February 1846, driving a team for Parley P. Pratt. He married Evline P. Robinson on 27 July 1846 at the Garden Grove settlement. After spending the winter at Winter Quarters, George and his wife left in June of 1847, traveling with the Edward Hunter/Joseph Horne/John Taylor company to the Salt Lake Valley, arriving in October of 1847. In Utah he married Elizabeth Comish as a plural wife. He died in March 1907.

EMMELINE BLANCHE
WOODWARD WHITNEY WELLS

Emmeline Blanche Woodward was born in Petersham, Franklin County, Massachusetts, 29 February 1828, to David and Diadama Hare Woodward. After attending the New Salem Academy and teaching for a period, she married James Harris 29 July 1843 and traveled with James and his parents to Nauvoo the following year. She was thrilled to meet the Prophet Joseph Smith, shortly before his death, but Nauvoo held many disappointments for her. Her firstborn son died a few weeks after his birth; her parents-in-law apostatized from the Church, leaving the young couple on their own in Nauvoo; and in the fall of 1844 James left Emmeline, ostensibly to find work in St. Louis or some other river town, but never to return. Emmeline taught school in Nauvoo until she married Bishop Newel K. Whitney as his first plural wife, in 1845. She traveled with his family to the West. In 1852, two years after Bishop Whitney's death, Emmeline married Daniel H. Wells. These two marriages gave Emmeline five daughters. A talented writer, she edited the Mormon women's paper, the *Woman's Exponent*; published a volume of poetry; and authored several short stories. She was active in the woman's suffrage movement, representing LDS women at the annual conventions of the national association. She organized several women's literary clubs and was the first woman to receive an honorary degree from Brigham Young University. A longtime Relief Society worker, she was appointed, at age eighty-two, general president, serving for eleven years. She died in April 1921.

Johanna Kirsten Larsen Winters

Johanna Kirsten Larsen Winters was born 22 August 1850 in Aalborg, Wisterhassing, Denmark, the daughter of Niels Larsen and Signe Jensen. After her conversion, she left Aalborg 5 May 1867, reaching New York Harbor in July. She traveled to the Salt Lake Valley with the Leonard G. Rich company of 1867 and moved to the Danish settlement in Ovid, Idaho. In July 1868, when she was eighteen years of age she married Franz Winters in Salt Lake City. The couple moved to Montpelier, Idaho, after their marriage. In connection with a Relief Society medical program to train midwives, Johanna was selected to go to Salt Lake City for a course in obstetrics. She served Montpelier and the surrounding areas as a practical nurse for many years. During this time she also managed to raise seven of her ten children, three of whom died as infants. She died at the age of eighty-nine.

William Wood, Sr.

William Wood, Sr., the son of William Wood and Elizabeth Gigseey, was born 1 May 1837 in Ostend, near Burnham, Essex,

England. In 1852 he moved to the Isle of Sheppy where he was apprenticed to a butcher. He was converted to Mormonism in 1855 and joined the Royal Navy the next year as a ship's butcher. He served on the crew of the *H.M.S. Retribution* and sailed to Peru, China, Japan, and Ceylon. He also helped lay the first submarine cable in the Red Sea. In 1860 he received his discharge and returned home. Two years later he emigrated to America with his fiancée, Elizabeth Gentry, and traveled to the Valley with the David P. Kimball freight train while she traveled with the James S. Brown independent company. They reunited in Salt Lake City and were married 7 November 1862. They had ten boys and three girls. He married Susan Parker in 1874 as a plural wife. In 1888, after both had died, he married Eliza Whytock. He worked in the cattle and meat business and ran a butcher shop in Salt Lake City. In 1867 he was called to the Muddy Mission, serving there and in Eagle Valley until 1872. He also helped settle Overton, Nevada. From 1880 to 1882 he served a mission to England. Following a second mission in 1892, he temporarily settled in Alberta, Canada, where he ranched. In 1913 he returned to Salt Lake City, where he died on 17 June 1916 in the butcher shop of his son, William Wood, Jr.

Information for these biographical sketches was taken from a variety of sources:

LDS Church Ancestral File, FamilySearch.
Bashore, Melvin L., and Linda L. Haslam. *Mormon Pioneer Companies Crossing the Plains, 1847–1868: Guide to Sources in Utah Libraries and Archives.* Salt Lake City: The Church of Jesus Christ of Latter-day Saints, 1989.

Bitton, Davis. *Guide to Mormon Diaries and Autobiographies.* Provo, Utah: Brigham Young University Press, 1977.

Black, Susan Easton. *Membership of The Church of Jesus Christ of Latter-day Saints, 1830–1848,* 50 vols. Provo, Utah: Brigham Young University Religious Studies Center, 1989.

Carter, Kate B., comp. *Hearth Throbs of the West,* 12 vols. Salt Lake City: Daughters of Utah Pioneers, 1939–1951.

———. *Our Pioneer Heritage,* 20 vols. Salt Lake City: Daughters of Utah Pioneers, 1958–1977.

———. *Treasures of Pioneer History,* 6 vols. Salt Lake City: Daughters of Utah Pioneers, 1952–1957.

Esshom, Frank. *Pioneers and Prominent Men of Utah.* Salt Lake City: Western Epics, Inc., 1966.

Jenson, Andrew. *Latter-day Saint Biographical Encyclopedia: A Compilation of Biographical Sketches of Prominent Men and Women in The Church of Jesus Christ of Latter-day Saints,* 4 vols. Salt Lake City: Andrew Jenson History Company, 1901–1935.

Wiggins, Marvin. *Mormons and Their Neighbors: An Index to over 75,000 Biographical Sketches from 1820 to the Present,* 2 vols. Provo, Utah: Harold B. Lee Library, Brigham Young University, 1984.

Various local community histories and biographies.

PICTURE CREDITS

All of the pictures of the journalists that appear in the volume were graciously loaned from the personal records of family members except for the following:

Lucy Meserve Smith: Used by permission of the Manuscripts Division, J. Willard Marriott Library, University of Utah, Salt Lake City, Utah.

Harriet Decker Hanks: Used by permission of the Daughters of Utah Pioneers Museum, Salt Lake City, Utah.

Sara Alexander: Used by permission of the Utah State Historical Society, Salt Lake City, Utah.

Ann Agatha Walker Pratt, Kersten Ericksen Benson, Leonora Cannon Taylor, Jane Snyder Richards, Emmeline Blanche Woodward Whitney Wells: Used by permission of the LDS Church Historical Department Archives, Salt Lake City, Utah.

Sarah Hancock Beesley: Photocopy from Stirling E. Beesley, *Kind Words, The Beginnings of Mormon Melody, Ebenezer Beesley, Utah Pioneer Musician*. Salt Lake City: Genealogical Research Foundation, 1980.

Barbara Ann Ewell Evans: Photocopy from *Bishop David Evans and His Family*. Provo, Utah: J. Grant Stevenson, 1972.

INDEX

Wood, William, Sr., 543: joins Church,
543–45; leaves England, 546–48;
arrives at Council Bluffs, 549; is
abandoned at Loop Fork, 550–51;
travels to Salt Lake Valley, 551–57
Woodbury, Catherine Haskell, 248, 252,
254
Woodbury, Joseph Jeremiah, 248
Woodbury, Mary Ann August, 248
Woodbury, Thomas, 247–18
Woodbury, William, 248, 254
Woodruff, Wilford: at Mt. Pisgah,
153–54; is hurt while cutting trees,
215; travels in first company to Salt
Lake Valley, 293; prays at
Independence Rock, 316–17; arrives
in Salt Lake Valley, 331, 333
Woodward, William, 639
Woodworth, Phoebe Watrous, 207, 254
Woolley, Edwin Delworth, 229, 233
Woolsey, Abigail Schaffer, 396
Woolsey, Thomas, 105
"Word and Will of the Lord," 311
Word of Wisdom, 532–33
Workman, Thomas, 357

Yerba Buena (San Fransisco), California,
23
York, A. M., 192
Young Lorenzo Sobieski, 309
Young, Adolphia, 329
Young, Brigham: agrees to move the
Saints west, 17–18; appears like
Joseph Smith, 398, 404; administers
endowments, 19, 21; is set apart to
lead Church, 273; advises Louisa
Pratt, 219; crosses Iowa, 60,
71–72,117, 120, 124–28; establishes
Garden Grove, 139–42; sends the
Mormon Battalion, 33–35, 155, 159,

187; helps Jane Richards, 260;
establishes Winter Quarters, 74–75,
77, 80–81; handles money from
Mormon Battalion, 245; makes treaty
with Indians at Winter Quarters, 255;
has dream of Joseph Smith, 292–93;
chooses vanguard company, 308–9;
receives D&C 136, 311; leaves Winter
Quarters, 293–94; admonishes
pioneers, 343; arrives in Salt Lake
Valley, 331, 349; returns to Winter
Quarters, 382; is sustained as
president of the Church, 47; travels
to Salt Lake Valley a second time,
237–38; greets new settlers in Salt
Lake Valley, 454, 540; establishes
Perpetual Emigration Fund, 586;
meets first handcart companies, 593,
606–7; sends rescuers for late
handcart companies, 634, 663–64,
667–68; speaks about the handcart
companies, 694
Young, Brigham H., 276, 284–86
Young, Brigham, Jr., 575–79
Young, Clara Decker, 263, 309–10,
384–85
Young, Edward Partridge, 97
Young, Emily Partridge, 32, 88
Young, Harriet Page Wheeler Decker,
263, 309–10, 384–85
Young, Isaac, 385
Young, John W., 320
Young, Joseph, 256, 294, 296, 549,
557–58
Young, Joseph A., 575, 579, 652, 660
Young, Lorenzo Dow, 121, 310
Young, Mary Ann, 19, 117
Young, Nancy Cressy Walker, 110
Young, Phineas, 276, 284–86
Young, Rhoda, 326, 329